Laurent Bugnion

Silverlight™ 4

UNLEASHED

SAMS | 800 East 96th Street, Indianapolis, Indiana 46240 USA

Silverlight™ 4 Unleashed

ISBN-13: 978-0-672-33336-1
ISBN-10: 0-672-33336-8

Library of Congress Cataloging-in-Publication Data

Bugnion, Laurent.
Silverlight 4 unleashed / Laurent Bugnion.
p. cm.
Includes index.
ISBN 978-0-672-33336-1
1. Silverlight (Electronic resource) 2. Multimedia systems. 3. Application software—Development. 4. Web site development. 5. Internet programming. 6. User interfaces (Computer systems) I. Title.
QA76.575.B839 2011
006.7'6—dc22

2010040175

Printed in the United States of America

First Printing October 2010

Trademarks

Warning and Disclaimer

Bulk Sales

Sams Publishing offers excellent discounts on this book when ordered in quantity for bulk purchases or special sales. For more information, please contact

U.S. Corporate and Government Sales
1-800-382-3419
corpsales@pearsontechgroup.com

For sales outside of the U.S., please contact

International Sales
international@pearsoned.com

Editor-in-Chief
Karen Gettman

Executive Editor
Neil Rowe

Development Editor
Mark Renfrow

Managing Editor
Kristy Hart

Project Editor
Andy Beaster

Copy Editor
Keith Cline

Indexer
Brad Herriman

Proofreader
Jennifer Gallant

Technical Editor
Peter Bromberg

Publishing Coordinator
Cindy Teeters

Book Designer
Gary Adair

Composition
Gloria Schurick

Contents at a Glance

Table of Contents

About the Author

Laurent Bugnion works as a senior user-experience integrator for IdentityMine, one of the leading companies committed to redefining the user experience and a Microsoft Gold Partner dedicated to easing the adoption and optimal use of Microsoft presentation technologies, including Windows Presentation Foundation (WPF), Silverlight, Windows Phone 7, Surface, and Windows 7.

Originally an electronics engineer, Laurent achieved postgrad credentials in software engineering in 1999. Before IdentityMine, he worked for Siemens for 13 years, introducing WPF and other .NET 3.5 technologies worldwide. His responsibilities involved developing with the previously mentioned technologies, training and coaching his colleagues, coordinating and integrating the graphic-design work, and fostering relationships with Microsoft. Before that, he wrote embedded C/C++, and then moved to desktop computers in Java, JavaScript, and eventually .NET (desktop and ASP.NET).

Privately, he codes in Silverlight, WPF, and ASP.NET. He blogs on http://blog.galasoft.ch and writes on http://www.galasoft.ch, where he publishes articles, prototypes, and demos related to the previously mentioned technologies. In 2008, he earned an MCTS for WPF. (In October of that same year, his book *Silverlight 2 Unleashed* was published.) This year, 2010, is his fourth year as a Microsoft MVP (Silverlight), and he was selected this year as Silverlight MVP of the year.

Laurent is based in Zurich, Switzerland, where he lives with his wife, Chi Meei, and his two daughters, Alise and Laeticia.

Dedication

Thank you Chi Meei for not killing me when I said
I wanted to write a new book.
Thank you for supporting me during the 11 months that it took.
I love you.

To my princesses Alise and Laeticia for bringing light in my life,
and for making me keep things in perspective.
I love you both so much.

To my parents and my grandparents,
for helping me become who I am today.

Imagination is more important than knowledge.
—Albert Einstein

Il nous faut écouter
L'oiseau au fond des bois
Le murmure de l'été
Le sang qui monte en soi
Les berceuses des mères
Les prières des enfants
Et le bruit de la terre
Qui s'endort doucement.
—Jacques Brel

Acknowledgments

Thanking everyone who helped me complete this book would probably take another 700 pages. So, to keep these acknowledgments concise, I want to generally thank everyone who helped in any way, while specifically calling out a few without whom I couldn't have completed this work.

The Silverlight community has been nothing short of fantastic. I received wonderful motivation every time I was about to throw in the towel (usually around 2 a.m.). I found documentation about the most cryptic topics in amazingly rich and detailed blog posts, and I had the best reviewers in the world, who did all that work with just the promise of a "thank you" and a beer next time I meet them. It is a wonderful time to develop software.

I especially want thank the following (in no particular order) and apologize to those I might have forgotten:

At IdentityMine: Nathan Dunlap, Josh Wagoner, Josh Smith, Andrew Whidett, and Jonathan Russ for teaching me all I know (or so it feels); Lu Silverstein, Mark Brown, Chad Brown, and Craig Jaris for encouraging me to write this book and dealing with the disturbance.

The designer dream team: Jonah Sterling, Javier Roca Garcia, Jamey Baumgardt, Stuart Mayhew, Lydia Bagwell, and more who help me to think differently. And all the others for making me part of the family. It is a privilege to work with you.

My dream team of reviewers: Corrado Cavalli, Laurent Kempé, David Gardner, Peter Bromberg, David Anson, Josh Smith, Shawn Wildermuth, Christian Schormann, Colin Blair, Tim Heuer, Rene Schulte, Walt Ritscher, and Glenn Block. Thank you so much.

A very special extra thank you to Laurent Kempé and Corrado Cavalli for jumping in at the last minute to review additional chapters.

At Microsoft: For building these fantastic frameworks and tools, and for answering my frequent pleas for help: Scott Guthrie, Ian Ellison-Taylor, Tim Sneath, Nikhil Kothari, John Gossman, Jaime Rodriguez, Laurence Moroney, Jesse Liberty, John Papa, Rob Relyea, Ted Hu, Stefano Malle, Ronnie Saurenmann, Sascha Corti, Pete Brown, Jeff Wilcox, David Anson, Christian Schormann, Pete Blois, Unni Ravindranathan, Kirupa Chinnathambi, Joanna Mason, David Teitlebaum, Tim Heuer, Glenn Block, Karen Corby, Mike Harsh, Joe Stegman, Rochelle Benavides, Grant Hinkson, Katrien de Graeve, Lisa Feigenbaum, Mark Boulter, Chad Royal, Chris Koenig, and all the others at the DevDiv.

The source of eternal inspiration and support: Dave Campbell, Adam Kinney, Robby Ingebretsen, Kevin Moore, Charles Petzold, Marlon Grech and all the WPF disciples, Shawn Wildermuth, Walt Ritscher, Justin Angel, Davide Zordan, David Yack, Don Burnett,

Erik Mork, Brian Noyes, Ward Bell, Rob Eisenberg, Dan Wahlin, Chad Campbell, John Stockton, Jonas Follesoe, Seema Ramchandani, Brian Henderson, Ian Smith, Scott Barnes, Jeremy Likness, Page Brooks, Rick Barraza, Cigdem Patlak, Michael Sync, Victor Gaudioso, David Kelley, Anand Iyer, all the Silverlight MVPs, and the whole vibrant and amazing Silverlight community.

The great team at Sams: And especially Neil Rowe (my editor, mentor, and friend since 2007), Andy Beaster, and Mark Renfrow.

We Want to Hear from You!

As the reader of this book, *you* are our most important critic and commentator. We value your opinion and want to know what we're doing right, what we could do better, what areas you'd like to see us publish in, and any other words of wisdom you're willing to pass our way.

You can email or write me directly to let me know what you did or didn't like about this book—as well as what we can do to make our books stronger.

Please note that I cannot help you with technical problems related to the topic of this book, and that due to the high volume of mail I receive, I might not be able to reply to every message.

When you write, please be sure to include this book's title and author as well as your name and phone or email address. I will carefully review your comments and share them with the author and editors who worked on the book.

Email: feedback@samspublishing.com

Mail: Neil Rowe
Executive Editor
Sams Publishing
800 East 96th Street
Indianapolis, IN 46240 USA

Reader Services

Visit our website and register this book at informit.com/register for convenient access to any updates, downloads, or errata that might be available for this book.

Foreword

The growth of Silverlight has been perhaps faster than any of us involved in its inception would have predicted. In less than three years, Microsoft has released four desktop releases, each packing a payload of hundreds of features in response to customer feedback. Silverlight is now deployed on somewhere approaching two-thirds of all Internet-connected PCs,[1] and it's the primary platform for general-purpose development on the new Windows Phone 7. Silverlight powers all manner of mainstream applications: from high-end media experiences like Netflix, NBC Sports, and Sky Player to the web version of Office. It's in use at top consumer websites like eBay and for mission-critical applications inside the firewall of numerous Fortune 500 companies.

In one sense, Silverlight is, of course, just an evolution of the .NET Framework that has been central to Microsoft's developer strategy for the past ten years. It stands on the shoulders of giants like Windows Presentation Foundation (WPF,) the big-sister technology that preceded it and laid the groundwork—with an architecture and XAML format that had already proved itself in real-world implementations.

When we started building Silverlight, one of the greatest constraints was size. We knew we needed something that was lightweight and easy to deploy without requiring a big download or dependencies on other prerequisites. At the same time, we wanted to ship a high-quality product as quickly as possible. There was a lot of debate internally about whether we should start with the existing .NET codebase and "take away" code or whether we should "build up" by starting with a clean slate and gradually adding features until we had an attractive product. In the end, we went with the latter approach, and I think it shows in the final product: Silverlight contains the key things that a developer needs while bringing little cruft along for the ride. For me, this is one key reason why Silverlight offers a unique sweet spot of power, flexibility, and easy deployment that suits it well for both consumer and business usage.

But a framework alone isn't sufficient for most pragmatic developers, who are less interested in history lessons or arcane details of internal architecture and more concerned with what they themselves can create quickly and efficiently. Over the last year or two since the last *Silverlight Unleashed* book was published, it's true that Silverlight has been expanded and enhanced; but even more important, the palette of tools available to a Silverlight developer has grown tremendously. In particular, the release of Visual Studio 2010 brought true WYSIWYG in-place editing to Silverlight, along with WCF RIA Services, a set of classes and design-time tools that offer major productivity gains to business application authors.

Beyond the core elements of Silverlight, a burgeoning community has sprung up over the past couple of years both inside and outside of Microsoft. The engineering team themselves have released a plethora of open source controls, components, and themes along with rich frameworks for media, extensibility, and analytics. Others have contributed libraries and components for everything from PDF creation to physics engines and full 3D support: CodePlex alone shows nearly 500 projects that are based on Silverlight. And of course, there is an endless supply of great content targeted at Silverlight developers, including the weekly Silverlight TV show at http://silverlight.tv.

What of the future of Silverlight? Some have argued that the rapid rise of HTML5 presents a new competitive threat to Silverlight. It's certainly true that the browser wars of old are back, with vendors duking it out to deliver the most advanced hardware-accelerated graphics platform for developers while delivering a stable and secure browser for a broader audience. It's also true that HTML in general has the most pervasive reach of any client platform. Indeed, the momentum behind Internet Explorer 9 shows that we at Microsoft are also putting a lot of energy into providing first-class support for "standards-based" web development.

A favorite business read among Microsoft executives is *Built to Last* by Jim Collins and Jerry Porras, which highlights how easy it is to be trapped by a false dichotomy (the "tyranny of the 'OR'"). The authors note how many strategic decisions are framed incorrectly as a choice between A or B (but *not* both). Yet often the correct answer is an *and* rather than an *or*.

In this vein, there need be no fork in the road between HTML5 and Silverlight. Both serve key needs that developers have, and both have powerful strengths. Even more important, many so-called Silverlight applications are in fact hybrid solutions that combine both technologies. Silverlight contains many useful bridging features to enable developers of both hues to access code and UIs written in the opposite framework. Silverlight developers should therefore feel confident that their skills have value for the indefinite future and that Silverlight itself has a rosy future.

I want to close this foreword by noting my delight to see this update to Laurent's popular predecessor title, *Silverlight 2 Unleashed*. I've had the privilege of knowing Laurent for some years now, and I can tell you that few in the Silverlight community command the respect that he does. He combines a passion for writing quality client software with a deep, practical, real-world knowledge of the tools and framework. He has had an insider's view of each release of Silverlight as it has been developed, and his feedback has shaped the product for the better. Laurent's own experience developing complex, large-scale Silverlight applications shines through, particularly in the more advanced topics toward the end of the book.

I heartily commend this book, both to newcomers to Silverlight as well as to those who already have experience with early releases of Silverlight and want to "upgrade" their knowledge with the latest advances.

—Tim Sneath
Senior Director, Client Platform Evangelism
Microsoft Corp.

---

[1] *As attested by our internal data and sites like riastats.com, which measure deployments of plug-ins based on millions of real-world users.*

Introduction

Silverlight 4, released to the public in April 2010, represents a major forward step in the history of this still-young technology. Although we'll certainly see later versions of the framework with additional features in the future, the current version is very mature and easy to work with. In addition, the tools used to develop Silverlight have also grown and offer the same level of maturity and ease of use.

It is interesting to take a good look at the extended Silverlight community today. From a niche topic, Silverlight has become the source of many discussions on Twitter and various blogs. Also, since days of Silverlight 2, we have witnessed the emergence of *design patterns* and of polished external frameworks. It is now possible to talk to Silverlight experts who have developed many professional applications, and who know what works best.

The book you have in your hands (or on your computer/e-reader/tablet/phone screen) tries to describe the current version of Silverlight version 4) as fully as possible. Doing so represents a difficult task, however, because of the multiple facets of this technology and the number of problems it can solve. You will find that this book goes into much more detail than *Silverlight 2 Unleashed*. That increased level of detail is intentional, and in fact, this book builds on the foundation presented in that earlier publication.

Honing Your Basic Skills

Silverlight is very much a story of continuity between versions. Most changes are in fact additional features. For developers who were already active in earlier versions of Silverlight, the skills that you already own are going to help you advance in Silverlight 4.

For developers who are completely new to Silverlight, we provide a free copy (as a PDF download) of *Silverlight 2 Unleashed*. This book was written with beginners in mind, and will bring you up to speed with fundamental concepts such as XAML, basic controls, transforms, animations, and more.

What Can You Learn from *Silverlight 2 Unleashed*?

The following chapters in *Silverlight 2 Unleashed* will help you to understand the basics of Silverlight 4:

> **TIP**
>
> If you are already experienced with Silverlight 2 or Silverlight 3, feel free to skip this step and jump right into Chapter 1.

- Chapter 1, "Introducing Silverlight," explains where Silverlight comes from. Although the landscape of web technologies evolved in two years, most of the information in this chapter is still very much valid. Note, however, that most demos described in Chapter 1 are not current anymore. In some cases, you will get errors, or the page will simply not be found anymore.

- Chapter 2, "Understanding XAML," is still valid. You can learn a lot about the fundamentals of XAML by reading this chapter.
- Chapter 3, "Playing with XAML Transforms and Animations," is still valid. All the transforms and animations present in Silverlight 2 work unchanged in Silverlight 4.
- Chapter 4, "Expression Blend," refers to Expression Blend 2. Many basic features are still valid, but we will cover Expression Blend 4 in this book.
- Chapter 5, "Using Media," is still valid and describes colors, vector graphics, and basic image and video handling.
- Chapter 6, "Blending a Little More," is still an interesting read, and provides an overview of functionalities that are still available in Expression Blend 4 (transforms, opacity masks, paths, clipping paths, grouping controls, and making user controls).
- Chapter 7, "Deploying to a Web Page," is still valid with minor changes. It shows you how to select a provider for your website and how to deploy your Silverlight application to that site.
- Chapter 8, "Programming Silverlight with JavaScript," is less relevant to Silverlight 4 than it was to Silverlight 2. However, JavaScript is an important skill to have for anyone who is involved into creating web applications.
- Chapter 9, "Understanding .NET," and Chapter 10, "Progressing with .NET," provide a tutorial from scratch about the most important constructs of the C# programming language and of the .NET framework. It is a good read for people who come to Silverlight from Flash, for instance, and have never worked in .NET before.
- Chapter 11, "Progressing with Animations" is still valid and will teach you how to create animations in Blend, how to start and stop animations in code, and other special kinds of animations. Silverlight 4 and especially Blend 4 build on this and offer additional features that you will discover in the present book.
- Chapter 12, "Encoding Videos with Expression Encoder," and Chapter 13, "Progressing with Videos," are based on Expression Encoder 2. The current version of this software (Expression Encoder 4) available today offers much of the same functionalities, with added features and a slightly different look and feel. Note, however, that the Microsoft Silverlight Streaming servers are unfortunately not available anymore.
- Chapter 14, "Letting Silverlight and JavaScript Talk," is less relevant to Silverlight 4, although most of the techniques will still work.
- Chapter 15, "Digging into Silverlight Elements," and Chapter 16, "Digging Deeper into Silverlight Elements," are still very much current. In fact, it is almost a must-read before starting to work in Silverlight.
- Chapter 17, "Using Resources, Styling, and Templating," is still valid; however, it is possible to store resources in external resource dictionaries in Silverlight 4, which was not the case in Silverlight 2.

- Chapter 18, "Data Binding and Using Data Controls," will be developed deeper in *Silverlight 4 Unleashed*. The section about the DataGrid is still an interesting read if you are working with this control. Note, however, that the DataGrid is now part of the core Silverlight framework.
- Chapter 19, "Creating User Controls and Custom Controls," overlaps in part with the present book's content. Controls are a very important part of the Silverlight framework, and it is important to understand how they are built and how they work.
- Chapter 20, "Taking Silverlight 2 One Step Further," and Chapter 21, "Taking Silverlight 2 Even Further," lists various topics, some of them overlapping with the present book's content.
- Chapter 22, "Connecting to the Web," overlaps in part with the present book's content, but also has some interesting techniques to download files and access their content.
- Chapter 23, "Placing Cross-Domain Requests and Handling Exceptions," contains information about the topic of cross-domain communication that is still current in Silverlight 4, as well as a tutorial about exceptions and how to handle them.
- Chapter 24, "Silverlight: Continuing the Journey," contains various information that can be interesting for Silverlight developers.

About Code in This Book

We tried to keep formatting as consistent as possible throughout this book and to make the code look like it does in Visual Studio. The source code is color-coded to help you to work faster and so that you can recognize key concepts in Visual Studio and in Expression Blend. Note that depending on the context where a keyword is used (XAML or C#, Visual Studio, or Expression Blend), the color code might differ.

The source code lines are numbered only where relevant (for example, when the text makes explicit reference to a line number).

The whole source code for this book is available online at http://www.galasoft.ch/SL4U/code. A translation of the C# code into VB.NET is being prepared at the time of this writing.

Adding a Reference to a Namespace

In some listings, classes from other namespaces/assemblies are added to the code. In some occasions, doing so might cause a compilation error with the following message:

The type or namespace name 'MyClass' could not be found (are you missing a using directive or an assembly reference?).

To correct this, make sure that the assembly in which `MyClass` is defined is added to the References folder in the Visual Studio Solution Explorer. If that is not the case, right-click this folder and select Add Reference from the context menu. In the Add Reference dialog, browse to the missing assembly and add it to the project.

If the error persists, you must add a reference to the namespace in which `MyClass` is placed in the source code file. You can do so by adding an entry at the top the current page, as follows (where `SilverlightApplication1.AnotherNamespace` is the namespace in which `MyClass` lives):

```
using SilverlightApplication1.AnotherNamespace;
```

In Visual Studio, this step can be automated by placing the cursor inside the name `MyClass` and pressing Ctrl+. (Ctrl and a dot) to open the context menu. Then, select the first entry of the menu to add a `using` directive.

Setting the Right Project as Startup

When an existing solution is opened, and this solution contains a web project hosting the Silverlight application (in the ClientBin folder), the web project should be set as Startup. This means that when Ctrl+F5 is pressed in Visual Studio, the Silverlight application will be executed in `http:` context, and not in the `file:` context that has more restrictions. To ensure that the web project is set as Startup, follow these steps:

1. Check in the Solution Explorer whether the web project is represented in bold. If that is the case, skip to Step 3.
2. If that is not the case, right-click the web project's name and select Set as StartUp Project from the context menu.
3. Right-click the HTML test page name (usually named [YourSilverlightApplication]TestPage.html or index.html) and select Set as Start Page from the context menu.

Using the `var` Keyword

Since Silverlight 3, it has been possible to use the `var` keyword to implicitly type a local variable. For example, in the following code, both expressions are exactly similar after the code is compiled:

```
var myVariable1 = new Button();
Button myVariable2 = new Button();
```

There is a lot of discussion in the .NET community about the usage of the `var` keyword. Choosing to use the keyword or not is very much a matter of personal preference, and there is unfortunately no way to please everyone in this matter. In this book, the `var` keyword is used consistently as shown here.

Happy Coding!

Now it's time to start! I wish you a successful journey in this book, and I am anxious to hear from you on Twitter (@LBugnion). I cannot promise to reply to every message, but I will definitely do my best, and I am very open to criticism (as long as it is constructive) and questions. Enjoy the trip, and happy coding!

Laurent

Stäfa, Switzerland, September 2010

CHAPTER 1

Three Years of Silverlight

IN THIS CHAPTER, WE WILL:

- Discuss what happened since Silverlight 2 Unleashed came out.
- Talk about cross-browser and cross-platform compatibility for Silverlight 4.
- Consider alternatives to Silverlight, both in the browser and out-of-the-browser.
- Look at the earlier versions of Silverlight 1.0, 2 and 3 and take a look into the future of this technology.
- Install Silverlight 4 as a user and explore a few demos.

In three short years, Silverlight has come a very long way. In this chapter, we review what Silverlight is, where it comes from, and try to peek into the future of this technology, illustrated by the "shiny logo" shown in Figure 1.1.

Discovering Silverlight 4

It seems like yesterday that we published *Silverlight 2 Unleashed* and introduced it at the Professional Developer Conference 2008 in Los Angeles just a few days after Silverlight 2 had been released to the Web. And yet here we are talking about Silverlight 4 already! In these less than two years, the Silverlight team at Microsoft has been very active listening to the community's feedback and implementing new features to transform what was an already solid, yet basic platform into a very rich framework, able to accommodate most client application developers' needs.

The very first public glimpse of Silverlight 4 beta was offered at the Professional Developer Conference 2009, when Scott Guthrie (Corporate Vice President, .NET Developer Platform, Microsoft) gave one of the exciting talks full of demos for which he is famous. Although still in beta stage, we were already able to clearly see the direction that the technology was taking. Even more important, we were told often that Silverlight is the future of client applications at Microsoft!

FIGURE 1.1
Silverlight logo.

With this new release, the border between web applications and desktop applications is becoming much thinner. For example, Silverlight 4 can now install applications "out of the browser," with a shortcut in the Start menu or on the desktop. Although these applications have fewer privileges and features than full-blown desktop applications, they have the huge advantage to be cross-platform (you can run them on Apple computers, too) and provide a very elegant way to offer rich functionality in online and also offline mode. We talk a lot more about out-of-the-browser applications in this book.

> **TIP**
>
> **What About Windows Presentation Foundation?**
>
> The richer (but running on Windows only) "big sister" of Silverlight called Windows Presentation Foundation (WPF) is still actively developed and extended by Microsoft, although in a maybe less-glamorous way. See the section "Alternatives to Silverlight," later in this chapter.

A lot of other features, which we discuss later too, help the developers to build so-called line-of-business (LOB) applications (for example, rich data applications for businesses, catalogs for products, data visualization screens, and many more). Silverlight is often mistaken for yet another media framework, when it is in fact much more than this. This new release makes the point very clear, and should help to put Silverlight in the focus of enterprise applications developers while continuing to build on the success it already has for multimedia applications.

Learning Silverlight Is Betting on the Future

With all this in mind, it is quite clear that learning Silverlight is a perfect way to advance in the future of client application development:

- For web developers, it adds important skills to your arsenal that will help enrich your web pages. Silverlight is not replacing classic web technologies such as Hypertext Markup Language (HTML), Cascading Style Sheets (CSS), and JavaScript, but it enhances them and plays an important role in the way that websites are evolving always more from document presentation to rich interactive applications.

- For "classic" desktop developers in the Windows world (with technologies such as Microsoft Foundation Classes [MFC] or Windows Forms), it teaches you a modern and exciting framework with revolutionary features such as the fantastic data binding system, rich animations and graphics, media integration, and so on.
- For WPF developers, you leverage a lot from what you already know and gain cross-platform compatibility for your applications, easy web deployment, and exposure to a wider audience.

One important thing to keep in mind is that Silverlight is not a replacement for HTML web pages, and will absolutely not kill HTML. Silverlight is here to enhance your web pages with richer content, and with the out-of-the-browser feature, to create lightweight applications that can function online or offline. Learning Silverlight does not mean that you should avoid writing HTML code, or that you should stop investing in technologies such as ASP.NET. But it means that you can now realize applications that were impossible (or very difficult) to do in HTML/CSS/JavaScript, and that you can use the same languages (and in some cases reuse code) on the server and on the client.

How Can They Be So Fast?

There are a few aspects that explain how new versions of Silverlight can hit the market so fast, and yet be so stable:

- Silverlight is developed in an agile manner. With short iterations and early releases, the team is able to react quickly when problems are found in the code or new features are suggested. This explains why we had three releases in less than three years.
- Silverlight is taking advantage of the experience gathered by the Windows Presentation Foundation team. Many features are similar, and some code can even be reused. Other features are re-implemented in a different way based on customer feedback. The teams are communicating to leverage the experience gained since WPF was released.
- The community is involved in an interactive manner. Your input counts! We will talk about ways to get involved in this chapter.

> **TIP**
>
> **The Community Counts!**
>
> Did you know that approximately 70% of the features requested by the Silverlight community have been implemented in Silverlight 4!

How About Compatibility with Older Versions?

An agile team at work for Silverlight provides a great basis for a rich feature set evolving very fast. With version 4, we can say that Silverlight is reaching maturity. There will, of course, be additional versions in the future, but it is obvious that versions 3 and 4 were major steps for this platform, which explains Microsoft's enthusiasm at the conferences where early versions were shown. Note, however, that a lot of effort has been put into backward compatibility:

- If you open a Silverlight 2 (or 3) project in the Silverlight 4 development environment, a lot of your code will work as is. Some of it will need to be updated, but the changes are, in general, painless ones. Note that the project files (*.CSPROJ) will be updated to the new environment, though.
- If you run a Silverlight 2 (or 3) application on a PC with Silverlight 4 installed, it will run without glitches, because the runtime environment is fully backward compatible.

In fact, your Silverlight 2 (or 3) applications should run even better in a Silverlight 4 runtime environment, because of the improvements brought to the core and to the plug-in. This history of backward compatibility is most certainly going to continue with future versions, so what you learn now is going to be a major skill for your future as a developer.

Cross-Browser and Cross-Platform Compatibility

The version of Silverlight developed by Microsoft is available on a wide variety of platforms, both on the Windows and Macintosh operating systems. This plug-in will run on all these platforms with the same feature set (with one exception that we will discuss in Chapter 18, "Drag and Drop, Full Screen, Clipboard, COM Interop, Duplex Polling, Notification Windows, and Splash Screens," namely the COM integration that is of course available only on Windows operating systems).

In addition, Novell is working on a version named Moonlight, available for certain distributions of Linux. The effort by Novell is encouraged by Microsoft but is conducted independently. This is why the version releases are not necessarily coordinated, and there might be some discrepancies in the feature set, too. However, a great effort is being expended to create a plug-in that is largely compatible with the one developed by Microsoft.

Finally, we will also take a look in Chapter 15, "Developing Navigation Applications and Silverlight for Windows Phone 7" at Silverlight for the mobile platform. After announcing that they wanted to support the mobile platform, Microsoft did not communicate much and encountered a few technical difficulties that took longer than expected to solve. This year, however, we finally heard much more about support for the mobile platform, and we will take a first look at what will be available in the near future.

In short, Silverlight is your best bet if you want to run .NET-based code on a large number of platforms!

Windows and Macintosh

The following table shows in detail what is and is not possible with the plug-in implemented by Microsoft.

TIP

Things Are Moving Fast

Table 1.1 is a snapshot at the time of this writing. The situation keeps changing, with new browsers and platforms being added. To get the latest information, make sure to visit the Silverlight.net website!

TABLE 1.1 Cross-Platform and -Browser Compatibility

OS	IE8	IE7	IE6	FF3	Safari3	Safari4	Chrome
Windows 7	Yes	Yes	n/a	Yes	n/a	n/a	Yes
Windows Vista	Yes	Yes	n/a	Yes	n/a	n/a	Yes
Windows Server 2008	Yes	Yes	n/a	Yes	n/a	n/a	Yes
Windows Server 2008 R2	Yes	n/a	n/a	n/a	n/a	n/a	Yes
Windows XP SP2 and SP3	Yes	Yes	Yes	Yes	n/a	n/a	Yes
Windows 2000 SP4[1]	n/a	n/a	Yes	n/a	n/a	n/a	n/a
Windows Server 2003	Yes	Yes	Yes	Yes	n/a	n/a	n/a
Mac OS 10.4.8 and later (Intel based)	n/a	n/a	n/a	Yes	Yes	Yes	Yes

1 *Windows 2000 requires the installation of an update (KB 891861) to execute Silverlight applications.*

Note the following restrictions:

- The Opera web browser is not officially supported at the time of this writing.
- PowerPC-based Apple computers support only Silverlight 1.0.

Linux

For Linux, FreeBSD, and Solaris operating systems, things are changing fast, so the best thing to do is to check the information on the Novell Moonlight website at http://www.galasoft.ch/sl4-moonlight.

Alternatives to Silverlight

Because Silverlight 4 can run inside or outside of the web browser, its alternatives cover a wider landscape. Interestingly, though, not many technologies allow you to program just once but run on multiple platforms and in multiple modes (offline/online, in the browser/out of the browser). In that sense, Silverlight is pretty unique.

In the Web Browser

Silverlight is traditionally a connected application running within a web browser. In that field, the landscape didn't really change much since Silverlight 2, with the exception maybe of XHTML, which is barely mentioned anymore and considered already obsolete now that HTML5 is becoming a trending topic.

Adobe Flash

This is the obvious contender, the one technology that is most often mentioned when Silverlight is compared to other frameworks. Adobe Flash is installed on a huge number of computers and various operating systems. It is also a well-known environment, and many companies develop applications in Flash for the Web.

As mentioned when Silverlight 2 was released, Flash is not going to be killed by Silverlight, and in fact this was never Microsoft's intention. Rather, Silverlight provides a welcomed alternative to firms who do not want to invest in two very different technologies for the desktop and the Web. In that sense, Silverlight is a great choice because it is developed with the same languages and the same tools as the well-known Windows Forms, ASP.NET, and WPF.

Silverlight and Flash are coexisting on the Web, sometimes even in the same web pages. Thankfully, this is easy to realize, and there is even a possibility to let these mixed applications communicate together through JavaScript. This allows a gradual modification of existing websites from Flash to Silverlight, without breaking the functionalities or forcing the users to adapt to large-scale changes. We actually saw some striking examples of this at Microsoft itself, with existing Flash applications being gradually converted to Silverlight without disruptions.

DHTML and AJAX

DHTML (Dynamic HTML) and AJAX (Asynchronous JavaScript and XML) are often used together on web pages to create a more interactive experience. This was made popular with web developers by the release of JavaScript frameworks such as jQuery.

The advantage of these frameworks is that they standardize the JavaScript functions by providing a layer on top of the various implementations available in different web browsers on different platforms. jQuery can be extended by plug-ins that are available for the user experience itself (for example, to create smoother animations), or at a lower level to enhance the communication with the web server, and so on. Also, they do not require an additional component in the web browser to run.

> **TIP**
>
> **Using jQuery in ASP.NET**
>
> Did you know that Microsoft supports jQuery development by contributing to this open source project, and including it in ASP.NET MVC (Model, View, Controller) projects in Visual Studio.

However, programming in JavaScript is not an easy task. The dynamic nature of the language makes it more difficult to offer advanced development tools (such as IntelliSense in Visual Studio) and to find and correct bugs. Also, the HTML platform is limited: Advanced and smooth animations with high frame rates are impossible to realize, it is impossible to create certain transformations for graphic elements, and so forth.

Note, however, that using Silverlight on a web page doesn't prevent you from using jQuery or another JavaScript-based framework—on the contrary. Here, too, these technologies complement each other.

HTML5

This new revision of HTML intends to provide a wide range of rich functionality, allowing developers to reduce the use of third-party plug-ins. In this matter, it positions itself as a concurrent of Adobe Flash and Microsoft Silverlight.

Although it is true that plug-ins cause problems, they also solve some. One big issue with HTML is that different web browsers have different implementations of the standard. This is a well-known issue: Testing a web page for all major web browsers on all major operating systems can be a real hassle. On the other hand, Silverlight as a plug-in is guaranteed to run the same in every supported web browser. It is the old "write once, run anywhere."

The major issue that HTML5 faces is that a wide adoption will take a lot of time. Also, if we learned anything from the past, it is that each browser is likely to offer a slightly different feature set. Some features will simply be missing from some browsers; other features will be implemented in a different manner. Compatibility will take a lot of time, if it is ever achieved. In the meantime, and until we know whether HTML5 really delivers what it promises, Silverlight offers a real alternative.

Out of the Browser

Running a Silverlight application out of the browser is similar to running a desktop application. Therefore, Silverlight can be seen as an alternative to any desktop technology, including "classic" MFC and Windows Forms applications on Windows or Mac applications on Mac OS. Let's just take a look at two modern desktop technologies.

Windows Presentation Foundation

When Silverlight functionalities are not enough to accomplish what you want, the answer is probably to look into WPF, Silverlight's "big sister." Even though the convergence is always greater between these two technologies, and Silverlight becomes richer and steps on WPF's playground, there are still some scenarios for which Silverlight is not suitable.

> **TIP**
>
> **Deploying WPF on the Web**
>
> Did you know that WPF applications can be deployed and installed from a web server using the ClickOnce technology? See http://www.galasoft.ch/sl4-clickonce.
>
> Also, a WPF application can be deployed and run inside some web browsers on Windows, and provide an interesting alternative to Silverlight. See http://www.galasoft.ch/sl4-xbap.

The biggest disadvantage of WPF with regard to Silverlight is that it runs only on Windows systems. Also, it requires the complete .NET framework (instead of the Silverlight subset), which is larger and takes more time to install on the target machine if it is not already present. Finally, although WPF is richer than Silverlight, this richness also makes it more complicated to learn. It is easier to start with Silverlight.

Note that thanks to the combined efforts of the Silverlight team and the WPF team at Microsoft, the compatibility between both technologies has never been greater, and it is in fact possible to convert a Silverlight application to WPF with a large portion of shared code. Generally speaking, however, and because Silverlight is a subset of .NET, it is easier to start in Silverlight and extend the application to WPF than the contrary. Similarly, it is also easier to start learning Silverlight and then to move to WPF.

Adobe AIR

A less well-known platform developed by Adobe is called AIR and allows creating desktop applications. As such, it is not a concurrent of "in-browser" Silverlight, but rather of the out-of-the-browser applications.

For users, AIR applications are known to be heavy in memory consumption, and require an additional framework that must be installed the first time you run an AIR application (even if you have Flash already installed). This can be a problem on corporate networks, where IT departments are often reluctant to install new components on users' PCs. Silverlight, on the other hand, is installed once and gets the out-of-the-browser capabilities immediately.

Legacy Technologies

Some technologies are still running inside some web browsers, but are becoming obsolete with time. The two mentioned in this section are not the only ones, but they are the best known, and it is possible that a developer starting a new project will be asked to consider these in the variant analysis.

Java Applets

Java as a plug-in is quite widespread and allows small applications known as applets to run in the web browser. Java was revolutionary in that way when it was released, but it suffers from a lot of issues:

- ▶ Java is notoriously slow. It's slow to install on a new computer, and especially slow to start.
- ▶ Java applets have a bad reputation when it comes to security. This claim might not be as true in newer versions as it used to be, but Java's adoption in the corporate world has suffered a lot from this concern.
- ▶ Java is cumbersome for .NET developers. The tools and the language are unusual and require additional training.

Silverlight addresses these concerns and offers a convincing alternative to Java applets. Perhaps the most compelling argument is that *Silverlight is .NET*. If your developers already know .NET-based client application technologies (WPF, Windows Forms, ASP.NET, and so on), they will feel at home very fast with Silverlight, and have a solid foundation to build on.

Microsoft ActiveX

Similarly to Java applets, ActiveX controls were once very popular to enrich a web page, but are rendered pretty much obsolete nowadays by the many improvements made to new technologies, and especially Silverlight. If you are a developer or maintainer of ActiveX controls, it is probably time to consider moving to the newer, richer, and safer platform that Microsoft is developing. ActiveX controls suffer from the same problems as Java applets regarding security and restrictions in the enterprise world; in addition, they run only on Windows-based operating systems, which prevents a large user base from using them.

Silverlight differs significantly from ActiveX, and converting existing applications to this new technology is not the easiest task a developer can dream of. With this step, however, you will offer a newer, richer, and much friendlier interface to your users, and make a big step toward the future of software development.

A Short History of Silverlight

The development of Silverlight has been consistently incremental. Silverlight 4 is a superset of Silverlight 3, which is a superset of Silverlight 2. Some of the code might not be completely compatible between versions, mostly because when some things were missing developers had to use workarounds. After a feature has been added in a later version, however, the workarounds might not work properly anymore, and it is time to upgrade the code to the proper implementation.

In some rare cases, the interface to some functionality might have changed because the team came up with a better implementation. These occurrences are rare, however, and upgrading an application to a newer version of Silverlight should be easy enough.

Silverlight 1.0

This early release of Silverlight (May 2007) was far from complete, and in fact did not support any .NET code; it had to be programmed in JavaScript. It did, however, support a small subset of XAML (eXtensible Application Markup Language), the language used to define the user interface of Silverlight applications.

> **TIP**
>
> **Video as an Incentive**
>
> Studies have shown that a user is most likely going to accept installing a new plug-in on his computer to watch videos. This is why the main focus has been put on video in Silverlight 1.0.

The main purpose of Silverlight 1.0 was to rapidly create a base of installation for the Silverlight plug-in. Other features were, however, supported in Silverlight 1.0. For example, you could already create some animations. There were no built-in controls (apart from the TextBlock), but using shapes, you could create buttons and other basic building blocks for your application that would trigger JavaScript-based code. For instance, some video players still available today on the Web are entirely written in Silverlight 1.0, without any .NET code.

> **TIP**
>
> **Code Name WPF/E**
>
> You might have heard the name Windows Presentation Foundation Everywhere, or WPF/E. This was the code name under which Microsoft developed Silverlight, in reference to Windows Presentation Foundation, the rich desktop programming framework included in .NET 3.0 and later. Very soon, however, this name was abandoned in favor of the catchier Silverlight.

Nowadays it is clear that Silverlight 1.0 was just a step on the road to rich interactive applications, and very soon the focus shifted to Silverlight 2, the first .NET-based version.

Silverlight 2

For a very short time, this version was named Silverlight 1.1, but considering the major changes implemented (and also to simplify the versioning process), it made sense to change the version number to a full digit instead.

Silverlight 2 (released shortly before the Professional Developer Conference in October 2008) was revolutionary because it brought for the very first time the .NET framework (as a subset) to other platforms than Windows. It also included a rich set of controls, enhanced video, new tool support, and many other exciting features.

When you study Silverlight 4, you will use a lot of features that were already available in Silverlight 2.

Silverlight 3

This version (again a full-digit increment) was released in July 2009, a mere nine months after Silverlight 2. In this short time, the team managed to bring Silverlight to a more mature version.

Controls and features were added, and the data layer extended to provide a stable foundation for more business-oriented scenarios. At the same time, the existing media layer was extended with new formats being supported, and new powerful effects (known as pixel shaders) being introduced. On the user experience level, it was now possible to transform 2D elements into the 3D space (what was sometimes called "pseudo 3D" or "2.5D"). Animations were pushed further, with smoother and more lifelike movement. Some steps were also taken to enable hardware acceleration (which is a real challenge on mixed platforms such as the ones supported by Silverlight).

It's also in Silverlight 3 that we saw the out-of-the-browser (OOB) feature for the first time. It was still rather incomplete: For example, the OOB application still couldn't get any additional permission, so it was pretty limited in its actions. It was also not possible to give a custom look and feel to the OOB window. Still, it was an intriguing first step, and the community's response was very encouraging.

In short, we wanted more...

And Silverlight 4...

And here we are! Silverlight 4 will not be the final version of this technology, but one thing is sure: If you were still hesitating to invest in Silverlight, now is a great time to start. We know a lot about what Silverlight is, what it can do and cannot do, and we have a quite clear vision of what will happen in the near future. We also have Silverlight experts with (in some cases) two or three years of experience with this technology.

Silverlight 4 is a very stable release. What we predicted when Silverlight 2 was published is proven true today: Silverlight is here to stay, and Microsoft is betting a lot on this technology. In these three years, it went from "Flash contender" to major user interface technology.

According to recent numbers, the Silverlight installation basis grew very fast since Silverlight 2 was released, and you can count on approximately 60% of all the connected computers having Silverlight 3 or Silverlight 4 already installed.[2]

Previewing the Future of Silverlight

The next burning question, of course, is where Silverlight is going. As usual, predicting the future of any technology is a difficult exercise, as the past few years have proven. The situation on the .NET front is a bit clearer now than it was two years ago, though; so what did we learn?

- Silverlight has strong support at Microsoft. They are pushing it very hard; they release new features at a fast pace, and managed in just a few years to create a very rich framework. This is not going to stop with Silverlight 4; more is coming.
- A convergence is occurring between Silverlight and WPF. More and more features are shared. The movement is toward compatibility, with Silverlight becoming a complete subset of WPF. Not just compatibility of interfaces, but also binary compatibility. We will probably see this happening in the next few years.

[2] *Source: http://riastats.com*

TIP

Not Completely Compatible Yet

Today, Silverlight is already in great part a subset of WPF in terms of interfaces. Many classes that are in Silverlight also exist in WPF. However, some new classes have been added to Silverlight 3 and 4; some of them have made it into WPF 4, some of them are still missing. The situation is not as clean as one would want.

Also, even though we see first steps in that direction, the binary compatibility is still limited.

- There is already a large adoption of Silverlight by developers and firms worldwide. We saw lots of interesting projects in the past few years, and more are coming. We also see a lot of firms that were reluctant to move to WPF embracing Silverlight for their rich application development because it is easier to learn.
- Finally, the installation base has literally exploded, going from approximately 25% for Silverlight 2 to 60% for Silverlight 3 and 4. The smooth update mechanism makes it painless to upgrade Silverlight if needed; and as new applications are being published on the Web, more users are installing Silverlight to access them.

Here's a quote from Pete Brown, who works for Microsoft as client application evangelist (http://www.galasoft.ch/sl4-convergence):

> In the future, it is very likely that both Silverlight and WPF will be a single technology with a single codebase.

So here it is, the probable future of Silverlight and WPF: A continuum framework that can be used on the desktop (very rich clients with full features / rich clients with fewer features and permissions) and in the web browser (very similar to what we have now, but with added functionality).

Installing Silverlight 4 as a User

Installing Silverlight 4 is very easy. For many users, a version of Silverlight might in fact be already installed on their computer. For instance, if you install one of the applications distributed under the label Windows Live (such as Live Messenger, Live Writer, and so on) and keep the default options, Silverlight will be installed on the target PC.

Similarly, Silverlight can be installed by the Windows Update program. This enables administrators to make sure that the latest versions of Microsoft applications are consistently installed in a corporate network. For home users, Windows Update is a great way to make sure that you get notified when a new version of a driver, an application, or a framework (such as Silverlight) is available.

That said, because it is so new, you might not have the latest version of Silverlight and will need to upgrade when you navigate to a Silverlight 4 application in your web browser. Or, you might not have Silverlight installed at all, and here too you will be notified when you reach the page you want to see.

Opening a Silverlight 4 Application

Silverlight applications are always embedded in an HTML page. Opening a Silverlight application for the first time is always a matter of navigating to a web page in a supported web browser.

With the possibility of saving Silverlight applications locally and to run them out-of-the-browser, the startup point might not be a web page anymore, but more classically a shortcut in the Start menu or on the desktop. However, an application may only be installed locally following a user action (for example, a click on a button or a right-click on the application and selecting Install from the Silverlight context menu). It always starts on the web page!

What to Do If Silverlight Is Not Installed?

If Silverlight is not installed at all on the computer you are using (not even an earlier version), you will see an image asking you to install Silverlight, as shown in Figure 1.2. Note, however, that this experience can be customized, and you might see different pages with elaborate designs.

FIGURE 1.2 Install Microsoft Silverlight.

Exploring Silverlight 4 Demos

Now that Silverlight 4 is a little older, it is possible to see some nice samples on the web. To see these demos, you just need to install Silverlight 4 and to navigate to a URL.

Deep Zooming the Matterhorn

The Matterhorn Deep Zoom application was developed by Microsoft Switzerland to celebrate their 20th anniversary in Switzerland. It features multiple gigapixel pictures stitched together and processed in order to be rendered by the DeepZoom technology. We already talked about DeepZoom in Silverlight 2 Unleashed: A composer application prepares a large image by splitting it into a collection of tiles. Multiple resolutions of each tiles are prepared. When the image is loaded in the DeepZoom viewer (powered by Silverlight), the user can zoom in or out (for example using the mouse wheel or, if he has a supported multitouch screen, with a "pinch" gesture).

When the image is zoomed, the DeepZoom viewer dynamically loads the corresponding tiles from the server. To render the experience more dynamic for the user, the tiles are loaded at low resolution first, and then gradually the image is rendered with a finer grain until the maximum resolution is reached.

To start the Matterhorn DeepZoom application (shown in Figure 1.3), navigate to http://www.galasoft.ch/sl4-matterhorn. Clicking on the demo sets the application in full screen. Select one of the pictures and use the mouse's wheel to zoom in. Notice how the zoom action is smooth, and how the tiles, blurry at first, become sharper as more information is loaded by the application. More information about the pictures can be seen by clicking on the "info" button, which is a nice way to enrich a presentation.

FIGURE 1.3 The Matterhorn DeepZoom application.

Getting Involved Socially with Sobees

In today's World Wide Web, social networks have gained in popularity to become an unavoidable part of the browsing experience. Many people, however, do not use the social websites but prefer to use a rich aggregator instead. Sobees offer such applications for multiple platforms, including one built in Silverlight 4 and running either in the browser or installed out-of-the-browser. The Sobees application can be used to visualize entries from Twitter, Facebook, MySpace, and LinkedIn within one single window. It is also possible to perform multiple searches on Twitter.

To run the Sobees Silverlight application (shown in Figure 1.4), navigate to http://sobees.com/web. Follow the instructions to connect to the services that you want to aggregate. In order to install the application and run it like a normal Windows (or Mac) application, right click anywhere on the application's surface and select Install Sobees web alpha onto this computer. After confirming the operation, this creates a shortcut in your Start menu and/or on your desktop that you can use to run the application without starting the web browser.

FIGURE 1.4 Sobees Silverlight application.

Navigating with Bing Maps Streetside and PhotoSynth

Bing maps and the Streetside application are an interesting way to navigate geographical maps and to immerse yourself in a city, either to discover it in advance or to remember where your steps took you. Note that the "classic" Bing maps application uses standard web technologies; to get the Silverlight version, follow the URL: http://www.bing.com/maps/explore.

After the application is loaded, use the mouse wheel to zoom into the map. Note the smooth loading of details, powered by Silverlight. As you zoom in, the level of detail changes, and switches from map view to satellite view. This can be controlled using the "+" and "-" buttons on the bottom of the page (shown in Figure 1.5).

Two additional features are available in selected areas: Streetside and PhotoSynth.

Exploring the Streets with Streetside

The idea behind Bing maps Streetside is not new but Silverlight provides a very smooth and innovative experience. First, you need to locate a region where Streetside is enabled. Click the second button from the right in the controls at the bottom of the page, as shown in Figure 1.5. This adds a number of blue areas to the map. Use the zoom controls to dive into one of these areas (for example the city of Seattle in the USA).

FIGURE 1.5 Bing maps controls.

After entering the Streetside view, you can use the mouse to click around your location and navigate the available area. It is interesting to see how the pictures are deconstructed and reconstructed to provide an impression of speed as the view advances along the streets. It is also possible to press and hold the mouse to pan the picture around, and the mouse wheel to zoom in and out. For example, the Seattle Aquarium building is shown in Figure 1.6.

FIGURE 1.6 Bing maps Streetside in Seattle.

Discovering a Landscape with PhotoSynth

The PhotoSynth technology uses Silverlight to combine multiple pictures taken around a same object (building, monument, landscape, and so forth). To dive into a PhotoSynth from the Bing Maps viewer, look for a small icon as shown in Figure 1.7.

FIGURE 1.7 PhotoSynth icons.

Once the PhotoSynth viewer is started, use the mouse to click on the panes shown in Figure 1.8, in order to see a different view of the same object. The view is composed of multiple pictures stitched together automatically. Silverlight is used to smoothly pass from one picture to another, providing an impression of 3D as the viewer navigates around the object. For more information about PhotoSynth, refer to http://photosynth.net/.

FIGURE 1.8 PhotoSynth of the Statue of Liberty.

Visualizing Information with the Pivot Viewer

The Silverlight Pivot viewer is an innovative way to display large quantities of information and to sort it. Some examples start being published on the Web, for example the page at http://www.galasoft.ch/sl4-pivot which represents all the editions of MSDN magazine since 2000. Using links or a search box, you can refine the search as shown in Figure 1.9 and Figure 1.10.

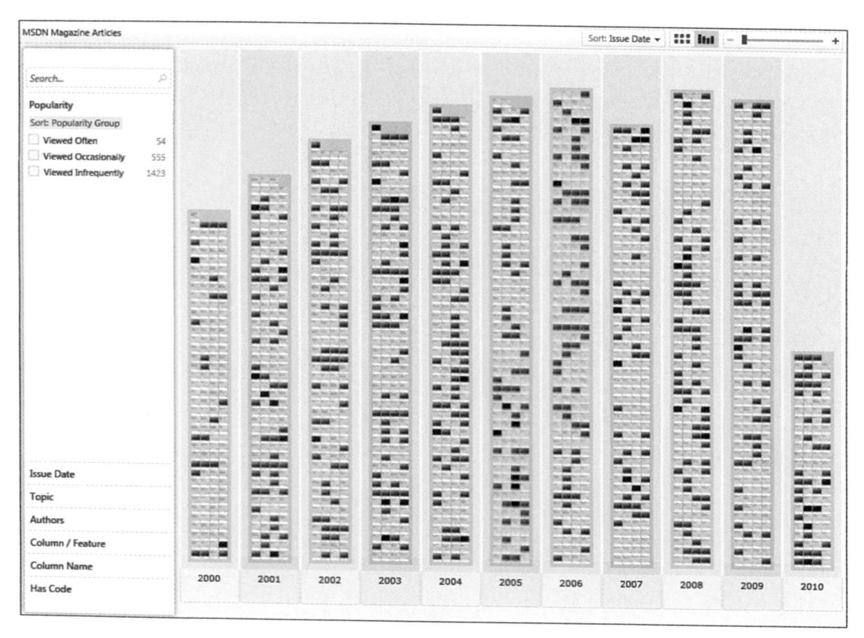

FIGURE 1.9 Pivot Viewer: All MSDN editions.

FIGURE 1.10 Pivot Viewer: MSDN editions by popularity, zoomed in.

The Pivot Viewer is but one possibility to represent information in a rich manner with Silverlight. In this book, we will work with data often and create rich connected business applications with Silverlight. The power of computation that Silverlight has over classic web solutions, as well as innovative representations such as shown in Figures 1.9 and 1.10 allow creating compelling experiences.

Drawing on the Web with Fantasia

The Fantasia drawing application demonstrates some advanced graphics features of Silverlight 4, such as using loading and modifying pictures, adding effects to a scene, opening pictures from Flickr directly, and saving the result as an image file locally on the computer. We will talk about many of these features, especially in Chapter 16, "Using Effects and Recording Media." The Fantasia drawing application shown in Figure 1.11 is a nice place to see all these in action, and to realize what advanced graphics features are included in this version of Silverlight. It is available at http://nokola.com/fantasia/.

FIGURE 1.11 The Fantasia Drawing Application.

How Can You Get Involved?

If you are (or want to become) an active Silverlight developer, there are ways to make yourself heard. You can collaborate with your local Microsoft development and platform evangelists, or participate in the forums at http://silverlight.net, the official home page of Silverlight, where you will get all the information needed to get started.

The Silverlight.net website (shown in Figure 1.12) is also where you will find even more information about Silverlight, compatibility, deployment tips, samples to help you get started, and so on.

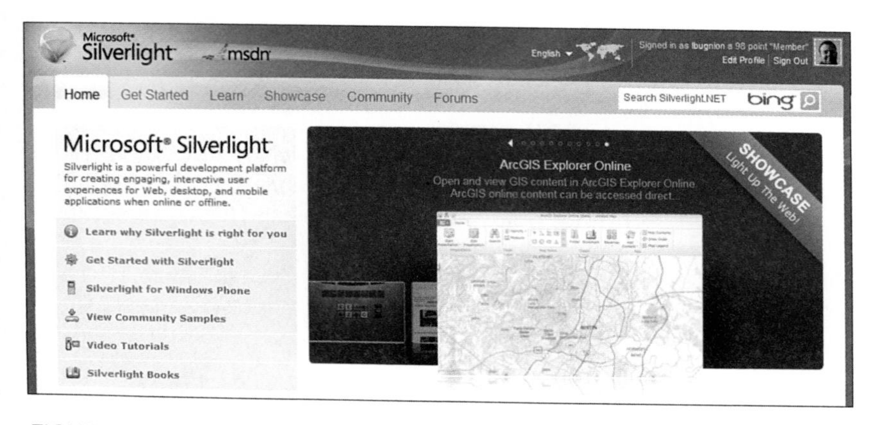

FIGURE 1.12 The Silverlight.net landing page.

Another great way to get involved in the Silverlight community is to participate in one of the many Silverlight user groups that have been created around the world. You can find more information about the Silverlight community at http://silverlight.net/community.

Finally, many Silverlight experts and members of the Microsoft Silverlight team are on Twitter. You will find their usernames at http://www.galasoft.ch/sl4-twittermvp and http://www.galasoft.ch/sl4-twittermsft.

Summary

This chapter explained what Silverlight has to offer for client application developers in terms of skills reuse (for .NET programmers) and cross-browser, cross-platform compatibility. We talked about a few alternative technologies, both in the web browser and outside. Then we saw how Silverlight evolved in the past few years to become Silverlight 4, and talked about the future. Finally, we installed Silverlight 4 (if it was not there already) and visited a few demos showing off some nice features available in the framework.

In the next chapter, we install the tools that we need to develop Silverlight applications, and take a tour of their features. This will be very important because we will spend many hours in those tools, both in this book and, should you like Silverlight, after you have finished reading.

CHAPTER 2

Setting Up and Discovering Your Environment

IN THIS CHAPTER, WE WILL:

- Install Visual Studio 2010 and the Silverlight tools for this Integrated Development Environment (IDE).
- Create a first Silverlight 4 application and inspect its files.
- Use the Visual Studio designer and understand the relationship between XAML and design.
- Install Expression Blend and use it to add an effect and an animation to the Silverlight application.

Before we start programming, we need to install and configure some tools. We will also take a short tour of the applications in which you are going to spend quite a lot of time while you read this book, and hopefully after you are done reading, too!

Installing Visual Studio

Nowadays, the line between design tool and development tool is a little more blurry than it used to be, with the addition of visual designers in Visual Studio and of code editors in Expression Blend. Still, some people tend to prefer one or the other for a given activity. The best is to try all the tools for yourself and to decide what you prefer depending on which activity you perform.

Visual Studio 2010

This is the (almost) unavoidable step for any .NET developer, and Silverlight is no exception. Installing Visual Studio will give you access to the full range of .NET technologies, server side and client side.

If you are an experienced developer in .NET, you probably already have Visual Studio installed on your PC. Unfortunately, it is not sure that you have the right version: You need Visual Studio 2010 to develop Silverlight 4.

Visual Studio can be downloaded from http://www.galasoft.ch/sl4-vs10.

If you have an MSDN subscription, Visual Studio is available to you as part of the subscription. Depending on your subscription, you might have a more- or less-elaborate version of Visual Studio, with more or fewer additional tools, but you don't need those to build Silverlight applications.

WARNING

Visual Studio 2010 Only

Silverlight 4 can be developed only in Visual Studio 2010, not in earlier versions. Note, however, that Visual Studio 2010 can be installed side by side with earlier versions without issues. Also, Visual Studio 2010 can be used to create and maintain applications in Silverlight 3 and in Silverlight 4.

Visual Web Developer Express

As with earlier versions of Silverlight, it is also possible to develop Silverlight 4 applications using the free edition of Visual Studio for the Web: Visual Web Developer Express. Of course, the free edition is more limited than the commercial one, but it provides a great place to start at no cost.

Visual Web Developer Express can be downloaded from this address: http://www.galasoft.ch/sl4-webexpress. In this book, we use Visual Studio 2010 for the samples, but you should be able to easily adapt the steps to Visual Web Developer Express.

TIP

Choosing a Programming Language

Silverlight can be programmed in Visual C# or in VB.NET. Depending on your past experiences, you may choose one or the other indistinctly. Other .NET languages are supported, too (for example, the dynamic languages IronPython and IronRuby).

Installing the Silverlight Tools for Visual Studio

Once Visual Studio (or the Express edition) is installed, you need additional tools for Silverlight 4 development, to be downloaded at http://www.galasoft.ch/sl4-tools (Silverlight 4 Tools for Visual Studio 2010).

These contain the following elements:

- **The Silverlight developer runtime**: This is a special version of the Silverlight plug-in that Visual Studio can attach a debugger to, to help you understand where issues come from, and to solve them.
- **New templates for Visual Studio**: These are used to create new projects and new items (pages, controls, classes, and so on) in your Silverlight application.

- **The Software Development Kit (SDK) for Silverlight**: This kit contains all the libraries you will need to create and deploy Silverlight applications, tools to create and package Silverlight application (for example, on a build server), and pointers to additional resources online such as the official Silverlight documentation.

After you have installed the Silverlight tools for Visual Studio, you are ready to create your first Silverlight application.

Verifying the Installation

The best way to verify the installation is to create a new Silverlight application. We will also use this opportunity to discover basic Silverlight-related functionality in the environment. Follow these steps:

1. Start Visual Studio 2010.
2. Select File, New, Project.
3. In the New Project dialog box, select the Silverlight category on the left, and create a new Silverlight Application named HelloSilverlight, as shown in Figure 2.1.

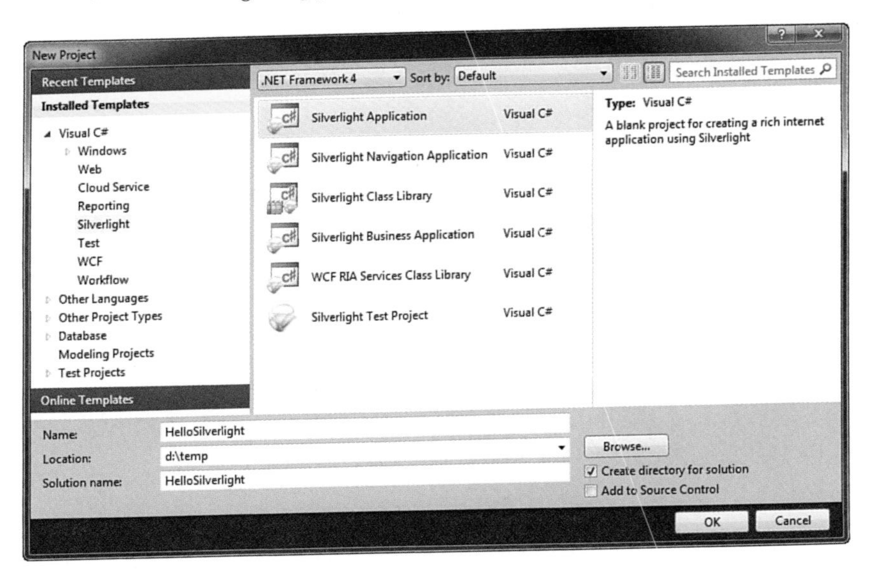

FIGURE 2.1 New Project dialog box.

4. In the next dialog box, shown in Figure 2.2, choose whether you want to create a new Web Application Project, a new ASP.NET Website, or a new ASP.NET MVC application to host the Silverlight application.

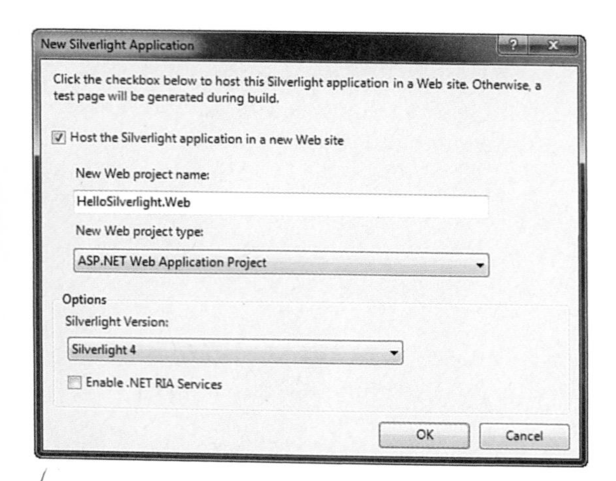

FIGURE 2.2 New Silverlight Application dialog box.

Choosing between web application project, website, or MVC application depends on what you want to achieve, personal preferences, what existing website you want to integrate your Silverlight application into, and so forth. The Silverlight application will be strictly the same, only the hosting web application will differ. The experience shows that web application projects are more flexible than ASP.NET websites, so this is what we will use in this book. ASP.NET MVC applications are also very interesting and offer a nice alternative to ASP.NET web applications. For more information about ASP.NET, check out the website at http://www.asp.net.

TIP

Creating a Web Project or Not

It is not compulsory to create a web project to host the Silverlight application. You can either create one later or attach your Silverlight application to an existing ASP.NET web project. You can also create the Silverlight application without any host, and run it from a simple HTML page. If you do not create a web project, Visual Studio and Blend will generate a test HTML page for you and open it in the web browser when you run the application.

To understand better what is happening, let's create a new web application project for this new application:

1. In the New Silverlight Application dialog box shown in Figure 2.2, check the first check box and make sure that ASP.NET Web Application Project is selected in the combo box. You can also enter a name for your web application and then click OK.
2. Make sure that Silverlight 4 is selected in the Silverlight Version combo box. Visual Studio 2010 allows creating Silverlight 3 applications without installing additional tools, and Silverlight 4 applications after you install the Silverlight tools for Visual Studio like we did earlier in this chapter.

3. Do not check the Enable .NET RIA Services check box for now. We cover this option in Chapter 13, "Creating Line-of-Business Applications."
4. Click OK.
5. To make sure that we have all the files ready, build the application by selecting Build, Build Solution from the menu.

Inspecting the Application

Based on the indications we gave, Visual Studio created two projects, as shown in Figure 2.3. It is indeed possible to mix Silverlight application and "full .NET" applications in a single solution.

Let's review the projects and the files:

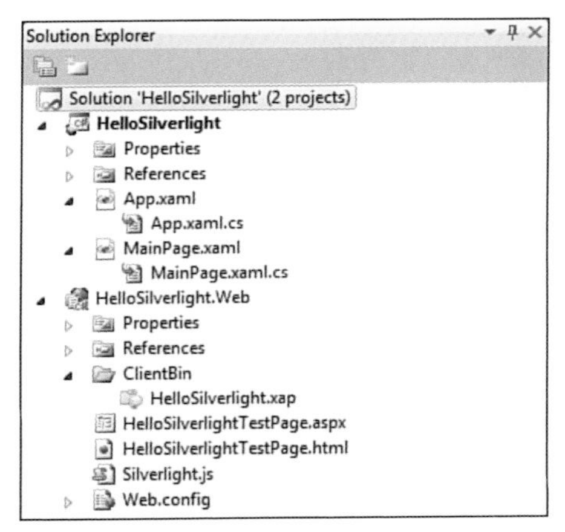

FIGURE 2.3 The created projects in the Solution Explorer.

- HelloSilverlight is the Silverlight application itself. It contains four important files:

  App.xaml and the attached App.xaml.cs contain the global application object, global event handlers, global resources, and so on. This is also the main entry point for the application.

  MainPage.xaml and the attached MainPage.xaml.cs are like the name indicates the main page for the application. You can have multiple pages in the application; the main page is the one that is created when the application starts.

- HelloSilverlight.Web is the web application, running on ASP.NET. It contains the files that will be downloaded to the web browser.
- ClientBin\HelloSilverlight.xap is a zip file with all the binary files needed to run the application in the plug-in (in our case, this is just HelloSilverlight.dll), and a file named AppManifest.xaml, called the application manifest. It contains information that the plug-in needs to start the application, as well as optional indication about the possibility to run the application out of the browser, and so forth.
- HelloSilverlightTestPage.aspx and HelloSilverlightTestPage.html are two generated test pages hosting the Silverlight application. If you open either file, you will see generated HTML and JavaScript code, including the `object` tag within which the Silverlight plug-in will run.
- Silverlight.js is a utility file with JavaScript functions that can be interesting to use within the HTML page. For example, there is a function helping you to check which version is installed on the client PC, and to react accordingly by alerting the user.

Unpacking an XAP File

If you want to look by yourself at the content of a XAP file, follow these steps:

1. Right-click the ClientBin folder in the Solution Explorer, and select Open folder in Windows Explorer from the context menu.
2. Make a copy of HelloSilverlight.xap and rename it to **HelloSilverlight.zip**.
3. If the operating system supports it (for example, in Windows 7), you can open the zip file just like any other folder and see the content.
4. On operating systems that do not support this function, you can use a zip tool to unpack the XAP file.

Note that if you want, you can recompress the XAP file with a higher level of compression and get smaller files to send to the web browser. The file will be transmitted faster, but it will take more time to unpack it to start the application.

Using the Visual Studio Designer

Open the file MainPage.xaml. If you didn't change the Visual Studio settings, you should now see some XAML code. XAML is an XML-based language used in Silverlight and Windows Presentation Foundation (WPF) to describe the user interface. There are other possible usages for XAML, and in fact it is really just a serialization language for .NET. If you want more information about XAML, you can refer to *Silverlight 2 Unleashed*, Chapters 2 and 3.

TIP

Opening in the Designer or in the Source Editor

By default, XAML files open in the Visual Studio designer. However, the designer takes some time to start. Many developers prefer to change the default by following these steps:

1. Right-click any XAML file.
2. Select Open With from the context menu.
3. In the Open With dialog box, choose Source Code (Text) Editor. If you want, you can set this as the default using the corresponding button.
4. Click OK.

Opening XAML files will be faster now, but you lose the designer functionality. To open a XAML file in the designer anyway, follow these steps:

1. Right-click the XAML file.
2. Select View Designer from the context menu.

With MainPage.xaml open in the designer, you should see tabs at the bottom, as shown in Figure 2.4.

On the other side of the bar, you will see three small buttons and a grip, as shown in Figure 2.5.

The buttons and the grip in Figure 2.5 and the tabs in Figure 2.4 are used to switch between XAML view and design view, or to split the editor window and have the XAML and the design on the same screen:

FIGURE 2.4 Bottom of the XAML editor.

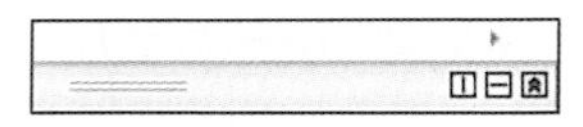

FIGURE 2.5 Grip and split buttons.

- Use the XAML tab to see the XAML code, and the Design tab to see the scene in the designer.
- Use the grip in Figure 2.5 to slide the separator up, and visualize the XAML code on top, and the design surface on the bottom.
- Using the buttons in Figure 2.5, you can split the editor vertically or horizontally and see the XAML and the design surface. The last button (with a double arrow) collapses or expands the design surface.

If you don't like to have the XAML on top, you can switch the XAML and the design surface by pressing the small button with two arrows located between the XAML tab and the Design tab, as shown in Figure 2.6. Note that this button is visible only when the window is split.

Another important element of the visual designer is the property editor. When one element is selected in the designer, the property editor shows all the element's properties that you can modify. You will learn how to use the property editor in the next section.

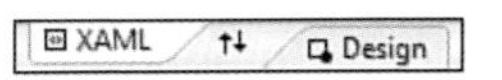

FIGURE 2.6 Switching XAML and Design view.

Implementing Hello Silverlight

To get to know Visual Studio a bit better, let's implement a simple application with the following steps:

1. Set a LinearGradientBrush in the main Grid by adding the XAML code from Listing 2.1 within the Grid tag. You must copy these lines between the opening tag <Grid x:Name="LayoutRoot"> and the closing tag </Grid>. You must also remove the Background property that was set in the Grid tag initially.

LISTING 2.1 Setting a *LinearGradientBrush*

```
<Grid.Background>
    <LinearGradientBrush StartPoint="0,0"
                         EndPoint="1,1">
        <GradientStop Offset="0"
```

```
                      Color="Red" />
        <GradientStop Offset="0.5"
                      Color="Red" />
        <GradientStop Offset="1"
                      Color="Orange" />
    </LinearGradientBrush>
</Grid.Background>
```

Checking the Properties Editor

If you are not quite sure what you are looking at and what a brush is in Silverlight, you can refer to *Silverlight 2 Unleashed*, Chapter 4.

With the visual designer open (in full-window or in split mode), you should now see the scene shown in Figure 2.7. In this figure, notice the bread crumb bar in the bottom, with the full path leading to the element that is selected in the XAML editor (in this case, the `LinearGradientBrush`). Passing your mouse on one of the elements in the path will display a small thumbnail of the element in question, which is very useful when you try to isolate a given element in a complex user interface.

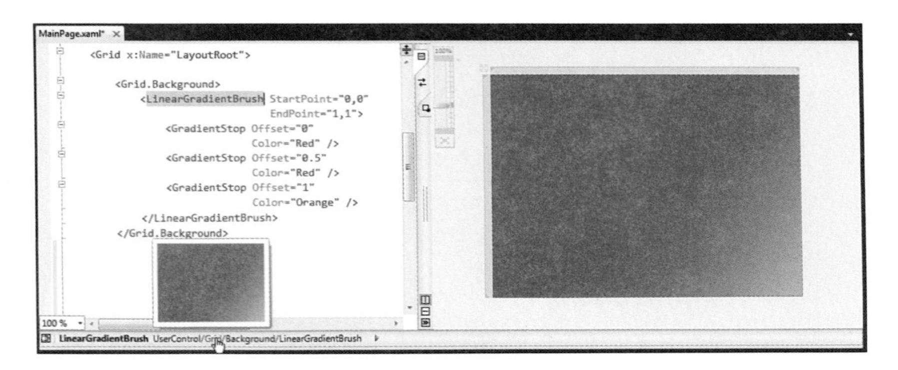

FIGURE 2.7 Grid background in the visual designer.

2. With the `LinearBackgroundBrush` selected in the XAML editor, press F4 (or select View, Properties Window from the Visual Studio menu).

3. You should now see all the properties of the brush in the Properties window, as in Figure 2.8; for example, notice the GradientStops collection, which define each "stop" where a color is applied. Silverlight then calculates the gradient between the different stops.

4. Click the small button shown in Figure 2.8 to open the GradientStops Collection Editor.

5. On the left of the Collection Editor, shown in Figure 2.9, select the GradientStop in the middle.

6. On the right, with the medium GradientStop selected, expand the Color property editor.

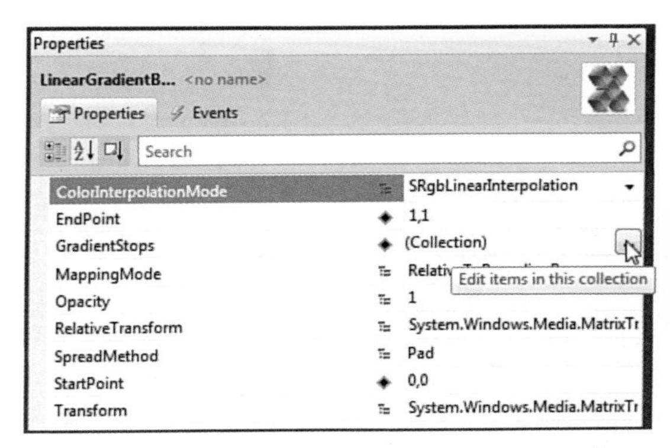

FIGURE 2.8 `LinearGradientBrush` properties.

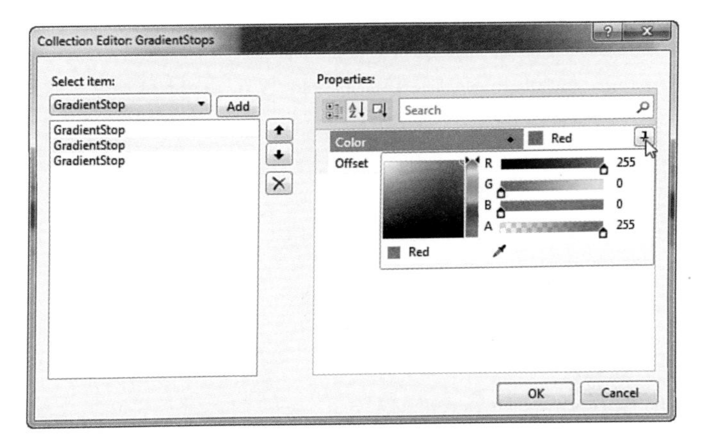

FIGURE 2.9 Collection Editor for the GradientStops collection.

7. Pick a new color for this gradient.

8. Using the Offset property, you can also move the gradient from the middle (it is now set at 0.5) to a different position.

9. Finally, using the Add button, you can set additional gradient stops with different colors, to create the brush that you desire.

There are many different ways to modify a property using the Properties editor, depending on the property's type. Everything you do in this editor is directly reflected in the XAML code. *There is nothing hidden*. Some developers prefer to edit the XAML markup, whereas others are more visual and prefer the property editor, or even Expression Blend that we will use later in this chapter. Most probably you will find yourself somewhere in the middle, and use both the XAML editor and the visual designer.

Finding a Property

When you have many properties in an element, it can be tough finding the correct one. Thankfully, the property editor helps you with the following functions:

- To sort the properties alphabetically and group them by category or by property source, use the small buttons on the left of the Search box in Figure 2.8.
- To look a property up, use the Search function. It is very useful because the search fragment may appear within the property name. For example, searching for the word *align* will show both the HorizontalAlignment and VerticalAlignment properties.

Creating Event Handlers

The Properties editor can also be used to create event handlers. To display all the events for a selected element, click the Events tab shown in Figure 2.8. In this case, we see all the events for the grid panel. Double-clicking in the field next to the event's name will add the event handler to the XAML code and implement the empty event handler in the code behind.

Alternatively, it is also possible to type the event name in XAML and use IntelliSense to create the event handler in the code behind automatically.

Adding Some Text

We will now add a text block to our scene by following the steps:

1. Make sure that the Toolbox is visible in Visual Studio. It should be visible on the far left of the Visual Studio window, just below the toolbars. If you do not see the Toolbox, select View, Toolbox from the menu.
2. If the Toolbox is collapsed, expand it by passing the mouse on the vertical Toolbox button, as shown on Figure 2.10.

> **WARNING**
>
> **Populating the Toolbox**
>
> It can take some time for the Toolbox to be populated with controls the first time that you expand it. If your Toolbox is empty when you expand it, give a little time to Visual Studio to scan the assemblies and add all the controls to it.

3. From the Common Silverlight Controls section in the Toolbox, drag a `TextBlock` and drop it on the grid in the visual designer.

4. With the new `TextBlock` selected, in the property editor, click the name textBlock1 just above the Properties and Events tabs. This allows you to edit the name. For now, we don't need a name for this text block, so you can just delete it.

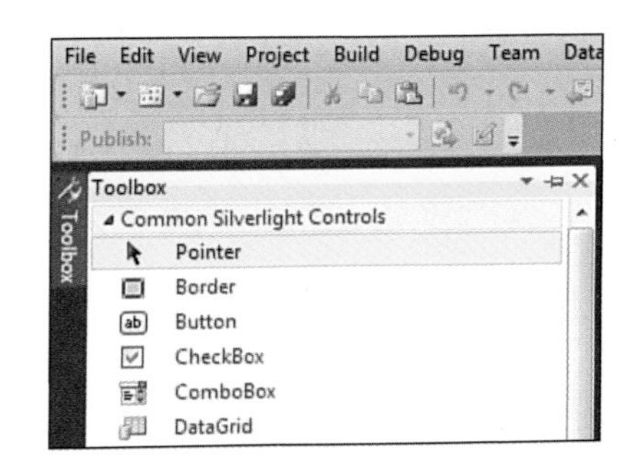

FIGURE 2.10 Toolbox.

TIP

Name, x:Name, or No Name

The `Name` property is available only on certain XAML elements. On the other hand, you can add `x:Name` to any element. (This is part of the eXtensibility in XAML.) Where available, the `Name` property is equivalent to the `x:Name` property.

Names are often not needed, except if the element is used in the code behind (for example, to set some properties programmatically). You also need a name if the element is the source of a binding, the target of an animation, and so forth. Names can be useful when you try to structure a very complex user interface with many nested elements. Adding a name will, however, have a small impact on performance, so it is recommended to avoid naming elements if possible.

If you do name an element, it is recommended to choose `x:Name` rather than just `Name`. Because `x:Name` is available everywhere, it brings more consistency to your XAML code.

5. Using the Properties editor or directly in XAML, find the `Text` property and set it to Hello Silverlight. Then change the following properties:

   - Set the `HorizontalAlignment` and `VerticalAlignment` properties to Center.
   - Set the `Margin` property to 0.
   - Set the `Width` and `Height` properties to Auto.
   - Set the `FontFamily` property to Verdana.
   - Set the `FontSize` to 72 and the `FontWeight` to Bold.
   - Finally, type **White** in the `Foreground` property.

After you complete these steps, you should see the image shown in Figure 2.11 in the visual designer.

TIP

Styles or Direct Values

In a real-world application, such formatting will be applied to an element using styles. You'll learn more about styles in Chapter 10, "Creating Resources, Styles, and Templates."

FIGURE 2.11 Text block with formatting.

Short Reminder About Colors in Silverlight

We talked a lot about colors in *Silverlight 2 Unleashed* (Chapter 5, "Using Media"). If you need to refresh your memory, you can check that chapter. Here is a quick reminder, though:

- Colors are coded in XAML using three or four hexadecimal numbers, each from 0 (#00) to 255 (#FF).
- The first two hexadecimal digits define the Alpha transparency of the color. #00 means that the color is completely transparent, and #FF completely opaque. These digits are optional. If they are omitted, the color is opaque.
- The second, third, and fourth positions define the Red, Green, and Blue channels. So, for example, the color blue is coded #FF0000FF (or #0000FF if you omit the Alpha channel).
- There is a large set of named colors available in Silverlight, using the same name as the named colors in HTML. There is a combo box below the color swatch that you can expand to show named colors, such as in Figure 2.12.

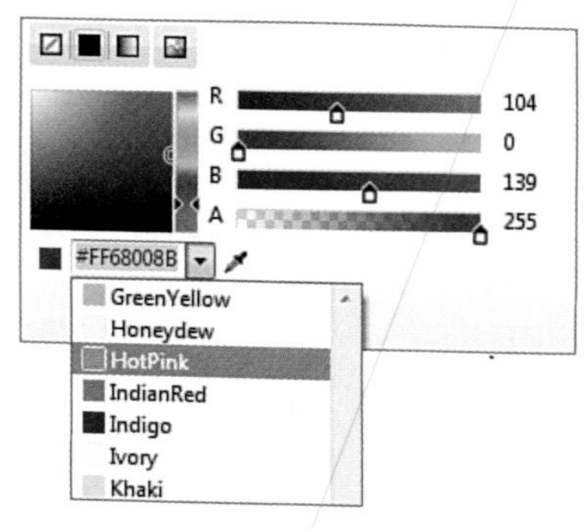

FIGURE 2.12 Named colors.

Using Design Time Width and Height

As you can see in Figure 2.11, the text block is too wide for the grid. In fact, neither the grid nor the `UserControl` containing it have any width and height. If you check these properties in the Properties editor, you will see that they are set to Auto, which is the default value. It means that the element will resize itself to fill the available space, depending on the size of its parent, on its content, on the alignment properties, and so forth.

In the application we are implementing now, because the user control does not have a size, it will take the size of the containing `object` tag in the HTML page. On the design surface in Visual Studio (and Expression Blend), however, there is no container, so the element would take the minimal size possible. In some cases, the automatic width and height can even be zero, which makes it impossible to design a background, for example.

To solve this problem, you can set the `DesignWidth` and `DesignHeight` properties in XAML. These two properties are defined (along with a few others) in the namespace assigned to the `d:` prefix in the current document.

The interesting thing with `d:` is that all these properties will be ignored when the application is running. They will be applied only on a design surface (for example, Visual Studio designer, or Expression Blend). This is a very convenient help for designers, who can visualize what they create without having to run the application. You'll see more examples of this in Chapter 11, "Mastering Expression Blend."

> **TIP**
>
> **Scrubbing Your XAML**
>
> The mechanism to ignore the attributes prefixed with `d:` involves two additional declarations: `xmlns:mc` and `mc:Ignorable`. If you decide not to use `d:DesignHeight` or `d:DesignWidth` (or any of the other `d:` attributes that we will talk about in this book), you can safely remove `xmlns:d`, `xmlns:mc`, and `mc:Ignorable` from your XAML code, as well as any attribute starting with the `d:` prefix.

To modify the design time width and height, you can either set these properties in the XAML code itself, or follow these steps:

1. Set the cursor in the `UserControl` tag in the XAML editor, or select the `UserControl` in the crumb bar.
2. There is a small icon indicating that the element is sized in design mode (Auto Size) or has a fixed width and height (Fixed Size), as shown in Figure 2.13.
3. Resize the `UserControl` in the designer. Switch from Auto Size to Fixed Size and back using the small icon, and observe the changes in the XAML code.

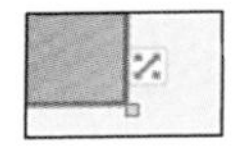
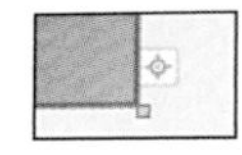

FIGURE 2.13 Auto Size and Fixed Size icons.

Saving the Application

In the next section, we use Expression Blend to refine the application and add movement to it. Because Expression Blend and Visual Studio work on the exact same files, it is important to remember to save all the files before you move from one environment to another.

The easiest way in Visual Studio to save all the files (including the project files) is by using File, Save All. Make sure that you remember where you saved the application, because we will extend it soon.

Installing Expression Blend

Blend is the tool used to visually design a Silverlight or WPF application. It is a very innovative tool, and might seem a little unusual to traditional software developers.

To develop Silverlight 4 (or WPF 4 for that matter), you will need the newest version of Blend, named Microsoft Expression Blend 4. You can download this version from the Blend website, http://www.microsoft.com/expression.

Note that there is currently no Express version of Expression Blend, only a commercial version is available. The price is $599 for a full version, part of a package called Expression Studio 4 Ultimate with a number of applications (including Expression Blend, Design, Web, and Encoder). If you have an MSDN Premium subscription, Expression Studio is included. If you work in a software development firm, you should check whether you have it already available!

WARNING

Blend 4 Only

Silverlight 4 can be developed only into *Microsoft Expression Blend 4*, and not in earlier versions. Note, however, that the latest can be installed side by side with earlier versions.

We take a quick tour of Expression Blend in this chapter, before diving deeper in Chapter 11.

Creating a New Silverlight Application

When you first start Expression Blend, you see the Welcome screen, as shown in Figure 2.14. This screen allows you to open an existing project or create a new one, to find some help before starting, or to open preinstalled samples. If you close the Welcome screen, you can always bring it back with Help, Welcome Screen.

The installed samples for Silverlight 4 are quite interesting because they help explain some of the capacities of Blend and of Silverlight. Don't hesitate to explore them. You can open any sample and run it by pressing F5 (or selecting Project, Run Project from the menu).

If you choose to create a new Silverlight 4 application, you must choose between a Silverlight 4 application (with or without website) and a Silverlight 4 control library, used to host controls that can be included in multiple applications. Just like in Visual Studio, selecting Silverlight 4 Application + Website will create an ASP.NET web application project with a link to the actual Silverlight application. Note, however, the following:

- In Expression Blend, you do not have the choice between ASP.NET Web Application, Website, or ASP.NET MVC.
- If you create a Silverlight application without a hosting website, you cannot add this application to another website in Blend. You also cannot create a new website in Blend without an attached Silverlight application.

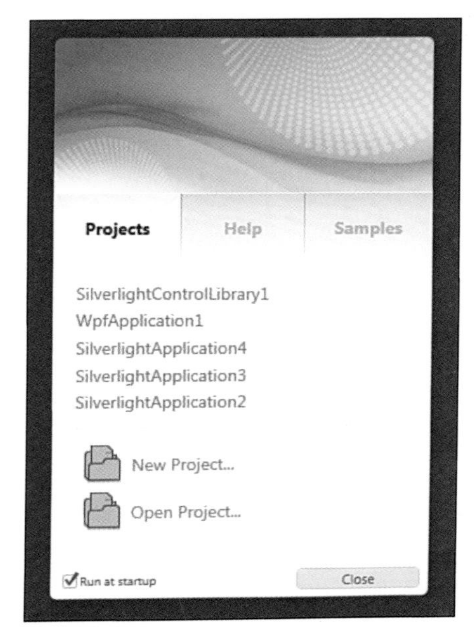

FIGURE 2.14 Expression Blend Welcome screen.

If you need more extended options when creating your application, you need to create it in Visual Studio. Because Expression Blend and Visual Studio use exactly the same solution files, project files, and code file, you can create an application in the environment of your choice and then modify it somewhere else. You can even open the projects in both environments at the same time, as you will see in Chapter 11 which is especially useful when you do design work on your application's screens.

Opening Hello Silverlight

We will refine our Hello Silverlight application and add some movement and effects. This is the perfect task for Expression Blend: Even though most of what you can do in Blend can also be done in Visual Studio (and vice versa), Blend is more suitable for design tasks, and Visual Studio for development tasks. It is really up to you to choose the tool that suits you the best.

To refine the application we created earlier in this chapter, follow these steps:

1. Select Open Project from the Welcome screen shown in Figure 2.14, or with choose File, Open Project/Solution from the menu.
2. Navigate to the folder in which you last saved the Hello Silverlight application.
3. Select the solution file HelloSilverlight.sln and open it in Blend.

Using Shortcuts to Open a Solution in Blend from Visual Studio

This way of opening an application is a bit slow, and there are ways to speed things up, by selecting one of the alternatives:

- In Visual Studio, right-click a XAML file, and select Open in Expression Blend from the context menu. This will start Blend and open the solution.

> **WARNING**
>
> **Choosing the Right Version**
>
> If you have Blend 3 and 4 installed side by side, chances are that the Open in Expression Blend context menu will pick the wrong version. In some cases, the menu might even be missing altogether. To correct this, refer to Tim Heuer's blog: http://www.galasoft.ch/sl4-integration.

- Right-click the solution in the Solution Explorer, and select Open Folder in Windows Explorer. Then in Windows Explorer, right-click the solution HelloSilverlight.sln and select Open With, Microsoft Expression Blend 4 from the Windows Explorer context menu.

Using Shortcuts to Open a Solution in Visual Studio from Blend

The same shortcut exists from Expression Blend, too: In Expression Blend, right-click the solution file, any project file, or any code file in the Projects panel, and select Edit in Visual Studio from the context menu.

After opening the solution and MainPage.xaml in Blend, you should be now seeing the exact same scene as in Visual Studio's designer. Only a few adorners are different. The design time width (`d:DesignWidth`) and height (`d:DesignHeight`) are also honored in Expression Blend!

Adding an Effect

We will now add a shadow effect to the Hello Silverlight text block. To do this, follow these steps:

1. Locate the `TextBlock` in the Objects and Timeline panel. This panel displays the tree of all the elements on the page, as shown in Figure 2.15: The `UserControl` (the page) contains a `Grid`, which contains a `TextBlock`.

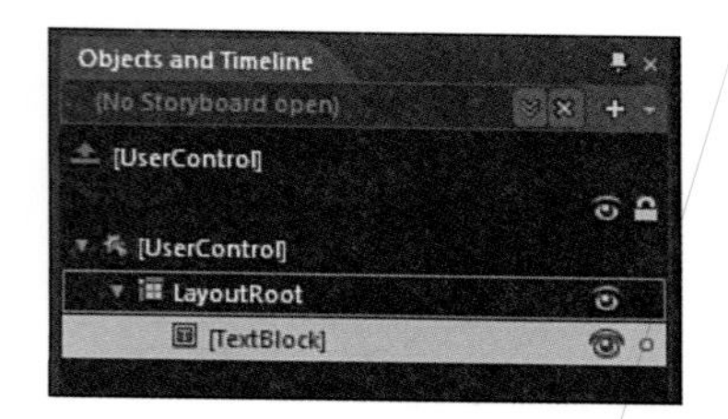

FIGURE 2.15 The elements tree.

2. Select the `TextBlock` and then copy and paste it. You can use the context menu for that, or Ctrl+C, Ctrl+V.

3. Click twice slowly on the first `TextBlock` in the tree to make its name editable, and change the name to **Shadow**.

> **TIP**
>
> **Working in Blend, Working in XAML**
>
> Just as with the Visual Studio designer, everything we do in Blend is immediately reflected in the XAML code: Open the page in split mode, using the Split button located on the top right of the main panel, as show in Figure 2.16. Then press Ctrl+Z to cancel the last operation, and then Ctrl+Y to repeat it. Observe how the XAML code is modified by Blend.

You should now see two text blocks in the Objects and Timeline panel: One is named Shadow, and the second doesn't have a name. However, both have exactly the same features, and therefore the front one is hiding the back one in the designer. Let's change this with the next steps:

FIGURE 2.16 Using the Split button.

> **TIP**
>
> **Understanding the Z-Order**
>
> Because the order in the tree reflects the order in which objects appear in the document, the Shadow (higher in the tree) appears behind the nameless `TextBlock`.

1. Select the Shadow element in the Objects and Timeline panel.
2. Make sure that the Properties panel is selected on the right side of the window, and using the brush editor, change the Shadow's foreground to black, as shown on Figure 2.17.
3. On the left of Blend's window, you should see the tabs Projects, Assets, States, and Parts. You'll learn more about all the panels in Chapter 11. For now, select the Assets tab. This is where you will find all the controls and effects that we can use in Silverlight.

FIGURE 2.17 Solid color brush editor.

4. Select the Effects category. You will see the two built-in effects in Silverlight 4: `Blur` and `DropShadow`.

TIP

Loading Additional Effects, Performance

Effects in Silverlight 4 are rendered by small components called *pixel shaders*. Although the default installation of Silverlight contains only two effects, you can find more online and add them to your application, as you will see in Chapter 16 "Using Effects and Recording Media."

For this effect, we will use a `Blur` effect applied to the `TextBlock` in the background. Note that we could also use the `DropShadow` effect available in Blend. However the `DropShadow` effect is slower than the `Blur` effect; if you can, it is recommended to use a `Blur` effect instead, as we do here.

5. Select the `Blur` effect and drag/drop it with the mouse on the Shadow `TextBlock` in the Objects and Timeline panel, as in Figure 2.18.
6. With the `BlurEffect` selected in the Objects and Timeline panel, check the Properties panel on the right of the window, and set the `Radius` property to 40. You should now see a shadow right behind the Hello Silverlight `TextBlock`.

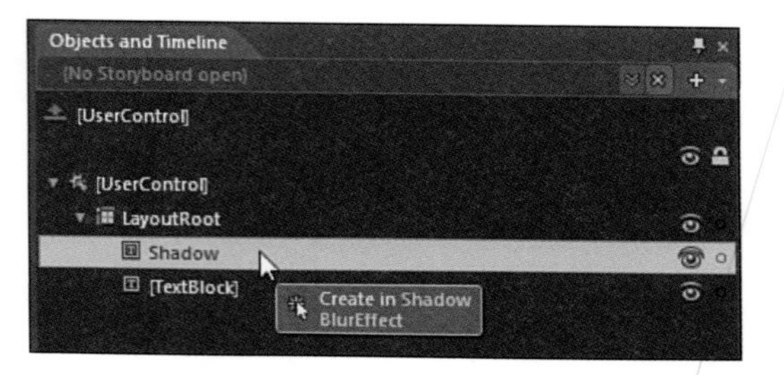

FIGURE 2.18 Dragging and dropping the blur effect.

Creating a Pulse Animation

We will now add some movement to the scene, by animating the Shadow when the `TextBlock` is clicked. Follow these steps:

1. In the Objects and Timeline panel shown in Figure 2.18, click the small plus sign (+) located on the top right of the panel to create a new storyboard.
2. In the Create Storyboard Resource dialog, name the storyboard **ShadowStoryboard**.
3. Notice how Blend turns in animation recording mode, with a red border signifying that the actions you perform now on the scene will be part of the storyboard.

TIP

More About Storyboards and Animations

For more information about storyboards and animations, you can jump into Chapter 3 of *Silverlight 2 Unleashed*.

4. Move the yellow vertical line (called the timeline) to 500 milliseconds, as shown in Figure 2.19.
5. Select the Shadow `TextBlock`.

6. Click the Record Keyframe button. This button is circled in orange in Figure 2.19.

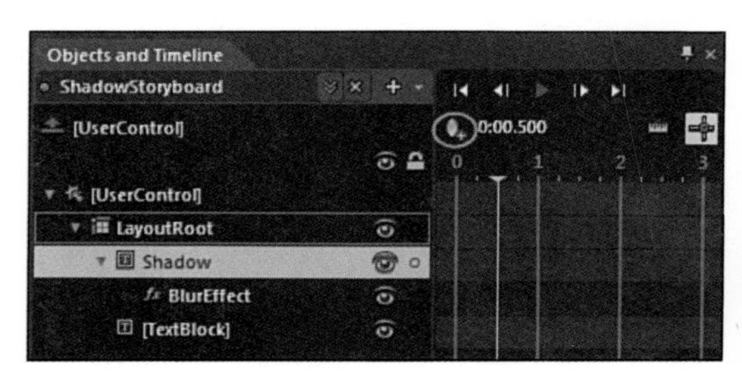

FIGURE 2.19 Recording a timeline.

This operation is adding a keyframe to the Silverlight scene at 500 milliseconds after the start of the storyboard. Now we need to modify the scene with the next steps to tell Silverlight what the user should see during these 500 milliseconds. We will also set a few properties on the storyboard itself. Silverlight will calculate the smooth transition to apply:

1. With the Shadow `TextBlock` selected, set the `Opacity` property to 0% in the Properties editor.
2. Click the name ShadowStoryboard in the Objects and Timeline panel. You should now see the storyboard's properties in the Properties panel.
3. Check the AutoReverse check box. This means that the storyboard will reverse automatically after 500 milliseconds and restore the scene to the original state.
4. Finally, set the `RepeatBehavior` to 3x. This means that the storyboard will run three times when triggered. Possible values are 1x, 2x, 3x, 4x, and so on. You can also enter **Forever**, meaning that the storyboard will never stop.
5. Close the storyboard by clicking on the small X button on the right of the name ShadowStoryboard.

Triggering the Storyboard

Now it's time to trigger the storyboard and to test it in the web browser. To do this, we will handle an event in C# code with the following steps:

1. Select the `TextBlock` in front of the scene (the one with no name).
2. To notify the user that something will happen if he clicks the `TextBlock`, set the `Cursor` property to Hand.
3. In the Properties editor, click the Events button, shown in Figure 2.20 (circled in orange). This displays the list of all the events for the `TextBlock` control.

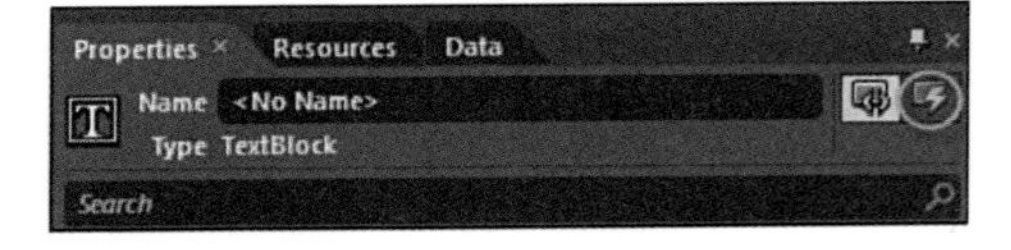

FIGURE 2.20 The Events button in the Properties editor.

4. Double-click in the field next to the name MouseLeftButtonDown. This event will be triggered when the user presses the mouse's left button on the `TextBlock` control. Depending on your settings, this opens a C# code file in Expression Blend's code editor, or in Visual Studio. You'll learn more about Blend options in Chapter 11. This code file is named the *code behind* file, and this is the location where event handlers and other methods for the Silverlight page are implemented.

The double-click action you performed in step 4 added a new event handler to the code file, named `TextBlock_MouseLeftButtonDown`. Modify this event handler as shown in Listing 2.2.

Listing 2.2 Implementing the Event Handler

```
1  private void TextBlock_MouseLeftButtonDown(
2    object sender,
3    MouseButtonEventArgs e)
4  {
5    var storyboard
6      = this.Resources["ShadowStoryboard"] as Storyboard;
7    if (storyboard != null)
8    {
9      storyboard.Begin();
10   }
11 }
```

- On lines 5 and 6, we get the storyboard we just created in Expression Blend from the resources. You'll learn more about resources in Chapter 10. If you check the file MainPage.xaml, you will see that Blend did create the storyboard within the `UserControl.Resources` section.
- Because the objects in the resources are stored with a type of `object`, we need to *cast* the object back to a `Storyboard` class, telling the compiler that we expect this object to be of this type, and that we will use the `Storyboard` methods and properties. This is what line 6 does.
- Finally, we check if the `Storyboard` has been found and cast properly on line 7, and then we start it on line 9 by calling the `Begin` method.

Testing the Application

Now it's time to run and test the application. You can do this in Expression Blend by pressing the F5 key (or selecting Project, Run Project from the menu); you can also do this in Visual Studio by pressing Ctrl+F5 (or selecting Debug, Start Without Debugging). If everything goes well, your default web browser should start, and you will see Hello Silverlight.

Pass your mouse over this text block (it should turn into a Hand cursor) and press the left mouse button. Observe how the shadow below the text block animates smoothly three times.

Summary

In this chapter, you saw how to install Visual Studio and Expression Blend, and how to start developing a simple Silverlight application. You will spend a lot of time in Visual Studio, so it is important to set it up correctly and to understand its features. For those interested in pushing the design of your application further than what the Visual Studio designer allows, Expression Blend is the perfect tool.

This chapter also got you started with a Silverlight application, and showed that creating a rich application using gradients, effects, and animations is quite simple with the right tools.

The next chapters cover Silverlight controls, especially the new controls (and related features) added in Silverlight 3 and 4. These are the building blocks for your application, and a good understanding of these elements is vital.

CHAPTER 3

Extending Your Application with Controls

IN THIS CHAPTER, WE WILL:

- Extend XAML documents with namespaces from the application.
- Understand what a user control is, and how they are created and used in Visual Studio and in Blend.
- Understand what a custom control is, what the parts and states are, and how templates are "wired" to the control.

Controls are the fundamental building blocks of your Silverlight 4 application. It is hard to imagine any user interface framework without a rich control set nowadays. In fact, we sometimes talk about "control ecosystem," because, as you will see in this chapter, in addition to the controls that are built in to the framework, multiple providers are offering controls for the Silverlight framework.

Extending XAML

One great feature of XML that also applies to XAML is its extensibility. This is in fact what the *X* in XML and XAML stand for (XAML means eXtensible Application Markup Language). Thus it is possible to import external elements into a document without breaking rules.

Mapping a Prefix to a CLR Namespace

Extensibility works in XML by defining a set of XML namespaces (`xmlns`). You can *map* a unique identifier to a prefix, thus notifying the XML parser that additional rules must be used when loading this document. Let's take a look at a simple example to illustrate this.

TIP

CLR Namespace and `xmlns`

When working in XAML, you are confronted with two different concepts: Common Language Runtime (CLR) namespaces and XML namespaces.

- CLR namespaces are used in .NET code (for example, C# or VB.NET) to group classes that logically belong together.
- XML namespaces (`xmlns`) are used to extend an XML document (in this case, XAML) with additional declarations.

In this book, we consistently talk about XML namespaces and CLR namespaces to try and reduce the confusion.

Let's imagine that you want to place a `Double` value in the document's resources. Because XAML is by default configured for user interface elements, the default XML namespaces do not map to the `Double` type. We need to import this type in the document by creating a new `xmlns` statement, with the following steps:

1. Create a new Silverlight application in Visual Studio and name it **DoubleInResources**.
2. Open MainPage.xaml.
3. In the `UserControl` tag (the root tag), add an `xmlns` statement mapping the prefix `sys` to the CLR namespace `System` in the assembly `mscorlib`. This assembly and this namespace are where the `Double` type is defined in .NET. The syntax to import this namespace and assembly is shown in Listing 3.1. The prefix you choose is free, but it must be unique within the XAML document, and must comply with the XML naming rules. (For example, there may not be a space or a period within such a prefix.)
4. Notice how Visual Studio helps you with IntelliSense: When you type the equals sign (=), quotes are added for you and a list of all the .NET namespaces defined in the application and in the referenced assemblies is proposed, as shown in Figure 3.1. This is very helpful because the syntax used to reference .NET namespaces in external assemblies is a bit difficult to remember.

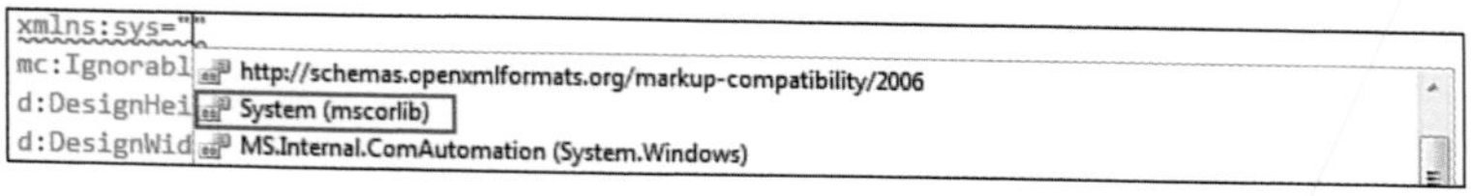

```
xmlns:sys=""
mc:Ignorabl   http://schemas.openxmlformats.org/markup-compatibility/2006
d:DesignHei   System (mscorlib)
d:DesignWid   MS.Internal.ComAutomation (System.Windows)
```

FIGURE 3.1 Adding a new `xmlns` statement with IntelliSense.

TIP

How to Find a .NET Type?

If you are not sure in which assembly and namespace a .NET type is defined, you will find this information on MSDN. For the `Double` type, point your web browser to http://www.galasoft.ch/sl4-typedoc. On top of this page, notice the lines pointing to the namespace (System) and the assembly (mscorlib).

`Double` is actually a structure and not a class, but both can be imported in XAML.

5. Add a `Double` value to the `UserControl`'s resources as shown in Listing 3.1, so that we can use that value from the XAML document. The resources are like a store for objects that can be reused later. You'll learn more about resources in Chapter 10 "Creating Resources, Styles, and Templates." They must be added within the `UserControl` tag, just before the `Grid` tag.

6. Finally, add a `Button` within the main `Grid` that uses the `Double` value from the resources.

LISTING 3.1 Adding a `Double` value to Resources and Using It

```
<UserControl
    x:Class="DoubleInResources.MainPage"
    xmlns="http://schemas.microsoft.com/winfx/2006/xaml/presentation"
    xmlns:x="http://schemas.microsoft.com/winfx/2006/xaml"
    xmlns:d="http://schemas.microsoft.com/expression/blend/2008"
    xmlns:mc="http://schemas.openxmlformats.org/markup-compatibility/2006"
    xmlns:sys="clr-namespace:System;assembly=mscorlib"
    mc:Ignorable="d"
    d:DesignHeight="300"
    d:DesignWidth="400">

    <UserControl.Resources>
        <sys:Double x:Key="ButtonsWidth">200</sys:Double>
    </UserControl.Resources>

    <Grid x:Name="LayoutRoot"
          Background="White">

        <Button Width="{StaticResource ButtonsWidth}"
                Content="Click me" />

    </Grid>
</UserControl>
```

Why Is a Prefix Not Always Needed?

Silverlight elements are defined into two namespaces. The first one is a Unique Resource Identifier (URI) mapped to the default `xmlns` (http://schemas.microsoft.com/winfx/2006/xaml/presentation).

In fact, multiple CLR namespaces (such as System.Windows.Controls, System.Windows.Shapes, and so on) are mapped to this URI. This allows us to use all the types within these namespaces without having to use a prefix. For example, we write `<Button Click="Button_Click" />` and not `<anyPrefix:Button Click="Button_Click" />`. Note that this URI is not a website's address, and entering it into a web browser will not lead you anywhere. It is just a Unique Resource Identifier, a unique name.

The other namespace used by Silverlight by default is http://schemas.microsoft.com/winfx/2006/xaml, another URI, which is mapped to the `x` prefix. Inside this namespace are defined additional properties that can be applied to any element. We already used the `x:Name` property in Chapter 2, "Setting Up and Discovering Your Environment."

Adding a Namespace to Any Element

In the example in Listing 3.1, we added the `xmlns:sys` mapping to the `UserControl` tag. In fact, you can add such a mapping to any element in your XAML code. For example, Listing 3.2 shows an `xmlns` mapping added to a `Button` tag.

LISTING 3.2 Adding an `xmlns` Mapping to a Local Element

```
<UserControl x:Class="MyApplication.MainPage"
             xmlns="http://schemas.microsoft.com/winfx/2006/xaml/presentation"
             xmlns:x="http://schemas.microsoft.com/winfx/2006/xaml">

    <StackPanel x:Name="LayoutRoot">

        <Button xmlns:controls="clr-namespace:MyApplication.Controls">
            <controls:MyControl />
        </Button>

    </StackPanel>
</UserControl>
```

Defining Your Own URI and Mapping CLR Namespaces

You can, if you want, map your own URI to a group of namespaces. This is useful because you can consolidate multiple CLR namespaces into one single URI, and also because it hides the CLR namespaces that your code is using. If you decide to refactor your application and move some classes to different CLR namespaces, you don't need to change the XAML code. Also, for companies, it brings your brand into the XAML code. To do this, follow these steps:

1. Open the file AssemblyInfo.cs. This file stores global information about the project, such as the title, copyright, version number, and so forth.
2. At the bottom of the file, add an `XmlnsDefinition` attribute mapping your URI to one CLR namespace, as shown in Listing 3.3. If you want, you can add multiple `XmlnsDefinition` attributes to map multiple namespaces to one or more URIs.
3. Build your application.
4. Then, in the XAML code, when you enter a new `xmlns:prefix` statement, you should now see the URI in the list of possible choices, as shown on Figure 3.2.

LISTING 3.3 Mapping CLR Namespaces to a URI

```
[assembly: XmlnsDefinition(
    "http://www.mycompany.com",
    "DoubleInResources")]
[assembly: XmlnsDefinition(
    "http://www.mycompany.com",
    "DoubleInResources.Controls")]
[assembly: XmlnsDefinition(
    "http://www.mycompany.com",
    "DoubleInResources.DataAccess")]
```

Importing CLR namespaces into your XAML document is very useful, and we will do this often. In this chapter, we use this feature to import new controls in our user interface. Later, we use it to create data objects and make data binding easier.

FIGURE 3.2 The new URI in IntelliSense.

What's a Control?

A control is an element of software encapsulating some functionality related to user interface. In Silverlight, there are two kinds of controls: user controls and custom controls.

User Controls

A *user control* is a logical group of other controls. It is typically used to separate a user interface in smaller parts that are easier to code and design. In fact, in Silverlight, all the pages of an application are user controls, as the following steps prove:

1. Create a new Silverlight 4 application in Visual Studio. For these simple examples, you do not need to create a web project to host the application.
2. Open the file MainPage.xaml. The page starts with the XAML code shown in Listing 3.4. Notice that the tag used for this page is `UserControl`.

3. Open the file MainPage.xaml.cs (the main page's code behind). Notice that the class `MainPage` derives from `UserControl`, as shown in Listing 3.5.

LISTING 3.4 UserControl Tag in MainPage.xaml

```
<UserControl x:Class="SilverlightApplication1.MainPage"
    xmlns="http://schemas.microsoft.com/winfx/2006/xaml/presentation"
    xmlns:x="http://schemas.microsoft.com/winfx/2006/xaml"
    xmlns:d="http://schemas.microsoft.com/expression/blend/2008"
    xmlns:mc="http://schemas.openxmlformats.org/markup-compatibility/2006"
    mc:Ignorable="d"
    d:DesignHeight="300" d:DesignWidth="400">
```

LISTING 3.5 MainPage Declaration in MainPage.xaml.cs

```
public partial class MainPage : UserControl
{
    public MainPage()
    {
        InitializeComponent();
    }
}
```

As mentioned earlier, the `App` class (defined in App.xaml and App.xaml.cs) is the main point of entry for the Silverlight application. This is also where the `MainPage` control is created and assigned, as you can see with the following steps:

4. In the Silverlight application we created in Step 1, open the file App.xaml.cs.

5. Check the event handler named `Application_Startup`. This method is executed when the application is loaded and ready to start. The implementation (provided in Listing 3.6) is very simple by default, and consists only of the creation of the `MainPage` user control and its assignment to the application's `RootVisual` property.

LISTING 3.6 Application_Startup Event Handler in App.xaml.cs

```
private void Application_Startup(object sender, StartupEventArgs e)
{
    this.RootVisual = new MainPage();
}
```

TIP

Renaming the `MainPage`

If you rename the `MainPage` control to a different name, you must also change the name in the `RootVisual` assignment, or else your application will not compile anymore. Thankfully, Visual Studio assists you in renaming objects with the Refactor menu.

WARNING

Assign RootVisual Only Once!

The `RootVisual` property can be set only once during the lifetime of the application. If you want to replace the scene with another one while the application is running, you must use other techniques, as you will see in Chapter 15, "Developing Navigation Applications and Silverlight for Windows Phone 7."

Creating a New `UserControl` in Expression Blend

Apart from splitting a complex user interface into multiple parts, creating a logical separation and making maintenance easier, user controls can also be reused at multiple locations in your application. This is an *encapsulation of functionality*. Properties and methods can be added to create additional functionality or to define variations between two instances of the same user control.

If you have Expression Blend, creating a new user control is very easy with the following steps:

1. Create a new Silverlight application in Expression Blend and name it NewUserControl. Here, too, you do not need to create a website to host your application.

2. With MainPage.xaml open, and `LayoutRoot` selected in the Objects and Timeline panel, add a button to the design surface. The `Button` control can be added from the toolbar at the far left of Blend's window.

3. Add other controls to the design surface from the toolbar. Note that additional controls can be revealed by pressing and holding some of the toolbar's buttons.

4. If you are not finding the control that you are looking for in the toolbar, check the Controls category in the Assets tab. Make sure to expand the Controls category to see all the available controls.

5. On the design surface, select all the controls that you want to "pack" in a user control. To select multiple controls, press the Ctrl key and click the controls on the design surface or in the Objects and Timeline panel. Figure 3.3 shows a `PasswordBox`, a `ComboBox`, and a `RadioButton` being selected. The `TextBlock` and the `Button` in Figure 3.3 are not selected.

6. Right-click one of the selected controls and select Make Into UserControl from the context menu, or select Tools, Make Into UserControl from Blend's menu bar.

7. In the next dialog box, enter a name for your user control and click OK.

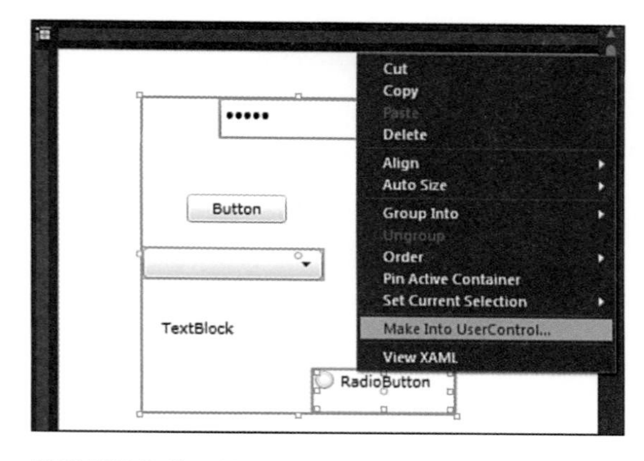

FIGURE 3.3 Making a `UserControl` in Blend.

Steps 1 through 7 create two new files into your project: one XAML file (the front end) and one code file (the code behind). In addition, this process adds one instance of the new `UserControl` to the `MainPage`. If you open MainPage.xaml in Blend again, you will see that the controls you selected are still there, although an orange border and an exclamation mark warn you that something is not correct (as shown in Figure 3.4). Let's correct that and investigate some more with the following steps:

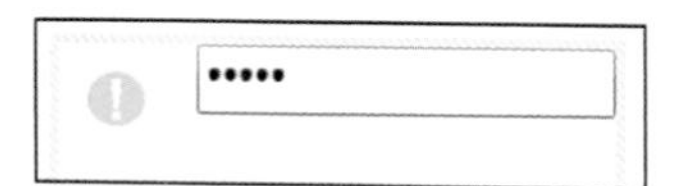

FIGURE 3.4 Uncompiled `UserControl`.

8. The orange border shown in Figure 3.4 indicates that the `UserControl` cannot be found in the application. This is correct, because even though it has been created, the application has not been built since then, and the control doesn't exist in any assembly. Build the application to correct this using Project, Build Project.

9. Pass your mouse over the group of controls. A blue border appears, marking the limits of the new `UserControl`.

10. Drag the new `UserControl` to a different location on the design surface. Notice how only the controls that we selected earlier in Step 5 move. They belong to the `UserControl`. The other controls are not part of the `UserControl`, and they do not move.

Adding a New `UserControl` in Expression Blend

As previously mentioned, the `UserControl` is not just grouping controls; it is also a way to duplicate functionality. You can add multiple instances of a `UserControl` to your scene by following these steps:

1. In the Assets tab, select the Project category. This contains all the assets that are included into your own application.

2. Select the `UserControl` you created in the previous section, and drag it onto the design surface.
3. Notice how an additional instance of the same `UserControl` has been added in the Objects and Timeline panel.

Of course, a `UserControl` created this way needs additional work: The layout is likely to be messed up when the control is resized. The steps described here, however, are a convenient way to create the new files and move the selected controls within.

Creating a New `UserControl` in Visual Studio

In Visual Studio, follow these steps to create a new `UserControl`:

1. Create a new Silverlight application named **NewUserControlVS** in Visual Studio.
2. Right-click the Silverlight project in the Solution Explorer.
3. Select Add, New Item from the context menu.
4. In the Add New Item dialog box, select the Silverlight category (under Installed Templates).
5. Select a Silverlight `UserControl`, enter a name (for example, MyNewUserControl.xaml), and click Add. This creates a new `UserControl` and its code behind file.
6. Open the file MyNewUserControl.xaml (either in the XAML editor or in the visual designer) and add a new button into the main grid. Set the button's margin to 20 pixels and leave all the other properties at their default. This will cause the button to be resized to occupy the whole grid's space, minus 20 pixels on each side. You can use the Properties editor to set the `Margin` property (as shown in Figure 3.5), or set it directly in XAML.

TIP

The `Thickness` Type

The `Margin` property is of type `Thickness`. This type is used for other properties, too, such as `BorderThickness`, `Padding`, and so forth. To enter a `Thickness` in XAML, define the left value first, and then the top, right, and bottom values (for example, `Margin="10,20,10,40"`). You can also specify the same value for all four sides (for example, `Margin="10"`) or the same value for left and right, and another value for top and bottom (for example, `Margin="10,20"`).

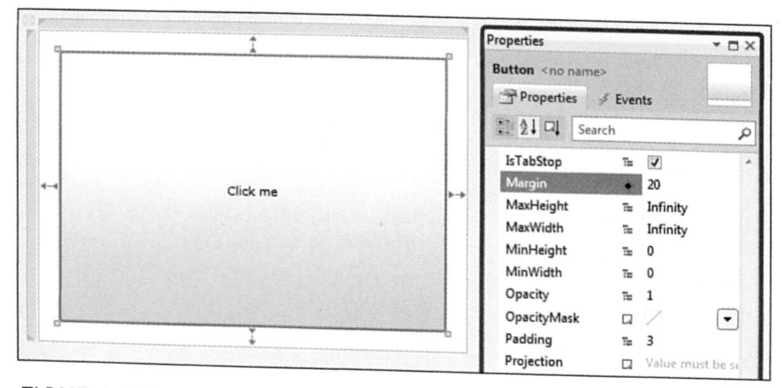

FIGURE 3.5 Setting the button's `Margin` property.

Now that the new `UserControl` is defined, you can use it in your main page, either in the visual designer or in XAML, as you will see in the next two sections.

Adding a New `UserControl` in Visual Studio

After you have created your new `UserControl`, you need to build your application by selecting Build, Build Solution from the menu. If the build is successful, the new `UserControl` will appear in the Toolbox, as shown in Figure 3.6. You can then drag it on the main grid (in the visual designer), which will create all the XAML code that you need.

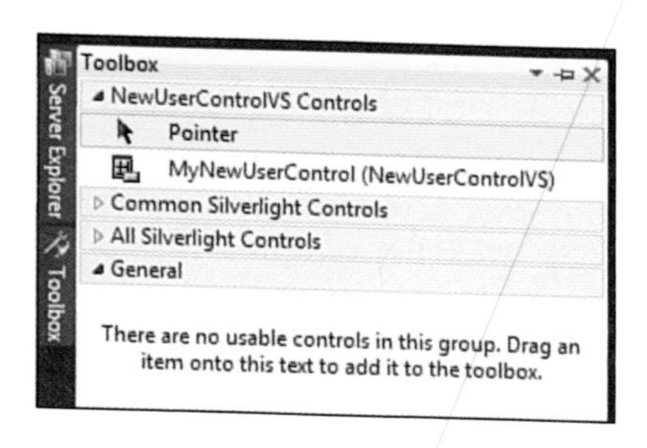

FIGURE 3.6 New `UserControl` in the Toolbox.

If you check the XAML code in the XAML editor now (by opening the XAML tab shown in Figure 2.4), you will see that Visual Studio added a new `xmlns` statement, named `xmlns:my`. This stands for "my controls," which might not be the best name ever. In the next section ("Adding a new `UserControl` in XAML"), we will rather use the prefix `local` for local controls, but as mentioned earlier, the prefix can be anything as long as it is valid in XML.

WARNING

Changing an `xmlns` Prefix

If you decide to change the `xmlns` prefix (for example, from `my` to `local`), you must be careful not to forget any place where this prefix is used. However, if you forget a location, your project will not compile anymore, which makes errors rather easy to find.

Adding a new `UserControl` in XAML

You can also add the new `UserControl` directly in the XAML file with a few manual steps. Of course, using the Toolbox is more straightforward, but typing XAML code is actually well supported in Visual Studio, and this is a good way to better understand what is happening under the hood. You should at least try it a few times before you decide which environment you prefer (XAML editor, visual designer, Blend). Follow these steps:

1. With MainPage.xaml open, add a new `xmlns` statement into the root tag, as shown in Listing 3.7. You must choose a unique prefix that will be mapped to the namespace that you are importing in the XAML document. In Listing 3.7, we map the prefix `local` to the CLR namespace `NewUserControlVS`.

LISTING 3.7 Adding a New xmlns Statement to the Root Tag

```
<UserControl
  x:Class="NewUserControlVS.MainPage"
  xmlns="http://schemas.microsoft.com/winfx/2006/xaml/presentation"
  xmlns:x="http://schemas.microsoft.com/winfx/2006/xaml"
  xmlns:d="http://schemas.microsoft.com/expression/blend/2008"
  xmlns:mc="http://schemas.openxmlformats.org/markup-compatibility/2006"
  xmlns:local="clr-namespace:NewUserControlVS"
  mc:Ignorable="d" d:DesignHeight="300" d:DesignWidth="400">
```

By adding this new `xmlns` statement, we can use the mapped .NET namespace in our XAML document.

> **TIP**
>
> **Reopening IntelliSense**
>
> If the IntelliSense window is closed, you can reopen it by pressing Ctrl+Space in Visual Studio. Of course, the cursor must be located in a place where IntelliSense is active. This tip works in XAML and also in code.

2. At the location in which you want to add the `UserControl`, enter the code shown in Listing 3.8. Again, notice how IntelliSense helps you: After you type the opening angle bracket, a list of elements and of prefixes is proposed. Select the `local` prefix and enter a colon. Visual Studio then proposes a list of elements available in the .NET namespace mapped to the `local` prefix.

LISTING 3.8 Adding the New UserControl in the Main Grid

```
<Grid x:Name="LayoutRoot"
      Background="White">
    <local:MyNewUserControl />
</Grid>
```

Setting Properties on the `UserControl`

The `UserControl` class (of which `MyNewUserControl` derives) defines a number of properties that you can set to modify its appearance (for example, the `Width` and `Height`, the `Margin`). All these properties can be set (either in XAML or with the Properties editor), and their effect is visible immediately.

Some other properties, however, are only defined as a "gateway" between the outside of the `UserControl` and the UI elements that compose it. The `Background` is such a property, and the following steps experiment with it:

1. Open MainPage.xaml in the Visual Studio designer. You should see the white main grid, and the instance of `MyNewUserControl` displayed as a button with a 20-pixel margin.
2. Select the main `Grid` and set its `Background` brush to red in the Properties editor.
3. Notice how the 20-pixel wide area around the button in `MyNewUserControl` displays the red background, too (as shown in Figure 3.7). The `UserControl`'s background is transparent.
4. Select the instance of `MyNewUserControl`.
5. In the Properties editor, set its `Background` property to yellow.

   Even with its `Background` property set to a solid color brush, `MyNewUserControl` displays the background below. The property is set, but does not have any effect; it is just a gateway to the inner elements of the `UserControl`.

FIGURE 3.7 Main grid with red background, transparent `UserControl`.

6. Open MyNewUserControl.xaml.
7. In the XAML editor, add the `x:Name` attribute to the `UserControl` root tag and set its value to `RootControl`.
8. In the main `Grid` tag, add a data binding on the `Background` property as shown in Listing 3.9. This will bind the value of the `Grid`'s `Background` to whatever is set on the `UserControl`'s `Background`. The `Grid` will be used to render the brush that has been set externally.
9. Go back to MainPage.xaml and build the application. As a result, in the designer, the 20-pixel wide area around the button into the instance of `MyNewUserControl` will be rendered yellow.
10. Drag another `MyNewUserControl` from the Toolbox to the `MainPage` in the designer, and this time set its `Background` property to blue. You should now see one yellow instance and one blue instance, as in Figure 3.8. We used a property of the `UserControl` to personalize each instance.

LISTING 3.9 UserControl's Inner Elements

```
<UserControl x:Class="NewUserControlVS.MyNewUserControl"
             xmlns="http://schemas.microsoft.com/winfx/2006/xaml/presentation"
             xmlns:x="http://schemas.microsoft.com/winfx/2006/xaml"
             xmlns:d="http://schemas.microsoft.com/expression/blend/2008"
             xmlns:mc="http://schemas.openxmlformats.org/markup-compatibility/2006"
             x:Name="RootControl"
             mc:Ignorable="d"
             d:DesignHeight="300"
             d:DesignWidth="400">
    <Grid x:Name="LayoutRoot"
          Background="{Binding ElementName=RootControl, Path=Background}">
        <Button Content="Click me"
                Margin="20" />
    </Grid>
</UserControl>
```

Note the following:

- We will talk a lot more about data binding in Chapter 6, "Working with Data: Binding, Grouping, Sorting, and Filtering" and later.
- If you use the Properties editor to add a name to `MyNewUserControl`'s root tag, the property `Name` rather than `x:Name` will be used. We discussed this in Chapter 2 (see the box titled "Name, x:Name, or No Name"). Generally, it is better to use `x:Name` rather than `Name`.

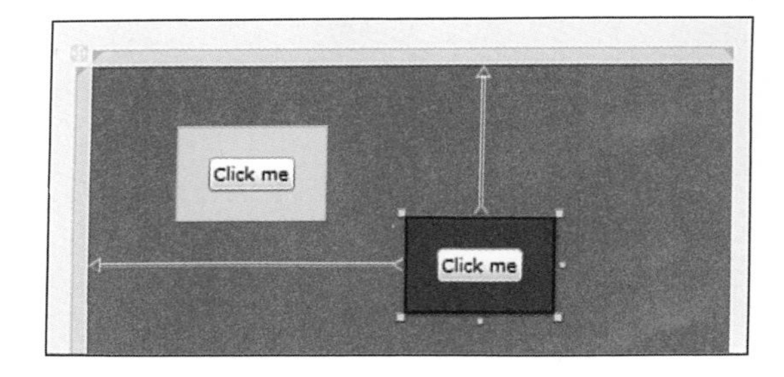

FIGURE 3.8 Two instances of `MyNewUserControl`.

Adding Custom Properties

For further customization of the new `UserControl`, you can add custom properties to the `UserControl`'s code behind. You can actually add any property to it, but if you want special functionalities (such as data binding, animation, and so on) to work with the properties, you should add a *dependency property*. We talk much more about this special type of properties in Chapter 5, "Understanding Dependency Properties." Follow these steps to add a new dependency property to `MyNewUserControl` and bind it to the `Button`'s `Content` property:

1. Open the file MyNewUserControl.xaml.cs. This is the `UserControl`'s code behind file.
2. Add the code in Listing 3.10 below the `MyNewUserControl` constructor. This defines the new dependency property named `DisplayTest`, of type `string`.

3. Open MyNewUserControl.xaml into the XAML editor and modify the `Button` tag as shown in Listing 3.11. This binds the `Content` property to the control's `DisplayText` property.
4. Build the application.
5. Open MainPage.xaml in the visual designer and select the first instance of `MyNewUserControl`. Observe how the `DisplayText` property is now visible into the Properties editor.
6. Set the `DisplayText` property to `"Hello world"` and observe how the text is now rendered into the button.
7. Select the second `UserControl` and set `DisplayText` to another value.

LISTING 3.10 Adding a Dependency Property in MyNewUserControl.xaml.cs

```
public const string DisplayTextPropertyName = "DisplayText";

public string DisplayText
{
    get
    {
        return (string)GetValue(DisplayTextProperty);
    }
    set
    {
        SetValue(DisplayTextProperty, value);
    }
}

public static readonly DependencyProperty DisplayTextProperty
    = DependencyProperty.Register(
        DisplayTextPropertyName,
        typeof(string),
        typeof(MyNewUserControl),
        new PropertyMetadata(string.Empty));
```

LISTING 3.11 Setting a `Binding` to the New Property in MyNewUserControl.xaml

```
<Button Content="{Binding ElementName=RootControl, Path=DisplayText}"
        Margin="20" />
```

Using built-in properties and custom properties, you can extend a `UserControl`'s functionality and customize instances. However, as mentioned earlier, `UserControls` are mainly used to encapsulate other controls. To create a control with brand new functionality, it is often preferable to use a custom control, as you will see in the following section.

Custom Controls

In contrast to user controls, which have a XAML front end and a code behind file, custom controls are made of only code, without any front end. We talk about *lookless controls*. In fact, all built-in controls in Silverlight are lookless. The custom control file defines only the control's functionality: Properties and methods form the control's interface, and its behavior is defined by its *states and parts*. You will see in just a moment what this means.

For the controls to be visible, a XAML front end must be defined, though. An invisible control is not very usable! One control can have multiple appearances, defined in as many *control templates*. We talk about a separation of concerns: The control's code defines its functionality; the control's template defines its appearance. Typically, a developer implements the control, whereas a designer *styles and templates it*.

Implementing the Custom Control

You'll learn more about templates in Chapter 10. For now, let's create a simple custom control with a *generic template*. The control we are building is used to represent a value, according to the following requirements:

- The user defines a threshold and a value, both of type `Double`.
- If the value is higher than the threshold, the control is in High state.
- If the value is lower than the threshold, the control is in Low state.
- If the value is equal to the threshold, the control is in Equal state.
- Both the threshold and the value can change dynamically, be data bound, animated, and so forth.
- The user can click one part of the control to increment the value by one unit, and another part to decrement by one unit.
- The control can be disabled, in which case clicking does not change the value.

TIP

Implementing a Control with Unit Tests

One big advantage of having a clear separation of concerns is that the control's functionality can be tested systematically with *unit tests*, as you will see in Chapter 22, "Advanced Development Techniques." This allows modifying the control (for example, by adding features) but at the same time making sure that the existing functionality is not broken: Just run all the unit tests again and make sure that none of them break.

TIP

Working with Designers

It is more and more common to have designers work on rich applications such as the ones we are building here. However, not every firm can afford a professional designer. When we talk about designers, we talk about the designer role, and not necessarily a professionally trained designer. That said, having a professional designer work on an application brings it to an unmatched level of usability.

Notice how these requirements do not state anything about the appearance of the control. They only define its functionality. The developer can start working, testing the control, and does not have to worry about the design of the control. This will be the work of a designer later.

Let's start with the following steps:

1. In Visual Studio, select File, New, Project from the menu.
2. In the Add New Project dialog, in the Silverlight category, select Silverlight Class Library.
3. Enter the name **CustomControlsLibrary** and click OK. Make sure that you select Silverlight 4 in the next dialog. This creates an assembly, a library that can be referenced in multiple applications but cannot be run on its own.
4. Delete the file Class1.cs in the Solution Explorer (because will not use it).
5. Right-click the CustomControlsLibrary project in the Solution Explorer, and select Add, New Item from the context menu.
6. In the Add New Item dialog, select the Silverlight, and then select a Silverlight Templated Control.
7. Enter the name **ThresholdControl.cs** and click Add.

Defining the Parts and States

These steps create a C# code file, a folder named Themes, and a XAML file named Generic.xaml. We will investigate this last file later; for now let's declare the *parts and states* for this control:

8. Open the file ThresholdControl.cs.
9. According to the requirements, the control has two state groups. We will call these the Common states (Normal, Disabled) and the Threshold states (High, Equal, Low). Note that the states within a state group are mutually exclusive; that is, the control cannot be simultaneously in Normal and in Disabled state. However, it can be Normal and High, or Normal and Low, and so forth. Defining the states and states groups is done with the `TemplateVisualState` attribute on the class, as shown in Listing 3.12.
10. The requirements also state that the control has two parts with a special meaning: Clicking them increments or decrements the value. Here too, we use an attribute to define the parts on the class: the `TemplatePart` attribute that is shown in Listing 3.12.

The type of the parts is chosen accordingly to the functionality that they must fulfil. It is a good practice to choose a type as generic as possible. In our case, we know that a part must react to a click. However, we do not want to constrain the designer too much, so we will choose the type defining the `MouseLeftButtonDown` event, which is more generic than the Click event: All the elements deriving from UIElement have the MouseLeftButtonDown event, while the Click event is only defined on the ButtonBase class and all the classes deriving from it (Button, ToggleButton, CheckBox, and so forth).

LISTING 3.12 Parts and States for the Threshold Control.

```
[TemplatePart(Name = "IncrementPart", Type = typeof(UIElement))]
[TemplatePart(Name = "DecrementPart", Type = typeof(UIElement))]
[TemplateVisualState(GroupName = "Common", Name = "Normal")]
[TemplateVisualState(GroupName = "Common", Name = "Disabled")]
[TemplateVisualState(GroupName = "Threshold", Name = "High")]
[TemplateVisualState(GroupName = "Threshold", Name = "Equal")]
[TemplateVisualState(GroupName = "Threshold", Name = "Low")]
public class ThresholdControl : Control
```


Defining Properties

Per the requirements, the control has two properties of type Double that the user can interface with: the Value and the Threshold. In addition, we know that these properties can be data bound, animated, and so forth. This hints that dependency properties should be used again.

At this point, it is important to remember that XAML is based on XML. When attributes are set on a XAML element, there is no guarantee as to the order in which these attributes are set. For example, the developer must accept that the Height property of a control can be set before or after the Width property.

Also, the XAML parser (like all XML parsers) requires an empty constructor to work. It is good practice to have only the default constructor for controls, and to set all the values through public properties, without setting a constraint on their order.

The Value property is shown in Listing 3.13. We will dig much deeper into dependency properties in Chapter 5, but notice an important addition: The method OnValueChanged will be called each time that the property's value changes. We will use this *property changed callback* (shown in Listing 3.14) to calculate the control's new state.

LISTING 3.13 The Value Dependency Property

```
public double Value
{
    get
    {
        return (double)GetValue(ValueProperty);
    }
    set
    {
        SetValue(ValueProperty, value);
    }
}
```

```
public static readonly DependencyProperty ValueProperty
    = DependencyProperty.Register(
        "Value",
        typeof(double),
        typeof(ThresholdControl),
        new PropertyMetadata(0.0, OnValueChanged));
```

The `Threshold` property is shown in Listing 3.14. Here, too, we use the same method property changed callback `OnValueChanged` to calculate the control's new state.

LISTING 3.14 The Threshold Dependency Property

```
public double Threshold
{
    get
    {
        return (double)GetValue(ThresholdProperty);
    }
    set
    {
        SetValue(ThresholdProperty, value);
    }
}

public static readonly DependencyProperty ThresholdProperty
    = DependencyProperty.Register(
        "Threshold",
        typeof(double),
        typeof(ThresholdControl),
        new PropertyMetadata(0.0, OnValueChanged));
```

The `OnValueChanged` method (shown in Listing 3.15) must be a static method, because of the static nature of dependency properties. To access the control that triggered the property changed event, we use the sender parameter after we cast it to a `ThresholdControl`. This way is is a bit cumbersome and confusing at first; we discuss it in more detail in Chapter 5. For now, simply remember that this method will be called each time that either the `Value` or the `Threshold` properties change.

LISTING 3.15 The OnValueChanged Property Changed Callback

```
private static void OnValueChanged(
    object s,
    DependencyPropertyChangedEventArgs e)
{
    var sender = s as ThresholdControl;
```

```
        if (sender != null)
        {
            sender.GoToThresholdState(true);
        }
    }
```

The `GoToThresholdState` method is shown in Listing 3.16. To change the control's state, we use the `VisualStateManager` class, built in Silverlight 4. This class is a useful helper that will take care of transitioning the control from one state to another. To do this, we use its `GoToState` method, which accepts the control itself as first parameter, the name of the destination state, and a `bool` indicating whether transitions (that is, animations) should be used when changing the control's state. We take a look at transitions when we cover control templates in Chapter 10.

LISTING 3.16 The GoToThresholdState Method

```
private void GoToThresholdState(bool useTransitions)
{
    if (Value > Threshold)
    {
        VisualStateManager.GoToState(this, "High", useTransitions);
    }
    else
    {
        if (Value < Threshold)
        {
            VisualStateManager.GoToState(this, "Low", useTransitions);
        }
        else
        {
            VisualStateManager.GoToState(this, "Equal", useTransitions);
        }
    }
}
```

Wiring the Parts

It is important to understand that the parts are optional. It is well possible that the designer chooses to omit one or all of them. The control's functionality should take missing parts into consideration, and react accordingly.

The wiring takes place in the `OnApplyTemplate` method, which is called by the custom control's base class, the `Control` class. We override this method and look for the named parts by implementing the `OnApplyTemplate` method shown in Listing 3.17.

LISTING 3.17 Implementing OnApplyTemplate

```
public override void OnApplyTemplate()
{
    base.OnApplyTemplate();
    var incremementPart
        = GetTemplateChild("IncrementPart") as UIElement;

    if (incremementPart != null)
    {
        incremementPart.MouseLeftButtonDown
            += IncremementPartMouseLeftButtonDown;
    }

    var decremementPart
        = GetTemplateChild("DecrementPart") as UIElement;

    if (decremementPart != null)
    {
        decremementPart.MouseLeftButtonDown
            += DecremementPartMouseLeftButtonDown;
    }

    GoToThresholdState(false);
}

void IncremementPartMouseLeftButtonDown(
    object sender,
    MouseButtonEventArgs e)
{
    Value++;
}

void DecremementPartMouseLeftButtonDown(
    object sender,
    MouseButtonEventArgs e)
{
    Value—;
}
```

The OnApplyTemplate method in listing 3.17 performs the following operations:

- First we call the base class's `OnApplyTemplate` method, to make sure that everything is set up correctly.
- Then, we use the control's `GetTemplateChild` method to check whether there is a part named `IncrementPart`, of type `UIElement`. If we find it, we add an event handler

to its MouseLeftButtonDown event. Notice that if the part is not found, the application does not crash (no exception is thrown), but the control will have less functionality.

- We proceed to do the same with the part named DecrementPart.
- At the end of the OnApplyTemplate method, everything is wired correctly, and we let the control go into the initial state. It is necessary, because otherwise the control would have an undefined state. Notice, however, that we do not use transitions for this initial state setting because we want it to happen as fast as possible.
- Finally we implement the MouseLeftButtonDown event handlers for the IncrementPart and the DecrementPart. Because of the preliminary work we did in the Value property (and its property changed callback), the event handlers are very simple: They just increment or decrement the control's Value.

At this point, our control is ready from a functionality point of view. We still need to create a visual representation (the template). However, even without a visual, we could already write unit tests for this control, and test whether the control switches to the correct state when the Value is above or below the Threshold.

Creating a Default Template

Even though this section's title starts with the word *creating*, what we really need to do is tweak the already existing default template that was created when we chose the Silverlight Templated Control in Visual Studio. The default template is available in the file Generic.xaml. When Silverlight is told to create a new ThresholdControl, the following operations take place:

- Silverlight checks whether a template for the TargetType CustomControlsLibray.ThresholdControl is available in the application that uses this control, or in a referenced assembly.
- If that is not the case, Silverlight looks for the file named Themes\Generic.xaml within the same assembly as the ThresholdControl.
- If this file is found, and it contains a default template for the control's type, this template will be used. This is a *fallback* mechanism.

Default templates are often kept quite simple, but should provide a way to visualize and test the control's functionality. In our case, we want to display the Value and the Threshold, visualize the state of the control (High, Low, or Equal), and provide two named parts to increment and decrement the Value. For now, follow these steps:

1. Open the file Themes\Generic.xaml.
2. Locate the template for the type local:ThresholdControl. There might be multiple templates in this file, if there are multiple controls in the assembly, but there should be only one template per control type.
3. Modify the ControlTemplate to look like Listing 3.18.

LISTING 3.18 Default ControlTemplate for ThresholdControl

```
1  <ControlTemplate TargetType="local:ThresholdControl">
2      <Border Background="{TemplateBinding Background}"
3              BorderBrush="{TemplateBinding BorderBrush}"
4              BorderThickness="{TemplateBinding BorderThickness}">
5          <Grid>
6              <Grid.ColumnDefinitions>
7                  <ColumnDefinition Width="30" />
8                  <ColumnDefinition Width="*" />
9                  <ColumnDefinition Width="30" />
10             </Grid.ColumnDefinitions>
11
12             <Border Background="Blue"
13                     x:Name="DecrementPart"
14                     Cursor="Hand">
15                 <TextBlock Text="-" />
16             </Border>
17
18             <StackPanel Grid.Column="1"
19                         Orientation="Vertical"
20                         Margin="10">
21                 <TextBlock Text="{Binding
22                     RelativeSource={RelativeSource TemplatedParent},
23                     Path=Value}" />
24
25                 <TextBlock
26                     x:Name="HighTextBlock"
27                     Text="&gt;" />
28                 <TextBlock
29                     x:Name="EqualTextBlock"
30                     Text="==" />
31                 <TextBlock
32                     x:Name="LowTextBlock"
33                     Text="&lt;" />
34
35                 <TextBlock Text="{Binding
36                     RelativeSource={RelativeSource TemplatedParent},
37                     Path=Threshold}" />
38             </StackPanel>
39
40             <Border Background="Red"
41                     x:Name="IncrementPart"
42                     Grid.Column="2"
43                     Cursor="Hand">
44                 <TextBlock Text="+" />
```

```
45                </Border>
46            </Grid>
47        </Border>
48    </ControlTemplate>
```

Let's review this XAML code:

- The template is defined with a `TargetType` of `local:ThresholdControl` (where the `local` prefix is mapped to the CLR namespace `CustomControlsLibrary`). It will be automatically applied for all instances of `ThresholdControl` (unless you explicitly overload the default template in your application, as you will see in Chapter 10.
- On line 2, 3, and 4, note the usage of the `TemplateBinding` keyword. This special kind of binding links the target property (here, the `Border`'s `Background`) to the source property (here, the control's `Background`); the source property is looked for on the control that this template represents. By setting the control's background to a brush, through the `TemplateBinding`, the `Border's Background` will be set and rendered.
- We use a `Grid` with three columns as the panel. For more information about grids and the flexible layout that they allow, you can refer to *Silverlight 2 Unleashed*, Chapter 15.
- A blue `Border` will be displayed in the first column (lines 12 to 16). Note that `Border`'s name: It is set to `DecrementPart`. Remember that this name has a special meaning for the `Threshold` control: It will be wired to decrement the `Value` when the `MouseLeftButtonDown` event is triggered.
- In the middle column (set by `Grid.Column="1"`) we have a vertical `StackPanel`.
- Its first child is a `TextBlock` that will be used to display the `Value` property. We get this value through a `Binding` on the `TemplatedParent` (in other words, the `ThresholdControl`).
- The three next `TextBlock` instances display the signs >, ==, and <. Note that since XAML is XML, we had to encode the > and < signs to `">"` and `"<"`, respectively to avoid errors in the XML document.
- The last child is another `TextBlock` used to display the `Threshold` property, again through a `Binding` on the `TemplatedParent`.
- Finally, in the third column (set by `Grid.Column="2"`), we have a red `Border` named `IncrementPart`, another meaningful name for the `ThresholdControl`.

Representing the Visual States

This control template does not take care of the control's state. Ideally, we want the three `TextBlock` instances with <, ==, > to be shown or hidden according to the state of the control. To do this, we will modify the template according to the `High`, `Equal`, and `Low` states. Add the XAML code in Listing 3.19 within the main `Border` tag (which is between lines 4 and 5 of Listing 3.18).

LISTING 3.19 Setting the Control Template's High State

```
1  <VisualStateManager.VisualStateGroups>
2      <VisualStateGroup x:Name="Threshold">
3          <VisualState x:Name="High">
4              <Storyboard>
5                  <DoubleAnimationUsingKeyFrames
6                      Storyboard.TargetProperty="(UIElement.Opacity)"
7                      Storyboard.TargetName="EqualTextBlock">
8                      <EasingDoubleKeyFrame
9                          KeyTime="0" Value="0" />
10                 </DoubleAnimationUsingKeyFrames>
11                 <DoubleAnimationUsingKeyFrames
12                     Storyboard.TargetProperty="(UIElement.Opacity)"
13                     Storyboard.TargetName="LowTextBlock">
14                     <EasingDoubleKeyFrame
15                         KeyTime="0" Value="0" />
16                 </DoubleAnimationUsingKeyFrames>
17             </Storyboard>
18         </VisualState>
19         <!--...-->
20     </VisualStateGroup>
21 </VisualStateManager.VisualStateGroups>
```

- The `VisualStateGroup` tag on line 3 groups all the states belonging to one group (in this case, the `Threshold` state group).
- On lines 3 to 18, we define a transition (in the form of a `Storyboard`) from any state to the `High` state. Two elements are targeted: The `EqualTextBlock` and the `LowTextBlock` are hidden. For example, the `EqualTextBlock`'s `Opacity` is set to 0 on lines 5 to 10, at a `KeyTime` of 0 seconds. This means that the transition is immediate. You could specify a different `KeyTime` (for example, `"0:0:0.2"`, which is 200 milliseconds) to have a smoother transition.
- Only the `High` state is represented in Listing 3.19. The other states (`Equal` and `Low`) are very similar and should appear instead of the XML comment at line 19. The complete source code is available at http://galasoft.ch/SL4U/Code/Chapter03.

As you can see in this chapter, creating control templates in Visual Studio is not an easy task, because of the amount of XAML code that is involved. Even a very simple template like the `ThresholdControl`'s default template requires a lot of manual work. This is why control templates are typically created in Expression Blend, which is a fantastic tool for this kind of work.

Summary

In this chapter, we discussed the extensibility of XAML documents, which is very useful to import all kind of objects into your user interface, from simple values to objects in resources to controls.

Then we discussed user controls, and how they are used to group and encapsulate other controls. With user controls, you can easily divide your user interface in smaller, more manageable pieces. You can also reuse these pieces in multiple places in your application. And of course, you can also add properties within to extend the user control's functionality.

Finally, we studied custom controls, what Silverlight coders call "lookless controls". These controls enforce a strict separation of functionality (in the code) and presentation (in a control template). The code is typically developed and tested by a developer, while someone in the role of a designer works on the template. In this Chapter we saw how to create a default template, useful to test the control's functionalities. In Chapter 10, we will see how more elaborate and complex templates can be created for existing controls.

CHAPTER 4

Investigating Existing Controls

IN THIS CHAPTER, WE WILL:

- Review some controls that were discussed in Silverlight 2 Unleashed, and that are still present and useful in Silverlight 4.
- See what changes Silverlight 4 brought to existing controls.
- Talk about new controls added to the core Silverlight framework.
- Explore the Silverlight Toolkit, a collection of controls provided by Microsoft independently from the core Silverlight framework.
- List some points that you should check before purchasing controls from third-party vendors.

In Chapter 3, "Extending Your Application with Controls," you saw how to create user controls and custom controls to extend your application with functionality. However, in many cases, you do not actually need to create controls yourself. Instead, you will use existing controls, either within the Silverlight framework itself or from external providers. In this chapter, we cover these controls, including what has changed since Silverlight 2 was released and where to find new controls.

Reviewing the Basics

In *Silverlight 2 Unleashed*, we spent two chapters talking about controls. First, we reviewed the Silverlight class hierarchy in Chapter 15. Understanding how objects and controls are composed is very important to master the framework. Further in the same chapter, we talked about panels (such as `StackPanel`, `Canvas`, and `Grid`), and when you should be choosing which panel to layout your application. We also spent some time talking about `ScrollViewer` and `Popup`, and finished with a section about the `Shape` class (such as `Rectangle`, `Ellipse` and `Path`).

Then, in Chapter 16 of *Silverlight 2 Unleashed*, we talked about the properties of the `Control` class, before reviewing some of the controls:

- The `TextBlock`, used to present and format text.
- The `TextBox`, used to let the user input and edit text.
- The `Button`, `CheckBox`, `RadioButton`, `HyperlinkButton`, `RepeatButton`, and `ToggleButton`, all deriving from the `ButtonBase` class used for all things that can be clicked.

- `Scrollbar` and `Slider`, two controls similar in the way they are built, both with a middle element that can be dragged along a track. The `Scrollbar` is used to scroll big areas, while the `Slider` is used to set a value (in steps or continuously) by dragging their middle part. We also talked about the `Thumb` control, very useful when you need something you can drag.
- The `GridSplitter` that can be dragged to resize a grid's cells.
- The `Calendar` and `DatePicker` controls, useful to input and edit dates in an application.
- The `InkPresenter`, a control that is used to allow the user to draw or write on the screen, ideally with a stylus or his fingers.

We then proceeded with an introduction to the `ItemsControl` (of which most data controls derive, such as `TabControl`, `ListBox`, `ComboBox`, and so on).

The chapter ended with a section about DeepZoom, an impressive feature that allows smooth zooming into high-definition pictures, allowing a fantastic experience such as demonstrated in the Matterhorn demo we sampled earlier.

Another good chapter in *Silverlight 2 Unleashed* about controls is Chapter 18, specifically the second half about data controls:

- That chapter covers how to use the `ListBox`, one of the most useful controls in the whole Silverlight framework to represent collections of data.
- We worked with the `ObservableCollection` class, a class made to hold a list of items and notify its users (for example, a data control) when items are added, removed, or when the order of these items changes.
- We studied the `DataGrid`, a powerful element to display, sort, group, filter, and edit data in business applications.

Few changes were made to all these controls since Silverlight 2 was released. It must be noted that all the controls that were into the Silverlight 2 Toolkit are now included into the code framework. In this chapter, we review changes that were made to existing controls, and we will talk about some of the new controls that were included in Silverlight 3 and 4.

Show Me Some Code!

To illustrate the features mentioned in this chapter, a sample browser can be downloaded from http://www.galasoft.ch/SL4U/code/chapter04.

The application uses sample data created by Expression Blend (a feature that we discuss in Chapter 11, "Mastering Expression Blend"). This is especially interesting when working with data controls because Blend creates a list of random items without the developer having to come up with complicated services or XML files. Another interesting feature of this Silverlight application is a navigation application, a special type of application that we will review in Chapter 15, "Developing Navigation Applications and Silverlight for Windows Phone 7."

In this sample application, we use the `Customers` collection in multiple samples. This collection (defined by Blend as a static resource in App.xaml) has a number of customers defined, each with a `Name` (`string`), `ContractNumber` (`integer`), and `IsActive` (`bool`) properties. Expression Blend generated the values. For instance, the XAML code in Listing 4.1 binds a control's `CurrentItem` property to the first customer in the collection. In Listing 4.2, we bind a data control's `ItemsSource` property to the list of customers.

LISTING 4.1 Binding to the First Customer

```
CurrentItem="{Binding Source={StaticResource Customers},
                      Path=Collection[0]}" />
```

LISTING 4.2 Binding to the List of Customers

```
ItemsSource="{Binding Source={StaticResource Customers},
                      Path=Collection}"
```

Changes in Existing Controls

All the controls that were available in Silverlight 2 and 3 are still available in Silverlight 4. There were a few changes to existing controls, though.

Mouse Wheel Support

The controls with a content that can be scrolled now automatically support the mouse wheel action. The controls in question are as follows:

- `ScrollViewer`
- `TextBox` (only when the `VerticalScrollBarVisibility` property is set to `Auto` or `Visible`)
- `ComboBox` (when the number of items is large enough)
- `Calendar` (to scroll the decades, years, months)
- `DatePicker` (to scroll the decades, years, months when the `Calendar` is open)

Localizing for Right-to-Left Languages

The story of localizing Silverlight applications is not perfect by a long shot, but a step in the right direction was taken with the introduction of support for right-to-left languages (for example, Hebraic or Arabic languages). Simply set the `FlowDirection` property on any `FrameworkElement` to `RightToLeft` for such languages. The default is `LeftToRight`.

Getting a Control Template's Current State

A control's template typically defines various state groups with states and transitions, as you saw in Chapter 3, "Extending Your Application with Controls." For example, a `Button` has the states `Normal`, `MouseOver`, `Pressed` and `Disabled` (in the state group `CommonStates`), and can transition from one to the other.

However, getting the control's current state programmatically was difficult, because neither the control nor the `VisualStateManager` class keeps track of which state the control currently is in. It is possible to build a custom class deriving from `VisualStateManager` and to assign it using `VisualStateManager.SetCustomVisualStateManager` static method. However, for small applications, this is too complex.

In Silverlight 4, this is corrected, with the addition of the `VisualStateGroup.CurrentState` property. Getting a control's current state to calculate the next transition in code is shown in Listing 4.3. This makes calculating the transitions easier because keeping track of the current state is not needed anymore.

LISTING 4.3 Getting a Control's State

```
1  var groups
2      = VisualStateManager.GetVisualStateGroups(background);
3
4  if (groups == null
5      || groups.Count == 0)
6  {
7      return;
8  }
9
10 VisualStateGroup group
11     = groups[0] as VisualStateGroup;
12
13 if (group == null)
14 {
15     return;
16 }
17
18 VisualState currentState = group.CurrentState;
19
20 // Calculate transition based on current state
```

- On line 2, the variable `background` is a `FrameworkElement` that is part of the control template, and on which the visual states are defined in XAML (as we did, for example, in Listing 3.19).

- Note that depending on how the control template is built, a given VisualStateGroup or a given state within that group might not be available. The code should take this fact into account, and be robust enough not to crash if that is the case, as in Listing 4.3 on lines 4 to 8.

Adding SelectedValue and SelectedValuePath

All controls deriving from the Selector class now have two new properties: SelectedValue and SelectedValuePath. In the Silverlight core framework, two controls derive from Selector: ComboBox and ListBox.

These properties work together to facilitate data binding in XAML. For instance, imagine that a ListBox displays a list of customers. Each Customer item has a Name property and a ContractNumber property. The ListBox is set to display the customer's name. However, by setting the property SelectedValuePath to "ContractNumber", you can then bind to the ListBox's SelectedValue property, as shown in Listing 4.4.

Note that another way to reach the exact same result would be to bind to the ListBox's SelectedItem.ContractNumber, as shown in Listing 4.5. Both expressions work the same. However, SelectedValuePath and SelectedValue are invaluable when all you have to identify the binding is a set of strings (for example, from a ComboBox, from a web service, or from a database).

LISTING 4.4 Using SelectedValue and SelectedValuePath

```
<ListBox x:Name="CustomersListBox"
         ItemTemplate="{StaticResource ItemTemplate}"
         SelectedValuePath="ContractNumber"
         ItemsSource="{Binding Collection}" />
<TextBlock Text="{Binding SelectedValue,
                          ElementName=CustomersListBox}" />
```

LISTING 4.5 Using SelectedItem

```
<ListBox x:Name="CustomersListBox2"
    ItemTemplate="{StaticResource ItemTemplate}"
    ItemsSource="{Binding Collection}" />
<TextBlock Text="{Binding SelectedItem.ContractNumber,
                          ElementName=CustomersListBox2}" />
```

Adding Command and CommandParameter

Commands were introduced in Windows Presentation Foundation (WPF) from the first version to implement a loosely coupled event-handling mechanism. When you implement an event handler for a Button control, for example, you create a very strong link between the XAML and the code behind. This can cause unexpected side effects, such as memory leaks, especially if you forget to unregister the event handler when the `Button` is disposed. You'll learn more about this in Chapter 21, "Optimizing Performance."

Another annoying effect with events is that the event handler must be located in the code behind. That can be an issue, especially when you create a template: Generally, the template is located in a resource dictionary that does not have any code behind (as you will see in Chapter 10, "Creating Resources, Styles, and Templates"). Using events creates a strong dependency between the XAML and the code behind that complicates the work of the designers.

To solve this issue, instead of a `Click` event, you can use the `Command` property (and an optional `CommandParameter` property) that will invoke a method on an object, not necessarily in the page's code behind. Note that the object must implement the `ICommand` interface that was already available in Silverlight 2 and Silverlight 3.

Until Silverlight 4 was released, it was quite difficult to use commands in Silverlight because most of the infrastructure was missing and a lot of manual work was involved. In Silverlight 4, however, we get (almost) the same support as in WPF, with the addition of the `Command` and `CommandParameter` properties on the `ButtonBase` class (of which `Button`, `RepeatButton`, `ToggleButton`, `CheckBox`, `RadioButton` derive) and on the `HyperlinkButton` control.

You'll learn more about commands in Chapter 7, "Understanding the Model-View-ViewModel Pattern." A short example is provided in the sample browser available at http://www.galasoft.ch/SL4U/code/chapter04. Listing 4.6 shows the C# code with the `ICommand` implementation, and the object that holds a property of this type. In Listing 4.7, you can see the XAML code that binds a `Button`'s `Command` property and its `CommandParameter` on the corresponding objects.

The `ICommand` interface specifies three compulsory members:

- The `Execute` method is called when the command is invoked. For the controls that have the `Command` property, clicking the control is the only way to actually invoke the command. In Chapter 19, "Authentication, Event to Command Binding, Random Animations, Multitouch, Local Communication, and Bing Maps Control," you will see other ways to invoke a command, without being limited to clicking the control. Note that the `Execute` method has a parameter (of type `object`). This parameter holds the value of the `CommandParameter` property on the invoking control. If `CommandParameter` is not set, then the parameter is `null`.

- The `CanExecute` method should return `true` if the command may be invoked, and `false` otherwise, depending on the value of the `CommandParameter` or of any other influencing factors. The control that the command is bound to will be enabled/disabled automatically according to the value returned by this method.

- The `CanExecuteChanged` event must be raised when the value of the `CanExecute` method changes. For example, imagine that the value of `CanExecute` depends on the value of an object's property. When this property changes, the `CanExecuteChanged` event must be raised manually to notify the user interface that `CanExecute` must be queried, and the controls enabled/disabled accordingly.

WARNING

Raising CanExecuteChanged Manually

Developers used to WPF will find puzzling that the CanExecuteChanged even must be raised manually in Silverlight. In the richer WPF, a class named CommandManager takes care of querying all the commands when something happens in the user interface (for example, when a user enters text, clicks an item, and so on). In Silverlight, this support does not exist.

LISTING 4.6 Implementing a Command and Using It as Property

```
1  public class ReceiveValueCommand : ICommand, INotifyPropertyChanged
2  {
3      public event EventHandler CanExecuteChanged;
4      public event PropertyChangedEventHandler PropertyChanged;
5
6      public string ReceivedValue
7      {
8          get;
9          private set;
10     }
11
12     public bool CanExecute(object parameter)
13     {
14         // Entering the words "Hello World" will disable the command!
15         return parameter != null
16             && parameter.ToString() != "Hello World";
17     }
18
19     public void Execute(object parameter)
20     {
21         // Command was invoked
22         if (parameter == null)
23         {
24             ReceivedValue = "Null";
25         }
26         else
27         {
28             ReceivedValue = parameter.ToString();
29         }
30
31         // Notify the bindings
32         if (PropertyChanged != null)
33         {
34             PropertyChanged(this,
35                 new PropertyChangedEventArgs("ReceivedValue"));
```

```
36          }
37      }
38  }
39
40  public class CommandSampleViewModel
41  {
42      public ICommand ReceiveCommand
43      {
44          get;
45          private set;
46      }
47
48      public CommandSampleViewModel()
49      {
50          ReceiveCommand = new ReceiveValueCommand();
51      }
52  }
```

- Line 3 declares the CanExecuteChanged event, as required by the ICommand interface.
- Note that the command also implements INotifyPropertyChanged. (Defined on line 1, and implemented on line 4, this interface defines only one event, PropertyChanged. We will raise this event a little later.) This is useful because we want to use data binding on the ReceivedValue property. However, having a command implementing INotifyPropertyChanged is a little unusual. We discuss better alternatives in Chapter 7.
- Lines 6 to 10 define a custom property that will store the value received when the Execute method is invoked, depending on the CommandParameter property on the Button control.
- Lines 12 to 17 define the CanExecute method that is executed when the command is bound to a control, each time that the CanExecuteChanged event is raised, or every time that the CommandParameter property's value changes. For example, in Listing 4.7, CommandParameter is bound to the ValueTextBox.Text property, so CanExecute will be executed when the user types something in the ValueTextBox.
- Lines 19 to 37 declare the Execute method, also required by the ICommand interface. This method simply stores the string value of the parameter into the ReceivedValue property.
- On lines 32 to 36, we raise the PropertyChanged event, thus notifying subscribers (for example, data bindings) that the ReceivedValue property changed. First we check whether the event is null (which would be the case if nobody subscribed to the event).

- From line 40, we declare a new class, called CommandSampleViewModel. This class is the *viewmodel* for the CommandSample page (also called the *view*). This is a simple implementation of the Model-View-ViewModel pattern, which we cover in more detail in Chapter 7.
- Lines 42 to 46 declare a property of type ICommand. The property is instantiated at line 50, by creating a new ReceiveValueCommand. We will bind the Button's Command property to this ICommand in Listing 4.7.

LISTING 4.7 Using the Command in XAML

```
1  <UserControl.Resources>
2      <vm:CommandSampleViewModel x:Key="CommandSampleViewModel" />
3  </UserControl.Resources>
4
5  <StackPanel x:Name="LayoutRoot"
6      DataContext="{Binding Source={StaticResource CommandSampleViewModel}}">
7
8      <TextBlock
9          Text="Enter the words Hello World to disable the command" />
10
11     <TextBox Text="Enter a value..."
12              x:Name="ValueTextBox" />
13
14     <Button Content="Click me"
15             Command="{Binding ReceiveCommand}"
16             CommandParameter="{Binding Text, ElementName=ValueTextBox}" />
17
18     <TextBlock Text="Received Value:" />
19     <TextBlock Text="{Binding ReceiveCommand.ReceivedValue}" />
20
21 </StackPanel>
```

On line 2, we create a new instance of the CommandSampleViewModel class in the UserControl's resources. Remember that resources are a store where you can keep any kind of object, not just styles and templates. In this case, the vm prefix is mapped to the CLR namespace SilverlightToolkitSamples.ViewModel, where this class lives. Then on line 6, we assign the instance of CommandSampleViewModel to the StackPanel's DataContext. From now on, the source for every Binding will implicitly be that instance, unless of course you specify otherwise explicitly.

Lines 11 and 12 define a TextBox named ValueTextBox. We will use this as the source for the CommandParameter. Further, line 15 assigns the ReceiveCommand property from the CommandSampleViewModel instance to the Command property of the Button. Because we do not define any source for this Binding, it automatically refers to the CommandSampleViewModel instance that we set as DataContext.

Line 16 assigns the Text property of ValueTextBox to the CommandParameter of the Button. We explicitly set the Binding's source (through the ElementName) to be the TextBox. In that case, the Binding's source is not the DataContext. Finally, line 19 displays ReceiveCommand's ReceivedValue property into a TextBlock.

Presenting and Editing Text with the RichTextBox

Until Silverlight 4 was released, the possibilities to present and edit rich text were quite limited. For presentation, it was possible to combine together some TextBlock elements with different formatting, but this was cumbersome. For rich text edition, nothing was available out of the box.

In Silverlight 4, the RichTextBox control was introduced to provide such a support, with the following features:

- The RichTextBox contains a collection of Block instances. These can be simple paragraphs, or formatted blocks such as Bold, Italic, and Underline. These elements can also be combined.
- You can add any element deriving from UIElement (such as shapes, images, panels, controls, and so on), using an InlineUIContainer wrapping it.
- The RichTextBlock provides the possibility to include Hyperlinks for navigation to web pages. However, the Hyperlinks are active only when the RichTextBlock is in read-only mode.
- Static text is formatted using XAML, as shown in Listing 4.8. Of course, as always in Silverlight, everything that can be done in XAML can also be done in code, which allows for dynamic formatting of the RichTextBox's content.
- The RichTextBox's Xaml property gives access to the formatted rich content expressed as XAML. This offers a convenient way to save the content of the box in a file, or to set it later.

LISTING 4.8 RichTextBox with Rich Content

```
<RichTextBox FontSize="14" Foreground="#FF646464"
              FontFamily="Verdana" TextWrapping="Wrap"
              IsReadOnly="{Binding IsChecked, ElementName=ReadOnlyCheck box}"
              VerticalScrollBarVisibility="Auto">

    <Paragraph FontSize="24">
        <Run FontWeight="Bold"
             Text="What Is Silverlight?"
             Foreground="#FF2400FF" />
    </Paragraph>

    <Paragraph>
```

```
        Silverlight is a <Bold>cross-browser, cross-platform and cross-device
        browser plug-in</Bold> that helps companies design, develop and
        deliver applications and experiences on the Web. Go to
        <Hyperlink NavigateUri="http://www.silverlight.net"
                   TargetName="_blank">Silverlight.net</Hyperlink>
        to learn more!
    </Paragraph>

    <Paragraph>
        <InlineUIContainer>
            <Image Source="/Assets/sl4bloglogo.png"
                   Width="200" Margin="10" />
        </InlineUIContainer>
    </Paragraph>
</RichTextBox>
```


Note the following:

- Setting properties on the `RichTextBox` itself will make these valid for the whole content. You can overload these properties (for example, the `FontSize` property) on an inner element.
- Notice the usage of the `Run` element to make a whole paragraph bold, and of the `Bold` element to make parts of the paragraph bold. You can combine these elements and others to achieve the desired formatting.
- As mentioned, the `InlineUIContainer` element can be used to add any `UIElement` to the content. The sample available at http://www.galasoft.ch/SL4U/code/chapter04 also shows a `MediaElement` playing a video.
- By default, the `RichTextBox` does not display any scrollbars, even if it is resized smaller than its content. Use the `VerticalScrollBarVisibility` and `HorizontalScrollBarVisibility` properties to change this.

Using these features, and with some code involved, it is possible to provide rich editing capabilities to your Silverlight application's users. A common usage for the `RichTextBox` is to combine it with a custom toolbar to format parts of the text and to add rich elements.

Zooming with the `Viewbox`

The `Viewbox` is a fantastic control when you need to zoom an area (or all) of your Silverlight application, or when you need to scale an element that was not made for it (for example a `Path`). For example, suppose that you want your application to fill the entire HTML host, whatever the size of this host is. This can be quite tricky and involve a lot of calculation and layout. However, in certain cases, it is much easier to design your application for a given size, and then to scale it up or down to fill the whole space.

> **TIP**
>
> **Watching Netflix with Silverlight**
>
> Our readers in the United States have probably heard of Netflix, the well-known DVD rental service. Netflix also has a streaming service over the Internet: Browse the list of available movies, select the one you like, and watch it instantly. The movie is *streamed* online: It is sent over the wire, buffered on the client computer, and as soon as enough of it is available, it starts playing. The Netflix application in Windows Media Center (on Windows 7) is scaled up or down depending on the size of the containing window. The application always looks proportional, whatever the size of the container, as shown in Figure 4.1.

To scale your application and fill the whole host, follow these steps:

1. Open your Silverlight application in Visual Studio or in Expression Blend.

2. Set a fixed size on the main panel. For example, you may want to design your application for a standard monitor size, such as 1024 x 768 pixels.

3. In XAML, wrap your main panel into a `Viewbox`. You do not need to set any property on the `Viewbox`, it will automatically fill the whole space.

FIGURE 4.1 Scaled Netflix window.

(Or)

In Expression Blend, right-click the main panel in Objects and Timeline, and select Group Into from the context menu. Select a `Viewbox`. This will wrap the main panel into the `Viewbox`. Make sure that the `Viewbox`'s `Width` and `Height` are set to `Auto`.

4. Test your application and resize the browser window. You should see the application's content being scaled up or down to fill the whole space.

WARNING

To Scale or Not to Scale

Choosing to scale or not an application depends a lot on the application's design. You have the following alternatives:

- Scale the application as demonstrated in this section. This can cause annoying effects, especially if the window is resized to a very small size (readability problem) or very large size (pixilation of images). Note that vector images, however, will not get pixilated. (See *Silverlight 2 Unleashed*, Chapter 5, for more information about scaling images.)
- Change the layout based on the application's size. For example, if you use a grid-based layout, you can let the columns be resized dynamically when the host's size changes (flow layout). Also, you can select different templates for your controls based on the control's size, in order, for example, to display fewer details when the application is smaller.

As mentioned, another frequent usage for a `Viewbox` control is the resizing of `Path` elements, for example when they compose a logo. `Path` elements cannot be resized easily, so wrapping them in a `Viewbox` and resizing this box instead is a better approach.

Opening a `ChildWindow`

The `ChildWindow` class was actually already present in Silverlight 3. It is a very useful class when you want to present additional information in a semi-modal way to the user. By "semi-modal," we mean that the user will not be able to access other controls on the Silverlight application as long as he didn't acknowledge the dialog; however, the application itself is not blocked, and continues to process information, to run animations, and so forth. The dialog is shown in an *asynchronous way*. To add a `ChildWindow` to your Silverlight application, follow these steps:

1. Right-click the project in the Solution Explorer, and then select Add, New Item from the context menu.
2. In the Add New Item dialog, select Silverlight Child Window; enter **MyChildWindow** as window's name, and click Add.
3. Customize the `ChildWindow`'s look and feel by modifying its XAML file. Note that you can also design the XAML into Expression Blend.
4. Set the `OverlayBrush`. As shown in Figure 4.2, the `ChildWindow`, when open, is appearing in front of your Silverlight application and prevents the user from clicking the controls below. The `OverlayBrush` is, as the name shows, a brush that can be set as you want (`SolidColorBrush`, `LinearGradientBrush`, `RadialGradientBrush`, and so forth). For more information about brushes, refer to *Silverlight 2 Unleashed*, Chapters 2 and 4.

WARNING

Setting the `OverlayBrush` to `Null`

You can set the `OverlayBrush` to `{x:Null}`, which means that no brush will be applied. Note, however, that all controls on the Silverlight page below the `ChildWindow` are disabled when it is open. This is, as mentioned previously, a pseudo-modal dialog. A better idea is to set the `OverlayBrush` to a light half-opaque gray (for example, #33999999).

5. If you want your user to input information, you can, for example, save the information in a dependency property, as shown in Listing 4.9.

6. Note that closing the `ChildWindow` is done by setting its `DialogResult` property, as you can see in Listing 4.9. As soon as the property is set, the window is closed automatically. In the default `ChildWindow`, the button OK sets `DialogResult` to `true`, and Cancel (as well as the X button in the title bar) sets `DialogResult` to `false`.

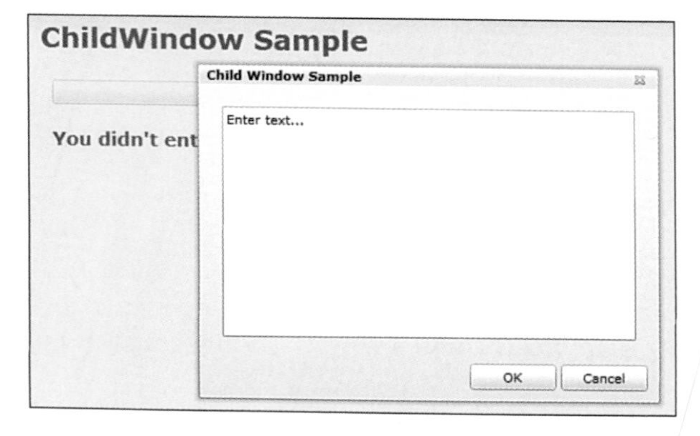

FIGURE 4.2 `ChildWindow` and overlay.

7. To open the `ChildWindow`, from any page in your application, instantiate a new `MyChildWindow` and call the `Show` method on the new instance, as shown in Listing 4.10.

8. To retrieve the information entered by the user after the window has been closed, you can handle the `Closed` event as shown in Listing 4.10. Again, this is an asynchronous pattern, and you need to handle the event to access the window's properties after it has been closed.

LISTING 4.9 The `ChildWindow`'s Code Behind

```
public partial class MyChildWindow : ChildWindow
{
    public const string InputPropertyName = "Input";

    public string Input
    {
        get
        {
```

```
            return (string)GetValue(InputProperty);
        }
        set
        {
            SetValue(InputProperty, value);
        }
    }

    public static readonly DependencyProperty InputProperty
        = DependencyProperty.Register(
        InputPropertyName,
        typeof(string),
        typeof(MyChildWindow),
        new PropertyMetadata("Enter text..."));

    public MyChildWindow()
    {
        InitializeComponent();
    }

    private void OKButton_Click(object sender, RoutedEventArgs e)
    {
        this.DialogResult = true;
    }

    private void CancelButton_Click(object sender, RoutedEventArgs e)
    {
        this.DialogResult = false;
    }
}
```

LISTING 4.10 Opening the Window and Handling Its Closed Event

```
private void OpenWindowButton_Click(object sender, RoutedEventArgs e)
{
    var window = new MyChildWindow();
    window.Closed += window_Closed;
    window.Show();
}

void window_Closed(object sender, EventArgs e)
{
    var window = sender as MyChildWindow;
    if (window != null
        && window.DialogResult == true)
    {
```

4

```
        InputTextBlock.Text = window.Input;
    }
}
```

Like all the controls in Silverlight, the `ChildWindow` can be styled and templated to change its appearance completely if needed.

Finding More Information

Because Silverlight 4 comes with such a large range of controls, it is materially impossible to detail all of them. Thankfully, when you install the Silverlight tools, you get a documentation file, too. You can download this file from http://www.galasoft.ch/sl4-offlinedoc.

The documentation is also available online. The page specific to the built-in controls' documentation is at http://www.galasoft.ch/sl4-onlinedoc.

Where to Find Additional Controls?

As soon as Silverlight 1.0 was released, third-party providers started creating controls to cover what was missing from the core framework. As Silverlight became more and more elaborate and powerful, many of the controls were made available to users of the core, and it is possible to create a very rich application without resorting to external providers.

Do You Really Need a Control?

An interesting side effect of the templates system in Silverlight is that it is now possible to change the functionality of an existing control in such a way that it fulfils your requirement even though it was not intended for this purpose at first.

For instance, the `CheckBox` and the `RadioButton` controls are essentially `ToggleButton` instances: This special kind of button has three states (`Checked`, `Unchecked`, and `Indeterminate`). Turning such a control into a `CheckBox` simply requires a different template to change the control's appearance, as shown in Figure 4.3. The functionality remains, for the most part, unchanged. Note that the default template for `RadioButton` and for `ToggleButton` do not differentiate the `Unchecked` and `Indeterminate` states. If you want a `RadioButton` that behaves differently, you will have to modify the template (as you will see in Chapter 10).

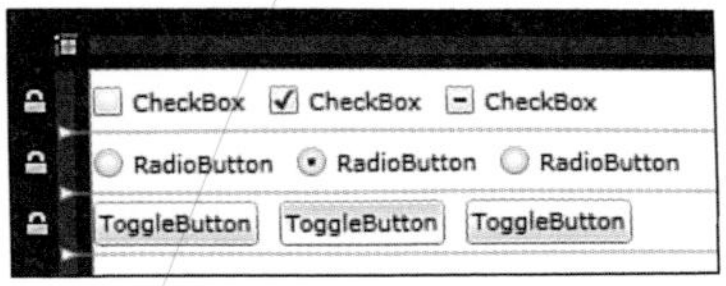

FIGURE 4.3 *CheckBox*, *RadioButton*, and *ToggleButton* in three states (in Blend).

Another example is the `ListBox`. This data control is used to represent a list of items. Thanks to the possibility to redesign an item's template (called `DataTemplate`) completely, as well as the `ListBox` 's template itself, it is a really versatile control that can be adapted to many uses.

The Silverlight Toolkit

As previously mentioned in Chapter 1, "Three Years of Silverlight," the Silverlight team works in a very agile manner. One of the principles of this software development methodology is to release small incremental versions, and to release them often. However, when you publish a framework as rich as Silverlight, there are limits to how often you can release new versions. Some important firms have large projects, and converting them to a new version of Silverlight takes time, costs money, and creates frustration. On the other hand, having new controls as soon as possible is very important for other customers. For this purpose, Microsoft is releasing new controls into a "staging area" called the Silverlight Toolkit. This is a CodePlex project (available at http://silverlight.codeplex.com) where a large number of controls are made available to the public, including the source code and unit tests. The Toolkit is a probably the first place that developers should check when they need a new Silverlight control.

An interesting aspect of the Silverlight Toolkit is that it defines four bands for the included controls:

- **The *Experimental* band, for controls in early development**: This band is used mostly to gather feedback. Controls in the Experimental band should not be used in production applications. Also, these controls may disappear from future versions of the Toolkit.
- **The *Preview* band, for controls that are ready for basic scenarios (alpha version)**: Some changes may affect the control's interface, so you might have to edit your code if you use these controls. Using controls from the Preview band in production application is risky, but might be okay, for example, if the application is not due for release before a certain time.
- **The *Stable* band, for controls that are ready for most scenarios (beta version) but might be subject to a few minor changes in the future**: Using these controls in a production application should not be critical, as long as you are aware of their beta-like quality.
- **The *Mature* band, for controls that are ready for production**: These controls might change in future versions (if security requires it, for example).

TIP

Moving Controls to the Core Framework

When a new Silverlight framework is released, Microsoft includes some of the controls from the Toolkit's Mature band into the core framework. Readers of *Silverlight 2 Unleashed* may remember that some of the controls we studied (such as the `Calendar`, `DatePicker`, `DataGrid`) were in the Toolkit at that time, and are now included into the core Silverlight framework. For the developer, converting a Silverlight 2 project to Silverlight 3 or 4 allows removing some external dependencies to assemblies and reducing the size of the application downloaded to the Silverlight plug-in.

Installing the Silverlight Toolkit

The Toolkit can be installed with an MSI installer, which you can download from the CodePlex site. By default, all the files get installed into C:\Program Files\Microsoft SDKs\Silverlight\v4.0\Toolkit\[DATE] (where [DATE] is the Toolkit's date; for example, Apr10). On Windows x64 machines, "Program Files" is replaced by "Program Files (x86)".

Note that the Toolkit is distributed under the MS-PL license, which is Microsoft's open source license. This grants you the right to modify the Toolkit's source code (included when you install it).

Using the Silverlight Toolkit in Visual Studio

After the Toolkit has been installed, you should see all the controls in the Visual Studio toolbox. Visual Studio assists you when adding controls to the page by referencing the correct DLLs and adding the required XML namespaces, as you will see with the following steps:

1. Create a new Silverlight 4 application.
2. Open MainPage.xaml in the Visual Studio designer.
3. Select the control that you want to add from the Toolbox and drag it onto the designer surface.
4. Customize the control using the Properties panel.

> **TIP**
>
> **If You Don't See the Controls in the Toolbox**
>
> Sometimes a control might be missing from the Toolbox. To set up what the Toolbox displays, follow these steps:
>
> 1. Right-click anywhere on the Toolbox panel.
> 2. Select Choose Items from the context menu. Opening this dialog can take quite a long time.
> 3. In the Choose Toolbox Items dialog, select the Silverlight Components tab. Then check or uncheck the controls you want to display or hide.
> 4. Click OK. The Toolbox should now be updated.

Note that you can also add a reference to the correct DLL manually, using the Add Reference context menu in the Solution Explorer. In that case, you must also add an xmlns statement pointing a prefix to the CLR namespace in which the control is located.

For instance, the `Accordion` control that we detail further in this chapter is included in the assembly System.Windows.Controls.Layout.Toolkit, in the namespace System.Windows.Controls. Therefore, the XAML code to add an `Accordion` control to the main grid looks like Listing 4.11. You can find the information about the control's DLL and its namespace in the Toolkit's documentation (and throughout this chapter).

LISTING 4.11 Adding an Accordion Control in XAML

```
<UserControl
  x:Class="SilverlightApplication7.MainPage"
  xmlns="http://schemas.microsoft.com/winfx/2006/xaml/presentation"
  xmlns:x="http://schemas.microsoft.com/winfx/2006/xaml"
  xmlns:toolkit="
http://schemas.microsoft.com/winfx/2006/xaml/presentation/toolkit">

    <Grid x:Name="LayoutRoot"
          Background="White">
        <toolkit:Accordion>
            <toolkit:AccordionItem Content="Item 1"
                Header="Header 1" />
            <toolkit:AccordionItem Content="Item 2"
                Header="Header 2" />
        </layoutToolkit:Accordion>
    </Grid>
</UserControl>
```

Using the Silverlight Toolkit in Expression Blend

In Blend, using a control from the toolkit is a quite easy, too, as the following steps show:

1. Create a new Silverlight 4 application in Blend.
2. In the Assets library, select the control or panel that you want to add to the scene, and drag it on the designer surface.
3. Blend takes care of adding all the references needed for you.

Exploring the Controls

Together with the Toolkit, a sample browser (shown in Figure 4.4) gets installed, allowing you to explore the controls included, understand how they can be used and get sample XAML, C#, and VB.NET code. The Toolkit sample browser can be started from the Microsoft Silverlight 4 Toolkit folder in your Start menu. The full source code is also installed on your machine and a link is available in the Toolkit folder in the Start menu.

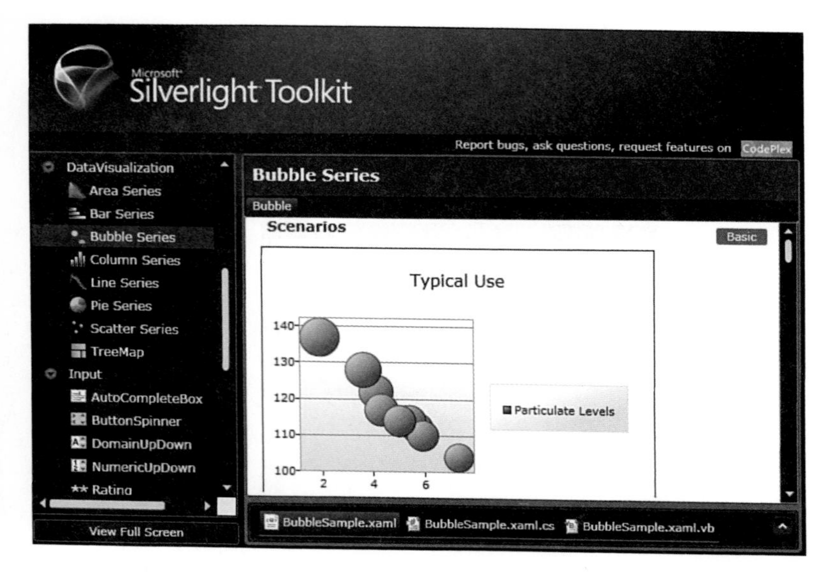

FIGURE 4.4 Toolkit sample browser with a bubble chart sample.

In the version of the Silverlight Toolkit that is current at the time of this writing, you will find the following controls:

- **`Chart`, `Rating`, `NumericUpDown`, `TimeUpDown`, `DomainUpDown`, `GlobalCalendar`, `TimePicker`, `Expander`, `Accordion`, `LayoutTransformer`, `TransitioningContentControl`, `DockPanel`, `WrapPanel`, `ContextMenu`**: These controls and panels are reviewed further in this chapter.
- **`DescriptionViewer`, `Label`, `ValidationSummary`, `DataForm`, `BusyIndicator`**: These controls are used in scenarios requiring data entry. You'll learn more about these controls in further chapters.
- **A large number of themes**: Themes can be applied to your application without you having to create styles and templates for the controls. The implicit theme will be picked up by all the controls in your application, unless of course you specify otherwise. You will see how to apply a theme to your application in Chapter 10.

Chart

Namespace: System.Windows.Controls.DataVisualization.Charting

Assembly: System.Windows.Controls.DataVisualization.Toolkit.dll

Charting is traditionally an area where third-party providers have been active and provide, in some cases, advanced solutions. However, for many smaller applications, the cost of such a professional solution can be prohibitive. This is why the Silverlight Toolkit's chart controls are a very interesting alternative.

At the time of writing, the following chart types are available in the Toolkit: Area, Bar, Bubble, Columns, Line, Pie, Scatter, and Stacked. Some of these chart types are shown in Figure 4.5.

The charts available allow a great level of flexibility, including the possibility to define multiple series, custom axis, and even dynamic data with the chart being animated as the data is changing.

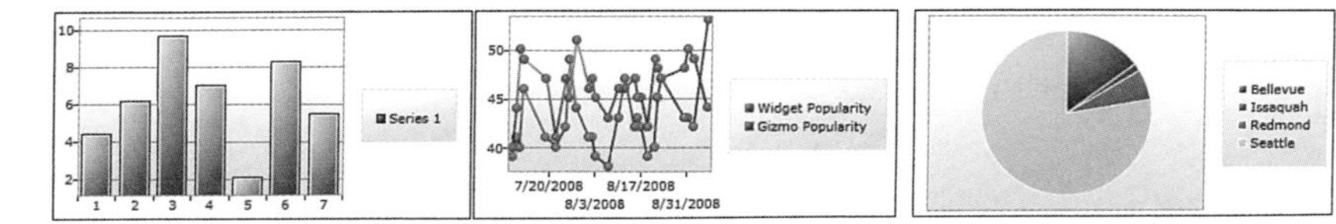

FIGURE 4.5 Three types of charts: Column, Line, Pie.

Rating

Namespace: System.Windows.Controls

Assembly: System.Windows.Controls.Input.Toolkit.dll

The `Rating` control is interesting when you want to allow your application's user to rate an article, a picture, and so forth. Like most of the controls in the Silverlight Toolkit, this control can be used with a default style or with a custom style/template, allowing an unlimited range of changes, as shown in Figure 4.6. Note that the number of items (stars, bullets, and so on) can be customized through a property; also, the rated value is a double, allowing for fractional values to be entered.

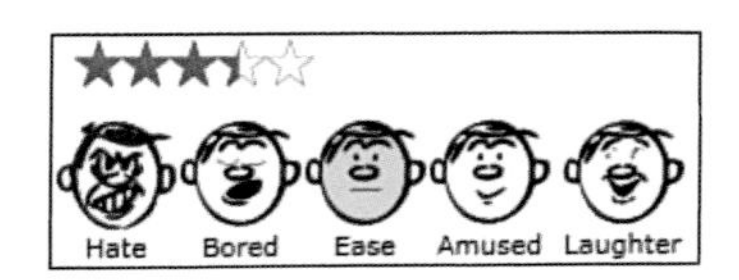

FIGURE 4.6 Rating control in default style, and with customized template.

`NumericUpDown`, `TimeUpDown`, `DomainUpDown`

Namespace: System.Windows.Controls

Assembly: System.Windows.Controls.Input.Toolkit.dll

These three controls all derive from the same base class named `UpDownBase<T>`. This is a generic control, and can be extended for additional types if needed. These controls have an input area and a spinner buttons. The buttons are used to increment the value, while the input area can be used to jump to a value by entering it using the keyboard. Because the Silverlight Toolkit comes with the source code, you can check how the team created these controls, and inspire yourself from that solution to create your own up-down control:

- `NumericUpDown` is used to "spin" numeric values. This is the simplest of the three controls.

- `TimeUpDown`, like the name shows, is used to "spin" time values. Depending on the location of the cursor in the control's input area, either the hours, the minutes, or (if available) the AM/PM indicator are spun. Note that you can change the time representation by using the `Culture` property (for example, en-US or fr-CH).
- `DomainUpDown` is the most complex of the three up-down controls available in the Toolkit. In fact, it is more of a data control: You can data bind its `ItemsSource` property to a collection of items. You can also customize the items' appearance by creating a data template and assigning it to the `ItemTemplate` property. Thus, the `DomainUpDown` is quite similar in its usage to a `ListBox`.

The Silverlight Toolkit's sample browser has many examples of up-down controls in the Input section. Make sure to check them out and review the source code to understand how they are configured.

`GlobalCalendar`

Namespace: System.Windows.Controls

Assembly: System.Windows.Controls.Toolkit.dll

A control very similar to the `Calendar` control that is available in the core framework, the `GlobalCalendar` can display years, months, and dates for a given culture. To change the culture of the `GlobalCalendar` to ja-JP (Japanese culture), use the code in Listing 4.12.

LISTING 4.12 Setting the `GlobalCalendar`'s Culture

```
MyCalendar.CalendarInfo
    = new CultureCalendarInfo(new CultureInfo("ja-JP"));
```

`TimePicker`

Namespace: System.Windows.Controls

Assembly: System.Windows.Controls.Input.Toolkit.dll

The `TimePicker` is complementary to the already well-known `DatePicker` that was available in earlier versions of the Toolkit, and as of Silverlight 3, inside the core Silverlight framework. It is composed of a `TimeUpDown` control (which we discussed earlier in this chapter) and a small button shaped as a clock. The clock displays a pop-up allowing selecting a time. Note that the pop-up can be customized to display a range control with sliders, as shown in Figure 4.7. Also, the `TimePicker` can be customized for a given culture (with the `ActualCulture` property) and for a given format (using the `ActualFormat` property).

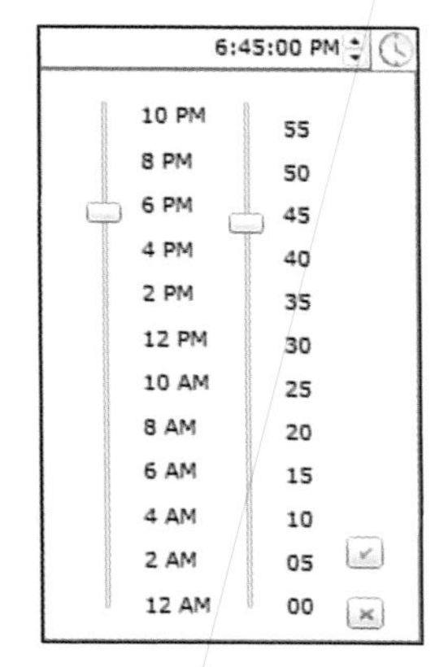

FIGURE 4.7 *`TimePicker`* with *`RangeTimePickerPopup`*.

`Expander`

Namespace: System.Windows.Controls

Assembly: System.Windows.Controls.Toolkit.dll

Accordion

Namespace: System.Windows.Controls

Assembly: System.Windows.Controls.Layout.Toolkit.dll

The `Expander` and `Accordion` controls are two controls used to hide/show their content to create flexible layout.

The `Expander` has one `Content` property that can be any object (as is usual for `ContentControls`). The `Content` will be expanded/collapsed when the user clicks the header, you we see in Figure 4.8:

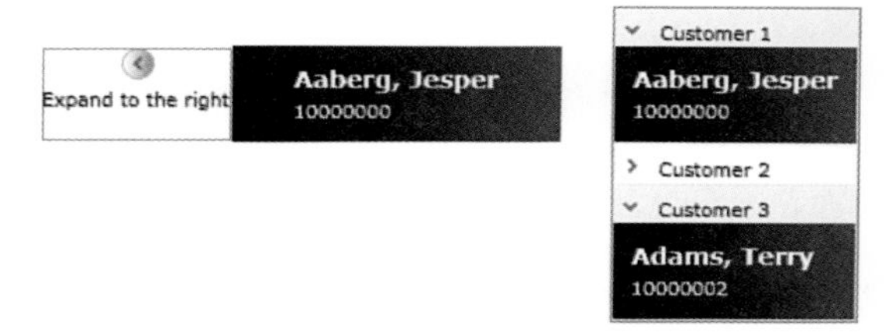

FIGURE 4.8 *Expander* and *Accordion* controls.

- If the `Content` is a string, a `TextBlock` will be used automatically for the display.
- If the `Content` is a `UIElement`, it will be rendered.
- For data items, you can set the `ContentTemplate` property to specify how the item must be rendered.

The `Accordion` control works a little like the `Expander`, but with multiple `AccordionItem` instances, each with a `Content` property and a `Header` as seen on Figure 4.8. You can either set the `AccordionItem` instances manually, or bind the `Accordion`'s `ItemsSource` property to a collection, like with other data controls.

Depending on the `SelectionMode` property, the `Accordion` may display one only of the items (automatically closing the others), or just leave them open/closed as the user activates them. Other properties such as `SelectionSequence` (`Simultaneous` or `CollapseBeforeExpand`) and `ExpandDirection` govern the way that the `AccordionItem` instances are expanded/collapsed, as shown in Listing 4.13.

LISTING 4.13 Expander and Accordion Controls

```
<toolkit:Expander
    ExpandDirection="Right"
    Header="Expand to the right"
    Content="{Binding Collection[0], Source={StaticResource Customers}}"
    ContentTemplate="{StaticResource ExpanderContentTemplate}" />

<toolkit:Accordion
    ContentTemplate="{StaticResource ExpanderContentTemplate}"
    SelectionMode="ZeroOrMore"
    SelectionSequence="CollapseBeforeExpand">
    <toolkit:AccordionItem
```

```
        Content="{Binding Collection[0],
                         Source={StaticResource Customers}}"
        Header="Customer 1" />

    <toolkit:AccordionItem
        Content="{Binding Collection[1],
                         Source={StaticResource Customers}}"
        Header="Customer 2" />

    <toolkit:AccordionItem
        Content="{Binding Collection[2],
                         Source={StaticResource Customers}}"
        Header="Customer 3" />
</toolkit:Accordion>
```

`LayoutTransformer`

Namespace: System.Windows.Controls

Assembly: System.Windows.Controls.Layout.Toolkit.dll

This control is quite specialized. WPF developers are familiar with the two types of transformations that this framework offers: `RenderTransform` (available in Silverlight) and `LayoutTransform` (not available in Silverlight). The main difference is that `RenderTransform` will modify the elements after the layout pass is completed. Other controls are not affected by a `RenderTransform`. This can create unwanted side effects. For example, Figure 4.9 shows three `Buttons` in a `StackPanel`. The middle button is transformed by a `RenderTransform` (45-degree `RotateTransform`).

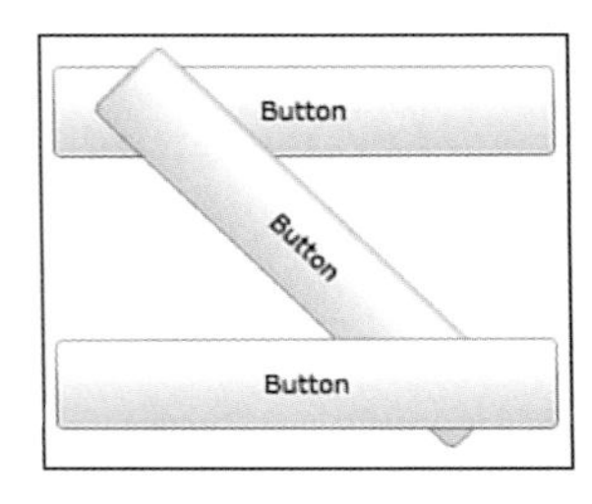

FIGURE 4.9 *RenderTransform* applied to a button.

On the other hand, the `LayoutTransform` is applied before the layout pass, which means that other controls' placement (and in some case their size) will be modified according to the transformed element (as shown in Figure 4.10).

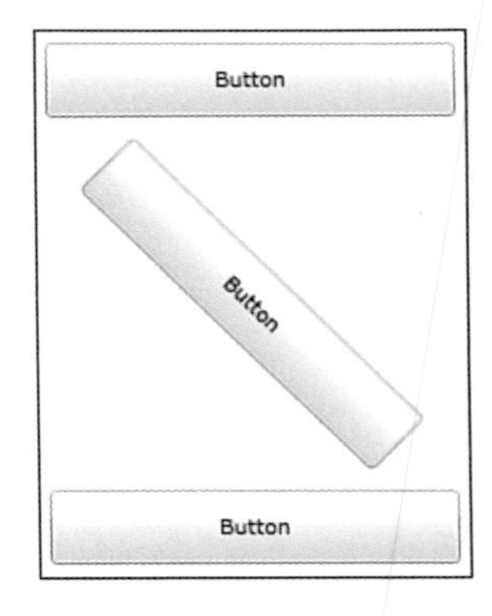

FIGURE 4.10 *LayoutTransform* applied to a button (with *LayoutTransformer*).

Because `LayoutTransform` is not available in the core Silverlight framework, however, using the `LayoutTransformer` instead solves the issue (see Listing 4.14). You can find more information about this control on its developer's blog, David Anson: http://www.galasoft.ch/sl4-layouttransform.

LISTING 4.14 LayoutTransform Applied to a Button (with LayoutTransformer)

```
<toolkit:LayoutTransformer>
     <toolkit:LayoutTransformer.LayoutTransform>
          <TransformGroup>
               <ScaleTransform/>
               <SkewTransform/>
               <RotateTransform Angle="45"/>
               <TranslateTransform/>
          </TransformGroup>
     </toolkit:LayoutTransformer.LayoutTransform>
     <Button Content="Button" Height="40" Width="213" />
</toolkit:LayoutTransformer>
```


`TransitioningContentControl`

Namespace: System.Windows.Controls

Assembly: System.Windows.Controls.Layout.Toolkit.dll

This control can be used in place of a standard `ContentControl` to create a smooth transition between two different contents. The transitions are specified using visual states. By default, the control knows the `"UpTransition"` (the old content shifts up before being replaced by the new content) and the `"DownTransition"` (the exact opposite). You can also specify different transitions using the `VisualStateManager`. You can find more information about the `TransitioningContentControl` on Jesse Liberty's blog, at http://www.galasoft.ch/sl4-transitioncontrol.

`DockPanel`

Namespace: System.Windows.Controls

Assembly: System.Windows.Controls.Toolkit.dll

The `DockPanel` is well known from WPF. It is useful to lay out your application by anchoring UI elements to various sides of the panel. To change which side of the panel an element is docked to, use the `DockPanel.Dock` attached property. Its value can be `Left`, `Right`, `Top`, or `Bottom`, as shown in Listing 4.15. For more information about attached properties, see Chapter 5, "Understanding Dependency Properties."

In addition,, you can specify whether the last element added to the panel must fill the rest of the space. Depending on the value of the `LastChildFill` property on the `DockPanel`, the layout will vary, as shown in Figure 4.11. The default for this property is `True`.

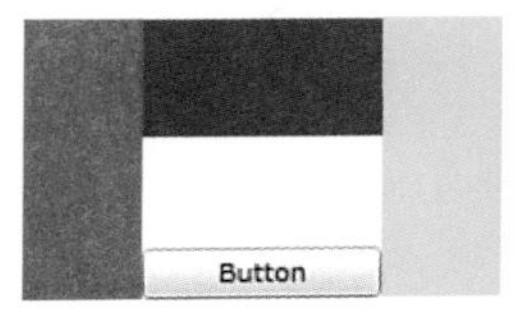

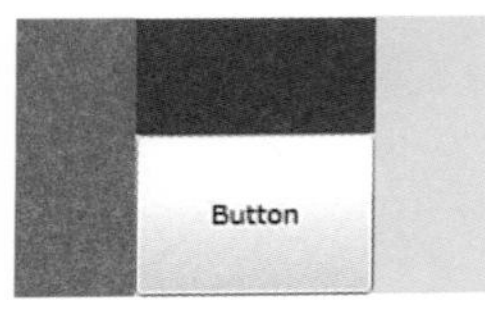

FIGURE 4.11 *`LastChildFill`* property set to *`False`* or *`True`*.

LISTING 4.15 Setting Elements in a DockPanel

```
<toolkit:DockPanel LastChildFill="False">
    <Rectangle Fill="Red" Width="50"
               toolkit:DockPanel.Dock="Left" />
    <Rectangle Fill="Yellow" Width="50"
               toolkit:DockPanel.Dock="Right" />
    <Rectangle Fill="Blue" Height="50"
               toolkit:DockPanel.Dock="Top" />
    <Button Content="Button"
            toolkit:DockPanel.Dock="Bottom" />
</toolkit:DockPanel>
```

`WrapPanel`

Namespace: System.Windows.Controls

Assembly: System.Windows.Controls.Toolkit.dll

`WrapPanels` are useful to display multiple items in a row, with the ability to wrap on the next line when the panel is resized. This ability is especially interesting when the `WrapPanel` is used as the presenting panel for a data control, such as a `ListBox`. To do this, just set the `ListBox`'s `ItemsPanel` property to a `WrapPanel`, as shown in Listing 4.16 and in Figure 4.12.

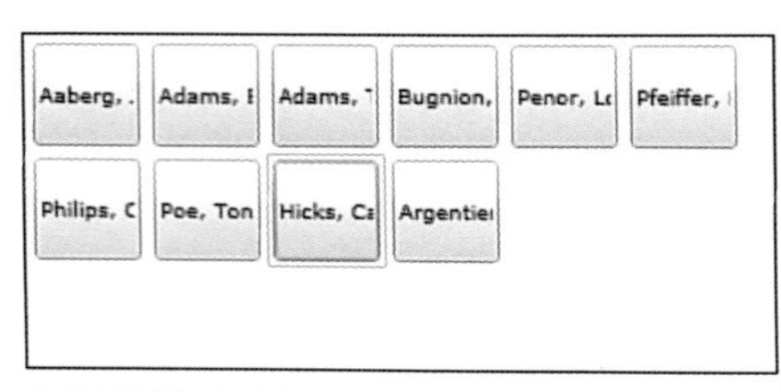

FIGURE 4.12 Using a *WrapPanel* as *ItemPanel* for a *ListBox*.

LISTING 4.16 Using a WrapPanel as ItemPanel for a ListBox

```
<ListBox ItemsSource="{Binding Source={StaticResource Customers},
                               Path=Collection}"
         ItemTemplate="{StaticResource MyItemTemplate}"
         Grid.Column="1"
         ScrollViewer.HorizontalScrollBarVisibility="Disabled"
         ScrollViewer.VerticalScrollBarVisibility="Disabled">
    <ListBox.ItemsPanel>
        <ItemsPanelTemplate>
            <toolkit:WrapPanel />
        </ItemsPanelTemplate>
    </ListBox.ItemsPanel>
</ListBox>
```

The ContextMenu

Until recently, the Silverlight developer did not have any control on what was displayed when the user right-clicks on the Silverlight application: The `MouseRightButtonDown` was unavailable for the developers, and reserved to display the Silverlight menu only.

In Silverlight 4, the MouseRightButtonDown event is now available and can be handled by your application, as we will see in Chapter 17, "New Transforms, Right Click, HTML Browser, WebBrowserBrush, and Isolated Storage." In the Silverlight Toolkit, a ContextMenu is even provided. It makes it very easy to build customizable context menus, for example with the code in Listing 4.17. Note that each menu item can also display icons if desired.

LISTING 4.17 Using a ContextMenu

```
<Image Source="../Assets/sl4bloglogo.png">
    <toolkit:ContextMenuService.ContextMenu>
        <toolkit:ContextMenu>
            <toolkit:MenuItem Header="Menu 1"
                              Click="Menu1Click" />
            <toolkit:MenuItem Header="Menu 2"
                              Click="Menu2Click" />
        </toolkit:ContextMenu>
    </toolkit:ContextMenuService.ContextMenu>
</Image>
```


Third-Party Providers

It is hard to keep track of all the third-party providers of Silverlight controls. It is also very difficult to recommend one or the other, because it really depends what problem you are trying to solve in your project.

The following checklist can be useful when trying to choose a third party provider for your controls:

- Check the provider's reputation online. Thankfully, with modern means of communication such as online forums or Twitter, users are more vocal than they used to be. It is fairly easy to find information online about a provider.
- However, remember that users are much more prone to voice negative comments than positive ones. So, take each comment online with a grain of salt. If you are in doubt about what really happened, do not hesitate to contact the person who wrote the comment to ask for clarification.
- If you don't find information about the provider you are interested in, post your questions about them, either on Twitter or on independent forums such as http://www.silverlight.net.
- Check what support plan the provider is offering. Will you get a guaranteed answer if you have an issue, and in what time frame? Many providers offer help through online forums on their website. Take some time to check the quality of the replies, and who wrote them: Is it a member of the support team? Is it the developer himself (in which case, it might mean that there is no dedicated support team)?

- Are the controls free or "cheap"? What does this imply in terms of quality? Although some free controls have a really good quality, and might totally fulfill your needs, do not underestimate the value of a good support team.
- What is your relationship with this provider? Did you have experience with other of their products? Many professional controls providers have offerings in other technologies too (such as ASP.NET, WPF, Windows Forms, and so on). Did someone in your firm work with them already?
- Is there a possibility to evaluate the controls? If yes, for how much time, and under which conditions?
- How good is the documentation? Is it easy to find information about the controls' interface? Can you find working samples?

In summary, plan enough time to evaluate carefully the different offerings. Remember that controls providers cater to a large audience, and their controls are designed to cover a large spectrum of uses. You are most probably going to have to customize the controls for your specific application. This is going to take some time, and you want to take precautions before you start coding.

Summary

Silverlight 4 is the most mature version of the framework. This maturity is clearly visible in the number of controls available, and in the means provided by the framework to build new controls.

In this chapter, we talked about various changes in the Silverlight framework to facilitate the creation of controls and their use in Silverlight applications. With these changes, the framework is becoming richer and more compatible with Windows Presentation Foundation and more able to support your needs as a developer and a designer.

With this maturity, we see the appearance of a large number of controls, within the framework and outside; so much so in fact that every developer intending to use controls in his project should plan enough time to evaluate the various offerings. We talked about the three main sources of Silverlight controls: the Silverlight framework itself, the Silverlight Toolkit, and third-party providers. We also reviewed some of the controls available, and you worked through an application with a number of samples. Additional samples for the Silverlight Toolkit are available in the toolkit sample browser that is provided when the toolkit itself is installed on a development machine.

CHAPTER 5

Understanding Dependency Properties

IN THIS CHAPTER, WE WILL:

- Discover the dependency property system and the DependencyObject class.
- See how dependency properties are registered.
- Talk about attached properties, another kind of dependency properties.
- See how attached properties can be used to become attached behaviors.
- Understand how a dependency property's value is calculated.

The dependency property system is probably one of the most important fundaments of Silverlight (and Windows Presentation Foundation, too). A lot of functionality is based on dependency objects and their properties (most important, data binding and the animation system).

In fact, many of the types used in the Silverlight framework derive from the `DependencyObject` class, as the following steps show:

1. Open the Silverlight 4 documentation (available offline, CHM file, from http://www.galasoft.ch/sl4-offlinedoc, or online at http://www.galasoft.ch/sl4-onlinedoc).
2. Navigate to a class (for example, the `ScrollViewer` control, in the namespace System.Windows.Controls).
3. Scroll down until you see the class hierarchy, as shown in Figure 5.1.
4. Notice how the second highest class in the hierarchy (directly under the `Object` class) is `DependencyObject`.

You are likely to encounter `DependencyObject` very often in Silverlight. For example, all the classes that derive from `UIElement` (that is, all the elements that can be drawn on the screen) are also `DependencyObject` instances. This shows how deeply the dependency property system is rooted in the Silverlight framework.

In *Silverlight 2 Unleashed*, Chapter 15, we explored the class hierarchy and explained what role the `object`, `DependencyObject`, `UIElement`, and `FrameworkElement` classes play. It is a good moment to refresh your memory if needed before we dive deeper.

⊟ **Inheritance Hierarchy**
System.Object
  System.Windows.DependencyObject
    System.Windows.UIElement
      System.Windows.FrameworkElement
        System.Windows.Controls.Control
          System.Windows.Controls.ContentControl
            System.Windows.Controls.ScrollViewer

FIGURE 5.1 *ScrollViewer* control class hierarchy.

Inheriting DependencyObject

The `DependencyObject` class serves two major purposes:

- Providing an interface to facilitate interaction between threads
- Hosting dependency properties

Threading

We will talk about threading in more detail in Chapter 22 "Advanced Development Techniques." What we need to remember for now is that most objects are owned by the thread that created them. In most cases, this is the main thread of the application (called the UI thread) that owns the objects (for instance, all the `UIElement` instances).

However, when long-running tasks are executed on the UI thread, all other activities are blocked until that task is completed. It means that animations will not run anymore, and the controls will not react to user input. This is a rather irritating effect that hinders the user experience.

In such a case, the best practice is to spawn a background thread (as we will do in Chapter 22). This way, the UI thread is not blocked and can process animations and user input. However, every access from the background thread to the objects owned by the UI thread (including all the `UIElement` instances, as mentioned previously) must be *dispatched* to avoid a crash in the application. The `DependencyObject` has two members to help you with that task:

- **The `Dispatcher` property**: Each thread has one instance of the `Dispatcher` class that manages the queue of operations to be executed on that thread. This is the class you use when you want to dispatch an operation from one thread to another. Do not let the fact that the `Dispatcher` class and the `DependencyObject.Dispatcher` property have the same name confuse you.
- **The `CheckAccess` method**: When an object calls this method on another object, the method returns true if direct access is allowed. If that is not the case, the operation must be dispatched.

In Chapter 22, we will work more with threading in Silverlight and spend more time with the `Dispatcher` object.

Accessing a Dependency Property's Value

Dependency properties are registered in a static manner, as you will see in "Registering Dependency Properties," later in this chapter. It means that the value for each different instance of a class is administrated by the dependency property system, and must be accessed using methods that are defined on the `DependencyObject` class:

- The `SetValue` and `GetValue` methods are used to set and get the value of a given dependency property.
- The `ClearValue` method is used to reset the property to its default value. (You will see in a moment how to define a default value for a dependency property.)
- Two methods, `ReadLocalValue` and `GetAnimationBaseValue` are used to get the dependency property's value in some special cases, as covered later in this chapter.

Now that you understand better what a `DependencyObject` does, let's talk about dependency properties themselves, and how to define new ones.

Using a `DependencyObject` as Data Item

The `DependencyObject` class itself is abstract in Silverlight and therefore cannot be instantiated. However, in Silverlight 4, it is possible to derive a class from `DependencyObject` to host dependency properties. You can then use instances of this class as data objects, as shown in Listing 5.1.

LISTING 5.1 `Customer` Class Inheriting `DependencyObject`

```
1  public class Customer : DependencyObject
2  {
3      public const string NamePropertyName = "Name";
4
5       public string Name
6      {
7          get { return (string)GetValue(NameProperty); }
8          set { SetValue(NameProperty, value); }
9      }
10
11     public static readonly DependencyProperty NameProperty
12         = DependencyProperty.Register(
13         NamePropertyName,
14         typeof(string),
15         typeof(Customer),
16         new PropertyMetadata(string.Empty));
17
18     public Customer(string name)
19     {
```

```
20            Name = name;
21        }
22    }
```

See the “Registering Dependency Properties” section for more details about Listing 5.1.

Using a Better Implementation for Data Items

Using full-blown `DependencyObject` instances to host data might not be the best idea. Using the dependency property system requires quite a lot of code, and if you do not explicitly need it, it is better to avoid creating a `DependencyObject` for this kind of purpose.

A better solution is to use *plain old CLR objects* (also known as POCO) implementing an interface called `INotifyPropertyChanged`. (You met this interface already in Chapter 4, “Investigating Existing Controls,” in Listing 4.6.) This is very convenient because data bindings will react when the `PropertyChanged` event that this interface defines is raised. However, raising the event must be done explicitly in code when the value of the property changes, while dependency properties do this automatically. Listing 5.2 shows an alternative implementation of the `Customer` object, with exactly the same features.

LISTING 5.2 Customer Class with `INotifyPropertyChanged`

```
 1  public class Customer : INotifyPropertyChanged
 2  {
 3      public event PropertyChangedEventHandler PropertyChanged;
 4
 5       public const string NamePropertyName
 6          = "Name";
 7
 8      private string _name = string.Empty;
 9
10      public string Name
11      {
12          get
13          {
14              return _name;
15          }
16
17          set
18          {
19              if (_name == value)
20              {
21                  return;
22              }
23
24              _name = value;
```

```
25                 RaisePropertyChanged(NamePropertyName);
26             }
27         }
28
29         public Customer(string name)
30         {
31             Name = name;
32         }
33
34         private void RaisePropertyChanged(string propertyName)
35         {
36             if (PropertyChanged != null)
37             {
38                 PropertyChanged(
39                     this,
40                     new PropertyChangedEventArgs(propertyName));
41             }
42         }
43     }
```

5

- Line 3 implements the `INotifyPropertyChanged` interface by declaring the `PropertyChanged` event.
- Line 5 declares the name of the property as a constant. String-based identifiers should be stored in constants to avoid errors when the identifier is used in another part of the code.
- Line 8 declares an attribute for the `Name` property value and initializes it.
- Lines 12 to 15 are a simple getter for the `Name` property.
- Lines 19 to 22 verify whether the property is actually changed by the object calling it. If it is unchanged, we simply return, to avoid raising the `PropertyChanged` event unnecessarily.
- Line 25 calls a utility method declared a little further in the code, which raises the `PropertyChanged` event.
- Lines 34 to 42 are declaring this utility method: First we check that the `PropertyChanged` event is not `null`. In .NET, events are `null` if no other object registered for them. That would be the case if no data binding and no other object used the `Customer` object. Raising the `PropertyChanged` event if it is `null` will crash the application.
- Finally, on line 38 to 40, we raise the `PropertyChanged` event. By convention, the first argument of this event (and all other events in .NET) is the event sender, which we set to this. The second argument is an instance of `PropertyChangedEventArgs`, which carries the name of the changed property as payload.

WARNING

Using "Magic Strings"

Many areas in Silverlight rely on what programmers in the Silverlight community call "magic strings." For example, registering a dependency property requires the name of this property to be passed as a string to the `DependencyProperty.Register` method. This is dangerous because if you want to modify the name of one of these identifiers, you must look everywhere in your code (and XAML!) to make sure that you changed it correctly. Using constants to store string identifiers (as on line 3) is a good step to avoid such errors. Unfortunately, this is not possible in XAML.

The implementations in Listing 5.1 and Listing 5.2 are equivalent from a data binding point of view. However, Listing 5.2 does not rely on the dependency property system at all. POCO objects like this one are easier to handle for other objects: They can be easily tested (for example, in unit tests), passed to web services, serialized for safekeeping, and so forth.

This is why it is usually better to rely on implementing `INotifyPropertyChanged` for data objects, and reserve `DependencyObject` instances for user interface objects such as controls, UI elements, and so forth.

Registering Dependency Properties

As you saw in Listing 5.1, a dependency property needs to be registered using the static method `DependencyProperty.Register`. Let's review Listing 5.1 and understand what we implemented:

- Line 3 stores the name of the property in a constant. Like when we implemented `INotifyPropertyChanged` in Listing 5.2, it is a good practice to store any string identifier in a constant to avoid errors when using this identifier.
- Lines 5 to 9 declare a getter and a setter for the `Name` property. The getter uses the method `GetValue` implemented by the `DependencyObject` base class. Similarly, the setter uses the method `SetValue`. The value of the property is not stored locally, but is instead stored within the dependency property system.

WARNING

Convenience Getter and Setter

In fact, the property getter and setter declared on lines 5 to 9 of Listing 5.1 are not used by the data binding system or the animation system to modify the property's value. They are only here for convenience: It is easier to use the `Name` property directly instead of having to call the methods `GetValue` and `SetValue` each time.

- Lines 11 to 16 are where the actual registration takes place. The static method `DependencyProperty.Register` takes four parameters:

  The name of the property that is registered. We use the constant we declared on line 3

  The type of the dependency property

  The type of the object to which the dependency property belongs

  An instance of the `PropertyMetadata` class, which we discuss in the "Defining Metadata" section, next.
- Note that the object returned by the `Register` method is saved, and used as an identifier for the dependency property. It is used in various occasions (for example, when a binding is created in code, as you will see in Chapter 6, "Working with Data: Binding, Grouping, Sorting, and Filtering."
- Finally, we declare a constructor for the `Customer` class. Notice how we use the convenience setter for the `Name` property on line 20.

Because the convenience getter and setter are public, other objects can use them to set and get the dependency property's value. Of course, depending on your implementation, you might want to restrict the getter's or the setter's visibility. You can even delete the `Name` getter and setter altogether and rely only on the methods `GetValue` and `SetValue` if you prefer.

Defining Metadata

The dependency property system requires a little more information during the registration process. We provide this information using an instance of the `PropertyMetadata` class.

TIP

Why Metadata?

The `DependencyProperty.Register` method was implemented first in Windows Presentation Foundation (WPF, Silverlight's richer counterpart for the Windows desktop). In fact, the `Register` method and the metadata system available in WPF are more complex than the ones in Silverlight, and allow for more functionality. The syntax available in Silverlight might seem a little cumbersome at times, but it is in fact there for reason of compatibility with the richer WPF framework.

Setting a Default Value

The `PropertyMetadata` constructor allows setting a default value for the property. Every time that an instance of the `Customer` object is created, the `Name` dependency property is set to `string.Empty`.

Handling a Property Change

As mentioned earlier, the data binding system as well as the animation system set a property's value through the base class's SetValue method, and not through the convenience setter. Because of this, the object you are implementing will not be notified if another object sets one of its properties.

To solve this problem, you need to use a different overload of the PropertyMetadata constructor and provide a PropertyChangedCallback delegate. To illustrate this, let's add a dependency property named NumberOfChanges to the Customer class. This property should be incremented every time that the Name property is modified. The registration for the Name dependency property becomes Listing 5.3.

LISTING 5.3 Modified Name Dependency Property with PropertyChangedCallback

```
1  public static readonly DependencyProperty NameProperty
2      = DependencyProperty.Register(
3      NamePropertyName,
4      typeof(string),
5      typeof(Customer),
6      new PropertyMetadata(string.Empty, UpdateNumberOfChanges));
7
8  private static void UpdateNumberOfChanges(
9      DependencyObject d,
10     DependencyPropertyChangedEventArgs e)
11 {
12     var sender = d as Customer;
13     sender.NumberOfChanges++;
14 }
```

- On line 6, notice that a different overload of the PropertyMetadata constructor is used: We provide a PropertyChangedCallback delegate.
- The delegate is implemented on lines 8 to 14. Such a delegate has two parameters:

  The DependencyObject instance that owns the property. This is needed because the delegate is static (like the rest of the dependency property system). We use the first parameter to set nonstatic properties or call nonstatic methods on the instance.

  An instance of DependencyPropertyChangedEventArgs. This class contains information about the property change: The OldValue, the NewValue, and the DependencyProperty object that changed. Note that OldValue and NewValue are of type object, and must be cast to the actual type of the property.
- On line 12, we cast the first parameter to a Customer object. It is not necessary to check whether the parameter is actually of this type; it is always the case.
- On line 13, we update the property NumberOfChanges on the Customer instance. Note that this property is not present on Listing 5.3 to keep things simpler. You can, however, download a working sample from http://www.galasoft.ch/sl4-inheritdo.

TIP

Casting an Element Using the `as` Keyword

The `as` keyword is used to cast an element from a type to another type (for example, from `DependencyObject` to `Customer`). However, the cast is only successful if the original type (`DependencyObject`) is a super class of the destination type (`Customer`). Should that not be the case, the `as` keyword returns `null`, but does not throw an exception. This provides a convenient way to make sure that an instance is of a given type without having to try/catch an exception.

Note that the `as` keyword cannot be used on value types (such as `int`, `double`, and so forth) or on `struct` types. For these types, the casting operator `()` must be used.

Because the `UpdateNumberOfChanges` method is defined within the `Customer` object, it is possible to call private methods and to set/get private attributes and properties on the `PropertyChangedCallback` delegate's first parameter, because it is also of type `Customer`. This can be a little confusing at first.

There are altogether three overloads to construct a `PropertyMetadata` instance in Silverlight 4. We saw the first one in Listing 5.1 and the second in Listing 5.3. The third overload accepts only the `PropertyChangedCallback` delegate, but no default value for the property. In that case, the property's type's default value will be used (for example, `false` for `bool`, 0 for `int`, `null` for `object`, and so forth.)

Initializing Dependency Objects

Because of the specificities of dependency properties, and because of the fact that often `DependencyObject` is used in XAML documents, some precautions must be taken when initializing them.

Choosing a Good Default Value

The default value for the dependency property must be chosen wisely: The `PropertyChangedCallback` delegate is only executed if the property's new value is different from the previous value. If your implementation of the delegate contains code that is critical for your object's initialization, you must make sure that it is executed.

One way to guarantee that this code will be executed is to choose a default value that the user will not use. It might also be a good idea to notify the user about this, to avoid unwanted side effects. An example is shown in Listing 5.10: The `InitialAngle` property can be set from 0 to 360 degrees. To guarantee that the `PropertyChangedCallback` is executed, the default value for this property is set to 400 degrees.

Defining a Default Constructor

You saw in Chapter 3, "Extending Your Application with Controls," that XAML (like all XML-based languages) requires that the objects it hosts implement a default constructor (that is, a constructor without any parameters). Because most dependency objects will be used in XAML (as UI elements, or as data objects), it is good practice to always define an empty constructor and rely on the properties for the dependency object's initialization.

Remember that in .NET you do not need to explicitly define a default constructor if there is no other constructor in the class. If you define one or more constructors with parameters, however, you must explicitly implement a default constructor (even if it does nothing) for your dependency object to avoid exceptions in XAML.

> **WARNING**
>
> **Understanding the Silverlight Error**
>
> When you attempt to create an object in XAML that does not have an empty constructor, an error message is displayed (see Figure 5.2).

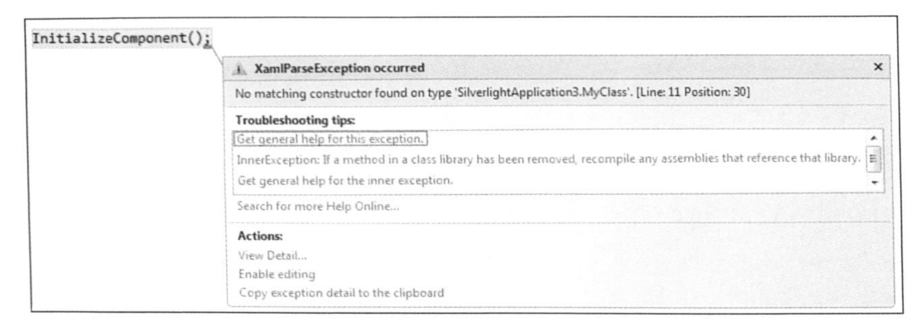

FIGURE 5.2 Error message for an object in XAML without empty constructor (shown in Visual Studio).

Protecting the Code When Properties Are Set

Similarly, remember that objects that are used in XAML can have their properties set in any order. Your `PropertyChangedCallback` code must take this into account. Listing 5.4 shows a `DependencyObject` that we will initialize in XAML. This object has two dependency properties, `Test1` and `Test2`. When one of these properties change, an attribute named `_lowerCaseStrings` is computed, by concatenating both dependency properties in lowercase format.

LISTING 5.4 Initializing a `DependencyObject`

```
 1  public class DataObject : DependencyObject
 2  {
 3      private string _lowerCaseStrings = string.Empty;
 4
 5      public const string Test1PropertyName = "Test1";
 6
 7      public string Test1
 8      {
 9          get { return (string)GetValue(Test1Property); }
10          set { SetValue(Test1Property, value); }
11      }
12
13      public static readonly DependencyProperty Test1Property
```

```
14          = DependencyProperty.Register(
15          Test1PropertyName,
16          typeof(string),
17          typeof(DataObject),
18          new PropertyMetadata(null, UpdateLowerCase));
19
20      public const string Test2PropertyName = "Test2";
21
22      public string Test2
23      {
24          get { return (string)GetValue(Test2Property); }
25          set { SetValue(Test2Property, value); }
26      }
27
28      public static readonly DependencyProperty Test2Property
29          = DependencyProperty.Register(
30          Test2PropertyName,
31          typeof(string),
32          typeof(DataObject),
33          new PropertyMetadata(null, UpdateLowerCase));
34
35      private static void UpdateLowerCase(
36          DependencyObject d,
37          DependencyPropertyChangedEventArgs e)
38      {
39          var sender = d as DataObject;
40
41          if (sender.Test1 == null
42              || sender.Test2 == null)
43          {
44              return;
45          }
46
47          sender._lowerCaseStrings
48              = sender.Test1.ToLower()
49              + sender.Test2.ToLower();
50      }
51  }
```

- Both `Test1` and `Test2` use the method `UpdateLowerCase` as their `PropertyChangedCallback` delegate.
- This method (defined on lines 35 to 50) uses the value of both properties to build the lowercase attribute. Lines 47 to 49 will throw a `NullReferenceException` if either one of the properties is `null`.

- To avoid the exception, we protect the method with lines 41 to 45 and simply exit if the properties are not set yet.
- Note that we didn't define any constructor for the DataObject class, which means that the default constructor is implicit.

This allows us to create a DataObject instance in XAML (in the resources) without worrying about the order of the properties, as shown in Listing 5.5.

LISTING 5.5 Creating Two DataObject Instances in XAML

```
<UserControl.Resources>
    <data:DataObject Test1="Hello"
                     Test2="World"
                     x:Key="TestDataObject1" />

    <data:DataObject Test2="Again"
                     Test1="Another"
                     x:Key="TestDataObject2" />
</UserControl.Resources>
```

Notice in Listing 5.5 how the order of the properties Test1 and Test2 differ. This is not a problem because we protected our code in Listing 5.4. In this case, we created a data object, but the same rules apply to controls and any other DependencyObject, such as controls, shapes, and so on.

Understanding Attached Properties

Using dependency properties is very convenient and powerful, but creating a new such property requires you to have access to the inner implementation of an object. Most of the time, however, this is not possible because you didn't implement the object in question.

One way to modify an existing object's behavior is to create a new class deriving from the original one, and add methods and properties. However, another less-invasive way is also possible: extending the existing class by attaching external properties to it. Such properties in Silverlight are called *attached properties*.

Using Attached Properties for Values

The most well-known usage for attached properties in Silverlight is to define a UI element's placement on a panel (for example, the Grid, the Canvas or the DockPanel). In such a case, the attached property is used as a store for a value that has relevance in only a certain context (when the element is placed onto a corresponding panel). The Grid defines four attached properties:

- Grid.Row and Grid.Column define in which cell of the Grid the element on which the properties are attached must be placed.
- Grid.RowSpan and Grid.ColumnSpan specify over how many rows or columns, respectively, the element must be placed. For instance, the XAML code in Listing 5.6 produces the placement in Figure 5.3 (seen in Expression Blend).

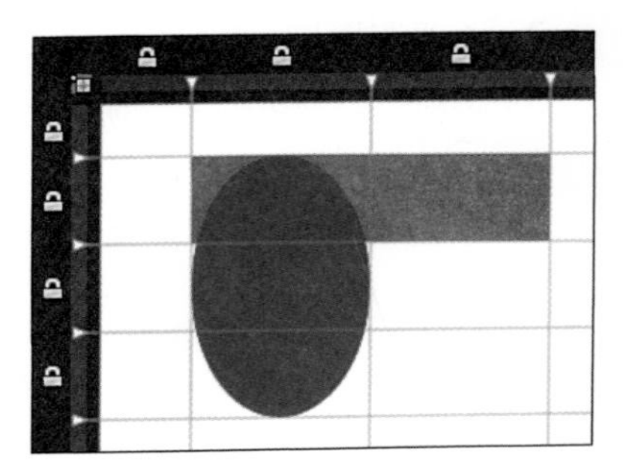

FIGURE 5.3 Setting elements on a *Grid* with attached properties.

LISTING 5.6 Setting Attached Properties in XAML

```
<Rectangle Grid.ColumnSpan="2"
           Grid.Column="1"
           Grid.Row="1"
           Fill="Red" />
<Ellipse Grid.Column="1"
         Grid.Row="1"
         Grid.RowSpan="3"
         Fill="Blue" />
```

Because attached properties are handled by the dependency property systems, the same interaction can be applied to them: data binding, animation, and so forth.

Registering an Attached Property

Attached properties can be defined on any DependencyObject, using the static method DependencyProperty.RegisterAttached, as shown in Listing 5.7. In this code, we create a special ChildWindow (which we examined in Chapter 4) to present a UIElement. We use attached properties to define additional presentation information directly on the element, which we will pass to our PresentationWindow class. When the method Present(UIElement) is called, the attached properties will be retrieved and used to configure the PresentationWindow.

LISTING 5.7 PresentationWindow Implementation

```
1  public partial class PresentationWindow : ChildWindow
2  {
3      public const string CaptionPropertyName = "Caption";
4
5      public static string GetCaption(DependencyObject obj)
6      {
7          return (string)obj.GetValue(CaptionProperty);
8      }
9
10     public static void SetCaption(DependencyObject obj, string value)
11     {
```

```
12            obj.SetValue(CaptionProperty, value);
13        }
14
15        public static readonly DependencyProperty CaptionProperty
16            = DependencyProperty.RegisterAttached(
17            CaptionPropertyName,
18            typeof(string),
19            typeof(PresentationWindow),
20            new PropertyMetadata(string.Empty));
21
22        public void Present(UIElement element)
23        {
24            PresentationGrid.Children.Add(element);
25
26            // Use attached property (if available)
27            var caption = GetCaption(element);
28            if (!string.IsNullOrEmpty(caption))
29            {
30                Title = caption;
31            }
32
33            Show();
34        }
35
36        public PresentationWindow()
37        {
38            InitializeComponent();
39        }
40
41        private void OKButton_Click(object sender, RoutedEventArgs e)
42        {
43            DialogResult = true;
44            PresentationGrid.Children.Clear();
45            Title = string.Empty;
45        }
46    }
```

- On line 3, we define the property's name in a constant. Here, too, we need a string identifier to register the property, and it is a good practice to use a constant for this.
- On line 5 to 8, we implement a method to get the value of the attached property. Note that this method is static. Also, in the contrary to the convenience properties used to access dependency properties, the `Get` and `Set` methods for attached properties are actually used by the system to set and get the value.

- Similarly, we define a static method to set the value of the property on lines 10 to 13. Note that these methods call the `GetValue` and `SetValue` methods defined on the `DependencyObject` class, just like we did in the getter/setter for a dependency property.
- Lines 15 to 20 show the registration itself using the static method `DependencyProperty.RegisterAttached`. It is very similar to registering a "standard" dependency property, and the parameters are the same:

  The attached property's name, which we retrieve from the constant on line 3

  The type of the attached property

  The type of the object to which the attached property belongs

  An instance of the `PropertyMetadata` class, used to define additional information (in this case, the default value)
- On lines 22 to 34, the `Present` method is defined. It accepts a `UIElement`.
- On line 24, we add the `UIElement` parameter to a `Grid` named `PresentationGrid`. This `Grid` is defined in the PresentationWindow.xaml, and simply occupies the whole content area. Note that `PresentationGrid` is cleared when the child window is closed, to avoid keeping references to unused elements.
- On lines 27, we use the `GetCaption` method to retrieve the value of the attached property `Caption` on the `UIElement` in question. Note that it is possible that this property has not been set, in which case `GetCaption` returns `null`.
- If the `Caption` attached property has been set on the `UIElement`, we set this value as the `PresentationWindow`'s title on line 30.
- Finally, we open the window on line 33.
- On lines 44 and 45, we clean up the window when it is closed: The `PresentationGrid` is cleared of elements, and the `Title` is reset.

Of course, we could use additional attached properties to define other properties of the `ChildWindow`; for example, the `OverlayBrush`, the number of buttons to be displayed (OK, Cancel, and so on), and so forth.

Note that the convenience methods are public, and can be used to access an attached property's value outside of the class defining this property. For example, Listing 5.8 shows a method incrementing the `Top` and `Left` properties on a `UIElement` placed into a `Canvas`.

LISTING 5.8 Getting and Setting Attached Properties in Code

```
public void Move(UIElement element)
{
    var x = Canvas.GetLeft(element);
    Canvas.SetLeft(element, x + 1);

    var y = Canvas.GetTop(element);
    Canvas.SetTop(element, y + 1);
}
```

Using Custom Attached Properties in XAML

You already saw in Listing 5.6 how attached properties are set in XAML. For attached properties on a custom class, the syntax is the same, but you need to prefix the reference to the class with the `xmlns` prefix as usual (exactly as you would do for custom controls, user controls, and data objects) For example, Listing 5.9 shows how the `PresentationWindow.Caption` attached property can be set on an `Ellipse` in XAML.

LISTING 5.9 Setting Custom Attached Properties in XAML

```
<Ellipse xmlns:local="clr-namespace:AttachedProperties"
         local:PresentationWindow.Caption="This is an ellipse"
         Fill="Red" Width="100" Height="100" />
```

Implementing an Attached Behavior

In the previous sections, you saw how attached properties can be used to attach a value to an object, even though the object does not implement the property. Another usage for attached property started to be popular not long ago in Silverlight and WPF: using attached properties to create an attached behavior.

When you create an attached behavior, you use the `PropertyChangedCallback` delegate to attach one or more events to the element on which the attached property is set. When the events are raised, the class hosting the attached behavior handles them. We did not just attach data to the element, but we attached actions, a *behavior*.

The following example demonstrates this. We implement an attached behavior that rotates any `UIElement` by 45 degrees every time that the mouse is pressed on the element. The attached behavior and the class hosting it are shown in Listing 5.10.

LISTING 5.10 ElementRotator Class and Attached Behavior

```
public class ElementRotator : DependencyObject
{
    public const string InitialAnglePropertyName = "InitialAngle";

    public static double GetInitialAngle(DependencyObject obj)
    {
```

```
        return (double)obj.GetValue(InitialAngleProperty);
    }

    public static void SetInitialAngle(DependencyObject obj, double value)
    {
        obj.SetValue(InitialAngleProperty, value);
    }

    public static readonly DependencyProperty InitialAngleProperty
        = DependencyProperty.RegisterAttached(
        InitialAnglePropertyName,
        typeof(double),
        typeof(ElementRotator),
        new PropertyMetadata(400.0, AttachToElement));

    private static void AttachToElement(
        DependencyObject d,
        DependencyPropertyChangedEventArgs e)
    {
        // See Listing 5.11
    }
}
```

The code in Listing 5.10 shows a standard registration of an attached property, as we did before. Notice, however, that the `PropertyMetadata` defines a `PropertyChangedCallback` delegate. The method is called `AttachToElement`, as shown in Listing 5.11.

LISTING 5.11 Attaching a Behavior to an Element

```
 1 private static void AttachToElement(
 2     DependencyObject d,
 3     DependencyPropertyChangedEventArgs e)
 4 {
 5     var element = d as UIElement;
 6     if (element == null)
 7     {
 8         return;
 9     }
10
11     if (e.NewValue == null)
12     {
13         Detach(element);
14     }
15
16     double initialAngle = (double)e.OldValue;
17
18     if (initialAngle >= 360.0)
```

```
19          {
20              // The element was not initialized yet.
21              // Attach the event handler.
22              element.MouseLeftButtonDown += RotateElement;
23              element.RenderTransformOrigin = new Point(0.5, 0.5);
24          }
25
26          element.RenderTransform = new RotateTransform
27          {
28              Angle = (double)e.NewValue
29          };
30      }
31
32      private static void RotateElement(object s, MouseButtonEventArgs e)
33      {
34          // See Listing 5.12
35      }
```

- On line 5, we cast the `DependencyObject` `d` to a `UIElement`: When you implement the `PropertyChangedCallback` delegate for an attached property, the first parameter is the element to which the property is attached. This provides a convenient way to attach event handlers or set properties on that element. Note that if the result of the cast is `null`, we just exit the method on line 8. That is the case if the object was `null` to start with, or if it cannot be cast to `UIElement`.

- On lines 11 to 14, we call a method named `Detach` that will clean up, as you will see in a moment.

- On line 16, we get the previous value of the property. As discussed earlier in this chapter, the `DependencyPropertyChangedEventArgs` class contains this information as well as the property's new value.

- On lines 18 to 24, we initialize the element. Detecting whether the element has been initialized already can be tricky, especially if you don't want to keep a list of subscribed elements. In this implementation, we initialize with a convention: The value of `InitialAngle` can be set between 0 and 360 degrees (not inclusive). But when we register the property, we set the default value to 400 degrees. This way, when the value is set for the first time, this is an indication that the `MouseLeftButtonDown` event should be registered, which we do on line 22. The event handler will be implemented in Listing 5.12.

- Notice that we also set the `RenderTransformOrigin` point on line 23. Even though this property's type is a `Point`, the values entered `(0.5, 0.5)` are *relative* to the element's size. In our case, the point is in the center of the element, 50% of the width and 50% of the height.

- On lines 26 to 29, we create a new `RotateTransform` with an `Angle` retrieved from the attached property's new value. The element is rotated according to the initial value of the attached property, as set by the user in XAML.

The next step is to implement what happens when the mouse is pressed on the element, as shown in Listing 5.12.

LISTING 5.12 Rotating the Element

```
1  private static void RotateElement(
2      object s,
3      MouseButtonEventArgs e)
4  {
5      var sender = s as UIElement;
6
7      if (sender == null)
8      {
9          return;
10     }
11
12     var transform = sender.RenderTransform
13         as RotateTransform;
14     if (transform == null)
15     {
16         return;
17     }
18
19     transform.Angle += 45;
20 }
```

- This method is a `MouseLeftButtonDown` event handler that takes two parameters: the event's sender (the element on which the attached property is set) and the `MouseButtonEventArgs` parameter, with information about the event and the mouse. We will not use this second parameter in the sample.
- On line 5, we cast the first parameter, of type `object`, to a `UIElement`. We exit the method on line 9 if the cast is `null`.
- On lines 12 and 13, we get the element's `RenderTransform` property, and cast it to a `RotateTransform`. Note that if the element has not been initialized correctly, the cast may not be successful. For example, the `RenderTransform` might not have been set at all, or it might be another type of transform (`TranslateTransform`, `ScaleTransform`, and so on) or even a `TransformGroup` containing multiple transforms. In that case, the cast will be `null`, and we exit the method on line 16.
- Finally, if all went well, we increase the `RotateTransform`'s `Angle` property by 45 degrees.

Cleaning Up to Avoid Memory Leaks

The last step we should take care of is giving the user a possibility to detach the element to avoid keeping it in memory. Even if, in this case, the event handler is static and thus does not cause a memory leak, detaching the event handlers when the attached behavior is removed is a good practice. In some cases (for example if the element to which the behavior is attached is stored in a collection for some reason), memory leaks can be created if the cleanup is not correctly executed.

Unfortunately, there is no way to automatically detect whether an object is disposed. We can, however, provide a way to unregister the event handler, as shown in Listing 5.13. The developer using the attached behavior should call the `Detach` method. This also resets the attached property to 400 degrees, to guarantee the element initialization if the property is reattached. The `Detach` method is also invoked if the attached property is set to `null`, as you saw in Listing 5.11, line 13.

Another way to solve this problem is to use the weak event pattern, which does not create a strong reference. For more information about this pattern, see http://www.galasoft.ch/sl4-weakevent.

LISTING 5.13 Detaching the Event Handler

```
public static void Detach(UIElement element)
{
    SetInitialAngle(element, 400.0);
    element.MouseLeftButtonDown -= RotateElement;
}
```

Using the Attached Behavior in XAML

Attaching this behavior on a `Rectangle` is as simple as shown in Listing 5.14.

LISTING 5.14 Attaching the Behavior in XAML

```
<Rectangle xmlns:ext="clr-namespace:AttachedBehaviour.Extensions"
           ext:ElementRotator.InitialAngle="15"
           Width="100" Height="100" Fill="Red" />
```

Attaching the `ElementRotator` behavior to an element is done by mapping a namespace and setting a property. From this moment onward, the element is rotated by 15 degrees, without us having to explicitly set a `RotateTransform`. Then, every time that the user presses the mouse's left button on the element, it is rotated by an additional 45 degrees.

Building on Attached Behaviors with Blend Behaviors

The Expression Blend team provided a library with a few classes that enable you to leverage the power of the attached behaviors that you saw here, but taking care of some of their inconveniences. Blend behaviors are one of the most innovative and exciting features that were added to Expression Blend 3: They provide developers with a way to cleanly encapsulate their code and to deploy it, making it reusable. At the same time, they allow designers to add interactive features to their XAML without having to type the code.

We will spend more time with Blend behaviors in Chapter 11, "Mastering Expression Blend."

Adding a New Property with Snippets

As you could see in the previous sections, adding a new dependency property or attached property involves a lot of repetitive code. Typing everything by hand is not the nicest task one can imagine, and is prone to errors.

Thankfully, Visual Studio provides an automated way to add chunks of code to a class, using so called *code snippets*. There are quite a few preinstalled code snippets, including a dependency property and an attached property for Windows Presentation Foundation. Unfortunately, the code created by these snippets will not compile in Silverlight without a few modifications.

Installing the Snippets for Silverlight

To make things easier, you can download two new snippets that do the same job for Silverlight, and install them with the following steps:

1. Download the snippets zip file from http://www.galasoft.ch/sl4-snippets.
2. Open Visual Studio 2010.
3. Select Tools, Code Snippets Manager from the menu.
4. In the Code Snippets Manager dialog, select Visual C# in the Language combo box.
5. Select the folder named My Code Snippets and copy the path shown in Figure 5.4.
6. Extract the zip file that you downloaded on step 1 to the path that you copied in Step 5.

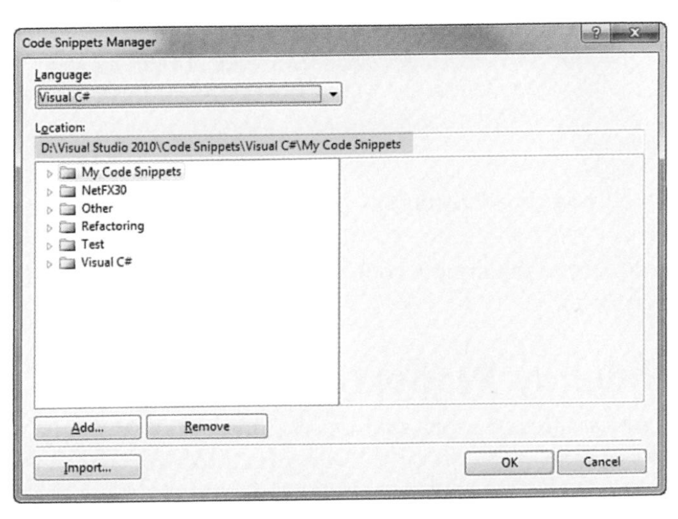

FIGURE 5.4 Getting the snippets' path.

Using the Snippets

With the snippets installed, you can now follow these steps to create a new dependency property:

1. Open a class deriving from `DependencyObject` in Visual Studio (for example, MainPage.xaml.cs, any `UserControl`, and so on).
2. At the location where you want to add the dependency property, type `slpropd`. You should see the item appear in the IntelliSense window. If it is not present, the snippet is not correctly installed. Close Visual Studio and repeat the steps to install the snippets correctly.
3. With `slpropd` selected in IntelliSense, press the Enter key, and then the Tab key. This expands the snippet and type most of the code for you.
4. You need to customize the snippet by entering a few identifiers. These are marked in the editor with a light green highlight, as shown on Figure 5.5. You can pass from one marker to the next by pressing the Tab key. When you reach the last marker, you can go back to the first one by pressing Tab again. The identifiers are as follows:
    - The name of the dependency property (default: `MyProperty`).
    - The type of the dependency property (default: `int`).
    - The owner class of the property. This is generally the class in which you are implementing it (default: `ownerclass`).
    - The default value (default: `0`).
5. Press the Escape key to finish editing the identifiers.

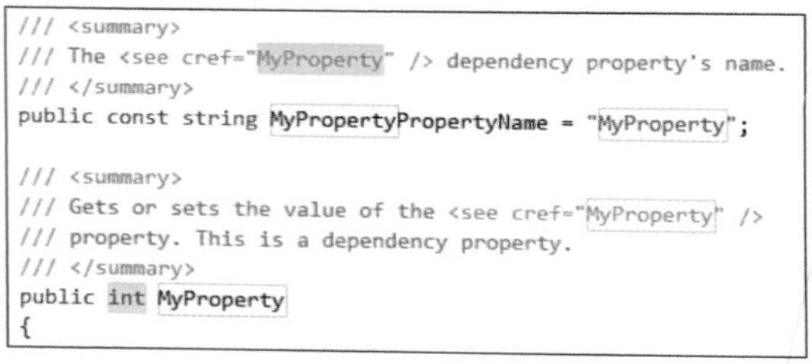

```
/// <summary>
/// The <see cref="MyProperty" /> dependency property's name.
/// </summary>
public const string MyPropertyPropertyName = "MyProperty";

/// <summary>
/// Gets or sets the value of the <see cref="MyProperty" />
/// property. This is a dependency property.
/// </summary>
public int MyProperty
{
```

FIGURE 5.5 Expanded snippet with marked identifiers.

Code snippets are very convenient to create boilerplate code faster. There is also a snippet for attached properties, named `slpropa`.

Calculating a Dependency Property's Value

A dependency property's value can be set from various sources. We already talked about the default value. You can also set the value in XAML or in code. Also, other mechanisms take advantage of the dependency property system (for example, data binding or animations).

Because of this, the value of the dependency property depends on multiple factors, and a system of priority, or precedence, must be established.

In Silverlight, the value can be set from the following sources (listed in order of precedence).

- (Highest) If an animation is setting the value, this has the highest priority. It is necessary because an animation must be able to change the value even if it has been set locally.

  Note that an animation may hold the value it was changing even if the storyboard is completed. To change this, the property `FillBehavior` can be set on the `Timeline` class (either the `Storyboard` or each separate animation). This property can be set to `HoldEnd` (the animated property's value will be kept by the animation) or to `Stop` (the animated property's value will be released by the animation when it is completed). Also, if multiple animations act on the same property, the property's value is a composite of all the animations' effect.
- Local value. The dependency property's value is set through a call to the `SetValue` method. You also saw earlier that the convenience setter for a dependency property is using `SetValue` in its implementation, so this is also a local value. The local value can be set in XAML or in code.
- If a control template or a data template is used to render an element (control, data item, and so on), certain properties can be set from within the template.
- If a style is applied to the element, certain properties can be set from within the style.
- Base style. As you will see in Chapter 10, "Creating Resources, Styles, and Templates," a style can be based on another style. If the base style sets a value, and the derived style sets another value for the same property, the derived style wins.
- Implicit styles. This is a new concept in Silverlight 4. These styles can be defined for a given type of control. For example, a style can be defined for all `Button` controls. If a value seems to be coming from nowhere, you should search the application and check whether an implicit style is defined for the control you are debugging. See Chapter 10 for more information about implicit styles.
- (Lowest) The default value defined when the dependency property is registered is the fallback value and will be applied if nothing else with a higher precedence occurs. Remember that if no default value was passed to the `PropertyMetadata`, the property's type's default value will be used.

This list is good to keep in mind when debugging a dependency object and trying to understand why a value is not corresponding to what was expected. The first step in such a search is to determine whether one or more animations are applied to the object, even if some of them are already completed.

Getting the Property's Base Value

It might be necessary to find out what the value of a dependency property would be if no animation were applied to it. For example, if an animation is running, and you need to prepare the application for the value that will be applied when the animation stops (if the FillBehavior is not set to HoldEnd), you can use the method GetAnimationBaseValue available on any DependencyObject.

The method takes a DependencyProperty as parameter, as shown in Listing 5.15. Note that the method returns an object, so it must be cast to the desired type.

The HeightProperty is defined on the FrameworkElement class. However, if you are executing this within a UserControl or another class deriving from FrameworkElement, you can omit the class name. Listing 5.15 shows multiple ways to get the base value for the Height property.

LISTING 5.15 Getting a Property's Base Value

```
double baseValue
    = (double)MyRectangle.GetAnimationBaseValue(
    FrameworkElement.HeightProperty);

baseValue
    = (double)MyRectangle.GetAnimationBaseValue(
    HeightProperty);

baseValue
    = (double)MyRectangle.GetAnimationBaseValue(
    Rectangle.HeightProperty);
```

Reading the Local Value

As mentioned earlier, the dependency property's value depends on a number of factors and their precedence. In the previous section, you saw how to get the base value, which is the value that would be applied to the property if it were neither animated nor held by a completed animation.

The base value is equal to the local value if the local value is set. However, this is not always the case. For instance, if you instantiate a Button and do not set its Height, the value of the HeightProperty is equal to DependencyProperty.UnsetValue. In that case, the base value depends on the priority setters with lower precedence (template, styles, default value).

In some scenarios, it is necessary to read the local value. To do this, use the method ReadLocalValue on objects deriving from DependencyObject. This method returns a value of type object, which can be either DependencyProperty.UnsetValue or can be cast to the desired type, as shown in Listing 5.16.

LISTING 5.16 Getting a Property's Local Value

```
double? rectangleHeight = null;
var localValue
    = MyRectangle.ReadLocalValue(HeightProperty);

if (localValue != DependencyProperty.UnsetValue)
{
    rectangleHeight = (double)localValue;
}
```

Summary

Dependency properties and attached properties are one very important pillar of the Silverlight framework. In this chapter, we talked about the purpose of the `DependencyObject` class, the base class for many of the Silverlight framework's types. Then we talked in depth of what is involved in registering a new dependency property.

Later, we created attached properties, allowing attaching data to another object without modifying it. We also talked about a very powerful way to attach functionality to an element with attached behaviors. Understanding how they work is important before we study Expression Blend behaviors in Chapter 11, to understand their mechanics.

This chapter also covered a convenient tool to create new dependency properties and attached properties with Visual Studio code snippets, which we installed to speed up the creation of such properties.

Finally, we talked about the precedence system and which factors influence the value of a dependency property, from animations to local values, templates, styles, and as a fallback, the default value.

In the next chapter, we examine one of the main reasons why dependency properties were introduced (data binding) and other data-related topics.

CHAPTER 6

Working with Data: Binding, Grouping, Sorting, and Filtering

IN THIS CHAPTER, WE WILL:

- Dive deep into data bindings and explore all their properties.
- Talk about various ways to validate data.
- Use Visual Studio and Blend's dialogs to create bindings.
- Debug data bindings and talk about ways to find errors.
- Group and sort data by using a CollectionViewSource.

An application would be nothing without data. In the early days of Silverlight, displaying and collecting data was not the major focus of the framework. Very soon, though, we saw the emergence of new controls, libraries, and services to make it easier to build a new kind of applications, the so called line-of-business (LOB) applications. These applications make it possible to handle large amounts of data in an efficient way, providing various advantages:

- The computational power of Silverlight makes it possible to treat larger amounts of data than with traditional web applications.
- Complex operations can be executed directly on the client computer (for example, for a first-stage validation of input). This reduces the traffic to the server because invalid data doesn't need to be sent back and forth. Of course, there should be additional validation on the server!
- It is possible to save data on the client computer and provide an offline mode for your application.
- Silverlight offers new graphics abilities allowing you to present data in innovative ways (charting, 3D, interactions, multitouch).

All these advantages and more open new possibilities for the information architects, the designers, and the developers to bring advanced user experience and increased productivity (and pleasure) in business applications.

Data is, of course, at the center of these applications, and therefore at the core of Silverlight, too. This chapter covers various low-level data-oriented topics, starting with a core fundament of Silverlight: data binding. We will end the chapter with a way to filter, group, or sort data from a collection with the `CollectionViewSource`.

Diving into Data Bindings

Data binding is not new in Silverlight or in client applications in general. In fact, other .NET-based technologies such as ASP.NET and Windows Forms already had some sort of data binding, although it was mostly limited to data controls (such as data grids).

The real innovation came into Windows Presentation Foundation (WPF), the rich desktop framework for client applications that is at the origin of Silverlight (and still used to build Windows desktop applications). With the dependency property system that we studied in Chapter 5, "Understanding Dependency Properties," and the introduction of the data binding framework, it became possible to bind the value of a property to the value of another property, on the same object or a different one, and to keep these properties synchronized.

Data binding was introduced in Silverlight, too, although with a slightly reduced scope. In Silverlight 4, we saw many improvements helping to make the data binding framework better and closer to the WPF framework.

We talked about the basics of data binding in *Silverlight 2 Unleashed*, Chapter 18. The concepts we studied there are still valid in Silverlight 4. In this section, we refresh these basic concepts and expand on them to explain the changes brought to the data binding framework since then.

Understanding a Binding's Elements

Before we dive deeper, it is interesting to understand what the elements of a binding are. For each binding, there is always a source (where the data comes from) and a target (where the data is sent).

Applying a binding to a Target

A binding is always applied to a *target*. In fact, data bindings can be applied only on a dependency property of a `DependencyObject` instance (or classes deriving from `DependencyObject`). Now you understand why so many classes in the Silverlight framework derive from this base class, as you saw in Chapter 5.

A binding can be applied in XAML or in code. The syntax is easier in XAML thanks to the use of a *markup extension*, expressed by an opening and a closing curly bracket as shown below. There are various markup extensions in Silverlight 4, such as `{Binding}` and `{RelativeSource}`, `{StaticResource}`, and so forth. In this example, the `Text` property of the `TextBlock` object is the target of the binding.

```
<TextBlock Text="{Binding ElementName=LayoutRoot,
                          Path=ActualWidth}" />
```

In code, the syntax is more complicated, and requires the use of the `BindingOperations` helper class, as shown in Listing 6.1.

LISTING 6.1 Setting a Binding on a Target in Code

```
var textBlock = new TextBlock();

var binding = new Binding
{
    ElementName = "LayoutRoot",
    Path = new PropertyPath("ActualWidth")
};

BindingOperations.SetBinding(
    textBlock,
    TextBlock.TextProperty,
    binding);
```

- The first parameter of the `SetBinding` method is the `DependencyObject` to which the binding must be applied (the target).
- The second parameter is the identifier for the dependency property to which the binding must be applied.
- The last parameter is the binding that will be applied.

Getting the Binding's Data from a Source

The source of a binding can be set by different means. Note that for each of these possibilities, the binding's source can be either the element itself, or a property within the element. Finally, remember that using a special syntax (that we will study further in this chapter), it is possible to dive into complex properties and access sub-properties, and so on. The source of the binding can be:

- A reference to a named element within the XAML document (with the `ElementName` property).
- A reference to an element stored in the resources (with the `Source` property).
- A reference to an element relative to the current element (with the `RelativeSource` property).
- Finally, if nothing else is specified, the source of the binding will be the *data context* in which the element is placed.

This last source is very important, because the data context is *inherited* from an element to all of its children. If the child's `DataContext` property is not set explicitly, then the parent's data context is used. This provides a very convenient way to define a common source for all the bindings within an element (such as a user control or a panel).

Understanding the Namescope

Silverlight relies on names for certain operations, such as identifying the source of a binding using the `ElementName` property (we will talk about this property a little later in this chapter). As usual when working with names, certain rules need to be enforced. Most important, names should not conflict with each other: A name must be unique within its scope.

However, conflicts are unavoidable when using control templates or data templates: Because the same template can be used on multiple elements in the `UserControl`, any named element within the template will appear multiple times. To solve this problem, Silverlight defines the concept of namescope. The following elements all have their own namescope:

- Data templates and control templates
- `UserControl`
- `ContentControl` and `ItemsControl`

This explains why the code in Listing 6.2 does not work: The binding attempts to access a `TextBox` defined within a `ControlTemplate`. The template's namescope is not the same as the `Button`'s namescope, and therefore the binding fails. It is important to remember where namescopes start and end when working with names, and to find workarounds when an element cannot be reached.

LISTING 6.2 Failed Attempt to Bind to an Element in Another Namescope

```
<Button Content="{Binding ElementName=InnerTextBox,
                          Path=Text}">
    <Button.Template>
        <ControlTemplate TargetType="Button">
            <StackPanel>
                <ContentPresenter Height="200" />
                <TextBox Text="Hello again"
                         x:Name="InnerTextBox" />
            </StackPanel>
        </ControlTemplate>
    </Button.Template>
</Button>
```

Setting the Source

When a binding is established, the data flows from a *source* to a *target* as you saw in the introduction. Note that any object and any property can be the source of a binding in Silverlight, not just dependency objects and dependency properties. However, a binding on "standard properties" (that is, properties that are not registered with the dependency property system) is not updated automatically unless you explicitly raise an event, as you saw in Listing 5.2.

> **WARNING**
>
> **Finding Binding Errors**
>
> Binding errors (for example, setting a binding in XAML on a nonexistent source) are silent and do not crash the application. For that reason, they can be hard to detect: There are no symptoms other than your application not working the way it should. You will learn how to debug these errors in the "Debugging Data Bindings" section, later in this chapter.

The `ElementName` Property

Probably the most direct way to set the source of a binding is through the `ElementName` property, which was introduced in Silverlight 3. This property enables the so-called *element-to-element binding*.

Here, the `Text` property of a `TextBlock` is set to a binding to the `Value` property of a `Slider`. Note that, thanks to the dynamic nature of data bindings, the text will be updated every time that the slider's cursor is moved. Of course, this element must be available in the target's namescope; otherwise, a data error will occur.

```
<TextBlock Text="{Binding ElementName=MySlider, Path=Value}" />
```

The `Source` Property

In Silverlight 2, the `Source` property was the only property you could use to set the source of the binding.

In XAML, the `Source` property is normally set to a resource available from the current position in the XAML document. Such a resource is defined in a resource dictionary. We will spend more time talking about the way that resources are resolved in a Silverlight application in Chapter 10, "Creating Resources, Styles, and Templates." For now, we will assume that the resource exists, and resolve it through a `StaticResource` extension, as shown here:

```
<TextBlock Text="{Binding Source={StaticResource MyDataObject}}" />
```

The `RelativeSource` Property

`RelativeSource` is a new property introduced in Silverlight 4. It provides a way to set the source of a binding relatively to the target element. Developers familiar with WPF already know the `RelativeSource` property, but there are only two modes in Silverlight:

- Self refers to the target element itself. You can use this if you need to pass the current UI element to the binding.
- TemplatedParent is used in control templates and data templates. It allows setting the source of a binding to the element (control or data item) that is represented by the template. For example, in a control template that will be applied to a Button, the TemplatedParent is the Button control itself. In a data template (for example, in a ListBox), the TemplateParent is the data item that is rendered by the data template.

The syntax in XAML (as shown below) is a bit confusing, due to the repetition of the word RelativeSource. The first (in red) is a property of the Binding class. The second (in brown) is the name of the markup extension that is used to set the RelativeSource property. The sample here displays the FontFamily property of a TextBlock in the TextBlock itself.

```
<TextBlock Text="{Binding RelativeSource={RelativeSource Self},
           Path=FontFamily}" />
```

Listing 6.3 shows a control template for a Button control where in addition to the content, the Button's name is shown using the TemplatedParent mode.

LISTING 6.3 Accessing the TemplatedParent

```
<Button x:Name="TestButton"
        Content="My content"
        Width="200" Height="100">
    <Button.Template>
        <ControlTemplate TargetType="Button">
            <StackPanel Background="#FFCCCCCC">
                <ContentPresenter />
                <TextBlock
                  Text="{Binding RelativeSource={RelativeSource TemplatedParent},
                                 Path=Name}" />
            </StackPanel>
        </ControlTemplate>
    </Button.Template>
</Button>
```

Binding to Implicit Data Context

The last way to set the source of a binding is to not set it! In that case, the source will be set to the data context of the target element's parent. Should that data context be empty on the parent, the parent's parent's context is used, and so forth. We talk about the *inherited data context,* also known as the *implicit data context.*

For example, the markup in Listing 6.4 sets a grid's DataContext to a Customer object contained in the resources. Further, a TextBlock is used to display the first name of the Customer.

LISTING 6.4 Binding to the implicit data context

```
<Grid x:Name="LayoutRoot"
      DataContext="{Binding Source={StaticResource MyCustomer}}">
    <TextBlock Text="{Binding Path=FirstName}" />
</Grid>
```

The implicit data context is extensively used in the Model-View-ViewModel pattern, which we discuss in Chapter 7, "Understanding the Model-View-ViewModel Pattern." In this pattern, an object (the *view-model*) is set as the `DataContext` property of a `UserControl` or any other UI element (the *view*). Because the `DataContext` is set on the root, it will be inherited by all the children elements in the tree, and bindings do not need their source to be set explicitly.

Because the source of a data binding may be empty, this even allows for "empty" bindings, where the binding is set to the current element's `DataContext`. An example shown in Listing 6.5 is used to send an element's `DataContext` to a command (we talked about commands in Chapter 4, "Investigating Existing Controls"). The full sample is available at http://www.galasoft.ch/SL4U/code/chapter06.

LISTING 6.5 Binding to the Implicit Data Context

```
1 <DataTemplate x:Key="MyDataTemplate">
2     <Border>
3         <Button Content="{Binding Path=Name}"
4                 Command="{Binding Source={StaticResource MainVM},
5                                   Path=DisplayItemCommand}"
6                 CommandParameter="{Binding}" />
7     </Border>
8 </DataTemplate>
```

- The data template in Listing 6.5 is used to render a data item. This data item (a standard CLR object) has a property named `Name`. Thanks to the Silverlight data framework, the data context of this `DataTemplate` is automatically set to be the data item in question. Because this `DataTemplate` is used in a `ListBox`, each row has a different data context, a different data item.
- On line 3, we bind the `Content` of the `Button` to the item's `Name` property. Notice that we do not specify the source of the binding, but only the `Path`. The implicit data context will be used.
- On lines 4 and 5, we bind a command named `DisplayItemCommand` to the `Command` property of the `Button`. Note that this command is not located on the implicit data context: The `Source` property is set explicitly! The `DisplayItemCommand` is set on an object named `MainVM`, available in the page's resources.
- The `CommandParameter` property is set to an "empty" binding. We pass the implicit data context itself to this property. The data item that this `DataTemplate` represents will arrive directly in the command for processing.

Refining the Path

Now that we figured the source of the binding, we can refine it by choosing a property on the source object. To do this, the `Path` property of the `Binding` object is used. Note, however, that you can create a binding without the `Path` property.

The `Path` property is of type `PropertyPath`. It is constructed in XAML or in code with a string following a special syntax.

> **TIP**
>
> **Using the Right `PropertyPath` Constructor**
>
> To construct a `PropertyPath` in source code, use the constructor `PropertyPath(object)`, and pass a `string` as the parameter. Do *not* pass a dependency property identifier because this doesn't work when used in a binding. (It works only when working with animations). Do not use the constructor `PropertyPath(string, object[])` either. This constructor is only here for compatibility with WPF, but the `object[]` parameter will be ignored in Silverlight.

The following scenarios are possible:

- If the source is a simple property, use `"MyProperty"`.
- If the source is a property nested inside the `MyProperty` object, use a dot syntax just like with objects: `"MyProperty.MyNestedProperty"`.
- If the source is an `ICollectionView`, you can use the dot syntax to access the data collection's current item. We talk about `ICollectionView` further in this chapter. For example: `"MyCollectionView.MyProperty"` will bind to `MyProperty` on the item currently selected in `MyCollectionView`. This is a shortcut equivalent to `"MyCollectionView.CurrentItem.MyProperty"`.
- If the source is an attached property, use `"(MyObject.MyAttachedProperty)"` where `MyObject` is the class that the attached property is declared on. Note that in XAML, you might have to use the `xmlns` prefix that you declared for the corresponding CLR namespace (for example, `"(myprefix:MyObject.MyAttachedProperty)"`).
- The parenthesis syntax can also be used within a template, when this template doesn't have a `TargetType`. This is a special case where you bind to a property which cannot be verified at compile time, but will be available when the template is applied to a control or to an item, for example, `"(TextBlock.FontSize)"`.
- If the source is an item within a collection, use square brackets to specify the index within the collection. Note that the index can be an integer (for example, `"MyArray[0]"`) or a string identifier (key). In that latter case, the key must be entered without quotes even if it has spaces within (for example, `"MyDictionary[My Key]"`, where `"My Key"` is the key of the wanted item in the dictionary).
- Finally, all these elements can be combined together to create a complex path.

WARNING

Using an Indexer in a `PropertyPath`

When the source of the binding is an item in a collection, an indexer can be used as you saw here, but with the following restrictions:

- The collection may only be one-dimensional.
- The collection must be of a type implementing the `IList` interface.
- When using an integer indexer, the indexer is always 0-based. `"MyCollection[0]"` represents the first element.

Listings 6.6 shows the way to set the `Path` of a `Binding` in code. Listing 6.7 shows various samples in XAML. Note that when used in XAML, you can omit `"Path="` if the `Path` identifier is the first element in the `Binding` expression, as shown in Listing 6.7, examples 2 and 3.

LISTING 6.6 Setting the `Path` in Code

```
var binding = new Binding
{
    Source = this,
    Path = new PropertyPath("Background.Color")
};
```


LISTING 6.7 Setting the `Path` in XAML

```
<!--(1) Binding to simple property-->
<TextBlock Text="{Binding ElementName=LayoutRoot,
                          Path=ActualWidth}" />

<!--(2) If the Path comes first, the qualifier can be omitted-->
<TextBlock Text="{Binding ActualWidth,
                          ElementName=LayoutRoot}" />

<!--(3) Binding to a property within a property-->
<TextBlock Text="{Binding Background.Color,
                          ElementName=LayoutRoot}" />

<!--(4) Binding to an attached property-->
<TextBlock Text="{Binding ElementName=MyRectangle,
        Path=(Grid.Column)}" />

<!--(5) Binding to an item in a collection-->
<TextBlock Text="{Binding MyCollection[1].Property1}" />
```

```
<!--(6) Binding to an item in a dictionary
    using a key with a space within-->
<TextBlock TextWrapping="Wrap"
           Text="{Binding MyDictionary[Index 1].Name}" />
```

Flowing in Two Directions

As mentioned earlier in this chapter, the data flows through a binding from the source to the target. However, it can sometimes be interesting to have it flow from the target to the source. For example, if the target is a `TextBox` displaying the value of a `Slider`, moving the `Slider`'s cursor will update the value in the `TextBox` (source → target). But if the user types a valid `double` value in the `TextBox`, the `Slider` should also be updated to reflect the new value (target → source).

To achieve this, you need to set the `Mode` property of the `Binding`. There are currently three possible values in the `BindingMode` enum in Silverlight 4:

- `OneTime`: This is the default when the source property is not a dependency property, but a normal CLR property. This value can also be set explicitly to the `Mode` property if desired.

  When a binding is in `OneTime` mode, it will be updated only once, when the XAML code is parsed. Any subsequent change on the source property will be ignored.

- `OneWay`: This is the default when the source property is a dependency property. In that mode, the changes will always flow from the source to the target, but never in the opposite direction.

- `TwoWay`: In that mode, the changes flow in two directions. This is the mode you need to use when the target may change and you want to keep the target and the source in sync. However, it is slightly less efficient than `OneWay`, so use it with care.

As with the other properties, the `Mode` can be set in code, or in XAML as shown below:

```
<TextBox Text="{Binding ElementName=MySlider,
                        Path=Value, Mode=TwoWay}" />
```

Converting the Values

Value converters are useful when you need to convert a value into another value through a binding. You can build your converters as you saw in *Silverlight 2 Unleashed* (Chapter 24, Listing 24.6): Simply create a new class implementing the `IValueConverter` interface, and implement the two methods:

- `Convert` for forward conversion.

- `ConvertBack` for backward conversion. This method is needed only if the value can be applied through a `TwoWay` binding. In many cases, the `ConvertBack` value is declared, but throws a `NotImplementedException`.

You can set a different culture for the converter through the ConverterCulture parameter, which should be set to the culture's code (for example, en-US, it-IT, and so on).

Finally, you can pass a ConverterParameter to the Convert and ConvertBack methods. This parameter cannot be set through a binding.

To use your own converters, remember to map an XML namespace to the CLR namespace in which the converter lives, as shown in Listing 6.8.

LISTING 6.8 Adding a Converter in the Resources and Using It

```
<Grid x:Name="LayoutRoot">
    <Grid.Resources>
        <conv:DoubleToGridWidthConverter x:Key="DoubleToGridWidthConverter" />
    </Grid.Resources>

    <Grid.ColumnDefinitions>
        <ColumnDefinition
            Width="{Binding ElementName=RootControl,
                    Path=ActualWidth,
                    Converter={StaticResource DoubleToGridWidthConverter},
                    ConverterParameter=100}" />
        <ColumnDefinition Width="*" />
    </Grid.ColumnDefinitions>

    <!--...-->
</Grid>
```


TIP

Naming the Converters with a Convention

It is good practice to name the converters according to a simple guideline: Use the name [OriginType]To[DestinationType]Converter (for example BooleanToVisibilityConverter, DoubleToGridWidthConverter).

Also, to make things easier, it is a good idea to use the converter's type name as its key in the resources, as we did in Listing 6.8.

Changing the Format

When you want to display a numeric value as a string in .NET, you typically want to format it according to the type of value it represents (monetary, time/date, number of decimals, and so forth.) and according to the culture of the user; for example, en-US (English in the United States) or fr-CH (French in Switzerland).

In Silverlight 3 and earlier, there was no way to change the format of a string set through a binding other than to build a converter for the binding. However, this is quite a lot of work, and a better solution was needed. In Silverlight 4, you can change the format of a string by using the StringFormat property of the binding. Note that if the binding also has a converter, the converter is executed first, and the `StringFormat` is applied to the output of the converter.

`StringFormat`'s syntax is the usual formatting syntax familiar to .NET programmers. Examples can be found in Listing 6.9, and a complete reference is at http://www.galasoft.ch/sl4-format.

LISTING 6.9 Various Formatting

```
<!--123.45678-->
<TextBlock Text="{Binding ElementName=RootControl,
                          Path=MyDouble}" />

<!--123.46-->
<TextBlock Text="{Binding ElementName=RootControl,
                          Path=MyDouble,
                          StringFormat=N2}" />

<!--$123.46-->
<TextBlock Text="{Binding ElementName=RootControl,
                          Path=MyDouble,
                          StringFormat=C}" />

<!--This percentage 12,345.68 % in a string-->
<TextBlock Text="{Binding ElementName=RootControl,
  Path=MyDouble,
  StringFormat=This percentage \{0:P2\} in a string}" />

<!--12.35E1-->
<TextBlock Text="{Binding ElementName=RootControl,
  Path=MyDouble,
  StringFormat=0#.##E0}" />

<!--0123-->
<TextBlock Text="{Binding ElementName=RootControl,
                          Path=MyInteger,
                          StringFormat=D4}" />

<!--1/16/2010 3:14 PM-->
<TextBlock Text="{Binding ElementName=RootControl,
                          Path=MyDateTime,
                          StringFormat=g}" />

<!--Saturday, January 16, 2010-->
<TextBlock Text="{Binding ElementName=RootControl,
                          Path=MyDateTime,
                          StringFormat=D}" />
```

Adding Some Text

As shown in Listing 6.9, the formatted parameter can be placed within a string. However, be careful because such text embedded in XAML is impossible to localize. If localization is needed, you need to set the `StringFormat` in code.

To embed the formatting information within a text, you need to add an index and enclose everything in curly brackets. However, in XAML, you need to escape the curly brackets to avoid confusing the XAML parser, because you are already in a `Binding` markup extension. The `StringFormat` property for a percentage becomes `\{0:P2\}` in a string.

Localizing the `StringFormat`

Even if the application's `CurrentCulture` and `CurrentUICulture` are set to a culture other than en-US, this will not be applied to the `StringFormat`. This annoying fact can be worked around by setting the `Language` property on the `UserControl` in which the binding is applied. The `Language` property can be applied in XAML or in code, as shown in Listing 6.10.

LISTING 6.10 Setting the `UserControl`'s Language

```
<!--In XAML-->
<UserControl
  x:Class="StringFormatSample.MainPage"
  xmlns="http://schemas.microsoft.com/winfx/2006/xaml/presentation"
  xmlns:x="http://schemas.microsoft.com/winfx/2006/xaml"
  Language="it-IT">
        <!--...-->
</UserControl>

// In code
Language = XmlLanguage.GetLanguage("it-IT");
```

TIP

Using Visual Studio to Format Binding Strings

The Visual Studio Silverlight designer can help you to create a string formatted like you want. In the “Using the Visual Studio Binding Dialog” section, later in this chapter, you will see how to set a binding and format it using this convenient tool.

Handling Special Cases

In some cases, the binding does not return a valid value. For example, the source property's name might be misspelled, in which case the application does not crash, but the bound value will be left blank. In other cases, the binding is valid, but the value returned is `null`.

In Silverlight 4, the `Binding` class has two properties taking care of these special cases:

- `TargetNullValue` is used in case the value returned by the binding expression is `null`.
- `FallbackValue` is used in case the binding is invalid.

Note that `TargetNullValue` is used only if the value of the binding is actually `null`. If the `Path` is complex, and one of the elements within the path (except the last one) is `null`, this is actually an invalid value, and `FallbackValue` is used instead.

Property Trigger

In `TwoWay` bindings, by default, the value of the source property is updated as soon as the target of the binding changes. In some cases, however, you might need to perform additional operations before notifying the source that it is changed, for instance if you need to perform multiple validation operations before you can confirm that the value is valid.

This can be done by setting the `UpdateSourceTrigger` property to `Explicit`. In that case, you must trigger the update in code with the help of the `BindingExpression` helper class, as shown below. This property is applicable only in `TwoWay` bindings, where the flow of data does not only go from the source to the target but also in the opposite direction.

```
BindingExpression expression
    = MyTextBox.GetBindingExpression(TextBox.TextProperty);
expression.UpdateSource();
```

Validating Input

Validation is used to verify that data is correct according to a set of rules. In Silverlight 2 and 3, the validation mechanism was basic and not very satisfying. In Silverlight 4, two new ways to handle validation errors were added, as you will see here.

In this section, we talk about the way that bindings handle validation errors. In Chapter 8, "Using Data Controls," we talk more about validation in relation to data controls.

`NotifyOnValidationError`

This property must be set to `True` on the `Binding` expression to trigger the validation mechanism. This property was already found in Silverlight 2 and 3. Listing 6.12 shows an example using this property.

After `NotifyOnValidationError` has been set to `True`, the developer of data objects can choose between three different ways to handle validation errors.

Using Exceptions with `ValidatesOnExceptions`

In Silverlight 2 and 3, the only way to notify a binding that data is invalid was to throw an exception. This is still available in Silverlight 4, so existing code will continue to work. Exception-based validation is also useful for the so-called DataAnnotations, which are covered in Chapter 8.

Listing 6.11 shows a view-model's property throwing an exception when the value entered by the user is either `null` or empty. Because this property is raising the `INotifyPropertyChanged` interface's `PropertyChanged` event, we can set a binding on this property in `TwoWay` mode.

LISTING 6.11 View-model's Property Throwing an Exception

```
1  public const string NamePropertyName = "Name";
2  private string _name = string.Empty;
3
4  public string Name
5  {
6      get { return _name; }
7
8      set
9      {
10         if (_name == value)
11         {
12             return;
13         }
14
15         if (string.IsNullOrEmpty(value))
16         {
17             throw new Exception("Name should not be empty");
18         }
19
20         _name = value;
21
22         if (PropertyChanged != null)
23         {
24             PropertyChanged(this,
25                 new PropertyChangedEventArgs(NamePropertyName));
26         }
27     }
28 }
```

Listing 6.12 shows how a `TextBox` control is bound to the `Name` property. When the user starts the application, the `TextBox` is empty and ready for input. If the user enters a name in the box, everything is fine. However, if the user then deletes the content of the `TextBox`, the exception will be thrown in the `Name` property's setter. This causes the `TextBox` control to react by displaying a red border with a small red corner, as shown in Figure 6.1. When the mouse is over the red corner, the exception's message is displayed in a ToolTip. Every Silverlight control that allows input is templated to display the error message when the state is invalid. You will learn more about this in Chapter 8.

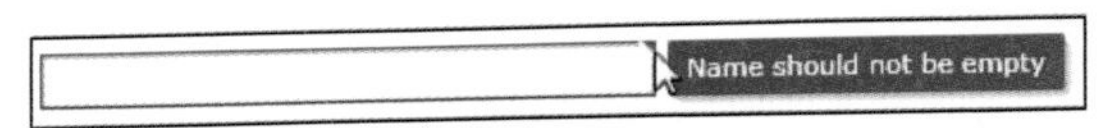

FIGURE 6.1 `TextBox` in invalid state.

LISTING 6.12 Binding a TextBox with Validation

```
<TextBox Margin="10,10,200,10"
         Text="{Binding Path=Name,
             Source={StaticResource ValidationViewModel},
             Mode=TwoWay,
             NotifyOnValidationError=True,
             ValidatesOnExceptions=True}" />
```

Working with exceptions for validation is simple, but is not following best practices. Exceptions should be reserved for exceptional cases, not just when a user makes a mistake when entering information. Also, the property on which the binding is applied is responsible for throwing the exception, which complicates the implementation of such properties.

Implementing IDataErrorInfo

A cleaner way to handle validation is to let the data objects implement the IDataErrorInfo interface that was introduced in Silverlight 4. This interface already exists in the full .NET framework for quite some time, and developers are used to this way of handling validation. Also, existing code using this interface can now be used in Silverlight.

This interface defines two members, but only one is used in Silverlight. The Error property is only here for compatibility with WPF; in Silverlight, we perform only property-based validation, with the help of the member this[string columnName] defined by IDataErrorInfo.

Listing 6.13 shows an implementation of the members defined by IDataErrorInfo within the viewmodel. Notice how the validation rules are neatly grouped within the this[] operator, instead of being mixed within the properties. For this to work, the binding pointing to the Name property must have its NotifyOnValidationError and ValidatesOnDataErrors properties set to True, while the ValidatesOnExceptions property may be removed.

With this implementation, the Name property defined in Listing 6.11 remains the same, except for lines 15 to 18, which are removed.

LISTING 6.13 IDataErrorInfo Members in the Viewmodel

```
public string this[string columnName]
{
    get
    {
        if (columnName == NamePropertyName)
        {
            if (string.IsNullOrEmpty(_name))
            {
                return "Name should not be empty";
            }
```

```
            }

            return null;
        }
    }

    public string Error
    {
        get { return null; }
    }
```

As mentioned before, the Error property is not used, and always returns null.

One difference between IDataErrorInfo and the exception-based validation we saw in the previous section is that the bindings will trigger the validation when the application starts. On the other hand, the exceptions are not queried by the bindings (that wouldn't work), but thrown by the property setters, which makes it much harder to set the Silverlight application in a validated state when it starts. This is yet another argument in favor of the IDataErrorInfo-based validation: Your user will know from the start which fields are compulsory.

Implementing INotifyDataErrorInfo

The INotifyDataErrorInfo interface was also introduced in Silverlight 4. It provides an additional way to handle validation for more complex scenarios than IDataErrorInfo allows. Note that this interface is specific to Silverlight for the moment, and does not exist in the full .NET framework.

INotifyDataErrorInfo defines three members:

- HasErrors is a bool property that should return true if the object has at least one error.
- GetErrors is a method returning a collection (of type IEnumerable). All the errors for a given property name should be placed in that collection and returned to the calling object.
- ErrorsChanged is an event that should be raised when new errors are detected on one property.

The ErrorChanged event takes an instance of DataErrorsChangedEventArgs. This class carries the name of the property for which the errors collection changed.

The main advantage of INotifyDataErrorInfo over IDataErrorInfo is the asynchronicity: The developer chooses when the consumer (in our case, the binding expression) should be notified that there are one or more errors. This makes complex validation scenarios easier to handle. Also, errors must not be strings anymore; they can be any object, in fact. This again enables more complex validation and notification scenarios than IDataErrorInfo.

Each property in an object can have multiple errors. For example, a requirement for the `Name` property could be to be longer than four characters and include at least one space.

> **TIP**
>
> **Returning Objects as Errors**
>
> Should you choose to returns objects rather than strings when the `GetErrors` method is called, the objects in question should override the `ToString()` method and use it to return the error message that the user interface will display.

For more information about `INotifyDataErrorInfo`, the Silverlight.net site has a good whitepaper and a sample application that you can download to understand better what this interface does. The whitepaper is available at http://www.galasoft.ch/sl4-indei.

Which Approach Is the Best?

Using exception-based validation is not recommended, for the reasons previously listed. Silverlight 4 still supports it for backward-compatibility reasons, but choosing one of the two validation interfaces is the better choice.

`IDataErrorInfo` is fairly simple to use, but has limitations, as mentioned earlier (notably, the fact that each property may have only one error at a time, and that validation must be synchronous can be an issue for complex validation scenarios). However, this interface is well known, is already used in other frameworks (such as Windows Forms, WPF, ASP.NET, and so on), and is quite easy to implement.

On the other hand, using `INotifyDataErrorInfo` in your Silverlight applications is probably a good idea for more complex scenarios. This interface is very scalable and suitable for larger applications. It is, however, more complicated to implement.

Using the Visual Studio Binding Dialog

We talked about the Visual Studio Properties editor in Chapter 2, "Setting Up and Discovering Your Environment." There is, however, one more aspect of this great helper that was not mentioned. It can be illustrated by following the steps:

1. Create a new Silverlight 4 application in Visual Studio.
2. Open MainPage.xaml in the Visual Studio designer.
3. From the Toolbox, add a `TextBox` and a `Slider` to the main `Grid` and arrange them on the surface.
4. Select the `Slider` control, and in the Properties editor, enter the name `MySlider` for it. (Reminder: The name can be entered by passing the mouse over the top of the Properties editor, next to the Slider label.)
5. Select the `TextBox` and locate the `Text` property in the Properties editor.

Next to the property's name, you will notice a small icon. This is a visualization of the origin of the property's value, and can take the shapes and colors illustrated in Figure 6.2.

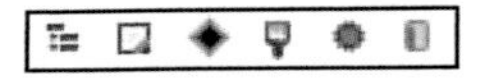

FIGURE 6.2 Property origin: Inherited, Default, Local, Resource, Style, Binding.

- **Inherited** means that the value is set somewhere on one of this element's ancestors (for example, the panel in which this element is placed, or the panel's parent, and so on).
- **Default** means that this property is not set and takes the default value defined in the element's implementation.
- **Local** means that the property is set on this property explicitly (for example, `Width="100"`).
- **Resource** means that this property is set through a `StaticResource` extension. You will learn in Chapter 10 how to create and set resources.
- **Style** means that the property is set through a style applied to the element.
- **Binding** means that this property is set through a data binding.

With the `TextBox` selected, open the data binding editor with the following steps:

1. Click the icon indicating the property's origin and select Apply Data Binding from the context menu.
2. In the Source section of the editor shown in Figure 6.3, select ElementName, and then the MySlider element.
3. In the Path section of the editor, select the Value property of the Slider.
4. If you need, use the next section, Converter, to select a value converter for the binding. We do not need one in this example.
5. Expand the Options section. Here you can set the string format in a friendly way, as well as the other options that we have discussed in this chapter.

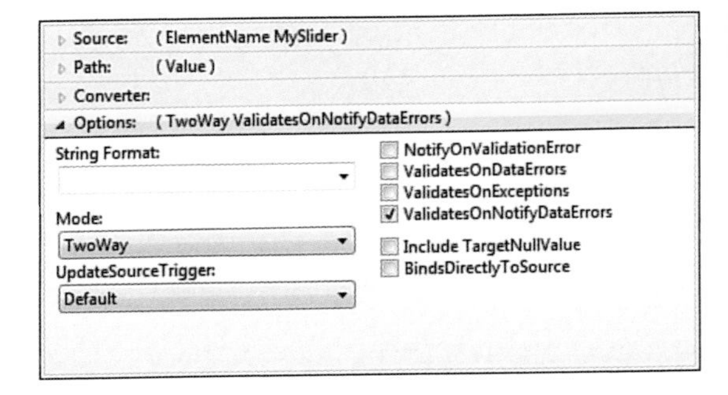

FIGURE 6.3 Data binding editor in Visual Studio.

6. Set the String format to {0:N2}, which is a numeric format with two decimal digits.
7. Make sure that the Mode is set to TwoWay.
8. Run the application and move the Slider's thumb. Check that the value is updated in the `TextBox`, in the correct format.
9. Then, enter a value between 0 and 10 in the `TextBox`, and check that the `Slider`'s value is updated accordingly.

Using the Expression Blend Binding Dialog

Expression Blend offers a similar functionality. To open the binding editor in Blend, follow these steps:

1. In Expression Blend, open the application we created in the "Using the Visual Studio Binding Dialog" section. The easiest way is to right-click MainPage.xaml in the Visual Studio Solution Explorer and select Open in Expression Blend from the context menu.

2. In Blend, select the TextBox and open the Properties panel.

3. Notice that the `Text` property's value is surrounded by an orange border. Also, the small peg next to the value is orange, too.

4. Click the peg and select Data Binding from the context menu. This opens the editor shown in Figure 6.5.

FIGURE 6.4 Property origin: Inherited/Default/Style, Local, Resource, Binding.

In fact, similar to what you saw earlier in Visual Studio, a visual indication for the property value's origin is coded in Blend, as shown in Figure 6.4.

Note that unlike in Visual Studio, Expression Blend does not differentiate between a value being set through inheritance, by default, or through a style.

The three tabs on top of the Blend binding editor allow selecting the source of the binding. If a property you want to select is missing from the Properties box in the editor, you should select All Properties from the Show combo box. Also, the bottom section can be expanded to display advanced properties for the binding.

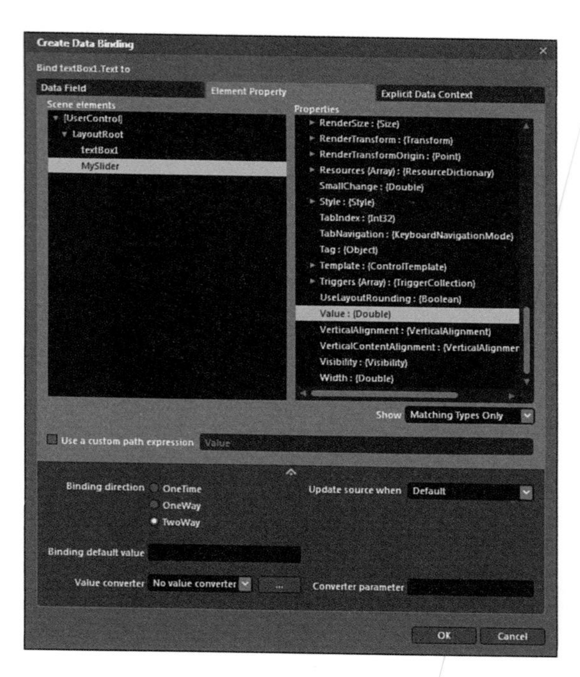

FIGURE 6.5 Data binding editor in Expression Blend.

Debugging Data Bindings

One issue when you develop applications using data bindings is that they are evaluated at runtime and sometimes fail silently. The application will not crash, but some features will not work as expected. Finding the cause of the error might be a little difficult. This section gives you a few tips that will help you when debugging.

Checking the Output Tab

Some information about the data error is shown in the Output tab. This can help you to find the cause of the issue. To witness this, follow these steps:

1. Create a new Silverlight application in Visual Studio 2010. Name it **DebuggingBindings**.
2. Replace the `LayoutRoot` grid in MainPage.xaml with the code in Listing 6.14.

LISTING 6.14 Scene with a Data Binding Error

```
<StackPanel x:Name="LayoutRoot" Background="White">

    <TextBlock Text="{Binding ElementName=MySlider, Path=Valu}"
               Margin="10" />

    <Slider x:Name="MySlider"
            Margin="10" />

</StackPanel>
```

3. Run the application in debug mode by pressing the F5 key. Note that the information about the binding error is shown only when the application runs in debug mode!
4. Select the Output tab in Visual Studio. If it is not visible already, select View, Output from the menu.

You should now see an error message similar to the one shown below. This message identifies the cause of the error precisely: The property name `Value` was misspelled as `Valu`. The property is not found, and therefore a data error is thrown. Note that if you had set a `FallbackValue` property on this binding, it would appear in the Silverlight application when the application runs.

```
System.Windows.Data Error: BindingExpression path error: 'Valu' property not found
on 'System.Windows.Controls.Slider Minimum:0 Maximum:10 Value:0'
'System.Windows.Controls.Slider' (HashCode=14993092). BindingExpression:
Path='Valu' DataItem='System.Windows.Controls.Slider Minimum:0 Maximum:10 Value:0'
(HashCode=14993092); target element is 'System.Windows.Controls.TextBlock'
(Name=''); target property is 'Text' (type 'System.String')..
```

Creating a Test Converter

The trick in the previous section works fine to solve simple issues. However sometimes it is not that easy: It is possible that the binding is valid, but the value is not what was expected.

Let's imagine the following scenario: We want to set a binding to current item in a list. However, the order of the items changes without notice. Suddenly the application displays the wrong information. The bindings are not in error, but they point to the wrong object.

To check which item is used for the binding, a temporary converter can be implemented, as shown in Listing 6.15.

LISTING 6.15 Test Converter for Debug

```
1  public class TempoDebugConverter : IValueConverter
2  {
3      public object Convert(object value, Type targetType,
4          object parameter,CultureInfo culture)
5      {
6          MessageBox.Show("We are in the debug converter");
7          MessageBox.Show("Current item name: "
8              + (value as DataItem).Name);
9
10         return value;
11     }
12
13     public object ConvertBack(object value, Type targetType,
14         object parameter, CultureInfo culture)
15     {
16         throw new NotImplementedException();
17     }
18 }
```

The test converter can be used in XAML, as shown in Listing 6.16.

LISTING 6.16 Using the Test Converter in XAML

```
<StackPanel x:Name="LayoutRoot"
            Background="White"
            xmlns:conv="clr-namespace:DebuggingBindings.Converters">
    <StackPanel.Resources>
        <conv:TempoDebugConverter x:Key="TempoDebugConverter" />
    </StackPanel.Resources>

    <Border DataContext="{Binding Source={StaticResource MyCvs},
            Path=CurrentItem,
```

```
            Converter={StaticResource TempoDebugConverter}}">
        <TextBlock Text="{Binding Path=ContractNumber}"
                   Margin="10" />
    </Border>
</StackPanel>
```

You can set a breakpoint in the `Convert` method of the test converter (for example, in Listing 6.15 on line 6), allowing you to inspect the source object. If the breakpoint is hit, it means that the binding expression is correct, and that the issue has another cause. You can also inspect some other parameters of the binding (for example, the current culture used to resolve the binding, passed to the fourth parameter).

Setting up a debug converter takes some time, but in some complex cases, it can be a real lifesaver.

Grouping, Filtering, and Sorting Data

Now that we talked in depth about data bindings, let's review other features of Silverlight 4 that makes working with large sets of data easier. Silverlight 3 introduced the possibility to modify the way data from a collection is presented without modifying the collection itself. This feature relies on the `ICollectionView` interface that a collection can choose to implement. This interface defines a number of events, methods, and properties that the collection should implement to provide a view of the data according to the criteria specified.

Built in the Silverlight core framework, there are two classes helping you to work with collection views: `CollectionViewSource` and `PagedCollectionView`.

Working with the `CollectionViewSource`

`CollectionViewSource` is a proxy class that takes a collection in its `Source` property, and exposes a `View` property of type `ICollectionView`. You can work in XAML with the `CollectionViewSource` very much as you would work with an `ICollectionView` directly. Note, however, that `CollectionViewSource` does not implement `ICollectionView`: It is not a view, but it provides a view.

> **WARNING**
>
> **Omitting `CollectionViewSource.View`**
>
> Working with `CollectionViewSource` in XAML or in code can be confusing: The `View` property must be omitted in XAML, but has to be used in code (as seen in Listing 6.17).

6

LISTING 6.17 Working with the CollectionViewSource in Code and in XAML

```
var cvs = Resources["MyCvs"] as CollectionViewSource;
MyDetailsBorder.DataContext = cvs.View.CurrentItem;
DataContext="{Binding Source={StaticResource MyCvs},
                      Path=CurrentItem}">
```

Current Item

One interesting feature of ICollectionView is that it keeps track of the current item in the collection. This can prove very useful when you have one data source used among multiple views. Note that the current item is saved directly in the ICollectionView instance, and not in the data control using it.

This scenario is often used in master/detail pages (that is, a page with a list of item on one side and the selected item's details on the other side). You can set the DataContext of the details panel as shown in Listing 6.17.

As a shortcut, the CurrentItem property of an ICollectionView can also be replaced by a dot, as shown here:

```
DataContext="{Binding Source={StaticResource MyCvs},
                      Path=.}">
```

The great advantage of using an ICollectionView to track the current item is that all your data controls will be synchronized automatically. For example, if you set a DataGrid and a ListBox to use the same CollectionViewSource, and the user selects an item in the ListBox, the same item will also be automatically selected in the DataGrid.

Sorting Items

Using CollectionViewSource, you can sort items according to a list of SortDescription instances. This structure can be built with a PropertyName (the property after which the data will be sorted) and a Direction (Ascending or Descending), as shown in Listing 6.18. You can define multiple SortDescription instances to allow multilevel sorting.

Note that the SortDescription structure is available in the namespace System.ComponentModel in the assembly System.Windows. When used in XAML, you need to map an xmlns prefix to this namespace.

Grouping Items

CollectionViewSource also allows grouping items according to a list of GroupDescription instances. Because GroupDescription is an abstract class, you need to provide a subclass that defines how the items should be grouped. In Silverlight, such a class is named PropertyGroupDescription and allows grouping the items according to a property's name.

Note that grouped items are rendered in a different way depending on the data control used. Figure 6.6 shows a list of items with each a bool property (MyBool), an int property (MyInt), and a string property (MyString). In the CollectionViewSource shown in Listing 6.18, the items are grouped according to the MyInt property and shown in a ListBox and in a `DataGrid`. Notice how the groups can be collapsed in the `DataGrid`, while the `ListBox` always shows all the items.

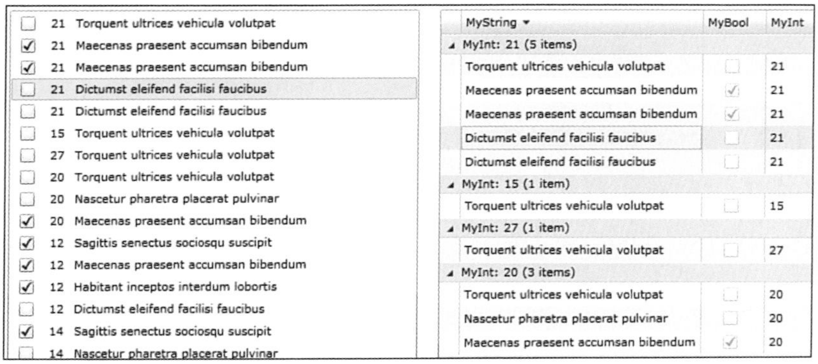

FIGURE 6.6 *`ListBox`* and *`DataGrid`* showing grouped items.

When Should You Use `CollectionViewSource`?

`CollectionViewSource` offers only limited interaction with the data, but it is more lightweight than the alternative `PagedCollectionView` that we will mention in the next section. Also, a `CollectionViewSource` can be constructed in XAML directly, whereas a `PagedCollectionView` requires code.

`CollectionViewSource` is a good choice when you need to quickly sort/group items in a data control. Listing 6.18 shows a `CollectionViewSource` in XAML with a `PropertyGroupDescription` and a `SortDescription`. The result is displayed in Figure 6.6 in a `ListBox` and in a `DataGrid`. Notice how the items are sorted alphabetically in descending order within each group.

LISTING 6.18 Creating a `CollectionViewSource` in XAML

```
<CollectionViewSource
    Source="{Binding Source={StaticResource SampleDataSource},
                     Path=Collection}"
    x:Key="MyCvs">
    <CollectionViewSource.GroupDescriptions>
        <PropertyGroupDescription PropertyName="MyInt" />
    </CollectionViewSource.GroupDescriptions>
    <CollectionViewSource.SortDescriptions>
        <scm:SortDescription PropertyName="MyString"
                             Direction="Descending" />
    </CollectionViewSource.SortDescriptions>
</CollectionViewSource>
```

Listing 6.19 shows a way to change the sorting order in code. The sorting order cannot be simply changed on an existing SortDescription, so instead we need to build a new one and add it instead of the old one. Of course, we can also change the sorting criteria or add multiple SortDescription instances to sort according to multiple criteria. We can also extend the code to change the grouping according to different PropertyGroupDescription instances.

LISTING 6.19 Changing the Sort Order of a CollectionViewSource

```
var cvs = this.Resources["MyCvs"] as CollectionViewSource;
cvs.SortDescriptions.Clear();

var sort = new SortDescription
{
    PropertyName = "MyString",
    Direction = (sortUp
        ? ListSortDirection.Ascending
        : ListSortDirection.Descending)
};

cvs.SortDescriptions.Add(sort);
```

Using a PagedCollectionView

PagedCollectionView is an implementation of ICollectionView that allows more interaction with the data than the CollectionViewSource does: grouping, sorting, filtering, and paging.

The PagedCollectionView class is typically used together with data controls such as the DataGrid and the DataPager. In Chapter 8. we will talk about data controls and see some samples using this ICollectionView.

Binding Directly to the Source

In this section, you saw how to use the CollectionViewSource class to act as a data provider and expose a property of type ICollectionView. You also learned that you can use the CollectionViewSource as the source of the bindings rather than the view itself because Silverlight will take a shortcut and get the data from the correct place automatically.

However, sometimes you want to actually bind to the data provider itself, instead of the ICollectionView it exposes, and the shortcut is actually a hindrance because it gets in the way of the properties you try to reach. In this case, set the property BindsDirectlyToSource to True. This value indicates to the binding that it should ignore the shortcut and get the desired value from the data provider directly.

Note, however, that Silverlight does part of the work for you: If you try to set a binding on a property that exists only on the data provider but not on the view that it exposes, the provider's property is used. Listing 6.20 shows an example where we use the shortcut to access the ICollectionView's CurrentItem property through the shortcut. If we set BindsDirectlyToSource to True on this binding, a data error occurs, because the CollectionViewSource class does not expose such a property: The shortcut is ignored because of this property.

LISTING 6.20 Using BindsDirectlyToSource to Ignore the Shortcut

```
<!--Success through the shortcut to ICollectionView-->
<TextBlock Text="{Binding Source={StaticResource MyCvs},
                  Path=CurrentItem.Property1}" />

<!--Shortcut is ignored, data error-->
<TextBlock Text="{Binding Source={StaticResource MyCvs},
                  Path=CurrentItem.Property1,
                  BindsDirectlyToSource=True}" />
```

Summary

In this chapter, we examined the Binding class in great detail, including the many improvements added to this class in Silverlight 4. The Binding class is not completely compatible with its Windows Presentation Foundation counterpart, but it has come a long way since the days of Silverlight 2.

Next, we covered the Visual Studio and the Expression Blend data binding editors. These tools enable you to create your bindings in a more visual way, and avoid errors when typing object and property names. Finally, we looked at some ways to debug data bindings in Visual Studio. Errors in bindings are quite difficult to find because they fail silently. However, with a few tricks and some practice, it is possible to detect and correct these errors.

Finally, we talked about data at a low level, explaining the mechanics of multiple classes involved in data processing: CollectionViewSource and ICollectionView for grouping, filtering, sorting, and paging.

In the next chapter, we cover higher-level usage of data in Silverlight applications, with the Model-View-ViewModel pattern. This pattern enables a clear separation between the user interface and the data model and provides a convenient place to prepare data for the user interface.

CHAPTER 7

Understanding the Model-View-ViewModel Pattern

IN THIS CHAPTER, WE WILL:

- Talk about design patterns and their utility.
- Review a few separation patterns and understand why separation is important in an application.
- Dive into the Model-View-ViewModel (MVVM) pattern and its usage in Silverlight.
- Study implementations of the MVVM pattern and build a sample application.
- Talk about helper components that help you to build decoupled and extensible application.

Ever since applications grew more complex than just a few lines of code, software developers have discussed the best way to organize them into components. More than anything else, modern developers love *separation*, *abstraction*, and *layers*. By defining small components with clearly defined responsibility, you make your application more readable, manageable, testable, and maintainable.

Client application developers came up with a number of *design patterns* to enhance their applications and to improve the process of making them. In this chapter, we briefly discuss design patterns, and then take a close look at the Model-View-ViewModel pattern, which is often used to structure Silverlight applications.

About Design Patterns

Design patterns are the software developer's solution to avoid reinventing the wheel. When a developer (or more likely, a community of developers) has a given problem to solve, he comes up with a solution to the issue. This can be an architecture answering to the particular constraint, a set of components, interfaces, and so on. When one solution is particularly good, it is interesting to modify it in a way that it can be reused in multiple places to solve similar problems. There is a process of *abstraction* (that is, taking the problem out of the given context, simplifying it by removing unnecessary detail, and turning it in something reusable in other places). These abstracted solutions are named *design patterns* or *software patterns*.

More than 20 of the most well-known design patterns are gathered into a book titled *Design Patterns: Elements of Reusable Object-Oriented Software*. Of course, 20 patterns are not all that is needed to build applications, so there are more books on the topic. Also, the book is a little outdated, and software development has evolved since it was released. It is, however, a good start to understand what a pattern is and how it can be used.

It is important to understand that design patterns are not sample code, and should not, in fact, propose an implementation. They should also not be tightly bound to a programming language or to a platform. This is why some people are arguing about the best implementation for a given pattern, and the discussions can get very passionate at times.

Separating the Concerns

Such discussions take place still now in the Silverlight and Windows Presentation Foundation (WPF) community about the best way to separate the user interface (the *view*) from the underlying layers of the application (the data, the services, and so on). These lower-level layers are often referred to as the *model*. In most applications, the view is a representation of the model.

Why Is Separation Good?

When a view is tightly bound to a model, some annoying issues can occur:

- It is hard to work on one part of the application without having the whole rest already in place. The application's components are *tightly bound*.
- It is difficult to modify one part of the application without impacting all the other parts, too. The application is not easily *maintainable*.
- It is hard to isolate one part of the application and test it to ensure that it works well in complex conditions. The application is not easily *testable*.
- It is very difficult or impossible to put the application in a given state without going through a lot of difficult steps. This makes the work of the designers difficult, because they need to see various parts of the view in various states to design the components. The application is not easily *designable*.

A better solution is to have multiple small-sized components that are loosely coupled. Each component should have a clear responsibility and should be able to reproduce this functionality even if it is in a different context. This allows putting each component in various states, testing these states with automated unit tests, and allowing designers to work on each component separately, but with a meaningful content.

Classic Separation Patterns

In the past few years of client application development, several separation patterns have been used in many applications.

The Model-View-Controller (MVC) Pattern

In this pattern, the model and the view are clearly separated: The model is completely view agnostic, and could even be used with multiple user interface technologies. The view is responsible for querying changes in the model, redrawing its invalidated parts, and notifying the controller when the user actuates an input. The controller prepares the data and updates the model. The interactions are shown in Figure 7.1.

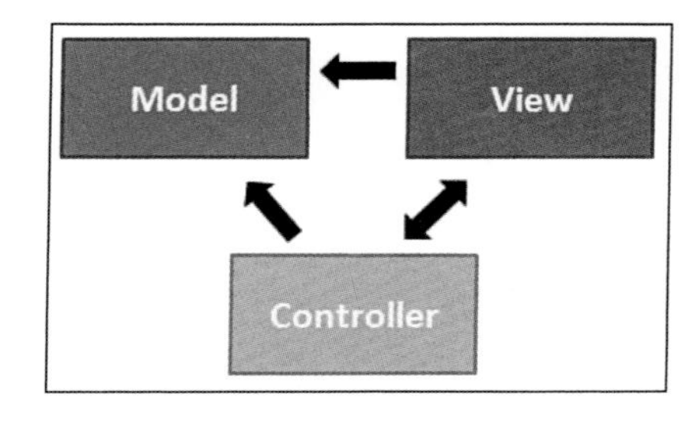

FIGURE 7.1 The MVC pattern.

In the .NET world, the MVC pattern is often used in Windows Forms application (a desktop framework that was popular before WPF offered a more modern alternative), and more recently in ASP.NET, with the ASP.NET MVC framework.

In this pattern, the view has an active role, which makes writing automated tests a little more difficult than it could be. Some user interface frameworks are not well suited for this kind of tests, and covering a large portion of the application's logic is difficult.

The Passive View Pattern

To make the application even more testable, Martin Fowler proposed a pattern named the Passive View, which is a variation of the MVC pattern where the view is completely passive and the controller is responsible for updating the view when the model changes, as shown in Figure 7.2. An application built according to this pattern is more testable because there is almost no intelligence in the view that must be tested. The automated unit tests do not depend on a user interface technology because the controller is view agnostic: It is "just code."

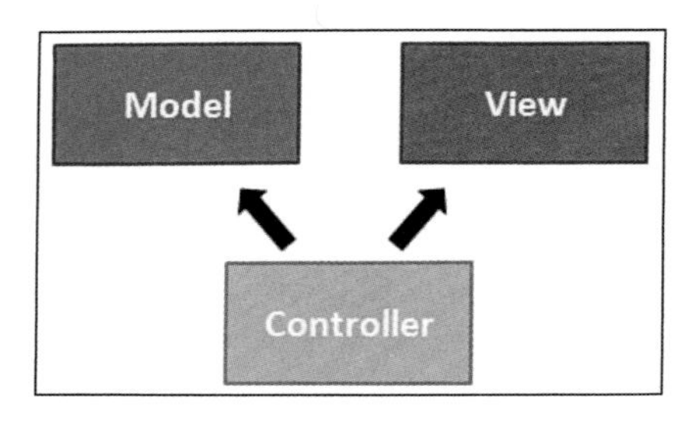

FIGURE 7.2 The Passive View pattern.

History of MVVM

Martin Fowler proposed yet another pattern named the Presentation Model pattern, where the controller is replaced by a number of objects (the presentation models), each having a state representing a view at all times. This is an intermediary object between the view and the model. Whenever something happens in the view, a synchronization mechanism updates the presentation model, which in turn updates the model if needed. On the other hand, when the model is updated, the presentation model is modified first, and then the changes are synchronized to the view.

In this pattern, the view is a little more active than in the Passive View pattern, because it must offer a synchronization mechanism, which can vary depending on the chosen user interface technology. Because the synchronization mechanism must be tested, too, the number of tests that must be written is greater.

Developing Expression Blend

At approximately the same time as the Presentation Model pattern was being developed, a team at Microsoft was working on the tool that we know today as Expression Blend. This tool was the first large application built entirely in WPF, which at the time was still a work in progress. The architects of Blend were faced by a number of new challenges, because the data bindings (discussed in Chapter 6, "Working with Data: Binding, Grouping, Sorting, and Filtering,") and the dependency property system (discussed in Chapter 5, "Understanding Dependency Properties") were changing the way that client applications are developed.

Expression Blend is a tool for designers, and therefore it must be able to display various components of the application in a given state, so that the designer can style and template them. This is why it is very interesting to use a pattern where the view is as disconnected from the model as possible, and where an intermediary object (the view-model) can be accessed and set in the state that the designer needs.

Presentation Model for WPF and Silverlight

WPF has one natural advantage when a synchronization mechanism is needed: The dependency property system and the binding framework are made exactly for this, and are built in to the framework. The developer does not need to test the synchronization mechanism; Microsoft did that work already. It was only natural to adapt the Presentation Model pattern to WPF, which became the Model-View-ViewModel pattern.

Expression Blend is built according to this pattern. This explains why MVVM works great with Blend. But there is more to MVVM than "Blendability": Because of the separation between the components, we also gain in testability, modularity, and maintainability.

Finally, when Silverlight was developed, many of the core concepts of WPF were ported over, and the same mechanisms are available, as you saw in Chapters 5 and 6. This makes MVVM the pattern of choice for Silverlight.

Architecture of MVVM

The MVVM pattern identifies three layers:

- The model is where the data comes from. It can be a gateway to web services, a data layer to a database, a file system manager, and so forth. It is completely ignorant of the view.
- The view-model is an intermediary layer, as shown in Figure 7.3, and is responsible for preparing the data that will be displayed in the view. We will talk about the implementation of this component later in this chapter.

- Finally, the view is the visual part of the application. In Silverlight, the view is XAML based. Note that most of the time the view also has some code (the code behind) to handle special view-related activities, such as starting or stopping animations, displaying messages to the user, and so forth.

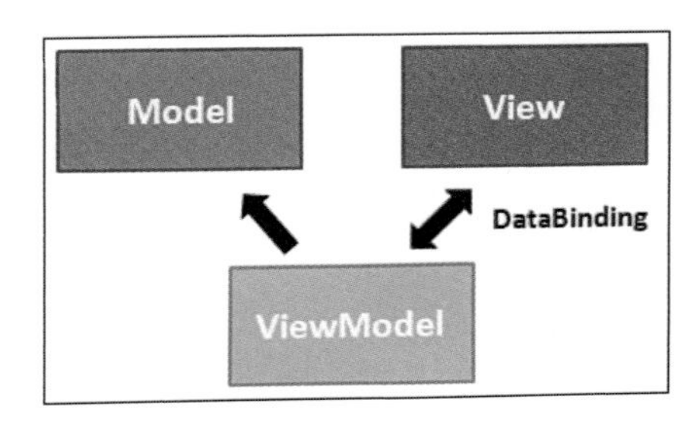

FIGURE 7.3 The Model-View-ViewModel pattern.

Figure 7.3 shows the three layers and their relationship. Note that the connection between the view and the view-model relies on data binding.

Translating to Silverlight

Now that we saw the theory of MVVM, we need to understand how to translate this to a real Silverlight application. First, let's review how these concepts are adapted in Silverlight before a sample application is implemented.

Getting Data Through the Model

The model is wherever the data comes from. In a Silverlight application, it is often a web service (through the `WebClient` class, a Windows Communication Foundation (WCF) service, an RSS feed, and so on). Sometimes data comes from files (XML or otherwise) on the local computer. For the client application, where the data comes from is not relevant, because the model is *abstracting and isolating* the source.

The model is usually one or more classes exposing methods with names such as `GetItems`, `SaveItems`, `CreateNewItem`, and so on. They should be developed in a way that protects the consumer (the view-model) in case the data layer changes. For example, if a WCF service gets converted into a Relational State Transfer (REST) service, the view-model and the view should not be modified at all. For more information about REST services, see http://www.galasoft.ch/sl4-rest.

Preparing the Data in the View-model

The raw data that is stored in the model is often not directly suitable for a Silverlight application. At the very least, changes in a property should raise the `PropertyChanged` event that is defined by the `INotifyPropertyChanged` interface, as you saw in Listing 5.2. This is why data items are often wrapped in their own view-models, as illustrated in Figure 7.4: a collection of `ItemVM` instances, where each wraps an instance of the `Item` class, which was retrieved from a service by the model.

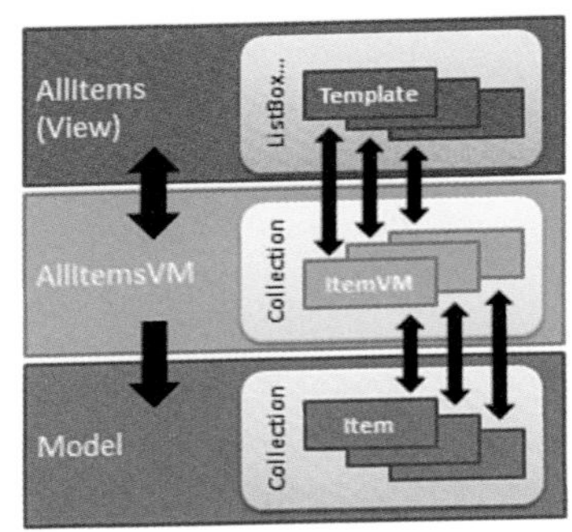

FIGURE 7.4 Organization of items, item view-models, and data templates.

This collection is owned by another kind of view-model, called `AllItemsVM` in Figure 7.4. This object will be bound to the `AllItems` user control later. In this class, we can also add properties that are directly related to the user interface. One such example is a property indicating that the application is busy with an asynchronous operation. Retrieving a list of customers from a web service or a database can take some time, and it is good practice to inform the user about what is happening. To do this, we can expose a property named `IsBusy` (of type `bool`) and set it to `true` when such an operation is happening. The view-model doesn't know what the view will do with this property; it is just providing it.

Two Kinds of View-models

It is important to understand the difference between the two kinds of view-models: The `ItemVM` class is used to represent data. It is typically stored in a collection and rendered by a `DataTemplate` in a data control (`ListBox`, `ItemsControl`, `ComboBox`, `DataGrid`, and so on).

On the other hand, the `AllItemsVM` class is bound to a `UserControl`. There is only one instance of this class per instance of the `AllItems` page. Its properties are rendered by various controls, such as `TextBlock`, `TextBox`, `RadioButton`, and so on. The `AllItemsVM` class owns the `ItemsVM` instances, typically in an `ObservableCollection`.

Rendering Items with a `DataTemplate`

As mentioned, items wrapped in a view-model and stored in collections are rendered through a data template and then displayed in a data control. The Silverlight framework automatically binds the implicit `DataContext` property of the data template to the item that it renders.

Rendering the View as a User Control

In Silverlight, a view is typically a `UserControl` with its `DataContext` set to a view-model. The *granularity* (that is, the size and complexity) of the view and of the view-model depends on multiple factors.

- If the view and the view-model grow too big, they become harder to maintain and test. It is a good time to refactor your application, and split the existing code base in multiple classes.
- If the view and the view-model are too small, you end up with a large number of classes to maintain, and your application code base can be confusing.

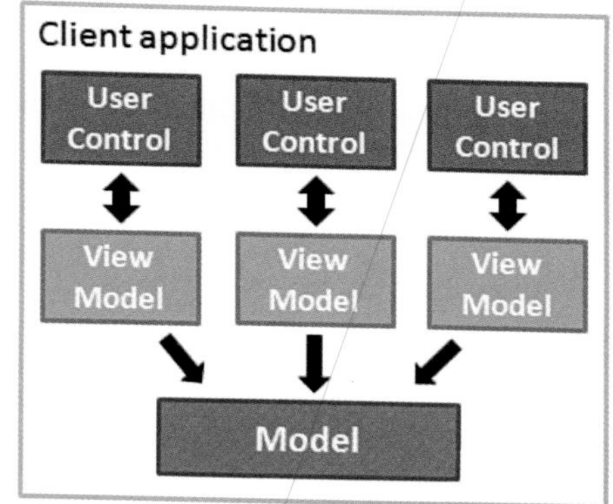

FIGURE 7.5 Splitting the application into model, view-models, and views.

It is often best to split a complex view in multiple user controls, each with its own view-model, as shown in Figure 7.5.

In contrast to data templates, the `DataContext` on a user control must be set manually to the corresponding view-model through a binding. There are multiple ways to do this, as you will see later in this chapter.

What About Custom Controls?

Custom controls can be seen as the smallest example of view/view-model pair in the Silverlight framework. As discussed in Chapter 3, "Extending Your Application with Controls," a custom control is made of a class with dependency properties and of a control template. The class is the view-model, and the template is the view, with data bindings to keep it synchronized with the view-model.

TIP

Binding the Data Template to the Model

If we follow Figure 7.4 strictly, a data template is completely disconnected from the item it represents, and all communication goes through properties and methods on the view-model. This is often not the best way because it implies duplicating most properties from the item. This is why it is often better to bind some elements from the data template directly to the corresponding properties on the item.

Note, however, that this is possible only if the items implement the `INotifyPropertyChanged` interface and raise the `PropertyChanged` event when their properties are updated. Otherwise, the bindings will not be notified when a property changes.

When the model is a WCF client, the *proxy* objects created by Visual Studio do implement this interface, and therefore can be used as the source for bindings on the data template directly.

Binding the View to the View-model

Once the view-model is implemented, it must be made available to the view, so that bindings can be set on properties. There are several ways to do that. Remember that MVVM is a pattern, and is subject to interpretation, depending on the goal that you want to achieve, on external constraints, and so forth. In this chapter, we expose a few ways to create view-models and to bind them to the view. However, it is possible to find other implementations on the Web, so do not hesitate to investigate more before deciding to use one or the other implementation.

Understanding the Data Context

The `DataContext` is a property defined on the `FrameworkElement` class. You saw in Listing 4.7 how it can be set to an object (in that case, a `StaticResource` defined in the view) through a data binding. Once the `DataContext` is set, the implicit source of every data binding on every child is automatically set to the `DataContext` object. Of course, you can still set the source of selected bindings to a different object (using one of the properties we saw in Chapter 6, in the "Setting the Source" section), but the `DataContext` offers a convenient shortcut.

Inheriting the Data Context

A user control set up as a view usually contains controls (buttons, check boxes, text blocks, and so on) and can also contain other user controls. All the elements within a view automatically inherit the view's data context.

The inherited context can be overwritten by setting a child element's `DataContext` property to something different (another view-model, another kind of object, or in the case of data templates, the data item that the template is rendering). This hierarchy of contexts and the corresponding user interface are represented in Figure 7.6.

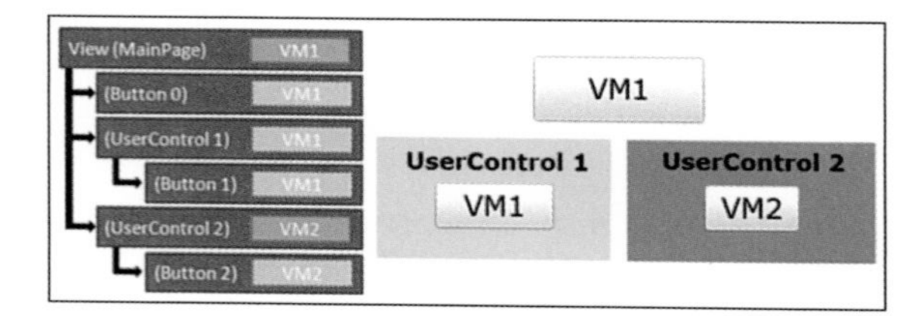

FIGURE 7.6 Logical tree and data context.

- In Figure 7.6, the data context of `MainPage` is set to the view-model named VM1.
- The data context is inherited to Button 0. Any binding set to the implicit data context will use properties within VM1.
- The same happens with User Control 1. This user control doesn't have a data context, so it inherits VM1.
- VM1 is also inherited to Button 1, which is within User Control 1.
- The data context of User Control 2 is set manually to VM2. This overwrites VM1. Any binding set to the data context within User Control 2 will use properties within VM2.
- VM2 is inherited to Button 2, which is within User Control 2.

Binding to the View

As mentioned a few times already, when the view is a `DataTemplate` used within a data control, the `DataContext` property is set automatically to the corresponding data item. In other cases, however, it must be defined manually.

There are multiple ways to do this, and as usual it depends what you are trying to achieve. In this section, we look at three ways to do so, which should cover most scenarios, and mention their advantages and inconveniencies. But this list is not exhaustive, and you will find additional implementations on the Web.

Creating the View-model in Resources

With this method, the view-model is made available in the view's resources. We mentioned earlier that the resources are a store, where any type of object can be placed for later usage. When an object is placed in the resources, it is created by the XAML parser if needed. Multiple consumers can use the same resource (for example, as the source of data bindings). Listing 7.1 shows a view-model in the view's resources, and the way that the `DataContext` is bound to this object.

LISTING 7.1 Binding to a View-model in Resources

```
1  <UserControl x:Class="SampleMvvm.MainPage"
2     xmlns="http://schemas.microsoft.com/winfx/2006/xaml/presentation"
3     xmlns:x="http://schemas.microsoft.com/winfx/2006/xaml"
4     xmlns:vm="clr-namespace:SampleMvvm.ViewModel">
5      <UserControl.Resources>
6         <vm:MainViewModel x:Key="MainViewModel" />
7     </UserControl.Resources>
8
9     <Grid x:Name="LayoutRoot"
10     DataContext="{Binding Source={StaticResource MainViewModel}}">
11    </Grid>
12 </UserControl>
```

- Line 4 defines an `xmlns` prefix pointing to our view-model's namespace.
- Line 6 creates an instance of the view-model in the page's resources.
- Line 10 sets the main `Grid`'s `DataContext` to the view-model in the resources through a binding.

Advantages

The whole interaction happens in XAML. It is much more localized and easy to find and to understand what happens. This way of doing works great with Expression Blend and the Visual Studio designer (as discussed later this chapter).

Disadvantages

There is no control about when the view-model is created. The XAML parser decides when the object is needed. There is also no way to pass parameters to the view-model constructor. The XAML parser uses the default constructor. Finally, there is no central location from which to get the view-model, for other objects that need to communicate with it.

This way of doing is great for very simple applications (for example, for demos or tests). In real-life applications, however, this is not convenient enough. A complete sample is available at http://galasoft.ch/SL4U/Code/Chapter07.

Using a `ViewModelLocator`

Another alternative that works great is to use an intermediary object called the `ViewModelLocator`. This object is in charge of creating, storing, and managing the view-models in the applications.

The `ViewModelLocator` instance is made available in the application's resources (into App.xaml). This makes it global for the whole application. The view-models are exposed through properties on this instance. Depending on the scenario, the view-model can be stored as a static attribute of the `ViewModelLocator`, or there might be multiple instances of a view-model (for example, for pop-ups). The `ViewModelLocator` is in charge of creating and deleting these instances.

Because the `ViewModelLocator` is stored in the global resources, it has to define an empty constructor, but this is usually not a big limitation. The view-models, on the other hand, can accept parameters (for example, services to handle data, settings).

Listing 7.2 shows a `ViewModelLocator` stored in App.xaml. A simple implementation is shown in Listing 7.3. Finally, Listing 7.4 shows the `DataContext` of the view being bound to the view-model through the `ViewModelLocator`'s `Main` property.

LISTING 7.2 ViewModelLocator in Global Resources

```
<Application.Resources>
    <!--Global View Model Locator-->
    <vm:ViewModelLocator x:Key="Locator" />
</Application.Resources>
```

LISTING 7.3 ViewModelLocator Implementation

```
public class ViewModelLocator
{
    private static MainViewModel _main;

    public ViewModelLocator()
    {
        var service = new CustomerServiceProxy();
        _main = new MainViewModel(service);
    }

    public MainViewModel Main
    {
        get
        {
            return _main;
        }
    }
}
```

LISTING 7.4 Binding the View's `DataContext` Through the `ViewModelLocator`

```
<UserControl x:Class="SampleMvvm.MainPage"
   xmlns="http://schemas.microsoft.com/winfx/2006/xaml/presentation"
   xmlns:x="http://schemas.microsoft.com/winfx/2006/xaml"
   DataContext="{Binding Source={StaticResource Locator},
                         Path=Main}">

</UserControl>
```

Advantages

A central location is responsible for the creation, storage, and deletion of the view-models. This is convenient, for example, when another object needs to get information from a view-model. Also, because the view-models are created in code, special cases are easy to handle. Finally, this solution works great with Expression Blend and the Visual Studio designer.

Disadvantages

The `ViewModelLocator` is an additional class to implement and maintain.

An implementation demonstrating this way to bind the view-model is also available at http://galasoft.ch/SL4U/Code/Chapter07.

Setting the Data Context in the Code Behind

Because the `DataContext` is a property of the view (it is available on every `FrameworkElement`), it can of course also be set in the code behind, in the view's constructor, as shown in Listing 7.5. Note how the view-model is constructed with a parameter: The service passed to the view-model is constructed in the view, and the view-model does not have to know whether this is a real implementation or just a dummy object for test purposes.

LISTING 7.5 Setting the `DataContext` in the View's Constructor

```
public partial class MainPage : UserControl
{
    public MainPage()
    {
        InitializeComponent();

        var service = new CustomerServiceProxy();
        var viewModel = new MainViewModel(service);
        DataContext = viewModel;
    }
}
```

Advantages

The view-models are created in code, so special cases are easy to handle, for example, calling a view-model's constructor with parameters for services, and so forth. There is no additional locator class to manage.

Disadvantages

No central location to get the view-models from. The creation and lifetime management is the responsibility of each view, which can cause certain confusion. Also, this doesn't work well in Expression Blend and the Visual Studio designer. The code behind is not executed when a view is loaded in Blend. The view-model will not be created, the data context is not set, and the view remains empty in Blend.

These two disadvantages can, however, be mitigated. A central location for the creation of view-models can be imported in the form of an inversion of control (IOC) container. These helper classes are very popular in the .NET world. For example, libraries such as Structure Map, Unity, NInject, the Managed Extensibility Framework (MEF), and others help to manage the lifetime of objects and services.

As for the design-time experience, a design time data context can be set in Visual Studio and Expression Blend, as you will see in Chapter 11, “Mastering Expression Blend.”

Building a Sample Application

In this section, we build a basic MVVM application to show some the advantages of this pattern in Silverlight 4. The application will use a WCF service to obtain data (a list of customers). Because the WCF service calls are made through the model, it is not relevant for the view-model and the view where the data comes from. This is one of the many advantages of a clean separation. In this section, we do not talk about the model, except to mention the interfaces we use to read data and save changes.

The sample application can be downloaded from http://galasoft.ch/SL4U/Code/Chapter07. You can download a “start” solution, containing the service implementation as well as the draft of the Silverlight application. There is also an “end” state, with the implementation as described in this chapter.

The Model’s Interface

The model exposes one interface named `ICustomerServiceProxy`, as shown in Listing 7.6.

LISTING 7.6 The `ICustomerServiceProxy` Interface

```
public interface ICustomerServiceProxy
{
    void GetCustomers(
        Action<IEnumerable<Customer>, Exception> callback);

    void SaveCustomers(
        IEnumerable <Customer> customers,
        Action<bool> callback);
}
```

- All the methods use an asynchronous pattern to access the service. In Silverlight, all web service calls are asynchronous (as you saw in *Silverlight 2 Unleashed*, Chapter 22). The consumer of the service passes an `Action` to the method. The `Action` class acts like a method, in the sense that it can be executed by another object. But it can be also passed as a parameter and saved for later. It is a *reference to a method*. This is perfect for asynchronous method calls because the service does not need to keep any reference to the consumer: When the web request is completed, simply execute the callback to inform the consumer.

- The method `GetCustomers` loads all the customers from the server. We use an `IEnumerable` collection, which is a simple interface that most collections in .NET implement. This gives the service a great freedom to change its implementation if needed without affecting the view-model.
- In the method `GetCustomer`'s callback, the second parameter is an `Exception`. This allows the service to notify the view-model if an error occurred when retrieving data. This `Exception` might be `null`, if all went well.
- The method `SaveCustomer` takes a collection of `Customer` instances as parameter and saves them to the server. It also uses a callback to indicate whether saving was successful.

These are the only two methods we will use in this simple application; of course, a real-life service will have additional methods (for example, to create a new customer or execute queries on the database).

There are multiple advantages in exposing the service through the `ICustomerServiceProxy` interface rather than a concrete class: The view-model does not depend at all on the service implementation. The interface is used as a *contract* between the consumer (the view-model) and the provider (the service implementation in the model). The class interaction from the view-model to the service can easily be unit tested: We can simulate the actions of the methods without having to use a complex web service. For example, we can implement a *mock* service (that is, a class implementing the `ICustomerServiceProxy` interface only for test purposes). For more information about mocking, see http://www.galasoft.ch/sl4-mock.

The service can easily be created by techniques known as inversion of control (IOC) and dependency injection (DI), which help creating complex applications and reduce the dependencies between the components. You can find more information about IOC and DI at http://www.galasoft.ch/sl4-ioc.

About the `Customer` Class

In this sample application, the `Customer` class is created by Visual Studio when we connect the Silverlight application to the WCF service. This is called a *proxy* (in other words, a client-side representation of the server-side object used by the service). An even better idea is to also use an interface `ICustomer` to completely decouple the view-model from the WCF service. In this simple application, however, we will just rely on the proxy. You will learn in Chapter 9, "Connecting to the Web," how to connect to a WCF service and use proxies.

The `Customer` class defined on the server is a pure data object with various properties, such as `FirstName`, `LastName`, a URI to a picture file named `PictureUri`, `Gender`, `AccountNumber`, and so forth. All these properties are also available on the client directly because the proxy is a representation of this server-side object and all the properties are populated when the WCF service call is made.

Building a CustomerViewModel

The Customer class is a WCF proxy object. Conveniently, the proxy generated by Visual Studio implements the INotifyPropertyChanged interface; this means that its properties can be used as the source for data bindings. This simplifies the development because we do not need to duplicate every property when we wrap the Customer class within the CustomerViewModel class. The Customer instance passed to the CustomerViewModel constructor is exposed in a public property, as shown in Listing 7.7.

LISTING 7.7 The CustomerViewModel Constructor and the Model Property

```
 1 public class CustomerViewModel : ViewModelBase
 2 {
 3     public Customer Model
 4     {
 5         get;
 6         private set;
 7     }
 8
 9     public CustomerViewModel(Customer model)
10     {
11         Model = model;
12     }
13 }
```

However, we need additional UI-specific properties. For instance, we want a property named DirtyVisibility to be set to Visibility.Visible when modified information must be saved to the server. Based on this property, we can modify the look and feel of the data template, and also find out which items must be saved to the server when such an operation is initiated by the user.

There are two steps needed to implement the DirtyVisibility property: First, we need a property that raises the PropertyChanged event, as shown in Listing 7.8. This event is raised by a method stored in a class named ViewModelBase of which all the view-models derive, and that we will reuse in other MVVM applications. The implementation of the ViewModelBase is shown later in this chapter, in the “Implementing a ViewModelBase Class” section.

LISTING 7.8 The DirtyVisibility Property

```
public const string DirtyVisibilityPropertyName
    = "DirtyVisibility";

private Visibility _dirty = Visibility.Collapsed;

public Visibility DirtyVisibility
{
    get
```

```
    {
        return _dirty;
    }

    set
    {
        if (_dirty == value)
        {
            return;
        }

        _dirty = value;
        RaisePropertyChanged(DirtyVisibilityPropertyName);
    }
}
```

The second step is to set the `DirtyVisibility` property to `Visibility.Visible` when a property changes in the `Customer` model. Because we know that this class raises the `PropertyChanged` event when a property is modified (either in code or through a binding), we can subscribe for this event. Whenever the event is raised, we can set `DirtyVisibility` as shown in Listing 7.9. This listing replaces lines 9 to 12 in Listing 7.7.

LISTING 7.9 Subscribing to the `PropertyChanged` Event

```
public CustomerViewModel(Customer model)
{
    Model = model;
    Model.PropertyChanged += (s, e) =>
    {
        DirtyVisibility = Visibility.Visible;
    };
}
```

Note that we use a *lambda expression* in Listing 7.9 to set the event handler. This is a shortcut allowing us to define an anonymous method. The parentheses contain the parameters of the method. Because the compiler knows what signature is expected, it is not necessary to set the parameters' types. The first parameter of the event handler is the sender `s`, and the second is the `PropertyChangedEventArgs` `e`. Then the arrow => indicates that what is following is the body of the method.

Lambda expressions seems a bit confusing when you first encounter them, but they are very convenient and, once you get used to them, very natural to write. You'll learn more about lambdas in Chapter 22, "Advanced Development Techniques."

7

Calling the Service in the `MainViewModel`

With the `CustomerViewModel` ready to be used, we can now implement the `MainViewModel` and call the service to get data, as shown in Listing 7.10.

LISTING 7.10 The `MainViewModel` Implementation

```
1  public class MainViewModel : ViewModelBase
2  {
3      private ICustomerServiceProxy _service;
4
5      public ObservableCollection<CustomerViewModel> Customers
6      {
7          get;
8          private set;
9      }
10
11     public const string ErrorMessagePropertyName
12         = "ErrorMessage";
13
14     private string _errorMessage = string.Empty;
15
16     public string ErrorMessage
17     {
18         get
19         {
20             return _errorMessage;
21         }
22
23         set
24         {
25             if (_errorMessage == value)
26             {
27                 return;
28             }
29
30             _errorMessage = value;
31             RaisePropertyChanged(ErrorMessagePropertyName);
32         }
33     }
34
35     public MainViewModel(ICustomerServiceProxy service)
36     {
37         Customers
38             = new ObservableCollection<CustomerViewModel>();
39         _service = service;
40         _service.GetCustomers(HandleResult);
```

```
41        }
42
43        private void HandleResult(
44            IEnumerable<Customer> result, Exception ex)
45        {
46            // See Listing 7.11
47        }
48    }
```

- On lines 5 to 9, we use an `ObservableCollection` to store the `CustomerViewModel` instances. This convenient collection class raises an event called `CollectionChanged` when its content is modified (either items added, removed, or the sorting order changed). When it is used as the source of a binding for a data control (for instance, the `ItemsSource` property of a `ListBox` control), the control's content will be automatically updated whenever something happens in the collection.
- Note that the `Customers` property does not raise the `PropertyChanged` event: It is created in the `MainViewModel` constructor, and then never changes. Only its content changes, which causes `CollectionChanged` to be raised.
- Lines 11 to 33 define a `string` property for error messages. This property raises the `PropertyChanged` event, so we can bind a `TextBlock` to it to show possible errors when getting or saving the data.
- The constructor (in lines 35 to 41) accepts an instance of `ICustomerServiceProxy` as parameter. Where this instance comes from is not relevant for the view-model. It might be a mock service used for tests, a design-time service used to provide data visualization in Blend, or a "real-life" service.
- On line 37, after creating the collection for the items and storing the service for later, we retrieve the data. Note the use of the `GetCustomers` method specified by the `ICustomerServiceProxy` interface (see Listing 7.6).
- The `GetCustomers` method accepts a callback method as parameter. This callback will be called asynchronously by the service when the data is ready. The method `HandleResult` is defined on lines 43 to 47 and accepts a list of `Customer` items (defined as an `IEnumerable`) and an `Exception` (which might or might not be `null`). This again corresponds to the contract that was shown in Listing 7.6

The `HandleResult` method's implementation is shown in Listing 7.11.

LISTING 7.11 Handling the Result

```
1  private void HandleResult(
2      IEnumerable<Customer> result, Exception ex)
3  {
4      Customers.Clear();
5
6      if (ex != null)
```

```
 7         {
 8             ErrorMessage = ex.Message;
 9             return;
10         }
11
12         if (result == null)
13         {
14             return;
15         }
16
17         foreach (var customer in result)
18         {
19             var vm = new CustomerViewModel(customer);
20             Customers.Add(vm);
21         }
22     }
```

- On line 4, we clear the `Customers` collection. Because this property does not raise the `PropertyChanged` event, we must be careful to clear the collection instead of creating a new one. If we were to create a new one, the bindings would not be notified, and the data would not be updated in the user interface!
- On lines 6 to 10, we check whether the `Exception` parameter is `null`. If that is not the case, we set the `ErrorMessage` property and stop handling the data.
- On lines 12 to 15 we make sure that the `result` parameter is not `null`. This would cause an error on line 17.
- Finally, on lines 17 to 21, we loop through the items. Because we know that the result is an `IEnumerable`, we do not need to worry about the concrete type that this collection is. We just know that we can enumerate the items. In case the underlying implementation of the service changes, the view-model code would not be affected.
- Note how we create a new `CustomerViewModel` on line 19, wrapping the `Customer` instance through the constructor.

Binding to Results

Our view-models are now ready to be used in the view. As you saw before, there are multiple ways to create an instance of the `MainViewModel` and to assign it to the `MainPage`'s `DataContext`. In this sample implementation, we choose to set the `DataContext` in the code behind (in MainPage.xaml.cs), as shown in Listing 7.12.

LISTING 7.12 Setting the `DataContext`

```
1  public partial class MainPage : UserControl
2  {
3      public MainPage()
```

```
4       {
5           InitializeComponent();
6
7           var service = new CustomerLocalService();
8           var vm = new MainViewModel(service);
9           DataContext = vm;
10      }
11  }
```

- Setting the `DataContext` must be done *after* the call to `InitializeComponent`. This method is defined in a file (called MainPage.g.cs) generated by Visual Studio. All the elements defined in XAML (including the `DataContext` property) will be available only after `InitializeComponent` has completed.
- Line 7 is where we create the concrete instance of the service. Because `CustomerServiceProxy` implements the `ICustomerServiceProxy` interface, we can use this instance to create the `MainViewModel` on line 8. Again, the `MainViewModel` does not need to know where the instance comes from. All it knows is that the `GetCustomers` and `SaveCustomer` methods are available.
- Finally, on line 9, we assign the newly created view-model to the page's `DataContext`.

> **TIP**
>
> **Generating Code from XAML**
>
> When a XAML file has the `x:Class` attribute, Visual Studio generates a code file for it. For the MainPage.xaml, this file is called MainPage.g.cs and is regenerated every time that the XAML is modified. In this file, the properties corresponding to named controls are defined, as well as the operations needed to parse the XAML code and create the corresponding objects. All the g.cs files can be found in your project folder under obj\Debug. Do not attempt to modify any of the generated files, because your changes will be overwritten immediately anyway.

From now on, the view is wired to the view-model, and we can set our bindings, as shown in Listing 7.13.

LISTING 7.13 Setting the Bindings

```
1  <UserControl x:Class="SampleMvvm.MainPage"
2       xmlns="http://schemas.microsoft.com/winfx/2006/xaml/presentation"
3       xmlns:x="http://schemas.microsoft.com/winfx/2006/xaml">
4      <UserControl.Resources>
5          <DataTemplate x:Key="CustomerTemplate">
6              <StackPanel Orientation="Horizontal">
7                  <TextBlock Text="*"
8                   FontWeight="Bold" Foreground="Red"
9                   Visibility="{Binding DirtyVisibility}"/>
```

```
10                  <TextBlock Text="{Binding Model.FirstName}" />
11                  <TextBlock Text=" " />
12                  <TextBlock Text="{Binding Model.LastName}" />
13              </StackPanel>
14          </DataTemplate>
15      </UserControl.Resources>
16
17      <Grid x:Name="LayoutRoot">
18          <Grid.ColumnDefinitions>
19              <ColumnDefinition Width="0.5*" />
20              <ColumnDefinition Width="0.5*" />
21          </Grid.ColumnDefinitions>
22          <Grid.RowDefinitions>
23              <RowDefinition Height="*" />
24              <RowDefinition Height="40" />
25          </Grid.RowDefinitions>
26
27          <ListBox x:Name="CustomersListBox"
28                   ItemsSource="{Binding Customers}"
29                   ItemTemplate="{StaticResource CustomerTemplate}" />
30
31          <StackPanel Grid.Column="1"
32           DataContext="{Binding ElementName=CustomersListBox,
33                                 Path=SelectedItem}">
34              <TextBox Text="{Binding Model.LastName, Mode=TwoWay}" />
35          </StackPanel>
36
37          <TextBlock Text="{Binding ErrorMessage}"
38           FontWeight="Bold" Foreground="Red"
39           Grid.Row="1" />
40      </Grid>
41  </UserControl>
```

- On lines 5 to 14, a `DataTemplate` is defined in the page's resources. It will be used to render the `CustomerViewModel` instances in the `ListBox` on line 29. Remember that Silverlight sets the `DataContext` of each rendered `DataTemplate` to the corresponding instance of a `CustomerViewModel`. Do not get confused: Everything that happens in the `DataTemplate` (between lines 5 and 14) is related to `CustomerViewModel`, and not to `MainViewModel`!

- On lines 7 to 9, we set a `TextBlock` displaying a red star. Its `Visibility` property is bound to the `DirtyVisibility` property on the `CustomerViewModel`.

- Note how in the template, on lines 10 and 12, the first and third `TextBlock`'s `Text` properties are bound on properties on the `Customer` class, through the `CustomerViewModel`'s `Model` property. As mentioned earlier, the `Customer` class raises `PropertyChanged` when its properties are updated, so the bindings will work.

- On lines 27 to 29, we set a `ListBox` in the first cell of the `Grid`. The `ItemsSource` is set through a binding to the `Customers` property on the `MainViewModel`. As seen in Listing 7.10, this property is an `ObservableCollection` of `CustomerViewModel` instances.
- On line 29, we assign the `DataTemplate` that we saw in the resources to the `ItemTemplate` property of the `ListBox`.
- On lines 31 to 35, we place a `StackPanel` in the `Grid`'s second cell. Notice how the `DataContext` of this panel is set to the `SelectedItem` of the `ListBox` on lines 32 and 33. When the user selects a different customer, the `StackPanel`'s data context changes and all the controls within the panel are updated with the new information.
- On line 34, we place a `TextBox`. Keep in mind that `SelectedItem` in the `ListBox` is a `CustomerViewModel`. We can now bind the `Text` property of the `TextBox` to the `Model.LastName` with a `TwoWay` binding: When the user edits the value in the `TextBox`, the customer will automatically be updated in the collection.
- Finally, we create a `TextBlock` on lines 37 to 39 to display a possible error message if there is one. The `ErrorMessage` property in the `MainViewModel` class was set in Listing 7.11, line 8.

Probably the most important fact to keep in mind when creating such a XAML user interface is what the data context is in the current section of the markup. Switching from `CustomerViewModel` to `MainViewModel` and back to `CustomerViewModel` can be confusing. However, the Visual Studio designer and Expression Blend assist you in this task when you use the data binding editors that were discussed in Chapter 6.

Testing the Application

The test application can be downloaded from http://galasoft.ch/SL4U/Code/Chapter07. Follow the instructions on that page to install and run the WCF service to which the Silverlight application will connect. The user interface is very crude, but the application demonstrates the interaction between view, view-model, and model. Follow these steps to test the sample:

1. With the application running, wait a moment until the data appears in the `ListBox`, as shown in Figure 7.7. Note that the customer information is obtained from a WCF service running locally. Loading the data can take a few seconds.
2. Select a customer in the list. Through the `SelectedItem` binding, the customer's last name will be displayed in the `TextBox` on the right side.
3. Edit the customer's last name and then press the Tab key to exit from the `TextBox`. Unlike in WPF, Silverlight bindings on a `TextBox` are updated only when the `TextBox` loses the focus.
4. Notice how the name is also updated in the `ListBox`, through the data bindings. Also, a red star indicates that the customer should be saved to the server.

Laurent Bugnion
Alise Bugnion
Laeticia Bugnion
Kathy Kam
*Dr WPF-Silverlight
Josh Smith
Walt Ritscher
Sacha Barber
Mike Brown
Tamir Khason

WPF-Silverlight

FIGURE 7.7 Sample MVVM application.

Bridging the Separation

Strictly speaking, the architecture that was exposed in the two previous sections is already an implementation of the Model-View-ViewModel pattern. However, a few additional components are needed to complete the picture.

Implementing a `ViewModelBase` Class

The `ViewModelBase` class stores code that is shared between all the view-model implementations. The most important method is the one raising the `PropertyChanged` event. If needed, additional shared methods and properties can be implemented in this base class, too. Creating a `ViewModelBase` class is often the first step in creating a MVVM framework!

A possible implementation for the `ViewModelBase` class is proposed in Listing 7.14.

LISTING 7.14 The ViewModelBase Class

```
1  public abstract class ViewModelBase : INotifyPropertyChanged
2  {
3      public event PropertyChangedEventHandler PropertyChanged;
4
5      protected virtual void RaisePropertyChanged(
6          string propertyName)
7      {
8          VerifyPropertyName(propertyName);
9
10         var handler = PropertyChanged;
11
12         if (handler != null)
13         {
14             handler(this,
15                 new PropertyChangedEventArgs(propertyName));
16         }
17     }
```

```
18
19        [Conditional("DEBUG")]
20        [DebuggerStepThrough]
21        public void VerifyPropertyName(string propertyName)
22        {
23            var myType = this.GetType();
24            if (myType.GetProperty(propertyName) == null)
25            {
26                throw new ArgumentException(
27                    "Property not found",
28                    propertyName);
29            }
30        }
31    }
```

Line 1 defines the class as being `abstract` and implementing `INotifyPropertyChanged`. The class can be derived from, but not instantiated directly. Line 3 defines the `PropertyChanged` event required by the `INotifyPropertyChanged` interface. Lines 5 to 17 implement a method named `RaisePropertyChanged` that each view-model deriving from this class can use to raise the `PropertyChanged` event, and actualize data bindings set on the corresponding property.

Because the `PropertyChangedEventArgs` class carries the property's name as a string, it is possible that errors happen (for example, typos in the property's name or copy/paste errors). To prevent these errors, the property's name is verified on line 8. Note, however, that the `VerifyPropertyName` method is executed only when the application runs in Debug configuration, as you will see in just a moment.

On line 12, we check whether the `PropertyChanged` event handler is `null`. This might be the case if no binding was set for this object and no other instance registered for the event. To avoid a crash, we need to check this before raising the event on lines 14 and 15.

Lines 19 to 30 define the `VerifyPropertyName` method, which is protecting the application from errors in the property's name. This method carries the `Conditional` attribute and is executed only when the application runs in Debug configuration. This can be changed in Visual Studio by using the Configuration Manager available in Visual Studio's toolbar, as shown in Figure 7.8. The `VerifyPropertyName` method throws an exception on lines 26 to 28 in case the property does not exist on the calling view-model. This gives the developer a clear sign that something is wrong, instead of having the binding fail silently as you saw in Chapter 6.

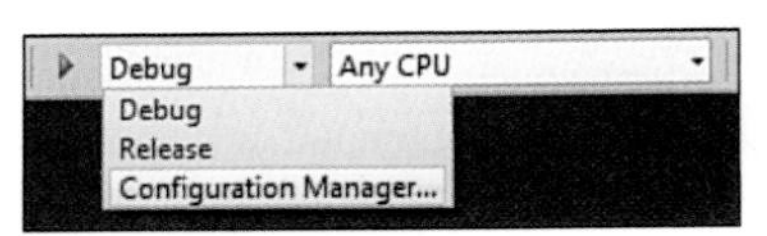

FIGURE 7.8 Configuration Manager in Visual Studio toolbar.

> **WARNING**
>
> **Debug or Release?**
>
> The Debug configuration is carrying additional information for the debugger. Normally, this configuration is used during the development, but not for the final deployment of the application. Applications built in Debug configuration are usually a little larger and slower than the same application in Release configuration.
>
> After you change the configuration to Release using the combo box shown in Figure 7.8, you will find a new XAP file in your project folder, under bin\Release. Note that Expression Blend always builds the application in Debug configuration.

Using Commands

Controls classically use events to execute a method when they are actuated. However, you learned in Chapter 4, "Investigating Existing Controls" (in the "Adding `Command` and `CommandParameter`" section) how having the event handler in the code behind causes issues, especially when the view is defined in a resource dictionary (as is often the case for data templates).

Having event handlers in the code behind also conflicts with one of the goals of the MVVM pattern, which is to reduce the amount of code that cannot easily be tested. Code behind is difficult to test automatically because it is very strongly tied to the user interface.

> **TIP**
>
> **Code Behind or No Code Behind?**
>
> Sometimes when the MVVM pattern is discussed, people say that the goal should be to have no code behind at all, and all the code should be in view-models. However, such a goal is very difficult to reach, and having a certain amount of code behind is okay, as long as it is related to the user interface. For example, starting or stopping animations, or displaying message boxes to the user, is not the responsibility of the view-model. Although reducing the amount of code behind is a respectable goal, software development often implies compromises if you want to ship your application in a reasonable time.
>
> In Chapter 11, you will see how it is possible to use objects called behaviors to reduce further the amount of code behind.

To execute methods on the view-model without resorting to event handlers, Silverlight proposes the `ICommand` interface and, as covered in Chapter 4, the `Command` and `CommandParameter` properties. This interface is very useful in the MVVM pattern because the `Command` property can be bound to a property of type `ICommand` on the view-model, as in Listing 4.7.

Note that `Command` and `CommandParameter` are available only on controls deriving from `ButtonBase` (`Button`, `ToggleButton`, `CheckBox`, and so on) and on the `Hyperlink` control. For all other controls and events, the core Silverlight does not have a corresponding property, but you will see in Chapter 11, "Mastering Expression Blend," how to use a Blend behavior to bridge that gap.

Relaying a Command

In Listing 4.6, a sample implementation of the ICommand interface is proposed. As shown in that listing, implementing such an interface requires quite a lot of code, and is not convenient.

To solve this issue, many MVVM frameworks offer a way to *relay a command* to a method: When the command is actuated, the method is executed directly in the view-model. The command is only there to serve as a gateway, as shown in Listing 7.16. In the sample MVVM application, the code for the RelayCommand class is included; however, in most cases it will rather be included in an external DLL.

To add a RelayCommand to the application, follow these steps:

1. In MainViewModel.cs, add the SaveCommand property as shown in Listing 7.15.

LISTING 7.15 Declaring the RelayCommand

```
public RelayCommand SaveCommand
{
    get;
    private set;
}
```

2. In the MainViewModel constructor, create the RelayCommand as shown in Listing 7.16. This replaces lines 35 to 41 in Listing 7.10.

LISTING 7.16 Creating the RelayCommand

```
1  public MainViewModel(ICustomerLocalService service)
2  {
3      Customers = new ObservableCollection<CustomerViewModel>();
4      _service = service;
5      _service.GetCustomers(HandleResult);
6
7      SaveCommand = new RelayCommand(SaveCustomers);
8  }
9
10 private void SaveCustomers()
11 {
12     var collection = new List<Customer>();
13
14     foreach (var customer in Customers)
15     {
```

```
16              if (customer.DirtyVisibility == Visibility.Visible)
17              {
18                  collection.Add(customer.Model);
19              }
20          }
21
22          if (collection.Count > 0)
23          {
24              _service.SaveCustomers(collection, AfterSave);
25          }
26  }
27
28  private void AfterSave(bool success)
29  {
30      if (success)
31      {
32          foreach (var customer in Customers)
33          {
34              customer.DirtyVisibility = Visibility.Collapsed;
35          }
36      }
37  }
```

- On line 7, the `RelayCommand` is created. The argument is a method, which is defined further on lines 10 to 26.
- In the method `SaveCustomers`, we start by checking among all `CustomerViewModel` instances which ones are dirty and must be saved. We store these dirty instances in a list.
- On line 22, we check whether any instance was found dirty. If that is the case, we call the `SaveCustomers` method on the service on line 24.
- The first parameter of the method is the list of `CustomerViewModel` instances. The method requires an `IEnumerable`, which the `List` collection implements.
- The second parameter is a callback method, which is defined by the interface as having one single parameter of type `bool` (see Listing 7.6).
- The callback method is defined on lines 28 to 37. If the operation was successful, the `DirtyVisibility` property is reset to `Collapsed` on each `CustomerViewModel` instances.

3. In MainPage.xaml, add the code in Listing 7.17 below the `TextBlock` showing the error message (see Listing 7.13; the code should be added between lines 39 and 40).

LISTING 7.17 Using the RelayCommand

```
<Button Content="Save customers"
  Command="{Binding SaveCommand}"
  Margin="10" Grid.Column="1" Grid.Row="1" />
```

Testing the Command

You can now run the application again, modify a customer's name, and then press the Save customers button. The method is invoked on the `MainViewModel` without any addition in the code behind. The resulting code is cleaner than if we had used an event handler. Also, when the view-model is tested in a unit test, the `SaveCustomers` method can be invoked and the results verified (for example, by using a mock service, as mentioned earlier in this chapter).

Enhancing the Application

This small sample is not perfect by far. There are several issues that should be improved: The user interface should display a message or an animation when an asynchronous operation is executed. This can be done by setting additional properties on the `MainViewModel` and observing these properties to start animations in the `MainPage`. Also, the user interface should be disabled while the application is saving the customers to the server. The user should not be able to make additional changes while an operation is in progress. Alternatively, a system of queues could be developed to allow parallel operations. Finally, the design of the application is very crude at this stage and should definitely be improved.

This is of course just the beginning of the MVVM journey, but this sample should give you a better understanding of this important pattern in Silverlight.

> **TIP**
>
> **Using Lambda Expressions**
>
> Much of the code presented in this chapter could be expressed as *lambda expressions*. The lambda syntax is a bit confusing at first, but simplifies the code greatly by allowing *anonymous methods* to be used as callbacks. To develop cleaner code, it is a good recommendation to study the lambda expression syntax, starting with http://www.galasoft.ch/sl4-lambda.

Sending Messages

With very loosely coupled components, it can be a challenge to send data from one view-model to another, for instance, or from the view-model to its view. Sometimes, it is necessary to handle special cases, as shown in the following two examples:

- A view-model might need some information from the user. However, displaying a dialog is really something that should be handled by the view because it is a user interface issue, something that a designer wants to optimize. In such a scenario, using a messaging system between the view-model and view is beneficial.

- In a complex application, the list of customers and the selected customer's details may be in different views. Binding to the `ListBox`'s `SelectedItem` as we did in Listing 7.13 is not possible in such a scenario. In that case, sending the selected item as a message from one view-model to the other is a good alternative.

These are only two examples where a messaging system comes in very handy. Although not directly related to the MVVM pattern, such a system is useful when developing loosely coupled applications. In Chapter 20, "Building Extensible and Maintainable Applications," you will learn about such a messaging system and study samples.

Using an MVVM Framework

When working with MVVM a lot, it can be interesting to use a framework to avoid repetitive tasks (whether you implement the framework yourself based on the recommendations and samples in this chapter or choose an existing framework developed by members of the Silverlight community). Chapter 20 covers frameworks that can help you develop faster in Silverlight.

What Could Be Better?

The MVVM pattern is very interesting because it helps separate the view from the data and increases the modularity of the components. This makes the application more testable and maintainable because each component is very loosely coupled to the others. The pattern also helps designers to style and template the user interface in Expression Blend, as you will see in Chapter 11.

However, not everything is perfect in this pattern. The major annoyance is the fact that so much code is needed to implement bindable properties. In Listing 7.10, for instance, we need about 20 lines of (formatted) code to declare a bindable property (in addition to the `ViewModelBase` class). Some third-party frameworks propose *code snippets* that make the task of writing such properties easier, but the code is still there and needs to be maintained.

In later versions of Silverlight, it is possible that raising properties will be much easier (for example, by placing an `[Observable]` attribute on each bindable property). Another alternative is explained at http://www.galasoft.ch/sl4-weaving, but it is very advanced and difficult to realize without a deep understanding of how a .NET application is compiled.

Summary

This chapter exposed where the Model-View-ViewModel pattern comes from, how it originates from other separation patterns such as the Model-View-Controller pattern, the Passive View pattern, and the Presentation Model pattern. We talked about the theory behind this pattern, what view-models are used for, and how the are rendered by views (`UserControl`, `DataTemplate`, and so on). This chapter explained the importance of the `DataContext` in this pattern and how it can be set and inherited by the children controls.

These concepts were illustrated by a sample application. Even though it is not all that complex, this sample is a good start to build a real-life data application, with a connection to a WCF service, building and handling view-models, and creating the beginning of a master-detail view in XAML.

The following chapter covers a series of data controls useful when an application has to deal with data (which is the case most of the time).

CHAPTER 8

Using Data Controls

IN THIS CHAPTER, WE WILL:

- Dive deeper into PagedCollectionView (which we first saw in Chapter 6, "Working with Data: Binding, Grouping, Sorting, and Fsiltering").
- Page through data with the DataPager control.
- Study data validation with IDataErrorInfo and with data annotations.
- Use the DataGrid control to present data in a rich manner.
- Use the DataForm control to build a master-detail view.

Silverlight 4 has come a long way since the days when it was used mostly to display videos and animate pictures to enrich a web page. It can still do that, and does it well, but with Silverlight 3 and especially Silverlight 4, the framework is now able to deal with data, lots of it, and to facilitate the creation of data applications (often referred to as line-of-business, LOB, applications).

Several parts of the Silverlight framework are built specifically to deal with data:

- Simple data controls such as the `ComboBox`, `ListBox`, or `ItemsControl`, making it easy to display lists of object. Thanks to dynamic collections (such as the `ObservableCollection` class) and views that can be applied on top of this data (such as the `CollectionViewSource` that we discussed in Chapter 6, and the `PagedCollectionView` that we will study in this chapter), it is easy to shape data and display it to the user.
- More complex controls (such as the `DataPager`, `DataGrid`, `DataForm`, and so on), allowing complex interaction with the data. We talk about these controls in this chapter.
- An improved validation framework (as discussed in Chapter 6) with which data controls can interact to inform the user when input is not valid.

- A strong communication layer allowing access to simple services (such as Relational State Transfer, REST, services) and to complex server-side applications based on Windows Communication Foundation (WCF). In Chapter 9, "Connecting to the Web," we talk about the communication stack and various ways to communicate with web servers and services.
- In addition, external frameworks facilitate the development of business applications. Chapters 13, "Creating Line of Business Applications," and Chapter 14, "Enhancing Line of Business Applications and Running Out of the Browser," cover the new WCF RIA Services, which enable the building of LOB applications fast with advanced support from Visual Studio.

Filtering and Paging with the `PagedCollectionView`

In Chapter 6, we talked about the `ICollectionView` interface, which defines events, methods, and properties enabling the following interactions with data. This interface (and the classes implementing it) enables grouping according to a property. Data controls that support this functionality (such as the `DataGrid`) can display the data in collapsed or expanded mode to allow the user to find data faster. It also enables sorting according to a property. The sorting can be modified in code during runtime, as shown in Chapter 6. Another feature is filtering according to criteria. In contrast to grouping and sorting, which can be done in XAML and in code, filtering can be done only in code. You will see a sample in this chapter. Finally, it is also possible to page through data according to a page size and page index. This allows you to display only parts of the data to the user, to make the user interface more responsive (because fewer objects need to be created on the screen).

To understand the `PagedCollectionView` better, we will build a sample application. The application in the initial state can be downloaded from http://www.galasoft.ch/SL4U/code/chapter08.

Preparing the Sample

The sample application is organized like the one in Chapter 6, with a server-side application named Customers offering services such as getting a list of customers and saving a list of customers back to the database; in this case, we do not use a real database, but a simple XML file. Follow the indications at http://www.galasoft.ch/SL4U/code/chapter08 to install and start the WCF service.

The application is organized according to the MVVM pattern that we studied in Chapter 7, "Understanding the Model-View-ViewModel Pattern." It interacts with the following objects:

- The `CustomerServiceProxy` (in the `Model` namespace), a high-level object that handles all the calls to the WCF service.

- The Customer object (nested inside the CustomerViewModel class) generated by Visual Studio as a proxy for the WCF data object; this class cannot be modified. The application uses its properties FirstName (string), LastName (string), and PictureUri (Uri).
- The MainViewModel class exposing an ObservableCollection of CustomerViewModel instances, and bound to the main view's DataContext in MainPage.xaml.cs.

In this sample, the data is shown in a DataGrid. Open the DataApplicationSample solution in Visual Studio and then follow these steps:

1. Open the file MainPage.xaml in the Visual Studio designer.
2. Open the Toolbox by selecting View, Toolbox from the menu.
3. Drag a DataGrid from the Toolbox to the design surface.

   The DataGrid is located in an assembly (System.Windows.Controls.Data.dll) that is not included in the Silverlight application by default. However, the Visual Studio designer added the corresponding reference automatically, as you can see if you expand the References folder in the Solution Explorer. It also added a new xmlns statement in MainPage.xaml, mapping the prefix data to the CLR namespace System.Windows.Controls in the assembly System.Windows.Controls.Data.

   The DataGrid needs to be customized to display the properties of the Customer object. When bound to the collection named Customers in the MainViewModel class (which we will do in just a moment), each row of the grid shows a CustomerViewModel instance. In this sample, the user interface should display the Customer's FirstName, LastName, and a picture. The first two properties are strings, so they are easy to display. The last one, however, is a URI pointing to the picture file on the server. To display the picture, an Image control is used.
4. Open MainPage.xaml in the XAML editor.
5. Modify the DataGrid according to Listing 8.1.

8

LISTING 8.1 Setting the DataGrid's Columns

```
1  <data:DataGrid Height="Auto"
2    HorizontalAlignment="Stretch"
3    Margin="10" Width="Auto"
4    Name="CustomersDataGrid"
5    VerticalAlignment="Stretch"
6    ItemsSource="{Binding}"
7    AutoGenerateColumns="False">
8
9      <data:DataGrid.Columns>
10         <data:DataGridTextColumn Header="Last name"
11           Binding="{Binding Model.LastName}" />
```

```
12            <data:DataGridTextColumn Header="First name"
13              Binding="{Binding Model.FirstName}" />
14            <data:DataGridTemplateColumn Header="Picture">
15                <data:DataGridTemplateColumn.CellTemplate>
16                    <DataTemplate>
17                        <Image Source="{Binding Model.PictureUri}"
18                          Height="100" />
19                    </DataTemplate>
20                </data:DataGridTemplateColumn.CellTemplate>
21            </data:DataGridTemplateColumn>
22        </data:DataGrid.Columns>
23
24    </data:DataGrid>
```

In listing 8.1, lines 1 to 7 set the `DataGrid`'s properties. Note on line 7 the `AutoGenerateColumns` property set to `False`. It means that the `DataGrid` control will not attempt to inspect the items and create columns automatically. Lines 9 to 22 define the `DataGrid`'s `Columns` collection.

Then, on lines 10 and 11, a `DataGridTextColumn` is added. The `Header` set to `"Last name"` will be displayed on top of the column. The content of the cell is bound to the `LastName` property of the `Model`. Because the implicit `DataContext` of the row is a `CustomerViewModel`, this all falls into place. On lines 12 and 13, the same is done for the `Customer's FirstName` property.

On lines 14 to 21, a more complex column is defined: The `DataGridTemplateColumn` allows creating a `DataTemplate` and displaying exactly what is needed. In our case, the `DataTemplate` uses an `Image` control with its `Source` property set to `Model.PictureUri`.

Before the application can be tested, the `DataGrid`'s `ItemsSource` must be set. One option would be to use the `Customers` collection directly. However, this class is limited and we want to configure the data for filtering and paging. This is why a `PagedCollectionView` is placed on top of the data.

Building the `PagedCollectionView`

The `PagedCollectionView` is located in yet another assembly. We need to add the reference to this assembly manually with the following steps:

1. In the Solution Explorer, right-click the DataApplicationSample project and select Add Reference from the context menu.

2. In the Add Reference dialog, choose the tab labeled Browse and navigate to C:\Program Files\Microsoft SDKs\Silverlight\v4.0\Libraries\Client. This path is where all the Silverlight assemblies are located. On Win64 machines, the folder is in Program Files (x86).

3. Select the assembly named System.Windows.Data.dll and click OK. This adds a reference to that assembly. Note that the assembly will also be added to your XAP file. This increases the size of the file that needs to be downloaded to the web browser, but at the same time it gives you access to the `PagedCollectionView` and its features.

4. In contrast to the `CollectionViewSource`, the `PagedCollectionView` class cannot be defined in XAML directly because it does not have a default constructor. To create it, open the file MainPage.xaml.cs in Visual Studio.

5. Modify the `MainPage` constructor as shown in Listing 8.2.

LISTING 8.2 Building a `PagedCollectionView`

```
public MainPage()
{
    InitializeComponent();

    var service = new CustomerServiceProxy();
    var vm = new MainViewModel(service);
    DataContext = vm;

    var pcv = new PagedCollectionView(vm.Customers);
    CustomersDataGrid.ItemsSource = pcv;
}
```

6. Make sure that the project DataApplicationSample.Web is set as startup project in the Solution Explorer. Its name should appear in bold. If this is not the case, the pictures won't be displayed because of a permission issue. We talked about this in *Silverlight 2 Unleashed*, Chapter 5, Table 5.3. To set the web application as startup, right-click the DataApplicationSample.Web project and select Set as StartUp Project from the context menu.

7. Run the application by pressing Ctrl+F5. After a small delay, the `DataGrid` shows a list of customers in three columns: First name, Last name, and a picture, as shown in Figure 8.1.

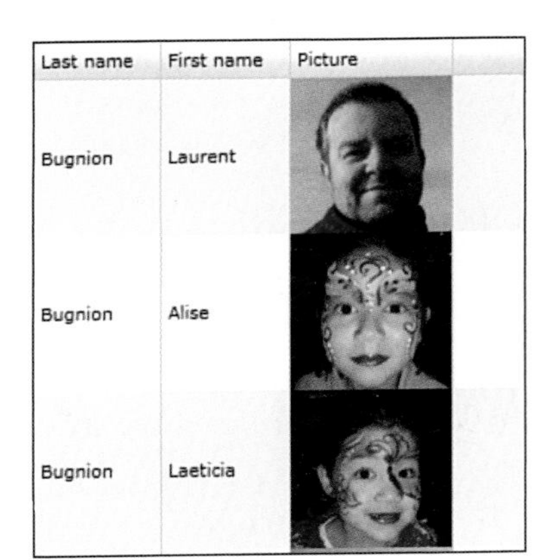

FIGURE 8.1 *`DataGrid`* with list of customers.

Filtering Data

In this section, the data should be filtered before display. After running the application we built in the previous section, some rows appear without a picture because the corresponding property is empty in the database. In this section, we are building a filter that removes customers without a picture with the following steps:

1. Open MainPage.xaml in the Visual Studio designer.
2. With the `Grid (LayoutRoot)` selected, pass the mouse on the side of the grid until the cursor turns into a cross, as shown in Figure 8.2.
3. At about 40 pixels from the bottom, click to set a new row in the grid.

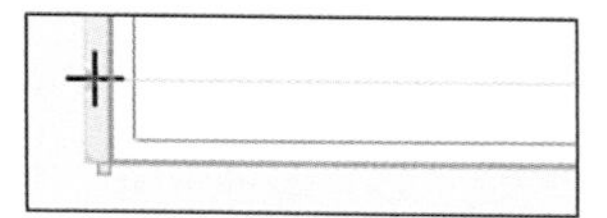

FIGURE 8.2 Setting a new row.

4. The grid's new row appears in the designer with its height in pixels indicated on the side. Pass again the mouse near the edge of the row until some icons appear, as shown in Figure 8.3. The first icon on top indicates a fixed height. Even when the window is resized, the row's height will not change. This is what you should click now. The second icon indicates a star height. It means that the row will take the rest of the height after all other rows have been calculated. If you have two or more rows with a star size, you can set for instance 0.4* and 0.6* and the rows will be sized proportionally. As for the last icon on the bottom, it indicates an Auto size. The height of the row depends on what the row contains. If the row is empty, its height will be set to zero.

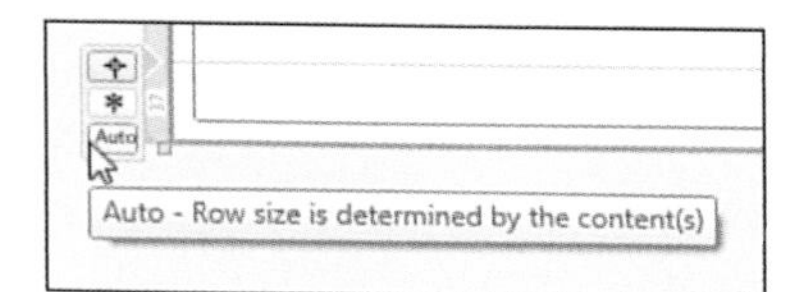

FIGURE 8.3 Setting the row's height.

5. Set the row to a fixed height of 40 pixels. If needed you can also change the value in XAML.
6. Select the `DataGrid` and change its `Grid.RowSpan` property to 1 in the Properties editor. This property has been set to 2 automatically when the new row was added. We need to free some space for the new UI elements.
7. Drag a check box from the Toolbox on the grid's new row. Set its properties so that it is aligned vertically in the center of the row.
8. Set the `Content` of the check box to `"With pictures only"`.
9. On top of the Properties editor, click the Events tab. Locate the `Click` event; double-click in the field next to the event's name. This adds a new event handler to the code behind and opens the file MainPage.xaml.cs.
10. Change the event handler's code to reflect Listing 8.3.

LISTING 8.3 Setting and Resetting the Filter

```
1  private void checkBox1_Click(
2      object sender,
3      System.Windows.RoutedEventArgs e)
4  {
5      var checkbox = sender as CheckBox;
6      var pcv = CustomersDataGrid.ItemsSource
7          as PagedCollectionView;
8
9      if (checkbox != null
10         && pcv != null)
11     {
12         if (checkbox.IsChecked == true)
13         {
14             pcv.Filter = c =>
15             {
16                 var customer = c as CustomerViewModel;
17
18                 return customer != null
19                    && customer.Model != null
20                    && customer.Model.PictureUri != null;
21             };
22         }
23         else
24         {
25             pcv.Filter = null;
26         }
27     }
28 }
```


- On line 5 we get the sender of the event and cast it to a CheckBox.
- On lines 6 and 7, we get the ItemsSource property of the DataGrid. It has been set to the PagedCollectionView into the MainPage constructor before. We can cast this property to a PagedCollectionView again.
- After making sure that the objects are not null and are casted correctly, we query the state of the Check box on line 12.
- If the check box is checked, we set the Filter property of the PagedCollectionView. The syntax used here is a *lambda expression*. You already saw a lambda in Chapter 7, Listing 7.9. The syntax here is a little bit different: We have only one parameter c (of type object), so we can omit the parenthesis around the parameter list.

- The filter block is defined after the arrow =>. The parameter c is casted to a CustomerViewModel on line 16. Then we check whether the parameter is null, if its Model property is null, and finally whether the PictureUri property is null. We only return true if all three conditions are false.
- Finally, if the check box is not checked, we reset the filter to null on line 25. This will automatically display all the rows in the grid again.

The framework executes the filter method when needed to decide which rows must be included in the result. The nice thing is that everything here is dynamic: Through the ObservableCollection, the PagedCollectionView and the data binding to the DataGrid, every change to the collection or to the filter will immediately be reflected in the user interface.

To test the filter, run the application, and then check/uncheck the check box. The rows without a picture disappear when the check box is unchecked.

Paging Through Data

As its name implies, the PagedCollectionView is also able to page through data. Paging is a great way to break the data into smaller chunks. This has the advantage of making the user interface more responsive (because less data has to be loaded before the user starts using the current page), and also making it easier for the user to find the row that he wants to handle.

Paging is done by setting the property PageSize. The PagedCollectionView will automatically deliver a set of data corresponding to this property. Moving through data is done with the methods MoveToFirstPage, MoveToLastPage, MoveToNextPage, MoveToPreviousPage, and MoveToPage. The events PageChanging and PageChanged are raised before and after the current page has changed, respectively, and the property IsPageChanging is set to true while the next page is calculated. This allows a control to display a small animation, for example. The PageIndex property indicates which page is currently displayed.

To test paging with the DataGrid, follow these steps:

1. Reopen the DataApplicationSample solution that we used earlier in this chapter.
2. In MainPage.xaml.cs, in the MainPage constructor, change the way that the PagedCollectionView is created according to Listing 8.4.
3. Run the application. After the initial loading time, only two rows are displayed, according to the page size.

LISTING 8.4 Setting the Page Size

```
var pcv = new PagedCollectionView(vm.Customers);
pcv.PageSize = 2;
CustomersDataGrid.ItemsSource = pcv;
```

Note the following:

- Even though only two rows are displayed, the initial loading time is the same as when all the rows were shown. The paging occurs on the client after all the data has been loaded from the server.
- There is currently no way to move to the next page. Additional user interface elements are needed to move through the pages. This could be done by adding a few buttons and text boxes, but there is also a convenient control that you will see a little later in this chapter: the `DataPager` control.

Optimizing Data Handling

The `PagedCollectionView` is very useful with complex data controls, but it also comes with a caveat: When you work with really large sets of data, it can be more efficient to implement paging on the server than on the client. Client-side paging implies that most of the data will be loaded initially before the user interface is shown to the user. This initial loading time can be very important and cause the application to take a long time to appear. Also, having the whole data on the client requires a lot of memory, which can be a problem on some limited platforms.

On the other hand, of course, having the whole data on the client makes the application more responsive after it has been loaded (because there are fewer client-server interactions).

Chapters 13 and 14 examine a way to build applications that get from the server only the amount of data needed, already sorted. As usual in software development, the right technology to choose depends on what your scenario is.

TIP

Using Endless Scrolling

Some data grids such as the one developed by XCeed offer endless scrolling: Once the user reaches the bottom of the loaded set of data, the grid automatically fetches more data and adds them to the display. This prevents the need to click on a "previous page" or "next page" button. This also speeds up the action because only the amount of data that is needed is kept in memory (data virtualization). Such a grid can be seen in action at http://demo.xceed.com/DataGrid_Silverlight/Demo/.

Implementing Custom Sorting

The `Customer` class returned by the WCF service has a `Gender` property. The value is taken from an enumeration with five possible values: `Male`, `Female`, `Boy`, `Girl`, and `Unknown`. It would be nice to be able to sort according to the gender (for example, `Female` and `Girl` first, then `Male` and `Boy`, and finally `Unknown`).

Unfortunately, custom sorting requires quite some manual work. You can find a good description about how to build a collection allowing custom sorting can be found at http://www.galasoft.ch/sl4-sorting.

Adding a `DataPager` Control

In the preceding section, you saw how to prepare a `PagedCollectionView` for paging, but did you also notice that something was missing? The `DataGrid` alone cannot page through the data. Additional UI elements are needed to display the data according to the user's needs.

One possibility is to create a custom user interface and to use the paging-related methods, properties, and events in the `PagedCollectionView` class. However, an easier way exists, with the `DataPager` control (available in the same assembly as the `DataGrid`: System.Windows.Controls.Data.dll), shown in Figure 8.4. This control can be added to our application with the following steps:

1. Open the SortingAndFitering application in VisualStudio.
2. Open the file MainPage.xaml in the XAML editor.
3. Modify the `RowDefinitions` of the `Grid` as shown in Listing 8.5.

LISTING 8.5 Creating a New Row

```
<Grid.RowDefinitions>
    <RowDefinition Height="*" />
    <RowDefinition Height="40" />
    <RowDefinition Height="40" />
</Grid.RowDefinitions>
```

4. After the `CheckBox` at the end of the `Grid`, add a `DataPager` control as shown in Listing 8.6.

LISTING 8.6 Adding a `DataPager` Control

```
<data:DataPager Source="{Binding ElementName=CustomersDataGrid,
                                 Path=ItemsSource}"
                Grid.Row="2"
                VerticalAlignment="Center"
                Margin="10,0,10,0" />
```

As shown in Listing 8.6, adding the `DataPager` is really very easy. The only property that is really needed is the `Source` property that must be set to the same `IEnumerable` as the `DataGrid`'s `ItemsSource` property. Once this is done, run the application. You should see the `DataPager` at the bottom of the page. Because we set the `PageSize` to 2 in Listing 8.4, only two rows of data are displayed.

To navigate to a different page, the buttons can be used (from left to right): Go to the first page, go to the previous page, go to any page according to an index, go to the next page, and go to the last page.

Customizing the Display

The default display can be customized using some properties and styles. The `DisplayMode` property can be set to various values, as shown in Figure 8.4 (copied from the Silverlight documentation).

When used with numeric buttons, additional properties can be used to customize the look and feel of the control:

- `NumericButtonCount` is used to set how many numeric buttons are shown in the control.
- `NumericButtonStyle` can be set to a `Style` and allows modifying the appearance of the numeric buttons without having to change the style and template of the whole `DataPager` control. The numeric buttons are `ToggleButton` controls, so the corresponding type must be used for the style (and the template if so desired).

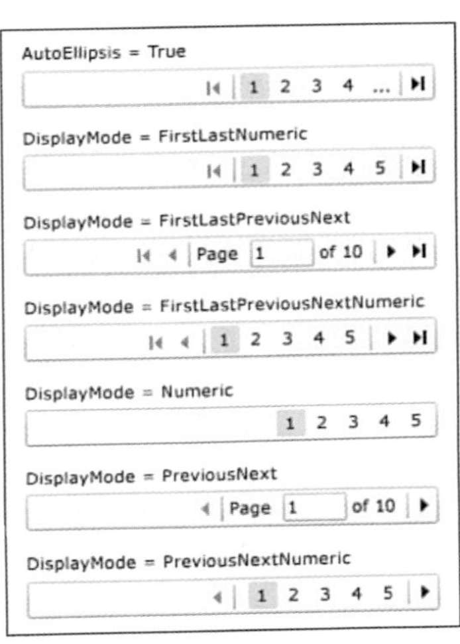

FIGURE 8.4 `DisplayMode` values (from the Silverlight documentation).

Finally, like for any control in Silverlight, the whole appearance of the `DataPager` control can be modified using its `Style` property and possibly a control template. In Chapter 10, "Creating Resources, Styles, and Templates," we will go through the process of retemplating controls.

Validating Data Input

Any data entered by a user should be validated. In the case of client/server applications, it is critical that a safe validation be executed on the server because client-side validation can always be hacked or worked around. However, this doesn't mean that client-side validation is bad, on the contrary. By validating input in the client application, the amount of invalid data that will fail validation on the server is greatly reduced. This puts less strain on the server-side application because this bad data never reaches it (and this can be very significant if you have one server and multiple Silverlight clients!). Also, less bandwidth between the client and the server will be wasted. Finally, validating on the client is faster than on the server, and creates a better user experience.

Using Interface-Based Validation

In Chapter 6, we talked about the two new interfaces added to Silverlight 4, `IDataErrorInfo` and `INotifyDataErrorInfo`, and showed how to use interface-based validation in an object used as the source of a data binding. We also showed how a simple `TextBox` control reacts when data entered is found to be invalid.

In the case of our sample application DataApplicationSample, the source of the data binding is a generated proxy object, the `Customer` class. As mentioned earlier, this generated class cannot be modified because changes will be lost when it is regenerated by Visual Studio. Because each `Customer` instance is wrapped into a corresponding `CustomerViewModel`, it is possible to create a gateway property with information about the validation. To demonstrate this, we will add a validation rule stating that the `LastName` property should not be empty and should start with a capital letter:

1. Open the DataApplicationSample application in Visual Studio.
2. Open the file CustomerViewModel.cs in the code editor.
3. Change the class declaration to make it an `IDataErrorInfo`, as shown in Listing 8.7. This interface requires a `using` statement to be added to the code file, pointing to `System.ComponentModel`.

LISTING 8.7 Declaring `IDataErrorInfo`

```
public class CustomerViewModel : ViewModelBase, IDataErrorInfo
```

4. Declare a new property in the `CustomerViewModel` class named `LastName`. This property is a gateway to the `LastName` property in the nested `Customer` model, as shown in Listing 8.8.

LISTING 8.8 Making a Gateway to `Model.Lastname`

```
public string LastNamePropertyName = "LastName";

public string LastName
{
    get { return Model.LastName; }
    set
    {
        if (Model.LastName == value)
        {
            return;
        }

        Model.LastName = value;
    }
}
```

5. Because the `LastName` property implemented in Listing 8.8 is just a gateway, we need to observe what happens in the proxy object and react when the `Model.LastName` is modified. This can be done in the method handling the model's `PropertyChanged` event. Modify the `CustomerViewModel` constructor as shown in Listing 8.9.

LISTING 8.9 Subscribing to Changes for the Model's `LastName` Property

```
 1  public CustomerViewModel(Customer model)
 2  {
 3      Model = model;
 4      model.PropertyChanged += (s, e) =>
 5      {
 6          DirtyVisibility = Visibility.Visible;
 7
 8          if (e.PropertyName == LastNamePropertyName)
 9          {
10              RaisePropertyChanged(LastNamePropertyName);
11              return;
12          }
13      };
14  }
```

6. Lines 8 to 12 are new: If the model raises the `PropertyChanged` event for its `LastName` property, the `CustomerViewModel` raises its own `PropertyChanged` event. This is needed because to switch the validation on, the data binding will be redirected to the view-model and not directly to the model like before.

7. In the body of the class, implement the `IDataErrorInfo` interface as shown in Listing 8.10.

LISTING 8.10 Implementing `IDataErrorInfo`

```
 1  public string Error
 2  {
 3      get { return null; }
 4  }
 5
 6  public string this[string columnName]
 7  {
 8      get
 9      {
10          if (columnName == LastNamePropertyName)
11          {
12              if (string.IsNullOrEmpty(LastName))
13              {
14                  return "The Last Name cannot be empty";
```

8

```
15                  }
16
17                  var firstChar = LastName[0];
18
19                  if (firstChar < 'A'
20                      || firstChar > 'Z')
21                  {
22                      return "The first character of the first name must be a capital
➥letter";
23                  }
24              }
25
26              return null;
27          }
28  }
```

- Lines 1 to 4 declare the `Error` property required by the `IDataErrorInfo` interface. However this property is not useful in property-based validation. (It is used only when the whole object is being validated in scenarios not related to data binding). Here the property simply returns `null`.
- Lines 6 to 28 are also required by the `IDataErrorInfo` interface. Depending on the property's name, the getter can return an error string if the property is not valid or `null` if everything is okay.
- In this case, the first test (on lines 12 to 15) checks whether the `LastName` property is empty, which is not valid.
- Then on lines 17 to 23, we make sure that the first character of this property occurs between `'A'` and `'Z'`. If this is not the case, an error string is also returned.

8. Finally, open MainPage.xaml in the XAML editor, and modify the `DataGrid`'s column with the `LastName` property, as shown in Listing 8.11.

LISTING 8.11 Validation in the Data Binding

```
<data:DataGridTextColumn Header="Last name"
    Binding="{Binding LastName,
        NotifyOnValidationError=True,
        ValidatesOnDataErrors=True}" />
```

The application can now be tested by pressing Ctrl+F5. Edit the first customer's last name and change it to violate the validation rules, and then press Tab to validate. As shown in Figure 8.5, the `DataGrid` should now display the validation summary with the error message that we defined in Listing 8.10.

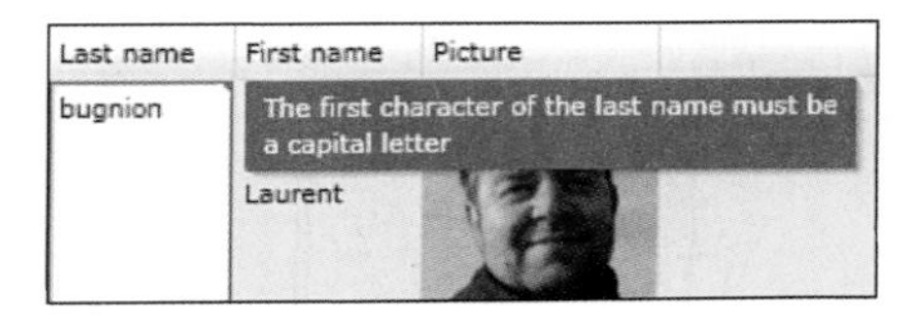

FIGURE 8.5 Validation summary in the *DataGrid*.

Validating with Data Annotations

Chapter 6 showed how data bindings react when the `ValidatesOnException` property is set to `True` and an exception is thrown in the property setter. We also mentioned that having to raise the exception in the property setter is not very convenient because each property mixes concerns with the addition of code responsible for the validation.

One way to minimize the validation code is to rely on validation attributes rather than code. In this scenario, each property that must be validated gets a set of attributes (from the `System.ComponentModel.DataAnnotations` namespace) defining the validation rules.

The interesting point with data annotations is that it is a fairly well-known validation mechanism in .NET. For example, data annotations can be used in ASP.NET MVC as shown in http://www.galasoft.ch/sl4-mvcannotations. Our sample can be modified to use validation attributes for the `LastName` property as follows:

1. Open the solution DataApplicationSample in Visual Studio.
2. Right-click the Silverlight project DataApplicationSample in the Solution Explorer, and select Add Reference from the context menu.
3. In the Add Reference dialog, select the Browse tab and navigate to C:\Program Files\Microsoft SDKs\Silverlight\v4.0\Libraries\Client.
4. Select the assembly System.ComponentModel.DataAnnotations.dll and click OK.
5. Open the file CustomerViewModel.cs.
6. Remove the `IDataErrorInfo` interface from the class declaration.
7. Remove the `Error` property and the operator `this[string columnName]`. Simply delete the lines shown in Listing 8.10.
8. Add a method to validate an arbitrary property. This method (shown in Listing 8.12) uses the `Validator` class to verify whether a property's value complies with the attributes that are defining the rules. You need to add a `using` statement for the namespace `System.ComponentModel.DataAnnotations` for this to work. Note that because the `Validate` method will be used in many properties and multiple objects, it would make sense to define it in a base class. The `ValidateProperty` method on the `Validator` object takes the value and an instance of the `ValidationContext` class. We use this class in a fairly simplified manner, with the two last parameters on the constructor set to `null`. The `ValidateProperty` method is used in multiple frameworks and multiple scenarios, which explains why it is more complex than what we really need here.

LISTING 8.12 Validating an Arbitrary Property

```
private void Validate(object value, string propertyName)
{
    Validator.ValidateProperty(value,
        new ValidationContext(this, null, null)
        {
            MemberName = propertyName
        });
}
```

9. Modify the `LastName` property as shown in Listing 8.13.

LISTING 8.13 Defining Attributes and Validating

```
 1  [Required(
 2      ErrorMessage="The last name must be entered")]
 3  [RegularExpression(
 4      "^[A-Z]+[a-zA-Z]*$",
 5      ErrorMessage="Only letters allowed, must start with a capital")]
 6  public string LastName
 7  {
 8      get { return Model.LastName; }
 9      set
10      {
11          if (Model.LastName == value)
12          {
13              return;
14          }
15
16          Validate(value, LastNamePropertyName);
17          Model.LastName = value;
18      }
19  }
```

Lines 1 and 2 of Listing 8.13 add the `Required` attribute to the property. For the validator, it means that `null` values and empty strings will be rejected. Note that you can customize the attribute to accept empty strings but reject `null` values for example. Lines 3 to 5 add another attribute: `RegularExpression`. This attribute is very versatile for string-based properties, and allows defining a validation rule based on a *regular expression*. In our sample, the regular expression `"^[A-Z]+[a-zA-Z]*$"` is a rather barbarian way to say "the string value must start with a capital letter, and must contain only letters."

Finally, the `Validate` method is called on line 16, before the value is saved into the proxy. Should the value not comply with the attributes, the `Validator` object will throw an exception and the validation fails before the value is even set.

TIP

Using Regular Expressions

Regular expressions are a very compact way to express a rule, but they are also using a syntax that is difficult to memorize. Thankfully, most of the time this is not needed: There are literally thousands of examples of regular expressions on the Web. For example, the one in Listing 8.13, line 4, is taken from http://www.galasoft.ch/sl4-regex.

Attributes in .NET can be customized with *named parameters*. For example, in Listing 8.13, line 2, we pass a parameter named `ErrorMessage` to the `Required` attribute. There are other named parameters for this attribute, but all named parameters are optional, so if they are not defined, the default value is used. All display and error messages are localizable.

There is one last step needed before testing the application: The data binding in MainPage.xaml must be modified with the `ValidatesOnExceptions` property, as shown in Listing 8.14.

LISTING 8.14 Modifying the Binding

```
<data:DataGridTextColumn Header="Last name"
    Binding="{Binding LastName,
        NotifyOnValidationError=True,
        ValidatesOnExceptions=True}" />
```

At this point, running the application and entering an invalid value in the Last Name column produces a result similar to Figure 8.5. The data is validated, and the application is protected.

Validating Before or After the Data Is Set

An interesting difference exists between interface-based validation and exception-based validation: The exception is thrown *before* the data is saved in the proxy object. On the other hand, if the application relies on `IDataErrorInfo` or `INotifyDataErrorInfo` for client-side validation, the data is already saved in the proxy object when the error is raised. Saving to the server must be explicitly disabled by the application so long as the state is not valid.

Validating on the Client and on the Server

One annoying side effect of client-side validation is that the server-side rules must often be repeated on the client. For example, a rule stating that the `LastName` property may not be empty can be set on the client, and should be checked on the server, too. This creates unnecessary work because the set of rules must be maintained in two different projects. If a rule changes, you must make sure that the change is made on the server and on the client, which increases the risk of errors.

The WCF RIA Services framework that we will examine in Chapters 13 and 14 proposes a solution: The validation attributes are defined on the server only, and are generated on the client. Even though this involves some code generation in Visual Studio (which can be cumbersome), having only one set of validation attributes to manage is an advantage.

Reviewing the DataGrid

We talked about the DataGrid control in *Silverlight 2 Unleashed*. The properties and methods described in this chapter are still active in Silverlight 4, and in fact the DataGrid control didn't change much, apart from optimizations in performance. We also saw in the sample earlier in this chapter how to add a DataGridTextColumn (to display a string) and a DataGridTemplateColumn (to display a custom column with any UI elements desired). For more information about the DataGrid and how to modify its appearance, refer to Chapter 18 of *Silverlight 2 Unleashed*. Another good place to find information about properties, styles, and templates to modify the DataGrid's appearance is http://www.galasoft.ch/sl4-datagrid.

Using the DataGrid with Automatic Columns

So far, we have used the DataGrid with the AutoGenerateColumns property set to False, and we added columns in XAML manually. This is probably the most frequent usage of the DataGrid for larger applications, where custom columns need to be defined in XAML. However, for smaller applications, it is possible to customize the DataGrid's columns directly in the data object. To illustrate this, get the sample named SimpleDataGrid available at http://www.galasoft.ch/SL4U/code/chapter08. Then, follow these steps:

1. Open the file MainPage.xaml and add the XAML markup in Listing 8.15 into the main Grid.

LISTING 8.15 Adding a DataGrid

```
<data:DataGrid ItemsSource="{Binding ElementName=MainRoot,
                                     Path=Items}"
               x:Name="MyDataGrid"
               AutoGenerateColumns="True"
               Margin="10" />
```

- The ItemsSource property is bound to the MainRoot through an ElementName binding. This name has been set on the main UserControl. This is a convenient way to data bind a property of the UI to a property defined in the code behind.
- Notice how the AutoGenerateColumns property is set to True.
- Open the file MainPage.xaml.cs and notice the Items property of type ObservableCollection<DataItem>. Also, note how the DataItem instances are created in the constructor and added to the collection.

- Open the file DataItem.cs located in the Data folder. This data object class has three bindable properties (in the sense that they raise the `PropertyChanged` event): `Name` (`string`), `ContractNumber` (`int`), `IsDirty` (`bool`).

2. Run the application. You should see the scene shown in Figure 8.6. Each of the three properties is automatically assigned to a column, and the property's name is used as the column header.

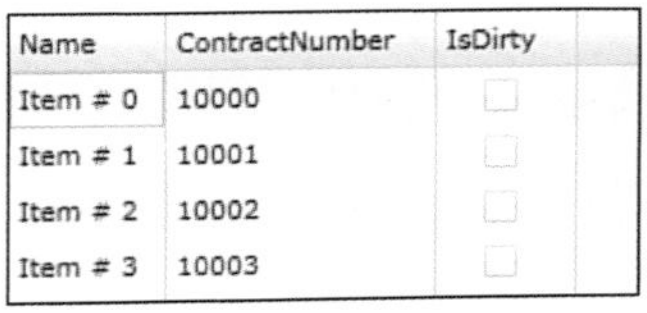

Name	ContractNumber	IsDirty
Item # 0	10000	☐
Item # 1	10001	☐
Item # 2	10002	☐
Item # 3	10003	☐

FIGURE 8.6 Autogenerated columns.

Multiple details should be changed, though: The ContractNumber column should actually be named Contract Number, with a space. Of course, spaces cannot be used in property names, so we need a special value for display. The contract number must be set between 10000 and 99999. Also, the IsDirty column should not be displayed. It is a utility property only. In addition, it would be great if the headers could be localizable.

Customizing with Attributes

All these requirements can be fulfilled with attributes similar to the ones we used earlier in this chapter in the "Validating with Data Annotations" section. Note that adding these attributes does not require changing the code itself; only metadata is added to the properties with the following steps:

1. In DataItem.cs, add the attributes shown in Listing 8.16 to the `ContractNumber` property.

LISTING 8.16 Customizing the `ContractNumber` Property

```
[Display(Name = "Contract Number")]
[Range(10000, 99999)]
public int ContractNumber
```

- The first attribute's `Name` parameter will be used as the column's header.
- The second attribute requires the input to fall between 10000 and 99999.

2. Add the attribute shown in Listing 8.17 to the `IsDirty` property.

LISTING 8.17 Customizing the `IsDirty` Property

```
[Display(AutoGenerateField = false)]
public bool IsDirty
```

8

3. Run the application and notice how the column header for the `ContractNumber` property changed. Also, the column for `IsDirty` is not displayed anymore. This is the result of the `AutoGenerateField` parameter set to false in Listing 8.17.

4. Try to enter an invalid number in the column for `ContractNumber` (either lower than 10000 or higher than 99999). An error message will display.

Localizing the Attributes

One nice feature offered with the attributes in data annotations is that they are easy to localize. Of course, localizing the attributes only makes sense if you are localizing the whole application! This process is explained in Chapter 22, "Advanced Development Techniques." The SimpleDataGrid application has been prepared with resource files that contain application texts in English and in French. These files can be found in the Properties folder. In Chapter 22, you will learn more about the resource files, how to create and use them.

It is now possible to modify the attributes to use the embedded resources rather than plain strings. We will also see how to modify the culture of the application to display localized texts with the following steps:

1. Open the file LocalizableTexts.resx in the Properties folder. This file has two values: `ContractNumberColumn` and `ContractNumberRangeError`.

2. Open the file LocalizableTexts.fr-FR.resx. The same values can be found, but this time translated in French.

3. Open DataItem.cs.

4. Modify the attributes as shown in Listing 8.18.

LISTING 8.18 Using Localized Values

```
1  [Display(
2      Name = "ContractNumberColumn",
3      ResourceType = typeof(Properties.LocalizableTexts))]
4  [Range(10000, 99999,
5      ErrorMessageResourceName = "ContractNumberRangeError",
6      ErrorMessageResourceType = typeof(Properties.LocalizableTexts))]
7  public int ContractNumber
```

- On line 2, instead of using a plain string as in Listing 8.16, we now use the `ContractNumberColumn` name from the resources. It is a little confusing that the same parameter (`Name`) is used as a plain string sometimes and other times as a resource name.

- The parameter ResourceType is also set, pointing the application to the class in which the resource can be found. This class is autogenerated when changes are done to the .resx file. You'll learn more about this in Chapter 22.
- The Range attribute can also be localized: Set the ErrorMessageResourceName and ErrorMessageResourceType parameters.
- The ErrorMessageResourceName is set to "The value for {0} must be between {1} and {2}" in the file LocalizableTexts.resx. The texts {0}, {1}, and {2} are placeholders that will be automatically replaced by, respectively, the header of the column, the lower-range value, and the upper-range value.

5. Run the application and enter an invalid value in the Contract Number column. The error message is shown in Figure 8.7.

Name	Contract Number
Item # 0	10000
Item # 1	3
Item # 2	10002

The value for Contract Number must be between 10000 and 99999

FIGURE 8.7 Error message in English.

6. Open the file App.xaml.cs.
7. Modify the Application_Startup event handler as shown in Listing 8.19. This sets the application to use the French (France) culture rather than the default English (United States).

LISTING 8.19 Setting the Application in French

```
private void Application_Startup(object sender, StartupEventArgs e)
{
    Thread.CurrentThread.CurrentCulture = new CultureInfo("fr-FR");
    Thread.CurrentThread.CurrentUICulture = new CultureInfo("fr-FR");

    this.RootVisual = new MainPage();
}
```


8. Run the application again and enter an invalid value in the column reading "Numéro de contrat". The error message and the column's header are now localized in French, as shown in Figure 8.8.

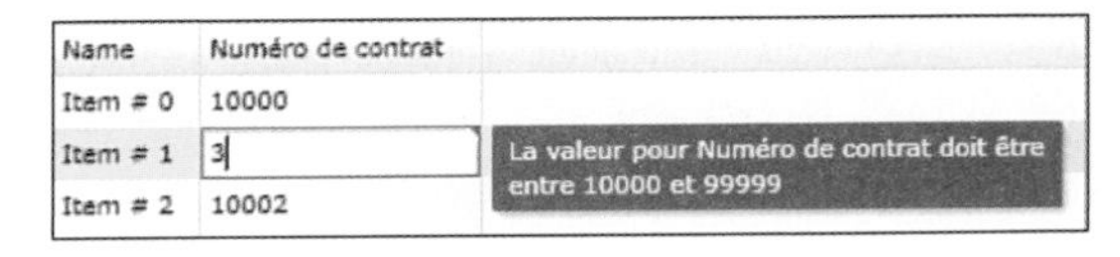

FIGURE 8.8 Error message in French.

Advantages and Disadvantages of Data Annotations

While very handy in certain cases, data annotations also have a few annoying side effects:

Advantages
Each data object is an enclosed entity and carries the information needed for its validation and its display. This can be very valuable when working on distributed applications with loosely coupled components like a client/server application.
The display attributes are easily localized.

Disadvantages
Attributes are sometimes criticized because even though they are metadata and not directly a part of the classes, methods, or properties that they decorate, they still require a recompilation of the application when they are modified.
Mixing user interface information with the data object is not complying with the separation of concerns that we mentioned a few times before.

Choosing Between `DataGrid` and `ListBox`

The `DataGrid` control is very powerful but does not offer a lot of creative freedom. Even after all the properties and styles are set, the data is still presented in columns and rows. For many purposes, using a `ListBox` instead with customized data templates can help present the data in more innovative ways and give to the graphics designers the freedom to invent a better user experience. If features such as sorting, grouping, moving, and resizing columns are not needed by the user requirements, looking at a `ListBox` first can be a good move.

Editing Data in the `DataForm`

Working with data annotations as you saw in the previous section can also be done with other controls than the `DataGrid`. The `DataForm` control (currently part of the Silverlight toolkit) provides a way to easily generate a data entry form based on data objects and their annotations. As before with the `DataGrid` and its `AutoGenerateColumns` property set to `True`, there are pros and cons to autogenerating a data entry form based on the data object. On one hand, it provides a very quick way to create data applications such as a master-detail view; on the other hand, however, autogenerated fields are hard to customize.

Note also that the `DataForm` is in the toolkit, in the Preview band. As you saw in Chapter 4, this band corresponds to an alpha stage of development, and the control may change in a further release.

In this section, you will see how to set up a `DataForm` and use it to display a `DataGrid`'s `SelectedItem` with the following steps:

1. Open in Visual Studio the SimpleDataGrid application that we created earlier in this chapter.

2. Right-click the References folder in the Solution Explorer and select Add Reference from the context menu.

3. Click the Browser tab, and navigate to the toolkit binaries' location: C:\Program Files\Microsoft SDKs\Silverlight\v4.0\Toolkit\[DATE] (where [DATE] is the toolkit's date, for example, Apr10). On Win64 machines, the folder is in Program Files (x86).

4. Select the assembly System.Windows.Controls.Data.DataForm.Toolkit.dll and click OK.

5. Open the file MainPage.xaml in the XAML editor.

6. Split the main grid in two columns by adding the column definitions shown in Listing 8.20.

LISTING 8.20 Splitting the `Grid` in Two Columns

```
<Grid.ColumnDefinitions>
    <ColumnDefinition />
    <ColumnDefinition />
</Grid.ColumnDefinitions>
```

7. Add an `xmlns` statement to the `UserControl` tag, as shown in Listing 8.21. This is mapping the `DataForm`'s namespace to the `form` prefix.

LISTING 8.21 Adding an `xmlns` Statement

```
xmlns:toolkit=" http://schemas.microsoft.com/winfx/2006/xaml/presentation/toolkit"
```

8. Add a `DataForm` in the main `Grid`, below the `DataGrid`, as shown in Listing 8.22.

LISTING 8.22 Adding a `DataForm`

```
1  <toolkit:DataForm ItemsSource="{Binding ElementName=MainRoot,
2                                          Path=Items}"
3                   CurrentItem="{Binding ElementName=MyDataGrid,
4                                         Path=SelectedItem,
5                                         Mode=TwoWay}"
6                   Grid.Column="1" />
```

- The `DataForm`'s `ItemSource` property takes a collection of items, just like the `DataGrid`. Even though the `DataForm` displays only one item at the time, the form has a `DataPager` control allowing moving through all the items of the collection. Setting the `ItemsSource` property is optional, and the `DataForm` can be used only with the `CurrentItem` property, as you will see in the section, "Making a Simple Property Editor," later in this chapter.

- To keep the DataGrid and the DataForm synchronized, we bind the DataForm's CurrentItem property to the DataGrid's SelectedItem with the TwoWay binding.

9. Run the application by pressing Ctrl+F5. In the DataGrid, select one of the items. The result is shown in Figure 8.9.

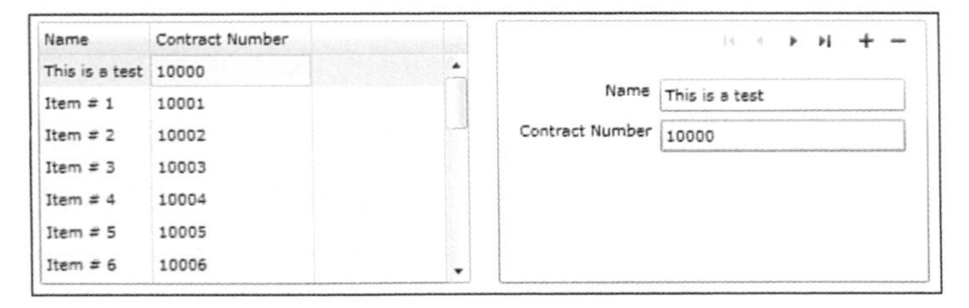

FIGURE 8.9 DataGrid and DataForm.

Notice the controls on top of the DataForm on the right. They allow paging or moving through the items. Because of the TwoWay binding we set up, moving to the next item using the DataForm's controls will also move the selection in the DataGrid.

On the far right, the + and – add or remove items from the collection. This operation is also provided automatically by the DataForm.

Adding a Description

In Figure 8.9, the labels Name and Contract Number are read from the display attributes that we created inside the DataItem class. If the culture is changed to French (as we did in Listing 8.19), the display will also be updated.

The Display attribute has another named parameter called Description. This is useful when displaying items in the DataForm, as in the following example:

1. Open the file LocalizableTexts.resx in the Properties folder.
2. Add a new line to the table: Set the Name to "DescriptionColumn" and the Value to "Set a unique value between 10000 and 99999", as shown in Figure 8.10.

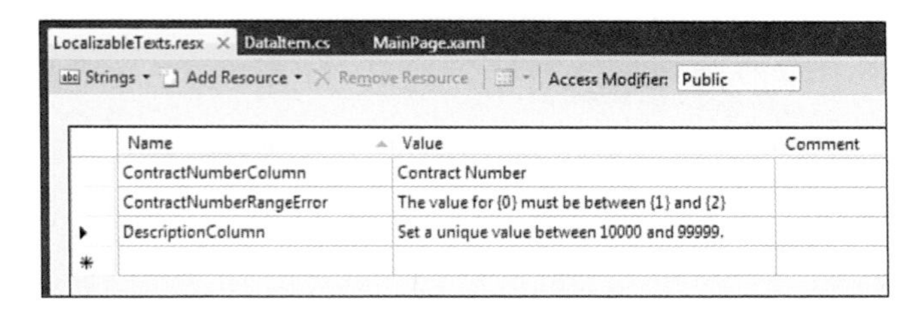

FIGURE 8.10 Adding a description to the resources.

3. Open the file DataItem.cs (in the Data folder).
4. Change the ContractNumber property's attributes as shown in Listing 8.23.

LISTING 8.23 Adding a Description

```
[Display(
    Name = "ContractNumberColumn",
    Description = "DescriptionColumn",
    ResourceType = typeof(Properties.LocalizableTexts))]
[Range(10000, 99999,
    ErrorMessageResourceName = "ContractNumberRangeError",
    ErrorMessageResourceType = typeof(Properties.LocalizableTexts))]
public int ContractNumber
```

5. Run the application again. Notice the small indicator next to the Contract Number field. Passing the mouse over it opens a ToolTip with the text we entered as `Description` for this property, as shown in Figure 8.11.

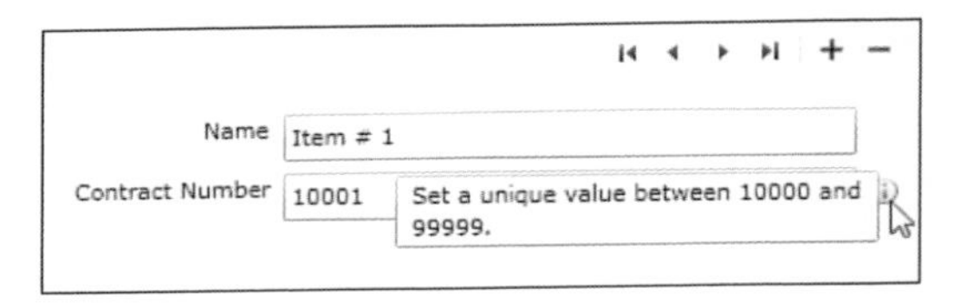

FIGURE 8.11 Showing the *Description*.

Validating the Input

The `DataForm` is also able to validate the input according to the exact same validation attributes that we already set in DataItem.cs. It is easy to test: Enter a value lower than 10000 in the Contract Number field and press the Tab key to exit the field. The `DataForm` shows the validation error, as shown in Figure 8.12.

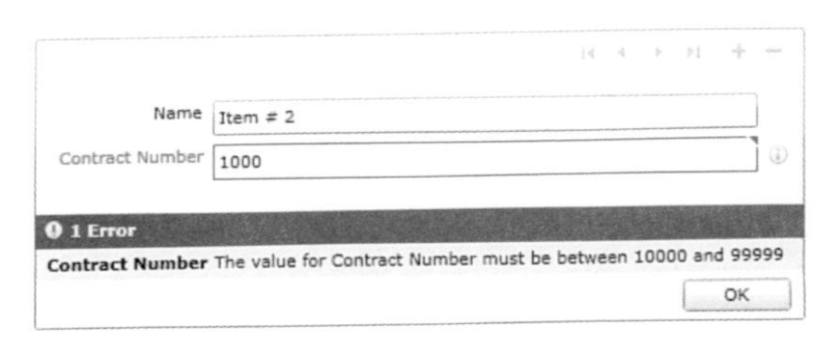

FIGURE 8.12 Showing a validation error.

Committing Changes Manually

With the application as it is implemented now, every change done by the user to a data item is immediately saved to the collection. Sometimes, however, this is dangerous: If the user clicks too fast, the change is committed and undoing it can be difficult. This can be shown by running the application, entering a different value in the selected item's Contract Number field, and then tabbing out of the text box: The value is immediately updated in the `DataGrid`, too.

A better idea, especially if the data item is complex and a lot of properties are shown, is to commit the data manually with the following steps:

1. Add the `AutoCommit` property to the `DataForm` tag, and set it to `False`. The default value for this property is `True`.

2. Run the application again and select an item.

3. Notice that a new button (OK) appears at the bottom of the `DataForm`. This button is disabled right now.

8

4. Edit the item's properties. The item does not change in the `DataGrid`. The changes are not committed yet.

5. Click the OK button. The `DataGrid` now displays the changes made in the `DataForm`.

Using a commit mechanism reduces the risk for minor errors such as typos to be saved into the model. These errors might not be caught by the validation, so committing the data gives the user a second chance to check the input.

Defining Fields Manually

If the automatic generation of fields does not fulfill the requirements, and a more complex user interface is needed, the fields can be defined manually using data templates. The `DataForm` accepts the following templates:

- `EditTemplate`: This template is used when the control is in edit mode.
- `HeaderTemplate`: Defines what is shown on top of the `DataForm`, next to the buttons allowing to page and move through the items.
- `NewItemTemplate`: Will be shown when the "new item" button is pressed. For example, you may want to allow the user to input some data when the item is created, but turn these fields read-only later.
- `ReadOnlyTemplate`: Shown when the `DataForm` is not in edit mode.

The templates can be set inline as shown in Listing 8.24 or stored in resources and referenced.

LISTING 8.24 Making an `EditTemplate`

```
<form:DataForm ItemsSource="{Binding ElementName=MainRoot,
                                     Path=Items}"
               CurrentItem="{Binding ElementName=MyDataGrid,
                                     Path=SelectedItem, Mode=TwoWay}"
               AutoGenerateFields="False"
               Grid.Column="1"
               Margin="10">
    <form:DataForm.EditTemplate>
        <DataTemplate>
            <StackPanel>
                <TextBox Text="{Binding ContractNumber}" />
            </StackPanel>
        </DataTemplate>
    </form:DataForm.EditTemplate>
</form:DataForm>
```

Making templates can be time-consuming and should not be underestimated. For example, the sample in Listing 8.24 does not display the validation summary anymore, so the user will not be informed when he enters invalid data. This work requires a certain experience, and using Expression Blend is probably a good idea to customize the experience precisely according to the user requirements.

Getting More Information

The DataGrid and the DataForm are among the most complex controls in the Silverlight framework (and the toolkit). There are many more properties, methods, and events in both controls. For more information about these members, refer to the corresponding documentation. Also, remember that all the controls in Silverlight can be styled and templated to modify their appearance and behavior. These controls allow rapid development of data applications if desired and, with more time and effort, precise customization to fulfill the requirements exactly.

Making a Simple Property Editor

As mentioned earlier, the DataForm doesn't necessarily need its ItemsSource property to be set. It is also possible to work with the CurrentItem property directly. For example, the following steps create a very simple property editor shown in Figure 8.13:

1. Create a new Silverlight application in Visual Studio.
2. Add a reference to the assembly System.Windows.Controls.Data.DataForm.Toolkit.dll, and an xmlns statement in MainPage.xaml, like we did earlier in this chapter.
3. Modify the LayoutRoot grid as shown in Listing 8.25.

LISTING 8.25 Simple Property Editor

```
<Grid x:Name="LayoutRoot"
      Background="White"
      Width="600" Height="400">
    <Grid.ColumnDefinitions>
        <ColumnDefinition />
        <ColumnDefinition />
    </Grid.ColumnDefinitions>

    <Rectangle Width="100" Height="200"
               Fill="Red" Stroke="Orange"
               StrokeThickness="4" />

    <controls:DataForm CurrentItem="{Binding ElementName=LayoutRoot,
                                             Path=Children[0]}"
                       Grid.Column="1"
                       Margin="10"/>
</Grid>
```

8

Through the data binding set on the CurrentItem property to the first child of the LayoutRoot grid (the red and orange rectangle), all its public properties are inspected and displayed in the DataForm on the right. Notice that enum values are displayed in combo boxes, and that some properties are read-only. Finally, some properties (such as the Fill) are of a complex type that cannot be edited in this simple view. However, the other simple properties can be edited at runtime, and will affect the way that the rectangle is rendered on the screen.

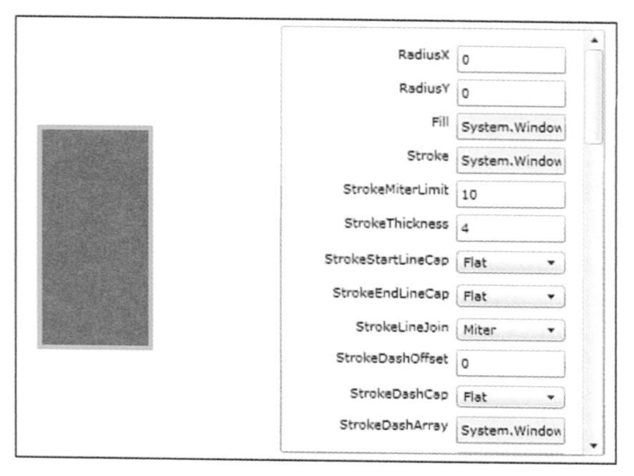

FIGURE 8.13 Simple property editor.

Summary

In this chapter, we took a closer look at the various elements that allow building data applications. We started with the PagedCollectionView, which offers additional functionality over the CollectionViewSource that we used in earlier chapters. We created a sample displaying a list of customers, and you learned how to filter them and page through them. The DataGrid and DataPager controls made this step quite easy and painless.

Later, we talked more about validation. After seeing how data bindings can be customized for validation errors in Chapter 6, you saw how the DataGrid and the DataForm controls react when such an error occurs. We also talked about data annotations, an exception-based way to validate data based on attributes set in the data object, on its properties.

We reviewed the DataGrid control and learned how to customize and localize autogenerated columns using data annotations. The next control we examined was the DataForm, and you learned how to autogenerate a detailed view of the bound item or to customize this view using templates.

All these data collections and controls are very useful to create line-of-business applications and allow rapid application development because of their ability to autogenerate columns and fields based on the data objects. This is, of course, only a more business-oriented aspect of Silverlight-based development. Depending on your scenario, Silverlight can be used to create a wide variety of applications.

The next chapter covers connectivity and web services, and you'll learn how to get data and information from the World Wide Web.

CHAPTER 9

Connecting to the Web

IN THIS CHAPTER, WE WILL:

- **Connect to cross-domain servers, talk about permissions and how to work around them.**
- **Place simple web requests (download and upload) with the `WebClient` class.**
- **Understand and handle networking errors.**
- **Send more complex requests with the `HttpWebRequest` class and talk about differences with the `WebClient` class.**
- **Discover the new networking stack and understand why it was needed.**
- **Handle XML and JSON-based responses.**
- **Set up and communicate with WCF services.**

Silverlight applications are historically tightly bound to the World Wide Web. After all, even in the case of the so-called out-of-the-browser applications that we will study in Chapter 14, "Enhancing Line of Business Applications and Running Out of the Browser," the very first contact that the user has with the application is through a web browser. Most Silverlight applications are online all the time.

When data or resources (such as videos and images) are needed by a Silverlight application, they can be included inside the XAP file and delivered together with the application. However, this can cover only a very small subset of the real-life scenarios. In most cases, the content of the application should be fetched online: Data is often dynamic (for example, in the form of RSS feeds, Twitter streams, stock exchange rates, and so on). Enclosing any of that in the XAP file would expose the application to stale information very fast. The developer cannot be expected to recompile the XAP file every time that the data changes.

Also, resources are often too big to be enclosed in the XAP. For example, videos should be left on the server and delivered to the Silverlight client via streaming (if available) or progressive download. Finally, new resources are added to the Web all the time with the explosion of social networks where people store images, videos, and files. It is simply impossible to enclose enough media to make the application interesting.

In fact, today's most common scenario for Silverlight developers is to implement some kind of client/server interaction. In this case, the application relies on the online data, and without this data, the application would barely make sense. Although these applications can, sometimes, be used offline (without connectivity), this is a special case where data is stored locally, and a synchronization mechanism is put in place.

With this in mind, this chapter covers the new developments in the domain of Silverlight connectivity since version 2 of the framework. The moment where a Silverlight application connects and retrieves data from the Internet is exciting even for experienced developers.

Getting Information from Cross-Domain Servers

One common issue that Silverlight applications encounter is the problem of *cross-domain access restrictions*. This occurs when a Silverlight application is served from a web server (for example, www.domain.com) and tries to access information on another domain (for example, www.anotherdomain.com). By default, such access is forbidden, and an exception occurs in the code trying to call the other domain.

The web server can allow access by using a cross-domain policy file. Silverlight checks for two files with a slightly different format. Note that the policy file must be placed at the root of the domain (for example, at www.anotherdomain.com/ClientAccessPolicy.xml):

- The file ClientAccessPolicy.xml is looked for first by the Silverlight application.
- Should the first file not be found, the Silverlight application tries to load another file named CrossDomain.xml.

These two files are described in *Silverlight 2 Unleashed*, Chapter 23, Listings 23.1 and 23.2. The CrossDomain.xml file is compatible with the Adobe Flash plug-in, and is available on a large number of web servers. However, its format is limited and does not allow for a very granular definition of the access policies. The ClientAccessPolicy.xml, on the other hand, was developed more recently and palliates some of the older file format's shortcomings. Because the Silverlight plug-in always looks for the newer file first, and then falls back to the older, it is possible to have both files in place if needed.

Checking Whether a Policy File Exists

Checking whether a policy file is in place on the server you attempt to access can be done before the application is implemented. For example, the following web page made by Silverlight expert Frank La Vigne can help you: http://www.galasoft.ch/sl4-crosscheck. Just enter the URL of the top domain that you try to access (for example, http://www.twitter.com). As shown in Figure 9.1, the tool informs you that there is no ClientAccessPolicy.xml in place. On the other hand, the CrossDomain.xml file exists, but the content (shown in Listing 9.1) allows access only from the Twitter.com domain. All the Twitter application programming interfaces (APIs) are restricted, and standard Silverlight or Flash clients cannot access it. You will see later in the "Working Around Cross-Domain Restrictions" section how a Silverlight application can access the restricted APIs.

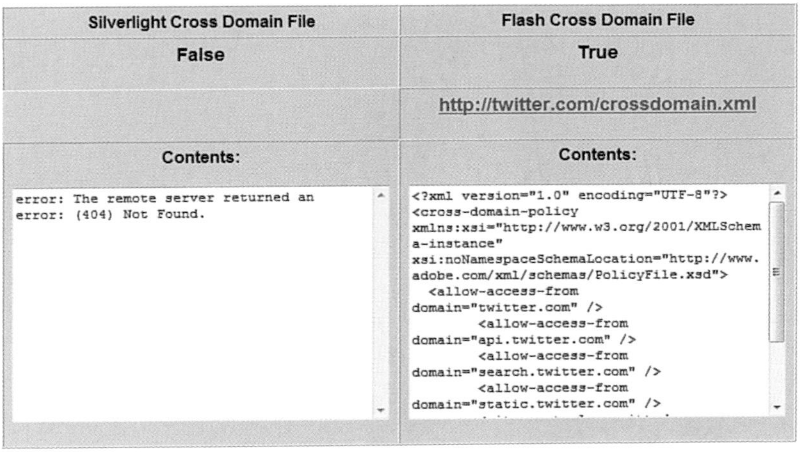

Silverlight Cross Domain File	Flash Cross Domain File
False	True
	http://twitter.com/crossdomain.xml
Contents:	Contents:
error: The remote server returned an error: (404) Not Found.	<?xml version="1.0" encoding="UTF-8"?> <cross-domain-policy xmlns:xsi="http://www.w3.org/2001/XMLSchema-instance" xsi:noNamespaceSchemaLocation="http://www.adobe.com/xml/schemas/PolicyFile.xsd"> <allow-access-from domain="twitter.com" /> <allow-access-from domain="api.twitter.com" /> <allow-access-from domain="search.twitter.com" /> <allow-access-from domain="static.twitter.com" />

FIGURE 9.1 Checking the Cross Domain Files for Twitter.com.

LISTING 9.1 The Twitter CrossDomain.xml File

```
<?xml version="1.0" encoding="UTF-8"?>
<cross-domain-policy
    xmlns:xsi="http://www.w3.org/2001/XMLSchema-instance"

xsi:noNamespaceSchemaLocation="http://www.adobe.com/xml/schemas/PolicyFile.xsd">
    <allow-access-from domain="twitter.com" />
    <allow-access-from domain="api.twitter.com" />
    <allow-access-from domain="search.twitter.com" />
    <allow-access-from domain="static.twitter.com" />
    <site-control permitted-cross-domain-policies="master-only"/>
    <allow-http-request-headers-from
        domain="*.twitter.com"
        headers="*"
        secure="true"/>
</cross-domain-policy>
```


By reading the policy file such as the one in Listing 9.1, the Silverlight developer can see what is allowed and what isn't, and decide on an alternative if needed.

Working Around Cross-Domain Restrictions

If your application needs to connect to a web server that forbids it (for example, www.twitter.com, as you saw earlier), there are two alternatives:

- Create a server application (a relay, or proxy) that will be contacted by your Silverlight application, and relay all the calls to the forbidden service. Server-side applications are not subjected to the same restrictions as the client-side Silverlight or Flash applications.

- Make your Silverlight application an out-of-the-browser application with elevated permissions. You will see in Chapter 14 what it means and how to do that.

Neither solution is perfect. The first one (the server proxy) requires quite a lot of additional code to relay the requests and the responses. Also, the server proxy needs to be hosted somewhere, which means additional costs and maintenance. One alternative is to host the server proxy on the Azure platform developed by Microsoft, which solves the issue of maintenance, but not the one of costs. You can find more information about Azure at http://www.galasoft.ch/sl4-azure.

As for the second solution, elevated applications are not subjected to the same restrictions as the standard Silverlight applications. However, depending on your scenario, an OOB application might not be possible at all.

Finally, a last possible solution is to contact the service provider and to respectfully request the addition of a cross-domain policy file. Some providers may have a good reason for denying this, but some others are open to this addition.

Placing Simple Calls

The simplest way to place calls to resources located on the web is to use the `WebClient` class. This class is optimized to be very simple to use, but also has limited abilities.

The `WebClient`'s methods are easy to use once the asynchronous pattern is understood. For each operation, there is a calling method (with the `Async` suffix) and an event handler (with the `Completed` suffix). Also available, the `CancelAsync` method will cancel the asynchronous operation that is currently pending.

> **WARNING**
>
> **Chaining Requests**
>
> The `WebClient` class does not queue requests. If an asynchronous operation is currently in progress, attempting to call another asynchronous method on the `WebClient` causes an exception. To work around this, either wait until one request is completed before placing the next, or use multiple `WebClient` instances.

Informing the User

To inform the user about progress in a download operation, the `WebClient` class's `DownloadProgressChanged` event handler can be used. This handler is called every time that part of the download completes. The `DownloadProgressChangedEventArgs` class contains three properties that can be used to create information messages: `BytesReceived` indicates how many bytes are already available on the client. `TotalBytesToReceive` indicates how many bytes in total need to be downloaded. `ProgressPercentage` is a convenient property that indicates the percentage completed. This value can be used immediately without conversion.

For upload operations, use the UploadProgressChanged event. It is called similarly to the DownloadProgressChanged event. The UploadProgressChangedEventArgs parameter passed to the event handler contains the same properties as the DownloadProgressChangedEventArgs class, with the addition of the BytesSent and TotalBytesToSend properties.

It can seem strange that the BytesReceived and the TotalBytesReceived properties are also available for an upload. However, when a server-side service receives a request, it always sends back a response, which is downloaded to the client.

Learning with a Sample

To understand the WebClient class better, a sample is available for download at http://galasoft.ch/SL4U/Code/Chapter09. The next sections make reference to the sample.

The Client-Side Project

This sample consists of two projects: The Silverlight application DownloadUpload offers a front-end page (MainPage.xaml) with a series of buttons, a textbox and an image. Each button triggers a different operation. For string download, a text file is read from the web server and displayed in a MessageBox. For binary download, an image file is read from the web server and displayed on the page. Note that a simpler alternative to this would be to set the Image control's Source property to a URL directly, and the content download would be triggered automatically. However, this does not provide fine control on the download like the OpenReadAsync method that we demonstrate here. In addition, this method can be used for any file, not just images.

For string upload, the user can enter a text in a textbox and send it to a service on the web server. A text file is created into the folder c:\temp (provided that the web server has write access to this directory of course). For binary upload, the user selects a JPG file on the client and sends it to another service on the web server. Here, too, the sent content is saved as is to a JPG file in the c:\temp folder.

The actual calls to the WebClient class are done in the DownloadUploadHelper class in the Helpers namespace. Creating a helper class for this is a good practice, and avoids mixing business logic code and UI code.

The Server-Side Project

The DownloadUpload.Web project is an ASP.NET web application. It serves the Silverlight application, and also provides content and services: MyFile.txt is used to demonstrate the string download. MyImage.jpg is used to demonstrate the binary download. UploadString.ashx is a generic handler, a service that we use to upload a string to the web server and create a text file. UploadImage.ashx is another service used to receive and save an image file from the Silverlight application.

Downloading Strings

The WebClient's DownloadStringAsync method and the DownloadStringCompleted event handler are used to place a request corresponding to a HTTP GET method on a URL and expect string content in return. This method is very convenient to get any string-based resource, such as HTML code, XML data, simple text or to trigger a service and get a text-based result (such as a string saying "OK").

In the DownloadUpload sample, the button titled Download string triggers the download. Its event handler `GetStringClick` calls the `DownloadUploadHelper` class's `GetString` method shown in Listing 9.2.

LISTING 9.2 DownloadUploadHelper.GetString Method

```
1  public static void GetString(
2      Action<string, Exception> callback)
3  {
4      var client = new WebClient();
5      client.DownloadStringCompleted += GetStringCompleted;
6      client.DownloadStringAsync(
7          new Uri(ServerPath + FileName),
8          callback);
9  }
```

- The only parameter of the `GetString` method is an `Action<string, Exception>`. This is a reference to a callback method, defined somewhere else, with two parameters (a `string` and an `Exception`). When the content is downloaded, the callback will be executed: Either everything went well and the `string` parameter is set to the text file's content (in which case the `Exception` is `null`), or there was an issue and the `Exception` parameter is set (in which case the `string` content is null). We will set these values in Listing 9.3. For the moment, we just store the callback for later use.
- Line 4 creates a new `WebClient`.
- On line 5, we assign an event handler to the `DownloadStringCompleted` event. This method is shown in Listing 9.3.
- Lines 6 to 8 are the actual call to the `DownloadStringAsync` method.
    - The first parameter is the URI of the text file to download. We construct this value from two constants defined in the `DownloadUploadHelper` class: the path to the web server, and the name of the file. In real applications, these values would probably be defined in a settings file.
    - The second parameter is the callback that the method received as parameter. We can actually pass any object to the `DownloadStringAsync` method, and this will be stored as a "user state" that can be retrieved in the `Completed` event as you will see in Listing 9.3.

The `DownloadStringCompleted` event is handled in Listing 9.3.

LISTING 9.3 DownloadStringCompleted Event Handler

```
1  private static void GetStringCompleted(
2      object sender,
3      DownloadStringCompletedEventArgs e)
4  {
5      var callback = e.UserState as Action<string, Exception>;
6      if (callback == null
7          || e.Cancelled)
8      {
9          callback(null, e.Error);
10         return;
11     }
12
13     if (e.Error != null)
14     {
15         callback(null, e.Error);
16         return;
17     }
18
19     // Everything OK
20     callback(e.Result, null);
21 }
```

- Line 5 retrieves the user state, which is the callback method that shall be called when the action is completed. This value is stored in the `DownloadStringCompletedEventArgs` parameter named `e`. This way of saving the operation's context is used very often in asynchronous methods in .NET, especially in the calls to web services.
- If the callback is `null`, the method can be aborted immediately, because we do not know what to do with the content. Similarly, the asynchronous operation might have been canceled by a call to the `WebClient`'s `CancelAsync` method; in that case, the `Cancelled` property is set to `true` in the `e` parameter. This is checked on lines 6 to 11.
- On lines 13 to 17, we check whether an error was encountered while executing the call. In that case, the `Error` property of the `e` parameter is passed to the callback.
- Finally, if everything went fine, we call the callback method with the file's content, and set the `Exception` parameter to null.

In MainPage.xaml.cs, executing this operation is shown in Listing 9.4.

LISTING 9.4 Triggering the Download

```
1  private void GetStringClick(object sender, RoutedEventArgs e)
2  {
3      Cache.Visibility = Visibility.Visible;
4
5      DownloadUploadHelper.GetString((result, error) =>
6      {
7          if (error != null)
8          {
9              HandleError(error);
10         }
11         else
12         {
13             if (result != null)
14             {
15                 MessageBox.Show(result);
16             }
17         }
18
19         Cache.Visibility = Visibility.Collapsed;
20     });
21 }
```

- On line 3, we display a `Cache` in front of the whole UI. This is a semitransparent `Border` placed in front of everything, and blocks the user while the operation is executed. This is not very user friendly, and in a real application a better user experience should be provided. The `Border` also displays a `TextBlock` in its center that we can use to provide information to the user, as you will see later.
- Lines 5 to 20 show the call to the `DownloadUploadHelper.GetString` method, and the callback operation. The callback is defined as a lambda expression.
- As you saw in Listing 9.2, the helper expects a callback method with two parameters, a `string` and an `Exception`. Here, these parameters are named `result` and `error`, and placed left of the => operator.
- On the right of the => operator, the body of the lambda expression is defined. This code will only be executed later, after the operation is completed! The status of the error is checked, and the method `HandleError` (defined in Listing 9.5) is called on line 9. If there was no error, the file content is shown to the user on line 15, and the `Cache` is hidden on line 19.

The asynchronous pattern of calling a method, providing a callback, saving this callback as user state, handling the `Completed` event, retrieving and executing the callback is used every time that asynchronous web calls are done. This can also prove convenient in other asynchronous operations, such as multithreaded code as you will see in Chapter 22, "Advanced Development Techniques."

Detecting Errors, Checking the Result

Accessing content online is a complex operation, and multiple issues can occur. You already saw in Listing 9.3 how to check the Error property available on the EventArgs parameter of the Completed event (DownloadCompletedEventArgs, OpenReadCompletedEventArgs, and so forth). In case anything happened that prevented the successful completion of the operation, the Error property contains corresponding information. Although this property is of type Exception, it can be casted to a WebException to get additional information about the server-side error, such as HTTP status code and status description.

If the Error property is not null, attempting to access the Result property of the EventArgs parameter will cause an error. Listing 9.5 shows the method HandleError that the application uses to inform the user.

LISTING 9.5 Handling the Error

```
1  private void HandleError(Exception error)
2  {
3      var message = error.GetType().FullName
4        + " " + error.Message;
5      var webError = error as WebException;
6      if (webError != null)
7      {
8          var response = webError.Response as HttpWebResponse;
9          if (response != null)
10         {
11             message += " (code " + response.StatusCode + ")";
12         }
13     }
14
15     MessageBox.Show(message);
16 }
```

- On lines 1 and 2, an error message is prepared, composed of the error type (for example, System.Security.SecurityException) and of the error message.
- In the case of a server-side error, however, the error message does not provide any information on what really happened. This is why we attempt to check the status code sent by the web server. First, the error is casted to a WebException on line 5.
- If the cast worked, and the error is indeed a WebException, we can use the Response property and cast it to an HttpWebResponse instance on line 8.
- If this cast was also successful, the StatusCode property can be accessed.

If the server application did not set the WebResponse's status code explicitly, a server-side error returns code 500 (internal server error). However, by default, the status codes are not passed to the Silverlight application. Instead, a 404 status code is passed, which means "not found" and can be confusing for the user. This limitation is due to the fact that Silverlight, by default, uses the web browser's communication stack, which limits the information that it passes to plug-ins about errors. To solve this issue, see the section "Discovering the New Networking Stack," later in this chapter.

The EventArgs parameter contains additional information on the operation: The Cancelled property is set to true if the operation has been canceled by the CancelAsync method on the WebClient class. The Result property, as the name shows, contains the result of the request. Depending on the operation, the Result property can be a string or a Stream. Finally, the UserState property (of type object) is a utility property that can be used to store temporary information while the asynchronous request is processed. It can be set when the operation is initiated on the WebClient class, as you saw when we used it to store the callback in Listing 9.2.

Opening a Resource for Reading

Although the DownloadStringAsync method can be used to easily get string-based content, it cannot be used for binary content. Another method is available on the WebClient for this: OpenReadAsync with its event handler OpenReadCompleted.

This method can be used to download any content. The Result parameter of the OpenReadCompletedEventArgs is a Stream that can be read, for example, with the BinaryReader class.

In the sample application, the code is very similar to what was shown for the DownloadStringAsync method, with a few notable differences: The DownloadUploadHelper.GetImage method requires two different callback methods. The first callback will be called, just like before, when the operation is completed. The first parameter is an ImageSource instance, instead of a string. This instance will be constructed from a Stream of bytes that we download from the web server. In MainPage.xaml.cs (in the method called GetImageClick), the ImageSource is assigned to the Source property of an Image control, which has the effect of displaying the image. The second callback is an Action<int> called progressCallback. This method is called when progress is made on the download, to inform the user. In MainPage.xaml.cs (in the method called GetImageClick), the int value is displayed as a percentage in the status TextBlock.

The DownloadProgressChanged event is handled by a method called GetImageProgressChanged. In this method, the value of the ProgressPercentage property is retrieved from the e parameter (of type DownloadProgressChangedEventArgs) and passed to the progressCallback that was stored as a static attribute. Note that using a static attribute for this is probably not the best practice, since it restricts the usage of DownloadUploadHelper to one concurrent operation. You will see a better way to store multiple objects in the user state in Listing 9.9.

As for the OpenReadCompleted event, it is handled by the method named GetImageCompleted. This method is very similar to GetStringCompleted that was shown in Listing 9.3. The ImageSource instance that is passed to the callback is constructed with three lines of code shown in Listing 9.6. The e.Result property is of type Stream; conveniently the SetSource method of the BitmapImage class accepts a Stream and translates that to an image. Because BitmapSource derives from ImageSource, we can use this code, and the result is displayed in the UI as shown in Figure 9.2.

FIGURE 9.2 Loading and Displaying an Image.

LISTING 9.6 Getting a Stream and Making a BitmapSource

```
var image = new BitmapImage();
image.SetSource(e.Result);
callback(image, null);
```

Uploading a String

Like we have a specialized method to download a string, there is also the equivalent method/event handler pair for uploading text-based content to the server. Although download operations are quite simple and do not require a special server-side endpoint, any upload operation requires a server-side service to accept the resource and save it. The easiest way to do this in ASP.NET is to use a so-called generic handler ASHX, as shown in Listing 9.7. To see this code, follow these steps:

1. Open the project called DownloadUpload.Web. This is an ASP.NET project (full .NET, not Silverlight).
2. Locate the file called UploadString.ashx and expand it in the Solution Explorer. The ASHX file is just an entry point. The code is located in the code-behind file.
3. Open the file UploadString.ashx.cs.

LISTING 9.7 Server-Side Generic Handler UploadString.ashx

```
1  public void ProcessRequest(HttpContext context)
2  {
3      var file = new FileInfo(@"c:\temp\receivedfile.txt");
4
5      if (!file.Directory.Exists)
6      {
7          file.Directory.Create();
8      }
9
10     var content = context.Request.InputStream;
11
```

```
12      if (content != null)
13      {
14          using (var writer = new StreamWriter(DestinationFile))
15          {
16              using (var reader = new StreamReader(content))
17              {
18                  writer.WriteLine(reader.ReadToEnd());
19              }
20          }
21      }
22
23      context.Response.ContentType = "text/plain";
24      context.Response.Write("OK");
25  }
```

- The `UploadString` handler implements the `IHttpHandler` interface, which defines two members: The `ProcessRequest` method will be called every time that the web server receives a request for this handler's URL. The `context` parameter contains all the information needed to handle the request and deliver a response. The other member, the `IsReusable` property is not used here. For more information about this property, refer to the ASP.NET documentation.
- Line 3 creates a new `FileInfo` at c:\temp\receivedfile.txt. Hard coding the path in the service is a very bad practice, only acceptable for this simple example. In real applications, the path would be saved in a settings file. Note that the server must have write-rights to that path, or else an error will occur. If needed, you can change the path in the code directly.
- On line 10, the content of the request is retrieved as a `Stream`.
- On lines 14 to 20, a `StreamWriter` is used to write the content of this `Stream` to a text file. The `using` statement on line 14 is very convenient: When used with disposable objects (such as `Stream`, `StreamReader`, `StreamWriter`, and such), these objects are created without having to worry about closing them or disposing them. This simplifies greatly the process of working with streams. The `StreamWriter` will automatically be closed and disposed on line 20 when the block under the `using` statement is left.
- Similarly, on line 16, a `StreamReader` is created in a `using` statement, and received the request's `Stream` as input.
- On line 18, the `StreamWriter` writes the content obtained from the `StreamReader`.
- Finally, on lines 23 and 24, a text saying "OK" is set in the response. This is a way to notify the client that everything went fine.

Back in the Silverlight application, calling the generic handler is very simple thanks to the `WebClient`'s `UploadStringAsync` method (in `DownloadUploadHelper.SendString`): Set the first parameter to the URL of the generic handler on the web server. (This is the location of the ASHX file expressed as a URL.) The second parameter is a string defining which HTTP method should be used. In this sample, the `POST` method is used. Note that the `PUT` method would cause an exception because it is not supported by default. You'll learn more about this and see a workaround in the section "Discovering the New Networking Stack," later in this chapter. The third parameter is the string content that should be sent. Finally, as usual, the last parameter is the user state, which we use to store the callback method.

The strings sent to the server are encoded using the UTF-8 format. If another format is desired, the `Encoding` property of the `WebClient` class should be set to another value (for example, Unicode).

Handling the `UploadStringCompleted` event is not compulsory if your application is not interested in the result. However, like for the download operations, the `Error`, `Cancelled`, `Result`, and `UserState` properties are available to provide information on the success or failure of the operation.

The `DownloadUploadHelper.SendString` method is called in MainPage.xaml.cs in the `SendStringClick` method. Just like before, the method is called with a callback expressed as a lambda expression. The content sent to the server is read from a `TextBox` named `MyText` in the XAML markup.

Opening a Resource for Writing

If the resource to upload is not a string, the method `OpenWriteAsync` can be used. This method uses a `Stream` as input, and sends the content to a server-side service (for example, a generic handler ASHX) using the `POST` method by default.

In contrast to the other methods available on the `WebClient` class, the `OpenWriteAsync` method is not straightforward, and does not offer a way to get a response from the web server, which can be inconvenient. The DownloadUpload sample provides a method uploading a picture to a service on the web server, with the following steps:

1. A picture needs to be chosen by the user. To do this, the `OpenFileDialog` provided by Silverlight is used, as shown in Listing 9.8. Note that there are certain security restrictions when using this dialog: Opening the file dialog must be triggered by the user. Silverlight will throw an exception if you attempt to open it programmatically somewhere else than in a `Click` or `MouseDown` event handler. Even in such an event handler, configuring and opening the file dialog is the first thing that you must do, or a `SecurityException` is raised.
   Also, the dialog uses the properties `File` (of type `FileInfo`) and `Files` (an array of `FileInfo` instances if multiselection was enabled) to give access to the chosen files. However, security prevents the application to access some of the `FileInfo` properties, such as `FullName`, `Directory`, `DirectoryName`, and so forth. Any information that hints where the file is located on the client computer causes a `SecurityException` when accessed.

LISTING 9.8 Selecting a File and Calling the Helper

```
private void SendFileClick(object sender, RoutedEventArgs e)
{
    var dialog = new OpenFileDialog();
    dialog.Filter = "JPEG files|*.jpg";

    if (dialog.ShowDialog() == true)
    {
        Cache.Visibility = Visibility.Visible;
        DownloadUploadHelper.SendImage(
            dialog.File,
            SendFileCallback);
    }
}
```

2. Before the file can be read and sent to the server, the `WebClient` needs to be opened for writing. This is also an asynchronous operation with a `Completed` event. Note, however, that when the `Completed` event is called, the request has not been sent yet. It is merely ready for writing. Listing 9.9 shows how to open the `WebClient` for writing.

LISTING 9.9 Opening the `WebClient` for Writing

```
 1 public static void SendImage(
 2     FileInfo content,
 3     Action<string, Exception> callback)
 4 {
 5     var client = new WebClient();
 6     client.OpenWriteCompleted += SendImageCompleted;
 7
 8     var info = new SendImageInfo
 9     {
10         Content = content,
11         Callback = callback
12     };
13
14     client.OpenWriteAsync(
15         new Uri(ServerPath + SendImageService),
16         "POST",
17         info);
18 }
19
20 private struct SendImageInfo
21 {
22     public FileInfo Content;
23     public Action<string, Exception> Callback;
24 }
```

- The Completed event handler is set on line 6 (and the code is shown in Listing 9.10). When this event is raised, the request is ready for writing, but has not been sent to the server yet.
- A lightweight object is used on lines 8 to 12 to store information while the asynchronous request is prepared. Because we need to store more than just the callback in the UserState, a struct (shown on lines 20 to 24) is used.
- The OpenWriteAsync method is called on lines 14 to 17. The POST HTTP method is used. This is not the most efficient way to send a file to a web server, but this is the only way available by default. Here, too, we will see a different way in the "Discovering the New Networking Stack," later in this chapter.

3. When the Completed event handler is called, the local file can be read using a BinaryReader, and then sent to the web server, as shown in Listing 9.10.

LISTING 9.10 Reading and Sending the File

```
1  private static void SendImageCompleted(
2      object sender,
3      OpenWriteCompletedEventArgs e)
4  {
5      if (e.Cancelled)
6      {
7          return;
8      }
9
10     var info = (SendImageInfo)e.UserState;
11
12     if (e.Error != null)
13     {
14         info.Callback(null, e.Error);
15         return;
16     }
17
18     var inputStream = info.Content.OpenRead();
19     var outputStream = e.Result;
20
21     ReadWriteFile(inputStream, outputStream);
22
23     // Everything OK
24     info.Callback("File sent, no server response to show", null);
25 }
```

- After retrieving the UserState on line 10, we check whether an error occurred while preparing the request, and abort the sending operation on lines 12 to 16 if that is the case.

- On line 18, we open the file for reading. This operation is allowed by security: the content of the file is accessible, only its location is concealed.
- On line 19, we get the output stream to which the content will be written.
- Line 21 calls a method called `ReadWriteFile` (shown in Listing 9.11) that will do the actual reading/writing operation. A separate method was created for this, because we will reuse this code in Listing 9.14 when using the `HttpWebRequest` to perform the same operation.
- Finally, even though we did not get any confirmation from the web server, the user is informed that as far as we know, the operation was successful.

4. The method `ReadWriteFile` is a utility method that reads the file's stream, and writes the bytes read into the request's stream that will be sent to the server, as shown in Listing 9.11. Note that as soon as the request's stream is closed, the request is sent to the web server.

LISTING 9.11 Reading and Writing the File's Content

```
public static void ReadWriteFile(
    Stream inputStream,
    Stream outputStream)
{
    using (var writer = new BinaryWriter(outputStream))
    {
        using (var reader = new BinaryReader(inputStream))
        {
            var stop = false;
            while (!stop)
            {
                var bytes = reader.ReadBytes(1000);
                writer.Write(bytes);

                if (bytes.Length < 1000)
                {
                    stop = true;
                }
            }
        }
    }
}
```

Accessing Headers

The WebClient class allows accessing the request's web headers, which can be useful if you need to send additional information to the web server. Note, however, that headers can be modified by all the actors involved on the way from the Silverlight client to the web server (such as routers, proxies, and so on).

The request's headers are stored in the WebClient's Headers property, which is a key/value collection.

The WebClient class does not allow retrieving the headers from the response, however. If the application needs this information, the HttpWebRequest class should be used instead, as you'll see in the following section.

Sending Complex Messages

The WebClient class is very convenient to place simple calls to a web server, either for download or upload. It fulfills most of the developer's needs and is relatively simple to use. If finer control is needed on the request and the response, the Silverlight framework offers the HttpWebRequest class. In fact, the WebClient class uses the HttpWebRequest class under the covers. The WebClient is a higher-level abstraction.

The main differences between the WebClient and the HttpWebRequest class are as follows: When sending a binary file to the web server, the WebClient ignores the response sent by the server (as you saw earlier in this chapter). If the response is important for that operation, the HttpWebRequest should be used instead. Also, the WebClient does not provide a convenient access to cookies like the HttpWebRequest does. Finally, the WebClient's methods and events are always executed on the initiating thread. For example, if you start a request on the UI thread, the response is automatically dispatched to the UI thread, too. In the case of the HttpWebRequest, however, the response arrives on a background thread and dispatching must be done manually, as you will see in Listing 9.15.

Posting a File to the Server with HttpWebRequest

The DownloadUpload sample provides a class sending a picture to the web server using the HttpWebRequest. The method is similar to the WebClient's one, but the actual code is more complex, as you can see in Listing 9.12.

LISTING 9.12 Storing Information While Sending

```
private struct SendImageInfo
{
    public WebRequest Request;
    public Action<string, Exception> Callback;
    public FileInfo Content;
    public SynchronizationContext MainThreadContext;
    public WebResponse Response;
    public Exception Error;
}
```

This structure expands on the one we used with the WebClient, and stores in addition the context on which the request is sent. We will need that later to dispatch the response from the worker thread created by the HttpWebrequest. We also prepare a field for the WebResponse, and one to store a possible Exception. We will need this later in Listing 9.15.

Listings 9.13 and 9.14 show how the request is prepared as an asynchronous operation with a callback method.

LISTING 9.13 Preparing the Request

```
 1  public static void SendImage(
 2      FileInfo content,
 3      Action<string, Exception> callback)
 4  {
 5      var request = (HttpWebRequest)WebRequest.Create(
 6          new Uri(ServerPath + SendImageService));
 7      request.Method = "POST";
 8
 9      var info = new SendImageInfo
10      {
11          Request = request,
12          Callback = callback,
13          Content = content,
14          MainThreadContext = SynchronizationContext.Current
15      };
16
17      request.BeginGetRequestStream(SendImageRequestCallback, info);
18  }
```

Note how the SynchronizationContext is stored on line 14. We will use that later. On line 17, the method BeginGetRequestStream is called. The callback method for this is shown in Listing 9.14. The user state is the info structure that was just created in lines 9 to 15.

LISTING 9.14 Sending the Request

```
 1  private static void SendImageRequestCallback(IAsyncResult result)
 2  {
 3      var info = (SendImageInfo)result.AsyncState;
 4      var request = info.Request;
 5
 6      var inputStream = info.Content.OpenRead();
 7      var outputStream = request.EndGetRequestStream(result);
 8
 9      DownloadUploadHelper.ReadWriteFile(inputStream, outputStream);
10
11      request.BeginGetResponse(ResponseCallback, info);
12  }
```

After retrieving the info structure on line 3, the streams are prepared: The file is open for reading on line 6, and the request's stream is obtained with the call to the EndGetRequestStream method. The streams are read and written using the method shown in Listing 9.11. Nothing changed here. Then, on line 11, the request is actually sent to the server. A callback is provided for the response, shown in Listing 9.15.

LISTING 9.15 Getting the Server's Response

```
1  private static void ResponseCallback(IAsyncResult result)
2  {
3      var info = (SendImageInfo)result.AsyncState;
4
5      try
6      {
7          var response = info.Request.EndGetResponse(result);
8          info.Response = response;
9      }
10     catch (Exception ex)
11     {
12         info.Error = ex;
13     }
14
15     info.MainThreadContext.Post(MainThreadCallback, info);
16 }
```

- The response (of type HttpWebResponse) is obtained from the Request object with the call to EndGetResponse. This class contains a Stream to the actual bytes sent by the web server (which we will decode in Listing 9.16) as well as other information about the operation, such as status code and description, response headers, cookies, length and type of the content, and so forth.
- On line 8, the response is stored into the info structure.
- The EndGetResponse method might throw an Exception if something went wrong on the web server. To avoid crashing the Silverlight application, this possible Exception is caught on line 10 and stored into the info structure.
- Because this method is executed on a worker thread, it needs to be dispatched to the main thread (this is one of the disadvantages of the HttpWebRequest class over the WebClient class). You'll learn more about dispatching in Chapter 22. Here, the dispatching is done by the SynchronizationContext instance that we stored earlier in Listing 9.13. The method that is being dispatched is shown in Listing 9.16.

LISTING 9.16 Executing the Callback

```
1  private static void MainThreadCallback(object state)
2  {
3      var info = (SendImageInfo)state;
4      if (info.Error != null)
5       {
6          info.Callback(null, info.Error);
7          return;
8      }
9
10     var response = info.Response as HttpWebResponse;
11     var stream = info.Response.GetResponseStream();
12
13     using (var reader = new StreamReader(stream))
14     {
15         var serverMessage = reader.ReadToEnd();
16         info.Callback(serverMessage, null);
17     }
18 }
```

This method concludes the complex operation of sending a file to the server. Because it has been dispatched, it can access the UI directly by using the callback that was stored in Listing 9.13. If an `Exception` was thrown by the server, the user is informed on lines 4 to 8.

On lines 13 to 17, the text sent by the web server is read with a `StreamReader` class. Of course, depending on the `ContentType` property of the `HttpWebResponse` class, other methods could be used to read and decode the bytes sent.

This sample shows that the `HttpWebRequest` class is more complicated to use than the `WebClient`, but also provides finer control over the request and the response objects. Note that for simplicity, the previous listings do not include much error handling code. A real application should be more careful when using these methods, to avoid crashes.

Discovering the New Networking Stack

In the early days, Silverlight's only way to communicate with a web server was to use the browser's networking stack in the background. Although this allowed Silverlight to be released faster (because a whole lot of functionalities didn't have to be rewritten), it also came with limitations.

Some of these have already been mentioned in this chapter (for instance, the fact that a request can only be sent with the HTTP methods `GET` or `POST`). Although many operations can be done with these two HTTP methods, additional methods such as `PUT` and `DELETE` should be made available, especially when using REST services.

Also, you saw that any server-side error translates to a 404 code (or "file not found") on the client. This is because the web browsers do not pass any additional information to the plug-ins they host. Implementing a clean error handling and informing the user is, of course, impossible in these conditions.

Another limitation is the fact that a Silverlight application cannot get or set cookies when it is using the default networking stack. Cookies can be used to send or receive additional information when communicating with the web server. If the web application relies on cookies, using the new networking stack may be the only way to go.

Using the Client HTTP Stack

The new HTTP stack (called the client HTTP stack, as opposed to the browser HTTP stack) is never used by default. The Silverlight application must opt in explicitly to use the new features. Opting in the new HTTP stack can be done at different levels.

For All Requests

Your Silverlight application can require all HTTP requests to be sent using the new stack, throughout the application, for both the `WebClient` and for the `HttpWebRequest` class. Listing 9.17 shows how the new stack can be required for all HTTP requests. Similar code can be used for HTTPS requests (secure HTTP communication, where the requests and responses are encrypted).

LISTING 9.17 Using the New Stack for All Requests

```
bool httpResult = WebRequest.RegisterPrefix(
    "http://",
    WebRequestCreator.ClientHttp);
```

For a Specific Domain

The `RegisterPrefix` method can also be used to force using the client HTTP stack for a given domain, as shown in Listing 9.18. All web requests to other domains will be done using the old browser stack.

LISTING 9.18 Using the New Stack for a Specific Domain

```
bool httpResult = WebRequest.RegisterPrefix(
    "http://www.galasoft.ch",
    WebRequestCreator.ClientHttp);
```

For a Specific Request

If the client HTTP stack should be used only for a specific request, but all others should be done with the default stack, you can create a new request specifically for the new networking stack. Listing 9.19 shows how the `WebRequestCreator` class's `ClientHttp` property is used to create a new `HttpWebRequest` instance. Once the instance exists, it can be used just like we did earlier in this chapter.

LISTING 9.19 Creating a Request for the New Stack

```
var request = WebRequestCreator.ClientHttp.Create(
    new Uri("http://www.galasoft.ch")) as HttpWebRequest;
```

Using Other HTTP Methods

Once the new stack has been obtained, either for the whole application, for a given domain, or for a given request, the calls can be placed just as you saw earlier in this chapter. The restrictions mentioned earlier are lifted, though. For instance, it is now possible to send a file to the web server using the HTTP method `PUT`, as shown with the following steps:

1. Open the DownloadUpload solution.
2. Open the file MainPage.xaml.cs.
3. Locate the lines shown in Listing 9.17 in the `MainPage` constructor, and uncomment them to make the code active. This requires using the new stack for all requests through the HTTP protocol.
4. Open the file DownloadUploadHelper.cs and locate the method named `SendImage`.
5. In the actual call to the `WebClient`'s `OpenWriteAsync` method, change the HTTP method from `POST` to `PUT`.
6. Run the application and send an image to the web server.

This last operation would cause an exception to occur if we had not requested the new networking stack. Note that even with the new networking stack, not all HTTP methods are supported for security reasons.

Using the `CookieContainer`

The new networking stack also allows using cookies, providing a mechanism to exchange small pieces of meta-information with the web server. In the web browser, cookies are also used to store information on the client. In Silverlight, however, a much more convenient and powerful storage facility exists, named the isolated storage. You'll learn more about this secure file system in Chapter 17, "New Transforms, Right Click, HTML Browser, WebBrowserBrush, and Isolated Storage."

To access the cookies, either to send them to the server or to read them from the response, the `CookieContainer` class is used, as shown in Listing 9.20, taken from the DownloadUpload sample (in the `CookieSample` class). The request does not create a `CookieContainer` by default, so a new instance must be set explicitly before the request is sent. A `Cookie` instance is always set for a given domain, with a key and a value.

LISTING 9.20 Sending a Cookie to the Server and Getting One Back

```
1  public static void SendCookie()
2  {
3      WebRequest.RegisterPrefix("http://", WebRequestCreator.ClientHttp);
4
5      var request = (HttpWebRequest)
6          WebRequest.Create(ServerPath + CookieService);
7
8      request.CookieContainer = new CookieContainer();
9
10     request.CookieContainer.Add(new Uri(ServerPath),
11         new Cookie("mycookie", "Hello"));
12     request.BeginGetResponse(ReadCallback, request);
13 }
14
15 private static void ReadCallback(IAsyncResult result)
16 {
17     var request = (HttpWebRequest)result.AsyncState;
18     var response = request.EndGetResponse(result)
19         as HttpWebResponse;
20     var stringValue = response.Cookies["mycookie"].Value;
21 }
```

- On line 3, the client HTTP stack is requested. Cookies can only be used with the new networking stack.
- On line 5 and 6, a new request is prepared. The `CookieService` constant contains the address of a server-side service that will simply read the value of the cookie and return one back after adding the word *success*.
- On line 8, a new `CookieContainer` is created. This step would be needed even if we didn't want to send cookies to the server, but only read those sent back instead.
- On lines 10 and 11, a new `Cookie` is created and added to the container. Note that we didn't specify additional properties in the `Cookie`, such as the expiration date.
- Finally, after the response has been received, the new value can be read from the response's `Cookies` collection.

Handling Responses

Often, web servers use XML or another text-based language called JavaScript Object Notation (JSON) to answer a query from a web client. These text-based protocols are very convenient:

- XML is very well known, and many tools and services have been using it for years. It is very well suited for HTTP communication. After all, HTML is very similar to XML in its structure (even though XML obeys stricter rules).
- JSON is also text based, and because it was developed more recently than XML, it answers some of the concerns that XML is causing. Most important, XML is a very verbose protocol, and a lot of text in an XML document is not actually carrying information. JSON, on the other hand, is very concise, and allows crafting messages that carry only very few formatting characters.

Silverlight is well equipped to decode both XML- and JSON-based messages. When a service exposes endpoints delivering both XML and JSON, it makes sense to prefer the JSON based one, to reduce the strain on the network. Decoding XML and JSON responses is quite easy using a technology called LINQ (Language INtegrated Query). This was already introduced in Silverlight 2 as an intrinsic part of the C# and VB.NET languages.

Handling XML Responses

Loading an XML document and accessing the content with LINQ-to-XML is done with the `XDocument` class. This class is available in an assembly that must be added to your Silverlight application with the following steps:

1. Right-click the Silverlight project in the Visual Studio Solution Explorer.
2. Select the Browse tab in the Add Reference dialog.
3. Navigate to C:\Program Files\Microsoft SDKs\Silverlight\v4.0\Libraries\Client and locate the DLL named System.Xml.Linq.dll.
4. Select this DLL and click OK.
5. The `XDocument` class is included in the namespace `System.Xml.Linq` that must be referenced with a `using` directive on top of the page.
6. Also add a `using` directive including the namespace `System.Linq`. This namespace contains multiple extensions methods that help parsing the XML elements.

Silverlight 2 Unleashed, Chapter 22, Listing 22.8, shows how to parse the XML result of a `WebClient`'s `DownloadStringAsync` method with LINQ.

Handling JSON Responses

Similarly, a JSON-formatted document can be parsed using LINQ-to-JSON, which is also a part of Silverlight. Often, JSON is not the default format returned by a web service, but must be requested explicitly. For example, the location service Foursquare exposes a set of API methods described at http://www.galasoft.ch/sl4-4sq. This is from the documentation:

> You can currently request output in XML (the default) as well as JSON. You should format the URL like this: http://api.foursquare.com/v1/user.json
> If your URL has no format extension, the default (XML) will be served up: http://api.foursquare.com/v1/user

Once the JSON formatted string is available in the application (for example, with a call to the `WebClient`'s `DownloadStringAsync` method), LINQ-to-JSON methods can be used to parse the results and convert them to C# objects. In *Silverlight 2 Unleashed*, Chapter 23, Listing 23.16 and subsequent listings show a JSON-formatted string obtained from the Flickr web services decoded by these means. It uses the `JsonObject` class, available in the `System.Json` namespace, in the assembly System.Json.dll, which must be referenced as we did in the previous section.

Communicating with WCF

Windows Communication Foundation (WCF) is an important pillar of the .NET framework. Before WCF was released, there were various communication frameworks based on the .NET framework, and used in various configurations. For example, sockets-based communication allows Windows applications to communicate at a low level, ASMX web services use an XML-based protocol (called SOAP, Simple Object Access Protocol) to exchange information with web applications, and so forth.

WCF groups and unifies all these various protocols and technologies. With mere configuration, it is possible to expose the same service as a TCP-based, binary endpoint, or as an HTTP-based endpoint delivering XML-based data. Of course, WCF is also a very complex framework, and many complete books are available for this technology. This section shows how to create a WCF service optimized for Silverlight and connect to it using a Silverlight application.

Setting Up a Service

A WCF service can be exposed in the same web server that is hosting the Silverlight application (same domain), or in a completely different web server. In this case, a cross-domain policy file may be needed to make sure that the Silverlight application can communicate with the service.

In this sample, we use the same web application to host the Silverlight application and the WCF service, with the following steps:

1. Create a new Silverlight application in Visual Studio, named **WcfServiceSample**.
2. Make sure that you host the Silverlight application in a new website named **WcfServiceSample.Web**.
3. Right-click the web project WcfServiceSample.Web and select Add, New Item from the context menu.
4. Select the Silverlight category, and then a Silverlight-enabled WCF Service. Name this new item **SampleService.svc**.
5. Right-click the web project again and select Add, Class from the context menu. Name this new item **DataItem.cs**. This class will be used to transport information from the web server to the web client.

6. Edit the `DataItem` class as shown in Listing 9.21. Note that the `DataContract` and `DataMember` attributes are into the namespace `System.Runtime.Serialization`. The corresponding `using` directive must be added. These attributes notify the WCF service that the class and properties are to be serialized and sent to the client.

LISTING 9.21 Implementing the `DataItem` Class

```
[DataContract]
public class DataItem
{
    [DataMember]
    public string Name
    {
        get;
        set;
    }

    [DataMember]
    public int ContractNumber
    {
        get;
        set;
    }
}
```

7. Open the file SampleService.svc.cs. The SVC file is the endpoint through which all calls are going; the implementation is into this code-behind file.

8. Set the `ServiceContract` attribute to a unique namespace (for example, `"http://www.mydomain.com"`). The namespace does not have to be a valid domain name; it is just a unique resource identifier.

9. Delete the method `DoWork` that had been generated, and instead implement the service, as shown in Listing 9.22. This is a simple method that takes an offset in hours and returns the server date/time minus the offset. Note the `OperationContract` attribute that is decorating the method, notifying WCF that this method should be exposed as a service.

LISTING 9.22 Implementing a New Method

```
[OperationContract]
public DateTime GetServerDateTime(int hoursMinusOffset)
{
    var now = DateTime.Now;
    return now - TimeSpan.FromHours(hoursMinusOffset);
}
```

To make sure that everything is okay, right-click the file SampleService.svc in the Solution Explorer, and select View in Browser from the context menu. This starts your favorite web browser and should display a web page with information about the service.

Using ASMX Web Services

Before WCF was released, web services were exposed as ASMX web services (so called because the extension of the service endpoint is .asmx). Because ASMX services use SOAP, Visual Studio is able to create proxy for these services, too. When creating a new service, however, it is recommended to rather choose WCF.

Connecting the Client Application

With the service created, we are ready to set up the client Silverlight application to connect to it. Follow these steps:

1. In the web browser window displaying the SampleService.svc page, copy the URL from the location bar. This URL shows the location of the SampleService.svc file on the web server. This is the endpoint through which our Silverlight application will connect.
2. In Visual Studio's Solution Explorer, right-click the WcfServiceSample project (the Silverlight project) and select Add Service Reference from the context menu.
3. Paste the URL you copied in Step 1 above in the Address field of the Add Service Reference dialog. Then click the Go button.
4. If all goes well, you should see the SampleService in the list of Services. Enter the name **MyService** in the Namespace field, and then click OK.

> **TIP**
>
> **Using the Discover Button**
>
> When the service is located in the same solution as the Silverlight application like here, you can also use the Discover button instead of copying/pasting the URL. If the service is remote, however, this doesn't work.

Visual Studio uses the information downloaded from the web service to create a new namespace (named `MyService`) and a set of *proxy objects* (that is, client-side representation of the server side objects). The `DataItem` class that we implemented on the server is now also present in the Silverlight application. For the WCF service, a client is created, exposing all the methods that had been marked with the `OperationContract` attribute.

1. Open the file MainPage.xaml and modify the user interface as shown in Listing 9.23.

LISTING 9.23 Setting the UI

```
<StackPanel x:Name="LayoutRoot"
      Background="White">
    <TextBox x:Name="OffsetHoursTextBox"
             Text="0"
             Margin="10" />

    <Button Content="Call service"
            Click="CallServiceClick"
            x:Name="MyButton"
            Margin="10" />
</StackPanel>
```

2. Right-click the event handler name `CallServiceClick` and select Navigate to Event Handler from the context menu. This opens the file MainPage.xaml.cs and sets the cursor in the corresponding event handler code.

Using the Client

Now that Visual Studio is set up to use the WCF client, sending asynchronous messages is as easy as calling a method and handling a `Completed` event. This event is raised when the response from the server comes back. The following steps show how to call the client, and use the `DateTime` instance returned by the service.

Modify the `CallServiceClick` event handler as shown in Listing 9.24.

LISTING 9.24 Calling the Client

```
1  private void CallServiceClick(object sender, RoutedEventArgs e)
2  {
3      var offset = Int32.Parse(OffsetHoursTextBox.Text);
4
5      var client = new MyService.SampleServiceClient();
6      client.GetServerDateTimeCompleted
7          += ClientGetServerDateTimeCompleted;
8      client.GetServerDateTimeAsync(offset, offset);
9  }
```

This event handler is called when the button is clicked. On line 3, the value entered in the `TextBox` is parsed. If the user entered an invalid value (not an integer number), this line will throw an exception, which should be handled. In this simple sample, we just leave it as is. On line 5, a new client is instantiated. Depending on the scenario, the client could be saved as a private member into the `MainPage` class. In this sample, the client is used and discarded. A new client is created the next time that the user clicks on the button.

On lines 6 and 7, the `Completed` event handler is assigned. The code is shown in Listing 9.25. Finally, on line 8, the `GetServerDateTimeAsync` method is called. There is an "async method / event handler" pair available for each method marked with the `OperationContract` attribute on the server. This pair is generated by Visual Studio in the client when the Add Service Reference operation is executed.

Note that we pass the `offset` variable twice to this method. Do not get confused:

- The first parameter is sent to the server-side method, and will be used in the calculation.
- The second parameter is optional. It is the `UserState` that we already saw earlier in this chapter. This parameter remains on the client, and will be used in the `Completed` event handler. This is just a convenient way to save information while the asynchronous call is executed.

Implement the `Completed` event handler as shown in Listing 9.25.

LISTING 9.25 Handling the Completed Event

```
1   void ClientGetServerDateTimeCompleted(
2       object sender,
3       MyService.GetServerDateTimeCompletedEventArgs e)
4   {
5       var offset = (int)e.UserState;
6
7       MyButton.Content = string.Format(
8           "Current date time on client: {0}"
9           + Environment.NewLine
10          + "Date time - {1} hours on server: {2}",
12          DateTime.Now.ToString(),
13          offset,
14          e.Result.ToString());
15  }
```

Line 5 retrieves the `offset` that the user had entered from the `UserState` property. Then, lines 7 to 14 set the text displayed by the button in the user interface.

On lines 8 to 10, we create a string with 3 placeholders `{0}` to `{2}`. The `string.Format` method uses these placeholders and replaces them with the arguments after the first parameter:

- The first placeholder is replaced by the current date/time on the client.
- The second placeholder is replaced by the `offset` that the user had entered.
- The last placeholder is replaced by the date/time sent by the server. The `e.Result` property is conveniently prepared by the WCF client, and its type corresponds to the type `DateTime` specified as the return value for the `GetServerDateTime` method in the server-side `SampleService` class.

9

At this point, you can run the application, enter an offset into the text box, and then press the button. After a short delay, a new text is displayed in the button.

Updating the Code on the Server

If changes are made on the server (such as adding or removing a method, changing the list of parameters on existing methods, and so on), the service reference must be updated. This is needed because the WCF client and all the proxy objects must be regenerated to reflect the changes. Visual Studio makes it easy to update the service reference, but this must be done every time changes are made on the server, as shown in the following steps:

1. Open the file SampleService.svc.cs in the WcfServiceSample.Web project.
2. Modify the name of the `GetServerDateTime` method to `GetServerDateTimeWithOffset`.
3. Build the application and run it. In the Silverlight page, click the button. This throws an exception because the client attempts to call a method that does not exist anymore on the server. The reference needs to be updated with the following steps:
4. In the Solution Explorer, expand the Service References folder in the Silverlight project.
5. Right-click the reference named MyService and select Update Service Reference from the context menu.
6. Wait until the references are updated, and then build the application.

The compilation fails now because the WCF client has been updated with the new method name. The Silverlight code needs to be changed accordingly, and then the application can be used.

Publishing the Service

Of course, getting the server date/time is not very exciting when the application runs on the same physical PC than the WCF service (which is the case while it is being developed). The WCF service should be published to a web server. This step is done in Visual Studio by right-clicking the web application and selecting Publish from the context menu. Depending on your web server configuration, you can choose Web Deploy, FTP, or another method to publish the code. For more information about what your web server supports, you should contact your Internet service provider.

After the service has been published, one step is needed in the Silverlight client. The URL of the SVC endpoint must be updated with the following steps:

1. In the Silverlight application, right-click the MyService reference (in the Service References folder) and select Configure Service Reference from the context menu.
2. Update the address of the SVC file in the Address field of the Service Reference Settings dialog (see Figure 9.3).
3. Compile the application after the reference has been updated.

The Silverlight application now connects to the remote WCF service when it is run. Do not get confused! Any changes made to the local WCF application will be ignored by the Silverlight client, at least as long the changes are not published to the web server.

Client
Address: http://localhost:6787/SampleService.svc
Access level for generated classes: Public
Generate asynchronous operations

FIGURE 9.3 Updating the endpoint URL.

Summary

Connecting to the Web is always an exciting step in a development project. Filling an otherwise empty UI with data, images, and videos and getting updated information continuously give life to your application. In this chapter, you saw how to use the `WebClient` class to connect easily to the Internet and download or upload text-based content as well as any binary content (files, videos, pictures, and so on). Then the `HttpWebRequest` was shown, as a way to access more complex services and to get finer control over the messages sent over the wire.

A bit further, we talked about the new HTTP stack introduced to overcome some of the shortcomings of the browser stack used as the default. This allowed us to use other HTTP methods (for example, to fully use REST-based services) and to access cookies.

We talked shortly about a way to handle text-based response from the web service, either using the XML or JSON protocols. Finally, you saw how to create and use a WCF service, which allows us to communicate with the server is a transparent way, just by calling methods and handling a `Completed` event.

In later chapters, we use this knowledge to build connected application and fully enjoy the advantages of the rich communication framework built in to Silverlight 4.

CHAPTER 10

Creating Resources, Styles, and Templates

IN THIS CHAPTER, WE WILL:

- Talk about resources and dictionaries.
- Use resources in Expression Blend.
- See why you should clean up unused resources, and how to do it.
- Create styles for controls and see what new features are available in Silverlight 4.
- Create templates for controls.
- Create custom easing functions for animations.
- Discover and use themes to easily customize Silverlight applications.

One of the most exciting features of Silverlight (and of its big sister Windows Presentation Foundation, WPF) is the ability to separate the functionality of a control from its appearance. This separation was already tested in other frameworks, such as HTML. The Cascading Style Sheets system (CSS) is used to describe the appearance of the page, while the HTML code itself is used to store the content of the page.

Such a separation makes a lot of sense because two very different roles are working on a user interface: The developer creates the functionality, while the designer works on the appearance of the page. In Silverlight, the same separation happens and the same roles work together to create beautiful applications.

Changing the appearance of the controls is done at two different levels in Silverlight:

- With styles, various properties of an element can be set. This is roughly equivalent to what CSS is offering: You can group property setters in a way that is isolated (so that a designer can work on them without disturbing the developer's work), and reusable (so that you have to define the looks of a set of similar controls only once).
- With templates, you can completely redefine the appearance of a control. This frees the designers completely because there are no limits anymore to what they create in their comps. Templates can be used to change the shape of a control and even to specify the transitions between various states that the control can have (such as `MouseOver`, `Pressed`, `Disabled`, and so on).

In this chapter, we first take a look at the resources system in Silverlight 4. Although not directly related, the resources system is used to store the elements that are needed to modify controls' appearance. Then we take a deep dive into the styles and templates system, and you'll learn how to create and modify them in XAML (in Visual Studio) and in Expression Blend.

Working with Resources in XAML

Resources can be thought of as a series of shelves, in which any element can be stored for later use. Although resources are used to define styles and templates, they can in fact store any element that can be expressed in XAML. For example, in Listing 2.2, a `Storyboard` was fetched from the local resources and started. This element had been placed there by Expression Blend when it had been created earlier. In Listing 3.1, a `Double` value was stored in the `UserControl`'s resources, and used further in XAML with the help of a `StaticResource` *markup extension*. In Listing 4.7, a whole view-model was stored in resources, and later used to set the `DataContext` of a `StackPanel`.

These few examples show how versatile a resource dictionary can be: As long as the element you want to store can be created in XAML, it can be placed in resources, and given a key for later use.

Using Local Resources

The `Resources` property is available on any `FrameworkElement`. Its type is `ResourceDictionary`, a specialized key/value collection. Each element it stores must have a key for identification.

> **WARNING**
>
> **Using `x:Name` in Resources**
>
> A particularity of Silverlight over WPF is that a name (set through the `x:Name` attribute) can be used when storing an element in resources, instead of `x:Key`. This is a remnant of Silverlight 1.0, when resource dictionaries were not implemented in a way compatible with WPF yet. Because using `x:Name` in a resource dictionary causes an error in WPF, it is recommended not to use this in Silverlight, but to use the `x:Key` attribute instead, with the possible exception of storyboards, where using `x:Name` actually facilitates the usage of such elements.

Listing 10.1 shows two `Border` elements in a `StackPanel`. Each `Border` stores a `SolidColorBrush` in its `Resources`, with the same key. Inside each `Border`, a `Button` element uses that key to set its `Background` property.

LISTING 10.1 Using Local Resources

```
<StackPanel>
    <Border Margin="10">
        <Border.Resources>
```

```
            <SolidColorBrush x:Key="MyBrush"
                             Color="Red" />
        </Border.Resources>
        <Button Background="{StaticResource MyBrush}"
                Width="100" Height="30" />
    </Border>

    <Border Margin="10">
        <Border.Resources>
            <SolidColorBrush x:Key="MyBrush"
                             Color="Green" />
        </Border.Resources>
        <Button Background="{StaticResource MyBrush}"
                Width="100" Height="30" />
    </Border>
</StackPanel>
```

- Because resources are searched bottom up, each `Button` uses the resource with the key `MyBrush` that is the closest to itself. This is why in Figure 10.1 the first button has a shade of red, whereas the second one has a shade of green. This is true also when using external resource dictionaries!
- Note that a `Button`'s default template uses a linear gradient as its background, which is why Figure 10.1 does not show a plain red or green background. You'll learn more about default templates later in this chapter.

FIGURE 10.1 Red and green buttons.

Merging Dictionaries

Silverlight 3 introduced the ability to use external resource dictionaries to store elements. This was a welcomed addition because it makes it possible to structure the resources in a more flexible way and to reuse whole dictionaries in various locations of the application (or even in other applications).

An external resource dictionary (as opposed to the local `Resources` property of a `FrameworkElement`) is defined in a XAML file. To create a new resource dictionary in a Silverlight application, follow these steps:

1. In the Solution Explorer in Visual Studio, right-click the Silverlight project and select Add, New Item from the context menu.
2. Select the Silverlight category and then Silverlight Resource Dictionary from the Add New Item dialog.
3. With the new dictionary selected in the Solution Explorer, show the properties by pressing F4. Notice that the Build Action for this element is set to Page, and that a custom tool is used to compile the XAML. This is needed to place the XAML file in the XAP file and make it available to the Silverlight application.

A new resource dictionary can also be added into Expression Blend, using the Add New Item dialog.

A simple external resource dictionary is shown in Listing 10.2. Notice that there is no x:Class attribute, because there is no code behind. Resources are defined in the external resource dictionary exactly in the same way than in local resources, with a key. Additional xmlns prefixes can be defined if needed.

LISTING 10.2 External Resource Dictionary

```
<ResourceDictionary
    xmlns="http://schemas.microsoft.com/winfx/2006/xaml/presentation"
    xmlns:x="http://schemas.microsoft.com/winfx/2006/xaml"
    xmlns:sys="clr-namespace:System;assembly=mscorlib">

    <sys:Double x:Key="ButtonWidth">100</sys:Double>

    <SolidColorBrush x:Key="ButtonBackground"
                     Color="Red" />

</ResourceDictionary>
```

From the Same Assembly

After one or more resource dictionaries have been added, they need to be merged into the application resources (global resources) or into a local element's Resources property (local resources). Typically, a Silverlight application has application-level resources, as shown in Listing 10.3 (for example, brushes, default styles, and templates that are used throughout the application), and page-level resources, such as in Listing 10.4 (for example, special styles and templates that are used only within the current page).

LISTING 10.3 Merging External Dictionaries in App.xaml

```
<Application.Resources>
    <ResourceDictionary>
        <ResourceDictionary.MergedDictionaries>
            <ResourceDictionary Source="Styles/GlobalResources.xaml"/>
            <ResourceDictionary Source="Styles/ButtonStyles.xaml"/>
            <ResourceDictionary Source="Styles/CheckboxStyles.xaml"/>
            <ResourceDictionary Source="Styles/SliderStyles.xaml"/>
        </ResourceDictionary.MergedDictionaries>
    </ResourceDictionary>
</Application.Resources>
```

LISTING 10.4 Merging External Dictionaries in MainPage.xaml

```
<UserControl.Resources>
    <ResourceDictionary>
        <ResourceDictionary.MergedDictionaries>
            <ResourceDictionary Source="Styles/MainPageStyles.xaml"/>
        </ResourceDictionary.MergedDictionaries>
    </ResourceDictionary>
</UserControl.Resources>
```

From a Different Assembly

Resource dictionaries can be included in external assemblies. This offers a neat way to create skins for an application, by grouping all the resources into a DLL. Later, the project used to compile the skin DLL can be passed to designers for a redesign. Also, such a DLL can be used in multiple applications (for example, to create a consistent corporate look and feel). A skin DLL can be created as follows:

1. Create a new Silverlight application in Visual Studio, named **SkinnedApplication**.
2. Right-click the SkinnedApplication solution in the Solution Explorer (the topmost node in the tree).
3. Select Add, New Project from the context menu.
4. Select a Silverlight Class Library from the dialog, and name it **SkinnedApplication.Skins**. Select Silverlight 4 as the target for this new project.
5. In this new project, delete the file named Class1.cs. We will not need this file.
6. Right-click the SkinnedApplication.Skins project in the Solution Explorer, and add a new Silverlight resource dictionary named **MainPageSkin.xaml**.
7. Add a new `SolidColorBrush` in MainPageSkin.xaml, and set its `x:Key` attribute to `LayoutRootBackgroundBrush`. Set its `Color` attribute to `Red`.
8. To use the external resource dictionary, a reference must be added in the main assembly. To do this, right-click the SkinnedApplication project in the Solution Explorer and select Add Reference from the context menu.
9. In the Add Reference dialog, select the Projects tab, then the SkinnedApplication.Skins project and click OK. This adds a reference to this project in the References folder. It will also copy the SkinnedApplication.Skins.dll assembly to the bin\Debug folder, and in the XAP file.
10. In MainPage.xaml, merge the dictionary from the external assembly with the markup shown in Listing 10.5.
11. Set the main `Grid`'s `Background` property as shown in Listing 10.5. Because the resources from the external resource dictionary have been merged, you can use them just as you would use local resources.

LISTING 10.5 Merging and Using a Dictionary from a Different Assembly

```
<UserControl.Resources>
    <ResourceDictionary>
        <ResourceDictionary.MergedDictionaries>
            <ResourceDictionary
                Source="/SkinnedApplication.Skins;component/MainPageSkin.xaml" />
        </ResourceDictionary.MergedDictionaries>
    </ResourceDictionary>
</UserControl.Resources>

<Grid x:Name="LayoutRoot"
      Background="{StaticResource LayoutRootBackgroundBrush}">
</Grid>
```

The syntax to reference elements in an external assembly is `/AssemblyName;component/Path/ElementName`, as follows:

- `AssemblyName` is name of the external assembly. This assembly must be available when the `Source` property is parsed. In general, it is a referenced assembly.
- `component` is a keyword specifying that the element referenced is within the external assembly.
- `Path` is the hierarchy of folders in which the element is located. In Listing 10.5, MainPageSkin.xaml is at the root of the assembly, so the path is empty.
- `ElementName` is the name of the referenced element.

The syntax shown for the `Source` property in Listing 10.5 is named *pack URI* syntax, and is very useful to reference elements in XAML. It can be used with XAML files (like here), but also with images, videos, or any other element that must be located within a referenced assembly in the Silverlight application. You can find more information about the pack URI syntax online at http://www.galasoft.ch/sl4-packuri. Note that even though this page talks about pack URIs for WPF, the information is also valid for Silverlight.

Using external resource dictionaries is very useful when you have a large application with hundreds of resources and need to structure them in an organized manner. Choosing to use external assemblies or not depends on multiple factors, such as your application's complexity, the developer-designer workflow in your firm, and so forth.

Merging a Dictionary Within Another Dictionary

It is also possible to merge one or more resource dictionaries within another resource dictionary, using the exact same syntax. This can be convenient to create skins for the application. Listing 10.6 shows a resource dictionary named Classic.xaml and merging resource dictionaries contained in a folder named Classic. The Classic.xaml dictionary can then be merged into the application's resources, as shown in Listing 10.7).

LISTING 10.6 Creating a “Summary Resource Dictionary”

```
<ResourceDictionary
    xmlns="http://schemas.microsoft.com/winfx/2006/xaml/presentation"
    xmlns:x="http://schemas.microsoft.com/winfx/2006/xaml">
    <ResourceDictionary.MergedDictionaries>
        <ResourceDictionary Source="Classic/GlobalResources.xaml" />
        <ResourceDictionary Source="Classic/ButtonStyles.xaml" />
        <ResourceDictionary Source="Classic/Check boxStyles.xaml" />
        <ResourceDictionary Source="Classic/SliderStyles.xaml" />
    </ResourceDictionary.MergedDictionaries>
</ResourceDictionary>
```

To create a different skin (for example, named Glass), follow these steps:

1. Create a new folder named **Glass**.
2. Copy all the resource dictionaries from the Classic folder into the Glass folder.
3. Update the resources into the Glass folder to create the new skin.
4. Create a new resource dictionary named **Glass.xaml** and merge all the dictionaries from the Glass folder into this resource dictionary.
5. In App.xaml, remove the merged dictionary pointing to Classic.xaml and replace it with Glass.xaml.

Thanks to the summary resource dictionary, only one entry needs to be changed in the application to apply the new skin.

Mixing Resources and Merged Dictionaries

It is also possible to mix resources and merged dictionaries, as shown in Listing 10.7. This allows refining a skin with additional resources specific to that application only. You can also overwrite a resource contained in a merged dictionary by defining a new local resource with the exact same key, but with a different content. Of course, it is important to make sure that the types are compatible. For example, a `SolidColorBrush` can be overwritten with a `LinearGradientBrush`, because both are deriving from `Brush`.

LISTING 10.7 Mixing Resources and Merged Dictionaries

```
<Application.Resources>
    <ResourceDictionary>
        <ResourceDictionary.MergedDictionaries>
            <ResourceDictionary Source="Styles/Classic.xaml"/>
        </ResourceDictionary.MergedDictionaries>
```

```
        <SolidColorBrush x:Key="MainTextBrush"
                         Color="#FF333333" />

    </ResourceDictionary>
</Application.Resources>
```

Resolving Resources

After resources have been created and stored in resource dictionaries (either through the `Resources` property or in a merged resource dictionary), they can be assigned to an element's properties. A resource can be used in XAML markup or in code. Note that it makes no differences at all if a resource has been defined locally into the `Resources` property of an element (or of the application) directly or if it has been merged.

Setting a `StaticResource` in XAML

XAML can be extended by using objects called *markup extensions*. We have already encountered some of these objects: `Binding`, `RelativeSource`, `TemplateBinding` are such elements. In XAML, a markup extension is delimited by curly brackets, `{}`. Unlike WPF, though, Silverlight does not support custom markup extensions; this means that only the ones available in the framework can be used.

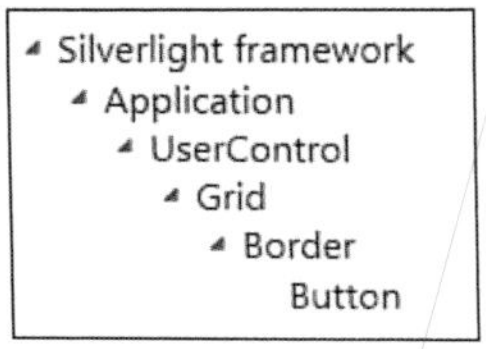

The `StaticResource` markup extension allows any property to be set to a resource in the XAML markup directly. An example was shown in Listing 10.5. When a `StaticResource` is set on a property, the XAML parser tries to locate the corresponding resource in the tree of elements, such as shown in Figure 10.2. When a property is set through a `StaticResource` in the `Button`, the XAML parser looks within the `Button`'s `Resources` property first for the given key. If the key is not found, the parser looks into the `Border`, then in the `Grid`, and then into the `UserControl`. If the resource is still not found, the application's global resources are searched. Finally, if nothing is found, the Silverlight framework itself contains default resources that can be searched. This method of looking into an element, then its parent, and then its parent's parent is called "walking the tree."

- Silverlight framework
  - Application
    - UserControl
      - Grid
        - Border
          - Button

FIGURE 10.2 Tree of elements.

WARNING

What About `DynamicResource`?

Developers coming from WPF and discovering Silverlight will notice that the `DynamicResource` markup extension is missing. Silverlight can only resolve resources statically, which makes dynamic skinning rather complicated. After a property has been set through a `StaticResource`, this resource cannot be modified anymore, and the only way to modify the property is by setting its value locally.

Using Default Styles and Templates

As mentioned earlier, the Silverlight framework contains a set of default resources. Most interesting, each standard control has a default style and template that defines its appearance. When these resources are not overwritten (as you will see later in this chapter), the default look and feel is used. There is a complete separation of functionality and appearance.

For custom controls, you saw in Chapter 3, "Extending Your Application with Controls," how to define their default appearance in a file named Generic.xaml included in the Themes folder. This is the same mechanism: The default style and template are resources that can be overwritten to modify the control's appearance.

Using Resources Set Later in the Markup

One limitation of the `StaticResource` markup extension is that it cannot "look forward" in the elements tree. For example, in Figure 10.2, if a resource is defined in the `Button`, a property of the `Border` cannot use it through `StaticResource`: When `Border` is parsed, the `Button`'s resources are not available yet to the parser. The resources must be structured in a way that prevents such "future reference" to occur.

Setting a Resource in Code

A resource can also be retrieved in code, by accessing a named element's `Resources` property directly. Similarly, the application's resources can also be searched, as shown in Listing 10.8.

LISTING 10.8 Accessing Resources in Code

```
1  public MainPage()
2  {
3      InitializeComponent();
4
5      TestButton.Background
6          = Resources["LightColorBrush"]
7          as Brush;
8      TestButton.Foreground
9          = Application.Current.Resources["MainTextBrush"]
10         as Brush;
11 }
```

- Lines 5 to 7 get a resource from the `UserControl`'s `Resources` property. If the resource does not exist, no exception is thrown. The property will simply be set to `null`.
- Lines 8 to 10 get a resource from the application's resources (defined or merged into the App.xaml file).

Note, however, that there is no built-in way to "walk the tree" and find resources defined in an element's parent, or its parent's parent, and so forth. In *Silverlight 2 Unleashed*, Chapter 24, Listings 24.25 and 24.26 show how to implement an equivalent to the WPF method `TryFindResource` that walks the tree and attempts to find a resource in the same way that `StaticResource` does. However, this recursive method can cause performance issues in the application. If possible, using `StaticResource` in markup is a better strategy, but it is not always possible.

Working with Resources in Blend

Expression Blend offers diverse features to facilitate operations on resources. When working in XAML, it is not easy to keep an overview of all the resources available in an application. Although Blend is not perfect yet and some resource management features are missing, the team is constantly working to improve the application and help users.

Merging a Resource Dictionary

Expression Blend makes it easy to merge a resource dictionary into an element's `Resources` property, as follows:

1. Create a Silverlight application in Expression Blend.
2. Right-click the Silverlight project in the Projects panel, and select Add New Item from the context menu.
3. Select a Resource Dictionary from the New Item dialog and name it **MainPageSkin.xaml**.
4. When a new resource dictionary is added into an application, Blend automatically merges it into the application's resources. However, we do not want this here; so, simply close the App.xaml file that Blend has opened, *without saving*.
5. Make sure that the MainPage.xaml is open and select the Resources tab in Blend.
6. Expand MainPage.xaml in the Resources tab and right-click the `UserControl`.
7. Expand Link to Resource Dictionary in the context menu and then select MainPageSkin.xaml, as shown in Figure 10.3.

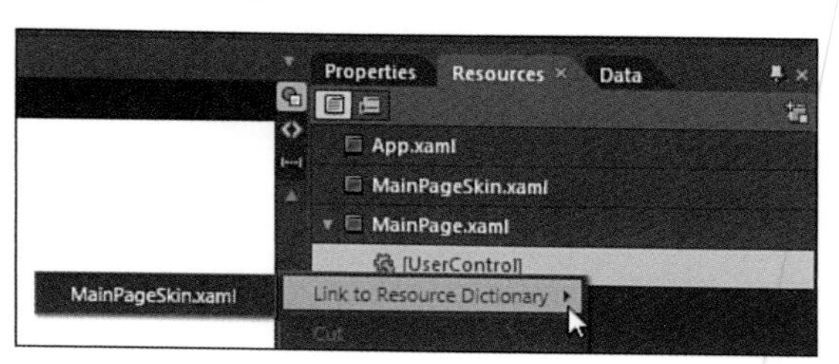

FIGURE 10.3 Merging resource dictionaries in Blend.

This creates the same markup in MainPage.xaml that you saw in Listing 10.4, and is a convenient way to merge multiple dictionaries. This method also works with dictionaries defined in referenced assemblies.

Resource dictionaries can also be merged into App.xaml or within another resource dictionary with the same context menu. Also, note that you can delete a link to a resource dictionary. To do this, expand the `UserControl` in the Resources tab, right-click the resource dictionary you want to remove, and select Delete from the context menu.

Creating New Resources

New resources can be created directly into Blend and saved to the resources of your choice (local or external) as follows:

1. Set the `Background` property of the main `Grid` (named `LayoutRoot`) to a `LinearGradientBrush`. If you are unsure how to do this, check *Silverlight 2 Unleashed,* Chapter 4.
2. In the Properties panel, with the LayoutRoot `Grid` selected, locate the `Background` property and click the small white peg next to the brush's preview. We saw this peg in Figure 6.4 and discussed its functionality.
3. Clicking the peg opens a context menu. Select Convert to New Resource from this menu.
4. In the Create Brush Resource dialog, enter a key for the new resource, and select a location to place it. This can be the Application, the current document (in which case you can select an element from the combo box as shown in Figure 10.4), or any resource dictionary merged into the current XAML file. You can even create a new resource dictionary directly from this dialog.

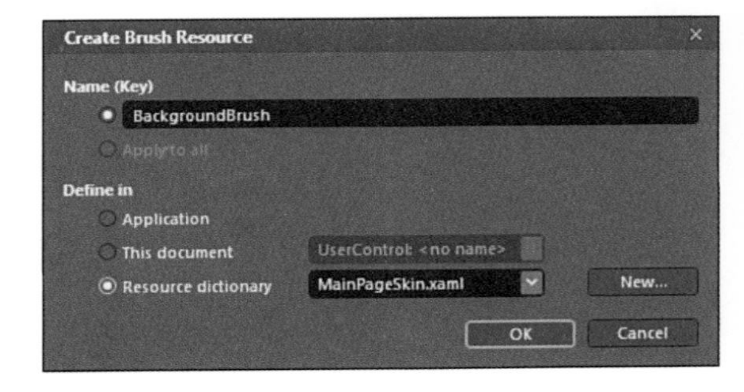

FIGURE 10.4 Creating a new resource.

This functionality is not limited to brushes. New resources can be created for properties of any type (as long as this type can be created in XAML), including styles and templates.

Selecting a Resource for a Property

The small advanced property peg allows selecting a resource for a given property: Locate the property in question in the Properties panel, click the peg to open a context menu, and then expand the Local Resources menu item. All the suitable resources from all the linked resource dictionaries are listed. However, there is no way to filter resources by name or to change the order in which they are sorted.

Using the Resources Panel

The way to manage resources in Blend is through the Resources panel. For example, if MainPage.xaml is open, the Resources panel displays MainPage.xaml, App.xaml, and a resource dictionary currently merged into MainPage.xaml and App.xaml. This offers a convenient view of all the resources that might be used by the current document.

Although the Resources panel speeds up work with resources, it also has a few shortcomings. For example, there is no way to search for a resource in this panel or to filter or sort the resources.

If you are unsure where a resource is located, use the Find in Files dialog (Ctrl+Shift+F). Also, when an element is selected in the Objects and Timeline panel, the small button circled in red in Figure 10.5 can be toggled to display only the resources used by the current element.

Editing Resources

Resources can be edited directly in the Resources panel. Figure 10.5 shows the editor used to modify a brush, but in fact many types of resources can be edited in this panel directly.

FIGURE 10.5 Editing resources in the Resources panel.

Renaming Resources

One of the most convenient features of the Resources panel is the ability to rename a resource and automatically update all the `StaticResource` references to that resource in the XAML markup. To do this, follow these steps:

1. Locate the resource you want to rename in the Resources panel.
2. Double-click the resource's name and edit the name as desired.
3. Press Enter.
4. Expression Blend displays a dialog shown in Figure 10.6. All the references to that particular resource are shown. You can choose to:

- **Update References**: This is the most common choice. Use this to automatically update all the references to the new name.
- **Break References**: This choice replaces the `StaticResource` extension by the explicit value where it was used. For example, for a `Background` property, the `Brush` is copied locally into the control that used the old resource.
- **Reset to Default Values**: The properties that used the old resource will simply be reset.
- **Don't Fix**: The existing `StaticResource` will keep using the old names. This is likely to break the application, but might prove useful in some scenarios.

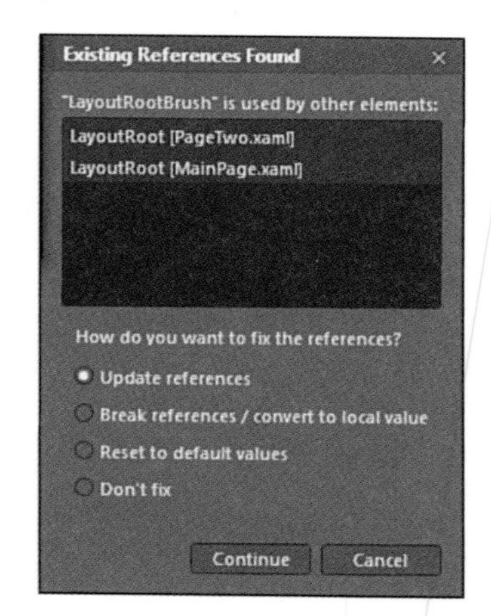

FIGURE 10.6 Updating a resource name.

If a resource is referenced in code (as you saw in Listing 10.8), it is not updated by Blend when the resource is renamed. If the application is using resources in code, a search-and-replace operation should be conducted.

Moving Resources

You can also use the Resources panel to move resources from one resource dictionary to another. This can prove quite useful to organize the application's resources in a more convenient way (for example, by moving local resources to an external resource dictionary).

To move a resource, just select it in the Resources panel, and then drag/drop it on the target dictionary. You can also reorder resources within a single dictionary (for example, grouping them by functionality).

Note that if a resource has XML comments for documentation purposes, they are not moved together with the resource. Generally speaking, it is better to avoid XML comments and to use meaningful resource names instead.

Cleaning Up Unused Resources

In large applications with many resources, a good way to improve the performance at startup and the memory usage is to remove unused resources from the application.

In Silverlight, unlike in WPF, all resources are instantiated and placed into memory at the time when they are parsed. For example, if the App.xaml file has multiple resource dictionaries merged into it, all the resources of all these dictionaries are created when the application starts. For a page, the creation occurs when the page is displayed. This can cause unnecessary delays. To improve this, analyzing your application's resources and removing the unused ones is a good practice.

Using the Pistachio Tool

The Pistachio tool was developed by Grant Hinkson and provides a visualization of XAML resources for Silverlight and WPF. Pistachio analyzes a CSPROJ file and the entire included XAML markup, and shows in which files each resource is used. It also helps to find unused resources that can be deleted safely, improving the performance without causing side effects in the application.

You can download Pistachio from http://www.galasoft.ch/sl4-pistachio. To install it, just unzip the content to a folder on your hard drive. Then start Pistachio.exe. To test the functionality, download a sample Silverlight application from http://www.galasoft.ch/sl4-resources.

To find out unused resources, follow these steps:

1. With Pistachio running, select the CSPROJ file containing the XAML files that you want to analyze.
2. Wait until the analysis is completed.

3. All the XAML files used in the application are shown, with a count of the resources as shown in Figure 10.7 (circled in red). The left number indicates the total number of resources; the right number is the number of used resources.

4. Select one of the XAML files. If a resource is used, its line can be expanded (as shown in Figure 10.7) and Pistachio shows in which XAML files it is in use.

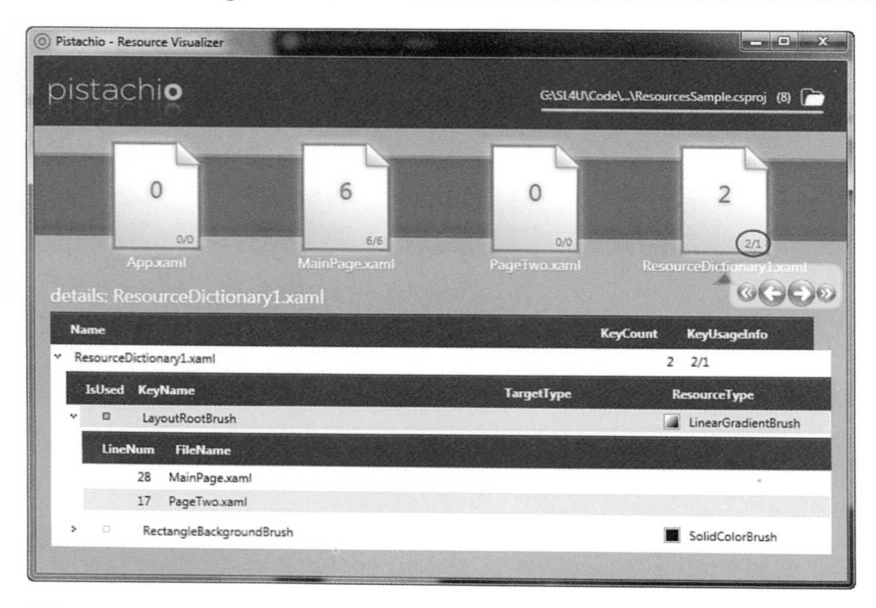

FIGURE 10.7 Pistachio.

Once an unused resource is located, it can be searched for in Visual Studio or in Expression Blend and deleted. Unfortunately, the current version of Pistachio lacks the ability to copy a resource name or to delete it directly from the tool. It does, however, speed up the process of looking for unused resources and understanding where each resource is used.

Styling a Control

As mentioned previously, there are a number similarities between Silverlight styles and the CSS that HTML pages are using. A `Style` in Silverlight contains a series of `Setter` elements, each with a dependency property name and a value. When the style is applied to a suitable element, the dependency properties defined in the style will have their value set correspondingly. One `Style` can be applied to multiple elements. However, in Chapter 5, "Understanding Dependency Properties," we discussed the system of precedence used to calculate the value of a dependency property. Styles are relatively low in the precedence list, so it is possible that the value of a `Setter` is overridden by another value of higher precedence.

Styles were already discussed in *Silverlight 2 Unleashed*, especially in Chapter 17, in the "Styling a Control" section. In this chapter, we concentrate on the additions made to the styling system in Silverlight 3 and 4.

Using Implicit Styles

Silverlight 4 introduces the possibility to create implicit styles. These styles are defined in resources like any other standard style, but they do not have a key, only a `TargetType` property. When an implicit style is available in the hierarchy of resources for a given control type (for example, a `Button`), it will automatically be applied to this control.

Although implicit styles can be handy to create a default look and feel for elements of an application, they also have a few inconveniencies:

- When implicit styles are applied, it can be really hard to find out where a given value comes from. This can make a designer's life really hard when he tries to "debug" a user interface and find out why the elements do not look like they should.
- In Silverlight, an implicit style cannot be used as the base for another style. (We will talk about `BasedOn` styles a little later in this chapter.) It is therefore impossible to define an implicit base style for all controls of a given type and then to refine a derived style for some of these controls.

For these reasons, implicit styles should be used with care in Silverlight.

Creating an Implicit Style in Blend

Expression Blend can be used to create an implicit style for a control, as follows:

1. Open a Silverlight application in Blend.
2. In the MainPage, add a `Button` control.
3. Make sure that the `Button` is selected in the Objects and Timeline panel, and then select Object, Edit Style, Create Empty from the menu.
4. In the Create Style Resource dialog, do not enter a key, but select the Apply to All radio button instead.
5. Select a location for the new implicit style and click OK.

Typically, implicit styles are placed in global resources (either in App.xaml, or in a resource dictionary that is merged into App.xaml) and thus made available for the whole application. An implicit style will be applied to a control only if the resource is "visible" from this control's location (through the hierarchy of resources that we discussed earlier in this chapter) and if no explicit style has been defined for that control.

Creating a Default Template

As mentioned, a Setter can be used to set any dependency property of an element, including the Template property, as shown in Listing 10.9.

LISTING 10.9 Implicit Style and Template

```
1  <Application.Resources>
2      <ControlTemplate x:Key="ButtonControlTemplate"
3                       TargetType="Button">
4          <Grid x:Name="Root">
5              <Ellipse x:Name="BackgroundEllipse"
6                       Fill="#FF930000"
7                       Stroke="#FFFF6B00"
8                       StrokeThickness="3" />
9
10             <ContentControl Content="{TemplateBinding Content}"
11                             VerticalAlignment="Center"
12                             HorizontalAlignment="Center"
13                             Foreground="#FFFF6B00"
14                             FontFamily="Showcard Gothic"
15                             FontSize="16" />
16         </Grid>
17     </ControlTemplate>
18
19     <Style TargetType="Button">
20         <Setter Property="Template"
21                 Value="{StaticResource ButtonControlTemplate}" />
22         <Setter Property="Cursor"
23                 Value="Hand" />
24     </Style>
25 </Application.Resources>
```

- The Style and ControlTemplate are placed into the application resources. This makes them global to the whole application. Unless they are overriden, this default look and feel will be used for all Button controls in the application.
- The ControlTemplate is defined before the Style. This is necessary, because a StaticResource is used on line 21 to set the Template property. As mentioned earlier, StaticResource can refer only to already parsed resources.
- Note that to keep things simple, this ControlTemplate does not specify any transitions from a state to another. In a real template, the XAML markup would be more complex.
- On line 19, the Style element is configured for a TargetType of Button. However, no key is entered. This is the only occasion where an element can be set in resources without a key. That makes it an implicit style.

Figure 10.8 shows a series of `Button` controls. Although they all use the same implicit `Style` and `ControlTemplate`, their `Height`, `Width`, and position are set individually.

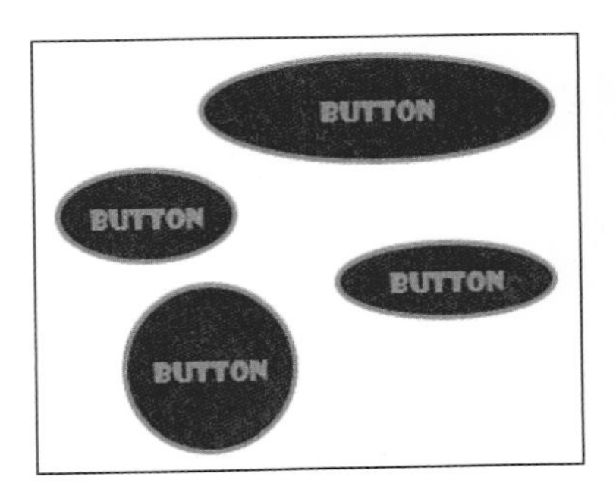

FIGURE 10.8 Buttons with implicit `Style` and `ControlTemplate`.

Creating a Hierarchy of Styles

A welcomed addition in Silverlight 3 was the possibility to base a style on another style, using the `BasedOn` property. This provides the possibility to create a base style for a control and then to refine it for various parts of the application. As mentioned earlier, however, an implicit style cannot be used as base style in Silverlight.

The `BasedOn` property can be set through a `StaticResource` as shown in Listing 10.10. In theory, there is no limitation to the depth of the hierarchy, but in practice it makes sense to avoid too many levels. Defining one basic `Style` and then one or two levels of refinement should suffice.

LISTING 10.10 Basing a `Style` on Another One

```
1  <ControlTemplate x:Key="ButtonControlTemplate"
2                   TargetType="Button">
3      <Grid>
4          <Ellipse Fill="{TemplateBinding Background}"
5                   Stroke="{TemplateBinding BorderBrush}" />
6
7          <ContentControl Content="{TemplateBinding Content}"
8                          VerticalAlignment="Center"
9                          HorizontalAlignment="Center"
10                         FontFamily="{TemplateBinding FontFamily}"
11                         FontSize="{TemplateBinding FontSize}"
12                         Foreground="{TemplateBinding Foreground}" />
13     </Grid>
14 </ControlTemplate>
15
16 <Style x:Key="ButtonStyle"
17        TargetType="Button">
18     <Setter Property="Template"
19             Value="{StaticResource ButtonControlTemplate}" />
20     <Setter Property="Background"
21             Value="Red" />
22     <Setter Property="BorderBrush"
23             Value="#FFF9A200" />
24     <Setter Property="Foreground"
25             Value="#FFF9A200" />
```

10

```
26       <Setter Property="FontSize"
27               Value="18" />
28       <Setter Property="FontFamily"
29               Value="Showcard Gothic" />
30   </Style>
31
32   <Style x:Key="ButtonDerivedStyle"
33          TargetType="Button"
34          BasedOn="{StaticResource ButtonStyle}">
35       <Setter Property="Background"
36               Value="#FF1800FF" />
37       <Setter Property="FontFamily"
38               Value="Snap ITC" />
39       <Setter Property="FontSize"
40               Value="24" />
41   </Style>
```

- The first `Style` defines a `ControlTemplate` and a set of properties defining the look and feel of a `Button` control. Note how, in the `ControlTemplate`, the `TemplateBinding` markup extension is used (for example, on line 4). This allows reusing the same template with different properties, when these are overridden in a derived `Style`.
- The second `Style` on lines 32 to 41 is based on the first `Style` (as set on line 34) and overrides the properties `Background`, `FontFamily`, and `FontSize`.
- Figure 10.9 shows two `Button` controls. The top one uses the first `Style`, while the second one uses the derived `Style`.

FIGURE 10.9 Base and derived styles for *Button* controls.

Creating a New Style in Blend

Expression Blend facilitates the creation of new styles for a given control, with the following steps:

1. In a Silverlight application, use local properties to give the control the desired look and feel.
2. When you are satisfied with this, create a new style by selecting Object, Edit Styles, Create Empty from the menu.
3. In the Create Style Resource dialog, enter a name for the new style, and place it within the current document.
4. Note that the Objects and Timeline panel now shows the `Style`, and not the UI elements hierarchy anymore. Any change you make in the Properties panel now applies to the `Style`, and not directly to the control.
5. Set Blend in split mode, using the button shown in Figure 2.16 (back in Chapter 2, "Setting Up and Discovering Your Environment").

6. Locate the control to which the `Style` is applied in the XAML markup.
7. Start moving the values from the control to the `Style`. For example, if the `Height` is set on the control directly, find the `Height` property in the Properties panel. Then click the Advanced Property Options peg and select Convert to Local Value from the context menu.

The last step creates a new `Setter` element in the `Style` for the `Height` property; it also removes the local `Height` attribute from the control. The value is now set through the `Style`, and not locally anymore. Repeat Step 7 until all the properties you want to move are now located within the `Style`. Note that some properties might need to remain local into the control element. Also, you might want to create a hierarchy of styles using the `BasedOn` property that was discussed earlier in this chapter.

TIP

In-Place or Out-of-Place Editing

Expression Blend does a great job editing controls when the style is located in the same document as the control it gets applied to. This allows "in-place editing," changing the appearance of the control in its context, next to all the other controls in the page, and with the background brush of the panel it is contained into.

When the style is located in an external resource dictionary, however, "out-of-place editing" is happening, and the control appears out of its context. This is much less convenient. To solve this, temporarily move the style from the external resource dictionary into the XAML file where the control is located. After the editing is done, you can move the style back where it belongs. This can be complicated and requires a lot of care.

Templating a Control

When a control's appearance should be changed radically, setting properties is not sufficient for the job. Instead, the `ControlTemplate` should be edited. *Silverlight 2 Unleashed* shows how to edit a relatively simple template, a `CheckBox` control into Expression Blend (Chapter 17, in the "Templating the Lookless Control" section). In the present chapter, you'll learn how to template a much more complex control, the `Scrollbar`. Then, we will see how to use a new feature of Expression Blend (introduced in Blend 3) allowing creating a control out of existing elements in the page.

Copying a Template in Blend

As mentioned before, the Silverlight framework comes with default styles and templates for all the controls it includes. This is the same for the Silverlight Toolkit and for any third-party controls set.

Creating a new template for a given control requires understanding the states and parts that this control presents. We already talked about this in Chapter 3. Creating a new template involves exposing the parts that the control will use to hook event handlers. In addition, a designer will create transitions between the states to improve the user experience.

Although it is possible to create a new control template completely in Visual Studio, it is a rather complex task. Expression Blend is the best-suited tool for the job, thanks to its ability to copy an existing template and modify it.

Checking Which States and Parts a Control Exposes

The states and parts are defined by attributes set on the class. You can learn how a control is built by checking the control's documentation in MSDN. For example, the Silverlight 4 `Scrollbar` control is documented at http://www.galasoft.ch/sl4-scrollbar. On this page, the states and the parts are documented as shown in Listing 10.11.

LISTING 10.11 States and Parts for the *Scrollbar* Control

```
[TemplateVisualStateAttribute(Name = "Disabled", GroupName = "CommonStates")]
[TemplatePartAttribute(Name = "HorizontalRoot", Type = typeof(FrameworkElement))]
[TemplatePartAttribute(Name = "HorizontalLargeIncrease", Type =
typeof(RepeatButton))]
[TemplatePartAttribute(Name = "HorizontalLargeDecrease", Type =
typeof(RepeatButton))]
[TemplatePartAttribute(Name = "HorizontalSmallDecrease", Type =
typeof(RepeatButton))]
[TemplatePartAttribute(Name = "HorizontalSmallIncrease", Type =
typeof(RepeatButton))]
[TemplatePartAttribute(Name = "HorizontalThumb", Type = typeof(Thumb))]
[TemplatePartAttribute(Name = "VerticalRoot", Type = typeof(FrameworkElement))]
[TemplatePartAttribute(Name = "VerticalLargeIncrease", Type = typeof(RepeatBut-
ton))]
[TemplatePartAttribute(Name = "VerticalLargeDecrease", Type = typeof(RepeatBut-
ton))]
[TemplatePartAttribute(Name = "VerticalSmallIncrease", Type = typeof(RepeatBut-
ton))]
[TemplatePartAttribute(Name = "VerticalSmallDecrease", Type = typeof(RepeatBut-
ton))]
[TemplatePartAttribute(Name = "VerticalThumb", Type = typeof(Thumb))]
[TemplateVisualStateAttribute(Name = "Normal", GroupName = "CommonStates")]
[TemplateVisualStateAttribute(Name = "MouseOver", GroupName = "CommonStates")]
public sealed class ScrollBar : RangeBase
```

Based on this listing, we learn a great deal about the control. For example, there are two different templates: one used for the `Scrollbar` in vertical orientation, and the other used when the `Scrollbar` is horizontal. We also learn that the horizontal template is composed of a root (of type `FrameworkElement`), four `RepeatButton` controls, and a `Thumb` control (the central element that can be dragged to modify the value).

Because the RepeatButton and Thumb control also have a default template, we can already foresee that creating a new template for the Scrollbar will also require new templates for these parts.

Copying the Template

A good way to start creating a new control template for a complex control is by copying and modifying the default template. You can do so easily in Expression Blend, as follows:

1. Create a new Silverlight application in Expression Blend and name it **ScrollbarTemplateSample**.
2. In the Assets tab, select a Scrollbar control and position it in MainPage.xaml. Note that the Scrollbar is vertical by default. Figure 10.10 shows the default appearance.
3. Right-click the control and select Edit Template, Edit a Copy from the context menu. A different option is to start with an empty control template. This, however, requires understanding already how the control works with its parts.
4. In the Create Style Resource dialog, enter the name **MyCustomScrollbarStyle** and click OK.

   Blend displays the new ControlTemplate that was just created and applied to the Scrollbar through the Style. No differences are visible on the screen because this is an exact copy of the default style and template. Figure 10.11 shows the vertical template expanded in the Objects and Timeline panel. A similar set of elements is available in the HorizontalRoot grid. Notice the small icon next to VerticalRoot, VerticalSmallDecrease, and other elements. This means that the element has been set as *a part* for this control. The names match the ones set through the TemplatePartAttribute in Listing 10.11. These parts have a special meaning for the control: For example, a Click event will be hooked to the VerticalSmallDecrease RepeatButton control.

5. Right-click the VerticalSmallDecrease element in the Objects and Timeline panel.

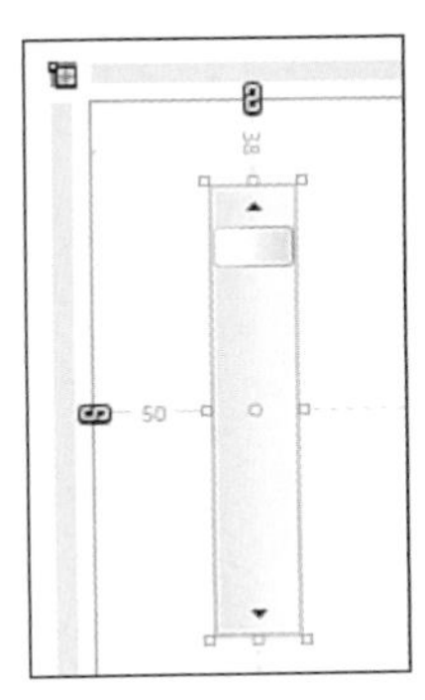

FIGURE 10.10 *Scrollbar* default template.

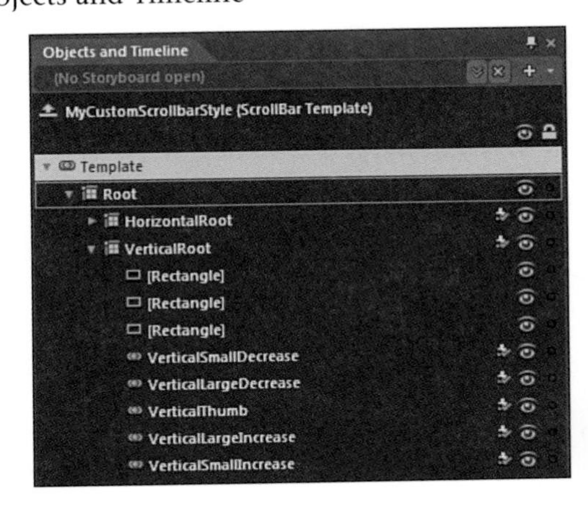

FIGURE 10.11 *VerticalRoot* grid and its elements.

6. Select Edit Template from the context menu. Notice that the menu item titled Edit Current is now available. This is because Blend didn't just copy the template for the `Scrollbar`, but also the template used by each part. In fact, if you check the XAML markup now, you will see that the copied style and all the templates represent about 660 lines of XAML.

7. Select Edit Current from the context menu. Blend now displays the `RepeatButton` control template in the Objects and Timeline panel.

> **TIP**
>
> **Setting the Template Through a Style**
>
> Expression Blend does not set the `Template` property of the `Scrollbar` directly, but instead creates a new `Style` with a `Setter` for this property. This is a good practice enabling designers to modify templates in an external resource dictionary without having to modify the MainPage.xaml file. Also, hooking the template through the style makes working visually in Blend much easier because changes to the style will automatically be visible on the template through the `TemplateBinding` elements.

8. Select the States panel in Blend.

9. On top of this panel, just below the pin and close buttons, click the button Turn on Transition Preview button (shown in Figure 10.12).

10. Select the `Rectangle` named `BackgroundMouseOver` in the Objects and Timeline panel.

11. Select the Normal state in the States panel, and then the MouseOver state. Notice how this `Rectangle`'s `Opacity` property changes from 0% to 100% in the Properties panel.

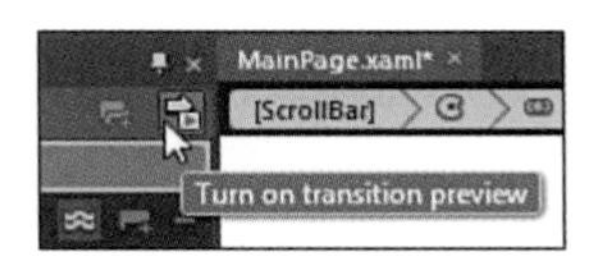

FIGURE 10.12 Turning on the transition preview.

12. Click the small arrow and plus sign (+) next to the Normal state, and select the Normal → MouseOver transition, as shown in Figure 10.13.

13. In the newly added transition, set a duration (for example, 0.2s, as in Figure 10.14).

FIGURE 10.13 Adding a transition.

14. Click the small EasingFunction button on the left of the duration text box. This is where you can select how the transition is played by Silverlight. By default, a linear transition is used, but you can select an acceleration or a deceleration for this transition. For example, Figure 10.14 shows a Cubic acceleration being selected.

15. Click the Normal state, and then click the MouseOver state. Observe how the transition is played by Blend. This allows you to select exactly which experience you want to create.

16. With the MouseOver state selected, modify the appearance of the `RepeatButton` to match the design that you want to implement. Blend records all the changes and creates an extrapolated transition matching the duration that was entered in Step 13.

FIGURE 10.14 Setting the transition duration and selecting an EasingFunction.

By editing all the templates and all the states/transitions in the `Scrollbar` control, you can completely modify its appearance. This is a long process that a designer (or what the Silverlight community calls an *integrator*; that is, someone sitting between a designer and a developer, and using Blend as his main tool) usually performs. Expression Blend helps a lot by displaying the visual representation of the control at all stages. Having at least one person on the team with a good knowledge of Blend is recommended if a custom user experience is desired.

Creating a Custom Easing Function

It is easy to implement a custom easing function with the following steps:

1. In the application, add a new class and name it MyOwnEasingFunction. You can do this in Expression Blend or in Visual Studio.

2. Modify the new class as shown in Listing 10.12. The custom function returns a power of the duration. The `Factor` property specifies which power will be used. Note that to use the `EasingFunctionBase` base class, you must add a **`using`** directive to `System.Windows.Media.Animation`.

3. Build your application, and then select the EasingFunction button shown in Figure 10.14.

4. Scroll to the bottom of the list. The new function should be visible.

5. Select the figure in the In column.

6. Modify the `Factor` property. Blend updates the preview of the function according to the value entered, as shown in Figure 10.15. This allows fine-tuning the transition.

FIGURE 10.15 Setting up the custom easing function.

LISTING 10.12 Custom Easing Function with a Property

```
public class MyOwnEasingFunction : EasingFunctionBase
{
    public double Factor
    {
        get; set;
    }

    protected override double EaseInCore(double normalizedTime)
    {
        return Math.Pow(normalizedTime, Factor);
    }
}
```

Making a Control in Blend

Another way to create a custom control template is to use the Make Into Control function available since Expression Blend 3. For example, a simple horizontal `Slider` control is easy to implement with the following steps:

1. Create a new Silverlight application in Expression Blend, name it **SliderTemplateSample** and open MainPage.xaml.
2. Create a horizontal `Grid`; set its `Height` to 30 and its `Width` to 450.
3. Create three columns in the `Grid`. Set the first column's `Width` to Auto, the second column's `Width` to 30 pixels, and the last column's `Width` to 1 Star. When you set the first column's `Width` to Auto, make sure that its `MinimumWidth` property is set to 0.
4. In the new `Grid`, create a thin `Rectangle` and set its `Fill` property to Gray, `Height` to 4 pixels, `Width` to Auto, `Column` to 0, `ColumnSpan` to 3, `HorizontalAlignment` to Stretch, `VerticalAlignment` to Center, and the `Margin` to 0.
5. In the same `Grid`, create an `Ellipse` and set its `Fill` property to Blue, `Height` and `Width` to Auto, `Column` to 1, `ColumnSpan` to 1, `HorizontalAlignment` and `VerticalAlignment` to Stretch, and `Margin` to 0.
6. Add a `RepeatButton` (available from the Assets tab, in the Controls/All category) to the first cell of the `Grid`. Set its `Opacity` to 0%, `Column` to 0, `ColumnSpan` to 1, `HorizontalAlignment` and `VerticalAlignment` to Stretch, and `Margin` to 0.
7. Add another `RepeatButton` to the last cell of the `Grid`. Set its `Opacity` to 0%, `Column` to 2, `ColumnSpan` to 1, `HorizontalAlignment` and `VerticalAlignment` to Stretch, and `Margin` to 0.
8. In the Objects and Timeline panel, right-click the new `Grid` and select Make into Control from the context menu.

The resulting group should look like Figure 10.16. The next step is to turn this Grid and its children into a Slider control, and to assign the parts, as follows:

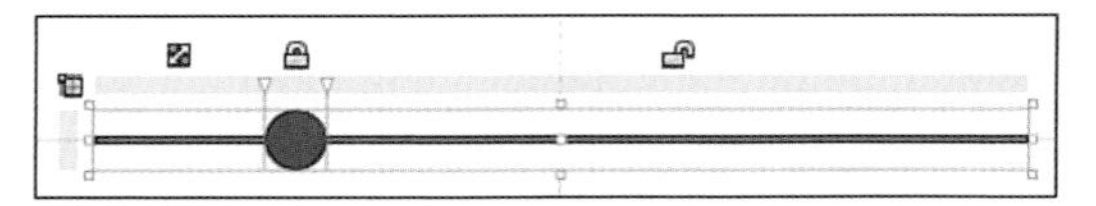

FIGURE 10.16 Grid and children.

9. In the Make into Control dialog, select a Slider control and enter the name **MySliderStyle**. As before, Blend creates a Style and set the Template property through a Setter.

10. Right-click the Grid and select Make into Part of Slider, HorizontalTemplate from the context menu.

11. Right-click the first RepeatButton and select Make into Part of Slider, HorizontalTrackLargeChangeDecreaseRepeatButton from the context menu.

12. Right-click the second RepeatButton and select Make into Part of Slider, HorizontalTrackLargeChangeIncreaseRepeatButton from the context menu.

13. Right-click the Ellipse and select Make into Part of Slider, HorizontalThumb from the context menu.

14. In the Make into Part dialog, enter the name **MyHorizontalThumbStyle** for the Thumb's Style, and click OK.

With Steps 13 and 14, Blend creates a new ControlTemplate for the Thumb control. This is why the procedure was slightly different than for both RepeatButton elements and for the Grid.

Blend's scope is now set into the Thumb template; return the scope to the MainPage by clicking twice on the "return scope" button (just below the Objects and Timeline panel title). The page now displays a Slider control where before the new Grid and its children were located. You can set the Slider's properties, such as the Maximum, Minimum, and Value. The Thumb control (templated as a blue Ellipse) moves according to these values. In addition, the application can be run and the Thumb be dragged to modify the Slider's Value.

Applying a Theme

Microsoft provides a number of themes that can be applied to an application. These themes are available in the Silverlight toolkit at http://www.galasoft.ch/sl4-themes.

Applying a theme to the whole application or to selected parts is easy following the indications provided on the themes' home page. Figure 10.17 shows 3 of the currently 11 available themes side by side: Expression Dark, Bubble Cream, and Rainier Orange.

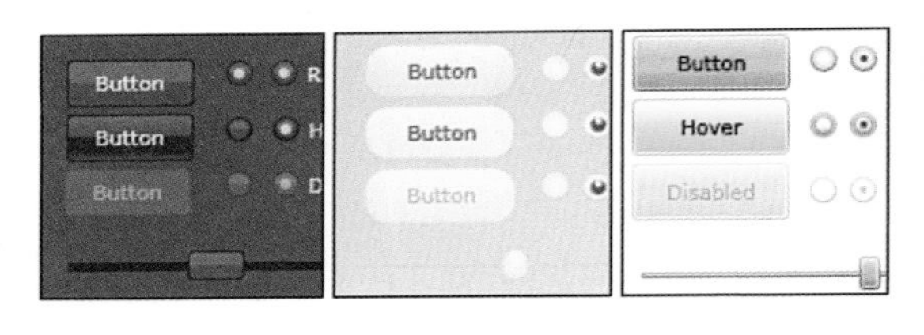

FIGURE 10.17 Three different themes.

Using a theme for a Silverlight application can be a good compromise when a designer is not available or when Expression Blend cannot be used to create a custom user experience. In addition, Microsoft regularly releases new themes in the latest versions of the Silverlight toolkit, which makes it really easy to change the application's appearance at less cost.

Summary

This chapter provided an overview of a Silverlight integrator's work with Visual Studio and especially Expression Blend.

First, we discussed resources and the new functionalities in Silverlight 3 and Silverlight 4, such as the ability to use external resource dictionaries, either in the same assembly or in an external DLL. You saw how resources are resolved in XAML and in code. Then we took a good look at resources in Expression Blend, a tool that offers a lot of helper functions to make this process easier.

We finished our overview of resources with the tool Pistachio, which helps to clean up unused resources and thus speeds up the startup of Silverlight applications and the opening of new pages.

Later, we talked about styles, in particular the new functions in Silverlight 3 and 4. The ability to create a hierarchy of styles with the `BasedOn` property was introduced in Silverlight 3. The implicit styles were added in Silverlight 4, and you saw how to use them to create a default look and feel for a type of controls.

Next, we discussed control templates, and how to copy a default template in Expression Blend to modify its parts and the transitions between the states. We also discussed how to create custom easing functions to animate the transitions according to any mathematical function. Finally, you saw how to use the Make into Control function introduced in Blend 3 to create a brand new `Style` and `ControlTemplate` for a control.

In the last section, we talked about the themes provided in the Silverlight toolkit that provide a way to change the appearance of an application. Although not allowing advanced customization of the user interface, it can be very useful for applications where a graphics designer or an integrator is not available.

In the next chapter, we continue our exploration of Blend and discuss advanced techniques to improve the Silverlight application user experience.

CHAPTER 11

Mastering Expression Blend

IN THIS CHAPTER, WE WILL:

- Understand what Expression Blend is and why using it is necessary sometimes.
- See how an application can be made "blendable," that is, how it can be developed to improve the experience in Expression Blend to the maximum.
- Talk about design time data and why it is important to improve the designer-developer workflow.
- Use and implement Blend Triggers, Actions and Behaviors.

In Chapter 10, "Creating Resources, Styles, and Templates," you saw how Expression Blend can be used to visually design styles and templates applied to controls and to manage resources. Blend is a fantastic visual tool, very different from the Visual Studio designer experience that "classic" application developers are used to (for example, in Windows Forms or ASP.NET technologies).

In this chapter, we take a deeper look at Expression Blend, and you'll learn some of the techniques that user experience integrators have developed in their profession.

To setup Expression Blend and its options, refer to *Silverlight 2 Unleashed*, Chapter 4.

What Is Blend, Exactly?

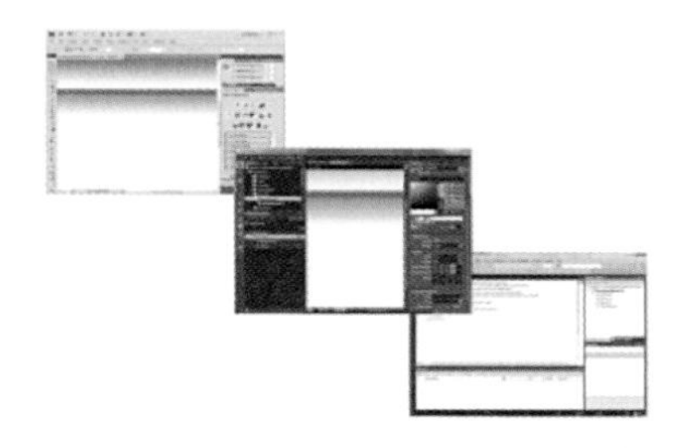

FIGURE 11.1 Expression Blend, between Photoshop and Visual Studio.

The position of Expression Blend in the designer-developer workflow is somewhat in the middle, as shown in Figure 11.1. Even though Blend was initially intended as a designer tool, it is fair to say that many developers are using it nowadays.

Working as a Tool for Integrators

In fact, many firms specializing in Silverlight development adopt a new role between the designer and the developer, dubbed the *integrator, user experience developer*, or *production designer*. Often, this role is fulfilled by a part-time developer with a good eye for design or by a part-time designer with a strong interest in code.

The integrator sits between the traditional designers and the developers and uses his skills to enhance the communication between these two very different professions. Expression Blend sits similarly between the designers' classic tools (such as Adobe Photoshop) and the developers' development environment (such as Visual Studio): It is used to visually design a client application, but it can also edit code, build and run the application, create simulated data, and so forth.

The tools that designers traditionally use to create comps are static and create deliverables that are completely separate from the final application. This used to make the process of *integrating* the visual assets (brushes, icons, shapes, and so on) cumbersome and difficult: The developer needs to run the application often to visualize the latest changes, which takes a lot of time, especially if he is working on a page that requires multiple steps to be displayed. Connecting the application to live data is not always possible in the development stage, either because it is too slow or because the services don't exist yet when the client is developed. In all these situations, Blend is an invaluable tool to assist the developer, the designer, and of course, the integrator.

Editing XAML Markup

Most important, the output that Blend creates is XAML markup. There is nothing hidden; every single tag and property can be visualized in the XAML editor (in Blend, in Visual Studio **or even in Notepad**) and modified manually if needed. In fact, Blend and Visual Studio work with the exact same files (SLN file for the solution, CSPROJ files for the C# projects, XAML and CS files for the markup and the code, and so on). The same project can be opened in Blend and in Studio at the same time, and you can switch from one environment to the other depending on the task at hand.

When Should You Use User Controls?

In Chapter 3, "Extending Your Application with Controls," you saw the difference between *custom controls* and *user controls*. The latter are typically used to separate a page is smaller, more manageable units. It is a good practice to split the application in smaller files and to edit these separately if possible.

Making an Application Blend

Silverlight applications work with data. There is a multitude of kinds of data, a thousand ways to represent this data, and a large number of possible data sources. For example, a video stream coming from a streaming server acts very differently than an XML document with customer information. During the integration process, Expression Blend will attempt to load and execute some of the code from the Silverlight application. In some cases, Blend is able to load the data and to display it correctly, as you already saw in previous chapters using the MVVM pattern.

In other cases, however, Blend fails at showing data. For example, sometimes the code behind is not executed at all, as you will see later in this chapter. Other sections of the code may cause an exception when run in the context of Expression Blend. In those cases, it is impossible to design the screens visually. We say that the application is not *blendable* anymore.

> **TIP**
>
> **Using the Visual Studio Designer**
>
> Because the Visual Studio designer shares much of its architecture with Expression Blend, the restrictions, patterns, and workarounds that are exposed here also apply to this editor.

Why Is Some Code Not Executed?

Even though Expression Blend loads and runs the XAML markup and some of the Silverlight code, the code behind of the user control that is being edited (the code file that is attached to most XAML files) is ignored by Blend (although Blend executes the code-behind when the control is used as part of another user control). If, for instance, a collection of items is exposed as a user control's property, initialized in the constructor, and data bound to a `ListBox` in XAML, the view will remain empty in Blend when the parent user control is being edited because the items are never created. Similarly, dependency properties in the edited user control's code-behind are not initialized.

This implementation choice can seem weird, but it prevents many issues (for example, when code-behind is used to trigger animations that would cause the user interface to get into an unwanted state in Expression Blend).

Why Does Some Code Fail?

Other code is, however, executed by Expression Blend:

- Custom controls are instantiated; their constructor and any method that it uses are run by Expression Blend.
- The resources placed in a page or a control are created by Blend. Here, too, the constructor is executed, as well as any methods that it uses.
- If a data binding uses a converter (as in Chapter 6, "Working with Data: Binding, Grouping, Sorting, and Filtering"), the `Convert` (or the `ConvertBack`) method is executed when the binding is evaluated.

In certain conditions, it is possible that this code causes an exception in Expression Blend but not when the application runs standalone. When Blend loads the application's code into its own context, some calls do not work the same. For instance, Blend does not allow calling a web service (such as Windows Communication Foundation, WCF) or executing web requests (through the `WebClient` class). Such code will cause an exception in the designer, as shown in Figure 11.2. There are other operations that will cause a similar exception in the design surface. All can be traced to the same cause: The context in which Blend executes the code is different from the runtime.

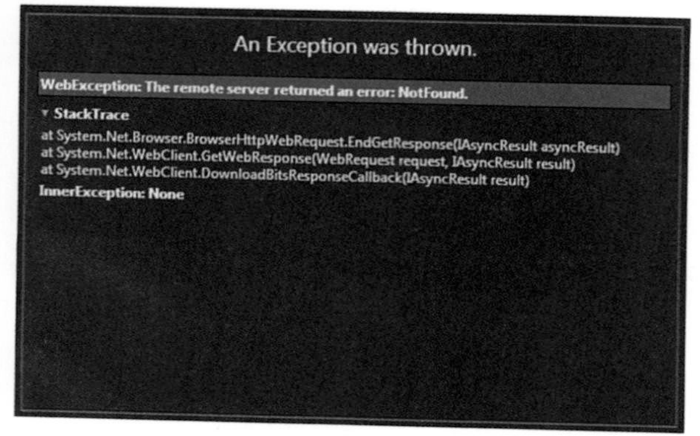

FIGURE 11.2 Exception in Blend's design surface.

Detecting the Cause of an Exception

To make the application *blendable* again (that is, to avoid the exception on the design surface), it is necessary to detect what code caused it, just as we would do when the application runs in the web browser. However, Expression Blend does not offer a debugger like Visual Studio does.

To find the cause of the error, we will take advantage of the fact that Blend is a WPF application and that the Visual Studio debugger can be attached to other processes, as the following steps show:

1. Close the page that is causing the exception in Blend.

> **TIP**
>
> **Setting an Image's `Source` Property**
>
> Even though Blend cannot execute web requests, an image's `Source` property may be set to a web URI, which will cause it to be downloaded and displayed on the design surface. This does not cause an error.

> **TIP**
>
> **Opening a Closed Panel in Blend**
>
> If an Expression Blend panel mentioned in this chapter (such as Assets, Objects and Timeline, Properties, and so on) isn't visible, you can reopen it through the Window menu.

2. (If the project was not open in Studio already) In Blend's Projects panel, right-click the Solution and select Edit in Visual Studio from the context menu. This starts Visual Studio and opens the exact same Solution and projects in Studio.

3. In Visual Studio, select Debug, Attach to Process. This opens the dialog shown in Figure 11.3.

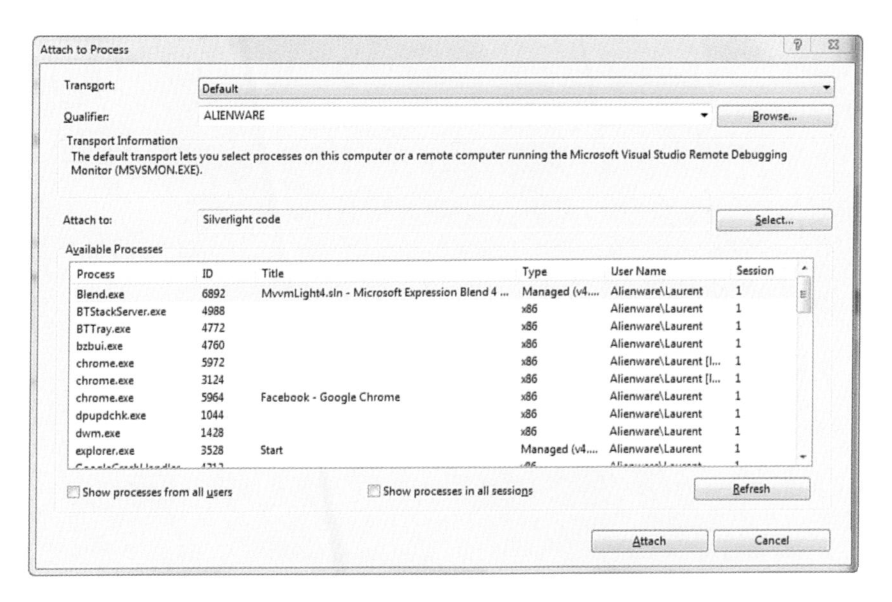

FIGURE 11.3 The Attach to Process dialog.

4. Locate the instance of Blend that has the exception. If you see multiple processes named Blend.exe, take a close look at the title to make sure that you select the correct one.

5. Make sure that the debugger is configured to be attached to Silverlight code. If this is not the case, click the Select button and choose Silverlight in the Debug These Code Types box.

6. Click the Attach button.

7. Set a few breakpoints in the code. If you use the MVVM pattern we discussed in Chapter 7, "Understanding the Model-View-ViewModel Pattern," a good entry point is the view-model's constructor. If your XAML page uses converters, you can also place a breakpoint in the `Convert` and `ConvertBack` methods. If there are custom controls on the page, and you have access to their code, place a breakpoint in the control's constructor, too.

8. Return to Expression Blend and open the page that was throwing the exception. This will cause the execution to break in Visual Studio. You can then debug the code step by step using the F10 and F11 keys. You can also inspect variables and properties and so forth.

This technique requires a bit of intuition and can be a kind of detective work, but at least it provides a modern debugging tool to assist you.

Isolating Code in Design Mode

After the offending code has been detected, it needs to be isolated in design mode. The Silverlight framework provides a convenient utility class to do this: the `DesignerProperties` class and its `IsInDesignTool` static property, as shown in Listing 11.1.

LISTING 11.1 Using the `IsInDesignTool` Property

```
1  public class MainViewModel : ViewModelBase
2  {
3      public const string HtmlStringPropertyName = "HtmlString";
4      private string _html;
5
6      public string HtmlString
7      {
8          get { return _html; }
9
10         set
11         {
12             if (_html == value)
13             {
14                 return;
15             }
16
17             _html = value;
18             RaisePropertyChanged(HtmlStringPropertyName);
19         }
20     }
21
22     public MainViewModel()
23     {
24         if (DesignerProperties.IsInDesignTool)
25         {
26             HtmlString = "<div>This is design time</div>";
27         }
28         else
29         {
30             var client = new WebClient();
31             client.DownloadStringCompleted += (s, e) =>
32             {
33                 HtmlString = ParseHtmlString(e.Result);
34             };
35
36             client.DownloadStringAsync(
```

```
37                    new Uri("http://www.galasoft.ch"));
38            }
39        }
40
41        private string ParseHtmlString(string html)
42        {
43            // ...
44        }
45    }
```

- This class is a view-model, as you saw in Chapter 7. However, the code used to make this class blendable can also be used in other classes, such as converters or custom controls.
- On lines 3 to 20, a bindable property is declared. In XAML, a text element (for example, the `Text` property of a `TextBox`) can be data bound to the `HtmlString` property. The UI will automatically be updated when `HtmlString` is changed.
- In the `MainViewModel` constructor on line 24, we check whether the code is running in Expression Blend or the Visual Studio designer. The `DesignerProperties.IsInDesignTool` property returns `true` if that is the case.
- On line 26, the `HtmlString` property is set to a dummy string. We talk about *design-time data*. This is the data that will be displayed in the design surface, and which will help the designer to visualize the changes that he is making.
- On lines 30 to 37, the `WebClient` class is used to fetch the content of a URL from the Web. This code would cause an error if run into Expression Blend. This is why it is isolated this way.

Note that to keep things simple, the `ParseHtmlString` method is not implemented here.

Improving the Separation

This implementation is handy for small applications because it rapidly provides design data for the integrator working in Blend. However, mixing design data (as we did on line 26 of Listing 11.1) with the runtime implementation is not very clean.

Instead, a cleaner implementation would use a high-level service abstracted by an interface (such as the `ICustomerServiceProxy` in Listing 7.6) and *injected* into the view-model's constructor (as in Listing 7.10).

Because the view-model knows only the interface and not the actual implementation of the service, it is easy to build a design time version of the service that does not cause the exception in Blend. This technique is very powerful because it allows creating any kind of data in code and provides a very lifelike visualization on Blend's design surface. For more information and a sample, check this author's session at MIX 2010 (http://www.galasoft.ch/sl4-mix10).

Creating Design Time Data in Blend

Creating a design-time service and passing it to the view-model works great when the data is quite complex. It does, however, require a developer to write code and takes some time to set up. Although it is very clean and creates a wonderful separation of concerns, it is not always applicable for a simple application, or when the team of developers is very busy with other tasks.

To solve this, Expression Blend 4 offers the possibility to create design-time data in three different ways.

Creating Design Time Data Manually

If the objects Blend needs to simulate at design time are fairly simple, the data can be created manually as follows:

1. Create a new application and name it **DesignTimeDataSample**.
2. Click the Data panel in Blend.
3. Click the small button on the top right of the Data panel showing a database with a plus sign (+). There are two such buttons; select the one circled in red in Figure 11.4.
4. From the context menu, select New Sample Data.
5. In the New Sample Data dialog, enter a name for the sample data source.
6. Choose where the sample data should be added. You can choose either the Project (in which case the sample data will be available in the whole application) or This Document (in which case it will be local to the current XAML file).

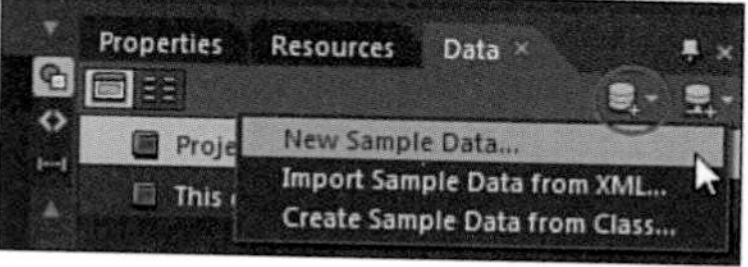

FIGURE 11.4 Creating new sample data.

7. If the design-time data should also be used at runtime, check the Enable Sample Data When Running check box. This is useful when the runtime data is not available yet but you want to test the application and visualize data in the UI anyway. For now, leave the check box checked.

   A new sample data source appears in the Data panel, as shown in Figure 11.5.

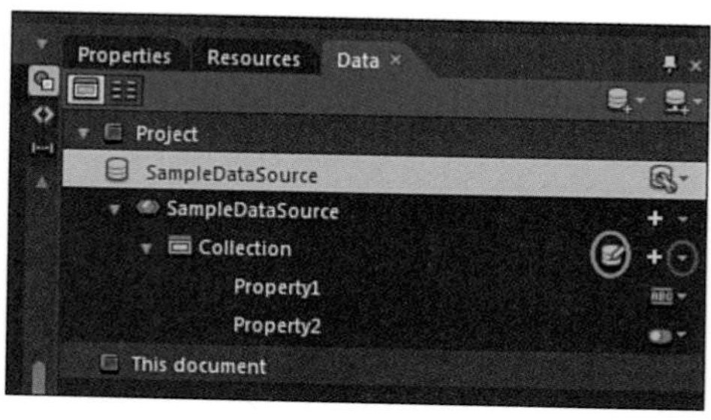

FIGURE 11.5 New sample data source.

The sample data source currently has one collection. Each item in this collection has two properties by default. The first (named Property1) is a string, and the second (Property2) is a Boolean. To add a new property to the collection, follow these steps:

1. Click the small arrow (circled in red in Figure 11.5) and open the menu.
2. You can select a simple property, a complex property (for example, to simulate an object containing other properties), or a collection of properties (to simulate arrays or lists). This allows you to simulate any kind and shape of data. For now, select a simple property.
3. Name the property **Birthday**.
4. Click the small ABC icon (the one that shows Change Property Type when you hover over it). This opens another menu in which the property can be configured. The following types are available:

   - **String**: Creates a text property in various formats: Lorem ipsum (random text), Address, Color, Company Name, Date, Email, Name, Phone Number, Price, Time, URL. For random text, the number of words and the maximum length of each word can also be specified.
   - **Number**: Generates a number according to the digits (length) specified. For example, a length of 2 creates numbers between 10 and 99.
   - **Boolean**: Generates true or false at random.
   - **Image**: Selects a random image from a folder. If no custom folder is specified, Blend adds a number of stock images to the project.

5. In this case, select the `String` type and change its format to be a `Date`.
6. Double-click the property name Property1 and change this to **CustomerName**. Then change the type of this string property to be a `Name`.
7. Double-click the property name Property2 and change this to **Gender**. We will use true for female, and false for male.
8. Add a new property and name it **Picture**. Change the property's type to be an `Image`. Do not specify a folder for the images, so that Blend uses the stock ones.
9. Drag the collection onto the design surface. Blend displays a ToolTip mentioning that it will create a new `ListBox` and data bind its `ItemsSource` property to the collection. After you drop the collection, a data template is automatically created and the `ListBox` displays the items as shown in Figure 11.6. The new `ListBox` can be set to fill the whole space by right-clicking on it and selecting Auto Size, Fill from the context menu.
10. The same data is used at runtime (as we specified), which can be verified by pressing F5 to run the application.

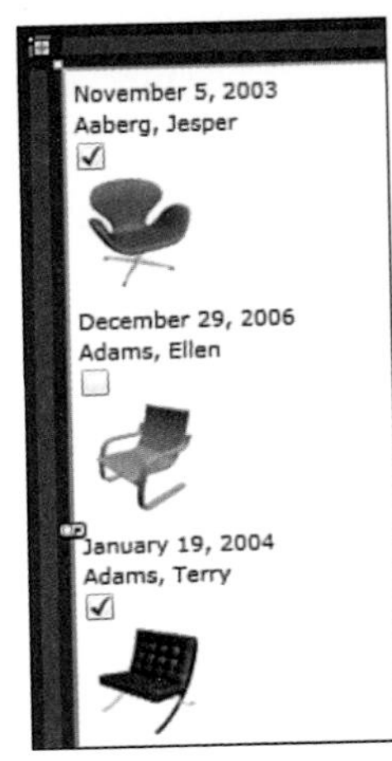

FIGURE 11.6 Design-time data in the `ListBox`.

Changing the Template

Obviously, the data template that Blend generated is not very satisfying. It is easy to change it with the following steps:

1. Select the `ListBox` in the Objects and Timeline panel.
2. Select Object, Edit Additional Templates, Edit Generated Template (ItemTemplate), Edit Current. This opens the data template in Expression Blend.
3. Modify the template to suit the needs of your application.

Changing the Data

It is also possible to edit the data even after the collection has been data bound, as follows:

1. In the Data panel, press the small database icon on the Collection line (circled in green in Figure 11.5). This opens a new dialog shown in Figure 11.7 where all the created sample data is visible.

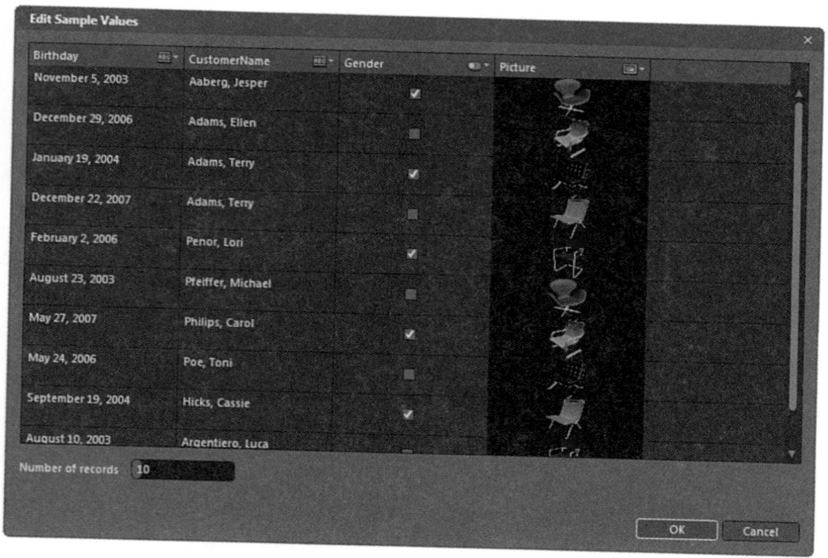

FIGURE 11.7 Editing the sample data.

2. To edit a string value (such as the Birthday or the CustomerName), select the value in the grid and type the new value.
3. To edit an image, double-click the image in the grid and select a new image. Note that you can also click the small picture icon in the grid's header and select a folder in which you placed sample images. Blend will add these images to the project and use them rather than the stock ones.

4. It is also possible to create more or fewer rows of data by editing the Number of Records field.

The Create Sample Data functionality enables a designer to create sample data in a fast way. However, if the data set is very complex, or if the shape of the data changes often, this is not the most efficient way to work.

Importing Design-Time Data from XML

Blend also offers the possibility to import sample XML data. This can be the output of an application or data created by a developer to help the design process. Such a sample XML file is shown in Listing 11.2.

LISTING 11.2 Sample XML Data File

```
<?xml version="1.0" encoding="utf-8"?>
<customers>
    <customer Name="Laurent Bugnion"
              Birthday="1971/4/13"
              Gender="false"
              Picture="pics/laurent.png" />
    <customer Name="Alise Bugnion"
              Birthday="2001/10/18"
              Gender="true"
              Picture="pics/alise.png" />
    <customer Name="Laeticia Bugnion"
              Birthday="2004/3/29"
              Gender="true"
              Picture="pics/laeticia.png" />
    <customer Name="Chi Meei Bugnion"
              Birthday="1969/12/25"
              Gender="true"
              Picture="pics/chimeei.png" />
</customers>
```

To import the data file, follow these steps:

1. Click the icon with the ToolTip Create Sample Data, located on top of the Data panel (shown in Figure 11.4).
2. Select Import Sample Data from XML.
3. In the Import Sample Data from XML dialog, browse to locate to XML file stored on your hard disk. Note that it is also possible to enter the URL of a web file or the path of an XML file already in your project.

4. Just as before, specify whether the data should be used when the application is running. You will learn later in this chapter how to replace the sample data with real data when it is ready.

5. When you click OK, a new sample data source is created in the Data panel. Drag the collection (named customerCollection after the customer item shown in Listing 11.2) onto the `ListBox` and drop it to bind its `ItemsSource` property to the list of data and to create a `DataTemplate`.

Note that the `Picture` property is not rendered by an `Image` control as it was before. Instead, a `TextBlock` is used. This is because Blend has no way to know in advance how to handle this string. Also, the corresponding pictures are not included in the project. This can be changed with the following steps:

1. In the Objects and Timeline panel, right-click the Silverlight project and select Add New Folder from the context menu.
2. Name the new folder **pics** just like the XML data shows.
3. Right-click the pics folder, and select Add Existing Item from the context menu.
4. Add four sample pictures and name them just like in the XML data file that was imported (in this case, Laurent.png, Alise.png, Laeticia.png and ChiMeei.png).
5. Select the `ListBox`, and then select Object, Edit Additional Templates, Edit Generated Template (ItemTemplate), Edit Current.
6. Select the last `TextBlock`, which shows the path to the picture for the selected customer, and delete it.
7. In the Assets tab, select the `Image` control. To find it easily, type the word **image** in the Search box.
8. Make sure that the root `StackPanel` is selected in the `ItemTemplate` in the Objects and Timeline panel, and then double-click the `Image` control in the Assets panel. This adds a new image to the template.
9. With the `Image` selected, open the Properties panel.
10. Locate the `Source` property, and click the small peg on the right of the field, with the ToolTip reading Advanced Properties.
11. In the menu, select Data Binding.
12. In the Create Data Binding dialog shown in Figure 11.8, select the Picture property and click OK. You should now see the pictures you added to the project appear in the `ListBox`.

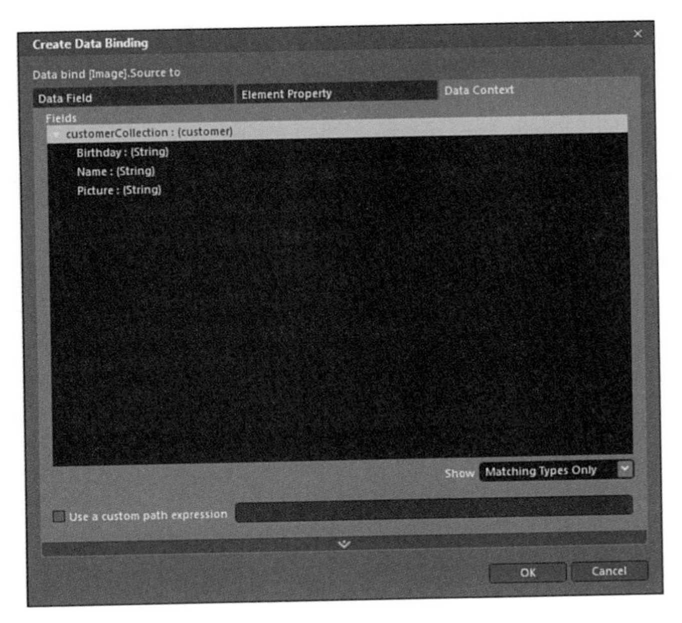

FIGURE 11.8 Create Data Binding dialog.

Creating Design-Time Data from a Class

The last possibility to create design-time data in Expression Blend was added in Blend 4. Instead of using a manual process or an XML file to create the data, it is possible to specify a data class to Expression Blend and to let it inspect that class and create design data accordingly.

This way of doing is very convenient when the application's user interface is data bound to data classes, especially when using the MVVM pattern discussed in Chapter 7. To test this, follow these steps:

1. Create a new Silverlight application in Blend and name it **DesignTimeClassSample**.
2. Right-click the Silverlight project in the Objects and Timeline and select Add New Folder from the context menu.
3. Name the new folder **ViewModel**.
4. Right-click the ViewModel folder and select Add New Item from the context menu.
5. In the New Item dialog, select a class and name it **ViewModelBase.cs**. Then click OK.
6. Implement the `ViewModelBase` class as shown in Listing 11.3. You need to add a `using` statement at the top of the page: `using System.ComponentModel`.

LISTING 11.3 ViewModelBase Class

```
public class ViewModelBase : INotifyPropertyChanged
{
    public event PropertyChangedEventHandler PropertyChanged;

    public void RaisePropertyChanged(string propertyName)
    {
        if (PropertyChanged != null)
        {
            PropertyChanged(
                this,
                new PropertyChangedEventArgs(propertyName));
        }
    }
}
```

7. Add a new class to the ViewModel folder and name it **MainViewModel.cs**. Implement this class as shown in Listing 11.4. Here, you need to add `using System.Collections.ObjectModel`.

LISTING 11.4 MainViewModel Class

```
public class MainViewModel : ViewModelBase
{
    public ObservableCollection<CustomerViewModel> Customers
    {
        get;
        set;
    }
}
```

8. Add another class to the ViewModel folder and name it **CustomerViewModel.cs**. The code for this class is shown in Listing 11.5.

LISTING 11.5 CustomerViewModel Class

```
public class CustomerViewModel : ViewModelBase
{
    public const string NamePropertyName = "Name";
    private string _name = string.Empty;

    public string Name
    {
        get { return _name; }
        set
```

```
        {
            if (_name == value)
            {
                return;
            }

            _name = value;
            RaisePropertyChanged(NamePropertyName);
        }
    }

    public const string BirthdayPropertyName = "Birthday";
    private DateTime _birthday = DateTime.MinValue;

    public DateTime Birthday
    {
        get { return _birthday; }
        set
        {
            if (_birthday == value)
            {
                return;
            }

            _birthday = value;
            RaisePropertyChanged(BirthdayPropertyName);
        }
    }
}
```

9. Build the application by pressing Ctrl+Shift+B.
10. Open MainPage.xaml. In the Data panel, press the icon circled in red in Figure 11.4, and select Create Sample Data from Class from the menu.
11. In the Create Sample Data from Class dialog, locate and select the MainViewModel class and click OK.
12. A new entry named MainViewModelSampleData is created in the Data panel. Expand this and the MainViewModel it contains, and locate the property named Customers (shown in Figure 11.9).
13. Drag the Customers collection onto the LayoutRoot grid in MainPage.xaml.

This last step creates a new `ListBox`, which is populated as before by design-time data, and a new `DataTemplate`. Note, however, the difference from the previous methods: The design data created by inspecting a data class is available only at design time. If you run the application now, the ListBox will remain empty. Also, Blend was not able to format the Name property as a name, and used random text instead. This can be changed in the Data panel.

Disadvantages of Using Expression Blend to Generate Design-Time Data

Using Expression Blend to generate design-time data (as opposed to creating the design data in a view-model or in a design data service) is a very nice automated way to provide data to the designer in charge of creating the user interface. However, there are a few disadvantages to this method:

- If the shape of the data changes often (for example, because the services are not completely implemented yet), it can be difficult to keep the design-time data and the runtime data in sync. In such a case, it is easier to leave the responsibility of the data in the hands of developers working in Visual Studio.
- If the data is complex, requiring that a designer generate it in Expression Blend can be a difficult matter. In such a case, too, it might be easier to leave a developer in charge of the data, runtime and design time.
- When design-time data is generated, Expression Blend adds files in the project. Removing these files in the production application is an additional step.

On the other hand, having a tool integrated in Expression Blend to create design data is an advantage for designers because they rely less on developers to make progress. This can help a lot, especially in the middle of the development process when developers are busy with other tasks.

Understanding the Design-Time Data Context

In the "Creating Design-Time Data in Blend" section, we always checked the check box (when applicable) requiring the design-time data to be made available at runtime, too.

Having design data displayed at runtime is convenient when the runtime services are not available yet (for example, because they are still being developed, or when using them is complex and requires a lot of setup). At some point, however, it is necessary to switch to real data. To understand how this is done, it is necessary to get the difference between design-time data context and runtime data context.

We've already discussed the DataContext property and explained that it is used to bind a UI element to a data class, so that the context is set for data bindings. The DataContext of an element is applied to its children (if it has any). Of course, it is possible to override a child's DataContext by setting it explicitly to a different object. We also saw that Silverlight sets a DataTemplate's DataContext implicitly, in which case the represented data item is used.

In addition to the standard DataContext property, Expression Blend, and Visual Studio 2010 use a different property named d:DataContext. You already saw properties starting with d: such as d:DesignHeight and d:DesignWidth. These properties are active only in

Expression Blend and the Visual Studio designer, and ignored at runtime, as explained in Chapter 2, “Setting Up and Discovering Your Environment.” To observe this, follow these steps:

1. Reopen the solution DesignTimeDataSample that we created earlier in this chapter and open the MainPage.xaml.
2. Select the `Grid` named `LayoutRoot` in the Objects and Timeline panel.
3. Set the designer surface in “split view” using the button shown in Figure 2.16, back in Chapter 2.
4. Observe in the XAML editor that the `Grid`’s `DataContext` is set to the `SampleDataSource` through a `Binding`.
5. In the Data panel, locate the SampleDataSource and click the small icon with the Data Source Options ToolTip, shown in Figure 11.9.
6. In the menu, uncheck Enable When Running Application.
7. Observe the XAML of the `LayoutRoot Grid` again. The `DataContext` property has now been replaced by `d:DataContext`.

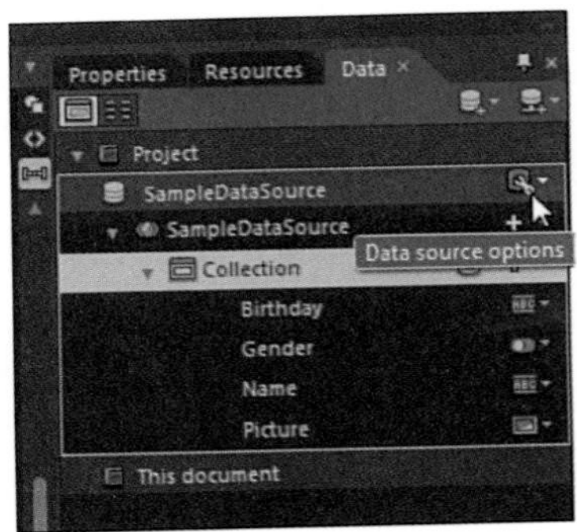

FIGURE 11.9 Sample data source options.

Because `d:DataContext` is now used, no data is displayed when the application runs. This can be changed by setting the `DataContext` property to an object that is created in runtime, as we did in Chapter 7. Note, however, that the names of the properties (such as the `Collection` property used to set the `ListBox’ ItemsSource`) must match in design time and in runtime, to avoid data errors.

You can find more information about design-time data in Blend and in Visual Studio on Karl Shifflett’s blog at http://www.galasoft.ch/sl4-designinstance.

Using Blend Behaviors

In Chapter 5, “Understanding Dependency Properties,” we discussed how to implement so-called “attached behaviors” (that is, attached properties that are used to add functionality to the object to which they are attached). Attached behaviors are very powerful and *encapsulated*. This is interesting for people without programming experience (for example, graphic designers) because they can reuse the encapsulated functionality without having to deal with the implementation. However, adding an attached behavior in XAML is annoying because Expression Blend cannot assist you in that task. The code must be written in XAML by hand. Also, if one attached behavior requires multiple properties to be set up, the syntax becomes cumbersome.

To propose a solution to these issues, the Expression Blend team developed Blend behaviors. Relying on the same principle as attached behaviors, Blend behaviors offer a friendlier interface and can be added in Expression Blend by dragging them from the asset library and dropping them on an element, as the following steps show:

1. Start Expression Blend and create a new Silverlight application named **UsingBlendBehaviors**.
2. Locate a few images in Windows Explorer, select a few of them, and then drag them into the main `Grid` in Blend. The images will be added to the Objects and Timeline panel and appear on the `Grid`.
3. Resize the images so that they do not fill the whole `Grid`, but overlap each other, as shown on Figure 11.10.
4. Select the Assets tab, and the Behaviors category. This shows all the behaviors that are installed with Expression Blend, and those that are included into the application and any referenced DLL.
5. Select the MouseDragElementBehavior and drop it on the first image. You can either drop it on the `Image` control in the Objects and Timeline panel or on the image in the visual designer itself. Notice how the behavior appears as a child of the `Image` control in Objects and Timeline.
6. With the newly added MouseDragElementBehavior selected, check the Properties panel. This simple behavior has only one common property: `ConstraintToParentBounds`. If set to `true`, this property will restrict the image's movement within the limits of the `Grid`. You can choose to turn this property on or off.
7. Repeat the Steps 4 to 6 for each of the images you added to the `Grid`.
8. Run the application by pressing F5. You can now press and hold the mouse on any of the images and drag them to another place on the `Grid`.

FIGURE 11.10 Preparing the scene for Blend behaviors.

Note that we didn't write any C# or VB.NET code for this to happen. The drag functionality is encapsulated into the `MouseDragElementBehavior`, and we reuse it in our project. To understand what happened, return to Expression Blend and open MainPage.xaml in XAML view. You should see two new `xmlns` statements on top of the page:

- `xmlns:i` pointing to the namespace `http://schemas.microsoft.com/expression/2010/interactivity`. This URI is mapped to a CLR namespace named `System.Windows.Interaction`, in the DLL of the same name. This is where the base classes for all Blend behaviors are defined.

- `xmlns:ei` pointing to the namespace `http://schemas.microsoft.com/expression/2010/interactions`. This URI corresponds to a few CLR namespaces, among which `Microsoft.Expression.Interactivity.Layout` in the assembly Microsoft.Expression.Interactions. This assembly contains the `MouseDragElementBehavior` implementation itself.

Note that neither of these two assemblies belongs to the core Silverlight framework. They will appear in the bin\Debug folder of your application, be packaged into the XAP file, and downloaded to the Silverlight client. This makes the XAP file larger, which is the price to pay to enjoy the benefit of the encapsulated functionality. They are, however, available as part of the Blend software development kit (SDK) at no cost, and do not require Expression Blend itself to be purchased or installed.

> **TIP**
>
> **Adding Multiple Behaviors to an Element**
>
> You can add multiple behaviors on each element. The actions of the behaviors will be combined.

The behavior is added with the XAML code in Listing 11.6.

Finding Behaviors Online

The current functionality is annoying because if you drag an image that is behind the others, it remains in the background. Ideally, you should have a way to set the image in front of the others. We will look for an existing behavior online and add it to our project by following these steps:

1. Download the behavior named BringToFrontBehavior from http://www.galasoft.ch/sl4-bringtofront. This behavior is also available on the Expression gallery (as well as many other behaviors) at http://gallery.expression.microsoft.com.

2. Download BringToFrontBehavior.zip and save it to your hard drive. As usual, unblock the file using the Properties dialog in Windows Explorer and the Unblock button (if available).

3. Extract the zip file and copy the DLL named BringToFrontBehavior.dll to a well-known place on your drive.

4. In Expression Blend, in the Projects panel, right-click the UsingBlendBehavior project and select Add Reference from the context menu. Navigate to the location where you just saved BringToFrontBehavior.dll and add it. Note that this DLL requires a reference to System.Windows.Interactivity.dll, but this assembly is already referenced in your project. Build the application to make sure that all assemblies are correctly referenced.

5. Select the Assets tab and the Behaviors category. You should now see the new BringToFrontBehavior listed.

6. Drag the behavior and drop it on the LayoutRoot grid in the Objects and Timeline panel.

7. Run the application again. Clicking an image should bring the image to the foreground when the mouse button is released. The drag behavior is still active, though.

> **TIP**
>
> **Using the Behaviors Included in Blend 4**
>
> Expression Blend 4 comes with a large number of behaviors, actions, and triggers that cover a wide range of user interaction. You can find a list of the included Blend behaviors, actions, and triggers in Chapter 12, "Sketching User Experience."

Other Blend behaviors can also be found on individual blogs, websites, and so forth. Note however that if these behaviors were compiled in an older version of Blend, they might not appear in the Assets library in Expression Blend 4 RTM. In that case, you need to download the source code (if possible) and rebuild in the current version of Blend.

Behavior, Trigger, or Action?

What is often referred to as a "Blend behavior" can in fact be a Behavior, a Trigger, or an Action. What is the difference?

Action

This is a rather general object: Its main feature is that it can be invoked, but the creators of the Action object did not set a constraint on what action it will perform. This allows for a great number of scenarios. For example, invoking an Action can play a sound, start an animation, set a control in a given state, and so forth. You can think of the Action as an actuator. Action objects should be designed to be as atomic and self-contained as possible: They should aim to fulfill one functionality only and should not rely on a state.

Trigger

On the other hand, a Trigger is an object that can be stimulated. Here, too, the way that it is stimulated is not constrained. It can be when an event is raised, when a storyboard is completed, and so forth. You can think of the Trigger as a sensor. A Trigger contains one or more Action instances, and when the Trigger is stimulated, it invokes all the Action instances.

You should consider Action and Trigger as building blocks. An Action should not expect to be invoked by a special kind of Trigger.

Behavior

The Behavior class is a little more specialized. Their intent is to add functionality to an element, as you saw before with the MouseDragElementBehavior. Behaviors often respond to multiple events (for example, MouseLeftButtonDown, MouseMove, and MouseLeftButtonUp) and modify the attached element accordingly.

Adding a Blend Behavior in Code

Of course, it possible to add a Blend behavior to an element in XAML markup and in C# code. For instance, the XAML code in Listing 11.6 and the C#code in Listing 11.7 are equivalent.

LISTING 11.6 Adding a Blend Behavior in XAML

```
<Image Margin="192,204,239,42"
       Source="el20100101006.jpg"
       Stretch="Fill">
    <i:Interaction.Behaviors>
        <ei:MouseDragElementBehavior />
    </i:Interaction.Behaviors>
</Image>
```

LISTING 11.7 Adding a Blend Behavior in C#

```
var uri = new Uri("el20100101006.jpg", UriKind.Relative);

var image = new Image
{
    Margin = new Thickness(192, 204, 239, 42),
    Source = new BitmapImage(uri),
    Stretch = Stretch.Fill
};

Interaction.GetBehaviors(image)
    .Add(new MouseDragElementBehavior());
```

Creating a New Blend Behavior

`Action`, `Trigger` and `Behavior` are made of code, so it is easier to implement them in Visual Studio. To avoid too strong a dependency on Expression Blend, the Blend team created the Expression Blend SDK that can be downloaded from http://www.galasoft.ch/sl4-blendsdk. Unfortunately, at the time of this writing, creating new Behaviors, Actions, or Triggers is not possible automatically in Visual Studio (unlike it was in a previous version of the Blend SDK). To work around this limitation, you can either create the classes in Expression Blend and edit them in Visual Studio (as we will do here), or do the work manually in Visual Studio alone.

Note that the SDK is also installed when you install the full Expression Blend, and Behaviors, Actions and Triggers are available as templates in Blend's New Item dialog. You can create a new `Behavior` as follows:

1. In Visual Studio, create a new Silverlight class library for Silverlight 4 and name it **MyOwnBehaviors**. This is not strictly needed and Blend behaviors can also be created directly in the application that uses them. Packing them in a class library makes them easier to reuse.
2. Delete the file Class1.cs.
3. Open MyOwnBehaviors.sln in Expression Blend.
4. Add a new item to the project in Blend. From the New Item dialog, select a Behavior and name it TextBoxListenerBehavior.cs. Then select File, Save All and return to Visual Studio.

The Behavior we will implement now as an example listens to the text entered in a TextBox and reacts if the text includes the string "hello" by displaying a MessageBox displaying the date and time. Continue the implementation with the following steps:

1. The Behavior is actually a generic class, and you must specify the type of the element that you expect. By default, the Behavior accepts any DependencyObject. In our case, we want to attach an event handler to the KeyUp event of a TextBox. Modify the class declaration to inherit from Behavior<TextBox> instead of Behavior<DependencyObject>.
2. Delete the commented lines in the TextBoxListenerBehavior constructor as well the commented lines further later in the object specifying an ICommand and the method named MyFunction. We will not need these for the simple example.
3. Add a dependency property to the TextBoxListenerBehavior as shown in Listing 11.8.

LISTING 11.8 Adding a Dependency Property

```
 1  public const string MessagePropertyName = "Message";
 2
 3  public string Message
 4  {
 5      get
 6      {
 7          return (string)GetValue(MessageProperty);
 8      }
 9      set
10      {
11          SetValue(MessageProperty, value);
12      }
13  }
14
15  public static readonly DependencyProperty MessageProperty
16      = DependencyProperty.Register(
17      MessagePropertyName,
```

```
18      typeof(string),
19      typeof(TextBoxListenerBehavior),
20      new PropertyMetadata("-empty-"));
```

There are two interesting methods to implement: OnAttached and OnDetaching. Remember when we implemented our attached behavior earlier in Chapter 5 we attached an event handler to the element. In the Behavior implementation, the act of attaching is done in the OnAttached method, which is defined on the Behavior class and overridden in your own implementation.

4. The attached element is saved automatically in the AssociatedObject property. Because this is a generic class, the AssociatedObject in our example is actually of type TextBox. Modify the OnAttached method to look like Listing 11.9. This method listens to every key pressed in the TextBox. If the letters form the word “hello”, a MessageBox is shown.

LISTING 11.9 Attaching to the KeyUp Event

```
protected override void OnAttached()
{
    base.OnAttached();
    AssociatedObject.KeyUp += TextBoxKeyUp;
}

private string _textEntered = string.Empty;
private const string ReferenceText = "hello";

private void TextBoxKeyUp(object sender, KeyEventArgs e)
{
    _textEntered += e.Key.ToString();

    if (ReferenceText.Equals(
        _textEntered,
        StringComparison.InvariantCultureIgnoreCase))
    {
        MessageBox.Show(
            string.Format("It is now {0}; your message is {1}",
            DateTime.Now,
            Message));
        _textEntered = string.Empty;
        return;
    }

    if (!ReferenceText.ToLower().StartsWith(
        _textEntered.ToLower()))
    {
```

```
        // Reset
        _textEntered = string.Empty;
    }
}
```

In Listing 5.13 of the attached behavior implementation, we provided a way to unregister the event handler and avoid memory leaks. However, we didn't have a guarantee that the developer using the attached behavior would call this method. For Blend behaviors, the solution proposed is cleaner: The method `OnDetaching` will be called when the `Behavior` is detached from the element. This is where the event handlers should be unregistered, as shown in Listing 11.10.

LISTING 11.10 Detaching the KeyUp Event Handler

```
protected override void OnDetaching()
{
    base.OnDetaching();
    AssociatedObject.KeyUp -= TextBoxKeyUp;
}
```

Using the Behavior

Using the new Blend behavior requires adding a dependency to the assembly named MyOwnBehaviors.dll, which is copied by Visual Studio in the bin\Debug folder of the MyOwnBehaviors project. Should you decide to reuse this `Behavior` in a different project or to release it to the public (for example, in the Expression Blend gallery where we found the BringToFrontBehavior), this DLL should be kept in a safe place so that it can be referenced later.

TIP

Adding More Behaviors to the DLL

Multiple `Behavior`, `Action`, and `Trigger` classes can be added to a single DLL. There is a compromise to be found between adding too many objects to a single DLL (in which case its size will grow, and finding an element will be more difficult) and adding too few of them (in which case, many projects and DLLs must be maintained).

It is also possible to use the `Behavior` through a project reference rather than a DLL reference, which is especially convenient when the `Behavior` must be tested. This can be done with the following steps:

1. Open the MyOwnBehaviors solution in Visual Studio.
2. Right-click the solution in the Solution Explorer.
3. Select Add, New Project from the context menu.
4. Select a new Silverlight application (not a class library, but a runnable application). Name the new project **MyOwnBehaviors.Test**.
5. Right-click the new Silverlight application in the Solution Explorer and select Set as StartUp Project.
6. Right-click the Silverlight application again, and select Add Reference.
7. In the Add Reference dialog, select the Projects tab.
8. Select the MyOwnBehaviors project and click OK.

   This adds a project reference to our Silverlight application. A project reference behaves very much the same as an assembly reference, but only works with projects located in the same Solution. Note, however, that the referenced project does not need to be located in the same folder as the project referencing it.
9. Save all the files by pressing Ctrl+Shift+S.
10. Right-click MainPage.xaml and select Open in Expression Blend from the context menu.
11. In Blend, open MainPage.xaml.
12. Add a `TextBox` to the page. Then, add a `Rectangle` next to the `TextBox`.
13. Build the application by selecting the menu Project, Build Project.
14. In the Assets tab, select Behaviors and locate the one named TextBoxListenerBehavior.
15. Drag the TextBoxListenerBehavior and drop it on the `TextBox`.

    In the Properties panel, notice the property named Message that was added in Listing 11.8. Because it is a dependency property, it can be data bound to another element or it can be set in a static manner in the Properties panel.
16. Enter a message in the Message text box in the Properties panel.
17. Run the application and enter a text in the `TextBox`. As long as you do not type the word "hello", nothing happens. If at any moment you do type this word, however, the `MessageBox` appears with the message you configured.
18. In Blend, try to drag another TextBoxListenerBehavior and drop it on the `Rectangle`. This does not work; Blend doesn't consider the `Rectangle` to be a valid drop target. This is because we defined that our `Behavior` can only be attached to elements deriving from `TextBox`.

Creating an Action

The Behavior we created in the previous section reacts to a TextBox.KeyUp event only. This is a much-encapsulated solution, but it is not very flexible. Using an Action instead makes it slightly less easy to configure and use, but more versatile. To create a DisplayMessageAction, follow these steps:

1. Reopen the MyOwnBehaviors solution in Blend.
2. Right-click the MyOwnBehaviors project in the Projects panel and select Add New Item from the context menu.
3. In the New Item dialog, select an Action. Name it **DisplayMessageAction.cs**, and then click OK. Save everything and go back to Visual Studio.
4. Change the base class from TriggerAction<DependencyObject> to TriggerAction<TextBox>.
5. Add the same dependency property named Message shown in Listing 11.8 to the DisplayMessageAction class.

   Important: On line 19 of Listing 11.8, replace the TextBoxListenerBehavior with DisplayMessageAction. This is the new owner for this dependency property.
6. Implement the method Invoke as shown in Listing 11.11.

LISTING 11.11 Implementing the Invoke Method

```
protected override void Invoke(object o)
{
    MessageBox.Show(
        string.Format("It is now {0}; your message is {1}",
        DateTime.Now.ToString(),
        Message));
}
```

Using the Action

After building the project, the new Action is visible in Expression Blend's Assets tab. Follow these steps to configure it:

1. Drag a DisplayMessageAction onto the TextBox on the main page.
2. In the Properties tab, notice that the Action is configured by default to work with an EventTrigger, a Trigger that reacts when an event is fired. This is shown in Figure 11.11.
3. For this sample, we will use another kind of Trigger, which reacts when a key is pressed on the target element. Click the New button next to the TriggerType property.

4. From the Select Object dialog, select a `KeyTrigger` (under Microsoft. Expression.Interactivity.Input) and click OK.

5. Configure the `KeyTrigger` to be fired on KeyDown. Set the Key property to PageDown and the Modifiers property to Control.

6. Expand the conditions. This section, available for every kind of `Trigger`, allows specifying a set of conditions to invoke the `Action` instances that the `Trigger` contains. When multiple conditions are defined, you can configure the `Trigger` to work when all the conditions are met, or only one of them.

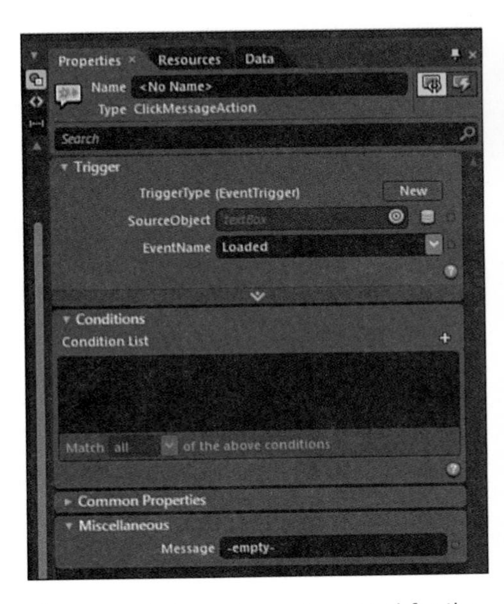

FIGURE 11.11 Properties panel for the `Action`.

7. To add a condition, press the small plus sign (+) button on the right of the Condition List title. This adds a ComparisonCondition to the list.

8. Use the small property peg next to the first value to create a new data binding.

9. In the Create Data Binding dialog, select the Element Property tab and select the `TextBox`.

10. Check the Use a Custom Path Expression check box and type **Text.Length** in the text box.

11. Set the combo box between the two values to GreaterThanOrEqual.

12. Set the second value to 10.

The configuration entered will fire the `Action` when the `TextBox` has the focus, when Ctrl+PageDown is pressed, but only if the string is at least 10 characters long. To test this, run the application and apply all these conditions, and then press Ctrl+PageDown. The `MessageBox` should appear.

Creating a Trigger

New `Trigger` classes can also be created in Visual Studio just as we created `Behavior` and `Action` classes. The process is fairly simple. After the `Trigger` is created and the application is built, the custom `Trigger` will appear in the Select Object dialog from which we selected the `KeyTrigger` in the previous section.

Finding More Information

In the version 4, Expression Blend grew to become an extremely rich tool, providing the user experience integrator with a very rich range of functionalities, so much so that it would be impossible to detail them all in just a couple of chapters.

For more information, we recommend *Expression Blend 4 Unleashed* that will be available at Sams Publishing in the beginning of 2011.

Also, a presentation given in March 2010 by this author is available for viewing online and shows tools and techniques used by Silverlight and WPF integrators to create customized user interfaces in collaboration with graphics designers. This video is available at http://www.galasoft.ch/sl4-integrator.

Summary

In this chapter, we took a deep dive into Expression Blend, one of the most innovative and surprising tools for Silverlight developers. Although the learning curve with Expression Blend is rather steep for traditional developers, the rewards are really outstanding when the user becomes more familiar with the functionalities. This chapter emphasized two areas where Expression Blend enhances radically the process of developing user interfaces and user experience: the creation of design-time data (so that the designer has something to design against), and the Blend behaviors, an encapsulation of functionality that is reusable and very friendly to configure.

There are multiple ways to create design-time data for Expression Blend (or the Visual Studio designer) and to make an application *blendable*. Although doing so requires a little additional work, the rewards are huge because a large portion of the user interface can be designed visually in Expression Blend.

Which option you choose to create design-time data is up to you, to the project's organization, to the size of the application, to the type of the services, and so forth. Whatever you choose, having design-time data in Expression Blend is going to help you tremendously to create a beautiful user experience. In the next chapter, we take a look at a different tool distributed as part of Expression Blend and used to create wireframes and prototypes in Silverlight 4: SketchFlow. Note that we will also see some features that are useful in Expression Blend itself, not just when prototypes are being developed. It is a recommended read even if you are not working in SketchFlow at all!

CHAPTER 12

Sketching the User Experience

IN THIS CHAPTER, WE WILL:

- Talk about the process of sketching and how it can be used to discover the requirements for an application.
- Talk about sketching, wireframing and prototyping, and how SketchFlow can assist you in these tasks.
- Create a prototype for a quiz application in SketchFlow, using states, transitions, mockups, animations and so on.
- Deploy and run the prototype.
- Collect and manage user feedback in the SketchFlow player.
- Talk about importing and exporting data to and from various applications.
- Integrate feedback and collaborate through Sharepoint and TFS.

A very important step in the creation of an application is the phase sometimes called envisioning, in which the requirements are gathered and the first sketches of the application are drawn. The information gathered during this step is used to shape the whole development process. It is important that this phase be executed as thoroughly as possible because any detail that is forgotten will end up costing time and effort to be integrated in the application later. In fact, forgotten details will cost more and more as the project reaches completion, until eventually it is not possible to make changes anymore without missing the deadline or killing the budget.

The envisioning, like all the phases of a software development project, is *iterative*. It is a succession of discussions with the end users, translating their ideas and inputs into requirements, sketching, and going back to the users for feedback. In fact, more than a phase, it is a process that is very active at the beginning of the project and then gradually less active as the development proceeds.

Sketching as a Discovery Process

The process of sketching is an important part of the envisioning. By simplifying an idea and representing it in a simple form, the focus is very much concentrated on this idea, and there are no other distractions. A user interface element should be represented in a simple manner, to convey only the functionality of the element, and to avoid confusing the user who is going to give feedback.

For example, a combo box control can be represented by a sketch, as shown in Figure 12.1. All the important parts are there (the drop-down, a scrollbar, items), but at the same time there is no overload of information:

- Colors are absent from the element because the user should not lose time discussing colors at this stage of the discovery process. This is way too early.
- The text is taken from Lorem Ipsum, and right now it doesn't quite matter what text will appear there. This question is discussed in later iterations.
- Similarly, the final application will probably not show pictures of chairs; their actual final content is not relevant at this stage.

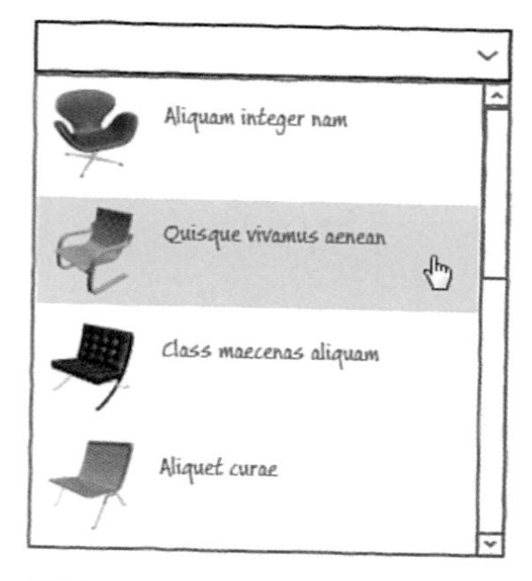

FIGURE 12.1 Sketched combo box.

By removing some visual information (such as the color), and by using data that is obviously a placeholder, the focus is removed from these questions and put on the functionality of the element only.

Using Sketching and Wireframing Tools

The deliverable resulting from the envisioning phase and from the sketching exercises are often named *wireframes* because the sketches look as if they were made of wires. Depending on the preference of the *information architect* in charge of the envisioning, various tools can be used:

- **Pen and paper**: It is often a great way to jot down ideas in a fast way, to be refined later. Most great ideas started as a quick sketch on a scrap of paper!
- **Whiteboard**: A refinement of the previous option, a whiteboard is a great way to sketch ideas in a more "social" way than with a piece of paper. Discussions in front of a whiteboard with end users or members of the team can be very lively and creative.

These two mediums are very useful but are somewhat difficult to archive and to iterate. Paper can be scanned, and whiteboards photographed for safekeeping, but past the initial discovery, it is better to move to more versatile mediums:

- Applications such as PowerPoint or Visio, where it is easy to draw blocks, shapes, and connections, can also be used to create wireframes. However, they are not very interactive. Although it is possible to add animations and even, in some of these applications, to react to user input, they were not made for this purpose, which can render their usage cumbersome at times. Also, there is no built-in way to gather feedback in an iterative manner.

- Wireframing tools are available in quite a large number on the Web. Some of them work online, some others can also be installed offline, some have integrated feedback abilities, and so forth. One such tool in particular is quite popular: Balsamiq Mockups (http://www.galasoft.ch/sl4-balsamiq).

All these tools have one major inconvenience: They are fairly static and do not allow much user interaction. Also, the wireframes are not running in Silverlight. There is a disconnection between the technology used in the early stages of the project and the final result. This can be an issue because some elements might be available in the wireframe and not in Silverlight, or some of the richness of Silverlight might not be easy to sketch in the chosen tool (for example, animations). Also, as the development process progresses, it will be more difficult to transition from the sketch to the application.

To solve these issues, the Expression Blend team developed a tool named SketchFlow, which we examine in this chapter. This tool creates applications in Silverlight and in Windows Presentation Foundation (WPF) just like Blend, but it provides a range of additional features and styles that allow rapid discovery and a sketch-like experience. More information about the genesis of SketchFlow can be found on Christian Schormann's blog at http://electricbeach.org/?p=332.

> **WARNING**
>
> **Installing SketchFlow**
>
> At the time of this writing, SketchFlow is installed together with Expression Blend 4. However, it is not impossible that, in later versions, SketchFlow may be deployed and installed as a separate setup.

Other Kinds of Sketching

For the sake of completeness, let's mention other kinds of sketching that SketchFlow does not handle. For example, it can sometimes be a good idea to create animations (cartoons) or animated videos to explore an idea or to explain a concept. The technique of *stop motion* is very interesting in that regard, and some amazing examples can be found on video sites such as Vimeo (http://www.vimeo.com). Of course, a good stop-motion video requires quite a lot of work, and it is not rare to see some of them becoming as beautiful and interesting as the final application that they are supposed to represent. In that case, it becomes difficult to talk about *sketching* as a supposedly rapid and iterative process.

> **TIP**
>
> **A Trace of Bill Buxton**
>
> Bill Buxton is present in SketchFlow in quite a personal manner: When you install the tool, a font named Buxton Sketch is also installed on your system. This font is used by default by all the SketchFlow controls as shown in Figure 12.2, and is included as homage to Bill Buxton. Because it is installed on your system, it can also be used in other applications.

A very inspirational book should be mentioned at this stage: *Sketching User Experiences*, by Bill Buxton (http://www.galasoft.ch/sl4-sketching). Bill is a computer scientist and designer working as a principal researcher at Microsoft. It is an interesting book, especially for nondesigners who try to understand and think a little more like a designer.

FIGURE 12.2 Buxton Sketch font in Expression Blend.

Discovering SketchFlow

The deliverables created by SketchFlow are, as mentioned before, made in Silverlight. For developers working in WPF, it is also possible to create WPF SketchFlow prototypes.

For a Silverlight developer, this is a great advantage because the same frameworks, controls and objects are used at all stages of the development process. This allows a faster, more efficient way to work. It also enables reusing parts of the prototype application in the final application, by gradually modifying and integrating them. Note that even though most of the SketchFlow application development happens in XAML directly, with no C# code involved, nothing prevents you from adding functionality in code. This is just a Silverlight application!

However, the SketchFlow application does not run as a standalone Silverlight application. Instead, it is executed in the *SketchFlow player*, which adds various functionalities, as you will see later in this chapter.

WARNING

A Prototype Is Not an Application

It is usually not a good idea to try to convert a prototype into a production application. A prototype should be made rapidly and explore multiple possibilities to implement some functionality. The developer should not be burdened by the thought of what will happen to the code after the prototype is completed. This is simply not the same kind of code. However, concepts and sometimes even parts of the SketchFlow application can be used to speed up the production application's development.

The SketchFlow documentation gives some directions to convert a SketchFlow prototype into a Silverlight application. However, we recommend against converting the SketchFlow prototypes.

Creating a New SketchFlow Application

In the following sections, we create the prototype of a quiz application, used to learn multiplications. According to first discussions with the marketing department, the user should be able to create a new quiz, to edit an existing quiz, and to take a quiz.

To create a new SketchFlow application, follow these steps:

1. Start Expression Blend.
2. Select File, New Project.
3. In the New Project dialog, select the Silverlight category, and then SketchFlow, Silverlight SketchFlow Application. Note that you can select which version of Silverlight the prototype should run on: Silverlight 3 or Silverlight 4.
4. Enter the name **Quiz.Prototype** and a location and click OK.

The new SketchFlow application is created, as is an initial screen.

Checking the Panels

Most of the panels used when creating a SketchFlow application are the same as for a standard Silverlight application in Blend. There are, however, a few specific ones. Should one of these screens be missing, they can be reopened through the Window menu:

- **The SketchFlow Map panel**: This important panel is used to create various screens, screen parts, and their connections. It provides a high-level overview over the application.
- **The SketchFlow Animation panel**: Here, frame-based animations for a given screen can be defined. This is a little different from states and transitions, as you will see later in this chapter.
- **The SketchFlow Feedback panel**: Used to import and manage user feedback.

These specialized panels are available only for SketchFlow applications. In addition to those, we will use all the well-known Blend panels to create the prototype. Expression Blend supports the concept of *workspaces* and it is possible to create and arrange the panels as you wish, and then to save this configuration. For example, a simplified workspace can be created with the indications at http://electricbeach.org/?p=238.

Creating and Connecting Screens

A good place to start creating a SketchFlow prototype is the Map panel. This is where the screens and their relations are defined. After creating the SketchFlow application, a screen is already available. Change its name by following these steps:

1. In the SketchFlow Map panel, double-click the blue item marked Screen1. This selects the panel's name.
2. Replace the name Screen1 with **Start**. Note that this changes only the name of the screen, but not the name of the XAML file. Changing the name of the XAML file is possible in the Projects tab, but it is not necessary.
3. Select a `TextBlock` from the toolbar and place it on the screen. Enter the text **Start** in the `Text` property of the `TextBlock`. Notice that the font family used is automatically set to the Buxton Sketch font that was shown in Figure 12.2.

Now we need to create new screens with the following steps:

1. Pass the mouse over the Start screen and pause until a small toolbar appears under it, as shown in Figure 12.3.
2. Click the first button on the left of the toolbar (with the ToolTip reading, "Create a Connected Screen"), and drag it to create a new screen below the Start screen. Note that the new screen is connected to the first one.
3. Name the new screen **CreateQuiz**.
4. In the CreateQuiz screen, add a `TextBlock` and set its `Text` property to CreateQuiz.
5. Right-click the connection line. This line represents the transition between the two screens. From the context menu shown in Figure 12.4, select Transition Style, Push.

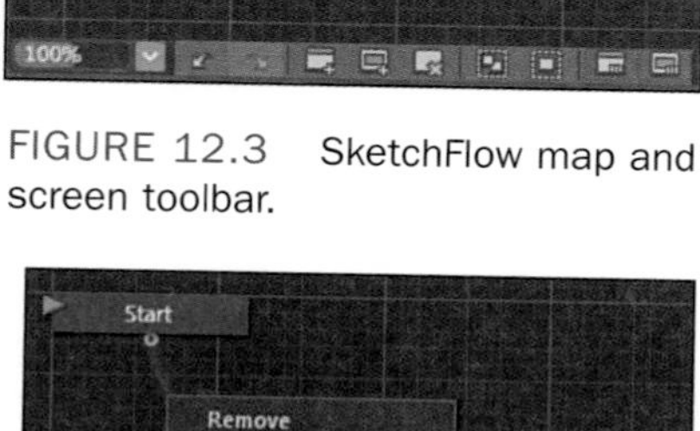

FIGURE 12.3 SketchFlow map and screen toolbar.

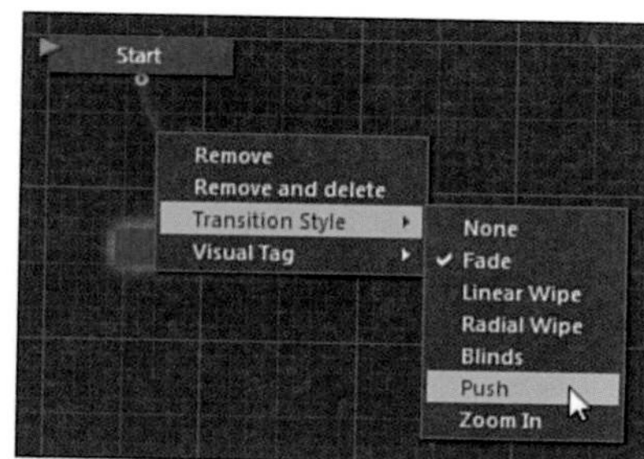

FIGURE 12.4 Changing the transition style.

Testing the Navigation

1. Press F5 to run the application. This starts your favorite web browser and displays the SketchFlow player with the Start screen, as shown on Figure 12.5. Notice that the SketchFlow player is simply a Silverlight application, and can therefore run on any platform supported by Silverlight 4. You'll learn more about the SketchFlow player later in this chapter.

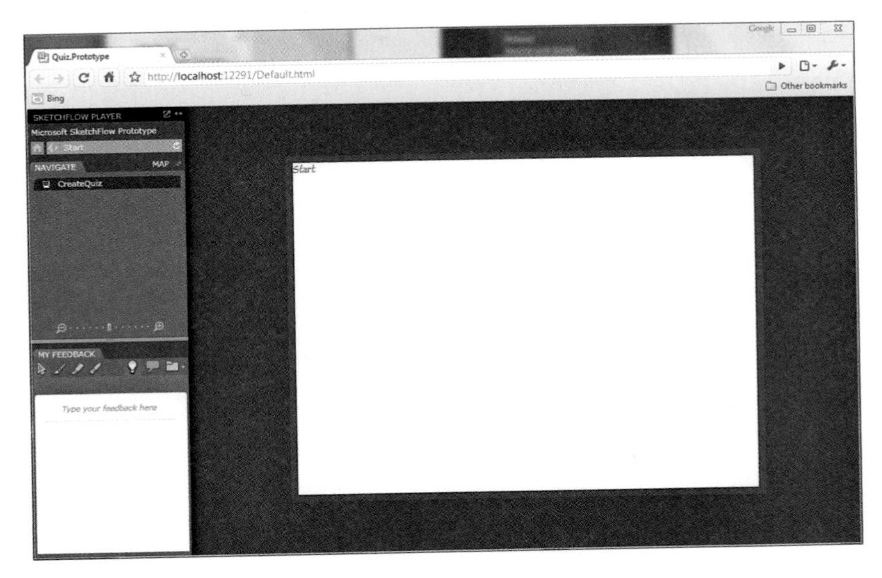

FIGURE 12.5 SketchFlow player in the Chrome browser.

2. On the left side, in the Navigate tab, select the CreateQuiz screen. The Push transition that was selected is played and the new screen is displayed.

   Now the Navigate tab does not show any screen name anymore. This is because the navigation was defined only from the Start screen to the CreateQuiz screen.

> **TIP**
>
> **Returning to the Home Screen**
>
> It is always possible to go back to the home screen (in this case, the Start screen) by clicking the Home button located below the Microsoft SketchFlow Prototype label (see Figure 12.5).

3. In Expression Blend, change the transition to a different one (for example, the Fade transition). Then press F5 and test the navigation again.

4. Go back to Expression Blend and add two more screens connected to the Start screen. Name them **EditQuiz** and **TakeQuiz**.

Connecting Existing Screens

We will now add a navigation path from the CreateQuiz screen to the TakeQuiz screen, and from the EditQuiz screen to the TakeQuiz screen, with the following steps:

1. Pass your mouse over the CreateQuiz screen in the SketchFlow map.

2. In the toolbar, click the button with the "Connect an Existing Screen" ToolTip (the second button from the left in Figure 12.3).

3. Drag the connection to the TakeQuiz screen.

4. Repeat the same operation to add a connection between the EditQuiz screen and the TakeQuiz screen.

5. Finally, add a connection between each of the three new screens (CreateQuiz, EditQuiz, TakeQuiz) and the Start screen. This will be useful to create a Home button.

The SketchFlow map should now look like Figure 12.6. The small green arrow on the Start screen indicates that this is the startup screen. This can be changed by right-clicking a different screen and selecting Set as Start from the context menu. This menu is also useful in case you need to duplicate, rename, or delete a screen. For complex maps, it is also possible to tag the screens or the transition lines visually by changing their color in the Visual Tag context menu.

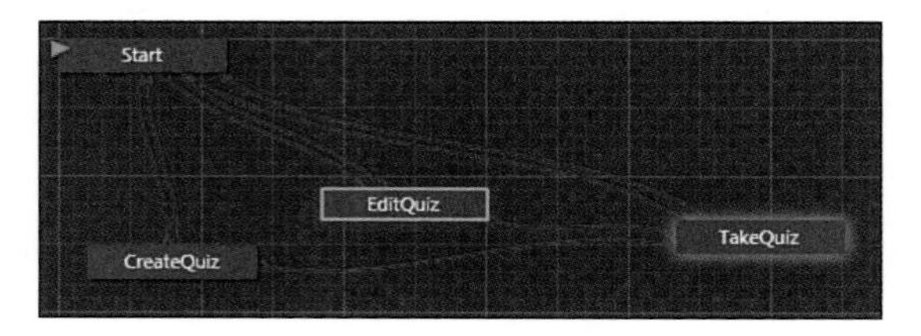

FIGURE 12.6 SketchFlow map of the quiz application.

Building the UI

Now that the screens and the navigation are established, it is time to start adding controls to the screens. First, let's add buttons to the Start screen to enable navigation to other screens, as follows:

1. Open the Start screen.

2. Delete the Start `TextBlock`.

3. Right-click the `LayoutRoot` grid and select Change Layout Type, StackPanel from the context menu.

4. Make sure that the new `StackPanel` is selected in the Objects and Timeline panel, and then double-click the button icon in Blend's toolbar. This adds a new button to the panel. Repeat the operation two more times, to have three buttons. Notice that the buttons have the sketch look and feel by default.

5. Select all three buttons in the Objects and Timeline panel and set their `Height` to 100px and their `Margin` to 10px on each side.

6. Set the first button's `Content` property to **Take Quiz**.

7. Right-click the first button (in Objects and Timeline or on the design surface) and select Navigate To, TakeQuiz from the context menu.

8. Expand the first button in the Objects and Timeline panel. Notice that an element named NavigateToScreenAction has been added. This is a Blend behavior that is in charge of screen navigation.
9. Repeat the operation for the second button, with **Create Quiz** as the Content and the CreateQuiz screen as the navigation target.
10. Finally, do the same for the third button, with **Edit Quiz** as the Content and the EditQuiz screen as the navigation target.
11. Run the application and click the first button. Doing so will display the TakeQuiz screen with the transition that was selected earlier in this chapter.

Notice that the Navigate tab in the SketchFlow player now shows a link to the Start screen, because this is how the navigation has been defined. Notice also that the CreateQuiz and the EditQuiz screens now offer a navigation path to the TakeQuiz screen. This can be confirmed by pressing on the Map button in the SketchFlow player, at the right of the Navigate tab (see Figure 12.5).

Creating a Component Screen

The navigation forward (from the Start screen to another screen) works well, but we should also offer the possibility, from any screen, to return to the Start screen. This is a shared functionality, which is what component screens are for.

You can think of a component as a user control (in fact, this is exactly how they are implemented in SketchFlow) that can be reused in multiple places. It is easy to build a component screen with the following steps:

1. Open the TakeQuiz screen.
2. From the Assets library, select a DockPanel. Note that such panels are actually part of the Silverlight Toolkit, which has to be installed on the developer's computer. (See Chapter 4, "Investigating Existing Controls," for more information about how to install the Silverlight Toolkit.) Because SketchFlow applications are really Silverlight applications, it is possible to use any Silverlight library to build the prototype.
3. Set the DockPanel's HorizontalAlignment to Stretch, VerticalAlignment to Bottom, and Height to 50 pixels. The Margin should be set to 0 pixels on all sides and its Width should be set to Auto.
4. With the DockPanel selected in the Objects and Timeline panel, add a TextBlock. Set its Dock property to Right, its VerticalAlignment to Center, its right Margin to 10px, and its FontSize to 24px. Set the Text property to **Back Home** and the Cursor to a Hand.
5. Right-click the TextBlock and select Navigate To, Start from the context menu.
6. In the Objects and Timeline panel, right-click the DockPanel and select Make Into Component Screen from the context menu.

7. In the Make into Component Screen dialog, enter the name NavigationPanel from the context menu. Then, click OK.

The SketchFlow Map now shows a new screen named NavigationPanel. There is a dotted line connecting this screen to the TakeQuiz screen, as shown on Figure 12.7. Notice also the navigation line from the NavigationPanel back to the Start screen.

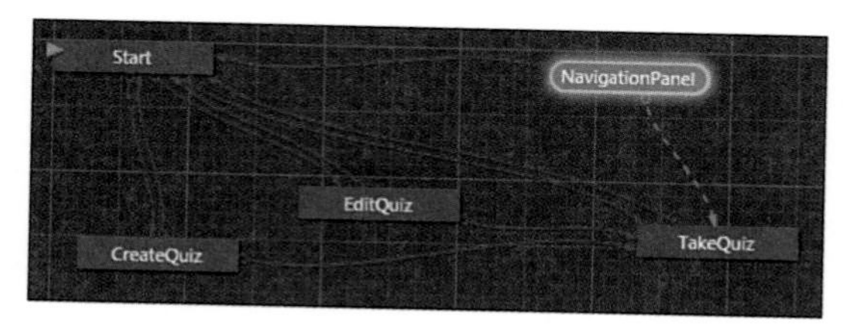

FIGURE 12.7 Map with component screen.

The creation of the NavigationPanel also caused a new XAML file named NavigationPanel.xaml (and its code behind) to be added to the project. This is in fact a standard `UserControl`:

1. With NavigationPanel.xaml open in the design surface, select the `UserControl` root and set the `Width` property to Auto.

2. Go back to the TakeQuiz screen. Notice that the NavigationPanel appears with an orange border and a warning sign. This means that the project should be rebuilt, so that the `UserControl` is added to the assembly properly. After you build, you should see the NavigationPanel in place.

Adding a Component to a Screen

The NavigationPanel must appear on the CreateQuiz and the EditQuiz screens, too. To do this, follow these steps:

1. In the SketchFlow map, drag the NavigationPanel onto the CreateQuiz screen. This creates a dotted line between the CreateQuiz screen and the component.

2. Open the CreateQuiz screen. You should now see the NavigationPanel added to the screen. Select this control in the Objects and Timeline panel and set its `VerticalAlignment` to Bottom and `HorizontalAlignment` to Stretch.

3. Repeat the Steps 1 and 2 with the EditQuiz screen.

4. Run the application. You should now be able to navigate from the Start screen to any other screen and back.

Using Sketch Controls

As you can understand from this chapter so far, the panels act exactly the same as in a "classic" Silverlight application. The controls, on the other hand, have a different look and feel, as if they were drawn by hand.

To create this look and feel, instead of creating new controls, the makers of SketchFlow simply relied on Silverlight's ability to use new styles and templates. For example, the `Button` controls we added on the Start screen use a style named Button-Sketch. This style can be found in the file named SketchStyles.xaml, which is automatically copied by SketchFlow in every new prototype.

Deriving a New Style

Note that the sketch styles are not implicit; that is, they are stored with a key. The Button-Sketch style is not automatically applied to all the buttons in the prototype. This is great for two reasons:

- It makes it easier to add "classic-looking buttons" to the application. For example, you might not want to use the sketch styles everywhere in the prototype. To add a "classic button" to a screen, just select a `Button` (not Button-Sketch) from the Assets library. This is also possible for all the other sketch controls.
- It is easy to define a new style based on a sketch style. Remember that we saw in Chapter 11, "Mastering Expression Blend," that styles cannot be based on implicit styles in Silverlight 4 (in contrast to WPF).

For example, the three navigation buttons in the Start screens all look the same. It is easy to define a common style for them as follows:

1. Open the Start screen.
2. Select the first button: Take Quiz.
3. Select Object, Edit Style, Create Empty.
4. In the Create Style Resource dialog, enter the name **NavigationButtonStyle** and select a location. If similar buttons are used in other places in the application, place the new style in the application (which means that it will be moved to App.xaml). Otherwise, leaving the style in this document is fine. Of course, you can also choose to create new resource dictionaries for your styles. In this case, select the current document.

After the new style is created, the `Button` appears with the default Silverlight ("classic") look and feel and not with the sketch look and feel anymore. To solve this, we need to specify that the new style derives from the sketch style. Unfortunately, there is currently no way to do that visually in Blend. Instead, the following steps must be completed:

1. Open the design surface in split view so that you can visualize the XAML markup.
2. Edit the XAML as shown in Listing 12.1.

Listing 12.1 Setting a Derived Style

```
<Style x:Key="NavigationButtonStyle"
       TargetType="Button"
       BasedOn="{StaticResource Button-Sketch}" />
```

Immediately after the `BasedOn` property is set, the appearance of the button in the designer changes to the sketch look and feel. The style can now be modified as we want with the following steps:

1. Select the style in the Objects and Timeline panel.
2. Click the small Advanced Options peg next to the `Height` property and select Convert to Local Value from the context menu. This creates a setter for this property in the style.
3. Do the same for the `Margin` property.
4. Set the `FontSize` property to 36 pixels.

> **TIP**
>
> **Using Points or Pixels**
>
> Expression Blend can use points or pixels as unit of measure for font size. However, Silverlight always uses pixels. This is why when you set a font size in points, the value in the XAML markup is different (for example, 20pts = 26.667px).
>
> To change the unit used, select Tools, Options, Units, Type Units and select points or pixels depending on your preference.

5. Click the small button circled in red in Figure 12.8. This sets the scope back to the main page.
6. Select the second and the third buttons.
7. Reset the `Height` and `Margin` properties for these two buttons by clicking the small Advanced Options peg and selecting Reset from the context menu.
8. Search for the `Style` property in the Properties panel.
9. Click the Advanced Options peg next to the `Style` property and select Local Resource, NavigationButtonStyle from the context menu.

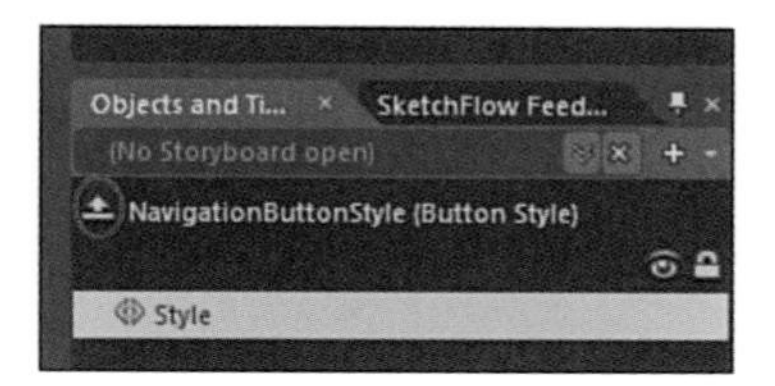

FIGURE 12.8 Setting the scope back to the main page.

> **TIP**
>
> **Applying a Style to Multiple Objects**
>
> Weirdly, Object, Edit Style, Apply Resource cannot be used when more than one element is selected. However, what we did in Step 9 works with multiple elements, too, which is convenient.

The three buttons should all look the same as before. However, changing all three of them is much easier than before because it is enough to just modify the style to apply the changes to all three controls simultaneously.

Exploring the Sketch Controls

By now, it is understood that there are no specific controls for SketchFlow, but only sketch styles and templates that are applied to standard Silverlight controls. This is great news because all these controls are well known by Silverlight developers: All the properties, events, and methods are strictly the same. In the current version of SketchFlow, the controls shown in Figure 12.9 are available as sketch elements.

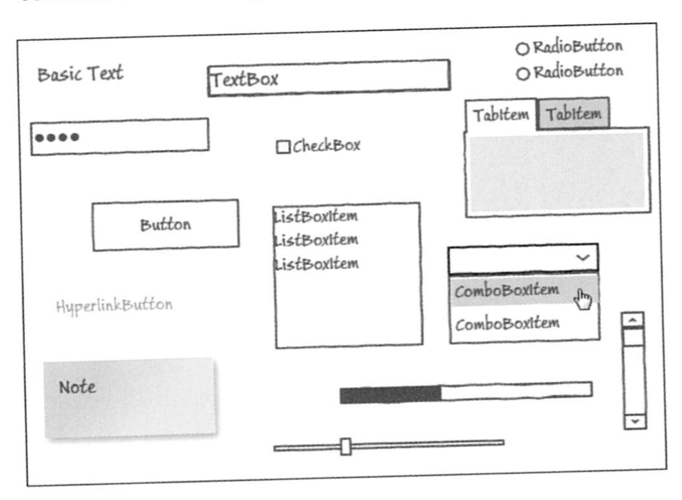

FIGURE 12.9 Sketch controls.

Should a control be missing in its sketch form, it is of course possible to modify a standard control's style and template to make it look like wanted. To do this, the sketch shapes described in the next section can prove useful.

Using Shapes

In addition to the controls we already talked about, Expression Blend 4 has a list of shapes in the Assets library (in the Shapes category) that can be very useful when building a user interface or a SketchFlow prototype. For SketchFlow, the shapes are also available with a sketch look and feel, as shown on Figure 12.10. Note that they can also be customized, for example, with different brushes, line thickness, and so forth.

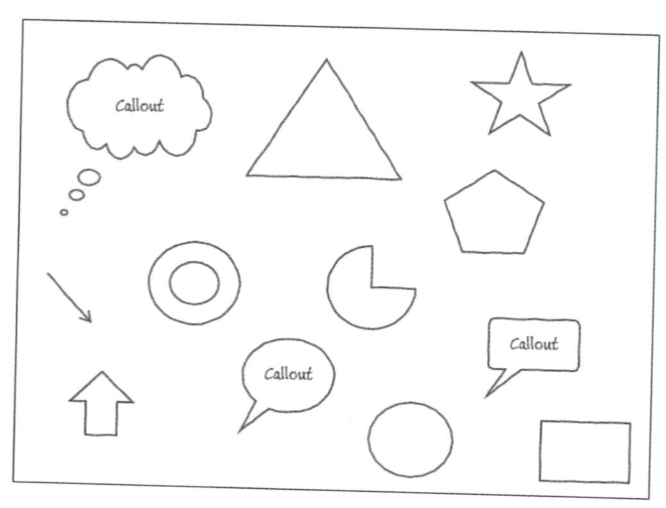

FIGURE 12.10 Sketch shapes.

Exploring the Behaviors

The standard Expression Blend has a list of included behaviors, actions, and triggers (elements discussed in Chapter 11). When working in a SketchFlow project, additional items are available.

Note that, as previously mentioned, these elements are not part of the standard Silverlight framework. The Blend behaviors are part of an external DLL named Microsoft.Expression.Interactions.dll. The SketchFlow behaviors are part of Microsoft.Expression.Prototyping.Interactions.dll. Should a behavior from one of these DLLs be used by your Silverlight application, the corresponding DLL will be added to the XAP file and downloaded to the web browser, which can be an issue in some cases (for example, if the target audience has a very low bandwidth).

The Blend and SketchFlow behaviors, actions, and triggers are as follows:

Actions

- **ActivateStateAction (SketchFlow)**: Sets a target screen in a given state. Note that this behavior works only with screens, and not with controls (for which the `GoToStateAction` should be used instead).
- **CallMethodAction**: Calls a method on a target object.
- **ChangePropertyAction**: Changes a property on a target object. Optionally, the property can be animated to the desired value.
- **ControlStoryboardAction**: Plays, stops, pauses, resumes (and so on) a target storyboard.
- **GoToStateAction**: Places a control in a given state.
- **HyperlinkAction**: Navigates to a given URL in a given web browser window.

- **InvokeCommandAction**: Invokes a command on a target object.
- **NavigateBackAction (SketchFlow)**: Navigates to the previous screen in the navigation history.
- **NavigateForwardAction (SketchFlow)**: Navigates to the next screen in the navigation history.
- **NavigateToScreenAction (SketchFlow)**: Navigates to a given screen.
- **NavigationMenuAction (SketchFlow)**: Used to implement navigation menus between the screens, in a manner that preserves the state of the component screen used as the navigation menu.
- **PlaySketchFlowAnimationAction (SketchFlow)**: Plays an animation in the current screen.
- **PlaySoundAction**: Plays a sound.
- **RemoveElementAction**: Removes an element from the page.
- **RemoveItemInListBoxAction (SketchFlow)**: Removes a list box item to simulate how a user action modifies a list.
- **SetDataStoreValueAction**: Modifies the value of a property in a DataStore. For more information about DataStores, see the "Using DataStores" note. The property change can optionally be animated.

> **TIP**
>
> **Using DataStores**
>
> In Chapter 7, "Understanding the Model-View-ViewModel Pattern," and in other chapters, you saw how to use the Data panel to include data into our Silverlight application in Blend. One option that was not mentioned is the possibility to create one or more DataStores for the application. These are a way to create and store small amounts of data (typically a few properties) and to reuse them throughout the application. Used together with the `SetDataStoreValueAction` behavior, this can prove useful in certain scenarios (for instance when building prototypes). In real-life applications, though, an object structure is used to store data rather than a DataStore.

All the actions mentioned previously are triggered by default by an `EventTrigger` (that is, an element that invokes its actions when a given event occurs). There are, however, other kinds of triggers:

Triggers

- **DataStoreChangeTrigger**: Fires when a given property changes in a DataStore.
- **DataTrigger**: Very similar to a WPF `DataTrigger`, this element fires when a data bound property reaches a given value.
- **PropertyChangedTrigger**: Fires when a data-bound property changes, regardless of the property's value.

- **TimerTrigger**: Fires once when a given event on a given element is raised, and then fires again for a given number of times after a given period.
- **KeyTrigger**: Fires when a given key combination is typed. We used this trigger in Chapter 11.
- **StoryboardCompletedTrigger**: Fires when a given storyboard is completed.

With a combination of triggers and actions, it is possible to compose a wide range of user interaction in Blend without resorting to code, in SketchFlow prototypes but also in Silverlight applications.

Expression Blend 4 also includes a few behaviors, as listed here:

Behaviors

- **DataStateBehavior**: Toggles an element between two states when a data-bound property reaches a given value. Note that if you want to toggle between more than two states, you should use a number of `DataTrigger` and `GoToStateAction` elements instead.
- **FluidMoveBehavior**: Allows you to animate an element's property between two non-double values in a fluid manner. For example, you can change the `Grid.Column` property on a UI element using a `FluidMoveBehavior`, which will cause the element to move smoothly from one column to the other instead of "jumping" in place. You can find more information about the `FluidMoveBehavior` at http://www.galasoft.ch/sl4-fluidmove.
- **FluidMoveSetTagBehavior**: Used together with the `FluidMoveBehavior`, it allows animating objects in special situations (for example, from a `ListBox` to a details view). More information about the `FluidMoveSetTagBehavior` and dynamic layout in general can be found at http://www.galasoft.ch/sl4-dynlayout.
- **MouseDragElementBehavior**: This behavior was already detailed in Chapter 11 and is used to drag an element on the page.

Using Mockups

When creating a prototype, it is interesting to use mockup elements to rapidly simulate a part of the user interface that is either out of the scope of the discovery process or not precisely defined yet. Expression Blend 4 has an interesting sample with a list of mockup controls and icons that can be reused in any Silverlight or SketchFlow application with the following steps:

1. Open a new instance of Expression Blend 4.
2. Should you not see the Welcome screen (shown in Figure 2.14), you can reopen it via Help, Welcome Screen.
3. Click the Samples tab and select the MockupDemonstration project.

Run the sample and familiarize yourself with the concept of mockups. To reuse the mockups in your own Silverlight or SketchFlow application, the DLL named Microsoft.Expression.Prototyping.MockupsSL.dll needs to be referenced into your application, which you can do as follows:

1. In the MockupDemonstration project, select the Projects tab and right-click the Solution.
2. Select Open Folder in Windows Explorer from the context menu.
3. In Windows Explorer, locate the folder MockupDemonstration\Libraries\Silverlight\Debug.
4. Copy Microsoft.Expression.Prototyping.MockupsSL.dll and the Design folder to a known location.
5. Reopen the solution Quiz.Prototype in Blend.
6. In the Projects folder, right-click the References folder under the project named Quiz.PrototypeScreens.
7. Select Add Reference from the context menu.
8. In the Add Reference dialog, navigate to the location where you saved Microsoft.Expression.Prototyping.MockupsSL.dll.
9. Select this DLL and click Open. This adds a reference to the DLL to the project. The assembly will also be added to the XAP file the next time you build the prototype.
10. You should now see the mockups in the Assets library, under the SketchFlow category. If you do not see them, build the application, and then search for the word *mockup* in the Assets library Search box.

TIP

Distributing References Together with the Source Code

When you clean up the source code to publish it (for example, as an open source project on CodePlex), the bin\Debug folder will be deleted. This can cause an issue, because any external DLL (such as Microsoft.Expression.Prototyping.MockupsSL.dll) will be deleted, too, and the next developer will be unable to build the application.

To avoid this, create a folder (for example, named External or References) at the root of your project (where the SLN file is located). Copy all the external assemblies in this folder, and point all the references from the project to the external assemblies located into this folder. When the source code is published, make sure that this folder is also copied. Such assembly references are relative and will work even when the source code is copied in a different environment.

It is now possible to use the mockups in the prototype, as follows:

1. In the Quiz.Prototype application, open the TakeQuiz screen.
2. In the Assets library, locate the `WebBrowserMockup` and double-click it to add one instance to the screen.

3. Resize the `WebBrowserMockup` so that it takes the whole width and height.
4. Select the NavigationPanel instance in the Objects and Timeline panel, and cut it (using Ctrl+X).
5. Expand the `WebBrowserMockup` instance, select the `Grid` it contains, and press paste (Ctrl+V). This places the NavigationPanel within the `WebBrowserMockup`, inside the `Grid` panel.
6. Set the properties so that the NavigationPanel appears on the bottom of the mockup web browser window, with a 0 pixels margin.

With these simple steps, we made our prototype look more realistic and added information (in this case, that the application will work in the web browser) but are still using sketch controls in the true spirit of sketching.

Creating States and Transitions

When a concept must be explained in a prototype, it is interesting to show exactly what states and transitions a given screen goes through. Expression Blend assists you in this task and makes the process very easy. For example, we will now start to implement the TakeQuiz screen of our prototype, with the following steps:

1. In the TakeQuiz screen, select the `Grid` in the `WebBrowserMockup` control and add a `TextBlock` to it.
2. Set the `TextBlock`'s `FontSize` property to 36 pixels.
3. Position the new `TextBlock` in the center of the screen, but set its bottom margin to 250 pixels.
4. Name the `TextBlock` **Q1**.
5. Copy the `TextBlock` Q1 and paste it in the `Grid`.
6. Name the copied `TextBlock` **A1** and set its bottom margin to -50 pixels.
7. Copy the `TextBlock` Q1 again and paste it twice in the `Grid`. Name the copies **Q2** and **Q3**.
8. Copy the `TextBlock` A1 and paste it twice in the `Grid`. Name the copies **A2** and **A3**.
9. Enter a question of your choice for Q1 and the corresponding answer for A1. For example, set the `Text` property of Q1 to **What is 8 x 9?** and A1 to **72**. Note that the screen gets messy with all the questions and answers overlapping, but you can use the small Eye button in the Objects and Timeline panel to hide or show each element.
10. Do the same for Q2, A2, Q3, and A3 with different questions and answers.
11. Select the `LayoutRoot` grid and open the States panel.

12. Click the button circled in red in Figure 12.11. This adds a new state group to the `Grid`. Name this state group **QuestionAnswerStates**. Note that states always get added to the `LayoutRoot` grid, even if another control or panel is selected when the Add State Group button is clicked!

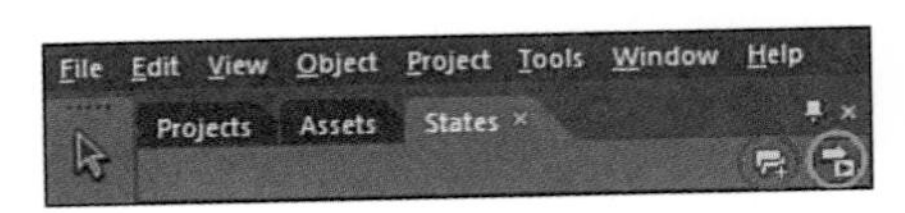

FIGURE 12.11 States panel buttons.

13. Click the small button circled in blue in Figure 12.12. This adds a new state to the `Grid`. Name this state **Normal**.

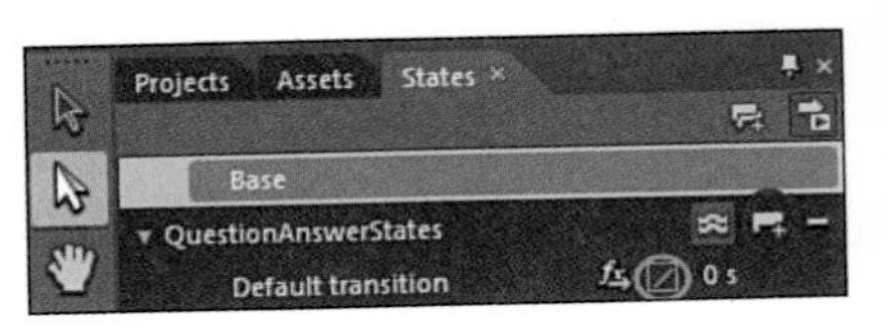

FIGURE 12.12 State buttons.

14. Click the button again and name the new state **Q1State**.
15. Repeat Step 14 five more times, and name the states **A1State**, **Q2State**, **A2State**, **Q3State** and **A3State**.
16. Select the Base state. Then select all the Q&A `TextBlock` elements in the Objects and Timeline panel.
17. Open the Transform category in the Properties panel. Select the Scale tab and set the `ScaleX` and `ScaleY` properties to 0.
18. Select the Q1State. Notice that Blend is now in recording mode, with a red border around the designer space.
19. Select the `TextBlock` Q1 and set its `ScaleX` and `ScaleY` to 1.
20. Select A1State. Then select the `TextBlock` elements Q1 and A1 and set their `ScaleX` and `ScaleY` properties to 1.
21. Select Q2State and set the `TextBlock` Q2's `ScaleX` and `ScaleY` to 1.
22. Repeat the steps until you went through all the states. Then select the Base state to exit the state recording mode.

All the states are ready now, but the transition needs to be defined. By default, the transition takes zero seconds, which is not a very good user experience. Change it with the following steps:

1. Next to the Default Transition line in the States panel (shown Figure 12.12), set the value to 1s.
2. Click the small EasingFunction button circled in green in Figure 12.12. This opens a choice where you can specify how the transition between the states should be set. Select the Elastic Out transition as shown in Figure 12.13.

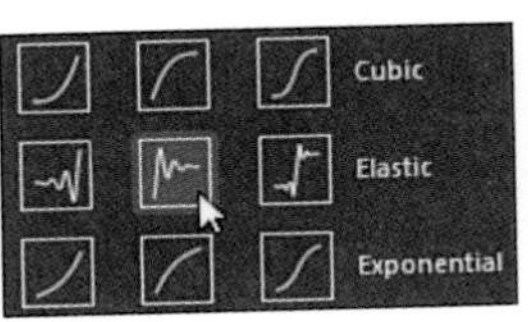

FIGURE 12.13 Setting the EasingFunction.

3. Turn on the Transition Preview by pressing the small button circled in green in Figure 12.11. Then, select the state Normal in the States panel, and then Q1State. Observe how the transition is played. Then, select A1State, Q2State, and so on.
4. Select the Base state to exit the recording mode.

Switching the States at Runtime

The screen needs to get to the correct state when the user interacts with the application. This is another good place to use a behavior. Follow these steps:

1. In the Assets library, select a `GoToStateAction` from the Behaviors category, and drag it onto `LayoutRoot`.
2. With the `GoToStateAction` selected, set the Trigger's `EventName` to **Loaded** in the Properties panel, and then the `StateName` property to **Q1State**.
3. Make sure that the UseTransitions check box is checked.
4. Drag a new `GoToStateAction` on the `LayoutRoot`. Set the Trigger's `EventName` to **MouseLeftButtonDown** and the `StateName` to **A1State**. Here, too, the `TargetObject` should be an `ElementName` binding to `LayoutRoot`.

   We want the `MouseLeftButtonDown` event of the Q1 `TextBlock` to be handled, not of `LayoutRoot`. This can be done by setting the `SourceObject` property of the `EventTrigger`. This is easy to do with the Artboard element picker shown in Figure 12.14.

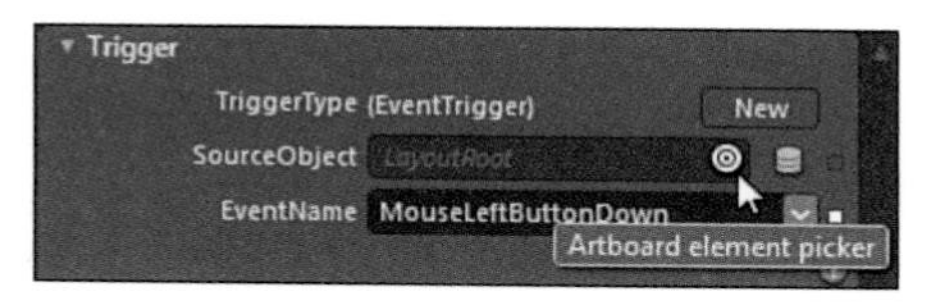

FIGURE 12.14 Artboard element picker.

5. Drag the Artboard element picker onto the Q1 `TextBlock` in the Objects and Timeline panel. This creates an `ElementName` binding to this `TextBlock`. Alternatively, you can use the Advanced Options peg menu to create a DataBinding to Q1.
6. Repeat Steps 4 and 5 for the `TextBlock` elements A1, Q2, A2, and Q3 with the corresponding state name (that is, Q2State for A1, A2State for Q2, and so on).
7. Run the application and load the TakeQuiz screen. The first question should appear when the screen is loaded. Then, click the first question to see the first answer, click the first answer to see the next question, and so on.

Using FluidLayout

We already talked about a behavior named `FluidMoveBehavior` that enables smooth movement even for non-double properties (such as `Grid.Column`, and so on). This is a convenient behavior, but it is sometimes a little cumbersome to set up. Another simpler way to enable smooth animation of non-double values is to use `FluidLayout` to toggle between states. The following steps show you how:

1. Select the element named TwoButtonDialogMockup in the Assets library and add it to the Grid within the WebBrowserMockup.
2. Position the mockup dialog in the middle of the web browser mockup window.
3. Click the OK button and set its content to **Yes**. Do the same with the Cancel button and set the content to **No**.
4. Select the dialog question and set it to **Your score is 4/8. Do you want to take the quiz again?**
5. Select the dialog explanation TextBlock and set its Visibility to Collapsed.
6. Select the DialogMockup and set its Visibility to Collapsed.
7. Add a new state named ContinueState to the QuestionAnswerStates group.
8. With the ContinueState selected and Blend in recording mode, select the DialogMockup and set its Visibility to Visible.

The transition from collapsed to visible is a sudden transition and cannot normally be animated. However, there is a way: Click the small button with the wave icon in Figure 12.12. This switches on the FluidLayout, which will calculate smooth transitions even for properties such as the visibility:

1. On the line of the A3State, click the small arrow with a plus sign (+) and the "Add Transition" ToolTip. Select the transition A3State → ContinueState from the context menu. This adds a specific transition just for this particular state change.
2. Set the duration to 0.7s and set the EasingFunction to Circle InOut.
3. Click the Base state to exit the recording mode.
4. Add a GoToStateAction to the LayoutRoot grid. Set the SourceObject to A3, and the StateName to ContinueState.
5. Run the application and take the quiz again. At the end, click the last answer. The dialog appears with an animation.

Building an Animation

In addition to the standard way of building animations using storyboards, SketchFlow also has the possibility to create animations in the Sketchflow Animation panel. The following steps show you how:

1. In the TakeQuiz screen, expand the WebBrowserMockup in the Objects and Timeline panel and then expand the NavBarContent.
2. Select the TextBox that is set within the NavBarContent and set its Text property to **http://www.myquiz.com**.
3. Set the TextBox's Opacity property to 0% and name it **UrlTextBox**.

4. Set the `Text` property of the new `TextBlock` to **http://www.myquiz.com**.
5. Set the `Opacity` property of the new `TextBlock` to 0%.
6. In the SketchFlow Animation panel, click the + button that creates a new SketchFlow animation.

In Figure 12.15, click the small clock button to display the time editors.

FIGURE 12.15 SketchFlow animation panel.

7. Double click the name SketchFlowAnimation and change the name to **OpeningAnimation**.
8. Set the duration of the transition between the Base and the first frame to 3 seconds. The `EasingFunction` is set to Cubic InOut by default, but it can be changed if you want.
9. Select the first frame. Blend is set in recording mode.
10. Select the `WebBrowserMockup` element. In the Properties panel, expand the Transform category. Click the Scale transform and set `ScaleX` and `ScaleY` to 2.
11. Select the Translate tab and set the `X` to 320 and the `Y` to 240.
12. Set the time inside the first frame to 0s.
13. Pass the mouse on the first frame, and click the small + button that appears. This adds a second frame.
14. Set the transition between the first and the second frame to 1s.
15. Select the second frame and set the UrlTextBox' `Opacity` property to 100%.
16. Add a third frame and set the transition to 3s. In the third frame, set the `ScaleTransform` and the `TranslateTransform` back as in the Base state.

When the animation is done, click the Base frame to exit the recording mode. Then, test by clicking the small play button shown in Figure 12.15.

The animation needs to be triggered now when the screen is loaded, and then the first question must be shown when the animation is completed. This can be done with the following steps:

1. In `LayoutRoot`, add a new behavior named `PlaySketchFlowAnimationAction` from the Assets library.
2. With the `PlaySketchFlowAnimationAction` selected, set the Trigger's `EventName` property to Loaded. Set the `SketchFlowAnimation` property to the OpeningAnimation that we just created.
3. Select the first `GoToStateAction` within the same grid. This is the one that was reacting on the `Grid`'s `Loaded` event.

4. In the Properties editor, click the New button next to the TriggerType.

5. In the Select Object dialog, select a `SketchFlowAnimationTrigger` and click OK.

6. Make sure that `FiredOn` is set to Completed, and select the OpeningAnimation as the `SketchFlowAnimation` property. Leave the other properties as is.

Run the application and select the TakeQuiz screen. You will see the animation being played, and then the application goes into the first state (as before).

Deploying the SketchFlow Application

Obviously, a lot more work needs to be done on the prototype. Because this is an iterative process, it is interesting to show the prototype to the end user early to gather feedback. Because this is, in fact, a Silverlight application, it is very simple to deploy:

1. In Blend, with the Quiz.Prototype solution open, select File, Package SketchFlow Project.

2. In the Package SketchFlow Project dialog, enter a location for the files and click OK.

3. Windows Explorer opens with all the files that you need to deploy to your web server.

Once the files are deployed, give the URL of the file Default.html to the end users who will test the prototype and provide feedback.

Running the Prototype

The SketchFlow prototype runs into the SketchFlow player, which is a Silverlight application shown in Figure 12.4. Even though this is a sketch-looking user interface, it is functional and, with its states and animations, conveys the functionality of the final application in a clear way. Note that because this is a Silverlight application, nothing needs to be installed on the tester's computer to see the prototype (apart, of course, from the Silverlight runtime).

The SketchFlow player has a few functionalities that help the user to explore the prototype, even if it is not completed:

- Each screen can be refreshed using the small circular arrow button next to the name of the screen above the Navigate tab. This is very useful to "replay a screen" and understand the interaction better. For example, for the TakeQuiz screen, this will reset the state and restart the OpeningAnimation.

- The Navigate tab has a list of all the screens that are accessible from the current screen, according to the SketchFlow map. This helps for the navigation, in case the developer of the prototype didn't add all the buttons and links yet.

- The Map button displays the SketchFlow map to help understand the navigation. Note that the map can be zoomed and also expanded to take the whole screen.
- Clicking screen names in the map navigates to the corresponding screen.

Giving Feedback

Maybe the most useful feature of the SketchFlow player is the ability to give feedback for each screen and pass the feedback to the developer. For example, in the TakeQuiz screen, the mouse needs to move too much to click the question, then the answer, and then the question again. Instead, it would be nicer to have one single button to progress through the questions and answer. Also, currently there is no way for the user to inform the application to mark an answer as correct or wrong.

Entering feedback can be done with the following steps:

1. With the prototype running in the web browser, navigate to the TakeQuiz screen.
2. Select Ink Feedback in the My Feedback tab shown in Figure 12.16 and select a color.
3. Draw a circle at the location where you would like to have the Next Question button, for example, above the Back Home link.
4. Click the Type Your Feedback Here text and enter feedback explaining what the button should do.
5. Click the small + button below the first feedback item to add another item.
6. Enter feedback explaining that there is no way to mark an answer as correct or wrong.
7. Press on the small folder icon in Figure 12.16 and select Export Feedback from the context menu.
8. Enter a name and initials.
9. Click OK. In the Save As dialog, navigate to a location where you can save the feedback file, enter a name for it, and click Save.

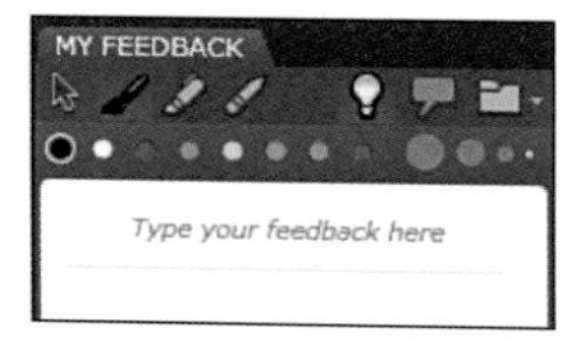

FIGURE 12.16
Feedback tab.

The next step is to send the feedback file to the developer so that he can review it and handle the suggestions.

Importing and Managing User Feedback

When the developer receives a feedback file, he can import it into the SketchFlow project as follows:

1. Open the Quiz.Prototype solution.
2. Select the SketchFlow Feedback panel. If it is not visible, open it by selecting Window, SketchFlow Feedback.
3. Click the small + button at the top of the panel.
4. Browse to the feedback file that you received, select it, and click Open.

Blend shows a list of revisions with information about the tester and the date/time of the feedback and the feedback items as shown in Figure 12.17. Notice how the ink on the screen appears in Blend, making it easy to understand where UI elements are faulty or missing.

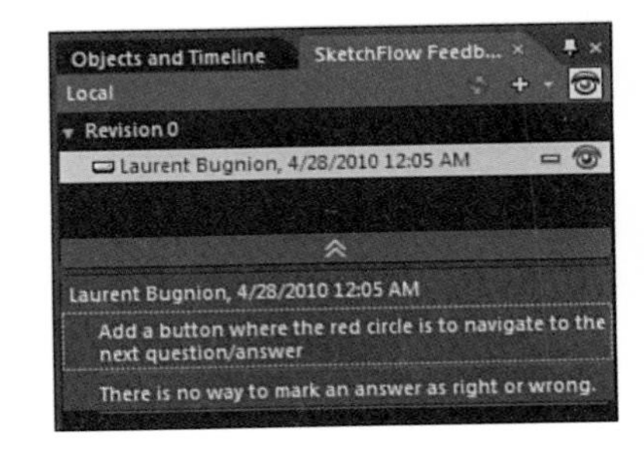

FIGURE 12.17 SketchFlow Feedback panel.

After corrections are made, the SketchFlow project can be packaged again as explained earlier in this chapter. This creates a new revision. When the testers send their feedback again, the feedback panel will clearly show which feedback items apply to which revision, making it easy to iterate and improve the prototype.

Note that the feedback files are imported into the project, in the folder named Feedback Files. It is possible to keep these files in source control and have a full history of every iteration.

> **TIP**
>
> **Archiving Revisions**
>
> It is a good idea to archive exported revisions to be able to explore various paths and to keep a history of the project. When you package the SketchFlow application, export the files to a folder on the web server named (for example) Rev1, Rev2, and so on This way it is immediately clear from the URL which version the tester is currently working with.

Importing and Exporting

Another interesting functionality is the ability to import graphics from Adobe Photoshop, Adobe Illustrator, and from Microsoft PowerPoint, and to export a complete report about the prototype to Microsoft Word. All these commands are available in the File menu.

Importing from Photoshop and Illustrator

Expression Blend (and not just SketchFlow) offers the possibility to import shapes, brushes, texts, and so on from Adobe Photoshop and Adobe Illustrator directly in XAML. For more information about this feature, refer to the presentation at http://www.galasoft.ch/sl4-integrator and to the tutorials at http://www.galasoft.ch/sl4-blendtutorial.

Importing from PowerPoint

This feature is available only in SketchFlow. It offers the possibility to load a series of slides into SketchFlow. However, the feature has limited functionality:

- Each imported slide is converted into a new screen.
- The slide is converted into an image (PNG format).
- It is not possible to interact with the slide's elements. It is, however, possible to simulate interactivity by placing controls on top of the image.

Exporting to Word

In addition to the possibility to let the end user test the prototype "live," it is also possible to create a Microsoft Word document with all the screens and their states, and then to edit this document to add information. This is a very convenient way to pass additional information to the user, as well as document an existing prototype.

To export to Microsoft Word, follow these steps:

1. Open the Quiz.Prototype solution in Blend.
2. Select File, Export to Microsoft Word.
3. In the Export to Word dialog, enter a name and a location for the new file. It is also possible to export the user feedback to this file and to use a custom template (for example, with your firm's header). Then click OK. Note that the export process can take a long time.

The generated file is very complete, with a table of contents and a table of figures. It displays the SketchFlow map, each navigation screen with all its different states, the component screens, and (optionally) the user feedback for each revision.

After the file has been generated, it can be edited to add explanations, other images, and so forth. Note, however, that your changes will be overwritten if you export to Word again using the same document location and name. Additions to the document must be handled manually.

> **WARNING**
>
> **Documenting the Animations**
>
> The SketchFlow animations are not exported to Microsoft Word, not even in a static form. This can be an issue if you want to document a specific animation for the end user.

Integrating and Collaborating

Expression Blend and SketchFlow can be integrated into team collaboration tools to make the collaboration easier.

Integrating into SharePoint

When multiple developers are collaborating on a SketchFlow prototype, it can be interesting to use a collaboration tool such a SharePoint. SketchFlow in Expression Blend 4 can be integrated with SharePoint (a part of Microsoft Office). In fact, publishing any Silverlight application to a SharePoint site is very easy: Simply copy all the files to your shared folders.

When the prototype is open into SketchFlow, it can be published as follows:

1. Select File, Publish to SharePoint.
2. In the Publish to SharePoint dialog, enter the path to the document library where the prototype should be copied and a name for the folder. Note that if the files are already available, they will be overwritten.
3. Click OK. The files are published, and then a dialog is displayed with a hyperlink starting the SketchFlow player.

The integration is also extended to the tester: When the feedback button is clicked in the SketchFlow player, an additional option allows copying the feedback to SharePoint instead of saving it as a file.

Once feedback is saved into SharePoint, the developer can simply refresh the feedback tab in SketchFlow (using the small refresh button visible in Figure 12.17) to see the new feedback available on SharePoint.

Integrating into Team Foundation Server

Expression Blend can handle source control integration in Team Foundation Server (TFS). There is nothing special to be done: If you open a project that is under TFS source control, Blend will automatically attempt to connect to the source server. When a file is being edited, it will be checked out, and so forth.

A nice feature in relation to SketchFlow is that it is possible to convert an item of feedback into a work item in TFS. Just right-click the feedback item and choose from the corresponding menu. This makes collaboration with other developers very easy.

Summary

When SketchFlow was first presented to the public, it opened a wide range of new ideas and processes to improve the discovery phase of an application. In Expression Blend 4, SketchFlow has been improved and extended and is more useful than ever. It must be underlined that it is not "just" a sketching tool, but that it helps to create mockups and prototypes that are functional. It also enables iterative discovery by making it easy for testers and end users to try the prototype and to deliver feedback.

This chapter concludes our incursion into Expression Blend and SketchFlow. In the next chapter, you will see how a new framework called WCF RIA Services helps Silverlight developers to build powerful business applications.

CHAPTER 13

Creating Line-of-Business Applications

IN THIS CHAPTER, WE WILL:

- See what layers are typically involved in a line-of-business application, and how WCF RIA Services helps to reduce the complexity.
- Prepare a server-side service and its database access.
- Create a Silverlight client that is not connected to WCF RIA Services, and then link the client and the server together.
- Take a good look at the DomainService class, a server-side class that is very important for WCF RIA Services.
- Create a UI with the visual designer and connect it automatically to the services.
- Refactor the sample to use the MVVM pattern instead, and avoid the problems that generated UIs can cause.
- Implement Create, Read, Update, Delete (CRUD) operations.
- Talk about validation in the context of WCF RIA Services.
- Create queries on the client and execute them on the server.

In this chapter, we investigate a new way to create data-oriented applications, also called line-of-business applications, or LOB. This kind of application works with a lot of data, typically located in a database on a server, through the means of various services. Because data is on the server and then brought to the client, this involves a lot of duplication. For example, consider the layers shown in Figure 13.1

From the bottom up in Figure 13.1, we see the following layers:

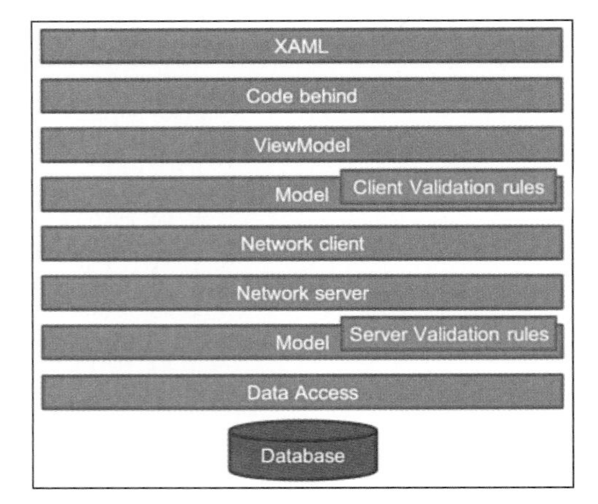

FIGURE 13.1 Layers in a traditional data application.

- The database in which the data is persisted.
- A data access layer. Depending on the database chosen and on the data access framework, this layer itself can be pretty complex (for example, involving stored procedures, SQL statements, and so on).
- A server-side object model with validation rules.
- A networking layer with server-side services and client-side access. For example, this can be a Windows Communication Foundation (WCF) service with the corresponding proxy objects on the client, or a thin REST service delivering an XML or JSON feed to the client, and so forth.
- On the client, the data is often rearranged into a client-side model. This model is similar to the server-side model previously mentioned.
- Validation rules are often available on the client, too, to avoid overloading the network with invalid data that will be refused by the server-side validation rules. The client-side rules are most often an exact match with the server-side rules.
- Silverlight applications often use the Model-View-ViewModel (MVVM) pattern covered in Chapter 7, "Understanding the Model-View-ViewModel Pattern." The view-model layer is preparing the data for the user interface.
- Finally, the Silverlight pages have an XAML markup front end and code behind.

All these layers render the development and especially the maintenance of the application complex and difficult. For instance, if the server-side validation rules are modified, the client-side rules must be changed, too. Also, the network layers (server and client) involve a lot of configuration, which can be difficult to handle.

The WCF RIA Services framework allows a great deal of simplification, as shown in Figure 13.2.

- The data access layer and the model are now using the Entity Framework to access the database. This greatly simplifies the data access by generating entities (data objects) and access methods.

- The network layers (server and client) are taken care of by WCF RIA Services. As the name shows, Windows Communication Foundation is used under the covers, but the developer does not need to worry about that.
- The client-side model is generated automatically. It is a client-side representation of the server-side model. Changes to the server-side model (for example, creating a new query or importing new tables) are automatically reflected on the client.

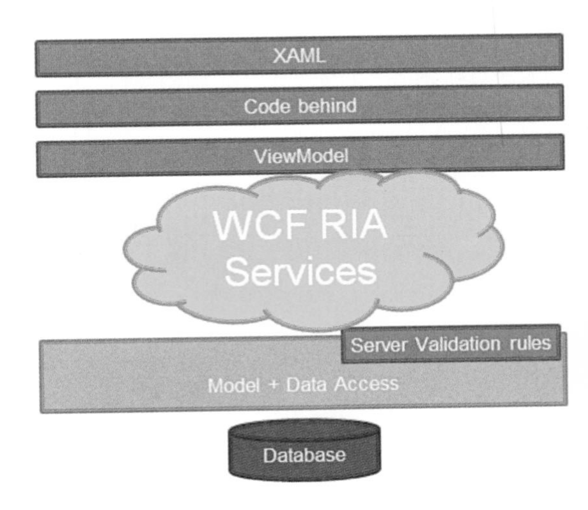

FIGURE 13.2 Layers in a WCF RIA Services application.

- The client-side validation rules are automatically generated, too. They are a replica of the server-side rules. Here, too, any change to the server-side rules is reflected automatically on the client.
- The top layers of the application remain, allowing us to work with the best practices (design time data, Blendability, testability of the view-model) that were already discussed in this book.

Visual Studio can also assist the developer to create the UI by dragging and dropping controls on the design surface, configure them with a property panel and automate connection to the data services. In this chapter, you will see how to do that; however this is often considered as a bad practice, except maybe for very small applications. This is why you will also see how to refactor such an application and use better patterns instead.

Preparing the Server-Side

A typical WCF RIA Service application gets its data from a SQL Server database, through the Entity Framework (EF). This Object-Relational Mapper (ORM) developed by Microsoft is in its version 4 nowadays, and has corrected many of the issues that plagued it in its first version. In this chapter, we will use EF as data access layer, however note that other data access technologies are also possible, such as LINQ-to-SQL.

Prerequisites

When you want to develop for WCF RIA Services, you need to install SQL Server 2008. Note that an Express version is available for free. It is installed together with certain versions of Visual Studio 2010 (if the corresponding option is chosen) or it can be installed as standalone from http://www.galasoft.ch/sl4-sqlex.

A SQL Server database is also needed. This can be set up in SQL Server directly or made available as a standalone MDF file. A sample file can be downloaded from http://www.galasoft.ch/sl4-northwind. (This is the notorious Northwind database that Microsoft created years ago.). To prepare for the rest of the chapter, download this file and extract it to a known location on your hard drive.

Preparing the Server-Side Application

When a new WCF RIA Services application is created, the server side and the client side are often created at the same time. This involves creating a web project to host the Silverlight application and checking the Enable WCF RIA Services check box shown in Figure 2.2. All the necessary assemblies are automatically referenced, and a link is established between the client and the server.

In this chapter however, we show how to create a new Silverlight application only after the server-side application has been prepared, which is a realistic scenario: This allows adding a Silverlight application to an existing website with database access. Proceed with the following steps:

1. Start Visual Studio and select File, New, Project.
2. In the New Project dialog, select Web, and then ASP.NET Empty Web Application. *Make sure that you select .NET Framework 4.0 in the combo box!* WCF RIA Services is not supported on .NET Framework 3.5 or earlier.
3. Enter a location and the name **MyNorthwind.Web**. Then click OK.
4. In Solution Explorer, right-click the MyNorthwind.Web project and select Add, New Item from the context menu.
5. In the Add New Item dialog, select the Data category, and then ADO.NET Entity Data Model. This is the Entity Framework ORM that we mentioned earlier. Enter the name **MyNorthwind.edmx** and click OK.
6. In the Entity Data Model Wizard, select Generate from Database, and then click Next.
7. In the next screen, click the New Connection button. This opens the Connection Properties dialog shown in Figure 13.3. Note that this step is needed only if you cannot already see the northwnd.mdf connection in the wizard's combo box. To make sure that the connection is correctly set up (for example, that the authentication is configured properly), click the Test Connection button. Then click OK.
8. Click the Next button in the Entity Data Model Wizard. If the wizard asks whether you want to copy the MDF file in the current project and modify the connection, say you do.

9. In the Choose Your DataBase Objects dialog, select the tables, views, or stored procedures that you want to use in the application. Select the tables Orders, Customers, and Employees and make sure that the two check boxes above the Model Namespace are checked. Then click Finish.

10. The Entity Framework takes a moment to generate the data access layer, and the model that will be used by the services. When this is done, the three tables and their relationships are displayed in a diagram. Make sure that everything looks okay and close the diagram.

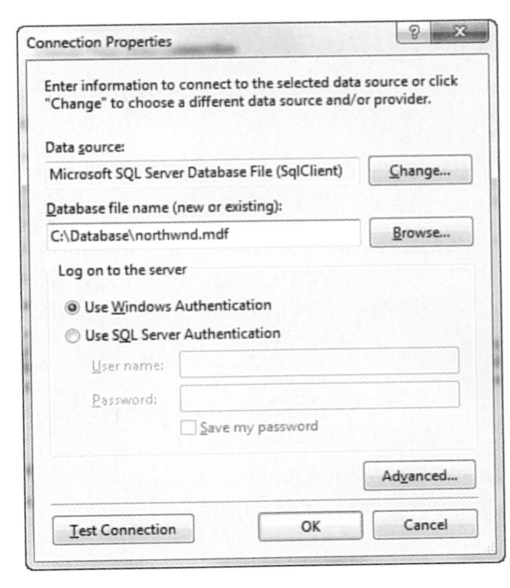

FIGURE 13.3 Connection Properties dialog.

At this point, the data layer is ready and could be used, for example, to create an ASP.NET web application. After the Silverlight application is created, we will connect the client and the server by the means of a new WCF RIA Services layer on top of the data layer.

Creating the Silverlight Client

Creating the client-side Silverlight application is similar to what we already did many times. Just follow these steps:

1. Right-click the MyNorthwind.Web solution in the Solution Explorer and select Add, New Project from the context menu.

2. In the Add New Project dialog, select the category Silverlight, and then a Silverlight application.

3. Name the new application **MyNorthwind.Silverlight** and click OK.

   In the New Silverlight Application dialog, there are options to host the application in the MyNorthwind.Web application (or in a new web application), and to enable the WCF RIA Services. You can also create a test page for the Silverlight application and enable Silverlight debugging. For now, however, we will not connect the Silverlight and the web application, because we want to demonstrate how to do that manually in a later step.

4. Uncheck the check box asking whether you want to host the Silverlight application in the MyNorthwind.Web project, and then click OK.

The new Silverlight application is created. It is still completely independent from the web application.

Bringing the Client and the Server Together

In this section, we link the client and the server applications, and create the WCF RIA Services dependencies. Follow these steps:

1. Right-click the Silverlight project in the Solution Explorer, and select Properties from the context menu.
2. In the Silverlight tab, set the WCF RIA Services combo box link to MyNorthwind.Web. This adds a few references to WCF RIA Services assemblies in the References folder.
3. Save the project properties and close the tab.
4. Right-click the web project in the Solution Explorer and select Properties from the context menu.
5. Select the Silverlight Applications tab.
6. Click the Add button.
7. In the Add Silverlight Application dialog, make sure that the Use an Existing Silverlight Project in the Solution radio button is checked, and that our Silverlight application is selected in the corresponding combo box.
8. Check the Enable WCF RIA Services check box.
9. Make sure to check Add a Test Page That References the Control and Enable Silverlight Debugging.
10. Click the Add button. This creates the well-known folder ClientBin in the web application. Build the application to create all the necessary assemblies and objects.

Adding a Domain Service

The last step adds a Domain Service class to the server application. This class is very important in WCF RIA Services because it creates a link between the client and the server. Now that everything is configured, adding such a class is very easy with the following steps:

1. Right-click the web project in the Solution Explorer and select Add, New Item from the context menu.
2. In the Add New Item dialog, select the Web category and then a Domain Service class. Enter the name **MyNorthwindDomainService**, and then click Add.

3. The Add New Domain Service Class dialog opens as shown in Figure 13.4. Make sure that the Entities in the list can be selected. If the check boxes are disabled, follow the instructions in the Enabling the Domain Service Entities box in this chapter.

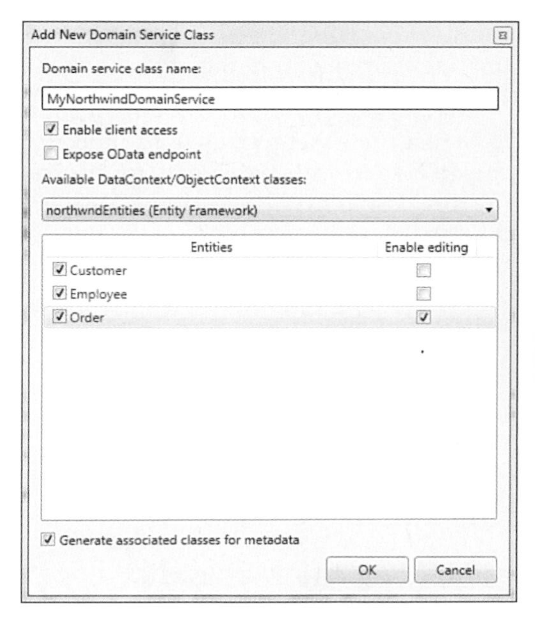

FIGURE 13.4 Add New Domain Service Class dialog.

4. Select the Customer, Employee, and Order entities, and enable editing for the Order entity only.
5. Make sure that Enable Client Access is checked, as well as Generate Associated Classes for Metadata. We will use the metadata later for validation purposes.
6. Click OK. The Domain Service class is generated.

13

WARNING

Enabling the Domain Service Entities

If the check boxes in the Entities list of the Add New Domain Service Class dialog shown in Figure 13.4 are disabled, it might be because you selected a wrong .NET version for the web application. WCF RIA Services is available only for .NET 4.0 on the web server. You can change the .NET version with the following steps:

1. Right-click the web project in the Solution Explorer and select Properties from the context menu.
2. In the Application tab, set Target Framework combo box to .NET Framework 4.
3. Save the project properties. The project is converted to the correct version of the framework.

Try again to add the Domain Service class.

Inspecting the Domain Service Class

A quick look reveals the methods that have been generated in the Domain Service class: Open the file MyNorthwindDomainService.cs. The following methods for the Orders table are available: `GetOrders`, `InsertOrder`, `UpdateOrder`, `DeleteOrder`. We get these methods because the Orders table was marked as editable in the Add New Domain Service Class dialog.

On the other hand, the Employees and Customers tables were not marked as editable, so they are read-only from the service point of view, and only `GetEmployees` and `GetCustomers` are generated.

Note that these methods all use a property of the Domain Service class named `ObjectContext`, which is a proxy for the database. This object has properties named after the three tables that we are importing: `Orders`, `Employees`, and `Customers`. Interacting with the database happens only through the `ObjectContext` property. No SQL statements are involved here.

Generated Class or Very Rich Template?

Even though a wizard is used to create the Domain Service class, it should not be considered as just another generated class. It is better to understand this file as a very rich template that you should not hesitate to modify after it has been created. In fact, the very first step done in most WCF RIA Services projects is to delete the generic data access methods (such as the GetOrders method that simply returns all the available orders in the database) and instead implement methods with more restricted criteria.

Inspecting the Metadata

In addition to the file MyNorthwindDomainService.cs, another file named MyNorthwindDomainService.metadata.cs has also been created by Visual Studio. It was created because we checked the Generate Associated Classes for Metadata check box in the Add New Domain Service Class dialog.

Open the metadata class. It contains the three entity classes (`Employee`, `Order`, and `Customer`) defined as `partial` classes. This keyword allows splitting a class definition among multiple files. An internal metadata class is added (for example, `OrderMetadata`). For each column of the database table, a property is available in this class. Later in this chapter, we use this class to define validation rules for the data.

Creating a New Server-Side Query

SQL is historically the language that has been used most often to access databases. A traditional approach would be to create SQL queries as strings, and then to pass this string to the data access layer, which will execute the query on the database. Although well-known and still widely used, this method is brittle and error prone: It is easy to mistype a SQL statement, and difficult to modify it and test what happens when it is executed.

Instead, .NET proposes an alternative way to create queries: LINQ (Language Integrated Query). We already talked about this language (or rather, this *part of the C# language*) in *Silverlight 2 Unleashed*, in Chapter 22. However, the source that we were targeting was different: We were talking about LINQ-to-XML. Later in Chapter 23, we used LINQ-to-JSON, again the same query language but this time used against a JSON (JavaScript Object Notation) formatted response returned by the popular photo service Flickr.

The variation of LINQ used to "talk" to the entity framework is called *LINQ-to-Entities*. Note that Silverlight cannot execute LINQ queries against the database directly. It needs to go through the web server, which is why we set up the WCF RIA Service.

To create a new query on the server, follow these steps:

1. Open the file MyNorthwindDomainService.cs.
2. Add a new method named `GetOrdersByCity`, as shown in Listing 13.1.

LISTING 13.1 Method `GetOrdersByCity`

```
1  public IQueryable<Order> GetOrdersByCity(string cityStart)
2  {
3      var orders = from o in ObjectContext.Orders
4                   where o.ShipCity.StartsWith(cityStart)
5                   select o;
6
7      return orders;
8  }
```

- On line 1, notice that the return type for the method is `IQueryable<Order>`. This interface is specific to LINQ and must be implemented by the various data providers (such as in LINQ-to-XML, LINQ-to-JSON, LINQ-to-Entities, and so on). Because `IQueryable` inherits `IEnumerable`, the result can be enumerated. However, `IQueryable` is special: The query will only be executed when the data is accessed.
- Lines 3 to 5 define the LINQ query that will be executed. The syntax is very similar to the one we used in *Silverlight 2 Unleashed* to parse an XML file. Here, data from the Orders table (accessed through the `ObjectContext.Orders` property) is filtered according to the name of the city the order is shipped to. The big advantage of this query versus a traditional SQL query is that the compiler checks the syntax when you build the application. Also, you get full IntelliSense. For instance, when you type a period after the variable `o`, all the properties of the `Order` entity are displayed in the IntelliSense menu, and you can pick the correct one.
- On line 7, the query is returned. Note that as we mentioned earlier, the query will not be executed before the result is accessed by the method's caller.

This method is created on the web server, but Visual Studio automatically generated the client-side equivalent, as you will see later in this chapter. The new method that was just created is automatically available on the client, too. Calling the client-side method causes the server-side query to be invoked. The developer does not have to worry about encoding/decoding the call and the returned value; instead, WCF RIA Services perform these tasks.

Working with the Visual Designer

One particularity of WCF RIA Services is that it is possible to create a fully functional application (almost) without typing code, simply by dragging and dropping elements from a designer onto the screen. Although this might seem attractive to some, such applications are notoriously difficult to maintain, extend and test. Drag-and-drop application development can probably be justified in some scenarios, but this is hardly a best practice, and caution is advised.

For the sake of completeness, this section shows how to create a view in the designer, with almost no source code, starting with the following steps. In the "Refactoring the Application to MVVM" section, we move to a better mannered application with a clean separation of concerns and Blendability.

1. Right-click the file MainPage.xaml in the Solution Explorer, and select View Designer from the context menu.
2. If the XAML markup is shown, select the Design tab (see Figure 2.4).
3. If the Document Outline window is not visible in Visual Studio, select View, Other Windows, Document Outline.
4. Select the `UserControl` in the Document Outline.
5. The small icon shown in Figure 2.13 appears in the lower-right corner. Make sure that the icon meaning "Auto Size" is used. Then, resize the `UserControl` at roughly 700 pixels in width and 500 pixels in height so that we have more space for the design. Note that this size is used only at design time. At runtime, the `UserControl` will automatically fill the whole space available.
6. In the Document Outline window, select the `LayoutRoot` grid.
7. Pass the mouse over the blue border above the top of the grid. The cursor turns into a cross. Position the cursor in the middle of the grid's width, and click. This creates two columns roughly of the same size.
8. Pass the mouse over the blue border on top of the right column. This displays a choice with three size options: Fixed, Star, or Auto. We already met these options when working with grids in Expression Blend. Select the Fixed option. The column on the right will always take approximately 350 pixels, while the column on the left will take the rest of the space. Note that if you need to be more precise, you can select the `ColumnDefinition` element in the Document Outline window and set the properties in the corresponding panel (or you can edit the XAML markup).
9. If the Data Sources window is not visible, open it with Data, Show Data Sources. You should see an object named MyNortwindDomainContext in this window. If the object is not visible, build the application.
10. Click the Order property below the MyNortwindDomainContext. This displays a combo box that you can expand as shown in Figure 13.5. In this pop-up, you can select if the table should be represented as a `DataGrid` or as a `DataForm`. We talked

about the DataForm control in Chapter 8, "Using Data Controls." For the moment, select the DataGrid. Note that other controls can be selected using the Customize menu.

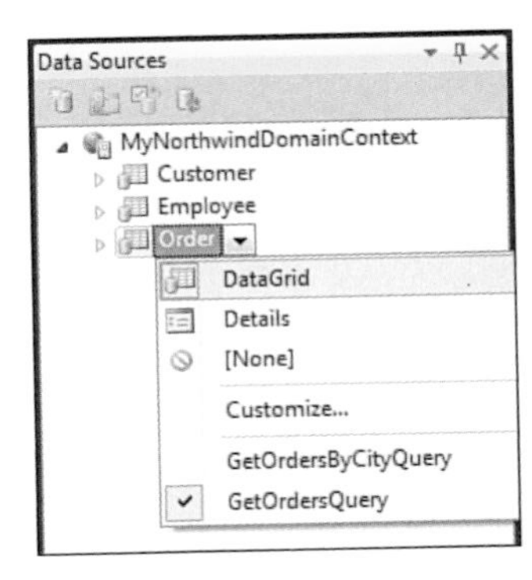

FIGURE 13.5 Configuring the data source.

11. Expand the Order in the tree. For each property, you can select if it should appear in the DataGrid, and with which control it should be represented. For example, click CustomerID, open the menu, and select None. Do the same for the EmployeeID property.

12. Similarly, click OrderDate and open the menu. Select a TextBlock for this property. The date will be displayed in the DataGrid, but won't be editable.

13. Drag the Order property from the Data Sources window onto the LayoutRoot grid in the designer. This creates a DataGrid on the designer surface.

14. Right-click the DataGrid in the designer and select Reset Layout, All from the context menu. Then, with the DataGrid selected, select the property Grid.Column in the Properties panel and set it 0. Set the property Grid.ColumnSpan to 1.

15. In the Solution Explorer, make sure that the web application is set as StartUp project. Then right-click the file MyNorthwind.SilverlightTestPage.html and select Set as Start Page from the context menu.

16. Run the application. The main page is shown with the DataGrid. After a short wait (due to the asynchronous loading of data), all the data rows are shown.

Understanding the DomainDataSource

Open MainPage.xaml in the XAML editor. Notice the presence of a DomainDataSource element. Even though it is placed on the user interface, it is invisible. This is the object responsible for interacting with the Domain Service class. Having this element in the UI makes its properties visible in the Properties Editor, which allows setting its parameters without typing C# code. However, as mentioned before, linking the user interface to the services in that manner is not a very good practice because it is a tight coupling that is not easy to maintain, test, or design.

Calling a Query with Parameter

Using the DomainDataSource, it is also possible to execute queries with parameters with the following steps:

1. Open MainPage.xaml in the Visual Studio Designer.
2. Select the LayoutRoot grid in the Document Outline window.

3. Add a new row on top of the grid by passing the mouse over the blue border on the left of the grid and clicking. Make this row 40 pixels high.

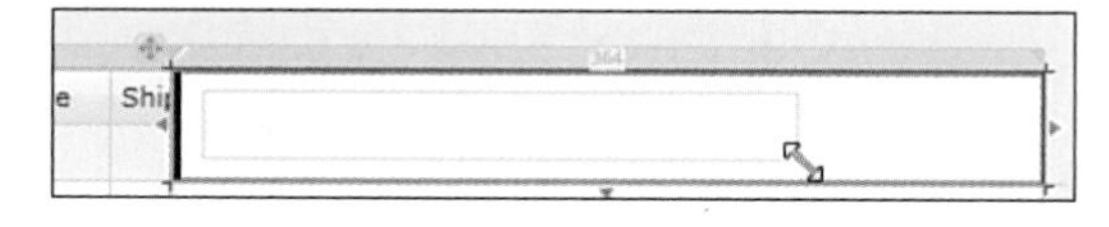

FIGURE 13.6 Drawing a TextBox.

4. Open the Toolbox. If this panel is not visible in Visual Studio, select View, Toolbox.

5. Select a `TextBox` in the Toolbox and draw it in the top-right cell, as shown on Figure 13.6. Set the `Width` property of the `TextBox` to 300, the `Height` to Auto and the `Margin` property to 0. Set the `HorizontalAlignment` and the `VerticalAlignment` to Center.

6. In the Properties Editor, change the name of the `TextBox` to CityStartTextBox. You can change the name by clicking the name textBox1 next on top of the Properties editor.

7. Select the `DomainDataSource` in the Document Outline.

8. In the Properties editor, enter the word *query* in the Search box. You should see `QueryName` and `QueryParameters`.

9. Modify the `QueryName` to GetOrdersByCityQuery. This is the name of the query targeting the method that was created in Listing 13.1. Note that if you mistype the name of the query, Visual Studio will display an error.

10. Click the button with the three dots in the `QueryParameters` field.

11. In the Collection Editor dialog, click the Add button to add a new query parameter.

12. Expand the Other section in the Properties and set the parameter's `ParameterName` property to **cityStart**. Here, too, an error is shown if you mistype the parameter name.

13. Click the small Advanced Properties sign (similar to Figure 6.4) in the Value field. Select Apply Data Binding from the menu.

14. Click `ElementName` and select the CityStartTextBox.

15. Click Path and select the Text property.

16. Then, close the Collection Editor dialog.

17. Run the application and enter the letter **L** in the `TextBox`. After a short delay (needed to send a new request and get the response), all orders shipped to a city starting with *L* are displayed. Note that the query is executed automatically, but only after a short delay when the text is modified, to avoid sending too many requests.

Sorting the Data

The DomainDataSource can also be used to sort the data according to sorting criteria, as follows:

1. Select the DomainDataSource in the Document Outline window.
2. In the Properties editor, find the SortDescriptors property.
3. Click the button with the three dots to open the Collection Editor.
4. In this dialog, click the Add button. Set the Direction to Ascending, and the PropertyPath to **ShipCity**. This is the property after which the data will be sorted.
5. Click OK to close the dialog and run the application. The data is now sorted according to the ShipCity.

Adding a Pager

When working with many rows of data, transmitting the items over the Internet and displaying them can take a very long time. The Silverlight controls are optimized to speed up the display of a large number of items by using so-called UI virtualization. You'll learn more about this in Chapter 21, "Optimizing Performance." However, this does not solve the delay needed to load huge numbers of data rows.

To make the application snappier, a good strategy is to add *paging* to the data controls. They will request only a small amount of data and keep track of which rows were loaded. The perfect element to handle this is the DataPager control that we already covered in Chapter 8. To add a DataPager to our application, follow these steps. Note that the paging operation will fail if the DomainDataSource does not have at least one SortDescriptor like we added in the previous section.

1. With MainPage.xaml open in the Visual Studio designer, add a row at the bottom of the page. Set this row's height to Auto.
2. Select the DataGrid in the Document Outline window. Then set the Grid.RowSpan property to 2.
3. Open the Toolbox and look for the DataPager. If you find it, skip to Step 7.
4. If you cannot find the DataPager, you must add it to the Toolbox. To do this, right-click the Toolbox and select Choose Items from the context menu.
5. Select the Silverlight Components tab in the Choose Toolbox Items dialog. Wait until all the components are loaded, and then scroll down to the DataPager control. If this element cannot be found, you need to install the Silverlight Toolkit first, as described in Chapter 4, "Investigating Existing Controls."
6. Select the DataPager and click OK. This control should now appear in the Toolbox.
7. Double-click the DataPager control in the Toolbox. This adds one instance to the page. Set the Grid.Row to 2, Grid.RowSpan to 1, Grid.Column to 0, and Grid.ColumnSpan to 2.

8. Then right-click the DataPager control and select Reset Layout, All from the context menu.

9. Locate the Source property for the DataPager in the Properties editor. Use the data binding editor to bind this property to the Data property of the DomainDataSource (named orderDomainDataSource).

10. With the DataPager element selected in the page, find the PageSize property in the Properties editor. It is set to 10 by default. Increase this number to 20.

11. Run the application again. Only 20 rows of data are loaded. The DataPager shows the current page number as well as the number of pages available. Using the controls, you can navigate to a different page, which will send a new request to the server.

Many other operations are possible using the visual designer and the Properties editor. At this point, however, we will move to a code-oriented approach and refactor the application.

Refactoring the Application to MVVM

Having the user interface tightly coupled to the service through the DomainDataSource is not very good practice. Instead, WCF RIA Services allow calling methods on the Domain Context class directly, which allows an intermediary layer: the view-model layer that we discussed in Chapter 7.

Adding a View-model

To refactor the application, follow these steps:

1. In the Solution Explorer, right-click the Silverlight project and select Add, New Folder from the context menu. Name this folder **ViewModel**.

2. Right-click the ViewModel folder and select Add, Class from the context menu. Name the new class **MainViewModel.cs**.

3. Implement the MainViewModel class as shown in Listing 13.2. This is a standard implementation of the INotifyPropertyChanged interface that we discussed in Chapter 7.

LISTING 13.2 MainViewModel Class

```
public class MainViewModel : INotifyPropertyChanged
{
    public event PropertyChangedEventHandler PropertyChanged;

    public void RaisePropertyChanged(string propertyName)
    {
        if (PropertyChanged != null)
```

```
        {
            PropertyChanged(this,
                new PropertyChangedEventArgs(propertyName));
        }
    }
}
```

4. Add a property named `IsBusy` that raises the `PropertyChanged` event as shown in Listing 13.3. We will use this property later to inform the user when an asynchronous operation is running.

LISTING 13.3 IsBusy Property

```
public const string IsBusyPropertyName = "IsBusy";
private bool _isBusy = false;

public bool IsBusy
{
    get { return _isBusy; }

    set
    {
        if (_isBusy == value)
        {
            return;
        }

        _isBusy = value;
        RaisePropertyChanged(IsBusyPropertyName);
    }
}
```

5. Add another property as shown in Listing 13.4. This is the collection of `Order` instances to which we will bind the `DataGrid`'s `ItemsSource` property. We use a `PagedCollectionView` class which is particularly well suited to work with WCF RIA Services, and add a `SortDescription` to make sure that the collection is always conveniently sorted.

LISTING 13.4 Orders Collection

```
private PagedCollectionView _orders;
public PagedCollectionView Orders
{
    get
    {
```

```
        if (_orders == null)
        {
            _orders = new PagedCollectionView(_context.Orders);
            _orders.SortDescriptions.Add(
                new SortDescription(
                    "ShipCity", ListSortDirection.Ascending));
        }
        return _orders;
    }
}
```

Finally, add the code in Listing 13.5 to the MainViewModel class.

LISTING 13.5 MainViewModel Constructor, Attributes, and Load Method

```
 1 private MyNorthwindDomainContext _context;
 2 private EntityQuery<Order> _currentQuery;
 3 private int _numberOfOrders = -1;
 4 private int _pageNumber = 0;
 5 private const int PageSize = 20;
 6
 7 public MainViewModel()
 8 {
 9     if (DesignerProperties.IsInDesignTool)
10     {
11         var list = new List<Order>
12         {
13             new Order { OrderID = 1234, ShipCity = "Zurich", Freight = 123 },
14             new Order { OrderID = 3456, ShipCity = "Lausanne", Freight = 42 },
15             new Order { OrderID = 4567, ShipCity = "Basel", Freight = 56 }
16         };
17         _orders = new PagedCollectionView(list);
18     }
19     else
20     {
21         _context = new MyNorthwindDomainContext();
22         LoadAllOrders();
23     }
24 }
25
26 public void LoadAllOrders()
27 {
28     IsBusy = true;
29     _pageNumber = 0;
30     _context.Orders.Clear();
```

```
31        _currentQuery = _context.GetOrdersQuery().OrderBy(o => o.ShipCity);
32        _context.Load(_currentQuery, LoadAllOrdersCompleted, null);
33  }
34
35  private void LoadAllOrdersCompleted(LoadOperation<Order> op)
36  {
37        IsBusy = false;
38  }
```


- Line 1 saves an instance of the Domain Context class named `MyNorthwindDomainContext`. This class gives us access to the server-side functionality without having to worry about the network layers.
- Line 2 saves the current query. We will use this attribute later for paging, as well as the attributes and the constant declared on lines 3 to 5.
- Lines 11 to 17 are executed only when the code runs into the designer tool (either Expression Blend or the Visual Studio designer). In this sample, we only create three rows of design-time data and assign dummy values to some of the columns.
- Lines 21 and 22 are executed when the code runs in runtime. A new instance of the Domain Context is created and stored. Then, we call the `LoadAllOrders` method. This method is defined on lines 26 to 32.
- On line 31, the query is prepared and requests all orders sorted according to the city's name.
- On line 32, the `Load` method is executed with the `_currentQuery`. Note that this last method returns only a query that will be executed on the server.
- The two other parameters of the `Load` method are a callback (executed when the data returns) and a state object. This can be useful to store information during an asynchronous request, as we already did before. In this case, we just leave it `null`.
- When the data returns, on line 37, we simply set the busy state to `false`. Note that thanks to the usage of the `PagedCollectionView`, we do not need to perform any additional step to update the UI.

Adapting the XAML Markup

1. Build the application, and then open MainPage.xaml in the Visual Studio designer.
2. In the `UserControl` tag, add a new `xmlns` prefix set to `xmlns:vm="clr-namespace:MyNorthwind.Silverlight.ViewModel"`.
3. Open the XAML tab and add the markup shown in Listing 13.6 to the `UserControl`. This creates a new instance of the `MainViewModel` class in the resources. Note that a better option is to use a `ViewModelLocator` like we did in Chapter 7.

LISTING 13.6 Creating the MainViewModel in the Resources

```
<UserControl.Resources>
    <vm:MainViewModel x:Key="MainViewModel"
      xmlns:vm="clr-namespace:MyNorthwind.Silverlight.ViewModel" />
</UserControl.Resources>
```

4. Select the Design tab. Click the `DomainDataSource` element in the Document Outline window. Then, right-click this selected element in the designer view and select Delete from the context menu.

5. Select the `LayoutRoot` grid in the Document Outline window. Locate the `DataContext` property in the Properties editor. Apply a data binding. In the data binding editor, select StaticResource, UserControl.Resources, MainViewModel. This binds the grid's `DataContext` property directly to the `MainViewModel` in the resources.

6. With the `DataGrid` selected, in the Properties editor, locate the `ItemsSource` property. Use the Apply a Databinding menu option for that property to open the data binding editor.

7. In the data binding editor, under Source, select DataContext. Notice that it is already set to the `MainViewModel`. This value is inherited to all the children of the `LayoutRoot` grid. Under Path, select the `Orders` property.

8. Remove the `DataPager` from the page. We will handle paging manually later.

Customizing the Columns

Because we took care of creating design time data in Listing 13.5, three rows of partially initialized data can be seen in the designer. This makes the process of designing the page more realistic. For example, the columns of the `DataGrid` can be customized by selecting the `Columns` property in the Properties editor. For each column, it is possible to specify a large range of properties, as follows:

1. Select the `DataGrid`'s `Columns` property in the Properties editor and click the button with the three dots to open the collection editor.

2. In the dialog, select the `OrderIDColumn` and move it on top of the other columns, to make it the first column.

3. Uncheck the check box in the `CanUserReorder` property for this column. This ensures that the `OrderIDColumn` is always the first column. Note that you can also prevent the user from sorting after a column or of resizing the column, should you want this.

4. Select the `ShipCityColumn` and move it after the `OrderIDColumn`. Notice that the change is reflected in the designer.

5. Select the `FreightColumn` and move it after the `ShipCityColumn` if needed. In the Properties, expand the Text section and set the `FontWeight` to Bold.

6. Expand the Layout section and set the `Width` property to SizeToCells. This ensures that the content of the cells is always visible. Note that other options are available (for example, SizeToHeader, Auto, entering a value in pixels, Star).
7. Click the `Binding` property for the `FreightColumn` and select Apply Data Binding from the context menu.
8. In the data binding editor, expand the Options.
9. Set the `StringFormat` to `{0:c}` (currency format). Then close the window.

TIP

Setting a Star Width for a DataGrid Column

Star width is a new feature in the `DataGrid` for Silverlight 4. Just as for a `Grid` panel, a star width column will take the rest of the available width. If two columns have, respectively, 0.3* and 0.7*, the first will take 30% of the available space and the second 70% of that space. This allows a much more flexibly column layout than in the earlier version of the `DataGrid`.

Localizing the User Interface

Note that the currency format used for the `FreightColumn` is U.S. based. To change this, a property can be added in the `UserControl`:

1. Select the `UserControl` in the Document Outline window.
2. Open the XAML editor. Unfortunately, this property cannot be set in the Properties editor.
3. In the `UserControl` tag, add the following property: `Language="fr-FR"`.
4. Build the application. The format of the `FreightColumn` should now display the euro currency sign.

Having to use the `Language` property on each page is annoying, but this can also be done in code. For example, the code in Listing 13.7 sets the application's and the page's culture to fr-FR (French in France). However, values set in the code behind are not applied in the visual designer.

LISTING 13.7 Setting the Application and Page Culture

```
public MainPage()
{
    Thread.CurrentThread.CurrentUICulture
        = Thread.CurrentThread.CurrentCulture
        = new CultureInfo("fr-FR");
    Language = XmlLanguage.GetLanguage("fr-FR");
    InitializeComponent();
}
```

We will talk more in details about localization in Chapter 22, "Advanced Development Techniques."

Adding a RelayCommand Class

In the next sections, we will bind a few commands from the view to the view-model. To make things easier, we will use the `RelayCommand` class that we already used in Chapter 7. To add this class to the project, follow these steps:

1. Download the file RelayCommand.zip from http://www.galasoft.ch/sl4-relaycommand and extract the content to a folder on your hard drive.
2. In the Solution Explorer, right-click the Silverlight project and select Add, New Folder from the context menu. Name the new folder **Helpers**.
3. From Windows Explorer, drag the two files RelayCommand.cs and RelayCommandGeneric.cs to the new Helpers folder. This adds the two files to the project.

In the next section, these classes are used to facilitate the creation of commands.

Executing the CRUD Operations in Code

In the world of business applications, CRUD stands for create, read, update, and delete, the four basic operations that one can perform against a database. Of course, these operations are supported by WCF RIA Services.

We already saw in Listing 13.5 how to *read* orders from the Domain Service class using the `GetOrdersQuery` method that is generated on the client.

Updating an Order

Updating an order can be done with the following steps:

1. Open MainViewModel.cs.
2. Add a property of type `RelayCommand` to the view-model, as shown in Listing 13.8. A `using` statement needs to be added on top of the page for the namespace `GalaSoft.MvvmLight.Command`.

LISTING 13.8 Adding a `SaveCommand`

```
public RelayCommand SaveCommand
{
    get;
    private set;
}
```

3. In the `MainViewModel` constructor, in the section executed during runtime (not design time), add the code in Listing 13.9.

LISTING 13.9 Creating the SaveCommand

```
SaveCommand = new RelayCommand(SaveChanges);
```

4. Finally, implement the delegate method that will be executed when the command is invoked, as shown in Listing 13.10.

LISTING 13.10 Executing the SaveCommand

```
public void SaveChanges()
{
    IsBusy = true;
    _context.SubmitChanges(SaveChangesCompleted, null);
}

private void SaveChangesCompleted(SubmitOperation op)
{
    IsBusy = false;
}
```

5. Build the application.
6. Open MainPage.xaml in the designer.
7. Add a `StackPanel` from the toolbox into the bottom-right column next to the `DataGrid`.
8. Right-click the `StackPanel` and select Reset Layout, All from the context menu.
9. Add a `Button` to the `StackPanel` and set its `Height` to 30, `Margin` to 10, `Width` to Auto and `Content` to Save.
10. Select the `Command` property in the Properties editor and select Apply a Binding.
11. In the Path section, select the `SaveCommand`. This command will be executed when the button is clicked. Should it not be visible in the data binding editor, build the application first.
12. Run the application and click the Order ID column header to filter all the orders in ascending sequence.
13. Edit the `Freight` value of the first order. Then, click the Save button.
14. In Visual Studio, select the window named Server Explorer. (If this window is not visible, open it with the menu View, Server Explorer.)
15. Expand the Data Connections tree and then the connection that your application is using (which should be northwnd.mdf1). This shows the tables and objects in the server-side database.
16. Expand the Tables folder.

17. Right-click the Orders table and select Show Table Data from the context menu.

18. Check the Freight column for the very first order. The cell should show the value that you just saved from the Silverlight application.

Creating an Order

New orders can also be added to the list and saved with the following steps:

1. Open MainViewModel.cs and add a using directive on top of the file to import the namespace System.Linq. This namespace defines extension methods that are very useful when dealing with collections of data.

2. Add a new RelayCommand named AddCommand to the MainViewModel, as in Listing 13.11.

LISTING 13.11 Adding an AddCommand

```
public RelayCommand AddCommand
{
    get;
    private set;
}
```

3. In the MainViewModel constructor, create the command as in Listing 13.12, just below the SaveCommand creation.

LISTING 13.12 Creating the AddCommand

```
AddCommand = new RelayCommand(AddOrder);
```

4. Implement the AddOrder method as shown in Listing 13.13.

LISTING 13.13 Adding an Order

```
 1 private void AddOrder()
 2 {
 3     var lastOrder = _context.Orders.OrderBy(o => o.OrderID).Last();
 4
 5     var newOrder = new Order
 6     {
 7         CustomerID = "ALFKI",
 8         EmployeeID = 1,
 9         Freight = 10,
10         OrderID = lastOrder.OrderID + 1
```

```
11        };
12
13        _context.Orders.Add(newOrder);
14        _numberOfOrders++;
15    }
```

- On line 3, we use LINQ extension methods to retrieve the last order of the list after sorting them by the `OrderID` property.
- Then, a new `Order` is created on lines 5 to 11. Notice that the `CustomerID` and the `EmployeeID` are set to hard-coded value. If these properties were missing, the database would throw an exception when the `Order` is saved! In this sample, the values are hard-coded, but in a real application, the user would need to enter the values (for example, with a `ComboBox` in the `DataGrid`).
- On line 13, the new `Order` is added to the `Orders` table in the Domain Context class. This will cause the `PagedCollectionView` to be updated automatically, as well as the UI.

5. Build the application.
6. Add a new button below the Save button in the `StackPanel` in MainPage.xaml. Just as we did before, give it the same size, and set the `Content` property to Add. Data bind the `Command` property to the `AddCommand` on the view-model.

Run the application now and add a new order. Fill the columns in the `DataGrid`, and then click the Save button. To check whether everything went well, reopen the Order table in the Server Explorer and scroll down until you see the new row and the value that were entered.

Displaying Messages from the View-model

Before we proceed, the application needs to be modified slightly to display messages to the user. This is a common problem when using the MVVM pattern because the view-model does not know anything about the view and should not be in charge of displaying dialog boxes. Instead, an *abstraction* should be offered, for example, with the following steps:

1. Right-click the ViewModel folder in the Silverlight project, and select Add, Class from the context menu.
2. Instead of a class, what is really needed is an interface, representing an abstraction of the functionality. Name the new item **IDialogService.cs**.
3. Replace the class's code with Listing 13.14.

LISTING 13.14 Adding an Interface

```
public interface IDialogService
{
    void ShowMessage(string message);
    bool AskConfirmation(string message);
}
```

4. The `MainViewModel` class needs to call the `ShowMessage` or the `AskConfirmation` method, but it should only know the `IDialogService` interface, to ensure a clean separation. Add a property of this type in the `MainViewModel` class, as shown in Listing 13.15.

LISTING 13.15 Adding an `IDialogService` in the `MainViewModel` Class

```
public IDialogService DialogService
{
    get;
    set;
}

public void ShowMessage(string message)
{
    if (DialogService != null)
    {
        DialogService.ShowMessage(message);
    }
}

private bool AskConfirmation(string message)
{
    if (DialogService != null)
    {
        return DialogService.AskConfirmation(message);
    }
    return true;
}
```

5. A class needs to implement this interface. In this simple example, the view can provide the functionality to display a message. Open MainPage.xaml.cs and modify the class declaration as shown in Listing 13.16.

LISTING 13.16 Modifying the `MainPage`

```
public partial class MainPage : UserControl, IDialogService
```

6. Implement the interface by adding the method shown in Listing 13.17 to the `MainPage`.

LISTING 13.17 Implement the `IDialogService`

```
public void ShowMessage(string content)
{
    MessageBox.Show(content);
}

public bool AskConfirmation(string message)
{
    var result = MessageBox.Show(
        message,
        "Are you sure?",
        MessageBoxButton.OKCancel);

    return result == MessageBoxResult.OK;
}
```

8. Finally, set the `DialogService` property on the `MainViewModel` from the `MainPage` class. The `MainViewModel` is the `LayoutRoot`'s `DataContext`, so the code in Listing 13.18 can be used.

LISTING 13.18 Setting the `DialogService`

```
public MainPage()
{
    InitializeComponent();

    var vm = LayoutRoot.DataContext as MainViewModel;
    if (vm != null)
    {
        vm.DialogService = this;
    }
}
```

The `MainViewModel` class is now able to display messages without having to worry about the actual way that the message is shown. If the designer decides to use a `ChildWindow` control rather than a `MessageBox`, the view-model does not need to change anything to its implementation. We have achieved a nice separation of concerns.

Deleting an Order

Deleting an order is a little more complex than creating or updating an order because of the dependencies between tables. The Northwind database has a table that was not imported in the application, named Order_Details. One Order can have multiple Order_Details; these are the products that were ordered by the customer. If an order is deleted, the application must take care of deleting the corresponding Order_Detail rows, too; otherwise, an exception will be thrown by the server. To retrieve the corresponding data, the Order_Details table needs to be imported in the application.

Another way to handle this would be to use a cascaded delete operation in the database. This is a more efficient way, but requires to understand quite well how the database works, which is out of scope here.

Modifying the Server-Side Model

To add the new table to the model, follow these steps:

1. In the Solution Explorer, expand the web project and double-click the MyNorthwind.edmx.
2. Right-click the diagram window and select Update model from DataBase in the context menu.
3. In the Update Wizard, select the Order Details table. Make sure that the two check boxes below the tree are checked, and click Finish.

The new schema is displayed, with a 1..n relation between the Order entity and the new Order_Detail entity.

Adding Queries

In this sample, it is not necessary to add queries to the Domain Service class. Should that, however, be needed after a modification to the EDMX model, the class `MyNorthwindDomainService` cannot be regenerated, or else all our changes would be lost. Adding new queries or metadata is a frequent operation when working on real-life applications. There are two ways to handle this issue:

- Generate a new, different Domain Service class and copy/paste the generated methods to the original Domain Service class. For clarity, it is even possible to use the `partial` keyword to split the original Domain Service class into multiple files. This option is detailed at http://www.galasoft.ch/sl4-domainservice.
- Adding the new queries and metadata manually. This is probably the easiest way for small changes.

Deleting the Order_Detail Instances

When an `Order` instance is deleted, the corresponding `Order_Detail` instances need to be found and deleted too. Follow these steps:

1. Open MyNorthwindDomainService.cs.
2. Find the DeleteOrder method and modify it as shown in Listing 13.19. This method now looks for and deletes all the Order_Detail objects corresponding to the Order instance that must be deleted.

LISTING 13.19 Modifying the Server-Side DeleteOrder Method

```
public void DeleteOrder(Order order)
{
    var orderDetails = from detail in ObjectContext.Order_Details
                       where detail.OrderID == order.OrderID
                       select detail;

    foreach (var detail in orderDetails)
    {
        ObjectContext.Order_Details.DeleteObject(detail);
    }

    if ((order.EntityState == EntityState.Detached))
    {
        this.ObjectContext.Orders.Attach(order);
    }
    this.ObjectContext.Orders.DeleteObject(order);
}
```


Deleting the Selected Order from the Client

Now that the server-side infrastructure is in place, the client-side application can be modified with the following steps to delete the order that is currently selected in the DataGrid:

1. Open MainViewModel.cs and add a new RelayCommand to this class. This time, the generic version of the class is used: RelayCommand<Order>. The CommandParameter will be set to the selected Order in the DataGrid. The command is shown in Listing 13.20.

LISTING 13.20 Adding a DeleteOrderCommand

```
public RelayCommand<Order> DeleteOrderCommand
{
    get;
    private set;
}
```

2. In the MainViewModel constructor, create the command as in Listing 13.21 below SaveCommand and AddCommand.

LISTING 13.21 Creating the DeleteOrderCommand

```
DeleteOrderCommand = new RelayCommand<Order>(DeleteOrder);
```

3. Finally, implement the client-side DeleteOrder method as shown in Listing 13.22.

LISTING 13.22 Implementing the DeleteOrder Method on the Client

```
1  private void DeleteOrder(Order order)
2  {
3      if (!_context.Orders.Contains(order))
4      {
5           return;
6      }
7
8      var confirmation = string.Format(
9          "Do you want to delete the order # {0}?",
10         order.OrderID);
11
12     if (AskConfirmation(confirmation))
13     {
14         IsBusy = true;
15         _context.Orders.Remove(order);
16         _context.SubmitChanges(DeleteOrderCompleted, order);
17     }
18 }
19
20 private void DeleteOrderCompleted(SubmitOperation op)
21 {
22     _numberOfOrders--;
23     IsBusy = false;
24 }
```

- On line 12, we use the AskConfirmation method that was implemented before (from the IDialogService interface).
- When SubmitChanges is called on line 16, the current Order is passed to the method as the user state. Later, when the asynchronous operation is completed, we can retrieve this object and finish handling it.
- The DeleteOrderCompleted callback is only executed when the operation on the server is finished.

4. Build the application.
5. Open MainPage.xaml in the designer and add a third button to the StackPanel on the right of the page, below the Save and Add buttons. Set the Content property to Delete.

6. With the Delete button selected, locate the `Command` property in the Properties editor and apply a data binding to the `DeleteOrderCommand` on the view-model.
7. The `DeleteOrderCommand` expects a parameter of type `Order`. Select the `CommandParameter` property of the Delete button and open the data binding editor.
8. In the Source section of the data binding editor, select ElementName and then the `orderDataGrid`.
9. In the Path section, select the `SelectedItem` property.
10. Run the application, select an item in the grid and click the Delete button. Then, load the Orders table data in the Server Explorer again, and check that the Order you just deleted is gone from the table indeed.

With this last method, the CRUD operations are implemented for the Orders table. In the remaining sections of the chapter, we add some features demonstrating various functions of WCF RIA Services, such as validation and client-side queries.

Validating the Values

The current state of the application allows entering invalid values. For example, try entering a negative amount in the `Freight` columns and clicking Save. The value is saved in the database, which is not acceptable. To solve this, validation rules should be added to the columns.

WCF RIA Services has an advanced validation mechanism that is also very easy to use thanks to the automatic duplication of the rules on the server and the client. To add range validation to the `Freight` column, follow these steps:

1. In the Solution Explorer, expand the MyNorthwind.Web project and open the file named MyNorthwindDomainService.metadata.cs. This file was generated when the Domain Service class was created, because we selected the corresponding option in the dialog shown at Figure 13.4.
2. Locate the class named `OrderMetadata` and the property named `Freight`. This value is a `Nullable<decimal>`, which means that it can take any value in the `decimal` range as well as the `null` value.
3. Modify the property by adding an attribute as shown in Listing 13.23.

LISTING 13.23 Adding a Validation Rule to the `Freight` Column

```
[Range(0, 10000)]
public Nullable<decimal> Freight { get; set; }
```

4. In addition, the `ShipCity` column should be compulsory. To do that, modify this property by adding a `Required` attribute, as shown in Listing 13.24.

LISTING 13.24 Adding a Validation Rule to the `ShipCity` Column

```
[Required]
public string ShipCity { get; set; }
```

5. Run the application and try setting a negative value in the `Freight` column of one of the orders. A validation error appears as shown in Figure 13.7.

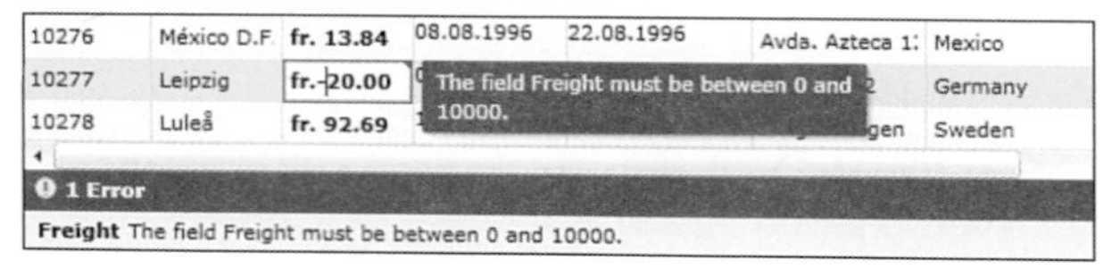

FIGURE 13.7 Validation error.

6. Correct the error. Then try deleting the `ShipCity` value. Another validation error is displayed.

Validation rules can easily be added on each property as needed, and combined. (For example, a `Required` attribute can be combined with a `Range` attribute.) Other validation rules exist, and custom ones can be added, as shown in the "Creating Custom Validation Rules" section of this chapter.

Detecting Errors When Saving

Even though the validation rules are active and detect errors, they do not prevent faulty `Order` instances from being saved. However, attempting to save faulty objects will cause an exception to occur on the server. To prevent this, it is necessary to check the entities and prevent saving if an invalid state is detected. The `SaveChanges` method that was implemented in the `MainViewModel` class in Listing 13.10 can be modified as shown in Listing 13.25.

LISTING 13.25 Checking Before Saving

```
public void SaveChanges()
{
    foreach (var entity in _context.Orders)
    {
        if (entity.HasChanges
            && entity.HasValidationErrors)
        {
            ShowMessage("Impossible to save");
            return;
        }
    }

    IsBusy = true;
    _context.SubmitChanges(SaveChangesCompleted, null);
}
```

To test this, run the application and set the Freight column of one of the orders to a negative value, and then click the Save button. The message should appear and the value is not saved to the server.

Providing More Validation

The following validation rules are available "out of the box." Remember that you saw some of them already in Chapter 8:

- Required: The property marked with this attribute must be present.
- StringLength: Specifies the length of a string property. This attribute can be used to specify the maximum and (optionally) the minimum length of a string.
- Range: For numeric values, specifies the minimum and maximum value for the property.
- RegularExpression: For string properties, allows specifying a regular expression that the value is checked against. Regular expressions are very versatile (and rather complex) expressions and allow for a large range of usage.

All the validation attributes can provide additional information to the user, in case the built-in error text is not satisfying. To do this, in the validation attribute, use the named parameter ErrorMessage, as shown in Listing 13.26.

LISTING 13.26 Providing a Custom Error Message

```
[Required(ErrorMessage="Please enter a name for the city"]
public string ShipCity { get; set; }
```

Creating Custom Validation

The built in validation attributes allow for a wide range of scenarios, especially the RegularExpression attribute for string values. Should your scenario not be covered by the built-in attributes, it is also possible to create your own. For more information about custom validation, check the following resources:

- Nikhil Kothari has a Silverlight TV interview about this specific topic at http://www.galasoft.ch/sl4-validationtv.
- Also by Nikhil Kothari, a very complete blog post about validation in WCF RIA Services is available at http://www.galasoft.ch/sl4-validationblog.

Generated Validation (Database Rules)

Even if no validation rules are entered explicitly, the WCF RIA Services import rules from the database and create the corresponding client-side rules. To see an example, follow these steps:

1. Start the MyNorthwind Silverlight application.
2. In the first row, try to change the `ShipCity` to any name with more than 15 letters and tab out of the field.
3. A validation error mentions that the field `ShipCity` may not be longer than 15 characters.
4. This validation rule is defined in the Domain Context class. To verify this, in the Solution Explorer, select the Silverlight project and then click the "Show All Files" ToolTip button in the Solution Explorer toolbar.
5. In the Generated_Code folder, open MyNorthwind.Web.g.cs. This is the client-side Domain Context class.
6. Find the `Order` class and the `ShipCity` property and notice that it has a `StringLength` attribute.

This attribute was generated because it is defined in the database, as shown by the following steps:

1. In Visual Studio, open the Server Explorer again.
2. Expand the northwnd.mdf1 connection, the Tables folder and the Orders table.
3. Click the `ShipCity` field and click F4 to display the Properties. The Length for this field is set to 15 characters.

Having the rules generated on the client helps to improve the user experience by minimizing the amount of data that must be transmitted to the server. By catching the error early, before the database rejects the value, the stability and the responsiveness of the application is improved.

At this point, the validation rules are defined on the server (and generated on the client in the data model). We will talk about displaying these errors in Chapter 14, "Enhancing Line-of-Business Applications and Running Out of the Browser."

Filtering the Data

An interesting feature of the WCF RIA Services is the ability to create a query on the client and to run it on the server. We can use this feature to refine the server-side query named `GetOrdersByCity` with additional criteria with the following steps:

1. Reopen the Northwind.Web solution that was created in earlier in this chapter, and then open MainViewModel.cs.
2. Add the method shown in Listing 13.27.

LISTING 13.27 LoadAllOrdersByCity Method

```
 1 public void LoadAllOrdersByCityAndShip(string cityStart)
 2 {
 3     IsBusy = true;
 4     _pageNumber = 0;
 5     var query = from o in _context.GetOrdersByCityQuery(cityStart)
 6                 where o.ShipName.StartsWith("V")
 7                 orderby o.ShipCity
 8                 orderby o.OrderID
 9                 select o;
10
11     _currentQuery = query;
12     _context.Load(query, LoadAllOrdersCompleted, null);
13     Orders.Filter = o =>
14     {
15         var order = o as Order;
16         return order.ShipCity.StartsWith(cityStart)
17             && order.ShipName != null
18             && order.ShipName.StartsWith("V");
19     };
20 }
```

- On lines 5 to 9, we create a new client-side query that leverages the server-side query implemented earlier. Note that this query is not executed yet, it is only defined. The query code will be sent to the server and executed there. No data is loaded until the `Load` method is called.
- On line 12, we call the well-known `Load` method on the service, and provide the query as parameter. Note that we reuse the `LoadAllOrdersCompleted` event handler to update the `DataGrid`.
- Lines 13 to 19 update the `Filter` property on the `Orders` `PagedCollectionView`. An alternative would be to clear the Domain Context before executing the query, but that is not a very good option, because the state of the data controls will be lost. Instead, using the `Filter` (while repeating the query's criteria) is a cleaner way to proceed.

3. Open MainPage.xaml in the Visual Studio designer.
4. Select the `CityStartTextBox` in the top-right corner.
5. In the Properties editor, click the Events tab.
6. Double-click in the `LostFocus` event. This adds an event handler in the code behind.
7. Modify the event handler as shown in Listing 13.28.

13

LISTING 13.28 Handling the LostFocus Event

```
private void CityStartTextBox_LostFocus(
    object sender, RoutedEventArgs e)
{
    var vm = LayoutRoot.DataContext as MainViewModel;
    if (vm != null)
    {
        vm.LoadAllOrdersByCityAndShip(CityStartTextBox.Text);
    }
}
```

8. Run the application, enter a search string in the `CityStartTextBox` (for example, **L**), and then tab out of the box. After a short delay, orders for cities starting with L and whose ship name starts with the letter V should be displayed.

TIP

Using Commands

Having to resort to code behind to handle the `LostFocus` event is not a big issue, but it would be even preferable to use a command on the view-model. Unfortunately, this is not possible out of the box in Silverlight because commands can only be placed on elements deriving from `ButtonBase` (`Button`, `CheckBox`, and so on), and the command will only be invoked when the element is clicked.

There is a way to use commands with any element and any event by the way of a Blend behavior. We talk about this in Chapter 19, "Authentication, Event to Command Binding, Random Animations, Multitouch, Local Communication, and Bing Maps Control."

Showing Feedback While Processing

To enhance the user experience, showing feedback to the user when an asynchronous operation is performed is a great idea. The view-model class already has a property named `IsBusy` that is set to `true` when an asynchronous operation is in progress. The `BusyIndicator` control can use this property to show feedback with the following steps:

1. With MainPage.xaml open in the visual designer, select the `BusyIndicator` control in the Toolbox. Should that control not be present, you must add it using the steps that are described earlier in this chapter, in the "Adding a Pager" section.

2. Make sure that the `LayoutRoot` is selected in the Document outline, and then drag the `BusyIndicator` on the main page.

3. Right-click the `BusyIndicator` and select Reset Layout, All from the context menu.

4. Set the `Grid.Column` to 0, `Grid.ColumnSpan` to 2, `Grid,Row` to 0, `Grid.RowSpan` to 3.

5. Using the data binding editor, bind the `BusyIndicator`'s `IsBusy` property to the `MainViewModel`'s `IsBusy` property.
6. Run the application. The `BusyIndicator` is now visible when an asynchronous operation is in progress.

Sharing Code

Before we move on to the next chapter, let's mention an interesting feature of WCF RIA Services allowing sharing code between the server and the client. This is especially useful if you have utility classes that are used on the server and want to include this code in the client application, too.

To share code in a WCF RIA Services application, just change the server-side code file's extension to .shared.cs. This will automatically force WCF RIA Services to generate the corresponding client-side file. However, note the following:

- It is a bit confusing that the shared file is not visible in the Solution Explorer. If not carefully documented, the shared feature is not immediately discoverable by the developer who uses it. A better way to share code is to use the linked files feature of Visual Studio: Select Add, Existing Item from the context menu, and then click the small arrow to the right of the Add button and select Add as Link. This creates a link to the physical file and appears as such in the Solution Explorer.
- Because the source code is shared between the server (.NET) and the client (Silverlight), only features available in both frameworks can be used.

Summary

WCF RIA Services went from interesting experiment to powerful framework before it was even officially released. It is also a framework that benefited from a lot of feedback from the developer community, and has been continuously improved since its inception. Although the information in this chapter will get you up to speed and allow you to build LOB applications, it is not possible to show all the framework's features in only one chapter.

In this chapter, we demonstrated some of the visual designer's features and the `DomainDataSource` element that allows creating data application with almost no code. Although this feature sounds very attractive at first and allows for very rapid application development, the experience shows that such tightly coupled applications are very hard to test, maintain, and extend. For this reason, the decoupled pattern shown in the second half of the chapter is preferable.

In the next chapter, we continue to enhance the application and see how we can also take it out of the browser and run it in a very similar fashion to a normal desktop application.

CHAPTER 14

Enhancing Line-of-Business Applications and Running Out of the Browser

IN THIS CHAPTER, WE WILL:

- Continue our discussion of line-of-business applications with WCF RIA services.
- Add server-side paging to our LOB application.
- Display errors when they occur.
- Talk about scenarios where multiple clients access the data and reconciling them.
- Show that Silverlight supports copy-paste operations.
- Implement printing in our application.
- Install, uninstall, debug and setup the application out-of-the-browser (OOB).
- Show how to check for updates and install them in OOB.
- Save files in isolated storage and in the My Documents folder.
- Run the application offline and check network connectivity.

In this chapter, we continue to work on the line-of-business application that we created in Chapter 13, "Creating Line-of-Business Applications."

In the second part of this chapter, we talk about taking Silverlight out of the browser and creating standalone applications that are very similar to the programs that we use every day on Windows and Macintosh.

Enhancing LOB Applications

The MyNorthwind application created in Chapter 13 is already able to connect to the WCF RIA Service to get and save data from and into the database. This is a nice start, but it needs to be enhanced to be more functional, with features such as server-side paging and printing.

Adding Paging

In Chapter 8, "Using Data Controls," we used the PagedCollectionView to page through large sets of data. In that case, the data was already available in the client application. In this section, we will see how to implement server-side paging with WCF RIA Services. The big difference is that instead of preloading all the data on the client and then paging through it, the pages will be fetched on demand from the server.

In the beginning of this chapter, we already implemented paging with a control called the DataPager working together with the DomainDataSource. After the DomainDataSource was removed, though, paging must be done in code.

There are two steps involved in creating a paging function in this application:

- Getting the total numbers of rows that a query is returning
- Using the current query, skip a number of rows (depending on the page which is currently displayed) and then taking a number of rows (depending on the page size)

Getting the Number of Rows

To get the total number of rows, a server-side method is added to the MyNorthwindDomainService class as shown in Listing 14.1.

LISTING 14.1 Server Side Method to Get the Numbers of Rows

```
public int GetNumberOfOrders(string cityStart)
{
    return GetOrdersByCity(cityStart).Count();
}
```

Once the method is added to the server, it can be called on the client in an asynchronous manner, as you will see in Listing 14.5.

Paging from the Client

To wire up buttons or menus to the page controls (back and forward), the best way is to declare commands in the MainViewModel class as shown in Listing 14.2, just as we did before for the Add, Delete, and Save operations. We also declare a Boolean flag named _isFilterApplied that we will use later to disable paging.

LISTING 14.2 Declaring the GoBackCommand and GoForwardCommand

```
public bool _isFilterApplied;

public RelayCommand GoForwardCommand
{
    get;
    private set;
}

public RelayCommand GoBackCommand
{
    get;
    private set;
}
```

These commands are created in the MainViewModel constructor as shown in Listing 14.3. (These lines are placed right after the SaveCommand, AddCommand, and DeleteCommand are created.)

LISTING 14.3 Initializing GoBackCommand and GoForwardCommand

```
1  GoForwardCommand = new RelayCommand(
2      GoForward,
3      () => !_isFilterApplied
4          && (_pageNumber + 1) * PageSize < _numberOfOrders);
5
6  GoBackCommand = new RelayCommand(
7      GoBack,
8      () => !_isFilterApplied
9          && _pageNumber > 0);
```


- On line 2, we assign a method named GoForward (defined in Listing 14.4 below) to the Execute delegate of the GoForwardCommand. Similarly, the method GoBack is assigned to the GoBackCommand's Execute delegate.
- The CanExecute delegate of the GoForwardCommand is calculated according to the current page number, the page size, the number of orders and if a filter (by city name) has been applied. Paging is only enabled when no filter is applied to the data. (These attributes and constant have been defined in Listing 13.5.) This will disable/enable the button using this command accordingly. The number of orders for the current query will be fetched from the server in Listing 14.5
- The CanExecute delegate of the GoBackCommand is easier to calculate (on line 7): This command can be executed if the page number is bigger than 0.

Finally, the GoForward and GoBack methods are shown in Listing 14.4.

LISTING 14.4 GoBack and GoForward Methods

```
1  public void GoForward()
2  {
3      var query = _currentQuery.Skip(++_pageNumber * PageSize)
4          .Take(PageSize);
5
6      _context.Orders.Clear();
7      _context.Load(query, LoadAllOrdersCompleted, null);
8  }
9
10 public void GoBack()
11 {
12     var query = _currentQuery.Skip(--_pageNumber * PageSize)
13         .Take(PageSize);
14
```

```
15         _context.Orders.Clear();
16         _context.Load(query, LoadAllOrdersCompleted, null);
17     }
```

- On line 3, we get the current query (depending on which method was executed, `LoadAllOrders` or `LoadOrdersByCity`). The query is extended by the `Skip` and `Take` methods, which "jump" to the correct page.
- On line 6, the current `Orders` table on the client is cleared.
- Line 7 loads the query, using the same `LoadAllOrdersCompleted` event handler that all other queries are using.
- The same happens for the `GoBack` method on lines 10 to 17.

The `LoadAllOrders` and `LoadAllOrdersByCity` methods used to perform the initial query on the data must also be modified as shown in Listing 14.5. The code in this listing replaces the original code in the existing application.

LISTING 14.5 Calling the Server-Side Method

```
 1  public void LoadAllOrders()
 2  {
 3      IsBusy = true;
 4      _pageNumber = 0;
 5      _isFilterApplied = false;
 6      _context.Orders.Clear();
 7      _currentQuery = _context.GetOrdersQuery().OrderBy(o => o.ShipCity);
 8      _context.GetNumberOfOrders(string.Empty, GetNumberOfOrdersCompleted, null);
 9      _context.Load(_currentQuery.Take(PageSize), LoadAllOrdersCompleted, null);
10  }
11
12  public void LoadAllOrdersByCityAndShip(string cityStart)
13  {
14      IsBusy = true;
14      _pageNumber = 0;
16      _isFilterApplied = false;
17      var query = from o in _context.GetOrdersByCityQuery(cityStart)
18                  where o.ShipName.StartsWith("V")
19                  orderby o.ShipCity
20                  orderby o.OrderID
21                  select o;
22
23      _currentQuery = query;
24      _context.GetNumberOfOrders(cityStart, GetNumberOfOrdersCompleted, null);
25      _context.Load(_currentQuery.Take(PageSize), LoadAllOrdersCompleted, null);
26  }
27
```

```
28  private void LoadAllOrdersCompleted(LoadOperation<Order> op)
29  {
30      Orders = new ObservableCollection<Order>(_context.Orders);
31      GoForwardCommand.RaiseCanExecuteChanged();
32      GoBackCommand.RaiseCanExecuteChanged();
33      IsBusy = false;
34  }
35
36  public void GetNumberOfOrdersCompleted(InvokeOperation<int> op)
37  {
38      _numberOfOrders = op.Value;
39      GoForwardCommand.RaiseCanExecuteChanged();
40  }
```


- Lines 7 and 24 have been added and require the current number of orders corresponding to the current query.
- Whenever a query is completed, the GoBackCommand and GoForwardCommand's CanExecuteChanged event is raised. This ensures that the state (enabled/disabled) of the command is recalculated, and the controls that are bound to these commands are enabled or disabled accordingly.
- Lines 36 to 40 are the callback for the asynchronous GetNumberOfOrders method. On line 38, the number of orders corresponding to the current query is saved in an attribute.
- On line 39, the GoForwardCommand's CanExecuteChanged is raised. This is necessary because the state of the command (enabled/disabled) depends on the number of orders, according to the calculation in Listing 14.3, lines 3 and 4.

To try paging, open MainPage.xaml and add two buttons (Prev and Next) below the Save, Add, and Delete buttons. Bind their Command property to the GoBackCommand and GoForwardCommand, respectively, on the MainViewModel.

The sample in this chapter is not the most sophisticated. To improve it, it would be nice to always preload one page in advance, and to cache the data. This way, the paging action would be faster. Another nice implementation is the endless scrolling already mentioned in Chapter 8.

Showing Errors

Many issues can occur between the client and the server. For example, it is possible that the server is down or that the client is not connected. In case an error occurs while data is fetched or saved, showing an error message to the client is absolutely necessary to avoid any confusion.

When an asynchronous operation is executed in WCF RIA Services, the callback receives one parameter with all the information about the result and (in case this is needed) what went wrong. We can use this information with the following steps:

1. Add a new method to the `MainViewModel` class as shown in Listing 14.6. This method uses the `IDialogService` to show the error to the user. Notice that the method `MarkErrorAsHandled` is called on the `OperationBase` parameter. If this is omitted, the application will crash.

LISTING 14.6 ShowError Method

```
private void ShowError(OperationBase op)
{
    IsBusy = false;
    if (op == null
        || op.Error == null)
    {
        ShowMessage("Unknown error");
        return;
    }

    ShowMessage(
        "There was an error:"
        + Environment.NewLine
        + op.Error.Message);
    op.MarkErrorAsHandled();
}
```

2. Modify the existing callbacks as shown in Listing 14.7.

LISTING 14.7 Modifying the Callbacks

```
private void LoadAllOrdersCompleted(LoadOperation<Order> op)
{
    if (op.HasError)
    {
        ShowError(op);
        return;
    }

    GoForwardCommand.RaiseCanExecuteChanged();
    GoBackCommand.RaiseCanExecuteChanged();
    IsBusy = false;
}

private void SaveChangesCompleted(SubmitOperation op)
{
    if (op.HasError)
    {
        ShowError(op);
```

```
            return;
        }

        IsBusy = false;
    }

    private void DeleteOrderCompleted(SubmitOperation op)
    {
        if (op.HasError)
        {
            ShowError(op);
            return;
        }

        _numberOfOrders--;
        IsBusy = false;
    }
```


Reconciling Data

A common scenario with client/server applications is that two or more clients access the data simultaneously. In this case, it is very important to prevent putting the database in an inconsistent state. For example, if the first client deletes a row of data, the second client should not be allowed to modify this entry after it has been removed from the database. WCF RIA Services watches the data for us and raises errors if an inconsistent operation is attempted. The following steps demonstrate this:

1. Start the application.
2. Copy the application's URL from the web browser's location bar.
3. Start a second window of the web browser (or another supported web browser) on the same computer and paste the address you copied in Step 2. This loads a second instance of the Silverlight application.
4. In the first Silverlight application, select the first row in the `DataGrid` and change the `Freight` column to 55. Then click the button Save.
5. Note that the display on the second application is not automatically updated. However, click the Next button (bound to the `GoForwardCommand`) to navigate to the next page, and then the Prev button (bound to the `GoBackCommand`). Notice that the `Freight` cell has now been updated to 55 as entered in Step 4.

   This case was not creating a conflict, and didn't leave the database in an inconsistent state. This is why it didn't raise an error. Of course, it would be nice if all the clients were notified when a row is modified. This doesn't occur automatically, but must be implemented manually (for example, with duplex polling, as you will see in Chapter 18, "Drag and Drop, Full Screen, Clipboard, COM Interop, Duplex Polling, Notification Windows, and Splash Screens").

6. In the first client, select the first row of data. Remember the Order ID, and then click the Delete button.

7. In the second client, try to change the `Freight` value in the order you just deleted (the row with the same Order ID). Then click the Save button.

This last step causes an error to be displayed. To identify precisely which entities are causing the issue, the `EntitiesInError` collection should be examined. For example, the `SaveChangesCompleted` method can be modified as shown in Listing 14.8.

LISTING 14.8 Detecting Conflicts and Refreshing the Data

```
private void SaveChangesCompleted(SubmitOperation op)
{
    if (op.HasError)
    {
        if (op.EntitiesInError != null
            && op.EntitiesInError.Count() > 0)
        {
            var ordersError = string.Empty;
            foreach (Order order in op.EntitiesInError)
            {
                ordersError
                    = string.Join(" ", ordersError, order.OrderID);
            }

            ShowMessage(string.Format(
                "Refreshing because of inconsistent data:{0}",
                ordersError));

            op.MarkErrorAsHandled();
            _context.Orders.Clear();
            _context.Load(
                 _currentQuery.Take(PageSize),
                 LoadAllOrdersCompleted,
                 null);
        }
        else
        {
            ShowError(op);
        }

        return;
    }

    IsBusy = false;
}
```

Copying and Pasting Rows

Silverlight 4 supports Clipboard access for the controls that have it enabled. For example, the `DataGrid` allows selecting rows and copying them to the Clipboard, as shown with the following steps:

1. Run the MyNorthwind Silverlight application and load some rows.
2. Select the rows that you want to copy. The `DataGrid` allows multiple selections by pressing the Ctrl key while the mouse is clicked. Contiguous rows can also be selected by pressing the Shift key while clicking the rows.
3. Press Ctrl+C on the keyboard. This causes a prompt to appear. Note that the user can choose to save the permission, so that he will be prompted only once for the current application.
4. Open a new text file in a text editor (for example, Notepad) and paste the rows.

Copying and Pasting Without Prompt (Elevated Permissions Only)

If the application runs with elevated permissions (as it will later in this chapter), the Clipboard can be accessed without the user having to confirm the action.

Revoking the Clipboard Access

Should the user decide to deny Clipboard access after he had allowed it, the Permissions tab in the Microsoft Silverlight Configuration dialog shown in Figure 14.5 further in this chapter can be used. In this tab, the permissions for each application can be removed (in which case subsequent attempts will have to be confirmed again) or even denied (in which case any subsequent attempt will fail).

Next to the Clipboard access, the user is asked for permission when the application wants to stay open in full-screen mode even when it does not have the focus (for example, when multiple monitors are used) and when the webcam and microphone are activated. You'll learn more about these features in Chapter 16, "Using Effects and Recording Media."

Printing

Silverlight 4 introduces printing in a very customizable way. It allows creating a print view from scratch in XAML. It is thus possible to create a completely different view of the same data for the printer. In this section, we will modify our MyNorthwind application to add a friendly dialog, load a data set from the WCF RIA Service, and create a printed report.

Of course, printing is not just limited to data; any XAML tree can be sent to the printer. Note, however, that the output is bitmap based, which explains why the process is relatively slow. (One page represents a large number of pixels, and of kilobytes.) This will certainly be improved in further versions of Silverlight.

Adding a Child Window

The following steps add a new `ChildWindow` to the application and use it to load a different set of data from the service. We need a different set because paging on the printer is done in a different way than in the online application. The whole data set is needed on the client, and pages are created on demand, in an asynchronous manner. For large number of data rows, this can obviously last quite a long time. Also, the application is blocked while printing is processed. To add a new `ChildWindow` follow these steps:

1. Open the Northwind.Web application in Visual Studio.
2. In the Silverlight project, add a new item. From the Silverlight category in the Add New Item dialog, select a Silverlight Child Window and name it PrintWindow.xaml.
3. In PrintWindow.xaml, set the `Title` property to Printing, and then add the markup in Listing 14.9 to the `LayoutRoot Grid`.

LISTING 14.9 Adding a Message

```
<TextBlock HorizontalAlignment="Center"
           Margin="0,30,0,0"
           x:Name="MessageTextBlock"
           Text="Initializing..."
           VerticalAlignment="Top" />
```

4. In PrintWindow.xaml.cs, modify the `PrintWindow` constructor as shown in Listing 14.10. The constructor receives the filter with which the query will be executed, and loads the orders accordingly.

LISTING 14.10 Constructing the `ChildWindow`

```
private OperationBase _operation;
private bool _cancel;
private int _printedItems;
private IEnumerable<Order> _ordersToPrint;

public PrintWindow(string cityStart)
{
    InitializeComponent();
    OKButton.IsEnabled = false;

    if (string.IsNullOrEmpty(cityStart))
    {
        MessageTextBlock.Text = string.Format(
            "Loading all orders",
            cityStart);
    }
    else
```

```
    {
        MessageTextBlock.Text = string.Format(
            "Loading orders for {0}",
            cityStart);
    }

    LoadOrders(cityStart);
}
```

5. Implement the `LoadOrders` method and its callback `LoadOrdersCompleted` as shown in Listing 14.11.

LISTING 14.11 Loading the Orders

```
private void LoadOrders(string cityStart)
{
    var context = new MyNorthwindDomainContext();
    _operation = context.Load(
        context.GetOrdersByCityQuery(cityStart),
        LoadCompleted,
        null);
}

private void LoadCompleted(LoadOperation<Order> op)
{
    MessageTextBlock.Text = string.Format(
        "{0} orders loaded, ready to print",
        op.Entities.Count());

    _ordersToPrint = op.Entities;
    OKButton.IsEnabled = true;
}
```

6. Modify the `CancelButton_Click` event handler as shown in Listing 14.12. If a long-lasting operation (loading a large number of rows) is conducted, clicking this button cancels the operation and closes the `ChildWindow`.

LISTING 14.12 Canceling the Operation

```
private void CancelButton_Click(object sender, RoutedEventArgs e)
{
    _cancel = true;

    if (_operation != null
        && _operation.CanCancel)
    {
```

```
        _operation.Cancel();
    }

    DialogResult = false;
}
```

Opening the Print Window

To open the print window from the main page, follow these steps:

1. In the ViewModel folder, select Add, Class from the context menu and name the new class **IPrintService.cs**. (Here, too, this is actually an interface, but there is no Add, New Interface dialog.) Implement this new interface as shown in Listing 14.13.

LISTING 14.13 IPrintService Interface

```
public interface IPrintService
{
    void PrintOrders();
}
```

2. In MainViewModel.cs, copy the `GoBackCommand` declaration, paste it and rename the pasted copy **PrintCommand**.
3. Copy the `DialogService` declaration and paste it; change the copy's type to `IPrintService`, and rename it from `DialogService` to **PrintService**.
4. In the `MainViewModel` constructor, below the `GoBackCommand` instantiation, create a new `PrintCommand` with the code shown in Listing 14.14.

LISTING 14.14 Creating the `PrintCommand`

```
PrintCommand = new RelayCommand(
    () =>
    {
        if (PrintService != null)
        {
            PrintService.PrintOrders();
        }
    });
```

5. In MainPage.xaml.cs, add `IPrintService` next to the `UserControl` and `IDialogService` declarations (where the `public partial class MainPage` is declared).
6. In the `MainPage` constructor, below the line where the `vm.DialogService` is set to `this`, do the same for `vm.PrintService`.
7. In MainPage.xaml.cs, implement the `PrintOrders` method as shown in Listing 14.15. Then build the application.

LISTING 14.15 PrintOrders Method

```
public void PrintOrders()
{
    var printWindow = new PrintWindow(CityStartTextBox.Text);
    printWindow.Show();
}
```

8. In MainPage.xaml, below the Delete button in the `StackPanel` on the right side, add a button with the same properties; set the `Content` to Print and bind its `Command` property to the `PrintCommand` property on the `MainViewModel`.

9. Build and run the application. Click the Print button. This opens the `PrintWindow` and after a short delay shows a message indicating that a number of orders have been loaded. Click the Cancel button to close the window.

Printing the Loaded Orders

We will now prepare an XAML document to be sent to the printer. Note that this could be done completely in code. However, creating a separate `UserControl` as we do here has the huge advantage to allow editing the XAML markup in the Visual Studio designer or in Blend, which is a very convenient way to customize what will be sent to the printer. To do this, follow these steps:

1. Add a new item to the Silverlight project and select a Silverlight User Control from the Silverlight category. Name it **PrintedReport.xaml**.

2. In PrintedReport.xaml, add a `DataTemplate` in the `UserControl.Resources` as shown in Listing 14.16. This is the element that will used to render each `Order` that must be printed. Note that Expression Blend can be used to customize this template visually. (However, the Visual Studio designer cannot do this at this time.)

LISTING 14.16 Creating a `DataTemplate`

```
<UserControl.Resources>
    <DataTemplate x:Key="OrdersTemplate">
        <StackPanel Margin="10">
            <StackPanel Orientation="Horizontal">
                <TextBlock Text="Order ID: "
                    FontWeight="Bold" FontSize="14" />
                <TextBlock Text="{Binding OrderID}"
                    FontSize="14" />
                <TextBlock Text=" To: "
                    FontWeight="Bold" FontSize="14" />
                <TextBlock Text="{Binding ShipCity}"
                    FontSize="14" />
            </StackPanel>
            <TextBlock Text="{Binding Freight, StringFormat=\{0:C\}}"
```

```
                FontSize="36" />
            <Rectangle Fill="Blue" Height="2" />
        </StackPanel>
    </DataTemplate>
</UserControl.Resources>
```

3. Modify the `LayoutRoot Grid` as shown in Listing 14.17.

LISTING 14.17 Setting Up the `PrintedReport` Markup

```
<Grid x:Name="LayoutRoot"
        Background="White">
    <Grid.RowDefinitions>
        <RowDefinition Height="50" />
        <RowDefinition Height="*" />
        <RowDefinition Height="50" />
    </Grid.RowDefinitions>

    <TextBlock HorizontalAlignment="Center"
        TextWrapping="Wrap"
        Text="Printed Orders Report"
        VerticalAlignment="Center"
        FontWeight="Bold" />
    <TextBlock HorizontalAlignment="Center"
        TextWrapping="Wrap"
        Text="Placeholder"
        x:Name="FooterTextBlock"
        VerticalAlignment="Center"
        Grid.Row="2" />

    <StackPanel Grid.Row="1"
        x:Name="OrdersPanel" />
</Grid>
```

4. Open MainPage.xaml.cs and implement the method `PreparePage` and the property `NumberOfOrders` as shown in Listing 14.18. This is a very important part of the printing process.

LISTING 14.18 Implementing the `PreparePage` Method

```
1  public int NumberOfOrders
2  { get; private set; }
3
4  public void PreparePage(
5       IEnumerable<Order> orders,
```

```
6       int startIndex, Size pageSize)
7   {
8       OrdersPanel.Children.Clear();
9       UpdateLayout();
10
11      foreach (var order in orders.Skip(startIndex))
12      {
13          var content = new ContentPresenter
14          {
15              Content = order,
16              ContentTemplate = Resources["OrdersTemplate"] as DataTemplate
17          };
18
19          OrdersPanel.Children.Add(content);
20          UpdateLayout();
21
22          if (DesiredSize.Height >= pageSize.Height)
23          {
24              OrdersPanel.Children.Remove(content);
25              break;
26          }
27      }
28
29      NumberOfOrders = OrdersPanel.Children.Count;
30      FooterTextBlock.Text = string.Format(
31          "Orders {0} to {1}",
32          startIndex + 1,
33          startIndex + NumberOfOrders);
34
35      UpdateLayout();
36  }
```

- Lines 1 and 2 declare a property that will be used later to know how many orders are being printed on one page. This number depends on the size of the page, the height of one order, the height of the header and footer, and so forth.
- On line 8, the `OrdersPanel` is cleared. This is a `StackPanel` that was prepared in Listing 14.17.
- On line 9, the `UpdateLayout` method is called. This method is available on each `UIElement` and forces it to recalculate its size. Note that calling this method in code can lower the application's performance, especially for complicated elements, and should be used only where needed, like in this listing.
- On lines 11 to 27, each `Order` (after the orders already rendered were skipped) is rendered by a `ContentPresenter` using the `DataTemplate` declared in Listing 14.16.

- Line 20 calls `UpdateLayout` again. This is needed because we want to know the exact size of the document and decide when we stop adding orders to avoid being larger than a physical page.
- Lines 22 to 26 perform this check. The `pageSize` is received from the method's caller and compared to the `UserControl`'s `DesiredSize` (another property available on every `UIElement`). If the `DesiredSize` is too large, the last added element is removed, and the loop is interrupted.
- Line 29 sets the `NumberOfOrders` property before the page's footer is prepared on lines 30 to 33. This shows how the XAML markup can be customized on each different page.
- Finally, `UpdateLayout` is called one last time to ensure that the `UserControl` will be rendered properly.

- Open PrintWindow.xaml.cs and modify the `OKButton_Click` event handler as shown in Listing 14.19. The `PrintDocument` class is raising events when needed to obtain new pages from the application.

LISTING 14.19 Preparing the `PrintDocument`

```
private void OKButton_Click(object sender, RoutedEventArgs e)
{
    var printDoc = new PrintDocument();
    printDoc.BeginPrint += BeginPrint;
    printDoc.PrintPage += PrintPage;
    printDoc.EndPrint += EndPrint;
    printDoc.Print("OrdersReport");
}
```

WARNING

Opening Dialogs

Calling the `Print` method on the `PrintDocument` class triggers the client computer to display the print dialog. For security reasons, this operation must be initiated by the user (for example, in response to a click event, as shown in Listing 14.19). If too many intermediary operations are performed before the `Print` method is called, a `SecurityException` is thrown.

5. Implement the `BeginPrint`, `PrintPage`, and `EndPrint` events as shown in Listing 14.20. Note that a reference to the namespace `System.Windows.Printing` must be added to the `using` directives.

LISTING 14.20 Handling the Print Events

```
1  private void BeginPrint(object sender, BeginPrintEventArgs e)
2  {
3      _printedItems = 0;
4  }
5
6  private void PrintPage(object sender, PrintPageEventArgs e)
7  {
8      var printedReport = new PrintedReport();
9      e.PageVisual = printedReport;
10
11     printedReport.PreparePage(
12         _ordersToPrint,
13         _printedItems,
14         e.PrintableArea);
15
16     _printedItems += printedReport.NumberOfOrders;
17     e.HasMorePages = _printedItems < _ordersToPrint.Count();
18 }
19
20 private void EndPrint(object sender, EndPrintEventArgs e)
21 {
22     DialogResult = true;
23 }
```


- Lines 1 to 4 are called when the Print button is clicked on the computer's print dialog. It signals the application that the print operation is started.
- Lines 6 to 18 are called every time that a new page is needed by the printer.
- Lines 8 and 9 create a new instance of the `PrintedReport` `UserControl` and assign it to the `PageVisual` property on the `PrintPageEventArgs` parameter. The `PrintDocument` will render this element and send it to the printer.
- Lines 11 to 14 call the `PreparePage` method on the `PrintedReport` control. Note the use of `e.PrintableArea`, which is the `Size` of the page available on the printer, after the margins have been removed.
- After the page has been prepared, the `NumberOfOrders` is retrieved and saved for later.
- Finally, line 17 checks whether additional pages are needed to render all the orders and sets the `HasMorePages` property accordingly.
- Lines 20 to 23 are called when the printing operation is finished, and simply close the `PrintWindow`.

To test this feature, run the application and click the Print button. To avoid killing trees while testing, use the Microsoft XPS Document Writer or a PDF writer if available. This will reproduce the printing experience digitally instead of using paper.

Printing is very useful for data applications, but it is of course also available for any other Silverlight application thanks to the `PrintDocument` class, inside or outside of the browser and without elevated permissions. Because the print dialog must be user initiated, and because the print operation cannot be started without the user explicitly giving his consent, security is respected.

Taking Silverlight Out of the Browser

Since Silverlight 3, it has been possible to install a Silverlight application on the user's hard drive and to run it in standalone mode, out of the browser (OOB), with or without an internet connection. This creates an experience very similar to running a standard Windows application. However, it has a few advantages:

- If the target PC does not have Silverlight installed, the setup experience is the same as for Silverlight in the browser. The same framework is used! The install experience is very fast and smooth, better than if the user had to install the full .NET framework.
- The framework is the same in the browser and out of the browser. If the application is installed with elevated permissions, additional features are available out of the browser, but generally speaking it is exactly the same framework, and what you already learned applies to this new kind of applications, too.
- The application can be run out of the browser on Apple computers, too. If the computer supports Silverlight, your application can be installed and run. This is the first time that standalone .NET applications can be installed on a Mac.

On the other hand, a Silverlight OOB application has fewer features than a Windows Presentation Foundation (WPF) application. For example, there is no true 3D framework in Silverlight (though the projection transform that we discuss in Chapter 17, "New Transforms, Right Click, HTML Browser, WebBrowserBrush, and Isolated Storage" allows some 3D-like effects), access to the host computer is limited, there is no real document presentation framework, and so on.

The decision to go Silverlight OOB or full WPF for a new application is not a very easy one. Generally speaking, if there is no "killer feature" that is unavailable on Silverlight, it is easier to start with a Silverlight OOB application, even if it needs to be converted to WPF later. Note, however, that the conversion mechanism is not completely straightforward and requires some effort.

> **WARNING**
>
> **Updating the OOB application**
>
> Unlike in browser applications, OOB applications are not updated automatically when a new version is available. This can be a little confusing at first. Further in the "Updating the Application" section, you will see how the application's version can be checked and an update triggered if needed.

Setting Up the Application

Installing the application out of the browser must be user initiated and requires additional settings. By default, your Silverlight application will not be installable out of the browser. To check whether the application is set up for this kind of installation, just right-click the application surface while it is running in the browser. If a context menu shows "Install [name] out of the browser" as shown in Figure 14.1, the application is ready for installation.

If this is not the case, however, the project properties need to be modified as follows:

1. Reopen the WCF RIA Services application that we created in Chapter 13 and modified in the first half of this chapter. This will be our basis for the next exercises. If you want to avoid changing this application, copy the folder containing it to another location before opening it.
2. In the Solution Explorer, right-click the Silverlight project and select Properties from the context menu.
3. Select the Silverlight tab. Then, check Enable Running the Application Out of the Browser check box.
4. Run the application and right-click the page. Note that you must make sure that you click the Silverlight surface, and not on the HTML page. For the sample application created in Chapter 13, the whole surface is filled by the Silverlight application, so there is no confusion possible.
5. In the context menu shown in Figure 14.1, select Install MyNorthwind.Silverlight onto this Computer.
6. In the Install application dialog shown in Figure 14.2, check both check boxes confirming the shortcut locations: Start menu and Desktop. Then click OK.

FIGURE 14.1 Installing the Silverlight application out of the browser.

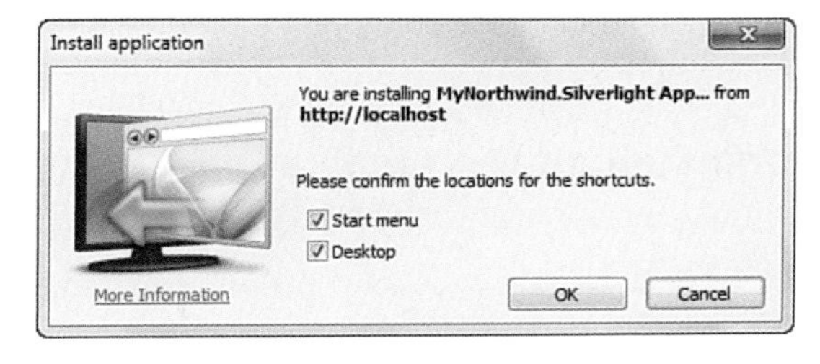

FIGURE 14.2 Install Application dialog.

The application opens in standalone mode, in its own window. The web browser remains open, but you can now close it. The `DataGrid` and the rest of the UI that was created in Chapter 13 are visible, and the data is loaded in the grid: Even though the application is running out of the browser, it connects to the WCF RIA server and offers exactly the same functionality as before.

One major difference is immediately visible though: the web browser's chrome (with the location bar, the back and forward buttons, the bookmarks, and so on) is gone. Instead, the application looks like a standard Windows or Mac application, with a title bar and borders. The icon in the title is also different, and looks like the one in the Install Application dialog shown in Figure 14.2.

Another difference is that a shortcut is now available on the desktop and also in the Start menu. Double-click the shortcut on the desktop to start the application again. The same application is started, and after a short delay the data appears again.

Making Sure That the WCF Server Is Running

The Silverlight application is now decoupled from the web server. However, it uses WCF RIA Services to connect and fetch data. This is obviously only possible if the server is up and running. To verify whether the development server is running while testing, follow these steps:

1. Open the web application's properties in Visual Studio.
2. On the Web tab, in the Servers section, write down the number appearing next to the Specific Port radio button.
3. In the Windows notification area, check whether a small icon similar to the one shown in Figure 14.3 is visible. If it is, pass the mouse over it and check whether the port displayed is the same than the one you wrote down in Step 2.

   If such an icon is available for the port you are looking for, the development web server is already running and the WCF service is available. If that is not the case, use the following checklist:

FIGURE 14.3 Development web server icon.

4. Open the web application in Visual Studio.
5. Right-click Default.aspx and select View in Browser from the context menu.

This last step starts the development web server integrated in Visual Studio 2010, which displays the message shown in Figure 14.4.

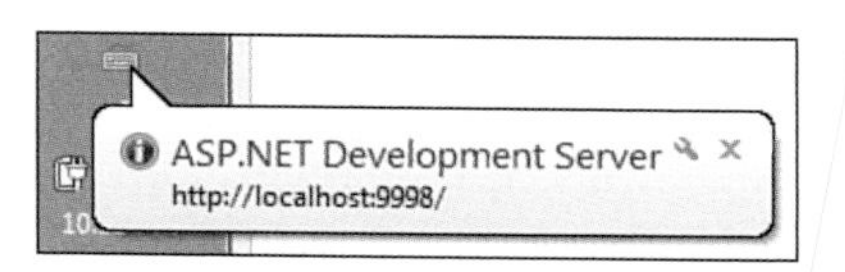

FIGURE 14.4 Starting the development web server.

Uninstalling the Application

Should the application need to be uninstalled, two ways are possible:

- With the application running, right-click its surface and select Remove This Application from the context menu.
- Open the Programs and Features control panel. Locate the application named MyNorthwind.Silverlight and click the Uninstall button.

Deleting the Isolated Storage

When the application is uninstalled, all the associated files are deleted, except the files saved in the isolated storage. (We talked about the isolated storage in *Silverlight 2 Unleashed*, Chapter 10.) To delete the isolated storage, the user has the possibility to use the following steps:

1. Right-click any Silverlight application and select Silverlight from the context menu.
2. In the Microsoft Silverlight Configuration dialog, select the Application Storage tab shown in Figure 14.5.

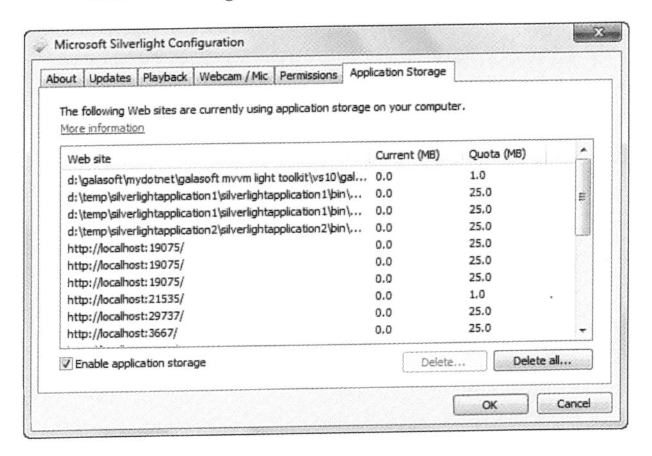

FIGURE 14.5 Microsoft Silverlight Configuration dialog.

3. Locate the application whose files you want to delete and click the Delete button. Alternatively, it is possible to delete all isolated stores, for example, to clean the host computer.

Debugging the OOB Application

Normally, the application is hosted into an HTML page:

- If no web application was created to host the Silverlight application, an HTML page is generated, and the Silverlight application runs within it. The HTML test application is created in the folder bin\Debug.
- If a web application was created as a separate project in the Solution, this web application should be set as start project, and the test HTML (or ASPX) page within it as start page.

In both cases, when the application is started from Visual Studio (by pressing the F5 or Ctrl+F5 keys), the HTML page is displayed in the web browser. To debug the application in OOB mode, the following steps are needed:

1. In the Solution Explorer, right-click the Silverlight project and select Properties from the context menu.
2. Select the Debug tab.
3. Set the Start Action to MyNorthwind.Web. It is a little confusing that to debug the OOB application MyNorthwind.Silverlight the choice must be set to MyNorthwind.Web. In most cases, however, there is only one choice in the combo box anyway.
4. Make sure that the Silverlight project is set as startup project in the Solution Explorer. The project name should appear in bold. If that is not the case, right-click the project name in the Solution Explorer and select Set as StartUp Project from the context menu.
5. Click F5 to run the application. If the dialog shown in Figure 14.6 appears, click the Yes button.
6. The OOB window appears and breakpoints can be placed within the code.

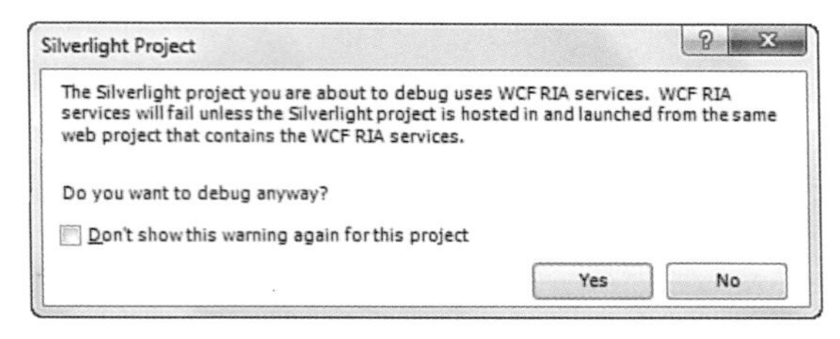

FIGURE 14.6 Warning dialog.

> **TIP**
>
> **Accessing Third-Party Web Servers**
>
> The OOB application is subject to the same restrictions as a Silverlight application running within the browser when it comes to cross-domain access: If the third-party server does not have a cross-domain file in place (as explained in Chapter 9, "Connecting to the Web"), the call will fail.
>
> Note, however, that applications with elevated permissions may access any server without restrictions.

Looking Under the Hood

Even though the Silverlight application runs in a standalone window, it is in fact hosted by a process, just like when it was running inside the web browser. This process is called sllauncher.exe and appears in the task manager when the OOB application is running. This is different from when you create a WPF application, where the process name is different for each application because it is not running into a host. This means that the Silverlight OOB application is not completely standalone.

Accessing the Host

When the application is running in OOB mode, there is no possibility for it to access its host like we did in *Silverlight 2 Unleashed*, Chapter 14. Access to the host computer is possible through specific APIs (and with the corresponding permissions, as you will see later in this chapter). For the Silverlight developer, it appears as if the application was completely independent.

Locating the Application Files

Another interesting fact about OOB applications is that, even though they appear in the list of installed applications in the Programs and Features control panel, the application files are not copied into C:\program files like for standard standalone applications. Most of the time, it is not relevant where the Silverlight OOB application is in fact copied, but do not get confused when looking for these files. Note that the application itself has no ways to know where its files are installed. This would be a security violation (revealing information about the directory structure of the host computer).

Should you however need to find the applications files, look into C:\Users\[name]\AppData\Local\Microsoft\Silverlight\OutOfBrowser, where [name] is your Windows user name. The files are installed there in subfolders with encoded names such as 1246460991.localhost.

Changing the Settings

A number of settings change the way that the OOB application behaves. To modify the settings, open the Silverlight project properties as we did before in this chapter. Then select the Silverlight tab and click the button labeled Out-of-Browser Settings.

WARNING

Making Sure That Changes Are Applied

Because of the way that the Silverlight OOB applications are cached, it is possible that changes to the application's properties (or even to the application in general) sometimes do not immediately appear when the application is run. To improve this behavior, try the following steps:

1. Run the application using the web project as the startup project.
2. Right-click and uninstall the OOB application.
3. Right-click the solution in the Solution Explorer and select Clean Solution from the context menu.
4. Click the Silverlight project and then on the second button from the left (the "Show All Files" button). This displays the folders that are not included in the project. Make sure that the folders named bin, obj, and Generated_Code are deleted.
5. Expand the web application in the Solution Explorer and delete the XAP file in the ClientBin folder.
6. Right-click the solution and select Rebuild Solution from the context menu.
7. Run and reinstall the application

Unfortunately, even these steps sometimes fail to refresh the changes. In that (rather rare) case, rebooting your computer is the last resort.

Setting the Window's Title, Shortcut Name, and Description

The Out-of-Browser Settings dialog allows entering a title, shortcut name, and a description for the application.

- The title will appear in the title bar and in the Windows application bar when the application is running.
- The shortcut name is used in the context menu shown in Figure 14.1 and in the dialog shown in Figure 14.2. It is also the name of the shortcut that is placed on the user's desktop and in his Start menu. Note that like with normal Windows application shortcuts, this name can be changed by the user.
- The description is shown when the user passes his mouse over the application shortcut on the desktop and in the Start menu. It is also shown in the comments of the Programs and Features control panel.

Setting the Window's Size and Position

The Out-of-Browser Settings dialog also allows setting the OOB window's initial size and position. These values are used every time that the user starts the application.

A better user experience strategy would be to save the window's current position and size when the user quits the application (for example, in the isolated storage). This must be done in code, however.

Setting Different Icons

Still in the Out-of-Browser Settings dialog, the icons for the application can be defined. Note that, in contrast to normal Windows applications, the icons are expected in the PNG format. ICO files will not work, because of the cross-platform compatibility needs. This is actually a good thing, because PNGs are easier to create than ICOs and have all the necessary features, such as transparency. You need, however, four different files (instead of having all four sizes embedded into one single ICO file).

To create icons for your application, follow these steps:

1. (If the application is already installed) Uninstall the application as explained in the "Uninstalling the Application" section of this chapter.
2. Create four different PNG files with dimensions 16 x 16, 32 x 32, 48 x 48, and 128 x 128 (in pixels). You need all four dimensions! To create the files, most drawing applications will work just fine. If you don't have a drawing application already, the free Paint.NET (running on the .NET framework) is a great drawing tool. For best results, make sure that your icons have a transparent background.
3. In the Solution Explorer, create a folder in the Silverlight project and name it **Resources** (or Icons, or any relevant name you prefer).
4. Right-click the new folder and select Add, Existing Item from the context menu.
5. Select the four PNG files and add them to the folder.

6. Open the Out-of-Browser Settings dialog and select the four icons files in the corresponding fields from the folder that was just created.
7. Click OK and install the application.

The icons are used in multiple places in the application: in the dialog shown in Figure 14.2, on the user's desktop and in his Start menu, in the application's title bar (and in the Windows taskbar). This is a great way to differentiate your application and to give it a specific identity.

Debugging the Icons

If the icons do not work as expected, check that all four PNG files are included correctly with the following steps:

1. In the Solution Explorer, click one of the PNG files and press F4 to show the Properties panel (or select the menu View, Properties Window).
2. Check that the Build Action is set to Content, and the Copy to Output property is set to Copy if Newer.
3. Repeat Steps 1 and 2 for all four PNG files.

Adding an element with the Content build action copies it into the XAP file but does not place it inside the DLL. If you rename the XAP file with a .zip extension, and open this file in a zip application, you can see that it contains the Resources folder and the four PNG files. On the other hand, a build action of Resource places the element *inside the assembly*. Although this is desired in some cases, if even just one of the four PNG icons has the wrong build action, the icons will not show properly in your application.

Using the Wrong Size

If an icon has the wrong size (for example, if you use a 64 x 64 PNG file for the 48 x 48 icon), it will be resized for the display. Note, however, that the icon may appear heavily pixilated in this case. It is better to use the correct sizes.

Using GPU Acceleration

Checking the corresponding check box in the Out-of-Browser Settings dialog enables GPU acceleration for the OOB application. For more information about the GPU acceleration, check the corresponding section in Chapter 21, "Optimizing Performance."

Show the Install Menu

The Show Install Menu check box controls what is displayed in the context menu when the user right-clicks the Silverlight application. By default, the context menu is set up as shown in Figure 14.1. You can, however, remove the Install menu item by unchecking this check box. This can be desired if you only want the user to install in certain circumstances or with a specific user experience. In that case, check the "Installing from the Code" section, later in this chapter.

Installing with Elevated Trust

Another check box allows to install with elevated permissions (elevated trust). This enables additional features in the application, as you will see in the "Running with Elevated Trust" section. The style of the host window can be set here, too: Default (with standard title bar and borders), No Border (without title bar or borders, with square corners), and Borderless Rounded Corners, as shown in Figure 14.7.

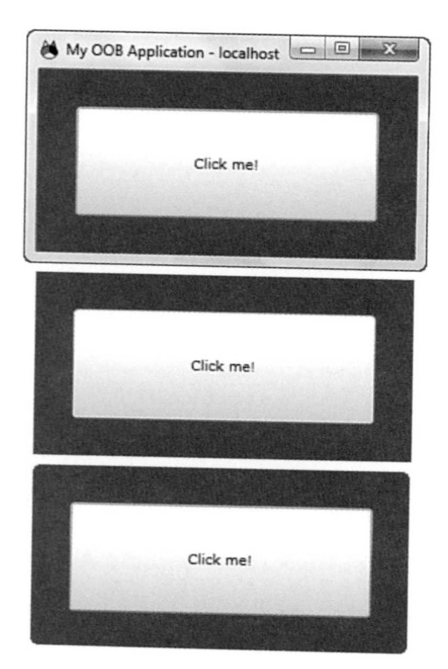

Figure 14.7 Window with borders, borderless, borderless rounded corners.

Note that even if the main `UserControl`'s background is set to `Transparent`, the Silverlight application will get a white background. Unlike in WPF, it is not possible to make transparent windows.

When an application is installed with elevated permissions, a different prompt is shown to the user (see Figure 14.8), similar to the Windows UAC (User Account Control) prompts. This signals the user that his action implies a security risk. Note that the dialog can be made much friendlier (as shown in Figure 14.9) by signing the Silverlight XAP file with a certificate such as the ones sold by Verisign and other firms. For more information about signing XAP files, check http://www.galasoft.ch/sl4-xapsign.

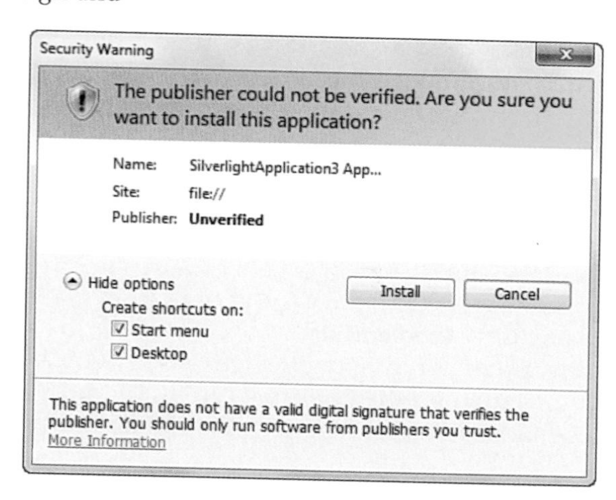

Figure 14.8 Security warning for unsigned application.

The following features are available with elevated permissions:

- Saving and reading documents in the user's folders such as My Documents, My Pictures, My Videos, and so forth. For more information, see the "Saving on the Hard Drive" section, later in this chapter.
- Accessing cross domain servers (even if they do not have a cross-domain access file).
- Accessing the Clipboard without prompt.
- Interoperability with COM.

- Hosting HTML in the Silverlight application.
- Displaying notification windows.

These three last features are detailed in Chapter 18.

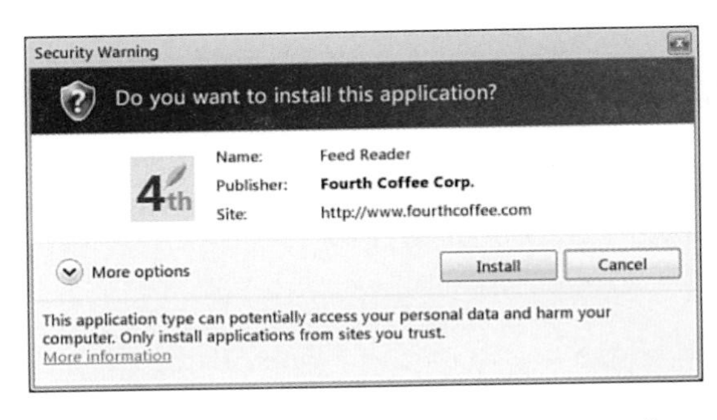

Figure 14.9 Security warning for signed application (from the Silverlight documentation).

Editing the Settings

The out-of-browser settings can also be seen in the file named OutOfBrowserSettings.xml in the Properties folder. This file's content is copied to the application manifest (AppManifest.xaml), which is enclosed in the XAP file. When the application is started, the Silverlight plug-in reads all the settings from this file and configures the out-of-browser application correspondingly.

Updating the Application

When Silverlight applications run within the web browser, they go through the exact same caching mechanisms as all other web materials: When the browser receives the order to load an element (web page, image, video, Silverlight XAP file, and so on), it checks first if the element is available in the cache. If it is found, a request is sent to the server to ask what is the last modified date of the server version. If a newer version is available on the server, the element is downloaded. If not, the cached version is used.

For the developer, it makes publishing a new version of a Silverlight application very easy: Just copy the XAP file to the web browser, and it will be downloaded by the web browser the next time that the application is run on the client computer.

With OOB applications, it is not as simple anymore: All the files are copied locally to a folder on the hard drive, and there is no automated way to check on the server whether a newer version exists. The application must perform the check manually. This can be triggered by the user when he clicks a Check Update button, for example, or even when the application starts, as shown in Listing 14.21 (to be placed in App.xaml.cs).

LISTING 14.21 Checking and Downloading an Update

```
1  private void Application_Startup(object sender, StartupEventArgs e)
2  {
3      if (IsRunningOutOfBrowser
4          && MessageBox.Show(
5              "Do you want to check for an update?",
6              "Check update?", MessageBoxButton.OKCancel)
7                  == MessageBoxResult.OK)
8      {
9          CheckAndDownloadUpdateCompleted += UpdateCompleted;
```

```
10            CheckAndDownloadUpdateAsync();
11        }
12        else
13        {
14            RootVisual = new MainPage();
15        }
16    }
```

- On line 3, we check whether the application runs outside of the browser. There is no point checking for an update if the application runs inside of the browser!
- On lines 4 to 7, we ask for confirmation from the user. Because a restart of the application is required to load the update, it is good practice to request confirmation before the download is initiated. Note, however, that it is not strictly required.
- On line 10, the check and update is initiated. The callback is the `UpdateCompleted` method defined in Listing 14.22.
- If the user chooses not to check for an update, the `MainPage` is loaded in the `RootVisual`, which starts the application with the normal UI.

WARNING

Checking at Every Occasion

Unfortunately, there is no way currently to check for a new version without automatically downloading and installing the updated version. Asking for the user's confirmation every time that the application starts is not very satisfying for the user experience. Another option is to let the user initiate the action by clicking a button, but there is a risk that the user never updates the application.

Another, perhaps more interesting solution is to let the application check for a new update (for example, by downloading a text file with the version number), and only asking the user to download the new application if there is a new version.

LISTING 14.22 UpdateCompleted Callback

```
1  private void UpdateCompleted(
2      object sender,
3      CheckAndDownloadUpdateCompletedEventArgs e)
4  {
5      if (e.UpdateAvailable)
6      {
7          var grid = new Grid
8          {
9              Background = new SolidColorBrush(Colors.Red)
10         };
11
```

```
12          var text = new TextBlock
13          {
14              Text = "An update has been downloaded, restart the application",
15              FontSize = 40,
16              TextWrapping = TextWrapping.Wrap,
17              Foreground = new SolidColorBrush(Colors.White),
18              VerticalAlignment = VerticalAlignment.Center,
19              HorizontalAlignment = HorizontalAlignment.Center
20          };
21
22          grid.Children.Add(text);
23          RootVisual = grid;
24      }
25      else
26      {
27          if (e.Error != null
28              && e.Error is PlatformNotSupportedException)
29          {
30              MessageBox.Show(
31                  "You need a new version of Silverlight for the update"
32                  + "Visit the application's homepage to upgrade");
33          }
34
35          RootVisual = new MainPage();
36      }
37  }
```

- Line 5 checks in the `EventArgs` if an update was available. If the `UpdateAvailable` variable is `true`, the update has been downloaded already. There is, however, no way to restart the application automatically, which is why an ad hoc UI is prepared on lines 7 to 23. This is a good example of how the `RootVisual` property can be set manually.
- If `UpdateAvailable` is `false`, it can be because the update requires a new version of the Silverlight framework. In that case, the user is warned that he should visit the website from where the application was installed.
- Finally, the application is started on line 35.

Installing from the Code

In addition to the Silverlight context menu shown in Figure 14.1, it is also possible to trigger the installation of the application from the code. This must be in response to a user interaction, such as a button click. In addition, the call to the `Install` method must happen as soon as possible after the first operation after the button is clicked. For example, consider the code in Listing 14.23.

14

LISTING 14.23 Installing the Application in Code

```
1  private void Button_Click(object sender, RoutedEventArgs e)
2  {
3      try
4      {
5          // MessageBox.Show("Installing now");
6
7          if (App.Current.IsRunningOutOfBrowser)
8          {
9              MessageBox.Show("Already installed");
10             return;
11         }
12
13         App.Current.Install();
14     }
15     catch (InvalidOperationException)
16     {
17         MessageBox.Show("The application is already installed");
18     }
19 }
```

- On line 7, we check whether the application is already running out of the browser, in which case a message is displayed. An even better user experience would be to check the state of the application when it starts, and to hide or disable the install button accordingly.
- On line 13, the application is installed.
- If the application is already installed on the current machine, an `InvalidOperationException` is thrown. This can happen if the user is unaware that the application is already installed, runs the Silverlight application from the website, and tries to install it again. In that case, the exception is caught on line 15, and an error message is shown.
- If line 5 is uncommented and made active, the installation will fail. No exception is thrown, but the application is not installed. This happens because the call to `App.Current.Install` occurs too late in the function.

Displaying a Custom UI Requiring the User to Install the Application

If the application makes sense only out of the browser (for example, if every operation requires elevated permissions), a custom UI can be displayed to require that the user installs before he proceeds. This is very similar to the steps we took

> **WARNING**
>
> **Setting the `RootVisual`**
>
> Through the `RootVisual`, you have control over what your application displays. Note, however, that the `RootVisual` can be set only once!

in Listing 14.22, lines 7 to 23. The custom UI will be shown if `IsRunningOutOfBrowser` is `false`. In this case, construct a `Grid` with a `TextBlock` and a `Button`, and wire the `Button`'s `Click` event to the event handler defined in Listing 14.23.

Saving Files

Silverlight 4 provides more possibilities to save documents on the client machine than ever. Saving locally can be done in the isolated storage, in the user's local folders. It is also possible to save to new documents created through COM automation (Windows only, as we will see in Chapter 18) or with the SaveFileDialog that we will discover in Chapter 16, "Using Effects and Recording Media."

Saving in the Isolated Storage

We already saw how to use the isolated storage in *Silverlight 2 Unleashed*, Chapter 10. In this book, Chapter 17, we talk more about new features implemented in the isolated storage in Silverlight 4.

When the application is running out of the browser, the isolated storage default quota is set to 25MB rather than 1MB in the browser. Note, however, that additional storage can be requested, as you will see in Chapter 17.

Saving in My Documents (Elevated Permissions Only)

The isolated storage is very convenient to save documents that are used internally by the application (for example, settings, temporary documents, and so on) but it is not very user friendly. It is not very convenient for the user to go and look for files in this rather hidden location.

Instead, Silverlight 4 applications with elevated permissions may save and read documents in the user's folders (My Documents, My Videos, My Music and My Pictures).

For example, the current page of data in the Northwind application can be saved to a text file using the following steps:

1. Reopen the Northwind.Web application in Visual Studio.
2. In the `MainViewModel` class, add a new command next to the existing `SaveCommand`, `AddCommand`, `DeleteOrderCommand`, `GoForwardCommand`, `GoBackCommand` and `PrintCommand`, as shown in Listing 14.24

LISTING 14.24 SaveToFileCommand

```
public RelayCommand SaveToFileCommand
{
    get;
    private set;
}
```

- In the `MainViewModel` constructor, initialize the `SaveToFileCommand` with the code shown in Listing 14.25, to be placed below the other commands' initialization.

LISTING 14.25 Creating the SaveToFileCommand

```
SaveToFileCommand = new RelayCommand(
    SaveToFile,
    () => App.Current.IsRunningOutOfBrowser
        && App.Current.HasElevatedPermissions);
```

- The Execute delegate is set to a method named SaveToFile, which is defined in Listing 14.26 below.
- The CanExecute delegate only returns true if the application is running out of the browser with elevated permissions. If that is not the case, the control bound to the command will be disabled.

3. Implement the SaveToFile method as shown in Listing 14.26.

LISTING 14.26 SaveToFile Method

```
1  public void SaveToFile()
2  {
3      if (!App.Current.IsRunningOutOfBrowser
4          || !App.Current.HasElevatedPermissions)
5      {
6          ShowMessage("Unavailable");
7          return;
8      }
9
10     var filePath = System.IO.Path.Combine(
11         Environment.GetFolderPath(
12             Environment.SpecialFolder.MyDocuments),
13         "NorthwindFiles\\Northwind.txt");
14
15     var fileInfo = new FileInfo(filePath);
16     if (!fileInfo.Directory.Exists)
17     {
18         fileInfo.Directory.Create();
19     }
20
21     if (fileInfo.Exists)
22     {
23         fileInfo.Delete();
24     }
25
26     using (var writer = new StreamWriter(fileInfo.FullName))
27     {
28         foreach (var order in _context.Orders)
```

```
29                 {
30                     writer.WriteLine(string.Format(
31                         "Order {0} to {1}, shipped on {2}",
32                         order.OrderID,
33                         order.ShipCity,
34                         order.ShippedDate));
35                 }
36             }
37     }
```

- On lines 3 to 8, we make sure that the application is running out of the browser and has elevated permissions. Even though the command that invokes this method will be disabled if that is not the case, the method is public and could be called by other means. It needs to be protected, to avoid a `SecurityException` to be thrown.
- On lines 10 to 13, the path to My Documents folder is retrieved with a call to the method `Environment.GetFolderPath`, with the argument `Environment.SpecialFolder.MyDocuments`. Note that all other special folders (such as the Desktop folder, the ApplicationData folder, and so on) are available in this enumeration. However, attempting to get any other value than `MyDocuments`, `MyVideos`, `MyPictures`, and `MyMusic` throws a `SecurityException`.
- The new file named Northwind.txt will be saved into a folder named NorthwindFiles within the My Documents folder.
- On line 15, a new instance of the `FileInfo` class is created. This class (as well as the `DirectoryInfo` class) in the `System.IO` namespace are very helpful to manipulate files and directories.
- On lines 16 to 19, the NorthwindFiles directory is created, in case it was not already existing.
- Lines 21 to 24 delete the file in case it was already existing.
- On line 26, a `StreamWriter` is created. There are multiple readers and writers depending on the type of file you want to read or save. The `StreamWriter` class is ideal to save text files. Note the usage of the `using` statement, which will automatically take care of closing and disposing the `StreamWriter` when the save operation is completed.
- Finally, on lines 28 to 35, we loop through all the orders in the `Orders` table of the Domain Context class (corresponding to the page currently displayed by the `DataGrid`) and save their `OrderID`, `ShipCity`, and `ShippedDate`.

4. To test the functionality, open MainPage.xaml in the Visual Studio designer; add a button below the Save, Add, and Delete buttons; and bind its `Command` property to the `SaveToFileCommand` property we added in Listing 14.24.

To check the result, open Windows Explorer and navigate to the My Documents folder. The folder NorthwindFiles should be present and contain one file named NorthwindFile.txt, with the list of saved orders.

Working Offline

A Silverlight application can detect the state of the network connectivity by using the code in Listing 14.27.

LISTING 14.27 Testing Network Connectivity

```
1  public MainPage()
2  {
3      InitializeComponent();
4      NetworkChange.NetworkAddressChanged += NetworkChanged;
5      CheckApplicationState();
6  }
7
8  private void NetworkChanged(object sender, EventArgs e)
9  {
10     CheckApplicationState();
11 }
12
13 private void CheckApplicationState()
14 {
15     if (NetworkInterface.GetIsNetworkAvailable())
16     {
17         // Online
18     }
19     else
20     {
21         // Offline
22     }
23 }
```

- Line 4 assigns an event handler to the `NetworkChange.NetworkAddressChanged` event that is raised every time that the network connectivity changes.
- The `CheckApplicationState` method calls the `NetworkInterface.GetIsNetworkAvailable` method. This returns `true` if network connectivity is available, `false` otherwise.

To enable a pure offline mode, the following features must be implemented:

- The application must be able to save data to the isolated storage.
- A synchronization mechanism must be implemented.

At the time of this writing, there is no officially available synchronization framework for Silverlight. However, Microsoft is perfecting its Sync Framework and modifying it to work with Silverlight. When it is available, it will allow applications to store data in the isolated storage, go offline, modify this data while being offline, and then to synchronize the changes back to the server when the application goes back online.

You can find more information about the Sync Framework and its application to Silverlight at http://www.galasoft.ch/sl4-sync.

Summary

This chapter and the previous showed how to develop applications that are not necessarily associated with Silverlight by people discovering the technology. Although the media and animation features are very enticing, having the possibility to develop rich business applications with Silverlight, in or out of the browser, is an exciting prospect for a large number of enterprise developers.

Even after so many pages, only some aspects of WCF RIA Services were covered. For example, we didn't talk yet about authentication and authorization, which will be handled in Chapter 19, "Authentication, Event to Command Binding, Random Animations, Multitouch, Local Communication, and Bing Maps Control." However, these pages should already get you started to handle a wide range of data scenarios!

In the second half of this chapter, we talked about taking Silverlight out of the browser and running the application standalone, in a manner very similar to any standard Windows or Mac application. Finally, you saw how elevated permissions can be given to the application, to allow operations that can present a security risk.

In the next chapter, we talk about Silverlight navigation applications and about the Windows Phone 7 applications running on Silverlight, another exciting usage of the Silverlight framework.

CHAPTER 15

Developing Navigation Applications and Silverlight for Windows Phone 7

IN THIS CHAPTER, WE WILL:

- Manually implement a simple application with pages, and understand why this is not ideal.
- Discover the concept of navigation built into Silverlight, and discuss when you should use it.
- Build a sample navigation application and talk about features such as routes, deep linking and the navigation service.
- Discover the brand new Silverlight for Windows Phone 7.
- Talk about the phone experience and default styles.
- Install the Windows Phone 7 tools.
- Develop a connected MVVM application in Silverlight for the desktop and for Windows Phone 7.

So far in this book, we've always started by creating a "standard" Silverlight application in Visual Studio or Expression Blend's New Project dialog (shown in Figure 2.1). Although this project template covers many requirements, this chapter talks about another application template called the Silverlight navigation application that is especially well suited to create applications where the web browser's Back and Forward buttons should be enabled or when a link (as a bookmark or copied and pasted in a document or an email) should lead the user directly to a specific screen in the application (commonly referred to as "deep linking").

In the second part of this chapter, we take an early look at the Windows Phone 7 devices and the way to develop applications for this mobile platform using Silverlight. Although the tools, framework, and devices for Windows Phone 7 are still in beta stage at the time of this writing, it is very interesting to see how Silverlight is used on this platform, allowing us to leverage what we learned to develop mobile applications.

Navigating with Silverlight

One big issue with rich application frameworks such as Silverlight or Flash is that they are difficult to navigate and not well integrated with the web browser history journal. For example, try the following steps:

1. Create a new "standard" Silverlight application in Visual Studio.
2. Edit the XAML markup of the LayoutRoot grid as shown in Listing 15.1. This creates two "pages" (implemented as Grid panels) on top of each other.

LISTING 15.1 Grid with Two "Pages"

```
1   <Grid x:Name="LayoutRoot"
2           Background="White">
3
4       <Grid x:Name="Page1"
5                Background="Red">
6           <TextBlock Text="Page 1" />
7
8           <Button Content="Forward"
9                   VerticalAlignment="Bottom"
10                  Click="ForwardButton_Click"
11                  Margin="10"
12                  Height="100"
13                  Width="200"/>
14      </Grid>
15
16      <Grid x:Name="Page2"
17              Background="Blue"
18              Visibility="Collapsed">
29          <TextBlock Text="Page 2" />
20
21          <Button Content="Back"
22                  VerticalAlignment="Bottom"
23                  Click="BackButton_Click"
24                  Margin="10"
25                  Height="100"
26                  Width="200" />
27      </Grid>
28  </Grid>
```

3. Right-click the event handler name ForwardButton_Click on line 10 of Listing 15.1, and select Navigate to Event Handler from the context menu. This creates the corresponding event handler in the code behind.
4. Select the MainPage.xaml again, and right-click the event handler name BackButton_Click on line 23 of Listing 15.1. Again, select Navigate to Event Handler from the context menu.
5. In MainPage.xaml.cs, implement both event handlers as shown in Listing 15.2.

LISTING 15.2 Navigating Back and Forth

```
private void ForwardButton_Click(
    object sender,
    RoutedEventArgs e)
{
    Page2.Visibility = Visibility.Visible;
    Page1.Visibility = Visibility.Collapsed;
}

private void BackButton_Click(
    object sender,
    RoutedEventArgs e)
{
    Page1.Visibility = Visibility.Visible;
    Page2.Visibility = Visibility.Collapsed;
}
```

6. Run the application and click the button marked Forward in the red page. This displays the blue page. Then click the button marked Back on the blue page to get back on the red page.

This very simple example implements a primitive navigation system. By putting the content of the pages in external `UserControl` files, we could even achieve separation of concerns, and have a fairly simple navigation application. However, there are two major issues:

- Depending on your web browser's history before you started the application, the browser's Back button might not be enabled at all. Or, if it is enabled, clicking it will stop the application, unload the whole Silverlight application and instead load the previous page (probably HTML) that was visible in the browser before you started the Silverlight application. There is no integration with the web browser's history.
- Sometimes you want a user to start directly on the blue page instead of having to go through the red page. In theory, you could add a query string to the HTML page's address, and implement custom parsing to load the correct "page" when the application starts. However, this is not straightforward; also, the URL with query string has a rather cumbersome format, not very user readable.

These issues are crippling most rich applications and breaking the model of the World Wide Web in which each Unique Resource Locator (URL) should lead to a unique resource, and each different resource (for example, Page1 and Page2) should have a different URL.

To solve these issues, the Silverlight framework has a different application template named the Silverlight Navigation Application that provides the initial plumbing to create an application that follows these navigation patterns, fully integrated with the web browser's journal and supporting deep linking.

Should You Always Use a Navigation Application?

Because of the advantages of the Silverlight navigation application, it is tempting to always use this kind of application. However, it is not always the best suited for the job.

By studying the requirements you need to implement, it should be possible to decide yourself for one or the other type. Note that switching from a standard application to a navigation application (or the reverse) involves some manual work (as shown in the "Adding Navigation to a Non-Navigation Application" section, later in this chapter). If possible, this decision should be taken before the start of the development.

- For applications that are more like a website, with multiple pages and defined navigation between the pages, a navigation application is the better choice.
- If you need to start the application on a specific page, the navigation application will help you by automatically displaying the page corresponding to a unique URL.
- On the other hand, if the Silverlight application is more like well-known desktop applications such as Microsoft Word or Excel, starting with a standard Silverlight application is better. This doesn't mean that standard applications cannot navigate between screens (for example like a wizard with a flow of content), but this might not be their main intent.

> **WARNING**
>
> **Handling Multiple Points of Entry**
>
> For certain applications, it can be a disadvantage to have multiple points of entry, like the navigation applications offer. For example, sometimes the user must go through a login page before entering the application. Every time that a different page is accessed, the application must check whether the credentials have been entered correctly. This is not very complicated, but requires more manual work than with an application with a single point of entry.

Creating a New Navigation Application

To create a new navigation application, select the corresponding template in Visual Studio, as shown with the following steps:

1. In Visual Studio, select File, New, Project.
2. In the New Project dialog, under the category Silverlight, select a Silverlight Navigation Application.
3. Enter the name NavigationSample for the application and select a location, then click OK.
4. A website to host the application is not needed; simply uncheck the corresponding check box in the New Silverlight Application dialog and click OK.
5. In the Solution Explorer, notice that two folders that we never saw before can be found: Assets and Views. To understand what these folders and the documents that they contain do, press Ctrl+F5 to run the application. The Home page is opened, as shown in Figure 15.1.

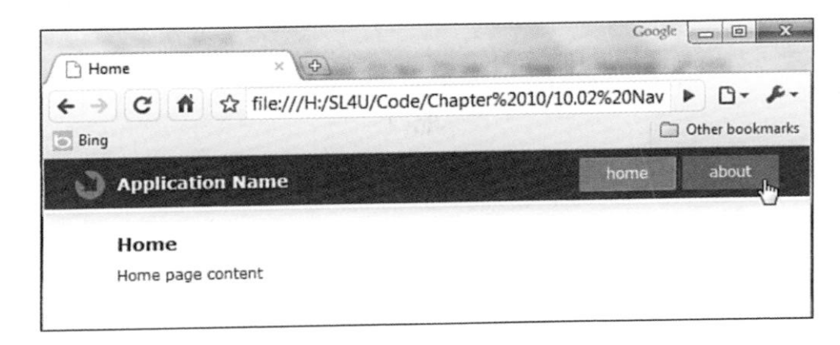

FIGURE 15.1 Navigation application with Home and About pages.

6. Click the About link on the top right of the application. The About page is displayed.
7. Click the web browser's Back button. The Home page is displayed again, and the browser's Forward button is enabled. Clicking this button now would show the About page again.

This small sample shows that the navigation between the Home and the About pages is *integrated into the web browser's history*. This makes the Silverlight navigation application very similar to a standard website for the end user, while providing all the comfort of development that the Silverlight tools provide.

Understanding the Structure

Open the file MainPage.xaml. This is the *navigation host* where all other pages are displayed. This page consists of well-known Silverlight controls, with one exception: the `navigation:Frame` and its content shown in Listing 15.3. (The prefix `navigation` represents the namespace `System.Windows.Controls` in the assembly System.Windows.Controls.Navigation.dll. Note that this assembly is not part of the core Silverlight framework, and it will be added to your XAP file.) This component is responsible for the whole navigation in the application, and for the integration with the web browser's navigation.

LISTING 15.3 Navigation `Frame` Element

```
1  <navigation:Frame x:Name="ContentFrame"
2                    Style="{StaticResource ContentFrameStyle}"
3                    Source="/Home"
4                    Navigated="ContentFrame_Navigated"
5                    NavigationFailed="ContentFrame_NavigationFailed">
6      <navigation:Frame.UriMapper>
7          <uriMapper:UriMapper>
8              <uriMapper:UriMapping Uri=""
9                                    MappedUri="/Views/Home.xaml" />
10             <uriMapper:UriMapping Uri="/{pageName}"
11                                   MappedUri="/Views/{pageName}.xaml" />
```

```
12            </uriMapper:UriMapper>
13        </navigation:Frame.UriMapper>
14    </navigation:Frame>
```

- On line 3, the `Source` property defines which page will be displayed first in the host. This is a URI that will be resolved using the entries in the URI mapper.
- On lines 4 and 5, two important events are handled: `Navigated` and `NavigationFailed`. We will talk about navigation events in the "Handling Navigation Events" section.
- On lines 6 to 13, the URI mapper is defined. This very important element is mapping all the URIs entered in the navigation bar of the web browser to the corresponding page. We talk about the mapping in the "Deep Linking to Pages" section.

Another interesting section is the `LinksStackPanel` shown in Listing 15.4. This panel contains two `HyperlinkButton` elements that can be clicked for navigation. The `NavigateUri` property will be set in the web browser's navigation bar, which causes the `UriMapper` to display the corresponding page in the host.

LISTING 15.4 Navigation with a `HyperlinkButton` Control

```
<StackPanel x:Name="LinksStackPanel"
            Style="{StaticResource LinksStackPanelStyle}">
    <HyperlinkButton x:Name="Link1"
                     Style="{StaticResource LinkStyle}"
                     NavigateUri="/Home"
                     TargetName="ContentFrame"
                     Content="home"/>

    <Rectangle x:Name="Divider1"
               Style="{StaticResource DividerStyle}"/>

    <HyperlinkButton x:Name="Link2"
                     Style="{StaticResource LinkStyle}"
                     NavigateUri="/About"
                     TargetName="ContentFrame"
                     Content="about"/>
</StackPanel>
```

Note that other elements can also be used for the navigation, such as the `Hyperlink` control, as shown in Listing 15.5.

LISTING 15.5 Navigation with a `Hyperlink` Control

```
<RichTextBox IsReadOnly="True">
    <Paragraph>
        Click here to go to
        the <Hyperlink NavigateUri="/About">About
        page</Hyperlink>
    </Paragraph>
</RichTextBox>
```

TIP

Using a `TargetName`

Note that even though the `HyperlinkButton` elements in Listing 15.4 are using the `TargetName` property, this is not strictly needed. The code also works without this property because there is only one `Frame` on the page. If you have multiple `Frame` elements, the `TargetName` property should be set to specify which host must display the page.

Deep Linking to Pages

The `UriMapper` element also allows deep linking; that is, the ability to navigate directly to a given page by clicking on a hyperlink (for example, embedded in an email) or a bookmark. To understand how this works, let's observe the URL that the web browser's navigation bar displays. Depending how your environment is configured, it could look something like this:

```
file:///C:/Code/NavigationSample/Bin/Debug/NavigationSampleTestPage.html#/Home
```

Or if the application is executed from a web server (and not in debug mode in Visual Studio), it could be something like this:

```
http://www.mypage.com/NavigationSampleTestPage.html#/Home
```

The important part here is what comes after the # character: The string `/Home` will be mapped by the `UriMapper`. In this case, the expression defined on line 10 of Listing 15.3 is used. The parameter `pageName` is replaced in the URI on line 11, and the page `Views/Home.xaml` is displayed in the host.

Note that another mapping is defined: If the page name parameter is missing from the URL, the expression on line 8 of Listing 15.3 is used and the page `Views/Home.xaml` is displayed, too.

Creating New Pages

Adding new pages to the application is fairly easy as shown with the following steps:

1. With the NavigationSample application open in Visual Studio, right-click the Views folder in the Solution Explorer, and select Add, New Folder from the context menu. Name this new folder **Shop**.

2. Right-click the Shop folder and select Add, New Item from the context menu.
3. In the Add New Item dialog, select the Silverlight category and add a new Silverlight Page named Catalog.xaml.

The new page is a `navigation:Page`. The rest of the XAML markup looks very similar to a standard Silverlight page (which is a `UserControl` as we saw before). Adding elements and styling the UI works exactly as for a normal page.

To define the mapping, follow these steps:

1. Reopen the file MainPage.xaml.
2. Change the `HyperlinkButton` elements as shown in Listing 15.6.

LISTING 15.6 Changing the `HyperlinkButton` Elements

```
<StackPanel x:Name="LinksStackPanel"
            Style="{StaticResource LinksStackPanelStyle}">
    <HyperlinkButton Style="{StaticResource LinkStyle}"
                     NavigateUri="/Shop/Beds/King"
                     Content="King Size Beds"/>

    <Rectangle Style="{StaticResource DividerStyle}"/>

    <HyperlinkButton Style="{StaticResource LinkStyle}"
                     NavigateUri="/Shop/Beds/Queen"
                     Content="Queen Size Beds" />
</StackPanel>
```

In the `UriMapper`, add a mapping as shown in Listing 15.7.

LISTING 15.7 New URI Mapping

```
 1  <uriMapper:UriMapper>
 2      <uriMapper:UriMapping Uri=""
 3        MappedUri="/Views/Home.xaml" />
 4      <uriMapper:UriMapping Uri="/Shop"
 5         MappedUri="/Views/Shop/Catalog.xaml" />
 6      <uriMapper:UriMapping Uri="/Shop/{category}/{filter}"
 7      MappedUri="/Views/Shop/Catalog.xaml?cat={category}&amp;filter={filter}" />
 8      <uriMapper:UriMapping Uri="/{pageName}"
 9        MappedUri="/Views/{pageName}.xaml" />
10  </uriMapper:UriMapper>
```

- Two URIs were added to the list: If the user navigates to `/Shop`, the page named Catalog.xaml will be displayed without specific information, as mapped on lines 4 and 5.
- If the user navigates for example, to `/Shop/Beds/QueenSize`, the URI will be mapped into `/Views/Shop/Catalog.xaml?cat=Beds&filter=QueenSize` as mapped on lines 6 and 7. The URI entered by the user is much shorter and less cryptic than the one it is mapped to. Also, the mapping helps reorganizing the application: It is easy to move the file Catalog.xaml to a different folder; the bookmarks saved by the user must not be updated; only the URI mapping needs to be changed.
- The order in which the mappings are placed in the list is very important. Some mappings are greedier than others. For example, the mapping on lines 4 and 5 is included in the mapping in line 8 and 9. If the `/{pageName}` mapping was placed before the `/Shop` mapping, the latter would never be called because the `/Shop` URI would be caught by the more generic one.

The concept of mapping a URI to another also exists in other frameworks such as ASP.NET MVC. In this framework, they are referred to as "routes."

Working with Query String Parameters

The page named Catalog.xaml needs to retrieve the query string parameters named cat and filter, and to display the corresponding information, for example, after a call to a web service. Retrieving the query string parameter can be done with the following steps:

1. Open the file Catalog.xaml.cs.
2. Modify the method `OnNavigatedTo` as shown in Listing 15.8. Note that this method (called when the Catalog page is loaded into the navigation host) is actually implemented on the `Page` class (which is the base class of all our navigation pages) and overridden in Catalog.xaml.cs. Of course, instead of showing a `MessageBox`, the final implementation must set the user interface in the state corresponding to the request. Note the use of the `NavigationContext` class, which provides handy access to the parsed `QueryString` parameters neatly arranged in a key-value dictionary.

LISTING 15.8 Method `OnNavigatedTo`

```
protected override void OnNavigatedTo(NavigationEventArgs e)
{
    if (!NavigationContext.QueryString.ContainsKey("cat")
        || !NavigationContext.QueryString.ContainsKey("filter"))
    {
        MessageBox.Show("This is the Shop page");
    }
    else
    {
        MessageBox.Show(
```

```
            string.Format("You want the category {0}"
                + " and the product {1}",
            NavigationContext.QueryString["cat"],
            NavigationContext.QueryString["filter"]));
    }

    base.OnNavigatedTo(e);
}
```

3. Run the application and click one of the links in the top-right corner. The Catalog page is loaded, and the corresponding `MessageBox` is shown.

> **WARNING**
>
> **Decoding the Error Messages**
>
> Unfortunately, the error messages in Silverlight 4 are sometimes confusing. For instance, if an `Exception` is raised in the `OnNavigatedTo` method, the error window tells you that the page "/Shop" was not found. In fact, the page was found, but an error occurred in the code behind. If you are not sure what the cause of the error is, try commenting out the code in the `OnNavigatedTo` method, and add code to it gradually until the error occurs again.
>
> Another method is to temporarily mark the error as not handled. To do this, open MainPage.xaml.cs and remove the first line of the method `ContentFrame_NavigationFailed` (saying `e.Handled = true;`). This will cause a much better error description to be displayed in the error window. Do not forget to mark the error as handled again before releasing the application, to avoid having it crash.

Navigating to a Fragment

In addition to page-level navigation and to the query string, Silverlight supports fragment navigation. A fragment is whatever comes after the # character in the XAML URI (for example, http://www.mypage.com/Shop/Catalog.xaml#Overview).

Note, however, that, in contrast to navigation applications in WPF, the fragment does not have a specific meaning for the user interface, and does not have to be a named UI element. The fragment can be anything, and must be decoded by the application before an action is executed.

To retrieve the fragment and execute code, follow these steps:

1. In the NavigationSample application, open MainPage.xaml.
2. Remove the `Source` property of the `navigation:Frame`. This will ensure that the application starts with an empty XAML URI.
3. Modify the `UriMapping` for the empty URI as shown in Listing 15.9.

LISTING 15.9 Adding a Fragment to the URI

```
<uriMapper:UriMapping Uri=""
    MappedUri="/Views/Home.xaml#Welcome" />
```

4. Open Home.xaml.cs
5. Add an override for the method `OnFragmentNavigation` as shown in Listing 15.10.

LISTING 15.10 Overriding `OnFragmentNavigation`

```
protected override void OnFragmentNavigation(
    FragmentNavigationEventArgs e)
{
    if (e.Fragment == "Welcome")
    {
        MessageBox.Show("Welcome to our site!!");
    }

    base.OnFragmentNavigation(e);
}
```

6. Run the application. The empty `UriMapping` is executed, the page Home.xaml is loaded, and because the fragment is set to `"Welcome"`, the welcome message is shown.

This simple sample shows fragment navigation in Silverlight. Unfortunately, this feature is less advanced than in Windows Presentation Foundation (WPF), where a named element can be targeted and will be brought into view. The fragment in Silverlight has only a symbolic meaning, and must be decoded by the application.

Theming the Application

Another thing that is special in the application shown in Figure 15.1 is the theme that it uses by default. This is not the default look and feel for a Silverlight application.

The theme is provided in the file named Styles.xaml, located in the Assets folder. There are styles for the main page (the host) and styles for the pages. The XAML markup can be modified at will, either in the Visual Studio XAML editor, the Visual Studio Silverlight designer (as shown in Figure 15.2) or in Expression Blend. This makes changing the look and feel of a navigation application very easy. A lot of work has been put into theming by the Silverlight theme, and more information (as well as additional themes) are available at http://galasoft.ch/s14-themesdownload.

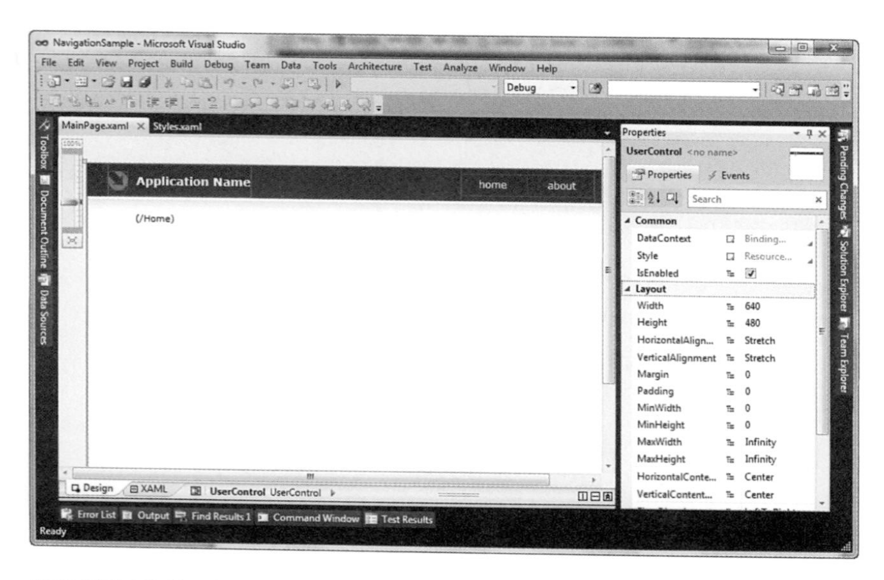

FIGURE 15.2 Silverlight navigation application in the Visual Studio designer.

Accessing Navigation Information

The navigation is handled by a navigation service, which in most applications is provided by default by the `Frame` control. Normally, you should be able to handle all the navigation scenarios simply by using this control.

Handling Navigation Events

Controlling the navigation can happen in two places: the host element (the `Frame`) and the hosted element (the `Page`).

For the `Frame` control, the following events can be handled (in the order in which they can occur):

- `FragmentNavigation`: Fired when navigation to a fragment occurs within the current page.
- `Navigating`: This event is fired before the content changes. Note that the event is fired even if the target `Page` does not exist.
- `NavigationFailed`: Fired when the target `Page` is not found, or when it throws an error before it is loaded. In the default navigation application, this event is used to display an error (using a `ChildWindow` control named `ErrorWindow`, and found in the Views folder).
- `NavigationStopped`: This event is fired when the application executes the `Frame.StopLoading` method (for example, in reaction to the user clicking a button to cancel the navigation). It is also fired when the user starts a new navigation before the previous one was completed.

- `Navigated`: This event is fired when the content changes, after the target `Page` has been found.

For the `Page` control, these events are not available directly, but the following methods can be overridden (shown in the order in which they can be called):

- `OnFragmentNavigation`: Called when a fragment navigation is taking place.
- `OnNavigatedTo`: Called when a `Page` becomes active in a `Frame`. This could be a good place to start an animation to show the `Page`'s content, for example.
- `OnNavigatingFrom`: Called before a `Page` is unloaded from a `Frame`, just before is stops being active. This would be a good place to execute an animation before the page changes, for example.
- `OnNavigatedFrom`: This method is called when the `Page` is unloaded from a `Frame` and is not active anymore. This is a good place to save the `Page`'s state to a file or a service, for example.

Using the Page's NavigationService

In addition to the methods exposed in the previous section, the `NavigationService` itself is exposed to the `Page` in the property of the same name. Useful information about the navigation can be found in this object:

- `CanGoBack` and `CanGoForward`: These Boolean properties can be used to enable/disable custom navigation buttons, for example.
- `CurrentSource`: Returns the URI of the `Page` that is currently displayed in the host.
- `Source`: This property can be set to force the navigation to a different `Page`.
- `GoBack`, `GoForward`, `Navigate`: These three methods can be used to navigate from a `Page` to another one.
- `Refresh`: This method reloads the current `Page`.
- `StopLoading`: This method cancels an ongoing navigation programmatically.

Finally, the same events already mentioned for the `Frame` class are available on the `NavigationService`. However, it is recommended to use the `OnXXX` methods on the `Page` class instead. This removes the need to unhook the event handlers when the `Page` is unloaded, which prevents potential memory leaks.

Providing Custom Navigation

Custom navigation can be useful if some special tasks need to be executed before or after the navigation is executed. Such scenarios can sometimes be enabled by handling the `Navigating` and the `Navigated` events. However, in some cases, these events are not enough, for example, if an asynchronous task must be fulfilled before the navigation can take place. One such example is the desire to navigate to pages that are not loaded in the application yet, but will be downloaded using the Managed Extensibility Framework (MEF). (We will talk about MEF and on-demand downloading in Chapter 20, "Building Extensible and Maintainable Applications.")

Custom navigation involves implementing the `INavigationContentLoader` interface in a custom class and providing an instance of this class to the `Frame.ContentLoader` property. By default, the `Frame` provides an `INavigationContentLoader` instance out of the box.

Should you need to implement a custom `INavigationContentLoader`, you can find more information in the Silverlight documentation, in the "Navigation Overview" section under Extending the Navigation System.

Adding Navigation to a Non-Navigation Application

You can add navigation to a non-navigation application as follows:

1. Open the non-navigation application in Visual Studio.
2. (If not available already) Add a reference to the DLLs System.Windows.Controls.dll and System.Windows.Controls.Navigation.dll. These two DLLs are found in the Add Reference dialog, in the .NET tab. On the hard drive, they are installed into the folder C:\Program Files\Microsoft SDKs\Silverlight\v4.0\Libraries\Client. On Windows 64 bits, the folder is in Program Files (x86).
3. Place a `Frame` in the Silverlight screen in which the navigation must take place.
4. Define the navigation by adding one or more `UriMapping` elements to the `Frame.UriMapper` property, as shown in Listing 15.3.
5. Move the content into one or more new `Page` elements that are loaded inside the `Frame`.

Integrating with the Web Browser Navigation

The integration with the web browser is given when you create a new Silverlight navigation application out of the box, but if you are looking to add navigation to an existing application, you need to pay attention to the following points:

- In Windows Explorer, locate the NavigationSample application's project files, and open the Bin\Debug folder. Open the file named NavigationSampleTestPage.html in a text editor. Near the bottom of the page, notice the presence of an HTML `iframe` element with the `id` set to `_sl_historyFrame`. Due to the semantic differences in browser history implementation, this `iframe` is used in some web browsers by the Silverlight application to integrate with the browser's navigation. If you are converting from a non-navigation application, you must add this `iframe` to the HTML page hosting the Silverlight application.
- Web-browser integrated navigation is only possible with a top-level `Frame`. If your application has nested `Frame` elements, their navigation will not be integrated.

- The `Frame` element shown in Listing 15.3 has a property named JournalOwnership (not shown in Listing 15.3). By default, the property is set to Automatic. This value means that, for a top level `Frame` (as opposed to a nested `Frame`) the navigation is integrated in the web browser's navigation. By setting the property to `OwnsJournal`, you can force the `Frame` to ignore the browser's navigation and instead have its own navigation journal.
- Browser-integrated navigation obviously doesn't work with out-of-the-browser applications, because the browser chrome is not visible.

Developing with Silverlight for Windows Phone 7

In February 2010, Microsoft's CEO Steve Ballmer gave the very first presentation of the new phone operating system Windows Phone 7. For quite some time already, leaks and rumors had been propagated on the Web, and it was interesting to follow the announcement and finally see whether these phones were going to hold their promise.

This first presentation was extremely well received by the observers. It is a groundbreaking change from existing Windows Mobile phones. The user interface and its design (codenamed "Metro") offer a welcomed alternative to existing smart phones such as iPhone, Nokia, Android, or BlackBerry devices. Metro is remarkably different and puts a lot of emphasis on typography and pictures, as shown in Figure 15.3. Heavily hardware accelerated, the animations displayed are very smooth and natural, and the multitouch-enabled capacitive screen responds very fast to the user's input.

FIGURE 15.3 Metro design, Zune, and Office applications.

Getting Hardware

At the time of this writing, some developers have started to receive actual phone devices to develop on. Prototypes have also been available at conferences and the user experience on these devices is excellent. If the stability and battery life of the commercial devices live up to the expectations, the first version (expected between October and November 2010) should encounter a great success.

If you are a developer and do not have access to a Windows Phone 7 device, the best way is to contact your local Microsoft Developer Platform Evangelist (DPE). Most of them have devices and can help you to get access.

Targeting a Specific Audience

Obviously, Windows Phone 7 is arriving in a market that is quite crowded already. To carve a piece of the market for themselves (and for the application developers), Microsoft is targeting a specific audience: active people in their late 30s who want to simplify their life by using a very powerful phone, but easy to use and intuitive. This phone is not primarily targeted at teenagers, for instance. Knowing the target audience will help you to develop successful applications.

Developing for Windows Phone 7

For Silverlight developers, probably the most exciting news is that Silverlight is a first-class citizen on the Windows Phone 7. In fact, application developers can choose between two frameworks: XNA (rather suited for games) and Silverlight (rather suited for applications).

Silverlight developers with experience on the desktop became phone application developers overnight. The learning curve will be less steep for existing Silverlight developers than for existing Windows Mobile developers. But don't fret if you are a Windows Mobile developer now, because learning Silverlight is a great adventure, and this book helps you in the task.

Silverlight for Windows Phone 7 is developed primarily in Visual Studio and in Expression Blend. The environment is well known, and the development experience is unsurpassed, including a very lifelike emulator running on the PC, and debugging on the device directly.

One interesting fact to mention is that it is possible to develop applications in Silverlight for Windows Phone 7 at no cost: The tools are available for free. There is a small fee to be paid to publish the applications on the Windows Phone marketplace, as you will see in the "Selling Your Applications" section, but it is reasonable. Anyone can become a Windows Phone 7 developer (if they know Silverlight or XNA, of course).

> **WARNING**
>
> **Disclaimer**
>
> The Silverlight tools for Windows Phone 7 are a work in progress and evolve very fast. It is possible that a version of the tools published after the time of this writing breaks some of the code in this chapter.

Developing for a Uniform Hardware Platform

Traditionally, developing for a mobile platform has given headaches to testers. With a large number of devices, all with their own features and incompatibilities, it was extremely difficult to make sure that the code was working consistently on every platform targeted.

Apple with the iPhone solved the problem in their own way, by locking down the hardware and forbidding any non-proprietary device to run the iPhone operating system. Of course, this is not very satisfactory. For example, some people prefer to have a phone with a hardware keyboard rather than the virtual on-screen keyboard. Others may want to spend more money to get a better camera, and so forth. Every customer has different needs and desires, and that is especially true when it comes to such a personal device as a mobile phone.

For Windows Phone 7, Microsoft is putting quite a lot of constraints on the device makers. For example, each phone running the Windows Phone 7 operating system must come with (at least) the following:

- A capacitive touch screen with 800 x 480 pixels. The screen must be able to recognize four touch points.
- Hardware acceleration built in. On the Windows Phone 7, Silverlight animations are always hardware accelerated to guarantee smooth movement.
- GPS, accelerometer, compass, location sensors.
- At least 5-megapixels digital camera.
- Start button, Back button, Search button as hardware buttons.
- Data connectivity with wireless networks and cellular networks.
- At least 256MB RAM and 8GB Flash storage.

Having this common set of features across all Windows Phone 7 devices facilitates the development of new applications. The developer knows exactly what to expect in his application. On the other hand, device makers are free to add a hardware keyboard, for example, a better camera with a flash, additional storage space, and so forth. This is an open platform with a minimum set of requirements.

Designing for the Phone

The Windows Phone 7 comes with a screen 480 pixels wide and 800 pixels high. A built-in accelerometer detects the orientation of the phone. If the application supports it, the screen will be rotated to display the application in portrait or landscape mode, as shown in Figure 15.4.

FIGURE 15.4 Web browser in portrait and landscape mode in the emulator.

Built-in default styles propose a consistent experience using the Metro design. This is leveraging the fact that Silverlight controls do not have a standard look and feel as you saw in Chapter 10, "Creating Resources, Styles, and Templates," but use styles and templates. On the desktop, the default styles and templates are different from those on the phone, which allows achieving a different look and feel without any design effort. For instance, the markup shown in Listing 15.11 is rendered differently as shown in Figure 15.5.

LISTING 15.11 UI elements in Windows Phone 7 and on the desktop

```
<StackPanel>
    <TextBlock Text="This is a label" />
    <TextBox Text="Enter some text here" />
    <StackPanel Orientation="Horizontal">
        <Button Content="Save" />
        <Button Content="Cancel" />
    </StackPanel>
    <RadioButton Content="I agree" />
    <RadioButton Content="I disagree" />
    <RadioButton Content="I don't know" />
    <Slider Minimum="0" Maximum="10" Value="5" />
    <CheckBox Content="Save results" />
</StackPanel>
```

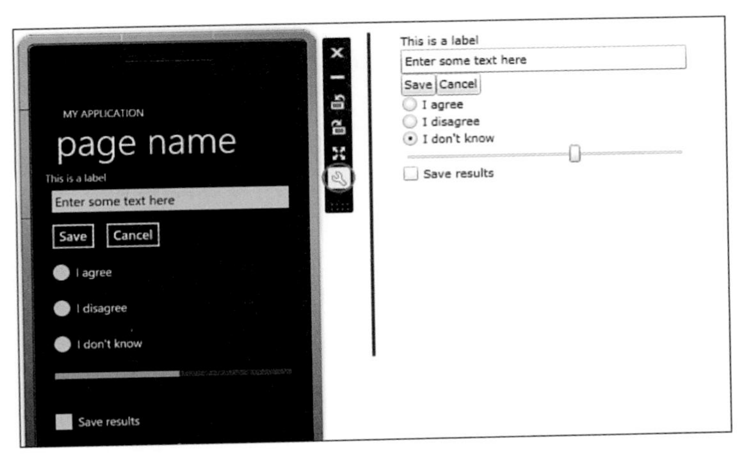

FIGURE 15.5 Default look and feel in Windows Phone 7 and on the desktop.

Nothing forces the developer or the designer to use the default styles and templates. If desired, a customized experience can be developed. However, be aware that designing for the phone is very different from designing for a desktop application. Because fingers are the main input "device," all the controls should be larger, with more space between them. Also, some controls are not available on the phone because they would be too difficult to handle with fingers (such as the combo box control).

To get a more realistic experience, it is recommended to zoom out in Expression Blend until the device has approximately the same size as a real phone. (For example, 66% zoom works quite well on a 1920 x 1200 screen.) Similarly, when the emulator is running, you can reduce the size on the screen using the Settings button in the side bar (circled in red in Figure 15.5).

Installing the Tools

The Windows Phone tools need to be installed separately from Visual Studio 2010. Note that these tools are currently in beta state, and not as stable as a production release. Also, a new version is released from time to time, and the developers should make sure to run the latest version of the tools.

To download the latest, go to http://developer.windowsphone.com and click the Get the Free Tools link. The beta version of the tools include all you need to create and run the samples in this chapter, including the Windows Phone Developer Tools for Visual Studio 2010 and the Microsoft Expression Blend for Windows Phone beta.

Using Multitouch in the Emulator

A good surprise for phone application developers owning a multitouch-enabled computer is that the Windows Phone 7 emulator supports gestures on multitouch screens. This enables a more lifelike testing for your applications before pushing them to the phone for real-life testing.

Developing in XNA

In addition to Silverlight, it is also possible to develop applications using the XNA framework, which is specialized for games but can also be used for other tasks. For more information about developing Windows Phone 7 applications with XNA, refer to http://www.galasoft.ch/sl4-wp7xna.

Selling Your Applications

To distribute his applications to users (against a fee or for free), a developer must be registered for the Windows Phone marketplace. This is the only way to install applications on a Windows Phone 7 device.

> **TIP**
>
> **Installing as a Developer**
>
> Although it is true that applications can be installed only through the marketplace, the developers will be able to register up to three devices where this restriction is lifted. This enables a developer to test his code on various devices (even though the uniform hardware profile should reduce the number of incompatible features between the various devices). Devices registered to test applications may be removed, allowing a different device to be registered instead.

Registering as a Developer

To publish applications, the developer must register on the Windows Phone developer site at http://developer.windowsphone.com. On this page, click the Register for the Marketplace link and follow the instructions. The registration costs $99 per year. This is, in fact, the only cost associated with Windows Phone 7 development, since the tools are free.

Registering for the marketplace involves registering with the Internal Revenue Service (IRS), which will tax the income from the sold applications. Note, however, that if you are a resident of a country other than the United States, and if your country has a tax treaty with the United States, you can apply for an Individual Tax Identification Number (ITIN), which can reduce or even lift the tax that the U.S. government will get. For more information, check the IRS's website at http://www.galasoft.ch/sl4-irs.

The registration process takes some time to be completed, and requires sending a document through snail mail (postal services) to Microsoft, and maybe even getting approved by the IRS. It is not very complicated, but make sure to start the process early enough to get your registration in time.

Building Compatible Applications for the Desktop and the Phone

In this section, we take an existing Silverlight desktop application and convert it to run on Windows Phone 7 devices.

The Silverlight application and its WCF service are available from http://www.galasoft.ch/sl4-wp7start. Download the CustomersManager-Start.zip file. Make sure that the zip file is unblocked by right-clicking it in Windows Explorer and selecting the file's properties. On the General tab, if the Unblock button is available, click it to avoid security issues later. Then, extract the zip file to a location on your hard drive.

Reviewing the Desktop Application

The existing application is a Silverlight 4 application connecting to a Windows Communication Foundation (WCF) service to get a list of customers. New customers can be added, and existing customers can be modified.

The application is built according to the principles of Model-View-ViewModel (MVVM) that you learned in Chapter 7, “Understanding the Model-View-ViewModel Pattern.” To make the developer’s life easier, the MVVM Light Toolkit is used; this is an open source toolkit developed and maintained by this author. You’ll learn more about this toolkit in Chapters 19, “Authentication, Event to Command Binding, Random Animations, Multitouch, Local Communication, and Bing Maps Control,” and 20, “Building Extensible and Maintainable Applications.” The MVVM Light Toolkit is available for Silverlight 4 on the desktop, and for Silverlight on Windows Phone 7, which helps creating compatible applications.

Configuring and Starting the WCF Service

To test the application, the WCF service needs to be started first. It is available as a separate application named Customers in the zip file you just downloaded. Follow the instructions at http://www.galasoft.ch/sl4-wp7start to open and start it. Having the WCF service in a separate solution forces you to explicitly start it when you want to test, but it also makes the deployment easier because there is no dependency between the Silverlight application and the WCF service.

Because the service runs in a different domain, accessing it from a Silverlight application is restricted (except if the Silverlight application runs with elevated permissions, as discussed in Chapter 14, “Enhancing Line-of-Business Applications and Running Out of the Browser”). To solve this, a clientaccesspolicy.xml file is in place in the root of the WCF application. This file enables access to all Silverlight applications in an unrestricted manner. When publishing the service to a production server, you may want to reduce the permissions. You can find more information about the cross-domain policy files in *Silverlight 2 Unleashed*, Chapter 23, Listings 23.1 and 23.2.

Once the WCF service is configured, right click on the file CustomerService.svc and select View in Browser from the context menu. An information page is displayed. Keep this window open, because you will need the URL of the page later in this chapter.

> **TIP**
>
> **Cross-Domain on the Phone**
>
> Windows Phone 7 applications are not subjected to cross-domain restrictions as are Silverlight desktop applications running in normal trust. A Windows Phone application can connect to any site or service.

Starting the Silverlight Client

To test the Silverlight application, follow these steps:

1. Open in Visual Studio the CustomersManager.sln solution that is found in the CustomersManager-Start folder.
2. Make sure that the CustomersManager.Web project is set as startup project, and the index.html page as startup page.

3. Press Ctrl+F5. The application starts and loads the list of customers is loaded from the WCF service. Using this application, it is possible to change the first name or last name of a customer, to change his gender (should that be needed), and then to save the changes back to the service. It is also possible to load a different picture for the user and upload it to the WCF server. Finally, you can also create a new customer.

Note that the Silverlight clients are not automatically notified when a customer changes or when a new customer is created. It would be possible to create such a functionality using the duplex polling networking feature that is discussed in Chapter 18, "Drag and Drop, Full Screen, Clipboard, COM Interop, Duplex Polling, Notification Windows, and Splash Screens."

This desktop application will not be detailed further here, but take some time to study the code. Of course, it is also fully Blendable with design-time data, thanks to the MVVM pattern.

Creating a New Windows Phone 7 Application

Now is time to expand our reach to customers by opening the application to the Windows Phone 7 platform. Thanks to the fact that Silverlight is used on both the desktop and the phone, and thanks to the MVVM separation pattern (and a few helpers to bridge the small differences between Silverlight on the desktop and on the phone), building a similar experience on the phone is very easy.

Of course, because of differences in the screen dimensions and in the more limited support that the phone platform offers, the experience will be less rich. In our sample, the phone user will be able to edit a customer's first name and last name. He will not, however, be able to create a new customer or to select a picture for the customer. Note that these features would be possible to implement on the phone, too, but we will keep it simple here. Let's start with the following steps:

1. With the CustomersManager solution open in Visual Studio, right-click the CustomersManager solution in the Solution Explorer and select Add, New Project from the context menu.

2. In the Add New Project dialog, under Silverlight for Windows Phone, select Windows Phone Application. If you do not see this template, you need to install the Windows Phone 7 tools as described earlier in this chapter. Name the new application **CustomersManager.WP7**, and then click OK.

3. Make sure that the phone application is selected as startup project, and then press Ctrl+F5 to start the emulator. This takes a few minutes. Do not close the emulator! After it runs, starting the application is much faster.

4. Right-click the CustomersManager.WP7 project and select Properties.

5. In the Application tab, set the Default Namespace to CustomersManager.SL instead of CustomersManager.WP7, as shown in Figure 15.6. We want to change the default namespace to share a maximum of code with the CustomersManager.SL project.

6. Right-click the References folder and select Add Reference. In the Browse tab, navigate to the folder named External that can be found in the CustomersManager-Start folder, next to CustomersManager.Web, CustomersManager.SL, and CustomersManager.WP7.

7. In the External folder, open the folder named WP7 and select the three DLLs that this folder contains. Click OK to close the Add Reference dialog and save everything using the File, Save All menu.

FIGURE 15.6 Changing the default namespace.

Adding a Service Reference

We need a service reference to the WCF project now with the following steps, just like we added one for the desktop Silverlight application.

1. In Visual Studio, right-click the References folder of the CustomersManager.WP7 and select Add Service Reference.

2. In the Add Service Reference dialog, paste the URL of the WCF service's web page that was displayed in the "Configuring and Starting the WCF Service" section. This is the URL of the CustomerService.svc file running in the development web server. Then click the button Go.

3. After the service information is done loading, change the Namespace in the Add Service Reference to be RemoteCustomersService, just as it is for the Silverlight 4 application. Here, too, to share code, we need to use the same name.

4. Save everything.

Sharing Code

Because both the Silverlight 4 and the Silverlight for Windows Phone 7 applications run Silverlight, it is possible to share code between both with the following steps:

1. Right-click the CustomersManager.WP7 project, and select Add, New Folder. Name this folder **Design**.

2. Right-click the Design folder and select Add, Existing Item. In the Existing Item dialog, navigate to CustomersManager-Start\CustomersManager.SL\Design\.

3. Select the file in this folder, and then click the small arrow in the Add button, as shown in Figure 15.7. Select Add as Link.

   The Add as Link operation adds a shortcut to the selected file in the WP7 project. There is no physical copy of the file on the disk, but the file will be compiled into the WP7 DLL anyway. This is a great way to share code between different platforms.

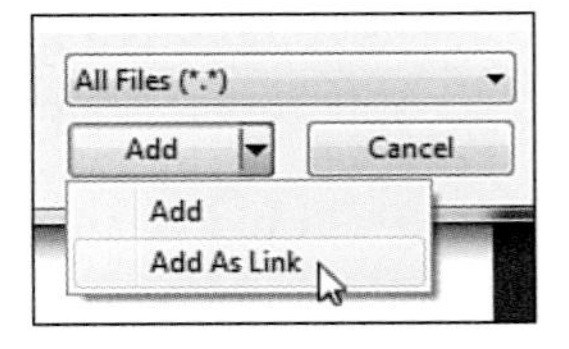

FIGURE 15.7 Adding as a link.

4. Repeat the Steps 1 to 3 for the folders Model and ViewModel. Make sure to link all the files in each folder.

5. Build the application. There should be one error mentioning that `ObservableCollection<CustomerViewModel>` does not have a constructor that takes one argument.

This error is due to a compatibility issue. In Silverlight 4, a new constructor (with one argument of type `IEnumerable<T>`) was added to the `ObservableCollection<T>` class. However, this overload of the constructor is not available in Silverlight 3, which is what the Windows Phone 7 is running. To solve this, we will use a conditional compilation symbol.

Using such conditional compilation is a little annoying because it makes the source code more complex to read. For small amounts of code, however, it is okay. Follow these steps:

1. Open the WP7 project properties and select the Build tab.

2. In the Conditional Compilation Symbols text box, notice the symbols **SILVERLIGHT;WINDOWS_PHONE**. This lets you use either symbol for the compilation.

3. Open MainViewModel.cs from the WP7 project. It is important to open it from there because opening the file from the SL project opens it in the context of Silverlight 4, while opening it from the WP7 project uses the phone context.

4. Locate the line in the `Refresh` method where the new `ObservableCollection<CustomerViewModel>` is created and change this line as shown in Listing 15.12. Note that depending on which context the file is open in (Silverlight 4 or Windows Phone) the corresponding lines are activated and colored in the editor, while the other lines are grayed.

LISTING 15.12 Creating the `ObservableCollection`

```
#if WINDOWS_PHONE
    Customers = new ObservableCollection<CustomerViewModel>();
    foreach (var customer in customers)
    {
        Customers.Add(customer);
```

```
    }
#else
    Customers = new ObservableCollection<CustomerViewModel>(customers);
#endif
```

5. Build the application again. This time it works fine.

Binding the View and the Viewmodel

We need to bind the application in an MVVM style by setting a `ViewModelLocator` in the App.xaml resources and then setting the `MainPage`'s `DataContext` to the `MainViewModel`, as follows:

1. Open App.xaml and modify the `Application.Resources` as shown in Listing 15.13.

LISTING 15.13 Creating a `ViewModelLocator`

```
<Application.Resources>
    <vm:ViewModelLocator x:Key="Locator"
        xmlns:vm="clr-namespace:CustomersManager.SL.ViewModel" />
</Application.Resources>
```


2. Open MainPage.xaml. In the `phoneNavigation:PhoneApplicationPage` root tag, set the `DataContext` property as shown in Listing 15.14.

LISTING 15.14 Setting the `DataContext`

```
DataContext="{Binding Main, Source={StaticResource Locator}}"
```

3. Check the XAML markup. Within the `LayoutRoot Grid`, there are two `Grid` elements named `TitleGrid` and `ContentGrid`. Set the two `TextBlock` elements in the `TitleGrid` to the application's name and to the page title.

4. Modify the `ContentGrid` as shown in Listing 15.15.

LISTING 15.15 Creating a Simple `ListBox`

```
<Grid x:Name="ContentGrid" Grid.Row="1">
    <ListBox ItemsSource="{Binding Customers}"
        ScrollViewer.HorizontalScrollBarVisibility="Disabled"
        SelectedItem="{Binding SelectedCustomer, Mode=TwoWay}" />
</Grid>
```

5. Run the application. If you see the image shown in Figure 15.8, everything is working fine! The connection to the WCF service worked perfectly, and a number of customers were returned. At this point, however, there is no `DataTemplate` able to

render these items. This is why, instead, the ToString method is called on each CustomerViewModel instance and the type name is returned by default.

Everything we did in this section is the same as we have done in Silverlight applications before. The same principles apply, and the MVVM pattern works great on the phone, too. In the next section, you will see that design-time data can also be created on the phone and that the application is Blendable.

FIGURE 15.8 Customers without a DataTemplate.

Creating the UI

At this point, it is possible to edit the UI either in the XAML editor, in the Visual Studio designer or in Expression Blend. It is really up to you to choose the tool you prefer. In this sample, we demonstrate how friendly Windows Phone 7 development is in Blend. As you saw when we installed the Windows Phone 7 developer tools, Expression Blend for the phone is free, so there is really no reason for not using it! Follow these steps:

1. Open the CustomersManager.sln solution in Expression Blend 4 for Windows Phone.
2. In the Projects panel, expand the CustomersManager.WP7 project and open the MainPage.xaml.
3. Notice that a number of customers (without a DataTemplate) are shown in the ListBox. These customers are created in design time by the class DesignCustomersService in the Design folder. This follows the sample shown at MIX 2010's "Understanding the MVVM pattern" talk, available as a video at http://www.galasoft.ch/sl4-mix10. By modifying this class, it is possible to change what Blend displays on the screen (after the application is recompiled).
4. Right-click the ListBox on the main design surface and select Edit Additional Templates, Edit Generated Items (ItemTemplate), Create Empty from the context menu.
5. In the Create DataTemplate Resource dialog, enter the name **CustomerTemplate** and click OK. Note that in Silverlight 3, external resource dictionary are not supported, so resources can only be placed in the page or in App.xaml.
6. In the Objects and Timeline panel, select the Grid in the ItemTemplate and set its Height to 130 pixels and its Width to 460 pixels.
7. Split the Grid in two columns by passing the mouse on top of the Grid's border in the designer surface and clicking. Select the first column, and in the Properties panel, set its Width to 130 pixels.

8. In the first column, add an `Image` control from the Assets library. Make it fill the whole cell, and set its `Margin` to 5,5,5,5.

9. Find the `Source` property for the `Image` and open the binding editor. You learned how to do this in Chapter 6, "Working with Data: Binding, Grouping, Sorting, and Filtering."

10. Because we are within a `DataTemplate` representing a `CustomerViewModel` instance, the implicit `DataContext` is automatically set to the `CustomerViewModel` class. In the data binding dialog, expand the Model property within the `CustomerViewModel`. This is a `Customer` instance as generated by the WCF service and wrapped into the `CustomerViewModel`.

11. In the `Customer` instance, select the `PictureUri` property and click OK.

    Notice how a picture (the logo of www.galasoft.ch) is appearing for each customer. To understand what is happening, inspect the `DesignCustomerService` class in the Design folder. For each design time customer created, the `PictureUri` is set to a remote URL corresponding to this picture. Blend is able to download this picture and display it on the design surface. At runtime however, a picture of the customer will be shown instead.

12. In the cell on the right of the `DataTemplate`, add a `StackPanel` and make it fill the whole space.

13. In the `StackPanel`, add two `TextBlock` elements.

14. Select the first `TextBlock` and create a data binding between its `Text` property and the Model's `FirstName` property. Then set its `FontSize` to 36px.

15. Select the second `TextBlock` and repeat Step 13, this time with the `LastName` property and a `FontSize` of 48px. If the font size is set in points (pt), remember that you can change it to pixels (px) with Tools, Options, Units.

16. Set the scope back to the page and run the application. After a short delay, you should see the list of customers and their picture in the emulator, as shown in Figure 15.9.

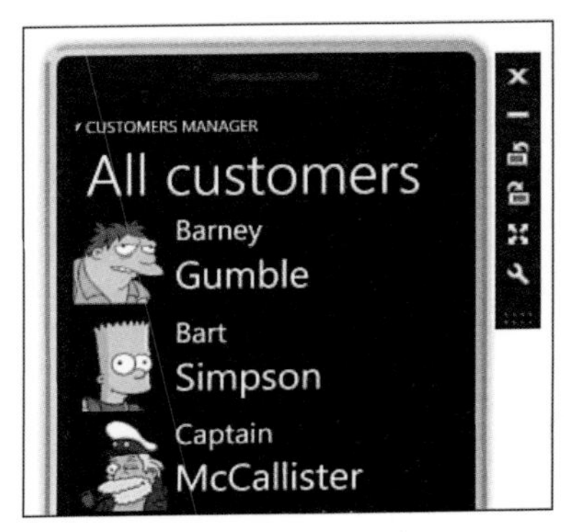

FIGURE 15.9 List of customers with `DataTemplate`.

Adding an Edit Panel

The CustomersManager Silverlight application for the desktop allows adding new customers, editing existing customers, and uploading a new picture. In this sample, we will allow editing the `FirstName` and `LastName` of a `Customer` on the phone, with the following steps:

1. In Blend, inside the `ContentGrid`, add a new `StackPanel` and make it fill the whole space. Name it `EditStackPanel`.

2. In the Objects and Timeline panel, move the StackPanel so that it appears behind the ListBox. It should be the first child of the ContentGrid.
3. Hide the ListBox by clicking the small Eye icon in the Objects and Timeline panel.
4. In the EditStackPanel, add a TextBlock, a TextBox, and the again a TextBlock and a TextBox.
5. Set the first TextBlock's Text property to "First Name".
6. Then, open the data binding editor for the first TextBox's Text property. The DataContext is now set to the MainViewModel, which is perfect. Select the SelectedCustomer.Model.FirstName property.
7. Expand the advanced properties section, and make sure that the data binding's Mode is set to TwoWay. We want the model to be updated when the user enter a text!
8. Repeat Step 5 for the second TextBlock and "Last Name".
9. Repeat Steps 6 and 7 for the second TextBox and the LastName property of the SelectedCustomer's Model.
10. Add a Button to the EditStackPanel and set its Content property to "Save".

Adding States

To switch from one view (the ListBox) to the other (the EditStackPanel), we need to add states and transitions. This is very simple in Blend, thanks to the visual design features, with the following steps:

1. Select the EditStackPanel and set its Opacity to 0.
2. In the Objects and Timeline panel, display the ListBox again by clicking on the small, hidden Eye icon.
3. Click the States tab. Add a new state group by pressing the corresponding button. Name the group **EditStates**.
4. In the EditStates group, add a new state named **Normal** and another state named **Edit**.
5. Set the default transition to 1s. You can also choose an easing function for this animation (for example, Cubic In).
6. With the Edit state selected, make sure that Blend is in state recording mode (with a red border around the design surface) and select the ListBox
7. Expand the Transform section in the Properties panel.
8. In the Projection section, select the Rotation tab and set the Y rotation to 76.6 degrees. Notice that the rotation happens with the Y axis in the middle of the ListBox's width, which is not what we want. The center of rotation needs to be moved.

9. Click the Base state to exit state recording mode. The center of rotation may not be edited while a state is recording, or else its value will only change for the corresponding state!
10. Select the Center of Rotation tab, and set the value of X to 0. The `ListBox` should now disappear completely due to the rotation angle.
11. Finally, select the `Edit` state again and set the `ListBox`'s `Opacity` to 0 and the `EditStackPanel's` `Opacity` to 100%. This way the transition will be smoother.
12. In the States panel, click "Turn On Transition Preview" (this is the tooltip of the small button just below the tabs). Then, click `Normal` and `Edit`, and see how the UI changes according to the defined transition.

Adding an ApplicationBar

To trigger the state transition, some controls are needed. However, we would like to lose as little "real estate" on the screen as possible, because of the small dimensions. A good solution is to use the `ApplicationBar`, a control specific to the Windows Phone 7 that ensures a consistent experience between all the applications. This control hosts a series of maximum four buttons and an optional menu. Unfortunately, at the time of this writing, Blend does not support adding and configuring an `ApplicationBar`, but it is easy to do so in XAML with the following steps:

1. Right-click the WP7 project and select Add, New Folder. Name the folder **Resources**.
2. Right-click the Resources folder and select Add, Existing Item.
3. In the Add Existing Item dialog, find the Resources folder inside the External folder where we got the external DLLs before. Inside the Resources folder, select the two PNG files and click Add.
4. Select the two PNG files in the Solution Explorer and press F4 to display their properties. Make sure that the Build Action is set to Content, and Copy to Output Directory is set to Copy If Newer.
5. In MainPage.xaml, uncomment the sample application bar markup at the bottom of the page, and then modify it as shown in Listing 15.16. Note that there can be only one `ApplicationBar` per page.

LISTING 15.16 Adding the `ApplicationBar`

```
<phone:PhoneApplicationPage.ApplicationBar>
    <shell:ApplicationBar
        IsVisible="True"
        IsMenuEnabled="True">
        <shell:ApplicationBarIconButton
            IconUri="/Resources/appbar.edit.rest.png"
            Text="edit"
            Click="EditButtonClick" />
```

```
        <shell:ApplicationBarIconButton
            IconUri="/Resources/appbar.cancel.rest.png"
            Text="cancel"
            Click="CancelButtonClick"
            IsEnabled="False"/>
        <shell:ApplicationBar.MenuItems>
            <shell:ApplicationBarMenuItem
                Text="Refresh"
                Click="RefreshClick" />
        </shell:ApplicationBar.MenuItems>
    </shell:ApplicationBar>
</phone:PhoneApplicationPage.ApplicationBar>
```

Listing 15.16 adds an `ApplicationBar` with one menu item titled `Refresh` and two buttons, Edit and Cancel. These controls are very primitive and have only a `Click` event. In fact, they are not even controls, but are a specific class of elements. This forces us to add code in the code behind, which is not a big problem but breaks a little the strict separation that we had until now.

8. Open MainPage.xaml.cs and add the event handlers shown in Listing 15.17.

LISTING 15.17 `ApplicationBar` Event Handlers

```
1  public enum IconButtons
2  {
3      Edit = 0,
4      Cancel = 1
5  }
6
7  public void EnableButton(IconButtons whichButton, bool enable)
8  {
9      (ApplicationBar.Buttons[(int)whichButton]
10         as ApplicationBarIconButton).IsEnabled = enable;
11 }
12
13 private void EditButtonClick(object sender, EventArgs e)
14 {
15     EnableButton(IconButtons.Edit, false);
16     EnableButton(IconButtons.Cancel, true);
17     VisualStateManager.GoToState(this, "Edit", true);
18 }
19
20 private void CancelButtonClick(object sender, EventArgs e)
21 {
```

```
22        EnableButton(IconButtons.Edit, true);
23        EnableButton(IconButtons.Cancel, false);
24        VisualStateManager.GoToState(this, "Normal", true);
25    }
26
27    private void RefreshClick(object sender, EventArgs e)
28    {
29        var vm = DataContext as MainViewModel;
30        if (vm != null)
31        {
32            vm.RefreshCommand.Execute(null);
33        }
34    }
```

- On lines 7 to 11, a method is enabling and disabling the `ApplicationBar` buttons. It uses the `enum` defined on lines 1 to 5. This is needed because the `ApplicationBarIconButton` elements cannot be referenced by name.
- On lines 17 and 24, note the usage of the `VisualStateManager` class used to set the page in the `Edit` or `Normal` states programmatically.
- On lines 29 to 33, the `RefreshClick` event handler retrieves the `DataContext`, casts it to `MainViewModel`, and then executes the `RefreshCommand`. This is a way to execute a command from the code behind when the controls used do not have a `Command` property.

15

Run the application. You should now see the `ApplicationBar` with its two buttons, Edit and Cancel (which is disabled). Select a customer and click the Edit button to observe the transition to the edit mode, and then click Cancel to go back to the `ListBox`. You can also open the menu by pressing on the three little dots in the application bar, and then click Refresh.

You can also expand the menu in the `ApplicationBar` and click the Refresh button. Any changes made in the meantime by the Silverlight desktop application will be reloaded on the phone.

Using Commands in Windows Phone 7

One thing is missing: The Save button in the edit panel doesn't work. It must be wired to the `SaveSelectedCustomerCommand` on the `MainViewModel` with the following steps:

1. Open MainPage.xaml in the XAML editor in Visual Studio and locate the `Button` with the `Content` set to `"Save"`.
2. Modify the `Button`'s markup as shown in Listing 15.18.

LISTING 15.18 Setting a Command on the Save *Button*

```
<Button Content="Save"
xmlns:cmd="clr-
namespace:GalaSoft.MvvmLight.Command;assembly=GalaSoft.MvvmLight.WP7"
cmd:ButtonBaseExtensions.Command="{Binding SaveSelectedCustomerCommand}" />
```

The markup in Listing 15.18 is using the `ButtonBaseExtension` class provided in the WP7 edition of MVVM Light Toolkit. This class (originally developed by Josh Smith) is handy because the `Button` control does not have a `Command` property in Windows Phone 7 (or in Silverlight 3 for that matter). By using the `ButtonBaseExtension.Command` and `ButtonBaseExtension.CommandParameter` attached properties, this functionality can be added to the `Button` control (and any other control driving from `ButtonBase`).

Run the application again, select a customer, and click the Edit button. You can now change the selected customer's first name, last name, and save the changes. In the Silverlight desktop application, click Refresh to see the changes made by the phone.

Continuing the Exploration

There is obviously much more to Windows Phone 7 than what was shown in these few pages, but this should give you a good head start with the technology. More information will be unveiled as the official release of the Windows Phone 7 devices becomes imminent. At the time of this writing, there are already multiple blog entries and even draft books related to Windows Phone 7 development available at no cost.

The official website for Windows Phone developers is http://developer.windowsphone.com. From there, the Resources link takes you to the section of MSDN dedicated to Windows Phone 7.

Finally, Sams has a Windows Phone 7 book in preparation titled *Windows Phone 7 Unleashed*. It should be available early 2011.

Summary

In this chapter, we talked about navigation with Silverlight 4 and Windows Phone 7 applications with Silverlight.

The first part of this chapter showed an interesting way to combine the richness of Silverlight applications with the navigation features of the web browser, normally associated with websites and web applications. The Back and Forward buttons were always an interesting feature of hypertext documents. Having this functionality available in a rich application makes it very versatile. However, we need to remember that this is a very different application model from the standard Silverlight application and plan the features accordingly.

The Windows Phone 7 platform is one of the most exciting developments for Silverlight because it allows reusing existing skills to build applications for a very different platform that should spread the usage of Silverlight to a larger population and to very different scenarios. This chapter offered a glimpse into the Windows Phone 7 development with Silverlight and how to reuse code between a Silverlight desktop application and a phone application.

In the next chapter, we will talk about effects and media in Silverlight 4: how to use pixel shaders to modify a picture, a video, or even a part of the user interface; how to take pictures and record sound using webcam and microphone; and how to create images on-the-fly and save them.

CHAPTER 16

Using Effects and Recording Media

IN THIS CHAPTER, WE WILL:

- Understand what pixel shaders are and how they work.
- Use the Shazzam tool to learn more about shaders and edit them.
- Integrate shaders in the Silverlight application and animate them.
- Access the webcam and microphone to enhance the interactivity.
- Use the OpenFileDialog to load files and the SaveFileDialog to save files to the local computer.
- Study the WriteableBitmap class and use it to save parts of the application as images.
- Learn how to save images in various formats from the Silverlight application.
- Use the WriteableBitmap to manipulate pixels of an image.
- Load the WriteableBitmapEx library from CodePlex and use some of its extended functionalities to combine images together.
- See a list of new features related to media in Silverlight 4.

In addition to the large topics such as MVVM, WCF RIA Services, new controls, and so on, Silverlight 4 is loaded with multiple improvements and new features that are maybe less extensive but contribute to making Silverlight a very rich platform.

In this chapter, we review features that have to do with media such as pixel shaders, webcams, and audio recording, before moving on to other features in the next chapter.

Creating Effects with Pixel Shaders

Pixel shaders are small programs that take each and every pixel of an element and process it. The color and transparency of the pixel can be modified (for example, based on the pixel's original color or its position). Pixel shaders can be applied to any visual on the screen (image, video, but also UI elements). Even better, they can have properties that can be data bound and/or animated. The range of effects is endless!

Shaders are written in a language named HLSL (High Level Shading Language), which is not related to Silverlight. In fact, it is possible to find pixel shaders online, and to apply them to a Silverlight element. Before they can be used by the Silverlight application, however, they need to be compiled, tested, and then included in the XAP file.

Writing, Finding, and Compiling Shader Files

Writing HLSL shaders often implies mathematic operations that can be quite complex. However, with so many shaders available online, it is often not necessary to write them but instead to find and parameter them. To understand how shaders work, let's write two small examples, starting with a simple monochrome effect shown in Listing 16.1, which removes the red and green components of each pixel and leaves only the blue and the alpha (transparency) components.

LISTING 16.1 Simple Monochrome Shader

```
1  sampler2D input : register(S0);
2
3  float4 main(float2 position : TEXCOORD) : COLOR
4  {
5      float4 color  = tex2D(input, position.xy);
6      return float4(0, 0, color.b, color.a);
7  }
```

- On line 1, a variable of type `sampler2D` is declared. This is the input of the pixel shader and corresponds to the visual to which the shader is applied (for example, an `Image` or a `UIElement`).
- Lines 3 to 7 are the `main` function, which is called once for every pixel. The return type is a `float4`, meaning that it is a register with four values (for the Red, Green, Blue, and Alpha channels). The only parameter is a `float2`, a register with 2 values (for the X and Y coordinates of the pixel). This method will be found in every shader.
- Line 5 uses the function called `tex2D`, which retrieves the color of a pixel in the input element based on its coordinates (normalized between 0 and 1). Notice the use of the `xy` property of the `position` parameter. `xy` allows to access both the X and the Y values in one pass, which speeds up the calculations. Pixel shaders work extremely well in parallel, but this makes them a little harder to understand. Next to `position.xy`, it is also possible to retrieve only `position.x` and `position.y` if needed.
- Finally, a new `float4` is constructed, but the values of the Red and Green channels are left to 0. In effect, this removes the Red and Green values and leaves only Blue and Alpha (transparency).

The shader in Listing 16.1 is processing pixels based only on their color. There is no distortion of the element to which the shader is applied. It is, however, possible to modify the color of a pixel based on its position, which creates a distorted output. For example, a well-known wave effect is shown in Listing 16.2.

LISTING 16.2 Wave Effect Shader

```
1  sampler2D input : register(S0);
2
3  float4 main(float2 position : TEXCOORD) : COLOR
4  {
5      position.y = position.y  + (sin(position.y*100)*0.03);
6      return tex2D(input, position.xy);
7  }
```

- Line 5 modifies the Y value of the position.
- Line 6 retrieves the color of the pixel at the same X coordinate than the original pixel, but at a different Y position. In effect, this replaces the color of the original pixel by the color of another pixel on the same element. This creates a distorted effect, which, because it corresponds to a sine function, looks like a reflection on water.

When applied to a picture, the shaders in Listing 16.1 and 16.2 create the output shown in Figure 16.1.

FIGURE 16.1 Unmodified picture, picture with monochrome shader, picture with wave shader.

Understanding the Restrictions

In Silverlight, the Shader Model 2 is supported, with a limit of maximum 64 arithmetic instructions and 32 texture sample instructions, as opposed to Windows Presentation Foundation (WPF) 4, which supports the Shader Model 3 with 512 instructions or more. When looking for shaders online, make sure that they are compatible!

Also, shaders in Silverlight are always executed on the CPU (as opposed to WPF, which runs the shaders on the GPU when possible). Note, however, that in case the client computer has multiple cores, the shader execution is parallelized, which speeds up things. Also, the CPU's fast SSE instruction set is used.

For more technical details about shaders, check http://www.galasoft.ch/sl4-shaders.

Creating and Modifying Shaders with Shazzam

Creating and testing shaders would be quite difficult if a great free tool didn't exist: Shazzam, the WPF/Silverlight Pixel Shader Utility. This application created by Walt Ritscher can be installed from http://shazzam-tool.com.

Configuring Shazzam

Make sure that the target framework selected is Silverlight. Shazzam is able to generate C# and VB.NET code that can be integrated in an application. You can also change the namespace that Shazzam uses to create the code (for example, to MyShaders).

Testing a Shader

To test the wave shader in Shazzam, follow these steps:

1. Use the menu File, New Shader File to create a blank shader.
2. In the New File Name dialog, select a location and name the new shader Wave.fx.
3. A void shader (without any effect) is generated by Shazzam. Delete the content of this file. Instead, enter the content of Listing 16.2 and save the file.
4. In the top panel of Shazzam, select one of the tabs with sample content.
5. Press F5. Shazzam compiles and applies the shader to the sample file.
6. Select the tabs to check the effect of the shader on various elements. Using the menu File, Open Image File and File, Open Media File, it is possible to select your own pictures and videos to test the shader.

Shazzam is a great tool and comes with a number of sample shaders that you can learn from.

Integrating Shaders in the Application

To integrate a pixel shader in a Silverlight application, two things are needed: the compiled shader file, and a Silverlight wrapper class that loads and exposes the shader to the application. When a shader file is compiled in Shazzam, the corresponding class is generated in C# and in VB.NET. To integrate and use the shader in a Silverlight application, follow these steps:

1. Create a new Silverlight application in Visual Studio and name it **ShaderTest**.
2. Open MainPage.xaml and place a few elements (UI controls, pictures, videos) in the `LayoutRoot Grid`. You can type the XAML markup, use the designer and the Toolbox, or use Expression Blend.
3. Add a folder named **MyShaders** to the Silverlight project.
4. With the Wave shader loaded in Shazzam, select Tools, Compile Shader.
5. Select Tools, Explore Compiled Shaders.
6. Locate the shader named Wave.ps and drag this file from Windows Explorer into the MyShaders folder in Visual Studio's Solution Explorer. This adds a copy of the Wave.ps file to the Silverlight project.
7. Select Wave.ps in the Solution Explorer and press F4 to show the Properties. Make sure that the Build Action is set to Resource.

8. In Visual Studio, create a new class into the MyShaders folder and name it **WaveEffect.cs**.
9. Replace the code in the `WaveEffect` class with the code in Listing 16.3.

LISTING 16.3 `WaveEffect` Class

```
1  public class WaveEffect : ShaderEffect
2  {
3      public WaveEffect()
4      {
5          var pixelShader = new PixelShader();
6          pixelShader.UriSource = new Uri(
7              "/ShaderTest;component/MyShaders/Wave.ps",
8              UriKind.Relative);
9          this.PixelShader = pixelShader;
10     }
11 }
```

10. In the XAML code, add an `xmlns` prefix to the `MainPage` `UserControl` tag mapping the prefix `xmlns:shaders` to `"clr-namespace:ShaderTest.MyShaders"`.
11. Add the `WaveEffect` to the `LayoutRoot` `Grid` with the markup in Listing 16.4.

LISTING 16.4 Adding the `WaveEffect`

```
<Grid x:Name="LayoutRoot">
    <Grid.Effect>
        <shaders:WaveEffect x:Name="MyWaveEffect" />
    </Grid.Effect>

    ...

</Grid>
```

At this point, the application can be run to see the effect. It is also applied when you look at the user interface in the Visual Studio designer or in Expression Blend.

TIP

Using Pack URIs

The URI at line 7 in Listing 16.3 is a *pack URI* used in Silverlight to reference elements in an assembly. Chapter 10, "Creating Resources, Styles, and Templates," briefly discussed this kind of URI. In their short form (without the name of the assembly), they instruct Silverlight to look for the element within the executing assembly. In the case of the shader, however, the full syntax must be used, even though the PS file is located inside the same assembly as the CS file. For more information about pack URIs, refer to http://www.galasoft.ch/sl4-packuri.

Adding the Effect into Blend

When an effect is included into the Silverlight assembly (or one of its referenced assemblies), Expression Blend shows it in the Asset library, in the Effects section. Opening the ShaderTest Silverlight application in Blend reveals the `WaveEffect` that was just implemented in the list of the available shaders. Adding the effect to an element is as simple as dragging the `WaveEffect` from the Assets library to the element to which it should be applied.

Combining Effects

A Silverlight element can accept only one effect. If multiple effects need to be applied, place the element with the first effect within a `Border` to which the second effect is applied. To test this, add the `SimpleMonochrome` effect of Listing 16.1 to the ShaderTest application, just like we did for the `Wave` effect. Then, modify the MainPage.xaml markup as shown in Listing 16.5.

LISTING 16.5 Combining Effects

```
<Border>
    <Border.Effect>
        <shaders:SimpleMonochromeEffect/>
    </Border.Effect>

    <Grid x:Name="LayoutRoot">
        <Grid.Effect>
            <shaders:WaveEffect x:Name="MyWaveEffect" />
        </Grid.Effect>
    </Grid>
    ...
</Border>
```

Adding Properties and Animating Shaders

Pixel shaders can also be configured with properties. For example, the amplitude of the `WaveEffect` can be modified by the Silverlight application, and even animated with the following steps:

1. Open Shazzam again.
2. In the Shader Loader section, if the Wave.fx shader is not visible, use the Change Location link to select the folder in which you saved the file.
3. Modify the shader code as shown in Listing 16.6.

LISTING 16.6 Modified Wave Shader

```
1  sampler2D input : register(S0);
2  float amplitude : register(C0);
3
4  float4 main(float2 position : TEXCOORD) : COLOR
5  {
6      position.y = position.y  + (sin(position.y*100)*amplitude);
7      return tex2D(input , position.xy);
8  }
```

- Line 2 declares an input variable, through the usage of the `register` keyword. Although `S0` is the input element (for example, the `LayoutRoot Grid`), `C0` is the first property applied to the shader. There can be multiple properties named `C0`, `C1`, `C2` and so forth.
- On line 6, the hard-coded value `0.03` is replaced by the variable named `amplitude`.

4. Compile the shader by selecting Tools, Compile Shader.
5. Replace the old Wave.ps file in Visual Studio with the newly compiled Wave.ps file from the GeneratedShaders folder that can be opened via Tools, Explore Compiled Shaders in Shazzam.
6. Modify the class WaveEffect.cs (from Listing 16.3) by adding a dependency property. Then use this property to configure the `PixelShader` as shown in Listing 16.7 by calling the method `UpdateShaderValue`. This method binds the `amplitude register` of the shader with the `Amplitude` dependency property.

LISTING 16.7 Modifying the `WaveEffect` Class

```
public static readonly DependencyProperty AmplitudeProperty
    = DependencyProperty.Register("Amplitude",
        typeof(float), typeof(WaveEffect),
        new PropertyMetadata((float)(0),
            PixelShaderConstantCallback(0)));

public float Amplitude
{
    get { return (float)GetValue(AmplitudeProperty); }
    set { SetValue(AmplitudeProperty, value); }
}

public WaveEffect()
{
    var pixelShader = new PixelShader();
    pixelShader.UriSource = new Uri(
```

```
        "/ShaderTest;component/MyShaders/Wave.ps",
        UriKind.Relative);
    this.PixelShader = pixelShader;
    UpdateShaderValue(AmplitudeProperty);
}
```

Because `Amplitude` is a dependency property, it can be animated; for example, with the animation shown in Listing 16.8 (to be added to MainPage.xaml) and started in the code behind in MainPage.xaml.cs, like in Listing 16.9.

LISTING 16.8 Creating an Animation in XAML

```
<UserControl.Resources>
    <Storyboard Storyboard.TargetName="MyWaveEffect"
                Storyboard.TargetProperty="Amplitude"
                x:Key="WaveAnimation">
        <DoubleAnimation To="0"
            AutoReverse="True" Duration="0:0:3"
            RepeatBehavior="Forever">
            <DoubleAnimation.EasingFunction>
                <CubicEase />
            </DoubleAnimation.EasingFunction>
        </DoubleAnimation>
    </Storyboard>
</UserControl.Resources>
```

LISTING 16.9 Starting the Animation in the Code Behind

```
public MainPage()
{
    InitializeComponent();
    var sbd = Resources["WaveAnimation"] as Storyboard;
    sbd.Begin();
}
```

Run the application and observe how the user interface is modified, as shown in Figure 16.2. This effect works nicely on images and videos (for example, to build a reflection), less nicely on controls, but it demonstrates how easily complex effects can be integrated in a Silverlight application.

FIGURE 16.2 ShaderTest application (animated).

Using Shaders for Transitions in the VSM

Expression Blend 4 allows using shaders for transitions between states. This is especially nice when large portions of the screen need to transition from one state to another, but it can also be used for small templates. Note, however, that not any kind of effect can be used for transitions: It must be a class deriving from `TransitionEffect` included in the namespace `Microsoft.Expression.Media.Effects`, in the assembly Microsoft.Expression.Interactions, which is installed with the Blend SDK.

To use shaders when implementing states and transitions in Blend, expand the choice with the small fx icon circled in green in Figure 16.3.

The shader will be applied to the active element during the transition from one state to the other, as shown in Figure 16.4. By activating the small button circled in red in Figure 16.3, you can visualize the transition in Expression Blend directly.

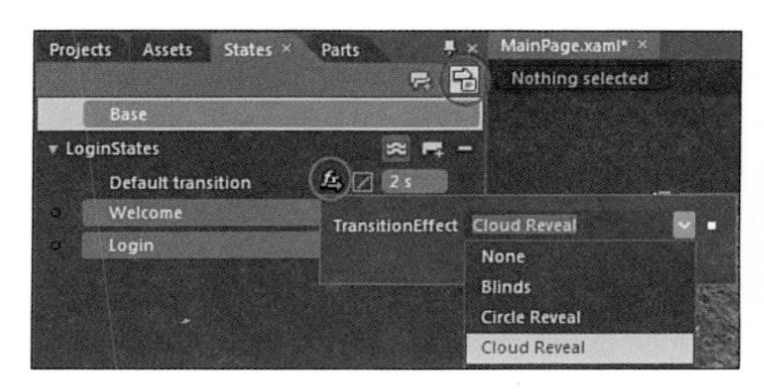

FIGURE 16.3 Selecting an effect for the transition.

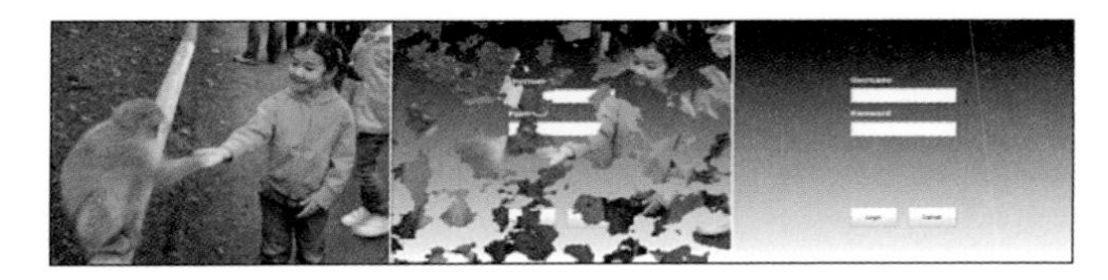

FIGURE 16.4 Screen before, during, and after transition with cloud reveal effect.

Accessing the Webcam and the Microphone

Silverlight 4 comes with extended access to the host computer, including a feature that everyone was eagerly awaiting: webcam and microphone access from the Silverlight application. At this time, unfortunately, there are no built-in encoders for the raw video and audio streams, which makes it very difficult to record and save videos. This is an improvement that we hope to see in a future version of Silverlight, to enable building videoconferencing systems.

In this section, we build a small application that creates greeting cards made of a picture, a frame and some overlay text and saves a short audio message. The initial state for this application named GreetingCardMaker can be downloaded from http://www.galasoft.ch/sl4-greeting. Download the zip file, and then right-click it in Windows Explorer and select Properties, the General tab, and then click Unblock. If the Unblock button is not visible, you can just unpack the files.

The start project is an MVVM application built with a view (MainPage.xaml), a `MainViewModel` class and a `ViewModelLocator`.

The interface IDialogService that was already used in Chapter 13, "Creating Line-of-Business Applications," is also included. The MainPage class implements this interface. As we did in Chapter 13, the MainViewModel has one property of type IDialogService that it uses to display messages to the user. This is a clean separation between intent (the MainViewModel wants to display a message) and implementation (the MainPage uses a MessageBox to show the message).

Getting the List of Devices

The first step to access a webcam and microphone is to detect which devices are available on the client computer. Some high-level classes allow doing this with the following steps:

1. Open the GreetingCardMaker application in Visual Studio, and then open the file MainViewModel.cs.
2. Add the two properties shown in Listing 16.10. These are ReadOnlyCollection instances (that is, collections that cannot be modified by the application).

LISTING 16.10 Collections of Video and Audio Devices

```
public ReadOnlyCollection<VideoCaptureDevice> WebCams
{
    get;
    private set;
}

public ReadOnlyCollection<AudioCaptureDevice> Microphones
{
    get;
    private set;
}
```

- Add a property shown in Listing 16.11, which will store an instance of the CaptureSource class. This object provides access to the functionalities of the video and audio devices.

LISTING 16.11 Storing a CaptureSource

```
public CaptureSource VideoAndAudioSource
{
    get;
    private set;
}
```

3. Add a property as shown in Listing 16.12 into the MainViewModel, to be notified when the user selects a video device. We will bind the SelectedItem of a ListBox to this property later.

LISTING 16.12 Selected Video Device

```
1  public const string SelectedWebCamPropertyName = "SelectedWebCam";
2  private VideoCaptureDevice _webcam;
3  public VideoCaptureDevice SelectedWebCam
4  {
5      get { return _webcam; }
6      set
7      {
8          if (_webcam == value)
9          {
10             return;
11         }
12
13         if (VideoAndAudioSource.State == CaptureState.Started)
14         {
15             VideoAndAudioSource.Stop();
16         }
17
18         _webcam = value;
19         RaisePropertyChanged(SelectedWebCamPropertyName);
20
21         if (_webcam != null)
22         {
23             VideoAndAudioSource.VideoCaptureDevice = _webcam;
24
25             if ((Microphones.Count == 0 || SelectedMicrophone != null)
26                 && (CaptureDeviceConfiguration.AllowedDeviceAccess
27                 || CaptureDeviceConfiguration.RequestDeviceAccess()))
28             {
29                 VideoAndAudioSource.Start();
30                 // StartAudioCommand.RaiseCanExecuteChanged();
31             }
32         }
33     }
34 }
```

- The property in Listing 16.12 raises the `PropertyChanged` event, so a data binding will be notified of changes to that property.
- In addition to the standard implementation of such a bindable property, lines 13 to 16 call the `Stop` method on the `CaptureSource` instance that we stored earlier. This is needed when selecting a new device to avoid issues with the hardware.
- On line 23, the selected video device is assigned to the `CaptureSource` instance. Note that it is also possible to select the DesiredFormat property. This can be useful if the webcam output is always used on a small surface. In that case, using a smaller format (for example 320 x 240) may speed up the operation.

- Lines 25 checks whether an audio device has been selected (but only if there are audio devices on the client computer).
- Line 26 checks whether the Silverlight application has permission to access the video and audio devices. This step is explained later in this chapter, in the "Enabling Access" section.
- If all these conditions are met, the CaptureSource instance is started. This switches the webcam on, and prepares the microphone.
- Line 30 is commented out for now. It will be used later to update the status of the command used to start an audio recording.

4. Copy Listing 16.12 and paste a copy underneath. Then make the following changes:

   On lines 1 and 19, replace SelectedWebCamPropertyName with SelectedMicrophonePropertyName.

   On line 1, replace "SelectedWebCam" with "SelectedMicrophone".

   On line 2 and 3, replace VideoCaptureDevice with AudioCaptureDevice.

   On line 2, 5, 8, 18, 21, and 23, replace _webcam with _microphone.

   On line 3, replace SelectedWebCam with SelectedMicrophone.

   On line 23, replace VideoCaptureDevice with AudioCaptureDevice.

   On line 25, replace Microphones with WebCams and SelectedMicrophone with SelectedWebCam.

5. In the MainViewModel constructor, initialize the two collections as declared in Listing 16.10. The CaptureDeviceConfiguration class is used to retrieve the list of video and audio devices available to record content, as shown in Listing 16.13.

LISTING 16.13 Retrieving Video and Audio Devices

```
WebCams = CaptureDeviceConfiguration
    .GetAvailableVideoCaptureDevices();
Microphones = CaptureDeviceConfiguration
    .GetAvailableAudioCaptureDevices();
```

Note that the CaptureDeviceConfiguration class also allows retrieving the default video and audio device, as configured by the user in the Silverlight configuration dialog (displayed by right-clicking any Silverlight application and choosing Silverlight from the context menu). This menu is shown in Figure 16.5.

6. In MainPage.xaml, add a DataTemplate to the UserControl.Resources as shown in Listing 16.14. This template will be used to represent one video or audio device by using its FriendlyName.

LISTING 16.14 Creating a DataTemplate

```
<UserControl.Resources>
    <DataTemplate x:Key="CaptureDeviceTemplate">
        <TextBlock Text="{Binding FriendlyName}" />
    </DataTemplate>
</UserControl.Resources>
```

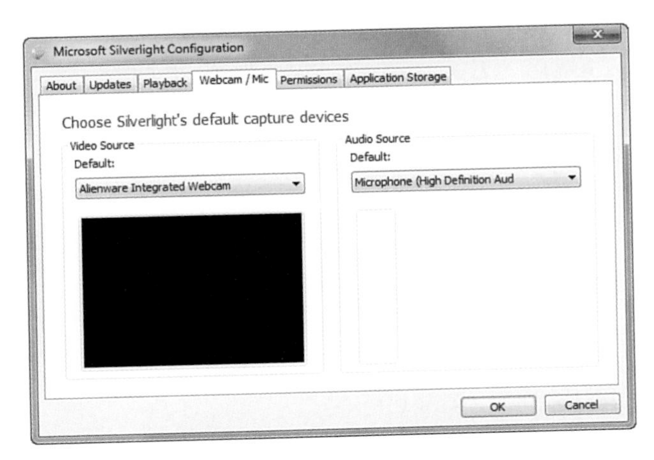

FIGURE 16.5 Default video and audio device.

7. Below the `Grid` named `CardImageGrid`, add two `ListBox` elements to display the list of devices, as shown in Listing 16.15.

LISTING 16.15 Two ListBox Elements

```
<ListBox Margin="10"
    Grid.Column="1"
    SelectedItem="{Binding SelectedWebCam, Mode=TwoWay}"
    ItemsSource="{Binding WebCams}"
    ItemTemplate="{StaticResource CaptureDeviceTemplate}" />
<ListBox Margin="10"
    Grid.Column="1"
    Grid.Row="1"
    SelectedItem="{Binding SelectedMicrophone, Mode=TwoWay}"
    ItemsSource="{Binding Microphones}"
    ItemTemplate="{StaticResource CaptureDeviceTemplate}" />
```

8. Run the application. You should now see the list of webcams in the upper `ListBox` and the list of microphones in the lower one.

Enabling Access

On line 26, Listing 16.12 checks whether the Silverlight application has permission to access the video and audio devices by checking the property `AllowedDeviceAccess` on the class `CaptureDeviceConfiguration`. This property is `true` if the user already gave his consent or if the application is running with elevated permissions.

If that is not the case, line 27 is executed, and the method `RequestDeviceAccess` is called. This causes the dialog shown in Figure 16.6 to be displayed. The user can store the permission, which will prevent the dialog of being shown the next time that the application is started. If needed, he can revoke it later using the Permissions tab in the Microsoft Silverlight Configuration dialog.

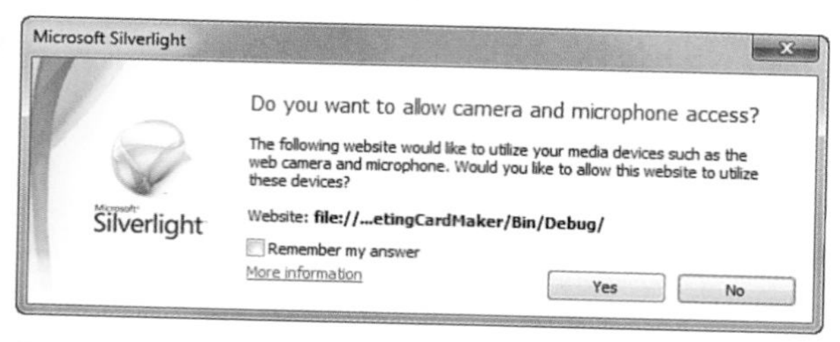

FIGURE 16.6 Camera and microphone access.

Displaying the Video Output

The output of the webcam is an instance of the class `CaptureSource`, which can be set as the source of a `VideoBrush`. We already used `VideoBrush` (and its static equivalent `ImageBrush`) in *Silverlight 2 Unleashed*, Chapters 5 and 6. Any element can be painted by this brush. In this case, we will use a `Rectangle`, as shown in Listing 16.16, that must be added within the `Grid` named `CardImageGrid`. Make sure that the `Rectangle` appears *before* the `TextBlock` that this `Grid` already contains. We want the `TextBlock` to be shown in front of the video. Note that this `Rectangle` can be transformed at will (for example, flipped horizontally to display a mirrored image, or rotated, skewed, and so forth).

LISTING 16.16 Rectangle and VideoBrush

```
<Rectangle Width="640" Height="480">
    <Rectangle.Fill>
        <VideoBrush x:Name="WebcamVideo"
                    Stretch="Uniform" />
    </Rectangle.Fill>
</Rectangle>
```

The `WebcamVideo` brush must be bound to the `CaptureSource` instance stored in the `MainViewModel` class. Unfortunately, the `VideoBrush` class does not have a `Source` property that can be handled in XAML. Instead, the `SetSource` method must be called. This is done in the `MainPage` class code behind: In the MainPage constructor, the `MainViewModel`'s

DialogService is set, like we already did in previous chapters. Modify this code as shown in Listing 16.17.

LISTING 16.17 Setting the Source of the VideoBrush

```
var vm = DataContext as MainViewModel;
if (vm != null)
{
    vm.DialogService = this;
    WebcamVideo.SetSource(vm.VideoAndAudioSource);
}
```

At this point, however, the CaptureSource instance is never initialized. This is solved in the MainViewModel class. Just add the line shown in Listing 16.18 to the MainViewModel constructor.

LISTING 16.18 Creating the CaptureSource

```
VideoAndAudioSource = new CaptureSource();
```

As soon as the VideoAndAudioSource is started in the MainViewModel, the output of the webcam is displayed in the Rectangle, which you can test by running the application, selecting the video and audio devices that you want to use, and confirming this action in the dialog shown in Figure 16.6.

Detecting Whether Other Applications Use the Device

Because of the way that webcams and microphones drivers are built, only one application at the time can access these devices. For instance, if the webcam is already active, an InvalidOperationException will be thrown on line 29 of Listing 16.12 (or in the equivalent line for the SelectedMicrophone property). To prevent the application from crashing, catch this exception as shown in Listing 16.19. This needs to be done in both the SelectedMicrophone and the SelectedWebCam properties.

LISTING 16.19 Catching the InvalidOperationException

```
try
{
    VideoAndAudioSource.Start();
    //StartAudioCommand.RaiseCanExecuteChanged();
}
catch (InvalidOperationException)
{
    DialogService.ShowMessage("Impossible to start the device");
}
```

Capturing Audio

At this point, the GreetingCardMaker application is able to display the output of a webcam, and the microphone is activated, but nothing much else happens. In this section, an audio stream will be recorded and saved to a WAV file on the user's hard disk.

Converting to a WAV File

The microphone's output is delivered in a raw format to the Silverlight application: The Pulse Code Modulation (PCM) format. It is a direct representation of the sound waves. The Silverlight application needs to convert this raw data into a usable format. This will gain space by compressing the raw data. Unfortunately, there are no built-in converters in Silverlight 4 (a situation which is likely to change in future versions). In the meantime, we can use an external class to convert PCM to WAV files. This is not the best format for audio because it creates quite large files, but the conversion from PCM to WAV is relatively simple.

In this sample, we will use the `WavManager` class created by Ondrej Svacina and available at http://www.galasoft.ch/sl4-pcmtowav. This static class has a single method `SavePcmToWav`, which takes care of the conversion.

Creating a Sink

Recording the raw audio is done by a class deriving from the abstract class `System.Windows.Media.AudioSink`. Here, too, there are no implementations of `AudioSink` in the Silverlight 4 framework at the moment. Implementing one is not very difficult, as shown by the following steps:

1. In Visual Studio, open the GreetingCardMaker application in the Solution Explorer, and then right-click the Helpers folder and select Add, Class from the context menu. Name the new class **WavAudioSink.cs**.

2. Derive the `WavAudioSink` class from `AudioSink` by changing its signature to `public class WavAudioSink : AudioSink`.

3. The abstract class `AudioSink` requires four methods named `OnCaptureStarted`, `OnCaptureStopped`, `OnFormatChange`, and `OnSamples`, as shown in Listing 16.20.

LISTING 16.20 Implementing an `AudioSink`

```
protected override void OnCaptureStarted()
{
}

protected override void OnCaptureStopped()
{
}
```

```
protected override void OnFormatChange(
    AudioFormat audioFormat)
{
}

protected override void OnSamples(
    long sampleTimeInHundredNanoseconds,
    long sampleDurationInHundredNanoseconds,
    byte[] sampleData)
{
}
```

4. On the top of the `WavAudioSink` class, add the three attributes shown in Listing 16.21. We will use them later.

LISTING 16.21 Three Attributes

```
private Stream _stream;
private AudioFormat _format;
private bool _isRecording;
```

5. Implement the `OnFormatChange` method as shown in Listing 16.22. This method is called at least once before the recording starts. It sets the format in which the recording takes place. Note that only PCM is supported at the moment.

LISTING 16.22 `OnFormatChange` Method

```
if (audioFormat.WaveFormat != WaveFormatType.Pcm)
{
    throw new ArgumentException(
        "Only PCM is supported",
        "audioFormat");
}
_format = audioFormat;
```

The `OnSamples` method shown in Listing 16.23 is the most important. It is called by the Silverlight framework as soon as sound samples are available in raw format, and periodically while the recording is going on.

LISTING 16.23 `OnSamples` Method

```
1 if (_stream == null)
2 {
3     _isRecording = true;
4     _stream = new MemoryStream();
```

```
 5   }
 6
 7  if (_isRecording)
 8  {
 9      _stream.Write(sampleData, 0, sampleData.Length);
10  }
```

- This method is called the first time when the recording is starting. It creates a new Stream if needed to store the audio samples.
- On line 7, the method checks whether recording is still active. This is needed because the Stream will be closed before saving it.
- Then, on line 9, the raw data is written into the Stream. Because a MemoryStream is used on line 4, the whole data is saved in the application's memory. For long recordings, this is not ideal, but for this kind of small greeting messages, it is okay.

6. Finally, add a new method named Save, shown in Listing 16.24. This method will take care of converting the PCM data to a WAV sound and writing the converted data to an output Stream.

LISTING 16.24 Saving the PCM Data to WAV

```
public void Save(Stream outputStream)
{
    _isRecording = false;
    CaptureSource = null;

    WavManager.SavePcmToWav(_stream, outputStream, _format);
    _stream = null;
}
```

Using the SaveFileDialog

We saw in Chapter 14, "Enhancing Line-of-Business Applications and Running Out of the Browser," how files can be saved to the user's folders (such as My Documents) if the application has elevated permissions. However, this is not possible when the application runs within the web browser. There is, however, another way using the SaveFileDialog class. Like all dialogs, this must be initiated by the user (for example, in response to a click a button). However the MainViewModel should not be in charge of displaying this dialog, because it should remain separated from the view. Instead, the IDialogService interface (in the ViewModel folder) can be extended as follows:

1. Modify IDialogService as shown in Listing 16.25. The method GetFile will take care of returning a Stream to a file selected by the user to save the audio recording.

LISTING 16.25 Extending the IDialogService Interface

```
public interface IDialogService
{
    void ShowMessage(string message);
    bool AskConfirmation(string message);
    Stream GetFile(string filter, string defaultExtension);
}
```

2. In the MainPage class (which implements the IDialogService interface), add the method shown in Listing 16.26.

LISTING 16.26 Getting a File with the SaveFileDialog

```
 1 public Stream GetFile(string filter, string defaultExtension)
 2 {
 3     var dialog = new SaveFileDialog
 4     {
 5         Filter = filter,
 6         DefaultExt = defaultExtension
 7     };
 8
 9     if (dialog.ShowDialog() == true)
10     {
11         return dialog.OpenFile();
12     }
13
14     return null;
15 }
```

- On lines 3 to 7, a new SaveFileDialog is created. The Filter property defines what kind of files the dialog can select. The DefaultExt property is used when a new file is saved without an extension. The content of DefaultExt will be used for this new file. For example, if the DefaultExt is .wav and the user types Test1 as the name of the file, the SaveFileDialog will create a file named Test1.wav.
- On line 9, the dialog is shown to the user. If the user clicks the Cancel button, the ShowDialog method returns false.
- If the user did select a file, the OpenFile method creates the file (if needed), opens it for reading or writing, and returns a FileStream (which is inheriting the Stream class).

Because the MainViewModel stores an instance of the IDialogService, it can now use this new method to get a Stream to save the audio file.

Using the Sink and Adding Commands

We already saw in previous chapters how to add commands on a viewmodel to trigger some actions. The RelayCommand and RelayCommand<T> classes that we already used before are available in the GreetingCardMaker application, in the Helpers folder. Add a StartAudioCommand and StopAudioCommand with the following steps:

1. In the MainViewModel class, add two properties and an attribute as shown in Listing 16.27: two commands to start and stop the recording, and an instance of the WavAudioSink class.

LISTING 16.27 Two Commands and a Sink

```
public RelayCommand StartAudioCommand
{
    get;
    private set;
}

public RelayCommand StopAudioCommand
{
    get;
    private set;
}

private WavAudioSink _sink;
```

2. Activate the call to the RaiseCanExecuteChanged method on the StartAudioCommand in the setter of the SelectedWebCam property as in Listing 16.12. Do the same for the SelectedMicrophone property. Just remove the comment signs in the beginning of the line.

3. In the MainViewModel constructor, instantiate the StartAudioCommand and StopAudioCommand as shown in Listing 16.28.

LISTING 16.28 Instantiating the Commands

```
1  StartAudioCommand = new RelayCommand(
2      StartAudio,
3      () => SelectedMicrophone != null
4          && _sink == null);
5
6  StopAudioCommand = new RelayCommand(
7      StopAudio,
8      () => _sink != null);
```

- On lines 2 and 7, the `Execute` delegates for these commands are declared. The `StartAudio` and `StopAudio` methods are shown in Listing 16.29 and 16.30.
- On lines 3 and 4, the `CanExecute` delegate for `StartAudioCommand` is declared. The command is enabled if the user selected a microphone and if the `WavAudioSink` has not been created yet. It means that the application is ready to record. When the recording starts (and the `WavAudioSink` is created), the `StartAudioCommand` should be disabled.
- On line 8, the `CanExecute` delegate for `StopAudioCommand` is declared. The command is enabled (and the recording can be stopped) if the `WavAudioSink` is available. The application will take care of setting this attribute to `null` when the recording stops.

4. Implement the `StartAudio` method as shown in Listing 16.29. This method is simple: It creates a new `WavAudioSink`, sets its `CaptureSource` property to the source that is currently active, and then refreshes the status of the two commands.

LISTING 16.29 `StartAudio` Method

```
private void StartAudio()
{
    _sink = new WavAudioSink
    {
        CaptureSource = VideoAndAudioSource
    };

    StartAudioCommand.RaiseCanExecuteChanged();
    StopAudioCommand.RaiseCanExecuteChanged();
}
```

5. Finally, implement the `StopAudio` method as shown in Listing 16.30.

LISTING 16.30 `StopAudio` Method

```
 1  private void StopAudio()
 2  {
 3      try
 4      {
 5          using (var outputStream = DialogService.GetFile(
 6              "WAV Files (*.wav) ¦ *.wav", ".wav"))
 7          {
 8              _sink.Save(outputStream);
 9          }
10      }
11      catch (IOException ex)
12      {
```

16

```
13             DialogService.ShowMessage(ex.Message);
14         }
15
16         _sink = null;
17         StartAudioCommand.RaiseCanExecuteChanged();
18         StopAudioCommand.RaiseCanExecuteChanged();
19     }
```

- On lines 5 and 6, the `GetFile` method of the `DialogService` is called. The filter is prepared in a format that is understood by the `SaveFileDialog` class: The string `WAV Files (*.wav)` will appear in the combo box used to filter files. As for `*.wav`, this extension is used to select the kind of files to display. This extension is also used as the default extension for new files.
- On line 5, a `using` statement is used to wrap the `Stream` operation. This will automatically close and dispose the `outputStream`, which will make the file available for later use.
- On line 8, the `Save` method is called on the sink and the `outputStream` is provided for saving.
- If the file that the user selected is open in another application, an `IOException` may occur. This exception is caught on line 11, and an error message is shown to the user on line 13.
- Finally, the sink is disposed, and the status of `StartAudioCommand` and `StopAudioCommand` is refreshed on lines 16 to 18.

Wiring the Commands

The user interface of the GreetingCardMaker application has two buttons: Start Audio and Stop Audio. These need to be wired to the corresponding commands. You can either do that in XAML directly, in the Visual Studio designer with the data binding editor, or in Expression Blend. After the binding is done, the buttons should appear in the XAML editor as shown in Listing 16.31.

LISTING 16.31 Start Audio and Stop Audio Buttons

```
<Button Content="Start Audio"
        Width="100"
        VerticalAlignment="Center"
        Margin="0,0,10,0"
        Command="{Binding StartAudioCommand}"/>
<Button Content="Stop Audio"
        Width="100"
        VerticalAlignment="Center"
        Margin="0,0,10,0"
        Command="{Binding StopAudioCommand}" />
```

Testing Audio Recording

To test the application, run it and select a webcam and a microphone. The output of the webcam should be displayed, and the Start Audio button should be enabled.

Click the Start Audio button to start the recording. Make some noise, and then click the Stop Audio button. The `SaveFileDialog` is displayed. You can either select an existing file (which will be overwritten) or enter a new name to create a new file.

After the file is saved, navigate to the folder you selected and play the file in a compatible sound player.

Writing to a Bitmap

After saving an audio file in the previous section, the output of the webcam also needs to be saved to a picture file. In fact, not just the webcam output, but also any element that is laid over it in the `CardImageGrid` can be saved in the picture file, thanks to the `WriteableBitmap` class.

This class allows manipulating images in multiple ways. In the GreetingCardMaker application, we are looking to convert a visual element (a `Grid` containing a `Rectangle` with a `VisualBrush` and a `TextBlock` over it) into a picture. The `WriteableBitmap` class makes this operation very simple with the following steps:

1. Open the GreetingCardMaker into Visual Studio.
2. In the `MainViewModel` class, add a command to capture the image currently displayed, as shown in Listing 16.32. Notice that this property is a `RelayCommand<UIElement>`, and that it expects the `CommandParameter` of the attached control to be set to the element that needs to be saved as an image.

16

LISTING 16.32 Adding the `CaptureCommand`

```
public RelayCommand<UIElement> CaptureImageCommand
{
    get;
    private set;
}
```

3. In the `MainViewModel` constructor, initialize the `CaptureImageCommand` by adding the line of code shown in Listing 16.33. The `CaptureImage` method is shown in Listing 16.34.

LISTING 16.33 Initializing the `CaptureImageCommand`

```
CaptureImageCommand = new RelayCommand<UIElement>(CaptureImage);
```

LISTING 16.34 CaptureImage Method

```
 1 private void CaptureImage(UIElement element)
 2 {
 3     try
 4     {
 5         var bitmap = new WriteableBitmap(element, null);
 6
 7         using (var outputStream = DialogService.GetFile(
 8             "PNG Files (*.png) ¦ *.png", ".png"))
 9         {
10             if (outputStream == null)
11             {
12                 return;
13             }
14
15             PngManager.SaveToImage(element, outputStream);
16         }
17     }
18     catch (IOException ex)
19     {
20         DialogService.ShowMessage(ex.Message) ;
21     }
22 }
```

- Line 5 captures the current state of the CardImageGrid and creates a WriteableBitmap with it. There are three constructors for this class: One takes a BitmapSource, for example, to manipulate images. Another constructor takes a width and a height and constructs an empty WriteableBitmap instance. The one we use here takes a UIElement and a Transform. For example, it would be possible to flip or rotate the UIElement before it is rendered to an image, or to scale it to create thumbnails. In our case, we don't want to transform the visual, so we just pass null.
- Lines 7 and 8 get a Stream from the DialogService using the GetFile method that was implemented earlier. This time, we are looking for a PNG file.
- On line 15, a class called PngManager is used to save the UIElement passed as parameter into a PNG file. This class will be implemented in the next section, "Saving the Picture to a PNG File."
- As usual when working with file streams, a using statement is used on line 7, and a possible IOException is caught and handled on lines 18 to 20.

5. Then, open MainPage.xaml and bind the Command of the Button with the Content set to "Capture Video" to the CaptureImageCommand we just created. The CommandParameter should be set through a binding to the CardImageGrid, the Grid that needs to be turned into an image (as shown in Listing 16.35).

LISTING 16.35 Binding the CaptureImageCommand

```
<Button Content="Capture Video"
        Width="100"
        VerticalAlignment="Center"
        Margin="0,0,10,0"
        Command="{Binding CaptureImageCommand}"
        CommandParameter="{Binding ElementName=CardImageGrid}"/>
```

Saving the Picture to a PNG File

Just like when we used an external encoder to convert the PCM sound stream to a WAV sound file, an external PNG encoder will be used to turn the raw picture bytes into a PNG file. To do this, we will use a `WriteableBitmap` and then an external library named ImageTools with the following steps:

1. The ImageTools library is an open source project hosted on CodePlex. It allows converting images to the PNG, GIF, JPG, and BMP formats. It also allows applying filters to images. Download the latest version from http://imagetools.codeplex.com and unpack the file in a known location on your hard drive. For more information about this very useful library, refer to the CodePlex site.
2. Open the GreetingCardMaker application in Visual Studio.
3. Right-click the References folder in the Solution Explorer and select Add Reference from the context menu.
4. In the Add Reference dialog, select the Browse tab and navigate to the folder which you just unpacked. Open the Bin folder and select the four following DLLs:

   ICSharpCode.SharpZipLib.Silverlight.dll, ImageTools.dll, ImageTools.IO.Png.dll, ImageTools.Utils.dll. Then click OK.

> **TIP**
>
> **Compressing and Packing**
>
> The DLL ICSharpCode.SharpZipLib.Silverlight.dll is very useful: It is another open source project (hosted at http://slsharpziplib.codeplex.com) that implements the zip protocol to compress and pack (or uncompress and unpack) zip files from your Silverlight application.

5. Right-click the Helpers folder and add a class named **PngManager.cs**.
6. In the `using` section of the `PngManager` class (at the top of the file), add `using ImageTools`.
7. In the `PngManager` class, implement the `SaveToImage` method shown in Listing 16.36.

LISTING 16.36 SaveToImage Method

```
1  public static void SaveToImage(
2      WriteableBitmap bitmap,
3      Stream outputStream)
4  {
5      var image = bitmap.ToImage();
6      image.WriteToStream(outputStream);
7  }
```

- Lines 1 to 3 declare the method's signature: The first parameter is a `WriteableBitmap`, which will be rendered to an image. The second parameter is a `Stream` to which the output will be written. Nothing here forces the caller to pass a `FileStream` (to save into a file). It could also be a `MemoryStream`, or the `Stream` of a web request to send the image to a web service, for example.
- Line 6 creates an `ImageTools.Image` by calling the `ToImage` method on the `WriteableBitmap`. Note that this method is an *extension method* that is added to the `WriteableBitmap` class by the ImageTools library. Extension methods extend the class they are attached to with additional functionality. For more information, see the "Creating Extension Methods" section in Chapter 22, "Advanced Development Techniques."
- Finally, line 7 serializes the image to the `outputStream`.

To test this feature, run the application and start the video and audio device. Enter a greeting text in the `TextBox` next to the Capture button, and then click that button. After you select a location for the file and save it, use Windows Explorer to retrieve the file and open it in your favorite picture viewer application.

Manipulating Pixels

`WriteableBitmap` offers a low-level interface to each pixel saved in an array. Note that the array is a single-dimension list of pixels, which can be a little confusing at first. For example, the example in Listing 16.37 loops through all the pixels of a `WriteableBitmap` and removes the Blue and Green components.

LISTING 16.37 Retrieving and Modifying Pixels

```
1  var bitmap = new WriteableBitmap(element, null);
2  int currentPixelIndex = 0;
3
4  for (var indexHeight = 0; indexHeight < bitmap.PixelHeight; indexHeight++)
5  {
6      for (var indexWidth = 0; indexWidth < bitmap.PixelWidth; indexWidth++)
7      {
8          int pixelValue = bitmap.Pixels[currentPixelIndex];
9
```

```
10          var color = Color.FromArgb(
11              (byte) (pixelValue >> 24),
12              (byte) (pixelValue >> 16),
13              (byte) (pixelValue >> 8),
14              (byte) pixelValue);
15
16          bitmap.Pixels[currentPixelIndex++] = color.A << 24 // A
17                                              | 0 << 16 // R
18                                              | 0 << 8  // G
19                                              | color.B; // B
20      }
21  }
```

- On line 4, a loop is created. This loop will enumerate all the rows of pixels. Note the use of the `PixelHeight` property, which returns the height in pixels of the `WriteableBitmap`.
- On line 6, an internal loop enumerates all the pixels in the current row, from left (index 0) to right. Here we use the `PixelWidth` property.
- On line 8, the current pixel is retrieved from the `Pixels` array. Because all the pixels are stored in one dimension only, we can simply use the `currentPixelIndex` counter, which is incremented on every pass of the loop (on line 16).
- Lines 10 to 14 get the A, R, G, and B components of the current pixel and create a `Color` instance. Because the pixel color is stored as an integer, we use the shift right operator to extract the components.
- On lines 16 to 19, a new value is assigned in the `Pixels` array. The A and B values are kept, but the R and G values are set to 0. Here the shift left operator is used to calculate the integer value out of the bytes.

The end effect is very similar to Figure 16.1, with the blue mask.

TIP

WriteableBitmap or Pixel Shader?

The effects that pixel manipulation in the `WriteableBitmap` instance are very close from what a pixel shader is doing. However, pixel shaders are much faster, especially on multicore machines (in which case, the mathematic operations are performed in parallel and use the CPU's fast SSE instructions.)

On the other hand, `WriteableBitmap` is great for in-process manipulation, or for combining multiple images, as you will see in the next section. Also, their number of operations is unlimited, whereas pixel shaders in Silverlight are limited to a maximum of 64 arithmetic instructions.

You can find more comparison data at http://www.galasoft.ch/sl4-bitmapvsshader.

Extending WriteableBitmap

Because every pixel can be modified individually, WriteableBitmap allows for a wide range of effects. However, addressing the pixels in the Pixels array is difficult and rather inconvenient. To solve this issue, Rene Schulte (a Silverlight MVP) created the WriteableBitmapEx library, which can be downloaded in Codeplex from http://writeablebitmapex.codeplex.com.

When this DLL is referenced in a Silverlight application, the WriteableBitmap class is extended with methods allowing higher-level manipulation of the pixels. For example, two images can be merged ("blitted") with the following steps:

1. In the GreetingCardMaker application, right-click the Silverlight project in the Solution Explorer and select Add, New Folder from the context menu. Name this folder **Resources**.
2. Download the image from http://www.galasoft.ch/sl4-frame. This image represents a frame, and all the inner pixels are transparent. Save the image to a known location on your hard drive.
3. Drag and drop the image from the location you saved it into to the Resources folder in the Solution Explorer. This adds the file to the Silverlight project.
4. With the file selected in the Solution Explorer, press F4 to display the properties. Make sure that the Build Action is set to Content and the Copy to Output Directory property is set to Copy If Newer.
5. In the PngManager class, add a using statement on top of the file: using System.Windows.Media.Imaging.
6. Modify the SaveToImage method as shown in Listing 16.38.

LISTING 16.38 New SaveToImage Method

```
1  public static void SaveToImage(
2      WriteableBitmap bitmap,
3      Stream outputStream)
4  {
5      var frameStreamInfo = Application.GetResourceStream(
6          new Uri("Resources/frame.png", UriKind.Relative));
7
8      var source = new BitmapImage();
9      source.SetSource(frameStreamInfo.Stream);
10     var frameBitmap = new WriteableBitmap(source);
11
12     var rectangle = new Rect(0, 0,
13         element.RenderSize.Width,
14         element.RenderSize.Height);
15     bitmap.Blit(rectangle, frameBitmap, rectangle);
```

```
16
17      var image = bitmap.ToImage();
18      image.WriteToStream(outputStream);
19  }
```

- Lines 5 and 6 retrieve the frame picture from the XAP file by using the `Application.GetResourceStream` method, which returns a `Stream` with the file's content.
- Lines 8 and 9 create a new `BitmapImage` and set its source to the `Stream` that was just retrieved.
- Then, on line 10 another `WriteableBitmap` is created with this image. Another constructor is used here, the one with a `BitmapSource` as parameter (`BitmapImage` inherits this abstract class).
- Lines 12 to 14 create a rectangle with the image's dimensions. Note that the `Rect` class is used, which is a pure geometric class, not the `Rectangle` class that is used in user interfaces. The `Rect` class simply defines a top-left point, a width, and a height.
- Line 15 uses the `Blit` extension method to combine the two bitmaps.
- Finally, lines 17 and 18 didn't change, and save the bitmap to the `Stream` in PNG format.

Test the application and save a capture to the hard drive. An example with the frame is shown in Figure 16.7.

FIGURE 16.7 Greeting card with text and frame.

WriteableBitmapEx has a number of very useful methods as well as some nice samples (including for Windows Phone 7) and is maintained and extended actively. This is a great addition to your arsenal of tools. For example, in addition to the blitting action that you saw in this chapter, there are also methods to draw on the bitmap directly, with various shapes and methods being supported. With WriteableBitmapEx, many of the operations that were possible in GDI+ are now possible in Silverlight. For more information about this extension class, make sure to check the CodePlex site.

Using the Open File Dialog

In this chapter, the Save File dialog was used to retrieve the Stream of a file in which content can be written. For security reasons, only the Stream is returned to the dialog's caller, and it is not possible to retrieve the filename. However, this dialog can be used even without additional permissions, which is very convenient.

The counterpart to the Save File dialog for reading files is also available: the OpenFileDialog class. This class can be used with the code in Listing 16.39. Note the presence of the Multiselect property. When set to true, the user can select multiple files that will be placed in the dialog's Files property. If Multiselect is false, only one file can be selected, and it will be placed in the File property.

LISTING 16.39 Using the OpenFileDialog Class

```
public IEnumerable<FileInfo> OpenFileForRead(string filter)
{
    var dialog = new OpenFileDialog
    {
        Filter = filter,
        Multiselect = true
    };

    if (dialog.ShowDialog() == true)
    {
        return dialog.Files;
    }

    return null;
}
```

This method can be used as shown in Listing 16.40.

LISTING 16.40 Getting Text Files and Reading Them

```
var files = OpenFileForRead("TXT Files (*.txt) | *.txt");

foreach (FileInfo file in files)
{
```

```
    using (var stream = file.OpenRead())
    {
        using (var reader = new StreamReader(stream))
        {
            var text = reader.ReadToEnd();
            // Do something with content of file
        }
    }
}
```

This dialog could be used in the GreetingCardMaker application to let the user select the frames for the pictures. In that case however, a `StreamReader` is not needed. Instead, simply use the result of `file.OpenRead()` on line 11 of Listing 16.38.

Learning About News in Media

Some new features are available in terms of media in Silverlight 3 and Silverlight 4:

- (Silverlight 4) Digital Rights Management systems (DRMs) are now available for the H264 media format. This popular format for video encoding can now also be protected by the Silverlight Digital Rights Management system, as was already the case for the VC1 format.
- (Silverlight 4) DRMs are now available for offline content. This is convenient for OOB Silverlight applications that are used to watch content on demand even when the client computer is not connected to the Internet.
- (Silverlight 3 and 4) In the earlier version of Silverlight, the support was added for new media formats such as H264 and AAC. This opens Silverlight applications to more popular content.
- (Silverlight 3 and 4) Together with Silverlight 3, smooth streaming for the Internet Information Services (IIS, Microsoft's web server). The resolution of the stream is automatically adapted to the speed of the Internet connection, in real time. If the speed drops temporarily, a lower resolution is sent to the client application, to avoid losing the stream and disrupting the experience. This was used in big events such as the Olympic games or in the transmission of conferences such as the Professional Developer Conference (PDC) 2009. For more information about smooth streaming, refer to http://www.galasoft.ch/sl4-smooth.
- (Silverlight 3 and 4) With these improvements, it is now also possible to stream high-definition (HD) content from a web server to a Silverlight application.
- Finally, Expression Encoder is now available in its version 4, with a lot of improvement to encode media.

Summary

In this chapter, you learned about multiple techniques that enable you to enhance Silverlight applications with effects and media.

With pixel shaders, the aspect of UI elements can be modified with external pieces of code that are applied in parallel to each pixel. This is very convenient when visual elements need to be modified dynamically (for example, to modify the aspect of a video that is playing) and very fast.

You also saw how to input media elements into the Silverlight application with video and audio devices. For the first time, Silverlight applications can be enhanced with images and sounds that the user himself records.

We talked about the `WriteableBitmap` class, another way to modify images dynamically, but this time within the Silverlight code directly. Although this method is a little slower than using pixel shaders, it is easier to configure and modify for Silverlight developers.

Finally, we listed a few additional improvements to the media features of Silverlight 3 and 4. In the next chapter, we continue our exploration of new features in Silverlight 4.

CHAPTER 17

New Transforms, Right Click, HTML Browser, WebBrowserBrush, and Isolated Storage

IN THIS CHAPTER, WE WILL:

- Discover the new PlaneProjection class that allows modifying elements in a 3D plane.
- Talk about a new easier way to compose transforms.
- Handle the right-click event on a Silverlight surface.
- Host HTML content within a Silverlight Out-of-the-Browser application.
- Paint elements with HTML content.
- Dive deeper into the isolated storage.

Continuing with the exploration of additions and changes brought to Silverlight 4, this chapter covers multiple improvements and new features.

Transforming Elements in a Projection

In *Silverlight 2 Unleashed*, Chapter 3, we talked in details about the basic transforms available in Silverlight (`TranslateTransform`, `ScaleTransform`, `SkewTransform`, `RotateTransform`) and about more complex transforms that combine multiple basic ones (`TransformGroup`, `MatrixTransform`). We also mentioned that all these transforms are *affine*; that is, that two parallel lines will remain parallel whatever transform is applied to the element, as shown in Figure 17.1.

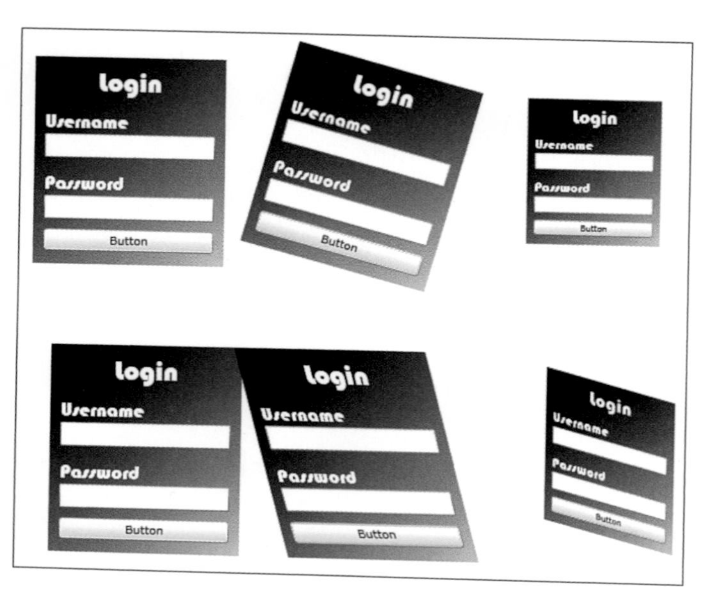

FIGURE 17.1 Affine transforms: Null, Rotate, Scale, Translate, Skew, `TransformGroup`.

Because of the constraint of the parallel lines, it was impossible to create 3D effects without resorting to external frameworks. In Silverlight 3, however, a new class named `PlaneProjection` was introduced and allows creating *perspective transforms*. Note, however, that in contrast to all the transforms mentioned before, `PlaneProjection` is not a `System.Windows.Media.Transform` descendant, but instead a `System.Windows.Media.Projection`.

By applying an instance of the `PlaneProjection` class to an element, it is possible to create a non-affine transform that gives an illusion of 3D. This is not true 3D; instead, the terms *3D-like effect* or *2.5D effect* are often used. In fact, `PlaneProjection` is really just a transform: No camera or lights are involved in the 2.5D scene, in contrast to "true 3D" as found in Windows Presentation Foundation (WPF).

`PlaneProjection` exposes a series of properties allowing moving the object in the 3D space. The most spectacular are `RotationX`, `RotationY` and `RotationZ` which, as the name shows, rotate the element along the X, Y, and Z axes as shown in Figure 17.2. In this figure, the Z axis is "coming out of the picture" and pointing at us.

FIGURE 17.2 `PlaneProjection` transform along the X, Y, and Z axis.

Of course, these rotations can be combined (as shown in Figure 17.3).

The easiest way to create a group of rotations in design mode is to use Expression Blend. A new group in the Properties panel shows an editor for the `PlaneProjection`. This includes the possibility to transform the element by clicking and dragging a rotation control (circled in red in Figure 17.4).

FIGURE 17.3 Composing the rotations.

Setting Additional Properties

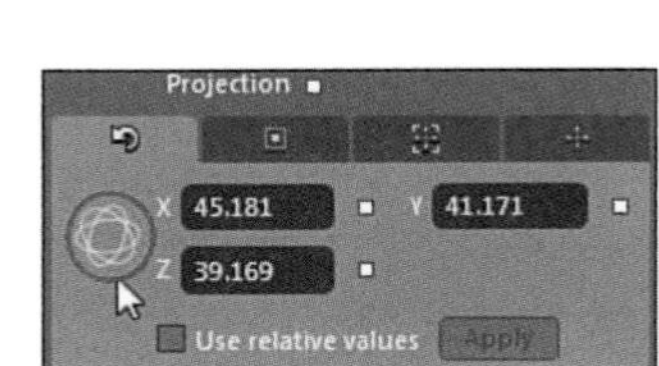

FIGURE 17.4 Using the Projection editor in Blend.

In addition to the three rotation angles, additional properties are used to customize the transformed element's appearance:

- `CenterOfRotationX`, `CenterOfRotationY`, `CenterOfRotationZ`: Sets the center point around which the rotations are applied. This is a *relative value* between 0 and 1, with (0, 0, 0) being the top left corner of the element. For the Z axis, values larger than 0 move the center of rotation toward the viewer (out of the picture) while negative values move it further away from the viewer (behind the picture).
- `GlobalOffsetX`, `GlobalOffsetY`, `GlobalOffsetZ`: These values are absolute (in pixels) and move the element along the X, Y, and Z axes, without considering the element's rotation. Figure 17.5 shows the global offset axis in red.
- `LocalOffsetX`, `LocalOffsetY`, `LocalOffsetZ`: With these values, the element is moved (in pixels) along the X, Y, and Z axes after these axes have been rotated along with the element. Figure 17.5 displays the local offset axis in green.

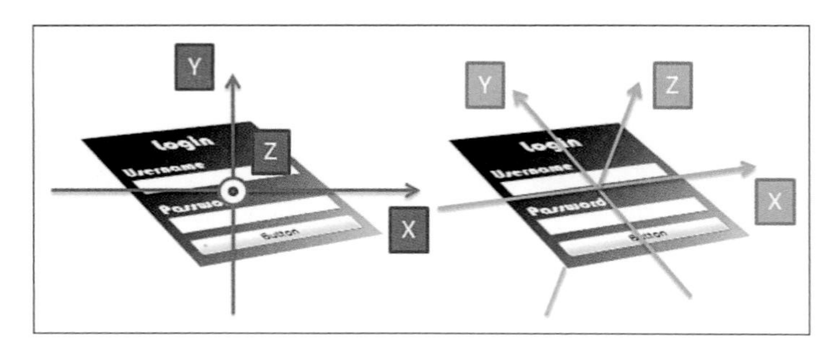

FIGURE 17.5 X, Y, and Z axes for global offset (red) and local offset (green).

Using a Matrix3DProjection

For more complex projections in the 3D space that the `PlaneProjection` cannot cover, the `Matrix3DProjection` class can help. Just like the `MatrixTransform` class that was shown in *Silverlight 2 Unleashed*, Chapter 3, the `Matrix3DProjection` is a matrix of parameters that modify the element's appearance. However, this matrix is more complex, since it takes place in the 3D space.

For more information about `Matrix3DProjection`, see http://www.galasoft.ch/sl4-matrix3d.

Animating the PlaneProjection

Because the `PlaneProjection`'s properties are dependency properties, they can be data bound and animated. In this section, we build a state transition in Expression Blend using the plane projection to create a nice effect. This is the same effect that the Windows Phone 7 uses for some of its transitions, and in fact what is shown here is applicable to phone applications, as well! Just follow these steps:

1. Start Expression Blend and create a new Silverlight 4 application. Name it **PerspectiveTransition**.
2. In the `LayoutRoot Grid`, add two additional `Grid` elements and name them **ContentGrid1** and **ContentGrid2**. Make sure that `ContentGrid1` is behind `ContentGrid2`. (It must appear first in the Objects and Timeline panel.)
3. Select the two new `Grid` elements in the Objects and Timeline panel and set their `Width` and `Height` to Auto, and the `Margin` to 0. Set the `VerticalAlignment` and `HorizontalAlignment` to Stretch.
4. Add a few controls and UI elements to `ContentGrid1`, and set the `Grid`'s `Background` to a nice linear gradient brush.
5. In the Objects and Timeline panel, hide the `ContentGrid1` by clicking the small Eye icon next to the element's name. Make sure that `ContentGrid2` is selected.
6. Set `ContentGrid2`'s `Background` to a plain white.

7. With ContentGrid2 still selected, find the Projection section (in the Transform category of the Properties panel). Select the Center of Rotation tab and set X to 0.5, Y to 0 and Z to 0. This places the point on the top border of the image, in the center of the width.

8. In Windows Explorer, select a picture and drag it on the designer surface. This adds the picture to the project, and adds an Image control to ContentGrid2. Make sure that the Image control is indeed a child of ContentGrid2 in the Objects and Timeline panel.

9. Resize the picture in the designer so that it fills the whole Width and Height. If needed, change the Stretch property, the HorizontalAlignment, VerticalAlignment and the Margin property until you are satisfied.

10. Display ContentGrid1 again by clicking on the small Eye icon next to its name in the Objects and Timeline panel.

11. Select the States panel and add a state group named **IntroStates**.

12. In the IntroStates group, add a new state named **Entrance** and another state named **Data**.

13. With the Data state selected, make sure that Blend is in state recording mode. A red border should be visible around the designer surface.

14. Select ContentGrid2. In the Projection section of the Properties panel, select the Rotation tab and increase the value of X until the panel disappears to the user's eyes. This should be a negative value of approximately -76.5.

15. With the Data state still selected and recording, set the Opacity of ContentGrid2 to 0.

16. Click the Base state to stop the recording. Set the Transition duration to 1.5 seconds.

17. Select an easing function for the transition (for example, the Cubic InOut easing).

18. Select a GoToStateAction in the Behaviors section of the Assets library and drag it onto ContentGrid2.

19. With the GoToStateAction selected, set the EventName to MouseLeftButtonDown in the Properties panel, and the StateName to Data. Make sure that UseTransitions is checked.

20. Drag another GoToStateAction, this time on ContentGrid1. Set the EventName to MouseLeftButtonDown, and the StateName to Entrance. Here, too, make sure that UseTransitions is checked.

21. Run the application and click the picture. The transition should be played in the 3D space as shown in Figure 17.6. Then click the Grid's background, which should reverse the animation and display the picture again.

17

Figure 17.6 Entrance state, transition, data state.

Composing Transforms

Another small but welcomed addition to the transform landscape is the introduction in Silverlight 4 of the new `CompositeTransform` class. This is just a simpler way to define a group of transforms without having to resort to a `TransformGroup` and its more complex syntax.

For example, the `TransformGroup` in Listing 17.1 can be expressed by the `CompositeTransform` in Listing 17.2. However, there is a small difference: In the `CompositeTransform`, the order of the transforms applied to the element are always: Scale, Skew, Rotate, and Translate. Should you want a different order for some reason, you need to use a `TransformGroup` instead. Another difference is that the `CenterX` and `CenterY` properties of the `CompositeTransform` are applied to each transform. With the `TransformGroup`, it is possible to specify a different center for each transform.

LISTING 17.1 Transform Composition with `TransformGroup`

```
<StackPanel.RenderTransform>
    <TransformGroup>
        <RotateTransform Angle="15" />
        <ScaleTransform ScaleX="0.7"
                        ScaleY="0.7" />
        <SkewTransform X="15" />
        <TranslateTransform X="20" />
    </TransformGroup>
</StackPanel.RenderTransform>
```

LISTING 17.2 Transform Composition with `CompositeTransform`

```
<StackPanel.RenderTransform>
    <CompositeTransform Rotation="15"
        ScaleX="0.7" ScaleY="0.7"
        SkewX="15" TranslateX="20" />
</StackPanel.RenderTransform>
```

Handling the Right-Click Event

In earlier versions of Silverlight, right-clicking on any element on the page would show the Silverlight context menu and nothing else. Although this is still the default behavior, the applications now have the possibility to handle the mouse right-click event and to perform a custom action.

The right-click event can be caught on any `UIElement`, and handled just like any other event. There is, however, one difference: If you want to prevent the default Silverlight context menu to be shown (for example, because you are displaying a custom context menu), the event must be marked as handled.

In the following sample, a custom right-click event is handled to remove a selected item from a `ListBox`. In the next section, we see how to use the context menu control from the Silverlight toolkit to perform the same operation. Start with the following steps:

1. Load the start application from http://www.galasoft.ch/sl4-rightclick. This is the frame of a Model-View-ViewModel (MVVM) application with a list of customers. For this simple sample, the data is simulated.
2. If needed, unblock the content by right-clicking on the zip file in Windows Explorer, selecting Properties from the context menu, and then clicking the Unblock button. If the button is not visible on the General tab, the content is already unblocked.
3. Extract the content of the zip file to a location on your hard drive, and then open the solution file in Visual Studio 2010.
4. Run the application. You should see a list of customers and their account number presented in a `ListBox`.

The customers are created in the `MainViewModel` class. This is just dummy data, and the source of this data is actually not relevant for this experiment. Each `Customer` instance is rendered in the `ListBox` by a `DataTemplate` located in the resources of MainPage.xaml. What is needed now is an event handler for the right-click event on the customers.

Handling a Routed Event

Because the right-click occurs on one of the elements displayed in the `ListBox`, it seems necessary to add an event handler in the `DataTemplate`. However, this is not convenient because it would make it impossible to move the `DataTemplate` to an external resource dictionary (which is very often needed to implement multiple skins or to facilitate the designer-developer workflow).

Instead, two possible solutions exist:

- Using commands. We already saw that a binding to a command is a loose coupling, and the binding is only resolved at runtime, when it is needed. That would be a very clean solution, however, there is one catch: In Silverlight (and WPF), only certain elements (`Button`, `ToggleButton`, `CheckBox`, `RadioButton`, and so on) have a

Command property. In Chapter 19, "Authentication, Event to Command Binding, Random Animations, Multitouch, Local Communication, and Bing Maps Control," we work around this limitation.

- Using a single event handler on the ListBox parent element.

A handler on the parent ListBox is able to catch and handle the MouseRightButtonDown event raised on the child because the event is *routed* (like many built-in events in Silverlight 4). It means that an event raised on any element in the tree will travel from this element to its parent, and the parent's parent, and all the way up to the main UserControl. This is very convenient because it allows us to place one single event handler that will catch the events raised by any of the ListBox's children. To demonstrate this, use the following steps:

1. Open MainViewModel.cs in Visual Studio and implement the DeleteCustomer method as shown in Listing 17.3. Because the Customers collection is an ObservableCollection, any change made to the items list (adding, removing, changing the sorting order) is automatically reflected by the user interface through the data binding.

LISTING 17.3 DeleteCustomer Method

```
public void DeleteCustomer(Customer toRemove)
{
    if (toRemove != null
        && Customers.Contains(toRemove))
    {
        Customers.Remove(toRemove);
    }
}
```

2. Open MainPage.xaml in the Visual Studio XAML editor and modify the ListBox tag as shown in Listing 17.4.

LISTING 17.4 Catching the MouseRightButtonDown Event in the ListBox

```
<ListBox Margin="30"
         ItemTemplate="{StaticResource CustomerTemplate}"
         ItemsSource="{Binding Customers}"
         MouseRightButtonDown="ListBoxMouseRightButtonDown" />
```

3. Right-click the ListBoxMouseRightButtonDown name and select Navigate to Event Handler from the context menu. This opens MainPage.xaml.cs.

4. Implement the event handler as shown in Listing 17.5.

LISTING 17.5 `ListBoxMouseRightButtonDown` Handler

```
1  private void ListBoxMouseRightButtonDown(
2      object sender,
3      MouseButtonEventArgs e)
4  {
5      var vm = DataContext as MainViewModel;
6      if (vm != null)
7      {
8          var element = e.OriginalSource as FrameworkElement;
9          if (element != null)
10         {
11             var customer = element.DataContext as Customer;
12             if (customer != null)
13             {
14                 vm.DeleteCustomer(customer);
15                 // e.Handled = true;
16             }
17         }
18     }
19 }
```

- Line 5 gets the `MainPage`'s `DataContext`. Because this property is of type `object`, it is necessary to cast it to the `MainViewModel` type.
- Line 6 checks whether the `vm` variable is `null`. This can be the case if the `DataContext` was not set yet, or if the `DataContext` is not of the `MainViewModel` type; in this case, the `as` operation returns `null`. This is a nice way to protect the application from a `NullReferenceException`.
- Line 8 gets the `OriginalSource` of the event. This is the element on which the mouse was actually clicked. Because the event is routed, it will eventually arrive in the `ListBox`. However, because the `ListBox` has many children, it is needed to know which element was clicked (and which `Customer` this item represents).
- Line 11 gets the `DataContext` of the clicked element. The Silverlight framework automatically sets the `DataContext` of a `DataTemplate` to the data item that this `DataTemplate` represents. In this case, the `DataContext` of each `DataTemplate` is one `Customer` instance.
- If the retrieved item is not `null` and has been casted successfully to the `Customer` type, the `DeleteCustomer` method on the `MainViewModel` is called on line 14.

TIP

Talking to the DataContext in Code

Getting the `DataContext` and using it to call methods or set properties on the viewmodel is a technique that is often used when there is no other way to address the viewmodel. In general, it is better to minimize the size of the code behind to increase the application's testability and maintainability, as discussed in Chapter 7, "Understanding the Model-View-ViewModel Pattern." However, this is not always possible, and code like that shown in Listing 17.5 is a perfectly acceptable workaround.

Run the application and right-click one of the elements. It should disappear from the list. However, the Silverlight context menu is displayed, which hinders further operation. We need to tell Silverlight that the right-click event was handled by our code, and that the Silverlight context menu should not be shown. To do this, follow these steps.

1. In MainPage.xaml.cs, in the `ListBoxMouseRightButtonDown` event handler shown in Listing 17.5, remove the comment sign (`//`) from line 15.
2. Run the application again and right-click a customer. This time, the Silverlight context menu is not displayed. Click the blue background of the `LayoutGrid`, and the default Silverlight context menu is shown.

Showing the Silverlight Context Menu

The Silverlight context menu should never be completely blocked by a Silverlight application because it offers convenient functionalities to the user: configuring permissions, checking and deleting isolated storage, configuring Silverlight updates, managing webcam and microphone. However, it is not possible at this time to display the Silverlight configuration dialog programmatically (for example, by adding a menu item to a custom context menu).

To allow the user to configure Silverlight, it is a good practice to never handle the right-click event on the parent element (the main `UserControl`), but instead to leave a border on which the user can right-click to display the configuration dialog.

Displaying a Context Menu

The usual function of a right-click event on an element is to display a context menu; that is, a menu whose content depends on the element that was clicked. Although the core Silverlight framework does not have such a control, there is one in the Silverlight toolkit. If the toolkit is not installed yet, follow the indications in Chapter 4, "Investigating Existing Controls," to make it available on your development computer, and then follow these steps:

1. Open MainViewModel.cs and add a `RelayCommand` as shown in Listing 17.6. Notice that the command expects a `Customer` instance as the `CommandParameter`.

LISTING 17.6 Adding the DeleteCustomerCommand

```
public RelayCommand<Customer> DeleteCustomerCommand
{
    get;
    private set;
}
```

2. In the MainViewModel constructor, instantiate the DeleteCustomerCommand as shown in Listing 17.7. This code uses a reference to the DeleteCustomer method that was defined in Listing 17.3. This works because DeleteCustomer expects one parameter of type Customer.

LISTING 17.7 Instantiating the DeleteCustomerCommand

```
DeleteCustomerCommand
    = new RelayCommand<Customer>(DeleteCustomer);
```

3. Right-click the References folder in the Silverlight application, in the Solution Explorer, and select Add Reference from the context menu.
4. In the Add Reference dialog, select the .NET tab and add a reference to System.Windows.Controls, System.Windows.Controls.Input.Toolkit, and System.Windows.Controls.Toolkit.
5. In MainPage.xaml.cs, delete the ListBoxMouseRightButtonDown event handler.
6. In MainPage.xaml, remove the MouseRightButtonDown property from the ListBox.
7. Locate the CustomerTemplate in the UserControl's Resources.
8. In the StackPanel within the DataTemplate, add the markup shown in Listing 17.8. In this listing, the input prefix stands for http://schemas.microsoft.com/winfx/2006/xaml/presentation/toolkit in the list of xmlns.

17

LISTING 17.8 Adding a Context Menu in XAML

```
1  <input:ContextMenuService.ContextMenu>
2      <input:ContextMenu Width="140">
3          <input:MenuItem Header="Delete"
4              Command="{Binding Source={StaticResource Locator},
5                                Path=Main.DeleteCustomerCommand}"
6              CommandParameter="{Binding}">
7              <input:MenuItem.Icon>
8                  <Image Source="Resources/DeleteIcon.png"
9                         Height="20" Width="20" />
10             </input:MenuItem.Icon>
```

```
11         </input:MenuItem>
12     </input:ContextMenu>
13 </input:ContextMenuService.ContextMenu>
```

- Line 1 uses an *attached property* defined in a class named the `ContextMenuService`. This class is currently in the Preview band of the Silverlight toolkit. It means that it is functional, but changes may well occur in future versions. Also, it is not fully tested, so some bugs might remain.
- The content of the attached property is set to a `ContextMenu` control, also defined in the Silverlight toolkit. This control is defined on lines 2 to 12.
- One `MenuItem` is added to the `ContextMenu` on lines 3 to 11. Its `Header` is set to `Delete`, which is the text shown in the menu item.
- Lines 4 and 5 bind the `MenuItem`'s `Command` property to the `DeleteCustomerCommand` on the `MainViewModel`. Notice that the `Source` of the `Binding` needs to be set explicitly. The implicit `DataContext` of the `DataTemplate` is the `Customer` item. The `DeleteCustomerCommand`, however, is defined in the `MainViewModel` class. This is where the `ViewModelLocator` comes handy.
- On line 6, the `CommandParameter` is set to an "empty binding." This means that the content of `CommandParameter` will be the *implicit* `DataContext` of the `MenuItem`. In this case, this is the instance of the `Customer` class that the `DataTemplate` represents. This is a convenient way to pass the `Customer` instance directly to the viewmodel.
- Finally, on lines 7 to 10, an icon is defined for the `MenuItem`, and set to a PNG image located in the Resources folder.

9. Run the application and right-click a customer in the `ListBox`. The custom context menu is shown as in Figure 17.7.

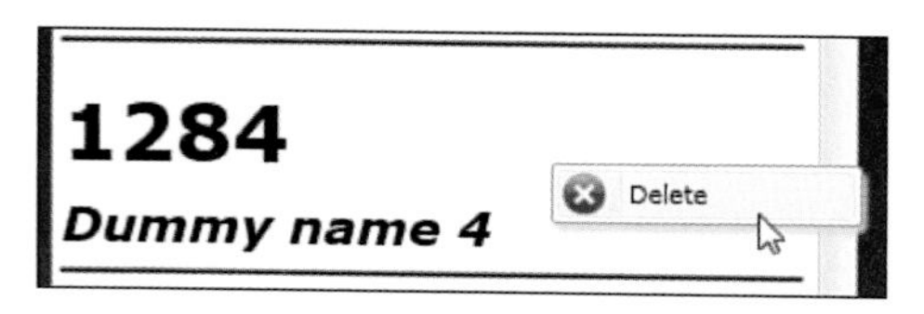

FIGURE 17.7 Custom context menu.

The `ContextMenuService` takes care of setting `e.Handled` to `true`, so the Silverlight context menu is automatically blocked when a custom context menu is used.

Hosting an HTML Browser (Out-of-the-Browser Only)

Until the out-of-browser (OOB) mode for Silverlight was developed, a Silverlight application was always running hosted in a web page. In some cases, the whole website was developed in Silverlight, with no visible HTML elements. In general, however, Silverlight elements are used to enhance the website with additional functionality or to improve the user experience.

Displaying HTML content within the Silverlight application was never intended for these scenarios. There are some third-party solutions relying on placing an HTML `iframe` element in front of the Silverlight plug-in. Although communication is possible between the Silverlight application and the HTML content, it is a cumbersome solution. However, for most applications, this was not critical because displaying HTML in Silverlight was a rare use case.

WARNING

Making a Site Fully in Silverlight

Developing a whole website in Silverlight, without any HTML elements, is generally speaking not a very good practice. Although Silverlight provides enhanced functionalities, it is not as ubiquitous as HTML/CSS/JavaScript. Running a Silverlight-only website on a mobile device, for example, is a challenge.

At the very least, alternative content for devices without Silverlight support should be offered.

With the advent of OOB applications however, this requirement becomes more frequent than before. Silverlight OOB applications are not hosted in an HTML environment anymore. The only way to display and interact with HTML elements is by hosting a web browser within the application. For example, if the OOB application wants to show a Twitter stream, an RSS feed, or even just an extract of a web page, hosting a web browser control is the only solution.

The `WebBrowser` control answers this concern. It can be embedded within a Silverlight application, and can navigate to a URI or render an HTML string. This leverages the capability of the computer's web browser (for example, to render PDF files or even Flash content within the Silverlight application), provides a viewer for rich content (for example, a Help file), integrates the HTML experience directly in the Silverlight application (instead of starting an external web browser), and so forth.

Understanding the Limitations

A few limitations must be taken in account:

- The `WebBrowser` control renders HTML content only when it is placed in an application running out of the browser. When the application runs in the browser, a warning message is displayed in the `WebBrowser` control, as shown in Figure 17.8.
- The `WebBrowser` control appears on top of every other element in the Silverlight application. It is not possible to change its Z-order, to transform it, or to change its `Opacity`. If you need to transform the HTML content, or display it under another element, check the "Painting with HTML" section, later in this chapter.
- When the OOB application runs in full screen, all navigation is disabled. The content cannot even be scrolled.

Building a Simple Web Browser

In this section, a simple web browser application is built in Silverlight to help us understand the features and limitations of the `WebBrowser` control. This application will then be extended with additional features. Follow these steps:

1. Download the starting point (named WebBrowserSample-Start) for this sample from http://www.galasoft.ch/sl4-webbrowser. Save the zip file on your hard drive, and then display the file's properties and (if needed) unblock its content by clicking the corresponding button.

2. Extract the content of the zip file and start the solution WebBrowserSample.sln in Visual Studio 2010.

   This application is prepared with a main page, and two `ChildWindow` elements that will be configured and used later. In addition, a web application is available to serve the Silverlight application and to provide same-domain content.

3. Open MainPage.xaml and add the markup shown in Listing 17.9 to the `LayoutRoot Grid`. This creates a `WebBrowser` control named `MyWebBrowser`. Note that the `WebBrowser` control is part of the core Silverlight framework, and does not need additional DLLs to be included in the XAP file.

LISTING 17.9 Creating the `WebBrowser` Control

```
<WebBrowser x:Name="MyWebBrowser"
            Grid.ColumnSpan="2"
            Margin="10,0,10,10"
            Grid.Row="1" />
```

4. Open MainPage.xaml.cs and add the code in Listing 17.10 to the `MainPage` constructor, after the call to `InitializeComponent`. This code adds an event handler to the `WebBrowser`'s `Completed` event, which is called when a navigation operation is completed. Note the usage of a lambda expression to declare an anonymous event handler. Note also that placing this call before `InitializeComponent` was called would fail because `MyWebBrowser` is available only after the XAML markup has been parsed.

LISTING 17.10 Handling the `Completed` Event

```
MyWebBrowser.LoadCompleted += (s, e) =>
    MyBusyIndicator.IsBusy = false;
```

5. Implement the `Navigate` method as shown in Listing 17.11. This method is called when the Navigate button is clicked.

LISTING 17.11 Navigate Method

```
private bool _isContentLocal;
private string _lastAddress = string.Empty;

private void Navigate()
{
    if (string.IsNullOrEmpty(LocationTextBox.Text))
    {
        return;
    }

    MyBusyIndicator.IsBusy = true;
    MyWebBrowser.Source = GetNavigationUri();
    SaveFileButton.IsEnabled = true;
    _lastAddress = MyWebBrowser.Source.AbsoluteUri;
    _isContentLocal = false;
}
```

6. Implement the method `GetNavigationUri` as shown in Listing 17.12. This method checks the `TextBox` on the main page and attempts to build a valid URI with its content.

LISTING 17.12 `GetNavigationUri` Method

```
 1  private Uri GetNavigationUri()
 2  {
 3      Uri nextUri;
 4
 5      if (LocationTextBox.Text.StartsWith("http://"))
 6      {
 7          nextUri = new Uri(LocationTextBox.Text, UriKind.Absolute);
 8      }
 9      else
10      {
11          var xapUri = App.Current.Host.Source;
12          var baseAddress = xapUri.AbsoluteUri.Substring(
13              0, xapUri.AbsoluteUri.IndexOf("ClientBin/"));
14
15          nextUri = new Uri(baseAddress
16              + LocationTextBox.Text, UriKind.Absolute);
17      }
18
19      return nextUri;
20  }
```

- Line 5 checks whether the address that the user entered starts with `http://`. If that is the case, the method considers that it is a remote address and creates an absolute `Uri` instance.
- If the address entered is relative to the Silverlight application's origin, a little more work is needed to create an absolute `Uri`. To understand why, check the "Using Relative URIs" section, later in this chapter.
- On line 11, the absolute address of the XAP file is retrieved.
- On lines 12 and 13, the base address of the website is extracted.
- Then, on lines 15 and 16, the absolute `Uri` is created.

Make sure that the WebBrowserSample.Web web project is set as the startup project, and that the page WebBrowserSampleTestPage.html is set as the start page. Then, run the application. Note that the `WebBrowser` control appears with a warning mentioning that HTML is enabled only in out-of-browser mode, as shown in Figure 17.8.

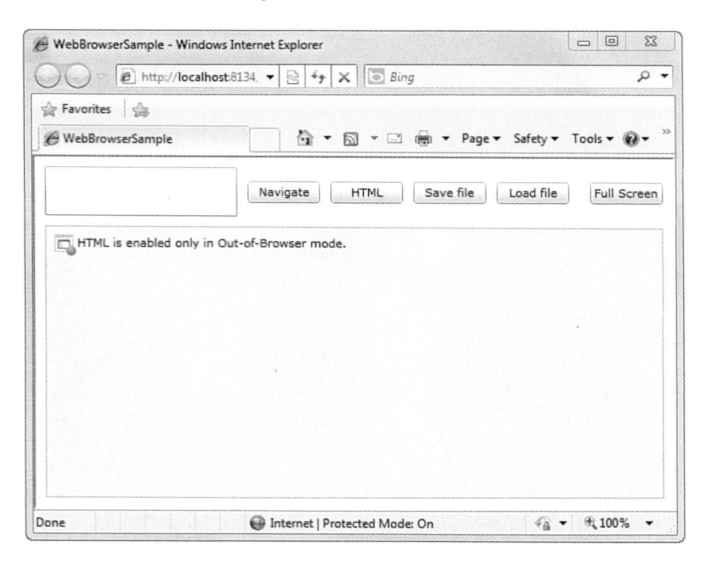

FIGURE 17.8 *`WebBrowser`* control in the browser.

Executing Out-of-the-Browser

To run the application out of the browser, follow these steps:

1. Close the application.
2. In Visual Studio, open the Silverlight project's properties.
3. In the Silverlight tab, check the Enable Running Application out of the Browser check box.
4. Run the application again.

5. Right-click the Silverlight application and select Install WebBrowserSample Application onto this computer. Then, close the web browser.

6. In the OOB application, enter the text `mypage.html` into the `TextBox` on top of the page, and then click the Navigate button.

mypage.html is a file located on the website from which the XAP file originates. It is a simple HTML file with a few links and a few text paragraphs. From here, click the Gutenberg link to be taken to the Project Gutenberg's website. This page is external to the site of origin, but it can be navigated anyway.

To run the OOB application from Visual Studio, select the Silverlight project properties. On the Debug tab, in the Start Action, check Out-of-Browser Application radio button and make sure that WebBrowserSample.Web is selected in the combo box. Then, set the Silverlight project as the start application in the Solution Explorer.

Exploring the Navigation Restrictions

By clicking various links in the `WebBrowser` control, we notice the following facts about navigation:

- All the content can be displayed, including images, Flash movies, and so forth. Scripts are executed.
- Cross-schema navigation (from HTTP to HTTPS or opposite) is not possible. No error is raised, but the navigation simply fails. Similarly, all the content displayed must be in the same schema.
- Content displayed in HTML `iframe` elements appears correctly, but only if both the page and the `iframe` run in the same schema (HTTP or in HTTPS).
- On Windows computers, right-clicking the `WebBrowser` control's surface displays the same context menu as in Internet Explorer.

Later, we will see that if the application runs with elevated permissions, there are no restrictions at all, and navigating from HTTP to HTTPS or opposite is enabled.

Using Relative URIs

Relative URIs in Silverlight must be handled with care. When trying to load a relative URI (for example, `new Uri("/Images/myimage.png", UriKind.Relative)`), Silverlight first checks within the XAP whether the PNG file can be found. If it is not the case, Silverlight checks relatively to the folder containing the XAP file (in general, that is the ClientBin folder). For example, if the web application's domain is www.mypage.com, and if the folder `/Images/myimage.png` cannot be found within the XAP file, the URI entered before resolves to the absolute URI www.mypage.com/ClientBin/Images/myimage.png.

To retrieve files placed outside of the ClientBin folder (on the root of the website or in a child folder), an absolute URI must be created, as shown in Listing 17.12.

Another difficulty is that in XAP, relative URIs must have a leading forward slash (/) character. For example, consider the following URIs set in XAML:

- `Source="Images/el20090906004.jpg"`

  Valid if the Images folder is in the ClientBin folder (not embedded in the XAP file)

  Invalid if Images is embedded in the XAP file

- `Source="/Images/el20090906004.jpg"`

  Valid in both scenarios

Finally, files embedded into the XAP file must have their Build Action set to Content, and the Copy to Output Directory property must be set to Copy If Newer or Copy Always.

Loading HTML Content from Memory

In addition to navigating to a URI, the `WebBrowser` control is also able to display HTML loaded from a `string`. This is very convenient, for example, to display richly formatted documents created by the Silverlight application (reports, articles, and so on) or to show documents when the application is offline. To test this, follow these steps:

1. Open MainPage.xaml.cs in Visual Studio.
2. Implement the event handler `ShowHtmlButtonClick` as shown in Listing 17.13.

LISTING 17.13 Navigating to a `string`

```
private void ShowHtmlButtonClick(object sender, RoutedEventArgs e)
{
    MyWebBrowser.NavigateToString(LocationTextBox.Text);
}
```

3. Run the application and enter HTML code into the `TextBox` (for example, the markup shown in Listing 17.14). Then, click the HTML button.

LISTING 17.14 Sample HTML Markup

```
<h1>This is a test</h1>
<div style="color: Red;">This works</div>
<a href="http://www.galasoft.ch">Go to GalaSoft</a>
```

In the “Saving to the Isolated Storage” section, later in this chapter, you will see how entire HTML files can be saved to memory and displayed later in offline mode, and what restrictions apply.

Invoking JavaScript

When a web page containing JavaScript functions is loaded into the `WebBrowser` control, Silverlight code can invoke the various methods by using the `InvokeScript` method, as shown in http://www.galasoft.ch/sl4-invokescript.

In the other direction, the script function can raise the `ScriptNotify` event on the `WebBrowser` control by calling the `window.external.notify` function and passing it a `string` parameter. This parameter can be retrieved in the `ScriptNotify` event handler of the `WebBrowser` class, as the `Value` property of the `NotifyEventArgs` parameter. You can find more information about `ScriptNotify` at http://www.galasoft.ch/sl4-scriptnotify.

Note that normal cross-domain restrictions apply, if the script is located in a different domain than the Silverlight application was loaded from.

Writing and Reading in the Isolated Storage

The isolated storage has been available to Silverlight applications since Silverlight 2. It is a location on the client computer organized like a file system with directories and files. However, the Silverlight application doesn't know where the files are located.

In *Silverlight 2 Unleashed*, the isolated storage was presented in Chapter 10. For the most part, the objects and restrictions remain the same in Silverlight 4. In this section, you'll see how to use the isolated storage to save HTML web pages locally for offline viewing.

Note the following restrictions for this sample:

- Only HTML markup is saved for offline viewing. Images and other content are not saved. This includes external CSS files, which will cause the HTML pages to appear "in the raw," without styling.
- At the time of this writing, some web pages cause the Silverlight application to crash when they are loaded from the isolated storage and displayed into the `WebBrowser` control. The cause of the crash seems to be related to external JavaScript files adding content dynamically to the web page.
- Some HTML files throw JavaScript errors when they are loaded offline. Unfortunately, there is no way to keep JavaScript errors like these silent.

Saving to the Isolated Storage

To turn this small sample into a full-blown offline viewer, a lot of additional work would be needed to "sanitize" the saved HTML pages. However, it shows how various features of the isolated storage can be used to enhance a Silverlight application, with the following steps:

1. Reopen the WebBrowserSample application in Visual Studio.
2. In the Solution Explorer, right-click the Helpers folder in the Silverlight project and add a class named **LocalFileHelper.cs**.

3. In this file, implement the `FileContent` property and the `SaveFile` method as shown in Listing 17.15.

LISTING 17.15 `FileContent` Property and `SaveFile` Method

```
 1  public string FileContent { get; set; }
 2
 3  public bool SaveFile(string fileName)
 4  {
 5       if (string.IsNullOrEmpty(fileName)
 6           || string.IsNullOrEmpty(FileContent))
 7      {
 8          return false;
 9      }
10
11      using (var isoStore = IsolatedStorageFile.GetUserStoreForApplication())
12      {
13          using (var stream = isoStore.OpenFile(fileName, FileMode.CreateNew))
14          {
15              using (var writer = new StreamWriter(stream))
16              {
17                  writer.Write(FileContent);
18              }
19          }
20      }
21
22      return true;
23  }
```

- Line 11 gets the isolated store for the application. Note that using the same class `IsolatedStorageFile`, it is also possible to get the store for the site of origin of the application. This is convenient if multiple Silverlight applications served from the same website need to exchange information about the client computer, or if some settings are shared.
- Line 13 opens the file in the isolated storage for writing. This line will fail if the file already exists. The caller of the method is responsible for checking this beforehand. Note the `using` statement, which will automatically close the `Stream` when the operation is completed.
- On line 15, a `StreamWriter` is created. This class is useful to write text content to a `Stream`. Here, too, a `using` statement takes care of closing the `StreamWriter` after the operation is finished.
- Line 17 writes the text saved in the `FileContent` property to the `Stream` before `true` (success) is returned on line 22.

Using Directories

Of course, it is also possible to use directories in the isolated storage to build a file structure. For more information about how to use directories, see http://www.galasoft.ch/sl4-isodirectories.

Note, however, that it is not possible to get a handle on the given directory, but only to work with the directory's name. To create a directory within another directory, the code in Listing 17.16 can be used.

LISTING 17.16 Creating a Directory Within Another Directory

```
isoStore.CreateDirectory("Directory1\\Directory2");
```

Requesting More Storage Space

The code in Listing 17.15 has one big issue: When the isolated storage is full, the save operation will fail. For an application with default permissions (in the browser or OOB), the default quota for isolated storage is 1MB. Applications with elevated permissions have a default quota of 25MB. However, after a certain time, the storage might not be sufficient to save an additional file.

To avoid this issue, add the content of Listing 17.17 between lines 12 and 13 of Listing 17.15. In this listing, additional storage is requested. For security, we request twice the size of the file that needs to be saved. Note that the user is free to refuse, in which case the operation is aborted on line 5.

LISTING 17.17 Increasing the Isolated Storage Quota

```
1  if (isoStore.AvailableFreeSpace < FileContent.Length)
2  {
3    if (!isoStore.IncreaseQuotaTo(isoStore.Quota + FileContent.Length * 2))
4    {
5       return false;
6    }
7  }
```

Checking Whether a File Exists

To check whether a given file already exists, the `LocalFileHelper` should be able to retrieve all the files from the isolated store, and then check whether the list of names contains the file that the user is looking for. This can be done with the following steps:

1. In LocalFileHelper.cs, add the code shown in Listing 17.18.
2. The `ToList` method used in the `FileExists` method is not available by default on the `string[]` array type (which is returned by `GetAvailableFiles`). To add this extension method to our toolbox, it is necessary to add the following statement to the top of the LocalFileHelper.cs file: `using System.Linq;`.

This statement adds a series of *extension methods* to the array class.

LISTING 17.18 Getting the List of Files and Checking Whether a File Exists

```
public string[] GetAvailableFiles()
{
    using (var isoStore
        = IsolatedStorageFile.GetUserStoreForApplication())
    {
        return isoStore.GetFileNames();
    }
}

public bool FileExists(string fileName)
{
    var list = GetAvailableFiles().ToList();
    return list.Contains(fileName);
}
```

Using the LocalFileHelper

To get information from the user and handle the file saving operation, a `ChildWindow` named SaveFileChildWindow.xaml will be used. This element is already present in the Silverlight project. Modify it as follows:

1. Open the file SaveFileChildWindow.xaml.cs in Visual Studio.
2. Modify the constructor as shown in Listing 17.19. This code creates a new `LocalFileHelper` as a private field, and then saves the content of the file in its `FileContent` property. The creator of the `ChildWindow` is responsible for passing the content of the file to this window.

LISTING 17.19 Modifying the `SaveFileChildWindow` Constructor

```
private LocalFileHelper _helper;

public SaveFileChildWindow(string fileContent)
{
    _helper = new LocalFileHelper
    {
        FileContent = fileContent
    };
    InitializeComponent();
}
```

3. Modify the `OKButton_Click` event handler as shown in Listing 17.20.

LISTING 17.20 Handling the OK Button

```
1  private void OKButton_Click(object sender, RoutedEventArgs e)
2  {
3      var fileName = FileNameTextBox.Text.ToLower();
4
5      if (_helper.FileExists(fileName))
6      {
7          MessageBox.Show("Already exists: " + FileNameTextBox.Text);
8          return;
9      }
10
11     if (_helper.SaveFile(fileName))
12     {
13         DialogResult = true;
14     }
15     else
16     {
17         MessageBox.Show("Problem when saving, try again or cancel");
18     }
19 }
```

- Line 3 retrieves the name that the user entered in the `TextBox` located in SaveFileChildWindow.xaml.
- Line 5 uses the `FileExists` method that was implemented in the `LocalFileHelper` class in Listing 17.18. If the file name is already used, a message is shown and the operation is aborted.
- Line 11 uses the `LocalFileHelper` to save the file in the isolated storage.
- If everything went well, the `DialogResult` is set to `true` on line 13. This closes the `ChildWindow`. The caller can retrieve the `DialogResult` property to check whether the operation was successful.

4. Open MainPage.xaml.cs and modify the `SaveFileButtonClick` event handler as shown in Listing 17.21.

LISTING 17.21 Handling the `SaveFileButtonClick` Event listing (17.21)

```
1  private void SaveFileButtonClick(object sender, RoutedEventArgs e)
2  {
3      try
4      {
5          var content = MyWebBrowser.SaveToString();
6          var window = new SaveFileChildWindow(content);
7          window.Closed += (s, args)
8              => MyWebBrowser.Visibility = Visibility.Visible;
```

17

```
 9            window.Show();
10
11            MyWebBrowser.Visibility = Visibility.Collapsed;
12        }
13        catch (SecurityException)
14        {
15            MessageBox.Show("Impossible to save, no permission");
16        }
17    }
```

- Line 5 calls the WebBrowser's SaveToString method. This method returns the HTML markup currently loaded into the web browser. Note, however, that this method may cause a SecurityException to be thrown, as you will see later in this chapter. This exception is caught on line 13, and a corresponding message is shown on line 15.
- Line 6 constructs a new SaveFileChildWindow and passes the content of the HTML file to it.
- Lines 7 and 8 define an event handler for the Closed event of the ChildWindow. The lambda expression used sets the WebBrowser control's Visibility to Visible. We will see in a moment why this is needed.
- Line 9 displays the ChildWindow.
- Finally, line 11 collapses the WebBrowser control.

Understanding the Restrictions of GDI

On line 11 of Listing 17.21, the WebBrowser control is hidden when the ChildWindow is displayed. This is necessary because of a restriction of the WebBrowser: the HTML content is rendered by the GDI graphics system (like many legacy applications) and not in DirectX (like modern application frameworks such as Silverlight). The rules of GDI apply to the WebBrowser control: This is why this control cannot be made semitransparent or transformed, cannot be animated and always appears on top of every other Silverlight element. This restriction is annoying but we will see a way to partly work around this in the section titled Painting with HTML. In the meantime, the WebBrowser is simply collapsed and restored when needed.

Testing the File Saving Operation

To test saving a file, run the application and enter the name mypage.html in the TextBox. Then click the Navigate button. After the page is loaded, click the Save File button. The operation should complete without errors.

You can also test the FileExists method of the LocalFileServer: Try to save a file with the same name that was just used. An error message should be displayed by the application.

WARNING

Making Sure That the Web Server Is Running

Because the pages mypage.html and secondpage.html are stored on a local web server, and because the OOB application runs independently, it is necessary to make sure that the web server is started before attempting to load the HTML page. You already saw how to do this in Chapter 14, "Enhancing Line-of-Business Applications and Running Out of the Browser," in the "Making Sure That the WCF Server Is Running" section.

Trying to Save Cross-Domain Content

Saving content served by the server of origin (in this case, the local web server) of the Silverlight application is not subjected to restrictions. However, attempting to save cross-domain content will cause an error to occur. To witness this, follow these steps:

1. Load mypage.html in the WebBrowserSample application. Then click the Gutenberg link to load the home page of the Project Gutenberg.
2. In the Project Gutenberg page, look for a book that you want to read offline and load it in the `WebBrowser`. After the book is loaded, click the Save button.
3. The error message we created in Listing 17.21, line 15 is shown. This is the result of the `SecurityException` being thrown.

Without elevated permissions, the `WebBrowser` control is allowed to display cross-domain web pages, but a call to the `SaveToString` method is not permitted for these pages. To solve this, the application needs to be installed with elevated permissions with the following steps:

1. Run the WebBrowserSample application.
2. Right-click the top of the page (on a Silverlight element) and select Remove This Application from the context menu.
3. In Visual Studio, display the Properties of the Silverlight project.
4. In the Silverlight tab, open the Out-of-Browser Settings dialog.
5. Check the Require Elevated Trust check box, and then close the dialog.
6. Set the WebBrowserSample.Web as the startup project.
7. Run the application and reinstall the Silverlight application on the computer.
8. Navigate to http://www.gutenberg.org and find the book you wanted to save. This time, the saving operation is successful.
9. Set the Silverlight project as the startup project in Visual Studio again.

This example shows the limitations of an OOB application without elevated permissions. For the rest of the chapter, we proceed with elevated permissions.

Reading from the Isolated Storage

Now that files are saved into the isolated storage, the application should offer them to the user for offline viewing with the following steps. As previously mentioned, only the HTML markup was saved; all the images, external Cascading Style Sheets (CSS), and other content are not available in this simple example. This explains why saved pages look differently from the original.

1. Reopen the WebBrowserSample application in Visual Studio.
2. In the `LocalFileHelper` class, add the code shown in Listing 17.22.

LISTING 17.22 Getting a File from the Isolated Storage

```
1  public bool GetFileContent(string fileName)
2  {
3      if (!FileExists(fileName))
4      {
5           return false;
6      }
7
8      using (var isoStore
9          = IsolatedStorageFile.GetUserStoreForApplication())
10     {
11         using (var stream = isoStore.OpenFile(fileName, FileMode.Open))
12         {
13             using (var reader = new StreamReader(stream))
14             {
15                 FileContent = reader.ReadToEnd();
16             }
17         }
18     }
19
20     return true;
21 }
```

- Line 3 checks whether the desired file actually exists in the store. If it cannot be found, the operation is aborted on line 5.
- Lines 8 and 9 retrieve the isolated store for the application, like we did before when saving a file.
- Line 11 opens the file for reading.
- Line 13 creates a `StreamReader`, the perfect class to read text content.
- Line 15 reads the whole content of the file, and place it in the `FileContent` property for later use.
- Line 20 notifies the caller that everything went fine.

3. A ChildWindow will be used to show the list of available files, and load the content. This element named LoadFileChildWindow.xaml is already available and partly implemented in the Silverlight project. Open LoadFileChildWindow.xaml.cs.

4. Create a new instance of the LocalFileHelper as shown in Listing 17.23. The FileContent property is a simple wrapper around the LocalFileHelper's property of the same name.

LISTING 17.23 Creating the LocalFileHelper

```
private LocalFileHelper _helper = new LocalFileHelper();
public string FileContent
{
    get { return _helper.FileContent; }
}
```

5. Modify the LoadFileChildWindow constructor as shown in Listing 17.24. The list of available files is simply retrieved thanks to the LocalFileHelper and an ObservableCollection is created to store the list.

LISTING 17.24 Retrieving the Files List

```
public LoadFileChildWindow()
{
    Files = new ObservableCollection<string>(_helper.GetAvailableFiles());
    InitializeComponent();
}
```

6. Modify the OKButton_Click event handler like in Listing 17.25.

LISTING 17.25 Getting the File's Content

```
 1  private void OKButton_Click(object sender, RoutedEventArgs e)
 2  {
 3      if (FilesListBox.SelectedIndex < 0)
 4      {
 5          MessageBox.Show("Please select a file or cancel");
 6          return;
 7      }
 8
 9      if (!_helper.GetFileContent(
10          FilesListBox.SelectedItem.ToString()))
11      {
12          MessageBox.Show("Cannot get file content, try again");
13          return;
```

```
14     }
15
16     DialogResult = true;
17 }
```

- Lines 9 and 10 call the GetFileContent method on the LocalFileHelper. This loads the content into the helper's FileContent property for later. If an error occurs, an error message is shown, and the operation is aborted.
- Line 16 is reached if everything went fine, and the window is closed by setting DialogResult to true.

7. Open MainPage.xaml.cs and modify the LoadFileButtonClick event handler as shown in Listing 17.26.

LISTING 17.26 Loading the File

```
1  private void LoadFileButtonClick(object sender, RoutedEventArgs e)
2  {
3      var window = new LoadFileChildWindow();
4      window.Closing += (s, args) =>
5      {
6          if (window.DialogResult == true)
7          {
8              MyWebBrowser.NavigateToString(window.FileContent);
9              _lastAddress = LocationTextBox.Text = window.FileName;
10             _isContentLocal = true;
11         }
12
13         MyWebBrowser.Visibility = Visibility.Visible;
14     };
15
16     MyWebBrowser.Visibility = Visibility.Collapsed;
17     window.Show();
18 }
```

- On line 3, a new LoadFileChildWindow is created.
- The Closing event of the new window is handled on lines 4 to 14. First, if the operation was successful, the offline file content is loaded into the WebBrowser control on line 8. Then, the WebBrowser's Visibility is restored. These lines will be executed when the user closes the window later.
- Line 16 hides the WebBrowser control for the reason explained earlier in this chapter, to avoid that the browser remains in front of the ChildWindow.
- Finally line 17 shows the ChildWindow to the user.

Now it's time for testing: Run the application and click the Load File button. Retrieve the file that was saved in the previous section from the Gutenberg website and load it in the window. You can now build your library online, and use it even when the computer is offline later.

Deleting Files

After a book is read, it doesn't make much sense to keep it on the computer, seeing how it can be loaded again from the Gutenberg website later. Deleting files from the isolated storage is very easy with the following steps:

1. In the LocalFileHelper class, add the code shown in Listing 17.27. This method checks whether the file to be deleted is available in the store, and then calls the store's DeleteFile method.

LISTING 17.27 Deleting a File from the Store

```
public void DeleteFile(string fileName)
{
    if (FileExists(fileName))
    {
        using (var isoStore
            = IsolatedStorageFile.GetUserStoreForApplication())
        {
            isoStore.DeleteFile(fileName);
        }
    }
}
```


2. In LoadFileChildWindow.xaml.cs, edit the DeleteFile_Click event handler as shown in Listing 17.28. Notice that the file name is also removed from the Files collection. Because this property is an ObservableCollection, the ListBox will be notified of the change through the data binding and will automatically be updated.

LISTING 17.28 Implementing the DeleteFile_Click Event Handler

```
private void DeleteFile_Click(object sender, RoutedEventArgs e)
{
    if (FilesListBox.SelectedIndex < 0)
    {
        return;
    }

    var fileName = FilesListBox.SelectedItem.ToString();
    _helper.DeleteFile(fileName);
    Files.Remove(fileName);
}
```

3. Run the application and click the Load File button. You can now select a file from the list and delete it from the isolated storage.

Using the IsolatedStorageSettings

A nice improvement to the WebBrowserSample application would be to automatically reload the last page that was viewed before the application was ended. This is a nice touch that many web browsers offer nowadays. In this section, we use the `IsolatedStorageSettings` class, a façade class from the Silverlight framework that hides some of the complexity of the isolated storage and offers a simpler interface to the functionality that is needed to save key/value pairs. To add this functionality to the application, follow these steps:

1. Reopen WebBrowserSample in Visual Studio.
2. In LocalFileHelper.cs, add the constants from Listing 17.29 on top of the class.

LISTING 17.29 Constants for Settings

```
private const string IsContentLocalKey = "IsContentLocal";
private const string LastAddressKey = "LastAddress";
private const string SettingsFileName = "__LocalSettings";
```

3. To save the settings, add the method shown in Listing 17.30 to the `LocalFileHelper` class.

LISTING 17.30 Saving the Settings

```
public void SaveSettings(bool isContentLocal, string lastAddress)
{
    IsolatedStorageSettings.ApplicationSettings[IsContentLocalKey]
        = isContentLocal;
    IsolatedStorageSettings.ApplicationSettings[LastAddressKey]
        = lastAddress;
}
```

4. The method in Listing 17.31 loads the settings from the isolated storage and should be added to the `LocalFileHelper` class, too.

LISTING 17.31 Loading the Settings

```
public void LoadSettings(
    out bool isContentLocal,
    out string lastAddress)
{
    isContentLocal = false;
```

```
    lastAddress = string.Empty;

    if (IsolatedStorageSettings.ApplicationSettings.Contains(
            LastAddressKey)
        && IsolatedStorageSettings.ApplicationSettings.Contains(
            IsContentLocalKey))
    {
        lastAddress = IsolatedStorageSettings
            .ApplicationSettings[LastAddressKey].ToString();
        isContentLocal = (bool)IsolatedStorageSettings
            .ApplicationSettings[IsContentLocalKey];
    }
}
```

Both `SaveSettings` and `LoadSettings` use the `IsolatedStorageSettings.ApplicationSettings` table to store the settings. This works very much like other key/value settings tables (for example, in ASP.NET). Because the content of the value is of type `object`, any serializable content can be stored and the Silverlight framework will take care of serializing the values for you.

Filtering the Settings File

In Listing 17.29, a constant named `SettingsFileName` was declared. This is the name of the `__LocalSettings` file that Silverlight creates to store the settings. The `LocalFileHelper` should filter this file out when retrieving the list of all the files stored in the isolated storage, or else this name will appear in the `LoadFileChildWindow`'s `ListBox`. This is done by modifying the `GetAvailableFiles` method as shown in Listing 17.32, which uses a LINQ query to filter the settings file name out of the list. The `Where` method is an extension method for lists contained in the `System.Linq` namespace that was added to the top of the class file earlier.

LISTING 17.32 Filtering the Settings Filename

```
public string[] GetAvailableFiles()
{
    using (var isoStore
        = IsolatedStorageFile.GetUserStoreForApplication())
    {
        return isoStore.GetFileNames().ToList()
            .Where(n => n != SettingsFileName)
            .ToArray();
    }
}
```

Using the Settings in the Main Page

The MainPage class can now load and save settings with the following steps:

1. On top of the MainPage class, create a LocalFileHelper as shown in Listing 17.33.

LISTING 17.33 Creating a LocalFileHelper in MainPage

```
private LocalFileHelper _helper = new LocalFileHelper();
```

2. In the MainPage constructor, add an event handler (shown in Listing 17.34) for the Application.Exit event. This is raised just before the application is ended, without a possibility to cancel the shutdown. This is the last moment we can choose to save the settings.

Listing 17.34 also shows a call to a new method named LoadInitialPage. This method (shown in Listing 17.35) will restore the last visited page when the application is started.

LISTING 17.34 Saving the Settings When the Application Exits

```
Application.Current.Exit += (s, e) =>
    _helper.SaveSettings(_isContentLocal, _lastAddress);
LoadInitialPage();
```

Finally, the LoadInitialPage method is shown in Listing 17.35. This method is called by the MainPage constructor. It loads the settings, checks whether the navigation was local or not, and attempts to restore the state that the application had when it was exited.

Note the LoadSettings method uses out parameters. The value of these parameters will be overwritten by the LoadFileHelper's LoadSettings method. Although out parameters are convenient in such a case, one should be careful when using them because it is not always quite clear what happens.

LISTING 17.35 Restoring the Initial Page

```
private void LoadInitialPage()
{
    _helper.LoadSettings(out _isContentLocal, out _lastAddress);

    if (!string.IsNullOrEmpty(_lastAddress))
    {
        LocationTextBox.Text = _lastAddress;

        if (_isContentLocal)
        {
            if (_helper.GetFileContent(_lastAddress))
            {
                MyWebBrowser.NavigateToString(_helper.FileContent);
            }
```

```
            }
            else
            {
                Navigate();
            }
        }
    }
```

To test this new functionality, run the application and navigate to a web page. Then, close the application and reopen it. The same page should be loaded again. Repeat the test with a local file.

(Not) Detecting Internal Navigation in the `WebBrowser`

The page saved by the application in the settings is in fact not the last page that the user navigated to (by clicking links in the displayed web page), but the last address that was loaded in the `WebBrowser` control's `Source` property. Because of limitations in the `WebBrowser` control, it is impossible to detect internal navigation: No event is raised when the user clicks a link, and even though the `LoadCompleted` event is raised, it is not possible to find out which URI the user navigated to. At the time of this writing, it is not clear whether this limitation will remain in future versions of the `WebBrowser` control.

Trusting the Isolated Storage or Not

The isolated storage is a secure storage location, in the sense that the Silverlight application does not know where the files are actually located. However, it is secure only in one direction. A user of the client computer can very easily find where the files are actually stored with the following steps:

1. Run the WebBrowserSample application and save a web page in the isolated storage. Write down the name that you used. (Make sure to use a name that is unique; for example, myownsavedwebpage.)
2. In Windows Explorer, search for the file name myownsavedwebpage in C:\.

The search result should display the text file as well as the _LocalSettings file, which can be opened in a text editor. Neither the name nor the content are encrypted! *Isolated storage is not a good place to store confidential information.* Instead, a user's personal information must be stored on the web server, where it can be hidden from prying eyes.

Painting with HTML

As you saw, the `WebBrowser` control has all the restrictions that classic GDI components have: It cannot be transformed, clipped, or made transparent. It always appears on top of all the other Silverlight elements. In some cases, this is not acceptable, (for example, when an animation must be played on the Silverlight page, or when something must be shown on top of the `WebBrowser`).

In this chapter, the `WebBrowser` control is simply collapsed when a `ChildWindow` must appear in front of it. This is a little confusing for the user, however, because the whole web page disappears from sight. It is easy to change this with the help of the `WebBrowserBrush` with the following steps:

1. Reopen the WebBrowserSample solution in Visual Studio.
2. In MainPage.xaml, add the markup shown in Listing 17.36. This `Rectangle` must appear *behind* the `WebBrowser` control. Notice that the `Fill` property of the `Rectangle` is set to a `WebBrowserBrush`, which will use HTML to paint it.

LISTING 17.36 Adding a `Rectangle` and a `WebBrowserBrush`

```
<Rectangle Margin="10,0,10,10"
           Grid.Row="1"
           Grid.ColumnSpan="2">
    <Rectangle.Fill>
        <WebBrowserBrush x:Name="MyWebBrowserBrush"
                         SourceName="MyWebBrowser" />
    </Rectangle.Fill>
</Rectangle>
```

3. In MainPage.xaml.cs, place the call shown in Listing 17.37 just before the `WebBrowser`'s `Visibility` is set to `Collapsed` in `SaveFileButtonClick` and in `LoadFileButtonClick`,.

LISTING 17.37 Redraw the `WebBrowserBrush`

```
MyWebBrowserBrush.Redraw();
```

4. Run the application, load a web page, and then click the Save button. Unlike before, the HTML page is still visible in the background. This is in fact the painted `Rectangle`.

The `WebBrowserBrush` does not allow any interaction with the HTML content. It requires a `WebBrowser` control to render the HTML markup. Note that the `WebBrowser` control should not be collapsed when the call to `Redraw` is made on the `WebBrowserBrush`, or else the whole `Rectangle` will be black. It is okay, however, if the `WebBrowser` control is placed outside of the visible screen.

Unlike any other `Brush`, `WebBrowserBrush` is the only one where the `Redraw` method must be called explicitly when something changes in the `WebBrowser` control.

Handling CompositeTarget.Rendering

The WebBrowserBrush is also useful in other situations; for example, when HTML content should be transformed (for instance to display a reflection effect below the WebBrowser control) or animated. A sample of a reflection effect and of an animation can be found at http://www.galasoft.ch/sl4-webbrowserbrush.

Note that in the case of the reflection effect, it is necessary to keep the brush and the WebBrowser control in sync at all times. To do this, the CompositionTarget.Rendering event can be handled as shown in Listing 17.38. This event is very convenient when fast- paced animations must be handled in code, or when something (like the call to Redraw) must happen very often. Note, however, that calling complex methods often can have an impact on performance.

LISTING 17.38 Handling the CompositionTarget.Rendering Eevent

```
public Reflection()
{
    InitializeComponent();

    CompositionTarget.Rendering += (s, e) =>
        MyWebBrowserBrush.Redraw();
}
```

Summary

In this chapter, we talked about topics added to Silverlight 4 such as the new PlaneProjection transform allowing moving elements in the 3D space, handling the right-click event to display a custom context menu or execute other functions, and how the WebBrowser control and the WebBrowserBrush can be used to display HTML content in an OOB application.

We also spent time examining exactly how the isolated storage works. Although this is not a new feature of Silverlight 4 (it was already found in Silverlight 2), understanding the isolated storage is crucial when developing Silverlight applications, especially OOB applications that can run offline.

In the next chapter, we continue exploring advanced techniques to enhance Silverlight applications.

CHAPTER 18

Drag and Drop, Full Screen, Clipboard, COM Interop, Duplex Polling, Notification Windows, and Splash Screens

IN THIS CHAPTER, WE WILL:

- Use drag and drop to improve the user experience when opening external files.
- Talk about the enhancements brought to the full screen mode.
- Copy and paste using the Windows Clipboard.
- Get notifications from a WCF service using duplex polling.
- Display notifications windows to inform the user even when the application is not active.
- Improve the splash screen that is shown when the application starts.

In Chapter 17, "Transforms, Right Click, HTML Browser, WebBrowserBrush, and Isolated Storage," we talked about a number of topics that help the Silverlight developers to create a smooth and rich experience. In this chapter, we continue the exploration.

Dragging and Dropping

In Chapter 9, "Connecting to the Web," we used the `OpenFileDialog` to select files on the local computer and load them into the Silverlight application for processing. This method is well known by the user, but it is not very friendly: It requires clicking a button, disrupting the workflow by presenting a dialog, navigating into the `OpenFileDialog`, selecting one or multiple files, and finally closing the dialog.

Dragging Files on the Silverlight Application

A more user-friendly experience is dragging files from the file explorer or from the desktop and dropping them onto the Silverlight application. This is a much more natural manner of selecting files and passing them to Silverlight with much less disruption. Dragging and dropping was introduced in Silverlight 4, and is very easy to add to an application, as we will show with the following steps. Note that even though this sample is an OOB application, drag and drop in Silverlight works without any special permission, in and out of the browser:

1. Reopen the WebBrowserSample application that was created in Chapter 17. If you don't have this application anymore, you can download it from http://www.galasoft.ch/sl4-dragdrop.

2. Open MainPage.xaml and modify the opening tag of the `LayoutRoot` `Grid` as shown in Listing 18.1. The `AllowDrop` attribute notifies Silverlight that the `Grid` is a valid drop target, and that it should raise the `Drop` event.

LISTING 18.1 Setting `AllowDrop` and the `Drop` Event Handler

```
<Grid x:Name="LayoutRoot"
        Background="White"
        AllowDrop="True"
        Drop="HandleDrop">
```

3. In MainPage.xaml.cs, add the `HandleDrop` event handler shown in Listing 18.2.

LISTING 18.2 Handling the `Drop` Event

```
 1  private void HandleDrop(object sender, DragEventArgs e)
 2  {
 3      var files = e.Data.GetData(DataFormats.FileDrop) as FileInfo[];
 4
 5      if (files == null || files.Length == 0)
 6      {
 7          return;
 8      }
 9
10      var isFirst = true;
11      foreach (var file in files)
12      {
13          using (var reader = file.OpenText())
14          {
15              _helper.FileContent = reader.ReadToEnd();
16              _helper.SaveFile(file.Name);
17
18              if (isFirst)
```

```
19                {
20                    MyWebBrowser.NavigateToString(_helper.FileContent);
21                    LocationTextBox.Text = file.Name;
22                    isFirst = false;
23                }
24            }
25        }
26        MessageBox.Show(string.Format(
27            "{0} files saved in storage", files.Length));
28    }
```

- Line 3 retrieves the Data property (of type IDataObject) that the object initiating the drag operation prepared. In our case, the IDataObject was created by the Silverlight framework in collaboration with the operating system. The GetData method returns an object that can be casted to FileInfo[], an array of FileInfo instances.
- On lines 11 to 25, we loop through all the files.
- On line 13, the current file is opened for text reading. The method OpenText returns a StreamReader, which can directly be used to read the document's content. Note that if the file is binary (such as a picture, and so on), the OpenText works fine, but the ReadToEnd method returns a long string of unreadable characters. For image files, you must use a BinaryReader.
- On line 15 and 16, the content of the text file is read and saved to isolated storage thanks to the LocalFileHelper. This class was implemented in Chapter 17, Listing 17.15.
- On lines 18 to 23, if the current file is the first of the list, it is displayed in the WebBrowser control, and its name is shown in the LocationTextBox.
- Finally, a message is shown to the user to confirm that the action ran correctly.

To test the application, run it and select a few files on your hard drive. Note that because the WebBrowser's NavigateToString method expects HTML content, simple text files will be shown without any formatting, which is not a very good experience. Test HTML files can be downloaded from http://www.gutenberg.org or from http://www.galasoft.ch/sl4-dragdrop.

Dropping the files on the WebBrowser control's surface doesn't work. The Drop event is intercepted by the WebBrowser's content, which does not belong to the Silverlight application. The files must be dropped on a Silverlight element so that the Drop event is bubbled up to the LayoutRoot Grid, which handles it.

Drag-and-Drop Restrictions

Unlike in Windows Presentation Foundation (WPF), it is not possible to initiate a drag-and-drop operations for other objects than for files out of the box (for example dragging and dropping items within the Silverlight application). However, the Silverlight Toolkit has a component that allows this operation. More details are found on Tim Heuer's blog at http://www.galasoft.ch/sl4-droptoolkit.

Supporting the Mac and Windowless

Maybe the most annoying limitation of drag and drop is that it does not work for windowless Silverlight applications. We talked about windowless in *Silverlight 2 Unleashed,* Chapter 7. This parameter is set in the HTML page hosting the Silverlight plug-in, and removes the white background that is shown when every element's `Background` of the Silverlight application is set to `Transparent`. Although it allows a nicer integration of the Silverlight application in the hosting web page, it increases the cost in terms of performance and prevents files to be dropped on the Silverlight surface.

Because Silverlight on the Mac always runs in windowless mode (whereas this is rather the exception on Windows), it is necessary to implement a workaround with the following steps if the Silverlight application is used on Mac as well as Windows (which is a common scenario).

1. Load the application at http://www.galasoft.ch/sl4-dropwindowless, unblock and extract it like we already did a few times in this book, and then open the Solution file.

2. Publish the web application on a web server that you have access to. *Silverlight 2 Unleashed,* Chapter 7 talks about getting web space and publishing Silverlight applications to it.

3. Run the application on a Mac computer. Try to drag and drop files on the red `Grid`. In Windows, this works (the number of files is shown in a `MessageBox`), but it fails on Mac.

4. In DragDropWindowlessTestPage.html, add the JavaScript code shown in Listing 18.3 below the `onSilverlightError` function.

LISTING 18.3 JavaScript Code to Enable Drag and Drop on a Mac

```
function handleDragEnter(oEvent)
{
    oEvent.preventDefault();
    var success = silverlightControl.dragEnter(oEvent);
    if (success)
        oEvent.stopPropagation();
}
function handleDragLeave(oEvent)
{
    oEvent.preventDefault();
    var success = silverlightControl.dragLeave(oEvent);
    if (success)
        oEvent.stopPropagation();
}
```

```
function handleDragOver(oEvent)
{
    oEvent.preventDefault();
    var success = silverlightControl.dragOver(oEvent);
    if (success)
        oEvent.stopPropagation();
}
function handleDropEvent(oEvent)
{
    oEvent.preventDefault();
    var success = silverlightControl.dragDrop(oEvent);
    if (success)
        oEvent.stopPropagation();
}
```

5. Run the application again and try dropping files. The `MessageBox` should be displayed by the Silverlight application.

Working in Full Screen

Setting a Silverlight application in full screen is very easy, as you will see in this section. This was already possible in Silverlight 2. There are, however, two improvements brought in Silverlight 4 to enhance the full-screen experience.

Getting Keyboard Support in Full-Screen Mode (Elevated Permissions)

Before Silverlight 4, keyboard support was disabled when the application was running in full-screen mode. This made creating kiosk-type applications difficult. The full-screen mode was interesting only for media applications controlled by the mouse.

> **TIP**
>
> **Using Keyboard in Full Screen Without Elevated Trust**
>
> The only keys that are enabled in full-screen mode with normal trust are: Up, Down, Left, and Right arrows; Space, Tab; Page up, Page down; Home, End, and Enter; and the function keys.
>
> Some web browsers support full-screen operations for any web page (for example, clicking Alt-Enter in Internet Explorer sets the page in full-screen). However, the web browser chrome is still visible in this mode, so it is not a true "kiosk" application.

In Silverlight 4, if the application runs OOB with elevated permissions, keyboard support is enabled, as shown with the following steps:

1. Create a new Silverlight application and name it FullScreen.

2. In MainPage.xaml, add a `TextBox` and a `Button`.
3. Set the `Content` of the `Button` to `"Enter Full Screen"` and create an event handler for the `Click` event, named **FullScreenButtonClick**.
4. In MainPage.xaml.cs, implement the `FullScreenButtonClick` event handler as shown in Listing 18.4.

LISTING 18.4 Setting the Application in Full Screen

```
private void FullScreenButtonClick(object sender, RoutedEventArgs e)
{
    if (App.Current.Host.Content.IsFullScreen)
    {
        (sender as Button).Content = "Enter full screen";
        App.Current.Host.Content.IsFullScreen = false;
    }
    else
    {
        (sender as Button).Content = "Exit full screen";
        App.Current.Host.Content.IsFullScreen = true;
    }
}
```

5. Test the application by running it and clicking the button. The application is now shown in full-screen mode, and a message is shown mentioning that pressing Esc will exit full screen (as shown in Figure 18.1).

Press ESC to exit full-screen mode.
http://localhost

FIGURE 18.1 Press Esc to exit full-screen mode.

6. Try to enter text in the `TextBox`. This is not possible.
7. Press Esc to exit full-screen mode, and change the Silverlight project properties to enable running out of the browser.
8. Run the application again. Right-click and install it.
9. In the OOB application, click the full-screen button. The behavior is the same as before: The message is shown, and it is not possible to type in the `TextBox`. Right click to uninstall the OOB application.
10. In the Silverlight project properties, click the Out-of-Browser Settings button and request elevated trust for the application.
11. Run the application and install it again. Then, in the OOB application, click the full-screen button.

With elevated permissions, the message is not displayed anymore. In fact, pressing the Escape key does not end the full-screen mode anymore. The only way to end full-screen mode is now to click the full-screen button. This can be convenient for kiosk applications. In this kind of applications, the user should not be allowed to exit the full-screen mode by pressing the Escape key. Instead, only a user initiated action (for example a menu protected by a password) should be allowed to reset the application in the normal mode.

WARNING

User Initiated

Even with elevated permissions, setting the Silverlight application in full-screen mode must be initiated by the user (for example, by clicking a button). The application cannot spontaneously set itself in full-screen mode.

Using Full Screen on a Monitor While Working on Another

Nowadays, more and more users have multiple monitors connected to their computer. For these users, being able to run a Silverlight application in full screen on the second monitor while working on the primary one is very attractive. Until now, however, the full-screen mode would toggle back to normal as soon as the mouse was clicked out of the Silverlight surface. When an application with elevated permissions is set in full-screen mode (like the application created in the previous section), it remains in full mode even if the mouse is clicked on the first monitor. This is easy to test if you have two monitors connected to your computer.

When the application runs with normal permissions, however, it can request permission to stay in full screen on one monitor, with the following steps:

1. Uninstall the FullScreen OOB application.
2. Reopen the FullScreen Solution in Visual Studio.
3. In the Silverlight project properties, disable the elevated permissions for out of browser.
4. In MainPage.xaml.cs, in the `MainPage` constructor, enter the code shown in Listing 18.5. This modifies the `FullScreenOptions` for the plug-in.

LISTING 18.5 Setting the `FullScreenOptions`

```
App.Current.Host.Content.FullScreenOptions
    = FullScreenOptions.StaysFullScreenWhenUnfocused;
```

5. Run the application in the browser and click the full-screen button. A permission dialog is displayed, shown in Figure 18.2. The permission requested here (which does only appear in non-elevated mode) is for the application to stay in full-screen mode. Click yes.

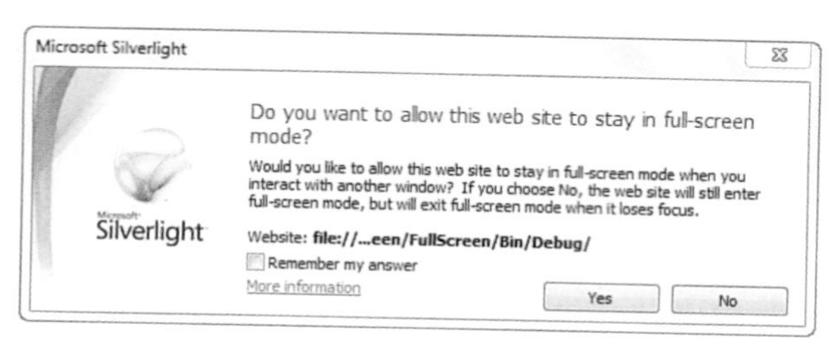

FIGURE 18.2 Permission dialog.

Try to type text in the `TextBox`: Text input is still disabled (because the application does not have elevated permissions anymore). Also, pressing Esc will exit full screen. The only thing that changed toward the normal application without any permission is that the application will stay in full screen on one monitor while you can use the mouse and keyboard in another monitor.

If the user chose to remember his answer in the permission dialog, he can revoke it in the Silverlight configuration dialog, just like he can manage webcam and microphone support.

Copying to and from the Clipboard

In Silverlight 3, Clipboard support was possible only by selecting text in a `TextBox` control, and using the keyboard shortcuts (Ctrl+C, Ctrl+X, Ctrl+V). This is still possible in Silverlight 4, of course.

What changed in Silverlight 4 is the possibility to access text operations on the Clipboard programmatically. We saw in Chapter 14, "Enhancing Line-of-Business Applications and Running Out of the Browser," how data rows can be copied from a `DataGrid` to a text file, for example, and how the Clipboard access can be revoked using the Silverlight configuration dialog. This is because the `DataGrid` control uses the Clipboard programmatically. With the following steps, it is easy to add Clipboard support to any Silverlight application:

1. Create a new Silverlight application and name it **ClipboardSample**.
2. Add two `TextBox` elements in MainPage.xaml. Name the first `TextBox` `FirstTextBox`, and the second `SecondTextBox`.
3. Run the application and type text in one `TextBox`.
4. Select the text with the mouse or the keyboard, then press Ctrl+C.
5. Place the cursor in the second `TextBox` and press Ctrl+V. The copied text is pasted. This is the support for the Clipboard that was already available in Silverlight 3. End the application.
6. In MainPage.xaml, add a `StackPanel` to the bottom of the page. Set its `Orientation` to `Horizontal` and add three `Button` controls to it. Set the first `Button`'s `Content` property to `"Copy"`, the second's to `"Cut"`, and the third's to `"Paste"`.

7. Add an event handler for the first Button's Click event and name it CopyButtonClick. Do the same for the second and third Button with respectively CutButtonClick and PasteButtonClick.

8. In MainPage.xaml.cs, implement the event handlers as shown in Listing 18.6.

LISTING 18.6 Copying, Cutting, and Pasting

```
private void CopyButtonClick(
    object sender, RoutedEventArgs e)
{
    Clipboard.SetText(
        "The first textbox says: " + FirstTextBox.Text);
}

private void CutButtonClick(
    object sender, RoutedEventArgs e)
{
    Clipboard.SetText(
        "The first textbox said: " + FirstTextBox.Text);
    FirstTextBox.Text = string.Empty;
}

private void PasteButtonClick(
    object sender, RoutedEventArgs e)
{
    if (Clipboard.ContainsText())
    {
        SecondTextBox.Text = Clipboard.GetText();
    }
}
```

9. Run the application and enter text in the first TextBox. Then click the Copy or Cut buttons and paste the text in the second TextBox.

Note that programmatic Clipboard operations are available only for text content. Like before, the permission dialog is shown the first time that the application tries to access the Clipboard. If the user chooses to remember the decision, he can manage the permission using the Silverlight Configuration dialog like for the webcam, microphone, and full-screen permissions. Also, if the application runs with elevated permissions, the user does not need to give his consent.

Working with COM (Elevated Permissions)

For data applications like we implemented in Chapters 13 and 14, creating reports is a very important feature. In general, this task is delegated to the web server on which the data is located. It is interesting, however, to offer a possibility to create reports locally, to speed things up. This way, the client/server interaction is reduced to nothing (except, of course, the initial task of loading data).

Silverlight 4 with elevated permissions offer an interesting possibility to interact with installed applications through the legacy COM interface. COM was a very widely used programming platform on Windows computers. Because it is an unmanaged programming environment, writing COM-enabled applications is not very easy. This is a low-level environment, where it is quite easy to create memory leaks or to crash the application. For this reason, COM is less actively developed nowadays than it used to be, but many Windows applications (including the Windows operating system itself) still offer COM interfaces to consume their services.

Understanding the Restrictions

Because COM is not available on Mac or Linux operating systems, only Silverlight on Windows can benefit from COM interaction. Because of this, COM interaction should be limited to environments where the client computers are well known (such as an intranet), or for functionalities that are not mission critical, but are enhancements to the Silverlight application.

Another important restriction is that COM interaction is available only to OOB applications running with elevated trust. Using COM, it is possible to access functionalities that a normal Silverlight application cannot perform. This is probably the feature of Silverlight that has the highest power, and therefore presents the highest risk. Because of this, it cannot be made available to applications running without elevated permissions.

Communicating with Microsoft Office

In this section, the WCF RIA Services application developed in Chapters 13 and 14 will be extended to communicate with Microsoft Office (if available) and create a new Excel file. Then, the user will be asked whether he wants to send the file as an attachment to a mail message in Microsoft Outlook.

The start point for this sample is the MyNorthwind.Web application as it was left after Chapter 14. If you didn't save this application back then, it can be downloaded from http://www.galasoft.ch/sl4-com. As usual, save the zip file on your hard drive, unblock the zip file using the File Properties dialog (if needed), extract the content, and open the MyNorthwind.Web.sln solution in Visual Studio.

This section assumes that Microsoft Excel and Microsoft Outlook are available on the client computer.

Creating and Filling an Excel Workbook

The first step is to create an Excel workbook and to fill it with values from the Order list with the following steps:

1. With the Northwind.Web solution open in Visual Studio, open MainPage.xaml.
2. In the `StackPanel` with all the `Button` controls on the right of the page, add a new `Button` with the same size and margins. Set its `Content` property to `"Email Excel Report"`, its `x:Name` to `EmailButton`, and its `Click` event to `EmailButtonClick`. This `Button` should not have a `Command` property.
3. In MainPage.xaml.cs, implement the `EmailButtonClick` event handler as shown in Listing 18.7. The `ReportingWindow` is a `ChildWindow` that will be implemented in the next steps.

LISTING 18.7 `EmailButtonClick` Event Handler

```
private void EmailButtonClick(object sender, RoutedEventArgs e)
{
    if (!App.Current.HasElevatedPermissions)
    {
        return;
    }

    var window = new ReportingWindow(
        orderDataGrid.ItemsSource as IEnumerable<Order>);
    window.Show();
}
```

4. Add a new `ChildWindow` to the Silverlight project and name it **ReportingWindow.xaml**.
5. Open ReportingWindow.xaml and add the markup in Listing 18.8 to the `LayoutRoot` `Grid`.

LISTING 18.8 Adding Input Elements

```
<StackPanel>
    <TextBlock Text="Name for Excel attachment (without extension)"
               Margin="0,10,0,0" />
    <TextBox x:Name="AttachmentNameTextBox" />
    <TextBlock Text="Recipient's email"
               Margin="0,10,0,0" />
    <TextBox x:Name="EmailTextBox" />
    <TextBlock Text="Email subject"
               Margin="0,10,0,0" />
    <TextBox x:Name="SubjectTextBox" />
</StackPanel>
```

6. Open ReportingWindow.xaml.cs and declare two constants, an attribute, and modify the constructor as shown in Listing 18.9. The two constants will be used later. The `_orders` attribute stores the list of `Order` instances that are passed to the `ChildWindow` when it is created. These are the orders that will be displayed in the Excel file.

LISTING 18.9 Initializing the Window

```
private const int MailItemTypeByValue = 1; // olByValue
private const int CreateItemTypeEmail = 0; // olMailItem
private IEnumerable<Order> _orders;

public ReportingWindow(IEnumerable<Order> orders)
{
    _orders = orders;
    InitializeComponent();
}
```

7. Modify the `OKButton_Click` event handler as shown in Listing 18.10.

LISTING 18.10 `OKButton_Click` Event Handler

```
 1 private void OKButton_Click(object sender, RoutedEventArgs e)
 2 {
 3     dynamic excelApplication =
 4         AutomationFactory.CreateObject("Excel.Application");
 5         excelApplication.Visible = true;
 6
 7     dynamic excelWorkbook = excelApplication.Workbooks.Add();
 8     dynamic excelSheet = excelApplication.ActiveSheet;
 9     dynamic excelCell;
10
11     excelCell = excelSheet.Cells[1, 1];
12     excelCell.Value = "Date";
13     excelCell.ColumnWidth = 25;
14     excelCell = excelSheet.Cells[1, 2];
15     excelCell.Value = "ID";
16     excelCell.ColumnWidth = 15;
17     excelCell = excelSheet.Cells[1, 3];
18     excelCell.Value = "Ship";
19     excelCell.ColumnWidth = 25;
20     excelCell = excelSheet.Cells[1, 4];
21     excelCell.Value = "To";
22     excelCell.ColumnWidth = 40;
23     excelCell = excelSheet.Cells[1, 5];
```

```
24      excelCell.Value = "Value";
25      excelCell.ColumnWidth = 25;
26      DialogResult = true;
27  }
```

- Lines 3 and 4 create an instance of Excel. The `AutomationFactory` class is the key to COM interaction. The parameter for the `CreateObject` method is the COM name (as a string) of Microsoft Excel. To find which name must be used, check the Microsoft Office documentation and look for COM automation.
- Notice the usage of the `dynamic` keyword on line 3. This is a new keyword in C# 4 that allows creating objects at runtime, the type of which is not known yet. Of course, IntelliSense does not work with `dynamic` objects because Visual Studio has no way to know what the actual type will be and what properties and methods will be available. This complicates the development.
- Line 5 notifies Excel that the workbook should be visible during processing. We will change this value later.
- Lines 7 and 8 create a new Excel workbook and a new worksheet.
- Then, on lines 11 to 26, the first row of the worksheet is prepared. Using the COM automation, it is possible to get a cell, set its size and its value, and many other attributes. For more information about Excel automation, check the Office documentation.

8. The `dynamic` keyword requires a DLL to be added to the Silverlight project references. Use the Add Reference context menu and from the .NET tab, add the Microsoft.CSharp assembly to the project.
9. Run the application and install it out of the browser. Click the Email Excel Report button after the first page is loaded, and then press OK in the `ChildWindow`. A new Excel document appears and the first row is filled.

> **WARNING**
>
> **Starting with 1**
>
> In the word of Office automation, just like in Visual Basic, the first index of the list is 1 and not 0 like in C#. Do not get confused!

Processing the Data

Adding data from the application to the Excel sheet is very simple, as shown in Listing 18.11, to be added between lines 25 and 26 of Listing 18.10. Of course, any additional calculation is possible. In Listing 18.11, some properties of each order are saved to the Excel file.

LISTING 18.11 Adding Data to the Excel Sheet

```
int index = 2;
foreach (Order o in _orders)
{
    excelCell = excelSheet.Cells[index, 1];
    excelCell.Value = o.OrderDate;
    excelCell = excelSheet.Cells[index, 2];
    excelCell.Value = o.OrderID;
    excelCell = excelSheet.Cells[index, 3];
    excelCell.Value = o.ShipName;
    excelCell = excelSheet.Cells[index, 4];
    excelCell.Value = o.ShipCity;
    excelCell = excelSheet.Cells[index, 5];
    excelCell.Value = o.Freight;
    index++;
}
```

Close the previous Excel file. Then, open the Silverlight project properties and in the Debug tab, set the Start Action radio button to Out-of-browser application. Set the Silverlight project as Startup project in the Solution Explorer, then run the application with Ctrl-F5. Click Email Excel Report again, press OK in the `ChildWindow` and witness how the values are added to the Excel worksheet.

Saving the Excel File

Now that the file is created, it needs to be saved. Also, it is not necessary to show this file to the user. Instead, the processing should take place in the background to avoid confusing the user. Follow these steps:

1. In MainPage.xaml.cs, change the line 5 of Listing 18.10 from `excelApplication.Visible = true;` to `excelApplication.Visible = false;` this will keep the workbook in the background, hidden from the user during processing.
2. Add the content of Listing 18.12 to the `OKButton_Click` event handler. This code must appear *before* the `DialogResult` property is set to `true`.

LISTING 18.12 Saving the File

```
1  var directoryPath = System.IO.Path.Combine(
2      Environment.GetFolderPath(Environment.SpecialFolder.MyDocuments),
3      "Northwind.Web.Temp");
4
5  if (Directory.Exists(directoryPath))
6  {
7      Directory.Delete(directoryPath, true);
8  }
9
```

```
10  Directory.CreateDirectory(directoryPath);
11
12  var fileName = System.IO.Path.Combine(
13      directoryPath,
14      AttachmentNameTextBox.Text + ".xlsx");
15
16  excelWorkbook.SaveAs(fileName);
17  excelApplication.Quit();
```

- Lines 1 to 3 get the path of the My Documents folder and append the name of a new directory that we will use as a temporary folder. This is possible because the application is running with elevated permissions.
- Lines 5 to 8 make sure that an old version of the temp folder is not left over. Note that this can be an issue if multiple versions of the same application run at the same time on the same computer. In this simple sample, it is assumed that it is not the case.
- Line 10 creates the temp folder in which the file will be saved.
- Lines 12 to 14 create the Excel file name depending on the user's input.
- Finally, lines 16 and 17 save the Excel file to the new location, and then quit the Excel application.

TIP

Using COM to Access the File System

Using COM automation, it is also possible to use the `Scripting.FileSystemObject` object that the `AutomationFactory` can create. This provides unlimited access to the whole file system. However, the syntax (with the `dynamic` keyword) is less comfortable to implement than using the proper file access provided in elevated trust by Silverlight.

3. Run the application and test the functionality. This time, you must enter a name for the Excel file! After it is completed, check that the file has been saved in My Documents\Northwind.Web.Temp\. This is a perfectly normal Excel file that can be opened and modified.

Emailing with Outlook

Microsoft Outlook also provides COM automation. We will use this to create a new email message, attach the Excel document, and show the message to the user so that he can send it. Note that even sending the message can be done automatically; however, it is relatively difficult to do so without any user interaction (such as selecting a folder in which the outgoing email message should be saved).

Sending an email with Outlook is probably not the most reliable solution. If a server-based alternative is available, it is probably better to use it for email. However, preparing the email message can be done with the following steps:

1. In MainPage.xaml.cs, in `OKButton_Click`, before `DialogResult` is set to `true`, add the code shown in Listing 18.13.

LISTING 18.13 Creating an Outlook Message

```
1  dynamic outlook = AutomationFactory.CreateObject("Outlook.Application");
2  dynamic mail = outlook.CreateItem(CreateItemTypeEmail);
3  mail.Recipients.Add(EmailTextBox.Text);
4  mail.Subject = SubjectTextBox.Text;
5  var now = DateTime.Now;
6  mail.Body = "Report generated on " + now.ToLongDateString()
7      + ", " + now.ToShortTimeString();
8  mail.Attachments.Add(fileName, MailItemTypeByValue);
9  mail.Save();
10 mail.Display(false);
11 Directory.Delete(directoryPath, true);
```

- Line 1 creates an instance of Outlook using the `AutomationFactory`.
- Line 2 creates a new mail message. The value of the `CreateItemTypeEmail` constant is found in the Outlook automation documentation at http://www.galasoft.ch/sl4-outlookdoc.
- Line 3 and 4 uses the input from the `ReportingWindow` to add a recipient and a topic.
- Lines 5 to 7 create a body mentioning when the report was created.
- Lines 6 to 8 add the Excel file as attachment. The value of the constant `MailItemTypeByValue` was found in the documentation at http://www.galasoft.ch/sl4-emaildoc.
- Lines 9 and 10 save the message and display it to the user. He is free now to review it before sending.
- Finally line 11 deletes the temp directory. Because the Excel file was added by value to the email message, we do not need to local copy anymore.

2. Test the application to make sure that everything works as expected. Note that communicating with the Office applications can take some time, especially if they were not running already.

Although COM automation opens the door to very powerful functionality, it is also more difficult to program than standard Silverlight code because the `dynamic` keyword does not provide any IntelliSense. Also, when a functionality does not work properly, the error messages are very cryptic and difficult to debug. Finally, the fact that this feature is available only on Windows computers makes it necessary to provide alternative means for the users that cannot use this feature. This makes COM automation a controversial feature and one that should be used with care. Used properly, however, it can make wonders to integrate your Silverlight OOB code with existing legacy applications and drivers.

Communicating over Duplex Polling

Client/server communication in the web world is most often done with a request/response mechanism where the request is initiated by the client. This can cause issues if the clients must be notified as fast as possible when something happens on the server: Because the request is initiated by the client, the only way to keep track of changes on the server is to poll the service repeatedly. However, polling can only be done every so often. To avoid running out of bandwidth, a client cannot reasonably send a request more than every few seconds at the very least.

In Silverlight 2, a perfect way to overcome this limitation was introduced: duplex polling. In this scenario, the client initiates a callback channel that the server can use to "push" information to the client. This avoids constant polling from the client and provides a way to notify clients immediately when something occurs on the server. In this section, we build a sample application that watches a folder on the server and notifies clients as soon as files are added or deleted from the server-side folder.

Implementing the Server-Side Service

The server-side application requires some manual configuration to enable duplex polling, as you will see with the following steps. Note that the code running in the web application, on the server, is implemented in the full version of .NET 4 and not in Silverlight.

1. Create a new Silverlight application in Visual Studio and name it **DuplexPollingSample**. Make sure to create the web application, too.
2. Right-click the Web project in the Solution Explorer and select Add Reference from the context menu.
3. Click the Browse tab and find the folder C:\Program Files\Microsoft SDKs\Silverlight\v4.0\Libraries. On Windows 64 bits, this folder is into Program Files (x86).
4. In the Server folder, select the System.ServiceModel.PollingDuplex.dll and click OK to add the reference to the Web application.
5. Right-click the References folder in the Silverlight application now, and select Add Reference from the context menu.
6. In the same folder as before, open the Client folder and add the System.ServiceModel.PollingDuplex.dll to the Silverlight application.

7. Right-click the Web application in the Solution Explorer and select Add, New Item from the context menu.

8. In the Web category of the Add New Item dialog, select a WCF Service and name it **FilesChangedService.svc**. This creates the SVC file, an attached code behind as well as an interface file named **IFileChangedService.cs**.

9. Modify the `IFileChangedService` interface as shown in Listing 18.14.

LISTING 18.14 `IFileChangedService` Interface

```
 1  [ServiceContract(
 2      Namespace = "http://www.mydomain.com",
 3      CallbackContract = typeof(IFilesChangedClient))]
 4  public interface IFilesChangedService
 5  {
 6      [OperationContract]
 7      void StartObservingFiles();
 8      [OperationContract]
 9      void StopObservingFiles();
10  }
```

- Lines 1 to 3 decorate the interface with the `ServiceContract` attribute. This tells the WCF infrastructure that the class implementing this interface should be exposed as a service. Because it is intended to support duplex communication, the `CallbackContract` parameter must be set. We will create the `IFilesChangedClient` interface a little later. Note that the `Namespace` parameter should be unique, but it does not have to be a valid URL of a website. This is just a unique name for the communication.

- Lines 6 and 7 declare the `StartObservingFile` method, decorated with the `OperationContract` attribute. The method will be exposed as a service method for remote clients.

- Lines 8 and 9 declare another service method, used to unregister a client from the notifications.

10. Add a new interface file to the Web application and name it **IFilesChangedClient.cs**. The code for this interface is shown in Listing 18.15. This is also a `ServiceContract`; however, the difference is that the method is declared with `IsOneWay=true`. This means that the communication is intended from the server to the client only.

LISTING 18.15 IFilesChangedClient Interface

```
[ServiceContract]
public interface IFilesChangedClient
{
    [OperationContract(IsOneWay=true)]
    void FileAdded(string fileName);
}
```

11. Open FilesChangedService.svc.cs. This is the actual implementation of the `IFilesChangedService` interface that is marked as `ServiceContract`. This class will be used to communicate with the Silverlight clients.

12. Implement the `FileChangedService` class as shown in Listing 18.16.

LISTING 18.16 Skeleton of the FilesChangedService Class

```
 1  [ServiceBehavior(
 2      InstanceContextMode = InstanceContextMode.PerCall)]
 3  public class FilesChangedService : IFilesChangedService
 4  {
 5      private static FileSystemWatcher _watcher;
 6      private static List<IFilesChangedClient> _clients;
 7
 8      private const string WatchedDirectory
 9          = "c:\\temp\\DuplexPollingSampleFiles";
10
11      public void StartObservingFiles()
12      {
13      }
14  }
```

- Line 5 declares an attribute of type `FileSystemWatcher`. This class will be used to observe the content of the watched folder and notify the service when something changes.
- Line 6 declares a list of all the clients that are interested to get notifications when the watched folder's content changes.
- Lines 8 and 9 declare the path of the watched folder. Change this value to match the folder that your Silverlight application should watch. Hard coding this path in the application is not ideal. Instead, it should be a setting in the Web.config file, but for this small sample it is okay.
- Lines 11 to 13 declare the `StartObservingFiles` method that is required by the `IFilesChangeService` interface.

13. Add the code from Listing 18.17 in the `StartObservingFiles` method.

LISTING 18.17 Getting a Request

```
1  if (_clients == null)
2  {
3      _clients = new List<IFilesChangedClient>();
4  }
5
6  var client = OperationContext.Current
7      .GetCallbackChannel<IFilesChangedClient>();
8
9  // Initial call
10 var dir = new DirectoryInfo(WatchedDirectory);
11 var files = dir.GetFiles();
12
13 foreach (var file in files)
14 {
15     client.FileAdded(file.Name.ToLower());
16 }
17
18 if (!_clients.Contains(client))
19 {
20     _clients.Add(client);
21 }
```

- Lines 6 and 7 get the calling client from the `OperationContext` class. The type for this instance is `IFilesChangedClient` according to what was declared before.
- Because the client should be notified of the initial state of the folder, lines 10 to 16 retrieve the current list of files in this folder, and call the `FileAdded` method on the client. This sends a series of notifications to the client, one for each file in the folder. We will see later how the client can react to the notifications.
- Lines 18 to 21 save the instance of the client in the list.

14. Below the code added in Listing 18.17 in the `StartObservingFiles` method, add the code from Listing 18.18. This creates a new `FileSystemWatcher` and registers for its `Created` event. Note that the watcher can also raise events when a file is deleted or renamed, or when a file's content changes. In this sample, we only handle files that are added. Later, you can extend the application to handle deleted and renamed files.

LISTING 18.18 Creating the `FileSystemWatcher`

```
if (_watcher == null)
{
    _watcher = new FileSystemWatcher(WatchedDirectory);
    _watcher.Created += OnWatcherCreated;
    _watcher.EnableRaisingEvents = true;
}
```

15. Implement the `OnWatcherCreated` event handler as shown in Listing 18.19.

LISTING 18.19 Notifying the Clients When a File Is Added

```
1  private void OnWatcherCreated(object sender, FileSystemEventArgs e)
2  {
3      var toRemove = new List<IFilesChangedClient>();
4
5      foreach (var client in _clients)
6      {
7          try
8          {
9              client.FileAdded(e.Name.ToLower());
10         }
11         catch (TimeoutException)
12         {
13             toRemove.Add(client);
14         }
15     }
16
17     foreach (var client in toRemove)
18     {
19         _clients.Remove(client);
20     }
21 }
```

- Line 3 creates a list. We will use this list to store clients that cannot be reached by the call (if any). This means that the corresponding clients are "dead," probably because the client application has been closed.
- On lines 5 to 15, we loop through every client that registered.
- Line 9 attempts to call the `FileAdded` method on the client and pass it the name of the file that has been added. If the client has been closed without notification, this will fail with a `TimeoutException` after one minute. This exception is caught on line 11. In this case, the faulty client is added to the list of clients to remove.
- Finally, on lines 17 to 20, the faulty clients are removed from the main collection.

Unregistering a Client

A client should be able to unregister itself from notifications. To do this, add the method shown in Listing 18.20 to the `FilesChangedService` class.

LISTING 18.20 Unregistering a Client

```
public void StopObservingFiles()
{
    var client = OperationContext.Current
        .GetCallbackChannel<IFilesChangedClient>();

    if (_clients != null
        && _clients.Contains(client))
    {
        _clients.Remove(client);
    }
}
```

Configuring the Service

A large part of the complexity of Windows Communication Foundation is configuration. Now that the service is ready, the Web.config file needs to be modified to expose the service with the correct configuration, with the following steps:

1. In the Web application, open the Web.config file.
2. Within the `system.serviceModel` section, before the `behaviors` are declared, add the markup in Listing 18.21. This registers the polling duplex infrastructure that we added earlier.

LISTING 18.21 Registering Extensions

```
<extensions>
    <bindingExtensions>
        <add name="pollingDuplexHttpBinding"
type="System.ServiceModel.Configuration.PollingDuplexHttpBindingCollectionElement,
      System.ServiceModel.PollingDuplex,
      Version=4.0.0.0,
      Culture=neutral,
      PublicKeyToken=31bf3856ad364e35" />
    </bindingExtensions>
</extensions>
```

3. Still in the same section and before the `behaviors`, add the markup in Listing 18.22. This defines the `pollingDuplexHttpBinding` that will be used by the service, and creates an `endpoint`, a point of entry for the service calls.

LISTING 18.22 Binding and Service

```
<bindings>
    <pollingDuplexHttpBinding />
</bindings>
<services>
    <service name="DuplexPollingSample.Web.FilesChangedService"
     behaviorConfiguration="DuplexPollingSample.Web.FilesChangedServiceBehavior">
        <endpoint
            address=""
            binding="pollingDuplexHttpBinding"
            contract="DuplexPollingSample.Web.IFilesChangedService">
        </endpoint>
    </service>
</services>
```

4. Then, modify the `behaviors` section as shown in Listing 18.23.

LISTING 18.23 Setting the Behaviors

```
<behaviors>
    <serviceBehaviors>
        <behavior name="">
            <serviceMetadata httpGetEnabled="true" />
            <serviceDebug includeExceptionDetailInFaults="false" />
        </behavior>
        <behavior name="DuplexPollingSample.Web.FilesChangedServiceBehavior">
            <serviceMetadata httpGetEnabled="true"/>
            <serviceDebug includeExceptionDetailInFaults="false"/>
        </behavior>
    </serviceBehaviors>
</behaviors>
```


To test whether everything is ready, right-click the FilesChangedService.svc file in Visual Studio's Solution Explorer, and select View in Browser from the context menu. A test page without errors should be shown in the web browser. If that is the case, the server is now ready, and the client can be implemented.

Implementing the Client

The Silverlight client must get a reference to the WCF service, and register for the notifications with the following steps:

1. Right-click the References folder in the Silverlight project in the Solution Explorer, and select Add Service Reference from the context menu.
2. In the Add Service Reference dialog shown in Figure 18.3, click the Discover button. The FileChangedService.svc should be shown.

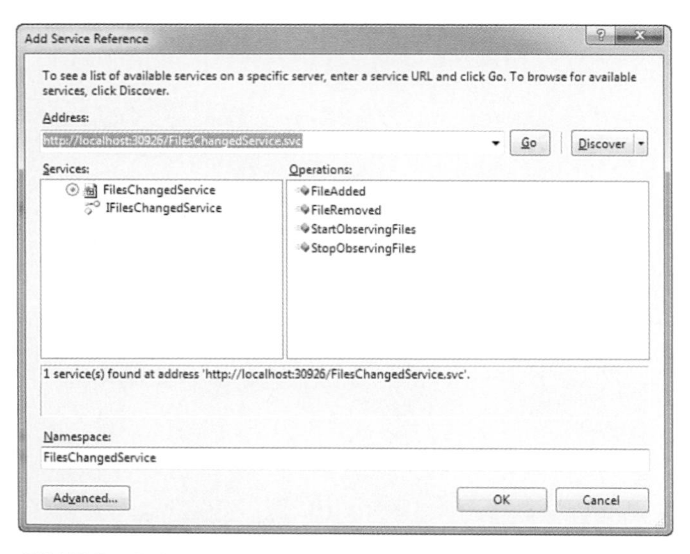

FIGURE 18.3 Add Service Reference dialog.

3. Click the Go button. The description of the service is downloaded and the service can be extended in the Services tree.

4. Enter the name **FileChangedService** in the Namespace text box and then click OK. Visual Studio creates all the objects needed for communication with the WCF service.

> **TIP**
>
> **Adding a Reference to an External Service**
>
> If the service is not in the same solution as the client, the Discover button does not work. In this case, copy the URL of the SVC file (for example, http://www.mydomain.com/FilesChangedService.svc) and paste it in the Add Service Reference dialog, and then click Go.

5. Open MainPage.xaml and set the `x:Name` of the main `UserControl` to `MyPage`.

6. Modify the `LayoutRoot Grid` with the markup shown in Listing 18.24.

LISTING 18.24 Setting the XAML

```
<Grid x:Name="LayoutRoot" Background="White">
    <Grid.RowDefinitions>
        <RowDefinition Height="*" />
        <RowDefinition Height="50" />
    </Grid.RowDefinitions>

    <ListBox ItemsSource="{Binding ElementName=MyPage, Path=Files}"
             Margin="10" />
```

```
    <StackPanel Orientation="Horizontal"
                Grid.Row="1">
        <Button Margin="10"
                x:Name="UnsubscribeButton"
                Content="Unsubscribe"
                Click="UnsubscribeButtonClick"/>
        <Button Margin="10"
                x:Name="ResubscribeButton"
                Content="Re-subscribe"
                IsEnabled="False"
                Click="ResubscribeButtonClick" />
    </StackPanel>
</Grid>
```

7. Open MainPage.xaml.cs. On top of the `MainPage` class, enter the attribute and the property shown in Listing 18.25. Note that the `FilesChangedServiceClient` is located in the namespace `DuplexPollingSample.FilesChangedService` that has been generated by Visual Studio, and that must be added to the list of `using` directives on top of the page.

LISTING 18.25 Declaring the Client and the List of Files

```
private FilesChangedServiceClient _client;
public ObservableCollection<string> Files
{
    get;
    private set;
}
```

8. Modify the `MainPage` constructor as shown in Listing 18.26.

LISTING 18.26 `MainPage` Constructor

```
 1 public MainPage()
 2 {
 3     Files = new ObservableCollection<string>();
 4     InitializeComponent();
 5
 6     var source = App.Current.Host.Source;
 7     var baseAddress = source.AbsoluteUri.Substring(
 8         0,
 9         source.AbsoluteUri.Length - source.AbsolutePath.Length);
10     var servicePath = baseAddress + "/FilesChangedService.svc";
11     var serviceAddress = new EndpointAddress(servicePath);
12     var binding = new PollingDuplexHttpBinding();
13
```

```
14      _client = new FilesChangedServiceClient(binding, serviceAddress);
15      _client.FileAddedReceived += FileAdded;
17      _client.StartObservingFilesAsync();
18  }
```

- Lines 6 to 10 get the absolute path of the service on the web server.
- Lines 11 and 12 declare an `EndPointAddress` and a `PollingDuplexHttpBinding` corresponding to the service we need to call.
- Lines 14 to 16 create the client and then subscribe to the `FileAddedReceived` event that is automatically created by Visual Studio when the reference to the service is configured. This event will be raised when the server sends a message to the client. Note that you can extend this with a method for when files are deleted, renamed, and so forth.
- Finally, line 17 starts the subscription by calling the `StartObservingFiles` method on the server. The call is asynchronous (like every web calls in Silverlight) and a corresponding `Completed` event exists in case the application is interested to the server's response. In this sample, the response is ignored.

> **WARNING**
>
> **Changing the Server, Refreshing the Client**
>
> Any change on the server-side service must be refreshed on the client by right-clicking the FileChangedService reference in the Service References folder in the Silverlight project and then selecting Update Service Reference from the context menu.

9. Implement the `FileAdded` event handler as shown in Listing 18.27. The name of the added file can be retrieved from the `FileAddedReceivedEventArgs` parameter.

LISTING 18.27 Receiving a New File

```
private void FileAdded(
    object sender,
    FileAddedReceivedEventArgs e)
{
    if (!Files.Contains(e.fileName))
    {
        Files.Add(e.fileName);
    }
}
```

Unsubscribing and Resubscribing

It is good practice to unsubscribe from the service when it is not needed anymore. The service offers the `StopObservingFiles` method to cleanly remove the corresponding client from the list. Note, however, that there is no guarantee that a client will unsubscribe cleanly, which is why the `TimeoutException` is caught in Listing 18.19.

> **WARNING**
>
> **Unsubscribing on Exit**
>
> Ideally, the Silverlight application should unsubscribe from the service before it is ended. However, there is no reliable way to send a message to a service when the application shuts down. For instance, if the message is sent from the `Application_Exit` event handler (in App.xaml.cs), the message is never sent because it is already too late in the application's lifetime.
>
> To implement a clean shutdown sequence, check the article at http://www.galasoft.ch/sl4-shutdown. However, this does not work when the user navigates to a different application by clicking a link or closes the browser window. In that case, the `TimeoutException` on the server is the only way to handle a client's "death."

To unsubscribe and resubscribe, implement the event handlers in the MainPage class shown in Listing 18.28.

LISTING 18.28 Unsubscribing and Resubscribing

```
private void UnsubscribeButtonClick(object sender, RoutedEventArgs e)
{
    _client.StopObservingFilesAsync();
    UnsubscribeButton.IsEnabled = false;
    ResubscribeButton.IsEnabled = true;
}

private void ResubscribeButtonClick(object sender, RoutedEventArgs e)
{
    Files.Clear();
    _client.StartObservingFilesAsync();
    UnsubscribeButton.IsEnabled = true;
    ResubscribeButton.IsEnabled = false;
}
```

Testing the Application

To test the application, open the folder you defined in the web application in Listing 18.16, lines 8 and 9. Add a few files in this folder, and then run the application. The `ListBox` in the Silverlight window should show the names of the files you just added. Then, while the application is running, add a few new files to the folder and observe how their names appear in the `ListBox`.

To test multiple clients, open a new web browser and copy/paste the location of the Silverlight application. This starts a new client that also subscribes to the service. Changes to the watched folders are reflected in both clients at the same time.

To test the timeout, close the first client, and then add files to the watched folder. The remaining client's `ListBox` remains unchanged until the timeout on the server occurs (one minute by default). Only then will the remaining client be updated again.

Finally, try unsubscribing and resubscribing to the service. To be complete, extend the service and the client with calls when files are deleted or renamed.

> **TIP**
>
> **Resetting the Web Server**
>
> When the Silverlight application is closed, the web server sometimes continues to run. To start testing with a clean slate and avoid confusion due to timeouts and so on, check whether the web server is still running: In the notification area of Windows, check whether the icon shown in Figure 14.3 can be seen and has the same port number as defined in the web application's project properties. If you can see this icon with the right port, stop the web server by right-clicking it and selecting Stop from the context menu. This will reset the whole situation on the server and enable you to restart testing cleanly.

Displaying Notification Windows

In the preceding section, you saw how the web server can send notifications to the client. If the Silverlight application is visible on the desktop, the changes are immediately noticeable. If the window is minimized (or simply behind another window), however, the changes may go unnoticed.

To solve this, Silverlight 4 introduces the `NotificationWindow` that is well known by computer users. These are the small "toasts" that appear (typically in the bottom right of the screen) when something happens in an application (for example, in Outlook when an email is received).

Understanding the Restrictions

There are a few restrictions that apply to notification windows:

- They are available only when the Silverlight application runs out of the browser.
- They are always square and fully opaque.
- The location of the `NotificationWindow` cannot be modified, only its size can be set.
- Content within a `NotificationWindow` cannot be edited by the user. Only mouse events are handled.
- There can only be one `NotificationWindow` open at a time for an application.

Adding a Notification Window

In this section, the DuplexSampleApplication we implemented in the previous section will be modified to run out of the browser and to display notification windows. If you didn't save this application, the initial state can be downloaded from http://www.galasoft.ch/sl4-notificationstart and modified with the following steps:

1. After unblocking the zip file and extracting the content, open the DuplexPollingSample solution in Visual Studio.
2. Add a new `UserControl` to the Silverlight project and name it **NotificationContent.xaml**.
3. Open Notification.xaml and set the `UserControl`'s `Height` to 80 and its `Width` to 350.
4. Enter the markup shown in Listing 18.29.

LISTING 18.29 Notification `UserControl`

```
<Grid x:Name="LayoutRoot"
      Background="#FFC4C4FF">
    <HyperlinkButton Content="Close"
                     HorizontalAlignment="Right"
                     Margin="0,10,10,0"
                     VerticalAlignment="Top"
                     Foreground="#FF3F3F3F"
                     Click="CloseButtonClick" />
    <TextBlock HorizontalAlignment="Left"
               Text="A file change was detected"
               FontSize="20"
               VerticalAlignment="Top"
               Margin="10,10,0,0" />
    <TextBlock Text="Click to show the application"
               Margin="10,45,10,10"
               FontStyle="Italic"
               FontSize="14" />
</Grid>
```

5. In NotificationContent.xaml.cs, handle the `HyperlinkButton`'s `Click` event as shown in Listing 18.30. This raises a custom event requesting to close the `NotificationWindow`.

LISTING 18.30 Requesting to Close

```
public event EventHandler CloseRequested;

private void CloseButtonClick(object sender, RoutedEventArgs e)
{
```

```
    if (CloseRequested != null)
    {
        CloseRequested(this, EventArgs.Empty);
    }
}
```

6. In MainPage.xaml.cs, add the code from Listing 18.31 in the bottom of the class.

LISTING 18.31 Displaying a NotificationWindow

```
 1  private bool _isNotificationOpen;
 2
 3  private void ShowNotification()
 4  {
 5      if (_isNotificationOpen
 6          || !App.Current.IsRunningOutOfBrowser)
 7      {
 8          return;
 9      }
10
11      var win = new NotificationWindow();
12      var uc = new NotificationContent();
13      win.Width = uc.Width;
14      win.Height = uc.Height;
15      win.Content = uc;
16      win.Closed += (s, e) => _isNotificationOpen = false;
17      uc.MouseLeftButtonDown += (s, e) => App.Current.MainWindow.Activate();
18      uc.CloseRequested += (s, e) => win.Close();
19      _isNotificationOpen = true;
20      win.Show(5000);
21  }
```

- On lines 5 to 9, we check whether a NotificationWindow is already open. If that is the case, or if the application is not running OOB, the operation is aborted.
- On lines 11 to 20, a NotificationWindow is prepared. After creating it on line 11, a new UserControl is instantiated on line 12. This is the content of the window. The Height and Width of the UserControl are assigned to the NotificationWindow, and then the UserControl itself is assigned to the window's Content on line 15.
- On line 16, the Closed event of the window is handled. This resets the _isNotificationOpen attribute so that a next NotificationWindow can appear.
- Line 17 handles the MouseLeftButtonDown on the NotificationWindow. This line uses the access to the MainWindow (in which the OOB application is hosted) to activate it and bring it in front. Note, however, that if the main window is minimized, this line will not restore its state.

- Line 18 handles the custom `CloseRequested` event raised by the `UserControl` when the `HyperlinkButton` is clicked. The `NotificationWindow` is closed.
- Finally, the window is showed on line 20 for a duration of 5,000 milliseconds.

7. Add a call to the `ShowNotification` method in the `FileHandled` method in Listing 18.27, just after the filename has been added to the `Files` collection. If you have also implemented a `FileDeleted` and `FileRenamed` method, you can also add the call to `ShowNotification` in those methods.
8. Open the Silverlight project properties and enable the application to run out of the browser. Then, run it and observe how the `NotificationWindow` appears in the bottom right of the screen when a file change is detected, as shown in Figure 18.4.

FIGURE 18.4 Showing a Notification Window.

Queuing Notification Windows

As mentioned in the section about restrictions, there can be only one `NotificationWindow` open for a given application. In the sample, we checked whether such a window is open, and we just blocked the new `NotificationWindow` if that was the case.

> **TIP**
>
> **Running the Web Server**
>
> Remember that the web server might have to be started manually when the application runs in OOB. Chapter 14 already explained how to do this, in the "Making Sure That the WCF Server Is Running" section.

On his blog, Tim Heuer (Silverlight Program Manager at Microsoft) has a suggestion to queue `NotificationWindow` elements, in case it is important that all the messages are shown. This is, for example, what happens with Microsoft Outlook, where one notification after another is shown when multiple emails are received. You can find more information about this at http://www.galasoft.ch/sl4-notificationqueue.

Interacting with the Main Window

Clicking the `NotificationWindow` activates the main window, the window that hosts the OOB application. Activating will attempt to put the window in front of all others, in case it was not minimized.

With normal trust, the interactions allowed are limited. With elevated permissions, however, it is possible to modify the state of the `MainWindow` (for example, `Minimized` or `Maximized`) and to change its size and position.

Making sure that the window is visible when the `NotificationWindow` is clicked can be achieved with the following steps:

1. Run the OOB application and uninstall it.

2. In the Silverlight project properties, enable elevated trust in the Out-of-Browser Settings.

3. Open MainPage.xaml.cs and modify line 17 of Listing 18.31 as shown in Listing 18.32.

LISTING 18.32 Restoring the Main Window

```
uc.MouseLeftButtonDown += (s, e) =>
{
    if (App.Current.MainWindow.WindowState == WindowState.Minimized)
    {
        App.Current.MainWindow.WindowState = WindowState.Normal;
    }

    App.Current.MainWindow.Activate();
};
```

4. Run the Silverlight in-browser application again and install it with elevated trust.

5. Minimize the OOB application and change a file in the watched folder. When the `NotificationWindow` appears, click it to restore the window.

Notification windows are a great way to interact with the user and add a desktop-like touch to the OOB Silverlight application, with or without elevated trust.

Creating a Custom Splash Screen

The Silverlight loader screen (also known as splash screen) is the very first thing that anyone accessing your application sees. Although the default progress counter shown in Figure 18.5 was original when Silverlight was first launched, it should really be replaced in your application by something that prepares the user to the original experience they will get.

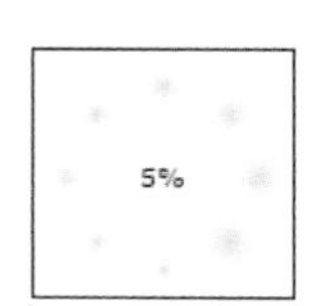

FIGURE 18.5 Default loader screen.

Because the Silverlight application is not loaded yet at the time where the splash screen is displayed, the code driving the animations cannot be written in .NET, but must be JavaScript and XAML only. This is a return to the early days of Silverlight 1.0! Preparing a custom splash screen can be done as follows:

1. Create a new Silverlight application and name it **CustomSplashTest**. Make sure to create a Web application to host it.

2. Because loading a XAP file on the local computer is very fast, add a large file to the Silverlight project (for example, a video), and set its Build Action to Content in the Properties panel, and Copy to Output Directory to Copy If Newer.

3. Right-click the Web application and select Add, New Item from the context menu. Select a Text file and set its name to **Splash.xaml**.

4. Select the Splash.xaml file, press F4 to show its properties, and make sure that the Build Action is set to Page.

5. Open Splash.xaml and set its content as shown in Listing 18.33.

LISTING 18.33 Splash Screen in XAML

```
<Grid xmlns="http://schemas.microsoft.com/winfx/2006/xaml/presentation"
      xmlns:x="http://schemas.microsoft.com/winfx/2006/xaml">
    <StackPanel HorizontalAlignment="Center"
                VerticalAlignment="Center">
        <TextBlock Text="Please wait..."
            FontSize="36" Margin="0,0,0,10" />

        <Border Width="300" Height="15"
            BorderBrush="#FFC4C3C3"
            CornerRadius="4"
            BorderThickness="1"
            x:Name="ProgressBorder">
            <Rectangle x:Name="ProgressRectangle"
                RadiusX="4" RadiusY="4"
                HorizontalAlignment="Left"
                Fill="#FFC4C3C3" />
        </Border>

        <StackPanel Orientation="Horizontal"
                    HorizontalAlignment="Right">
            <TextBlock x:Name="PercentageTextBlock"
                Text="32" FontSize="24"
                FontStyle="Italic"
                FontWeight="Bold"
                Foreground="#FFC4C3C3" />
        </StackPanel>
    </StackPanel>
</Grid>
```

6. Right-click the Web application and select Add Reference. In the dialog, select the .NET tab and then the three assemblies PresentationCore, PresentationFramework, and WindowsBase. Click OK to add them to the project.

7. Open CustomSplashTestTestPage.html and add the JavaScript function shown in Listing 18.34 below the `onSilverlightError` function.

LISTING 18.34 Updating the Progress

```
 1 function onSourceDownloadProgressChanged(sender, e) {
 2   var host
 3     = document.getElementById("SilverlightPlugIn");
 4   var progressBar
 5     = host.content.findName("ProgressRectangle");
 6   var progressBorder
 7     = host.content.findName("ProgressBorder");
 8   var percentTextBlock
 9     = host.content.findName("PercentageTextBlock");
10
11   var progress;
12   if (e.progress)
13     progress = e.progress;
14   else
15     progress = e.get_progress();
16
17   progressBar.Width = progress * progressBorder.Width;
18   percentTextBlock.Text
19     = "" + Math.round(progress * 100) + "%";
20 }
```

- Lines 2 and 3 get the host, the Silverlight plug-in.
- Lines 4 to 9 retrieve elements from the XAML content.
- Lines 11 to 15 retrieve the progress value (a numeric value between 0 and 1) from the e parameter. Depending on the platform, either line 13 or 15 will be executed.
- Line 17 sets the Width of the ProgressRectangle in the XAML. This will create a progress bar effect, where the filled region grows together with the progress value.
- Finally, lines 18 and 19 set the text of the PercentageTextBlock in the XAML.

8. Modify the HTML object tag as shown in Listing 18.35. This gives a name to the object, and adds two parameters instructing Silverlight to use the custom splash screen. The rest of the tag should remain unchanged.

LISTING 18.35 Naming the Object Tag and Adding Parameters

```
<object id="SilverlightPlugIn"
        data="data:application/x-silverlight-2,"
        type="application/x-silverlight-2"
        width="100%" height="100%">
    <param name="splashscreensource" value="Splash.xaml"/>
    <param name="onSourceDownloadProgressChanged"
```

```
            value="onSourceDownloadProgressChanged" />
...
</object>
```

9. Make sure that CustomSplashTestTestPage.html is the start page. Build and run the Web application. You should see the splash screen being updated as the XAP file is being downloaded.

Even with this super simple screen, the first impression on the user is already completely different from with the default loader screen. Creating custom splash screens is really easy and sets your application apart from others.

Summary

In this chapter, we continued our exploration of features of Silverlight that help create improved user experience and advanced functionalities.

Dragging and dropping files on the Silverlight UI, for example, is not a mission-critical feature, but it does improve the user experience over the classic `OpenFileDialog`.

The possibility to run in full screen allows creating kiosk applications that are very easy to deploy. With the new changes in Silverlight 4 OOB applications with elevated trust, interacting with kiosk applications is possible using the keyboard. For OOB applications, even without elevated trust, the possibility to run in full screen on a second monitor while the user works on the primary monitor increases the appeal of media applications such as video players, for example.

Working with COM is a new feature that is available only on Windows platforms. Very powerful, it allows nearly any interaction with the host computer, and therefore is available only to OOB applications with elevated permissions. Interacting with Microsoft Office, for example, adds value to line-of-business applications, as you saw in this chapter.

Duplex polling is an advanced communication mechanism that provides fast feedback from the server to any client that subscribed to the callback channel. Although a little complex to configure and implement, it allows creating very responsive applications even in a client/server scenario.

Notification windows are a feature that improves the user's comfort in OOB scenarios by showing feedback even when the application is in the background. We also saw how to interact with the main window hosting the OOB application (only with elevated permissions).

Finally, creating custom splash screens is a nice touch that helps differentiate your user experience from the very first contact that the user has with your application.

In the next chapter, the exploration continues with a range of new features: Authentication, advanced commanding, random animations, multitouch, local communication and the Bing maps control will be presented.

CHAPTER 19

Authentication, Event to Command Binding, Random Animations, Multitouch, Local Communication, and Bing Maps Control

IN THIS CHAPTER, WE WILL:

- Use authentication to log into a Silverlight application with a username and password.
- Bind events to commands directly without using code-behind.
- Build animations in XAML and then access them in code to randomize them.
- Talk about multitouch gestures in Silverlight.
- Let Silverlight applications "talk" to each other on the local computer, without going through the web server.
- Use the Bing maps control to add mapping to a Silverlight application.

In the two previous chapters, we talked about multiple improvements that were implemented in Silverlight 3 and 4 to make this platform more powerful and user friendly than ever before. In this chapter, we continue the series with additional features and learn to use them to create powerful and beautiful applications.

Logging In with Authentication

In this book, some useful techniques were shown to build data applications (also known as line-of-business applications). In these applications, however, every user was able to access the entirety of the application without any restriction. Obviously, this is not a good way to manage a business.

In this section, we show how to use the ASP.NET authentication services to verify and restrict access to some users. That Silverlight can leverage the existing security framework installed with ASP.NET is obviously making the developer's life much easier. This can be, however, an issue when the website from which the Silverlight application originates is not an ASP.NET website running on the Internet Information Services (IIS) server. In those cases, a custom security management system must be built.

Note that in addition to Visual Studio and the Silverlight tools, you need to install SQL Server Express to be able to create users. This database system also needs to be available on the web server where the Silverlight application is deployed (server only).

Creating a New Website

ASP.NET has two main kinds of server applications: web applications (including ASP.NET MVC application) and websites. Usually, using a web application as the host for the Silverlight application is preferable, because they are easier to configure than websites. However, configuring a web application for authentication is less straightforward in Visual Studio.

To keep things simple, we show how to use an ASP.NET website to host the application, configure the access rights, and verify access without leaving Visual Studio. For more information about configuring ASP.NET Security, check the book *Professional ASP.NET 2.0 Security* by Stefan Schackow (available at http://www.galasoft.ch/sl4-aspsecurity).

To create a new website, follow these steps:

1. Download the file AuthenticationSample-Start.zip from http://www.galasoft.ch/sl4-authentication. Unblock the downloaded file using the file's Properties dialog and clicking the Unblock button on the General tab (if available).
2. Open the solution AuthenticationSample.sln in Visual Studio.
3. Right-click the AuthenticationSample solution and select Add, New Web Site from the context menu.
4. In the Add New Web Site dialog, select ASP.NET Empty Web Site.
5. Enter a location for the new website. You can select File System, HTTP, or FTP. It is recommended to keep the website on the file system during development, and to copy it to the web server only after it has been tested. Note that the website does not need to be near the Silverlight application (although it is probably a good idea to keep them together).
6. Click OK.
7. As done before, we need to establish a link between the Silverlight application and the website. To do this, right-click the new website and select Property Pages from the context menu.
8. In the Property Pages dialog, select the Silverlight Applications category.
9. Click the Add button. In the Add Silverlight Application dialog, select the AuthenticationSample application and click the Add button. Then close the Property Pages by clicking OK.
10. Set the new website as StartUp Project and the page AuthenticationSampleTestPage.html as Start Page.

Adding and Managing Users

To check the user's identity, the web server needs to have some information about the users and their role. To do this, we use the ASP.NET configuration tool with the following steps:

1. In Visual Studio, select any file in the website, and then select Web Site, ASP.NET Configuration. This starts the configuration tool in a web browser, as shown in Figure 19.1.

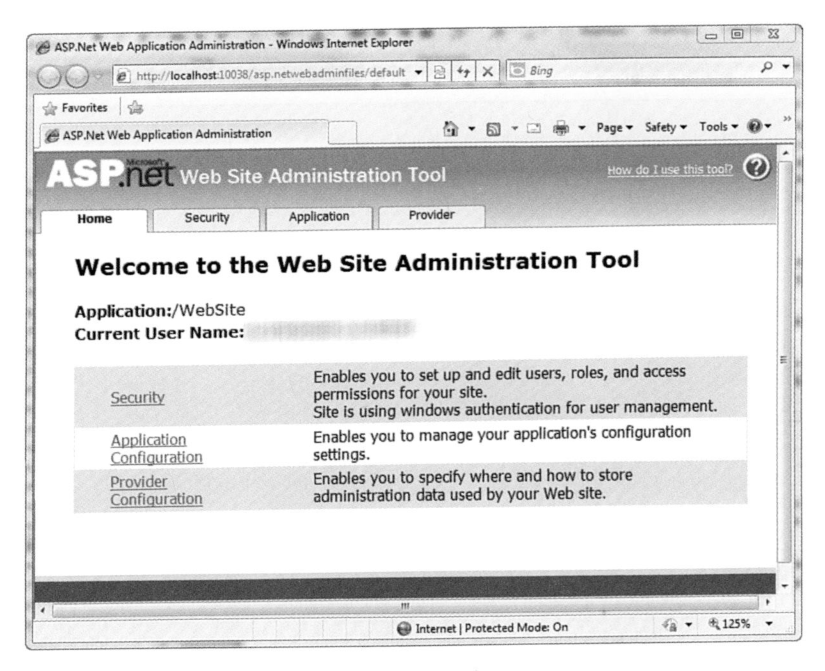

FIGURE 19.1 ASP.NET configuration tool.

2. In the configuration tool, click the Security tab.
3. In the Security tab, click Use the Security Setup Wizard link to configure security step-by-step.
4. Click Next to reach the Select Access Method screen.
5. Select the access method From the Internet and click Next.
6. Click Next again to reach the Define Roles screen.
7. Check Enable Roles for this Web Site check box. This is not absolutely compulsory, but using roles to manage access to various parts of the website is easier than to manage permissions on a user basis.
8. On the Add New Roles screen, add two roles named **manager** and **employee**. You can have as many roles as you need. Then click Next.

9. On the next screen, add two users. You can use any name, password, email, security question, and answer. Make sure to write down the username and the password; we will need them later.
10. Once the users are created, click Next to reach the New Access Rules screen. In this step, you can choose to enable or disable access automatically to some sections of the website. We will not need this feature here. click Next.
11. Finally in the last step, click Finish.
12. Click again on the Security tab, and then select Create or Manage roles.
13. In the list, click the Manage link next to the employee role.
14. Search for one of your users, and then check the User Is in Role check box.
15. Click the Back button and repeat steps 13 and 14 for the manager role and the other of your employees.

The website is now configured for access. You can close the configuration tool.

Configuring the Authentication Web Service

To authenticate the user and check his access rights, we will need two Windows Communications Foundation (WCF) services. However, we will implement only one. The other one is already implemented and part of ASP.NET. We just need to provide an endpoint for this service. Follow these steps:

1. Right-click the website, and add a new item.
2. In the Add New Item dialog, select a text file and enter the name **AuthenticationService.svc**. Because the service is built-in ASP.NET, we just need a façade file for the service.
3. Enter the markup shown in Listing 19.1 in the new file.

LISTING 19.1 AuthenticationService Endpoint

```
<%@ ServiceHost Language="C#"
Service="System.Web.ApplicationServices.AuthenticationService" %>
```

4. Open the file web.config on the web server and enter the configuration information shown in Listing 19.2. This goes within the configuration tag.

LISTING 19.2 Configuring the Service

```
1 <system.serviceModel>
2     <behaviors>
3         <serviceBehaviors>
4             <behavior name="AppServicesBehavior">
5                 <serviceMetadata httpGetEnabled="true"/>
```

```
6               </behavior>
7           </serviceBehaviors>
8       </behaviors>
9
10      <bindings>
11          <basicHttpBinding>
12              <binding name="userHttp">
13                  <security mode="None"/>
14              </binding>
15          </basicHttpBinding>
16      </bindings>
17
18      <services>
19          <service
20              name="System.Web.ApplicationServices.AuthenticationService"
21              behaviorConfiguration="AppServicesBehavior">
22              <endpoint
23                  contract="System.Web.ApplicationServices.AuthenticationService"
24                  binding="basicHttpBinding"
25                  bindingConfiguration="userHttp"
26                  bindingNamespace="http://asp.net/ApplicationServices/v200"/>
27          </service>
28      </services>
29      <serviceHostingEnvironment aspNetCompatibilityEnabled="true"/>
30  </system.serviceModel>
31
32  <system.web.extensions>
33      <scripting>
34          <webServices>
35              <authenticationService
36                  enabled="true"
37                  requireSSL="false"/>
38          </webServices>
39      </scripting>
40  </system.web.extensions>
```


WARNING

Choosing the Right Security

On line 13 of Listing 19.2, the security is set to `None`. Although this makes things easier during development, it is of course recommended to choose a better security mode when publishing the application to the server, depending on the security modes that your web server supports.

Checking the Access

The authentication service was available "in the box" and merely needed to be exposed and configured. Checking access for a group of employees can also be implemented as a service with the following steps:

1. Add a new item to the website again. This time, select a Silverlight-enabled WCF Service. Name the new service **CheckAccessService.svc**.
2. Implement the `CheckAccessService` class as shown in Listing 19.3. This method checks the currently authenticated user and his role and returns `true` if the user is a manager.

LISTING 19.3 `CheckAccessService` Class

```
[ServiceContract(Namespace = "http://www.mydomain.com")]
[AspNetCompatibilityRequirements(RequirementsMode
    = AspNetCompatibilityRequirementsMode.Allowed)]
public class CheckAccessService
{
    [OperationContract]
    public bool CanAccessManagerZone()
    {
        if (HttpContext.Current.User.IsInRole("manager"))
        {
            return true;
        }

        return false;
    }
}
```

Adding References to the Services

The Silverlight application needs to access the WCF services. We already saw that Visual Studio is able to create proxies for the services with the following steps:

1. Right-click the References folder of the Silverlight project and select Add Service Reference from the context menu.
2. Click the Discover button. Both services are shown in the Add Service Reference dialog.
3. Select AuthenticationService; enter the name **AuthenticationService** in the Namespace field, and then click OK.
4. Repeat Steps 1 to 3, but this time select CheckAccessService.

With these steps, the services are known from the Silverlight application and can be used. Note that if changes are made on the server, they will be visible only in the Silverlight client after right-clicking the reference and selecting Update Service Reference from the context menu.

Implementing the Client

Now it's time to interact with the user on one hand and with the service on the other hand. Follow these steps:

1. Open MainPage.xaml. This page has a `StackPanel` in the middle of the page named `LoginPanel`, with a `UserNameTextBox` and a `PasswordTextBox`. Also available are two `Button` elements (`Login` and `Cancel`) and a `MessageTextBlock` to inform the user.
2. Open MainPage.xaml.cs.
3. Modify the `LoginClick` event handler as shown in Listing 19.4.

LISTING 19.4 `LoginClick` Event Handler

```
1  private void LoginClick(object sender, RoutedEventArgs e)
2  {
3      MessageTextBlock.Text = "Logging in";
4      var client
5          = new AuthenticationService.AuthenticationServiceClient();
6      client.LoginCompleted += client_LoginCompleted;
7      UserNameTextBox.IsEnabled = false;
8      PasswordTextBox.IsEnabled = false;
9      client.LoginAsync(
10         UserNameTextBox.Text,
11         PasswordTextBox.Password,
12         string.Empty,
13         true,
14         UserNameTextBox);
15 }
```

- On lines 4 and 5, a new client is created for the `AuthenticationService`. This client was generated when the service reference was added.
- Line 6 sets an event handler (implemented in Listing 19.5) for the `LoginCompleted` event. This is where the application will find out whether the username and password are valid.
- Lines 9 to 14 call the service in an asynchronous manner, passing the username and the password. Note that since we didn't add security to the configuration (such as Secure Sockets Layer [SSL]), the username and password will be sent in clear text to the web server. This is, of course, not acceptable for a production environment.

4. Implement the `LoginCompleted` event handler shown in Listing 19.5.

LISTING 19.5 LoginCompleted Event Handler

```
 1 void client_LoginCompleted(
 2     object sender,
 3     LoginCompletedEventArgs e)
 4 {
 5     if (e.Result)
 6     {
 7         MessageTextBlock.Text = "Logged in, Checking access";
 8
 9         var client
10             = new CheckAccessService.CheckAccessServiceClient();
11         client.CanAccessManagerZoneCompleted
12             += client_CanAccessManagerZoneCompleted;
13         client.CanAccessManagerZoneAsync();
14     }
15     else
16     {
17         MessageTextBlock.Text = "Access denied";
18     }
19 }
```

- The result of the authentication is a `bool` flag that can be `true` (success) or `false` (failure). This is the content of `e.Result` that is checked on line 5.
- If the authentication is successful, the access rights for the current user are checked with the `CheckAccessService` created and called on line 9 to 13.

5. Implement the `client_CanAccessManagerZoneCompleted` event handler (called when the `CheckAccessService` call is completed) as shown in Listing 19.6.

LISTING 19.6 client_CanAccessManagerZoneCompleted Event Handler

```
 1 void client_CanAccessManagerZoneCompleted(
 2     object sender,
 3     CheckAccessService.CanAccessManagerZoneCompletedEventArgs e)
 4 {
 5     LoginPanel.Visibility = Visibility.Collapsed;
 6
 7     if (e.Result)
 8     {
 9         ShowManagerPage();
10     }
11     else
12     {
13         ShowEmployeePage();
14     }
```

```
15  }
16
17  private void ShowEmployeePage()
18  {
19      MessageBox.Show("Employee");
20  }
21
22  private void ShowManagerPage()
23  {
24      MessageBox.Show("Manager");
25  }
```

- After the `CheckAccessService` returns, the `LoginPanel` should be hidden, because the user is authenticated already. Depending on the result, we will display the manager zone user interface or the employee zone.
- The `CanAccessManagerZoneCompletedEventArgs` class is generated by Visual Studio when the Add Service Reference dialog is closed. Its `Result` property is of the same type as the `CanAccessManagerZone` method on the service.
- The service returns a `bool` that is checked on line 7. Depending on the value, the method `ShowManagerPage` or `ShowEmployeePage` is called.

These methods are not implemented here and just show a `MessageBox`, as you will see by starting the application and entering one of the usernames and passwords you defined. Depending on the type of application, the methods could navigate to a different page (in a navigation application), or hide/show/enable/disable some controls, and so forth.

This method of authentication is named Forms Authentication and is quite simple. It is a bit annoying to have to define all the users on the server, though, when some existing services can be leveraged. For example, using Windows Live ID is possible. An example for RIA Services is shown at http://www.galasoft.ch/sl4-windowslive. Nonetheless, the sample in this chapter shows how Silverlight leverages existing ASP.NET infrastructure to handle authentication.

Binding an Event to a Command

We talked a lot about commands and how they can be used to bind a click event on certain controls (`Button`, `CheckBox`, `RadioButton`, and so on) to a property of type `ICommand` (such as a `RelayCommand` or another custom implementation). Although the `Command` property (and its `CommandParameter` companion) was absent of Silverlight 3 entirely, it has been added to Silverlight 4. However, having this property only on certain controls and only for a `Click` event is very limiting. It would be great to be able to bind, for example, the `SelectionChanged` event of a `DataGrid`, or the `LostFocus` event of a `TextBox` to a command on a viewmodel.

Thankfully, this is possible by using an `Action` attached to an `EventTrigger`. We talked about these helper classes in Chapter 11, "Mastering Expression Blend," and saw how to implement and use a trigger/action pair to encapsulate functionality in a developer-friendly, reusable way. We also saw how to attach them to an element in XAML and in Expression Blend.

There are currently two main implementations of an `Action` allowing invoking an `ICommand`:

- The Expression Blend team implemented an `Action` named `InvokeCommandAction`. It can be added from the Assets library in Blend onto an element.
- The open source MVVM Light Toolkit that was mentioned already in Chapter 15, "Developing Navigation Applications and Silverlight for Windows Phone 7," has an `Action` named `EventToCommand` that aims to the same functionality but with a few more features.

Adding either `InvokeCommandAction` or `EventToCommand` to your application adds a dependency on external DLLs that will be added to your XAP file:

- System.Windows.Interactivity.dll is the base assembly for all behaviors, triggers, and actions. It is very often used by Silverlight developers, and there is a good chance that it has in fact already been added to your Silverlight application's dependencies.
- For `EventToCommand`, the MVVM Light Toolkit is needed in addition. This toolkit contains more than `EventToCommand`, and provides helper classes to help implement loosely coupled application, as you already saw in this book, and will again in Chapter 20, "Building Extensible and Maintainable Applications."

Choosing between `InvokeCommandAction` and `EventToCommand` depends on the functionality that you want to achieve. Although both components are overlapping for the basics, `EventToCommand` offers more features, such as disabling the attached control based on the value of the `ICommand`'s `CanExecute` method, and a possibility to pass the triggering event's `EventArgs` down to the `ICommand`'s parameter, to handle special cases such as drag and drop (as explained at http://www.galasoft.ch/sl4-e2cblog).

Executing a Command When a TextBox Loses Focus

`EventToCommand` can, for instance, be used to execute a saving operation when a `TextBox` loses the focus with the following steps:

1. Download, unblock, and extract the start application from http://www.galasoft.ch/sl4-e2c.
2. In the folder you just extracted, start the solution named TextBoxHandling.sln in Visual Studio.

Take a look at the application. It is an application built with the MVVM Light framework that is explained in more detail in Chapter 20, and very much similar to other MVVM applications we covered earlier in this book:

- In MainPage.xaml, two `TextBox` elements are defined and bound to a customer's `FirstName` and `LastName`. The customer itself is defined as a `CustomerViewModel` class.
- An `Ellipse` is also present in MainPage.xaml, with an animation (named `WaitAnimation`). This animation should be started when a saving operation is active.
- To start/stop the animation, an `IAnimationService` is defined in the ViewModel folder. The `MainPage` class implements this interface, and is responsible for finding, starting, and stopping the animation.
- In the Model folder, an `INetworkService` interface is defined with a single method `Save`. Because it is an asynchronous operation, a `callback` parameter must be passed to the `Save` method. We already used this asynchronous pattern in Chapters 7, "Understanding the Model-View-ViewModel Pattern," 9, "Connecting to the Web," and later chapters.
- The `INetworkService` interface is implemented by the `NetworkService` class in the Model folder. To simulate a busy network, every `Save` operation starts a background thread and lets it sleep for 5,000 milliseconds. You'll learn more about multithreading in Chapter 22, "Advanced Development Techniques." After these 5,000 milliseconds, the callback is executed.
- The `MainViewModel` class is responsible for holding the `CustomerViewModel` instance to which the two `TextBox` elements are data bound.

This is a fairly common setting for MVVM applications in Silverlight. Now, a command should be added that saves the data to the network when both the `FirstName` and the `LastName` have been entered. During a save operation, both `TextBox` elements should be disabled, and the animation should run. To perform this functionality, follow these steps:

1. In the `MainViewModel` class, add a command as shown in Listing 19.7. The `RelayCommand` class used here is part of the GalaSoft.MvvmLight.dll assembly, which is referenced by the sample application. We already used this class in other listings in this book.

LISTING 19.7 Adding a Command

```
public RelayCommand CheckAndSaveCommand
{
    get;
    private set;
}
```

2. Add a property named `IsSaving` as shown in Listing 19.8. This property raises the `CanExecuteChanged` on the `CheckAndSaveCommand` property. As you will see in Listing 19.9, the state of `CanExecute` for this command depends on the value of the `IsSaving` property. In addition, the property orders the `IAnimationService` to start or stop the animation.

LISTING 19.8 IsSaving Property

```
private bool _isSaving;
public bool IsSaving
{
    get { return _isSaving; }

    set
    {
        if (_isSaving == value)
        {
            return;
        }

        _isSaving = value;
        CheckAndSaveCommand.RaiseCanExecuteChanged();

        if (AnimationService != null)
        {
            if (_isSaving)
            {
                AnimationService.StartAnimation(WaitAnimationName);
            }
            else
            {
                AnimationService.StopAnimation(WaitAnimationName);
            }
        }
    }
}
```

3. Instantiate the `CheckAndSaveCommand` property by modifying the `MainViewModel` constructor as shown in Listing 19.9.

LISTING 19.9 Instantiating the Command

```
1  public MainViewModel(INetworkService networkService)
2  {
3      _networkService = networkService;
4      CurrentCustomer = new CustomerViewModel();
```

```
5
6       CheckAndSaveCommand = new RelayCommand(
7           CheckAndSave,
8           () => !IsSaving);
9   }
```

- On lines 6 to 8, the command is created.
- Line 7 assigns the method CheckAndSave (defined in Listing 19.10) to the Execute delegate. This method will be executed when the command is invoked.
- Line 8 is the CanExecute delegate, and returns true if the MainViewModel is not saving and false otherwise. This will determine the state of the two TextBox elements in the UI: enabled or disabled.

4. Define the CheckAndSave method as shown in Listing 19.10.

LISTING 19.10 CheckAndSave Method

```
1   private void CheckAndSave()
2   {
3       if (CurrentCustomer != null
4           && !string.IsNullOrEmpty(CurrentCustomer.FirstName)
5           && !string.IsNullOrEmpty(CurrentCustomer.LastName))
6       {
7           IsSaving = true;
8           _networkService.Save(SaveCompleted);
9       }
10  }
11
12  private void SaveCompleted(bool sucess)
13  {
14      IsSaving = false;
15  }
```

- On lines 3 to 5, the state of the CurrentCustomer is checked. If both the FirstName and the LastName have been filled, the operation can continue.
- The IsSaving property is set to true on line 7. This will trigger the animation in the UI and cause it to reevaluate the state of the CheckAndSaveCommand as we saw in Listing 19.8.
- Line 8 calls the Save method in the INetworkService class and passes if the SaveCompleted method defined on lines 12 to 18 as a callback.
- When the operation is completed and the callback is called by the NetworkService class, the IsSaving property is set back to false on line 14.

Setting an EventToCommand in XAML

The EventToCommand action can be added in XAML or in Blend, as usual. For completeness, we will see how to perform both operations. For XAML, follow these steps:

1. Open MainPage.xaml and add the xmlns prefixes shown in Listing 19.11. This maps the i prefix to System.Windows.Interactivity, which is the assembly where the behavior infrastructure is located. The cmd prefix is mapped to GalaSoft.MvvmLight.Command in the GalaSoft.MvvmLight.Extras.SL4 assembly. This is where the EventToCommand action is located. Both assemblies are into the External folder and referenced in the application.

LISTING 19.11 Adding xmlns Prefixes

```
xmlns:i="clr-
namespace:System.Windows.Interactivity;assembly=System.Windows.Interactivity"
xmlns:cmd="clr-
namespace:GalaSoft.MvvmLight.Command;assembly=GalaSoft.MvvmLight.Extras.SL4"
```

2. Find the TextBlock with the binding to CurrentCustomer.FirstName. Modify its markup as shown in Listing 19.12.

Listing 19.12 Adding EventToCommand in XAML

```
 1  <TextBox Margin="10,0,10,10"
 2           FontSize="20"
 3           Text="{Binding CurrentCustomer.FirstName, Mode=TwoWay}" >
 4      <i:Interaction.Triggers>
 5           <i:EventTrigger EventName="LostFocus">
 6               <cmd:EventToCommand
 7                    Command="{Binding CheckAndSaveCommand}"
 8                    MustToggleIsEnabled="True"/>
 9          </i:EventTrigger>
10      </i:Interaction.Triggers>
11  </TextBox>
```

- On lines 4 to 10, the attached property named Interaction.Triggers is defined. This is a collection of Triggers that can hold multiple ones.
- Lines 5 to 9 define an EventTrigger that reacts to the LostFocus event of the TextBox. We already talked about EventTrigger in Chapter 11 and mentioned that when a Trigger is fired, it invokes the list of Action elements that it contains.

- Lines 6 to 8 add an `Action` of type `EventToCommand` to the `EventTrigger`. Its `Command` property is data bound to the `CheckAndSaveCommand` property on the `MainViewModel` class (which is set as the `DataContext` of the whole page).
- Line 8 sets the `MustToggleIsEnabled` to `true`. This instructs the `EventToCommand` class that the `IsEnabled` property must be set according to the `CanExecute` method of the command. This is what allows disabling and enabling the `TextBox` elements based on the state of the `Save` operation.

Setting an `EventToCommand` in Blend

In Expression Blend, the same operation requires no hand coding, thanks to the user friendliness of behaviors. Follow these steps:

1. Save everything, build the application and open the solution in Blend.
2. Select the Assets tab and the Behaviors category.
3. Drag an `EventToCommand` element from the Assets library onto the second `TextBox` in the Objects and Timeline as shown in Figure 19.2.

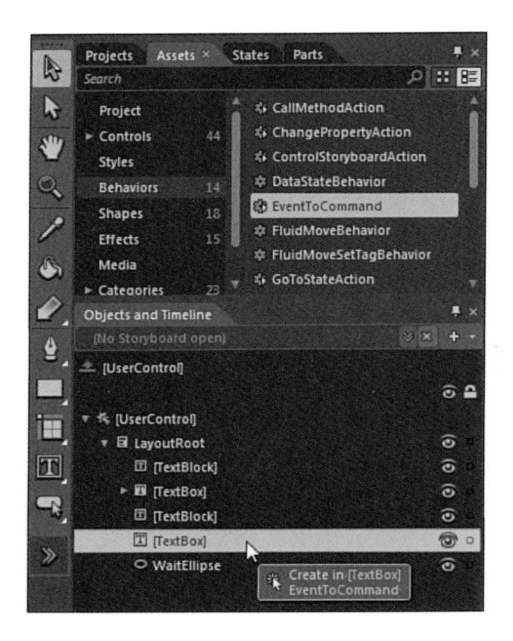

FIGURE 19.2 Setting the `EventToCommand` in Blend.

4. In the Properties panel, set the `EventName` property to `LostFocus`.
5. Using the data binding editor, set a binding between the `Command` property and the `CheckAndSaveCommand` property of the `MainViewModel` class as shown in Figure 19.3. Then close the dialog by clicking OK.

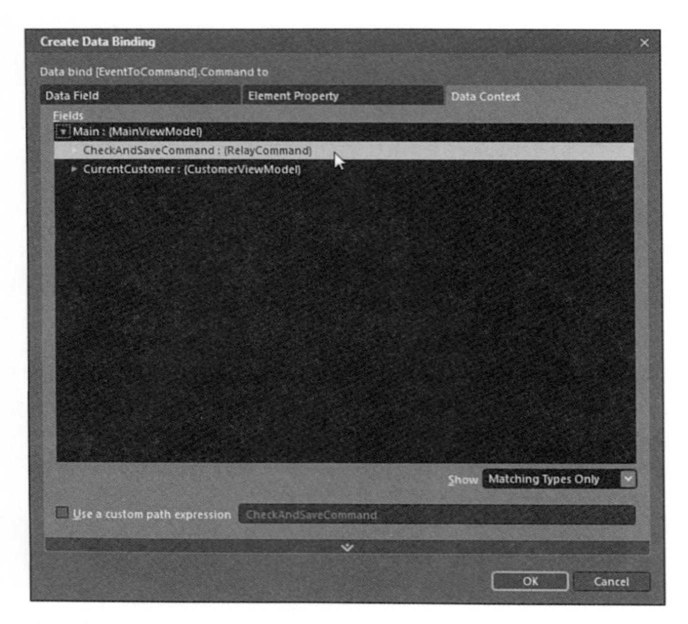

FIGURE 19.3 Setting a binding on the `Command` property.

6. Finally, in the Properties panel, check the MustToggleIsEnabled check box.

Testing the Application

Run the application, either from Expression Blend or from Visual Studio. Enter your first name and last name, and then click the Tab key to cause the second `TextBox` to lose the focus. This triggers the save operation for five seconds, starts the animation, and disables the two `TextBox` elements during this time.

`EventToCommand` is a powerful addition to the toolbox of the developer wanting to create rich decoupled applications. It builds on the concept of commands and allows extending it to any event of any UI element.

Building Random Animations

When a rich UI experience is created, it is often desirable to create random animations. For example, this could be a simulation of snowflakes falling according to a random path, bubbles or balloons floating on the screen, and so forth. In this section, you will learn how to build a random animation in Blend and in code.

Creating the Base Animation in Blend

To start, it is a good idea to create a base animation in XAML. Building animations in code from scratch is possible, but it is a long process, and hard to test because of the need to run the application to visualize every little change. By using Blend, it is much easier to visualize the animation's parameters. Later, code will be used to randomize them. Follow these steps.

1. Download the zip file named RandomAnimationSample-Start.zip from http://www.galasoft.ch/sl4-random. As usual, unblock the file with the Unblock button in the file Properties dialog (if available), and extract the content to your hard drive.
2. Open the solution RandomAnimationSample.sln in Expression Blend.
3. Click the small + button on top of the Objects and Timeline panel, as shown on Figure 19.4.

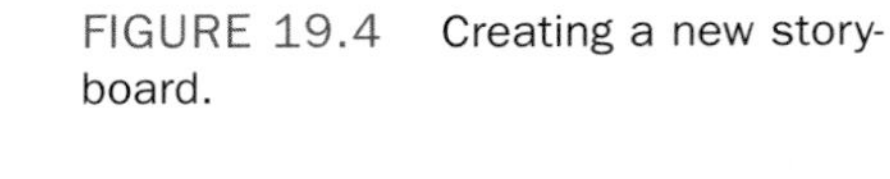

FIGURE 19.4 Creating a new storyboard.

4. In the Create Storyboard Resource dialog, enter the name **RandomAnimation** and then click OK. Blend turns in animation record mode. If you want, you can press the F6 key to toggle between Animation workspace and Design workspace, and back.
5. On the Objects and Timeline panel, place the yellow timeline on 2 seconds.
6. Select the `Grid` named `Ellipses` and click the Record Keyframe button shown in Figure 19.5.

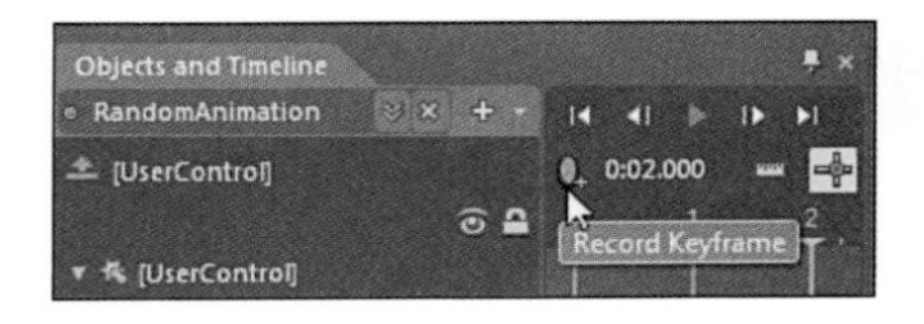

FIGURE 19.5 Record keyframe button.

7. In the Properties panel, in the Transform section, select the Scale tab and set X and Y to 0.5.
8. Select the Rotate tab in the Transform section of the Properties panel and set the Angle to 360 degrees.
9. Click the keyframe indicator on the yellow timeline in the Objects and Timeline panel, as shown in Figure 19.6.

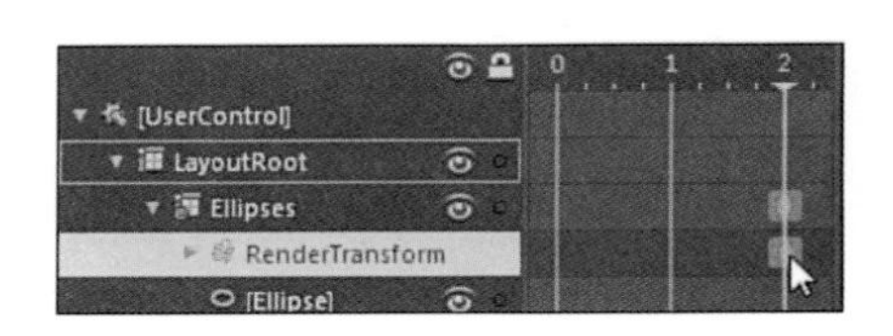

FIGURE 19.6 Selecting the keyframe.

10. In the Properties panel, select an EasingFunction for the animation (for example, Exponential InOut).
11. Play the animation using the controls in the Objects and Timeline panel. You can tweak it until you are satisfied. Then, select File, Save All.

Randomizing the Animation

Now that the base animation is ready, code needs to be written to randomize its parameters and start it with the following steps:

1. Open the same solution in Visual Studio.
2. Open MainPage.xaml.cs and modify the `MainPage` constructor as shown in Listing 19.13.

LISTING 19.13 Getting the Animation in Code

```
1  private readonly Storyboard _randomAnimation;
2  private readonly Random _random;
3
4  public MainPage()
5  {
6      InitializeComponent();
7
8      _random = new Random();
9      _randomAnimation = Resources["RandomAnimation"] as Storyboard;
10     _randomAnimation.Completed += (s, e) => StartNextAnimation();
11     StartNextAnimation();
12 }
```

- Line 1 declares an attribute to store the animation that we retrieve from the resources on line 9.
- Line 2 declares an attribute of type `Random`. This class is very useful to calculate pseudo-random numbers. This attribute is created at line 8.
- Line 10 handles the `Completed` event of the animation. It simply calls the `StartAnimation` method again, so that the movement never ends. This code will be executed only when the animation is completed.
- Then line 11 begins the first animation cycle by calling the `StartNextAnimation` method shown in Listing 19.14.

LISTING 19.14 `StartAnimation` Method

```
1  private void StartNextAnimation()
2  {
3      // Calculate target size
4      (_randomAnimation.Children[0] as DoubleAnimation).To
5          = (_randomAnimation.Children[1] as DoubleAnimation).To
6          = (double) _random.Next(4, 20) / 10;
7
8      // Calculate target angle
9      (_randomAnimation.Children[2] as DoubleAnimation).To
10         = _random.Next(0, 720);
11
12     // Calculate duration
```

```
13          _randomAnimation.Duration
14              = TimeSpan.FromMilliseconds(_random.Next(800, 2000));
15          _randomAnimation.Begin();
16      }
```

- Lines 4 to 6 calculate the target size for the `Ellipses Grid`. The `Random` class' `Next` method is used to calculate the new value between 0.4 and 2. Note that the animation is retrieved by its index, which is dangerous, as explained in the "Finding the Right Animation" box.
- Lines 9 and 10 calculate a random angle between 0 and 720 degrees.
- Finally, lines 13 and 14 calculate the duration for the animation between 800 and 2,000 milliseconds, before the animation is started on line 15.

WARNING

Finding the Right Animation

Unfortunately, there is no good way to retrieve an animation included within a `Storyboard`. In Listing 19.14, the index within the `Children` collection of the `Storyboard` is used, which is dangerous: If someone changes the order of the animations in the XAML markup, the code will not work anymore. This is the first thing you should look for in case the animation does not work as expected!

3. Start the application and watch how the animation plays.

With this simple code, it is possible to give a lifelike feel to an application by making it less predictable. Of course, this is not applicable to all the animations in the application, but depending on the scene you are building, this can come very handy.

Implementing Multitouch in Silverlight

Multitouch computing is one of the most exciting developments in modern-age client application development. Controlling a computer with one's fingers is not really new, and touch devices have existed for many years already (such as the Palm devices), but multitouch is something different:

- Contrary to these classic devices, multitouch computers can recognize multiple points of contact. Typical multitouch screens nowadays can handle up to four points of contact, sometimes more.
- Instead of using "taps" on the screen with the finger or a stylus, multitouch applications react to *gestures*, normally executed with the fingers. For example, Internet Explorer can react to different *flicks* (that is, a swiping movement with the fingers). One finger can create multiple actions depending on the direction of the flick. Also, the speed of the flick is relevant and influences the action.

- Multitouch is now found on many devices, ranging from very small (smartphones for instance) to quite large (such as the Microsoft Surface device) to very large (multitouch walls found in some venues). The cost of multitouch displays is dropping, so enabling multitouch on new devices is becoming less of a luxury. This is a cascading effect: People are confronted to multitouch more often, so they are more likely to purchase a multitouch device, which makes the technology more affordable for others.
- More and more research is put in making multitouch a first-class citizen, and even replacing the mouse devices in certain cases (tablet computers, kiosk applications, and so on). Eventually, it is possible that the (physical) keyboard will also be replaced by touch input, although this is more difficult.

TIP

Using Multitouch on a Microsoft Surface Device

Microsoft Surface is a project from Microsoft Research that made its way to a device: A computer is enclosed in a table with a large unpolished glass top. In the table, a computer running a multitouch shell on top of Windows Vista is driving the functions of the table. Infrared cameras placed within the table detect the presence of touch devices: fingers, shapes, or "blobs" (that is, larger objects that can be a hand, a glass, and so forth). Because the object detection is visual thanks to the infrared cameras, it allows the table to be completely enclosed, which protects it from spills and dirt. This is perfect for a table that is often used in bars, restaurants, and hotel lobbies.

Applications for Microsoft Surface are written in Windows Presentation Foundation (WPF), and a lot was learned from that experience: a device with a new form factor, used with fingers and interacting with its environment. This experience flows into Silverlight and Windows Phone 7 devices. Most important for the developer, developing multitouch experiences for Surface, WPF, Silverlight, and Windows Phone 7 is very similar!

Microsoft Surface is a relatively expensive device, but can be found nonetheless in many conference venues, hotels, and restaurants. It is a very convivial and innovative device that up to five or six people can use at the same time.

Getting the Right Computer

To develop a multitouch application, it is really recommended to use a multitouch computer. Although certain solutions exist to emulate multitouch input with multiple mouse devices, it is cumbersome at best. To understand the experience that the user is facing in your application, it is really better to use a touch-enabled computer.

Nowadays, buying a touch-enabled laptop is quite easy and not very expensive if the screen size is reasonable. Some developers have a main computer on which they develop (for example, a desktop or a powerful laptop) and a second, smaller touch-enabled computer on which they can test their multitouch applications. This is a nice combination that is acceptable in terms of price. Of course, there are also high-end computers that are touch enabled.

Another lesser-known solution is to apply a touch-enabled overlay on a normal display. For example, firms such as NextWindow (http://www.galasoft.ch/sl4-nextwin) produce overlay touch screens that can be mounted on top of any large plasma or LCD monitor with a PC running Windows 7. This is a way to get multitouch input without having to purchase a new monitor or a new laptop.

WARNING

Using the Right Operating System

At the moment, Silverlight supports multitouch operations only on operating systems that promote touch events to the applications running on it. This is the case for Windows 7, but other operating systems do not support Silverlight multitouch at the moment, unless specific touch devices are used.

Unfortunately at this time, multitouch is not supported when the application runs in full screen. Simple touch events are supported (for example, tapping on a button), but scale, rotate, and translate manipulations do not work in that mode.

Investigating Existing Elements

Some existing controls in Silverlight 4 support basic touch gestures. Most notably, the following controls react to touch:

- The Silverlight framework promotes taps on the Silverlight application to `MouseLeftButtonDown` and `MouseLeftButtonUp` events. For controls deriving from `ButtonBase` (such as `Button`, `ToggleButton`, `CheckBox`, `RadioButton`, and so on), this translates to a `Click` event. For other controls, the mouse events are raised.
- Tap and drag gestures are also supported automatically, so that a `Thumb` control can be dragged on the screen using a finger. For example, the `Thumb` of a `ScrollBar` can be dragged with a finger.
- A scale gesture (putting two fingers down on the Silverlight application and moving them away from each other or toward each other) is interpreted by the web browser and the Silverlight content is zoomed. However, note that this is not a feature of Silverlight proper, but of some web browsers. This feature is supported in Internet Explorer and Google Chrome on Windows 7 at least. Because this is not a Silverlight feature, availability depends on the web browser's implementation. Also, this is not supported when the application runs out of the browser.

Using Multitouch Libraries

Unfortunately, multitouch events are not first-class citizens in Silverlight 4 yet. Browsing through the documentation, you can see that some high-level multitouch events are available in the API: `ManipulationStarted`, `ManipulationDelta`, and `ManipulationCompleted` (with their corresponding `EventArgs`) are listed. However, do not get confused: These events are here only for compatibility with Windows Phone 7 and *should not be used in a Silverlight 4 application*. Trying to use them in code will not cause a compilation error. However, the events are not listed in Visual Studio IntelliSense, and they will not work as expected.

Instead, a low-level event is available. Its presence is less for direct consumption by a Silverlight application (although, of course, this is possible) than as the basis for future developments of higher level APIs to bring Silverlight (5 maybe?) up to par with WPF and (ironically) with Windows Phone 7 where some high-level gestures are supported (see the "Using Multitouch in Windows Phone 7 Applications" section, later in this chapter).

Using the Microsoft Surface Library for Silverlight

Thankfully, it is possible to build multitouch applications with high-level functionalities in Silverlight 4 by using helper libraries, such as the one published by the Microsoft Surface team at http://www.galasoft.ch/sl4-surface. Although the documentation on this page states that it is available for educational use only and without support, this is actually a pretty solid library that helps a lot when building applications by abstracting the low-level events. Be careful though, because the license does not allow commercial applications to be built with this library.

Using a Multitouch Behavior

Even the Microsoft Surface library is quite complex to use and understand, especially for simple applications. In many cases, only scaling, rotating, and translating are needed. (These operations are explained in the section of the same name.) In that case, a Blend behavior can be used to abstract the complexity even more. Davide Zordan (a Silverlight MVP) published such a behavior in open source on CodePlex (http://multitouch.codeplex.com/).

Scaling, Rotating, and Translating

The three basic manipulations in 2D are scaling, rotating, and translating, as shown in Figures 19.7, 19.8, and 19.9.

FIGURE 19.7 Scaling an element.

The manipulations can also be combined. In *Silverlight 2 Unleashed*, Chapter 3 explained that Silverlight has four affine transforms, three of which can be used to apply scaling, rotating, and translating to the element.

FIGURE 19.8 Rotating an element.

Detecting a Manipulation Frame

At the lowest level, Windows 7 reports the multitouch manipulations through an event named `Touch.FrameReported`. This event is fired every time that something relevant to multi-touch occurs: when one or more finger are pressed on the screen, when the fingers are moving, and when they are lifted up. To handle manipulations, the `TouchFrameEventArgs` class has all necessary information. The `TouchPoint` instances can be retrieved by calling `GetTouchPoints` and `GetPrimaryTouchPoint` on this class in the `Touch.FrameReported` event handler. This class has details about the number of fingers on the screen, their `Position`, `Size`, `Action` (`Down`, `Move` or `Up`) and a unique ID. Using math, it is possible to calculate all the transformations to be applied to the element.

FIGURE 19.9 Translating an element.

Using Inertia

When a physical object is dragged on a surface such as a table or a wooden floor, the movement does not stop immediately after the fingers are lifted and the object is let go. The translation will continue because of the momentum of the object. If the fingers had impressed a rotating movement on the object just before they were lifted, the rotation will also continue for a while.

To calculate the deceleration of an element, the `ManipulationDelta` event should be handled and the `ManipulationDeltaEventArgs.Velocities` property used in the calculations.

Implementing a Multitouch Application

A simple multitouch sample application can be created with the following steps:

1. Point your web browser to http://multitouch.codeplex.com.

2. At this time, the project does not have binaries for release for Silverlight 4. We will build the source code instead. Select the source tab.

3. On the right of the screen, find the Download link and click it.
4. Save the zip file on your computer. As usual, open the file Properties in Windows Explorer and unblock the file if needed. Then extract everything to a known location on your hard drive.
5. Create a new Silverlight application in Visual Studio or in Expression Blend and name it MultiTouchSample.
6. Right-click the solution in the Solution Explorer and select Add, Existing Project from the context menu.
7. In the Add Existing Project dialog, navigate to the location where you extracted the MultiTouch behavior code from CodePlex. The file you are looking for is inside the folder MultiTouch.Behaviors.Silverlight4 and is named MultiTouch.Behaviors.Silverlight4.csproj. Select this file and click Open.
8. In the Solution Explorer, right-click the References folder of the MultiTouchSample application, and select Add Reference from the context menu.
9. In the Add Reference dialog, select the Projects tab and the MultiTouch.Behaviors.Silverlight4 project, and then click OK.
10. Repeat Steps 6 to 9 for another project loaded from CodePlex named MultiTouch.ManipulationLib.Silverlight4. This is the Surface manipulation library for Silverlight mentioned earlier.
11. Build the application.

Adding the Behavior in Blend

Behaviors can be added in XAML or in Blend, as you saw in Chapter 11. Adding it in Blend is really much easier, as shown with the following steps.

1. Open the MultiTouchSample solution in Expression Blend 4.
2. In MainPage.xaml, right-click `LayoutRoot` in the Objects and Timeline panel and select Change Layout Type, Canvas from the context menu. The parent element for the transformed element is expected to be a `Canvas` panel.
3. Add a red `Rectangle` to the `Canvas`.
4. Open the Assets library and locate the `MultiTouchBehavior` in the Behaviors category. Drag and drop it on the red rectangle, either on the screen or in the Objects and Timeline panel.
5. With the behavior selected in the Objects and Timeline panel, check the Properties panel. You can select to enable scaling, rotation, translating, and/or inertia.
6. Run the application on a multitouch computer. Using one finger, you can translate the `Rectangle` on the screen. Using two fingers, you can rotate and scale it. Finally, note the effect of inertia: You can “throw” the `Rectangle` like you would a real object on a plane surface.

The multitouch behavior is a work in progress, and at the time of this writing it is going through changes. The bottom line is that in the current state of the affairs, multitouch is quite complex to use in Silverlight 4 because it is very low level, and that abstraction libraries are offering a welcomed help. Also, because the code is open source, you can learn a lot from browsing through the source on CodePlex.

Using Multitouch in Windows Phone 7 Applications

Ironically, even though Windows Phone 7 is based on Silverlight 3, the support for multi-touch in this framework is better than in Silverlight 4. This is in fact not surprising, considering that multitouch will be the main input mechanism on the phone, while it is still marginal for Silverlight applications on the desktop.

In Windows Phone 7, high-level multitouch manipulations are handled by using the `UIElement.ManipulationStarted`, `UIElement.ManipulationDelta`, and `UIElement.ManipulationCompleted` events. `ManipulationDelta` has all information you need to translate and scale a `UIElement`, using the `TranslateX`, `TranslateY`, `ScaleX`, and `ScaleY` properties of the `ManipulationDeltaEventArgs` class. Note, however, that manipulation events handle only scale and translate manipulations at this time and that inertia is not supported. For more advanced manipulations, using `Touch.FrameReported` is needed, or else downloading the multitouch behavior for Windows Phone 7 from CodePlex (http://multitouch.codeplex.com/).

Finding More Information

For more information about multitouch in Silverlight (and other technologies), Joshua Blake has a video presentation about NUI at http://www.galasoft.ch/sl4-joshnui, and is working on a book titled *Multitouch on Windows (NUI development with WPF and Silverlight)* that will be published at Manning in the end of 2010. This should be a great resource to dive much deeper into the wonderful world of the natural user interface.

Enabling Local Communication

There are multiple scenarios in which it is beneficial to have two Silverlight applications running on the same computer communicating together. In early versions of Silverlight, there were only very few options:

- Sending a message through the web server. The receiving application had to poll the server or use duplex polling until the message was sent by the sending application.
- (Only when both Silverlight applications run on the same web page) Using the HTML Bridge to communicate through JavaScript.

Neither solution was really satisfying. Thankfully, this is not an issue anymore, with the introduction of local messaging.

Understanding the Restrictions

Before a sample is implemented, it is necessary to talk about restrictions for this feature:

- Only `string` messages can be sent. Of course, this can be a serialization (in XML, JSON or any other protocol) of an object.
- The sent message can only be 40KB in size.
- A Silverlight application running in HTTP cannot send a message to an application running in HTTPS (or vice versa).

For most scenarios, these restrictions are not an issue, and it is fairly easy to enable local messaging, as you will see in the following sample.

Building a Receiver

The local messaging system uses a sender and a receiver and enables a one-to-one or one-to-many communication system. It is a targeted system, meaning that messages are sent and received with an identifier. Applications can register for local messages (sent from an application running in one network domain such as www.mydomain.com to another application running in the same domain) or global messages (sent from applications in any domain). Follow these steps:

1. Create a new Silverlight application in Visual Studio and name it **MessagingReceiver**.
2. Modify MainPage.xaml's `LayoutRoot` to look as shown in Listing 19.15.

LISTING 19.15 Receiver's User Interface

```
<StackPanel x:Name="LayoutRoot" Background="Red">
    <TextBlock TextWrapping="Wrap"
               Text="- no message yet -"
               x:Name="MessageTextBlock"
               Margin="20"/>
</StackPanel>
```

3. Then, modify MainPage.xaml.cs as shown in Listing 19.16.

LISTING 19.16 Subscribing and Receiving a Message

```
1  public MainPage()
2  {
3      var receiver = new LocalMessageReceiver(
4          "MessagingApplication2",
5          ReceiverNameScope.Global,
6          LocalMessageReceiver.AnyDomain);
7
```

```
 8         receiver.MessageReceived += receiver_MessageReceived;
 9         receiver.Listen();
10
11         InitializeComponent();
12     }
13
14     void receiver_MessageReceived(object sender, MessageReceivedEventArgs e)
15     {
16         MessageTextBlock.Text = e.Message;
17
18         e.Response = "Message received, thanks!";
19     }
```

- On lines 3 to 6, a `LocalMessageReceiver` instance is created. There are two overloads for this constructor, one allowing to receive local messages only (same network domain) and this one allowing to receive global messages (any domain).
- Line 8 subscribes to the `MessageReceived` event with an event handler defined on lines 14 to 19.
- Line 9 starts listening to messages.
- In the `MessageReceived` event handler, the message received is read on line 16. Optionally, a `Response` can be sent back to the sender with the code on line 18.

WARNING

Registering in the Global Namescope

When registering for global messages, the identifier used must be unique. In Listing 19.16, if another unrelated application registers with the identifier MessagingApplication2, an exception will be thrown. Keep that in mind when using global identifiers!

Building a Sender

The sender in this messaging system is equally easy to build, as follows:

1. Create another Silverlight application and name it MessagingSender. Because it is a separate solution in Visual Studio, running it in debug mode will use a separate domain name (for example, http://localhost:12345 versus http://localhost:98765). Silverlight considers these two domains to be unrelated, which is why the global namescope must be used here.
2. Modify MainPage.xaml's `LayoutRoot` as shown in Listing 19.17.

LISTING 19.17 Markup for the Receiver

```
<StackPanel x:Name="LayoutRoot"
            Background="Blue">
    <TextBox x:Name="SendingMessageTextBox"
             Text="Enter a message"
             TextWrapping="Wrap"
             Margin="20"
```

```
            Height="300" />

    <Button Content="Send"
            Click="SendClick"
            Margin="20" />

    <TextBlock TextWrapping="Wrap"
               Text="- no message yet -"
               x:Name="MessageTextBlock"
               Margin="20" />
</StackPanel>
```

3. Implement the sender in MainPage.xaml.cs as shown in Listing 19.18.

LISTING 19.18 Sending a Message

```
 1  private LocalMessageSender _sender;
 2
 3  public MainPage()
 4  {
 5      _sender = new LocalMessageSender(
 6          "MessagingApplication2",
 7          LocalMessageSender.Global);
 8      _sender.SendCompleted += _sender_SendCompleted;
 9
10      InitializeComponent();
11  }
12
13  void _sender_SendCompleted(object sender, SendCompletedEventArgs e)
14  {
15      if (e.Error != null)
16      {
17          MessageTextBlock.Text = e.Error.Message;
18          return;
19      }
20
21      if (!string.IsNullOrEmpty(e.Response))
22      {
23          MessageTextBlock.Text = e.Response;
24          return;
25      }
26
27      MessageTextBlock.Text = "Message sent";
28  }
29
30  private void SendClick(object sender, RoutedEventArgs e)
```

```
31  {
32       _sender.SendAsync(SendingMessageTextBox.Text);
33  }
```

- Line 1 declares a `LocalMessageSender`, the counterpart to the `LocalMessageReceiver` that we saw before.
- Lines 5 to 8 create a new instance with the same identifier in the global namescope as the receiver we built in the previous section. Then, an event handler is registered for the `SendCompleted` event. This is optional, but recommended to handle errors when sending the message, and also to receive the optional `Response`.
- Lines 15 to 19 handle errors, for example, what happens if no suitable receiver is found.
- Lines 21 to 25 handle the `Response`, which is a `string`.
- Finally, lines 30 to 33 send the message in an asynchronous manner.

Testing the Application

To test the application, run the sender first and click the button. An error message should appear, because no suitable receiver is found. Then, without stopping the sender, run the receiver and send the message again. This time the message appears in the receiver's window, and the response is shown in the sender's window. You can change the message and send again.

Sending and receiving messages works between applications running out of the browser, too, which provides a possible solution to some scenarios where multiple windows are needed. This is, of course, not as convenient as the possibility to open another window programmatically (as in WPF, for example), but is nonetheless good to keep in mind. Generally speaking, the messaging system is very useful to build distributed applications.

Mapping with the Bing Maps Control

Many applications nowadays can benefit from embedding geographical maps in their user interface: calculating driving routes, setting markers to pinpoint a location, showing a venue, and so forth. The Bing Maps team made this extremely easy by offering a free Silverlight control that can easily be added to any Silverlight application. There are samples available online, with a good starting point at http://www.galasoft.ch/sl4-maps. This section shows how to download and install the control, and how to create a very simple application with the following steps:

1. Before you start, it is necessary to register with the Bing Maps portal. Follow the instructions at http://www.galasoft.ch/sl4-bingmapsportal.
2. Download the Silverlight Bing Maps control from http://www.galasoft.ch/sl4-mapsdownload. Then run the MSI file.

The last step installs the binaries and documentation on your computer.

Adding the Map

Adding the map in XAML is very straightforward with the following steps:

1. Create a new Silverlight application named BingMapsSample. Note that the application must be hosted in a web application, to avoid cross-schema issues (from file protocol to HTTP).
2. Set the BingMapsSample.Web application as Startup and the BingMapsSampleTestPage.html as Startup page.
3. Right-click the Silverlight application's References folder in the Solution Explorer and add a reference to the Bing Maps DLLs that you installed in Step 2. These are Microsoft.Maps.MapControl.dll and Microsoft.Maps.MapControl.Common.dll and can be found in C:\Program Files\Bing Maps Silverlight Control\V1\Libraries. On Windows 64 bits, the folder is in Program Files (x86).
4. Open MainPage.xaml and add an `xmlns` prefix as shown in Listing 19.19.

LISTING 19.19 Adding an xmlns Prefix

```
xmlns:bing="clr-namespace:Microsoft.Maps.MapControl;assembly=Microsoft.Maps.MapCon-
trol"
```

5. Add the markup shown in Listing 19.20 within the `LayoutRoot`. Make sure that you replace the `YourAppIdHere` text with the ID you got from the Bing portal at Step 1.

LISTING 19.20 Adding a Map Control

```
<bing:Map CredentialsProvider="YourAppIdHere"
          x:Name="MyMap"/>
```

6. Run the application. You should see the Bing Maps control as shown in Figure 19.10.

The map control has a few built-in features that are very nice:

- Toggle between Road and Aerial (satellite) view
- Seamless zoom with the controls or with the mouse wheel
- Pan the map using the mouse

FIGURE 19.10 Bing Maps control.

Getting Location Information and Marking It

Interaction with the user is also possible (for example, getting a mouse click, adding a marker, and displaying location information), with the following steps:

1. Modify the MainPage.xaml.cs code as shown in Listing 19.21.

LISTING 19.21 Getting a Mouse Click and Adding Information

```
1  private readonly MapLayer _mapLayer;
2
3  public MainPage()
4  {
5      InitializeComponent();
6      _mapLayer = new MapLayer();
7      MyMap.Children.Add(_mapLayer);
8      MyMap.MouseClick += MapClick;
9  }
10
11 private void MapClick(
12     object sender,
13     Microsoft.Maps.MapControl.MapMouseEventArgs e)
14 {
```

19

```
15        var location = MyMap.ViewportPointToLocation(
16            e.ViewportPoint);
17
18        var marker = new Ellipse
19        {
20            Fill = new SolidColorBrush(Colors.Red),
21            Height = 10,
22            Width = 10,
23        };
24
25        var ToolTipPanel = new StackPanel();
26
27        ToolTipPanel.Children.Add(new TextBlock
28        {
29            Text = "Lat: " + location.Latitude
30        });
31
32        ToolTipPanel.Children.Add(new TextBlock
33        {
34            Text = "Lon: " + location.Longitude
35        });
36
37        ToolTipService.SetToolTip(
38            marker, ToolTipPanel);
39
40        var position = PositionOrigin.Center;
41        _mapLayer.AddChild(marker, location, position);
42    }
```

- Line 1 declares a layer that will be placed on top of the `Map` control. This is where you can draw any overlay. The `Map` control will take care of moving the markers as the map is zoomed or panned.
- This `MapLayer` is created and added to the `Map` on lines 6 and 7; a `Click` event handler is added on line 8.
- Lines 11 to 42 handle the `Click` event. First the `location` is retrieved on lines 15 and 16. This object has information about `Latitude` and `Longitude` at the mouse click.
- On lines 18 to 23, a new `Ellipse` is created. This will be a `marker` for the location.
- A `StackPanel` is created, and two `TextBlock` elements added to it on lines 25 to 35. The `TextBlock` elements display the `Latitude` and `Longitude`.

- The `StackPanel` is passed to the `ToolTipService`, a class that is in charge of displaying ToolTips when the mouse is passed over an element (in this case, the `marker` `Ellipse`).
- Finally, the `marker` is added to the `MapLayer` on lines 40 and 41.

Run the application, zoom and move to a location, and then click the map. A marker is displayed. Passing the mouse over it will show the location information.

Getting More Information

This small sample does not do justice to the Silverlight Bing Maps control, which has many more features. For more information, check the tutorials and documentation available at http://www.galasoft.ch/sl4-maps.

Summary

This chapter was the third of a series with a collection of features that are not large enough to fill a whole chapter but very important to help you enhance your Silverlight applications with advanced functionality. From authenticating your users to using the Bing Maps control, this chapter also showed how to bind any event to a command when using a loosely coupled architecture, build random animations that are more lifelike and less predictable, use multitouch in Silverlight, and enable local messaging between Silverlight applications. All these features come handy and represent a big progress to make Silverlight, a very rich application development platform.

In the next chapter, we talk about frameworks that help to build extensible Silverlight applications according to modern development techniques and architecture.

CHAPTER 20

Building Extensible and Maintainable Applications

IN THIS CHAPTER, WE WILL:

- Talk about frameworks allowing you to build applications that can easily be extended and maintained.
- Explain what dependency inversion is and use the Unity framework to build samples.
- Use the Managed Extensibility Framework MEF to split an application in components.
- Download XAP files on demand to enhance the user experience at startup and make it easy to add new functionalities in existing applications.
- Talk about the MVVM Light Toolkit, a framework making it easier to build decoupled applications.

In this chapter, we investigate three frameworks for Silverlight available at no cost and that allow building loosely coupled applications that are easy to maintain and extend:

- **Unity by Microsoft Patterns and Practices**: This dependency injection (DI) container allows building decoupled applications by providing a way to construct and retrieve objects according to certain criteria.
- **Managed Extensibility Framework (MEF)**: Used to extend and compose applications, this framework is relatively easy to use and quite lightweight. It is in fact part of the Silverlight SDK.
- **MVVM Light Toolkit**: We already used parts of this toolkit in previous chapters to build Silverlight applications according to the Model-View-ViewModel pattern.

Inverting Dependencies with Unity

Modern applications are often object oriented, and can be composed of a multitude of classes. Organizing them can get very confusing and lead to code that is impossible to maintain, modify, or test. To bring clarity, techniques and patterns were developed by software developers over the years. There are many discussions about the best way to implement a solution, and things are evolving constantly.

In this quest, people from the open source community such as Robert C. "Uncle Bob" Martin proposed a series of principles called SOLID. You can find more information about these five principles on Uncle Bob's website at http://www.galasoft.ch/sl4-solid.

The last letter of the acronym stands for dependency inversion. This principle recommends a cleaner implementation of complex classes by externalizing some of their tasks to other objects (low level components) that are then injected into higher level components. In addition, it recommends abstracting the low level components to avoid depending on a concrete implementation that would make it hard to use the high level component in another context.

One possible implementation of the dependency inversion principle is by using dependency injection (DI). For example, consider the code in Listing 20.1.

LISTING 20.1 View-Model Without Dependency Injection

```
 1 public class ViewModelWithoutDependencyInjection
 2 {
 3     public string ServiceAddressUri { get; set; }
 4     public ObservableCollection<Item> Items
 5     {
 6         get; private set;
 7     }
 8
 9     public ViewModelWithoutDependencyInjection()
10     {
11         Items = new ObservableCollection<Item>();
12         if (DesignerProperties.IsInDesignTool)
13         {
14             for (var index = 0; index < 100; index++)
15             {
16                 Items.Add(new Item());
17             }
18         }
19         else
20         {
21             var client = new WebClient();
22             client.DownloadStringCompleted += ClientDownloadStringCompleted;
23             client.DownloadStringAsync(new Uri(ServiceAddressUri));
24         }
25     }
26
27     private void ClientDownloadStringCompleted(
28         object sender,
29         DownloadStringCompletedEventArgs e)
30     {
```

```
31          Items = new ObservableCollection<Item>(ParseResult(e.Result));
32      }
33
34      private IEnumerable<Item> ParseResult(string serial)
35      {
36          var result = new List<Item>();
37          // Parse the result and return items
38          return result.AsEnumerable<Item>();
39      }
40 }
```

- Lines 14 to 16 create 100 "design-time items" and fill them into the `Items` `ObservableCollection`.
- Lines 21 to 23 are executed in "runtime mode" and connect to a web service.
- Lines 27 to 32 handle the `WebClient`'s `Completed` event, and parse the result using the `ParseResult` method defined on lines 34 to 39.

This class is not very complex, but already we see some issues:

- The class needs to know whether it is running in design or runtime mode.
- It needs to connect to a web service, and know how to parse the result. If the format used by the web service changes, the view-model class also needs to be updated.
- It is not easy to test because one single class handles too many scenarios. It is not a "single responsibility class" as recommended by the *S* in SOLID.

Developing this kind of "almighty objects" is a sure recipe for headaches later. When the developer comes back to the class a few weeks (or months or years) later, it is really hard to remember and understand everything that the class is doing.

Refactoring to Smaller and Simpler Classes

A better way is to decouple the dependencies by introducing abstraction in the application to help to extend the application later. We create smaller, more compact classes that fulfill one single role.

Defining a Contract

An interface is defined for a service in charge of getting the `Item` instances. Having an interface-based dependency decouples the objects. This is a contract expressing *what* the service can do, but not *how* it does it. We already mentioned these advantages in Chapter 7, "Understanding the Model-View-ViewModel Pattern." The `IDataService` is shown in Listing 20.2.

LISTING 20.2 IDataService Interface

```
public interface IDataService
{
    void GetItems(Action<IEnumerable<Item>> callback);
}
```

Because web communication in Silverlight is asynchronous, the `GetItems` method takes a *callback* that should be stored and executed later, when the web service sends the response. Thanks to the `Action` generic class, asynchronous programming is much easier than it used to be.

Injecting the Service

With these preparations, the view-model can be refactored to Listing 20.3. It does not need to know any more whether it is running in design or runtime mode; instead it gets a service whose interface is well known. Note also that we can build the view-model before the services are even built. All we know is the contract. This is beneficial when different teams work on different parts of the application.

LISTING 20.3 Injecting the Service

```
 1  public class ViewModelWithDependencyInjection
 2  {
 3      public ObservableCollection<Item> Items
 4      {
 5          get;
 6          private set;
 7      }
 8
 9      public ViewModelWithDependencyInjection(IDataService service)
10      {
11          service.GetItems(items =>
12          {
13              Items = new ObservableCollection<Item>(items);
14          });
15      }
16  }
```

- On line 9, the constructor now takes one parameter, of type `IDataService`. This is the *dependency injection* that we are talking about: The dependency on the functionality (getting the items) is not embedded within the view-model class anymore, it is injected into it.

Implementing for the Runtime

To get the actual items from the web service at runtime, the `DataService` class implements the `IDataService` interface as shown in Listing 20.4.

LISTING 20.4 DataService Implementation

```
public class DataService : IDataService
{
    public string ServiceAddressUri { get; set; }

    public void GetItems(Action<IEnumerable<Item>> callback)
    {
        var client = new WebClient();
        client.DownloadStringCompleted += ClientDownloadStringCompleted;
        client.DownloadStringAsync(new Uri(ServiceAddressUri), callback);
    }

    private void ClientDownloadStringCompleted(
        object sender,
        DownloadStringCompletedEventArgs e)
    {
        var callback = e.UserState as Action<IEnumerable<Item>>;
        callback(ParseResult(e.Result));
    }

    private IEnumerable<Item> ParseResult(string serial)
    {
        var result = new List<Item>();
        // Parse the result and return items
        return result.AsEnumerable<Item>();
    }
}
```

The DataService class is the most complex of the application. It does, however, only one single thing: It connects to the asynchronous web service and handles the result. This functionality can be tested extensively using automated tests, and it is easy to make sure that all the scenarios are working as they should.

Creating Another Implementation for Design Time

Because the interface introduces a neat separation between the consumer of the service and its provider, it is easy to isolate the design-time code in a separate class. In fact, with a little more work it would even be possible to move all design-time code to a separate assembly that is not shipped with the production application. The design time implementation is shown in Listing 20.5.

LISTING 20.5 DesignDataService Class

```
public class DesignDataService : IDataService
{
    public void GetItems(Action<IEnumerable<Item>> callback)
    {
```

```
        var items = new List<Item>();
        for (var index = 0; index < 100; index++)
        {
            items.Add(new Item
            {
                Message = "Dummy item #" + index
            });
        }
        return items.AsEnumerable<Item>();
    }
}
```

This class has the same `GetItems` method (as specified by the `IDataService` interface), but provides a very different implementation.

Using Other Implementations and Other Services

If needed, it is possible to create other implementations (for example, an implementation of `IDataService` used only when the view-model must be tested). In that case, the `TestDataService` class should offer the possibility to create different scenarios (for example, simulating offline mode or returning an empty list of `Item` instances).

Following this design makes it easy to identify, understand, and maintain service classes, each with a well-defined functionality.

Setting Up the Services

Listing 20.3 shows a view-model with an injected service. However, nothing shows who is injecting that service into the constructor. In applications, the creation of objects is typically handled ad hoc, where it is needed. It is difficult to create the objects in a consistent manner, taking in account all the dependencies. Also difficult is the *resolving* of the objects (that is, finding the right object to use its methods).

To solve these issues, the concept of *dependency injection container* (sometimes also called *inversion of control (IOC) container*) was developed. In short, it is a framework that handles the creation of objects and that acts as a registry to serve these objects to consumers. There are multiple dependency injection containers available as open source, such as the following:

- **NInject** (http://ninject.org), an open source project that is available for Windows Presentation Foundation (WPF), Silverlight, and recently for the Windows Phone 7.
- **CastleWindsor** (http://www.galasoft.ch/sl4-windsor) is a widely used IOC container.
- **StructureMap** (http://www.galasoft.ch/sl4-structuremap), another open source project that offers the basic functionality of a DI container plus a lot of additional features. StructureMap is best suited for large and complex applications.
- **Unity** (http://unity.codeplex.com) developed by Microsoft's Patterns and Practices group, which is lightweight and extensible.

There are also other DI containers available for Silverlight. The four mentioned here are probably the most used ones at the time of this writing.

Installing Unity

In this sample, the Unity DI container is used to show the principles of DI. A typical DI container works in two steps: setting up the objects and then resolving the objects. Let's see how to do that with Unity with the following steps:

1. Navigate to http://www.galasoft.ch/sl4-unityload and download the Unity 2.0 for Silverlight installer (an MSI file) from the Download section. Unity is distributed under the MS-PL license, which is very permissive. You are free to reuse, distribute, and modify the code as you want. The complete text of the MS-PL license can be found at http://www.galasoft.ch/sl4-mspl.

> **WARNING**
>
> **Using the Silverlight Version of Unity**
>
> The documentation available for Unity online often refers to the full .NET version, and not to the Silverlight version. Some features (such as XML-based configuration) are not available in the Silverlight version. Do not get confused!

2. Execute the MSI to install Unity.
3. Download the WhyDependencyInjection application's start state from http://www.galasoft.ch/sl4-whydi. Excerpts from this application are shown in listings 20.2 to 20.5. After the zip file is downloaded, unblock it by right-clicking it in Windows Explorer, selecting Properties, and clicking the Unblock button (if available). Then, extract all the files on your hard drive.
4. Start the WhyDependencyInjection.sln file in Visual Studio 2010.
5. Right-click the References folder and select Add Reference from the context menu.
6. In the Add Reference dialog, select the Browse tab and find the folder C:\Program Files\Microsoft Unity Application Block 2.0 for Silverlight\Bin. On Win64 machines, this folder is in Program Files (x86).
7. Select the DLL named Microsoft.Practices.Unity.Silverlight.dll and click OK.

Setting Up the Container

The DI container must be configured to know which object to return when certain conditions are met. We can setup the container within our `ViewModelLocator` class with the following steps:

1. In the folder ViewModel, open the file named ViewModelLocator.cs.
2. In the ViewModelLocator.cs file, add a `using` directive to the namespace `Microsoft.Practices.Unity` at the top of the page.
3. Modify the `ViewModelLocator` class as shown in Listing 20.6.

LISTING 20.6 `ViewModelLocator` Class

```
1  public class ViewModelLocator
2  {
3      public static IUnityContainer Container
4      {
5           get; private set;
6      }
7
8      public static void Setup()
9      {
10         if (Container != null)
11         {
12             // Setup already done
13             return;
14         }
15
16         Container = new UnityContainer();
17
18         // Setup the service
19         if (DesignerProperties.IsInDesignTool)
20         {
21             Container.RegisterType<IDataService, DesignDataService>();
22         }
23         else
24         {
25             Container.RegisterType<IDataService, DataService>();
26         }
27
28         // Setup the viewmodel
29         Container.RegisterType<ViewModelWithDependencyInjection>(
30             new ContainerControlledLifetimeManager());
31     }
32
33     public ViewModelWithDependencyInjection Main
34     {
35         get
36         {
37             return Container.Resolve<ViewModelWithDependencyInjection>();
38         }
39     }
40 }
```

- Lines 3 to 6 declare a `Container` of type `IUnityContainer`.
- Lines 8 to 31 perform the `Setup` operation. This method must be called once when the application starts. We will take care of that later in this chapter.

- Line 16 creates the new `UnityContainer` instance. This class implements the `IUnityContainer` interface.
- Line 21 is executed if the application is running in design mode (in Expression Blend or Visual Studio designer). It registers the concrete type `DesignDataService` for the interface `IDataService`. This instructs the `Container` to create and return an instance of `DesignDataService` every time that the `IDataService` interface is specified in the code.
- Line 25 registers the concrete type `DataService` for the same interface. This will happen at runtime.
- Lines 29 and 30 register the view-model type. Note that we do not use an interface here, because it is not strictly speaking necessary to abstract this simple viewmodel class.
- Line 37 *resolves* the instance of the `ViewModelWithDependencyInjection` class. To facilitate the work in Expression Blend, this instance is exposed through the `Main` property.

TIP

Using a Generic ViewModelLocator

It would be nicer to use a generic `ViewModelLocator` instead of declaring one property per view-model type. There is a lot of discussion and research going on in the programmer community around this topic. The most promising approach is one using indexers to resolve the view-model according to a key, in a generic manner. There is a bug in Silverlight 4 making this method cumbersome, as explained by John Papa (Silverlight evangelist) at http://www.galasoft.ch/sl4-vml. Also, some blendability is lost because Blend cannot display properties for the indexed view-models.

4. In MainPage.xaml, set the `DataContext` of the root `UserControl` to a data binding as shown in Listing 20.7. The `ViewModelLocator` is already available as a global resource (named `Locator`) in the file App.xaml.

LISTING 20.7 Setting the `DataContext`

```
DataContext="{Binding Source={StaticResource Locator}, Path=Main}"
```


Using a Lifetime Manager

Notice that line 30 of Listing 20.6 passes a new `ContainerControlledLifetimeManager` instance to the `Container`'s `RegisterType` method. This special class handles the lifetime of the `ViewModelWithDependencyInjection` instance. There are multiple lifetime managers available in Unity, such as the following (nonexhaustive list):

- TransientLifetimeManager: Instructs the Container to return a different instance of the registered object every time that Resolve is called. This is the default lifetime manager, and the one that is used when RegisterType is called without arguments.
- ContainerControlledLifetimeManager: Instructs the Container to register an object as a singleton instance. The same instance will always be returned when the Resolve method is called.
- ExternallyControlledLifetimeManager: Provides a way for external classes to control the object's lifetime.
- PerThreadLifetimeManager: Instructs the Container to return the same instance of the registered object every time that Resolve is called, within the same thread. Within another thread, another instance will be used. This lifetime manager can be especially useful to avoid cross-thread access exceptions. You'll learn more about these exceptions in Chapter 22, "Advanced Development Techniques."

Other Ways to Register

In addition to the RegisterType method used in Listing 20.6, it is possible to use the RegisterInstance method. This is useful when you already have an instance of the given type that was created somewhere else in the application, and you want to pass it to the Container so that consumers can resolve it.

Calling the Setup Method and Wiring Up

The application is now ready to call the ViewModelLocator's Setup method. This can be done as follows:

1. In ViewModelLocator.cs, add a static constructor as shown in Listing 20.8.

LISTING 20.8 Calling Setup

```
static ViewModelLocator()
{
    Setup();
}
```

2. Open MainPage.xaml and add a ListBox to the LayoutRoot Grid as shown in Listing 20.9.

LISTING 20.9 Adding a ListBox

```
<Grid x:Name="LayoutRoot"
        Background="White">
    <ListBox Margin="10"
                ItemsSource="{Binding Items}">
        <ListBox.ItemTemplate>
```

```
            <DataTemplate>
                <TextBlock Text="{Binding Message}" />
            </DataTemplate>
        </ListBox.ItemTemplate>
    </ListBox>
</Grid>
```

Run the application to test it. After a short wait (due to the asynchronous loading of a text file from the Internet, the parsing and populating of the `Items` collection), a series of words appear in the `ListBox`.

Testing in Blend

Thanks to the way that the view-model is set up in resources within the `ViewModelLocator`, and thanks to the `DesignDataService` class, design-time data can be seen in Expression Blend, making the work of the designer much easier. You can verify this by right-clicking the MainPage.xaml in the Visual Studio Solution Explorer and choosing Open in Blend from the context menu. The `ListBox` appears populated.

Discovering More About Unity

Unity has other interesting features, too, such as the following:

- The ability to register child containers to create a hierarchy of containers if needed
- Wiring up existing objects by using the `BuildUp` method
- Cleaning up existing objects by using the `Teardown` method
- And more

For more information about Unity and its features, start on the Codeplex site at http://unity.codeplex.com.

DI is a very useful mechanism to simplify the lifetime management of complex applications. In this section, we talked about the Unity DI container created by the Microsoft Patterns and Practices group, but this is not the only DI container. Make sure to do some research before you pick the best suited DI container for your needs!

Composing an Application with MEF

The Managed Extensibility Framework (MEF) is an effort from Microsoft similar to the Unity DI container. The goal of this innovative framework is to facilitate the composition of applications to make them extensible. This was developed in the first place to help the Visual Studio team with their task of rewriting parts of Visual Studio 2010 in Windows Presentation. MEF is not just for large applications like Studio, however, but also brings a lot of values to smaller WPF or Silverlight applications.

One interesting feature of MEF is the possibility to automatically discover components without needing a central object to do the setup, such as the `ViewModelLocator` class we implemented in the section about Unity. Instead, the information is passed to MEF using attributes.

Another great feature of MEF, especially when it comes to Silverlight, is the ability to download parts of the application on demand. Instead of packing all the components in a large XAP file that takes a long time to download, the user can load a basic framework first; then the application will download parts on demand and make them available to the user.

Exporting and Importing

Although MEF can be used to replace (at least partly) a DI container, it does not exactly work the same way, as shown at http://www.galasoft.ch/sl4-mefioc. MEF relies on an export/import mechanism, where exports are services that a component offers, and imports are services that a component consumes.

Using a Simple Export

To witness a simple export/import, follow these steps:

1. Create a new Silverlight application and name it **MefSample**.
2. Right-click the References folder, select Add Reference, and then select the .NET tab.
3. Select the two DLLs named System.ComponentModel.Composition and System.ComponentModel.Composition.Initialization, and then click OK.
4. Right-click the Silverlight project and select Add, Class from the context menu. Name the new file **IMessageService.cs**.
5. Implement `IMessageService` as shown in Listing 20.10.

LISTING 20.10 `IMessageService` Interface

```
public interface IMessageService
{
    void ShowMessage(string message);
}
```

6. Add a new class to the project and name it **MessageService.cs**. Its implementation is shown in Listing 20.11.

LISTING 20.11 `MessageService` Class

```
1  [Export(typeof(IMessageService))]
2  public class MessageService : IMessageService
3  {
4      public void ShowMessage(string message)
```

```
5         {
6             MessageBox.Show(message);
7         }
8     }
```

7. Modify the MainPage class as in Listing 20.12.

LISTING 20.12 Importing the Service

```
1  public partial class MainPage : UserControl
2  {
3      [Import]
4      public IMessageService MyMessageService
5      {
6          get;
7          set;
8      }
9
10     public MainPage()
11     {
12         CompositionInitializer.SatisfyImports(this);
13         InitializeComponent();
14         MyMessageService.ShowMessage("Page is created");
15     }
16 }
```

8. Run the application. The MessageBox should appear.

This small sample shows the heart of MEF: the import/export system. There are three important components:

- Line 1 in Listing 20.11 defines that the MessageService class is an import for the IMessageService interface. This is roughly equivalent to the way that we registered types in Unity in the previous section of this chapter.
- Lines 3 to 8 in Listing 20.12 declare a property of type IMessageService and specify that it must be imported.
- Line 12 in the MainPage constructor (Listing 20.12) composes the parts by calling the CompositionInitializer.SatisfyImports method.

When the CompositionInitializer is called, it searches all the referenced assemblies for parts that satisfy the import specification. In this case, it finds the MessageService class and calls the constructor on it.

Refactoring in Multiple Assemblies

The interesting thing is that it does not matter where the classes are located, as shown with the following steps:

1. Right-click the MefSample solution in the Solution Explorer and add a new project.
2. In the Add New Project dialog, select a Silverlight class library and name it **MefSample.Services**. Then click OK.
3. In MefSample.Services, delete the file Class1.cs.
4. Right-click the References folder of the MefSample.Services project and select Add Reference.
5. In the .NET tab, select the DLL System.ComponentModel.Composition.
6. Copy the MessageService.cs and IMessageService.cs files from MefSample to MefSample.Services. (You can just drag them in the Solution Explorer.) Then delete these two files in the MefSample project.
7. In MefSample, right-click the References folder and select Add Reference.
8. Select the Projects tab and add the MefSample.Services project to the references.

Run the application and see how the `MessageBox` appears again. Of course having the service in its own assembly barely makes sense for such a small application, but consider that the assemblies are now cleanly sorted according to their functionality. It is possible to have different teams working on each project without interference. Also, we didn't have to change the client application; the import/export mechanism works in exactly the same way.

Composing with Constructor Parameters

In the MefSample application, the default constructor of the `MessageService` class is called. This is very limiting; instead, it is possible to define a constructor with parameters. For instance, imagine that you have somewhere in the application a `Logger` class, implementing an `ILogger` interface and being exported (just like we export the `MessageService` class). This `Logger` can be passed to the `MessageService` constructor with the following steps:

1. With the MefSample application open in Visual Studio, edit the `MessageService` class as shown in Listing 20.13.

LISTING 20.13 Adding a Constructor to the `MessageService` Class

```
1  [Export(typeof(IMessageService))]
2  public class MessageService : IMessageService
3  {
4      private ILogger _logger;
5
6      [ImportingConstructor]
```

```
7       public MessageService(ILogger logger)
8       {
9           _logger = logger;
10      }
11
12      public void ShowMessage(string message)
13      {
14          MessageBox.Show(message);
15          _logger.Log(message);
16      }
17  }
```

- Lines 6 to 10 define the new constructor and mark it as the constructor to be used when importing this type. The class can have multiple constructors, but only one can be used for the import.
- On line 7, notice the parameter of type `ILogger`. When MEF composes the parts, it will check whether such a class is available for this contract in the catalog of exports.

2. Modify the `MainPage` constructor as shown in Listing 20.14.

LISTING 20.14 Using a Constructor with Parameters

```
1   public MainPage()
2   {
3       var catalog = new AssemblyCatalog(
4           typeof(IMessageService).Assembly);
5       var container = new CompositionContainer(catalog);
6       container.ComposeExportedValue(new Logger());
7       container.ComposeParts(this);
8
9       InitializeComponent();
10      MyMessageService.ShowMessage("Page is created");
11  }
```

- Lines 3 and 4 create an `AssemblyCatalog` that will be used to scan the assembly in which `IMessageService` is defined. (This is the MefSample.Services assembly.)
- Line 5 creates a new `CompositionContainer` for this assembly.
- Line 6 adds a `Logger` to the catalog of exports. This will be passed to the `logger` parameter in the `MessageService` constructor.
- Finally, line 7 composes the parts.

This way of doing is more flexible but also more complex. In fact, the `CompositionInitializer.SatisfyImport` is a shortcut that can be used for simple cases.

There are multiple kinds of catalogs, each able to scan different sources to get the classes corresponding to a given `Import` attribute: `AssemblyCatalog` scans an assembly; `DeploymentCatalog` (that we will use in the "Downloading on Demand" section) can download content from the web server; `AggregateCatalog` combines multiple catalogs; and more. Finally, should the built-in classes not be sufficient, you can also create your own catalog and container class.

Composing a Hierarchy of Objects

It is very common that an imported object also needs to import other objects. MEF can take care of this scenario quite easily, as shown with the following steps:

1. Download the MefHierarchy-Start.zip file from http://www.galasoft.ch/sl4-mef. Unblock it by right-clicking it, selecting file properties, and clicking the Unblock button (if available). Then, extract the files.
2. In this folder, open the MefHierarchy.sln solution in Visual Studio 2010.
3. The solution is similar to the application built before with Unity, but not exactly. For example, there is no setup in the `ViewModelLocator`, because MEF will take care of that.
4. The `DataService` is now an abstract class. We will see in a moment why. A concrete class deriving from `DataService` (which in turn implements the `IDataService` interface) is needed. Add a class to the ViewModel folder and name is **MorningDataService.cs**.
5. Implement the `MorningDataService` class as shown in Listing 20.15. It is essentially there just to provide the URI leading to a text file. The rest of the functionality is implemented in the abstract class `DataService`. `MorningDataService` is also marked as an `Export` for the `IDataService` interface.

LISTING 20.15 MorningDataService Class

```
[Export(typeof(IDataService))]
public class MorningDataService : DataService
{
    public override string ServiceAddressUri
    {
        get
        {
            return "http://www.galasoft.ch/sl4u/Code/Chapter20/sampleam.txt";
        }
    }
}
```

6. Open ViewModelWithMef.cs and add an Export attribute to this class, as shown in Listing 20.16.

LISTING 20.16 Adding an Export Attribute

```
[Export(typeof(ViewModelWithMef))]
public class ViewModelWithMef : INotifyPropertyChanged
```

7. In the ViewModelWithMef class, import the data service with the property shown in Listing 20.17.

LISTING 20.17 Importing the IDataService

```
[Import]
public IDataService CurrentService
{
    get;
    set;
}
```

8. Implement the GetItems method shown in Listing 20.18.

LISTING 20.18 GetItems Method

```
public void GetItems()
{
    CurrentService.GetItems(items =>
    {
        Items = new ObservableCollection<Item>(items);
    });
}
```

9. Open the ViewModelLocator and modify it as shown in Listing 20.19. This class is responsible for composing all the parts and then calling the GetItems method on the ViewModelWithMef class.

LISTING 20.19 ViewModelLocator Class

```
public class ViewModelLocator
{
    [Import]
    public ViewModelWithMef Main
    {
        get;
        set;
```

```
        }

        public ViewModelLocator()
        {
            CompositionInitializer.SatisfyImports(this);
            Main.GetItems();
        }
    }
```

10. Run the application. The content of the file gets loaded and parsed and then displayed into a `ListBox`.

Contrary to what happened before in the Unity sample, all the exports and imports were parameterized within the classes. This is an advantage of MEF: The configuration is less complex and more distributed than with class DI containers. On the other hand, modifying the configuration requires modifying the exported class.

Another thing to note is that `CompositionInitializer.SatisfyImport` was called only once by the `ViewModelLocator`. The import within the `ViewModelWithMef` class (which needs to import an `IDataService`) is handled automatically by MEF.

Importing Multiple Instances

MEF also offers the possibility to import multiple concrete classes for a given contract. This is very useful if you are not sure at design time which class is going to be picked at runtime. The following steps use metadata to define conditions. A lazy instantiation mechanism is used. This means that the classes will be created in memory on demand, and only if needed. Follow these steps:

1. Add an interface to the Model folder and name it `IDataServiceInfo` as in Listing 20.20. This interface will be used to define metadata information about the service, and allow us to pick the correct one. It specifies that one `bool` property must be available, named `IsForTheMorning`.

LISTING 20.20 `IDataServiceInfo` Interface

```
public interface IDataServiceInfo
{
    bool IsForTheMorning
    {
        get;
    }
}
```

2. Add a new class to the Model folder and name it **AfternoonDataService**. The implementation is shown in Listing 20.21.

LISTING 20.21 AfternoonDataService Class

```
1  [Export(typeof(IDataService))]
2  [ExportMetadata("IsForTheMorning", false)]
3  public class AfternoonDataService : DataService
4  {
5      public override string ServiceAddressUri
6      {
7          get
8          {
9              return "http://www.galasoft.ch/sl4u/Code/Chapter20/samplepm.txt";
10         }
11     }
12 }
```

- On line 1, the Export attribute is specified. It uses the same contract (IDataService) as the MorningDataService class.
- The ExportMetadata attribute is specified on line 2. Note that this attribute uses a string to specify the name of the metadata to export (in this case, the IsForTheMorning property that the IDataServiceInfo interface specified). Working with strings is easy but dangerous because of the risk of typos. It is also possible to use a custom attribute instead, as shown at http://www.galasoft.ch/sl4-metadata.
- Finally, the ServiceAddressUri property returns a different path than in the MorningDataService class. (The filename is samplepm, whereas it was sampleam for the morning!)

3. Add an ExportMetadata attribute to the MorningDataService class, too, as shown in Listing 20.22. This time the IsForTheMorning metadata is set to true.

LISTING 20.22 MorningDataService Class

```
[Export(typeof(IDataService))]
[ExportMetadata("IsForTheMorning", true)]
public class MorningDataService : DataService
```

4. In the ViewModelWithMef class, remove the CurrentService property and instead add the code shown in Listing 20.23.

LISTING 20.23 Importing the Services

```
1  [ImportMany]
2  public Lazy<IDataService, IDataServiceInfo>[] Services
3  {
4      get;
5      set;
6  }
```

- Line 1 specifies the `ImportMany` attribute. This is used when multiple instances can be found for a given contract. Note that in consequence, the property is an array.
- On line 2, the type of the content of the array is set to `Lazy<IDataService, IDataServiceInfo>`. The advantage of using the `Lazy` generic class is that the `IDataService` instance that the `ViewModelWithMef` class needs will be created on demand. This way the memory consumption and the performance are optimized.

5. Because multiple services implement the contract now, the `ViewModelWithMef` class needs to decide which instance to use, according to the metadata. This can be done with the code in Listing 20.24, to be added to the `ViewModelWithMef` class.

LISTING 20.24 Getting the Right Data Service

```
1  private IDataService CurrentService
2  {
3      get
4      {
5          IDataService currentService = null;
6
7          foreach (var service in Services)
8          {
9              if (DateTime.Now.Hour < 12)
10             {
11                 if (service.Metadata.IsForTheMorning)
12                 {
13                     currentService = service.Value;
14                     break;
15                 }
16             }
17             else
18             {
19                 if (!service.Metadata.IsForTheMorning)
20                 {
21                     currentService = service.Value;
22                     break;
23                 }
24             }
25         }
26
27         return currentService;
28     }
29 }
```

- Lines 7 to 25 loop through all the imported services.

- On line 9, the time of the day is read. If the code is executed in the morning, lines 11 to 15 are run. Otherwise, lines 19 to 23 are run.
- On line 11, the `Metadata` property of the `Lazy` class is used to get information about the type without actually creating it. The `IDataServiceInfo` interface is used for this, and the metadata that was exported by the `MorningDataService` and `AfternoonDataService` classes is read.
- If the condition is met, the `Value` property is used to get an instance of this class. It is only at this instant that the instance is created.
- The same happens on lines 19 and 21 for the afternoon.

Run the application and observe how a different file is displayed depending on the time of the day. You can simulate a different hour by changing the clock of your computer. Having the possibility to import multiple instances implementing a contract is a very handy feature, even more so thanks to the lazy instantiation. We will use this feature again in the "Downloading on Demand" section.

Using Other Kinds of Export

The export mechanism in MEF can be configured quite precisely (for example, with the following scenarios):

- In this sample, all the instances were created without any special policy. As a consequence, a different instance of the class is created every time that an import is taking place. This can be modified by adding a `PartCreationPolicy` attribute on the exported class. You can find more information about `PartCreationPolicy` at http://www.galasoft.ch/sl4-partcreation.
- Not just classes can be exported, but also single properties of a given class. This allows selecting precisely which properties are visible by the importer. Also, it allows exporting properties of a sealed class.
- Methods can be exported by using a type of `Action<T>` for the `Export` attribute's contract. The `Import` attribute must be placed on a property of the same `Action<T>` type.

More information about MEF and its configuration can be found on the Codeplex site at http://www.galasoft.ch/sl4-mefguide.

Using MEF in Blend (or Not)

Unfortunately, the export/import mechanism provided by MEF does not work in Blend. Because of this, it is not possible to use MEF to create a design-time service like we did in the section about Unity.

Using MEF to wire the views, viewmodels, and services is very convenient at runtime, however. To mitigate the issue in Blend and provide design-time data, consider using design-time data context as shown at http://www.galasoft.ch/sl4-datacontext or the

MEFedMVVM framework developed by Marlon Grech and available at http://mefedmvvm.codeplex.com. Another solution to consider is Glenn Block's Brook available at http://github.com/glennblock/Brook.

Downloading on Demand

In the previous pages, you saw one aspect of MEF: the export/import mechanism. Another great feature of the Managed Extensibility Framework is the ability to load and integrate parts on demand, even if these parts are located in other DLLs or even other XAP files. For Silverlight applications, this is very convenient: Imagine a large application with hundreds of screens. It is unlikely that a user always consumes all the screens. By splitting the application in multiple XAPs, the amount of data transferred is minimized: only the screens that are needed by the user are downloaded. This also reduces the initial loading time before the user can start using the application and improves the user experience. On the other hand, a delay will occur every time that a new XAP file is imported, and this can complicate transitions.

Any object can be exported/imported by MEF; it doesn't matter what the XAP file contains: XAML (for example, a `ResourceDictionary`), libraries, UI elements, pictures, and so forth. There are however a few caveats, listed at http://www.galasoft.ch/sl4-mefcatalog. In this sample, we build a search application with multiple plug-ins using the Bing API. Follow these steps:

1. Download the two files MefPlugins-Start.zip and MefPlugins.BingImageSearch-Start.zip from http://www.galasoft.ch/sl4-mef. As usual, unblock the zip files if needed (in the file properties dialog), and then extract all the files to your hard drive.

2. In the MefPlugins-Start folder, open MefPlugins.sln in Visual Studio.

3. To use the Bing API, an App ID is needed. This is a unique key that is passed to the web service with each call. To get an App ID, go to http://www.galasoft.ch/sl4-bingappid and follow the indications. Then, copy the App ID into BingTextSearch.xaml.cs in the MefPlugins.BingTextSearch project, where you see the text `"Copy your App ID here"`.

4. In the MefPlugins.BingTextSearch project, expand the Service References folder.

5. Right-click the BingSearchService reference and select Configure Service Reference from the context menu.

6. In the Service References Settings dialog, in the Address field, enter the same App ID in the URL, where the text `ENTERAPPID` is found. Then click OK. Note that you need to be online for this operation to succeed.

7. Check the code of the `BingTextSearch` class and see how the Bing service is used. For more information (and samples) about the Bing web service, refer to http://www.galasoft.ch/sl4-bing.

8. Set the MefPlugins.Web project as Startup project and the MefPluginsTestPage.html page as Start page; then run the application. Enter a search query in the TextBox, and then click the Search button. After a short wait, web results should be seen in the ListBox.

9. Note that building this application creates a new folder named Contracts where the two zip files were extracted in Step 1, and the MefPlugins.Contracts.dll assembly is copied into that folder.

> **TIP**
>
> **Using a Simpler Protocol**
>
> Using a SOAP based web service as in this sample is probably the easiest way to connect to Bing services, but it is not the most efficient. Other alternatives exist, such as using a JSON-based protocol (like we did in *Silverlight 2 Unleashed* with the Flickr services). For more information, refer to the Bing API documentation.

Refactoring to MEF

In the current state, the BingTextSearch plug-in is added in the MainPage.xaml markup as the fixed content of a tab item. This is not very flexible or extensible. Instead, we will now refactor the application to use MEF. Then, we will see how to create and load another plug-in dynamically.

1. In MainPage.xaml, find the TabControl named MyTabControl. Remove the TabItem that it contains so that the result is like Listing 20.25.

LISTING 20.25 Empty TabControl

```
<sdk:TabControl Margin="10,0"
                Grid.Row="1"
                x:Name="MyTabControl" />
```

2. In the MefPlugins project, add a reference to the two DLLs System.ComponentModel.Composition and System.ComponentModel.Composition.Initialization (with the Add Reference dialog's .NET tab). This last DLL is only needed when you want to call the SatisfyImports method or the ExportFactory class.

3. In MainPage.xaml.cs, modify the Engines property as shown in Listing 20.26. Note the usage of the ImportMany attribute with the AllowRecomposition parameter set to true. This allows reloading the list of plug-ins after the application has started. In this listing, we use a new class available in MEF for Silverlight 4, called Lazy. This class helps us by creating the ISearchEngine instances only when they are really needed (lazy instantiation).

LISTING 20.26 Importing the Engines

```
[ImportMany(AllowRecomposition = true)]
public Lazy<ISearchEngine>[] Engines
{
    get;
    set;
}
```

4. Note that the type of the contract used is `ISearchEngine`. This interface is defined in the MefPlugins.Contracts assembly, which is referenced by both the MefPlugins application and the MefPlugins.BingTextSearch plug-in assembly. It defines three members:

- `SearchType` (`string`, returns a description of the kind of search that the plug-in performs)
- `SearchView` (`UIElement`, a representation of the search results; for most plug-ins, this is simply a reference to `this`, the main `UserControl` itself)
- The `Search` method that performs the query.

5. Modify the `MainPage` constructor as shown in Listing 20.27. The manual initialization of the `Engines` library is removed. Instead, MEF is used to scan the referenced assemblies and load the local plug-ins.

LISTING 20.27 Initializing the Main Page

```
public MainPage()
{
    InitializeComponent();
    CompositionInitializer.SatisfyImports(this);
    Compose();
}
```

6. Implement the `Compose` method as shown in Listing 20.28.

LISTING 20.28 Compose Method

```
1  private void Compose()
2  {
3      foreach (var engine in Engines)
4      {
5          var found = false;
6          foreach (TabItem tab in MyTabControl.Items)
7          {
8              if (tab.Header.ToString()
9                  == engine.Value.SearchType)
```

```
10              {
11                  found = true;
12                  break;
13              }
14          }
15
16          if (found)
17          {
18              continue;
19          }
20
21          var newTab = new TabItem
22          {
23              Header = engine.Value.SearchType,
24              Content = engine.Value.SearchView
25          };
26
27          MyTabControl.Items.Add(newTab);
28      }
29  }
```

- Lines 3 to 14 inspect each engine that was loaded and compares their `SearchType` property to the `Header` of each `TabItem`. This avoids reloading engines that are already displayed in the `TabControl`.
- Should the inspected engine be new, a new `TabItem` is created on lines 21 to 25. The `Content` property of the `TabItem` is set to the `SearchView` property of the plugin (which in most cases returns the `UserControl` itself).
- Then on line 27 the new `TabItem` is added to the `TabControl`.

7. Modify the `SearchClick` event handler as shown in Listing 20.29.

LISTING 20.29 Modifying the `SearchClick` Event Handler

```
private void SearchClick(object sender, RoutedEventArgs e)
{
    foreach (var engine in Engines)
    {
        engine.Value.Search(QueryTextBox.Text);
    }
}
```

8. The `BingTextSearch` plugin needs to be adapted for MEF, too. First, in the MefPlugins.BingTextSearch project, add a reference to the System.ComponentModel.Composition assembly.

9. Open BingTextSearch.xaml.cs and add an `Export` attribute to the `BingTextSearch` class as shown in Listing 20.30. This class already implements the `ISearchEngine` contract, so nothing else needs to be changed.

LISTING 20.30 Exporting `BingTextSearch`

```
[Export(typeof(ISearchEngine))]
public partial class BingTextSearch : UserControl, ISearchEngine
```

10. Run the application again. The exact same functionality is reproduced, but this time MEF is integrated. Now we will modify the application to load an additional plug-in dynamically.

Preparing a Service

The application needs a service on the web server to deliver information about available plug-ins. This can be done with the following steps:

1. Right-click the MefPlugins.Web application. This is the web server that serves the Silverlight application.
2. Add a new item and select a generic handler from the Web section. Name this service **PluginsService.ashx**. This is a very simple Asp.NET service that can easily process simple requests.
3. Open PluginsService.ashx.cs and modify the `ProcessRequest` method as shown in Listing 20.31. This method scans the Plugins folder and returns a list of all the XAP files found in this folder. The format of the `Response` is very simple: It simply has one XAP file name per line. Note that the service could also have been implemented with WCF for example.

LISTING 20.31 `ProcessRequest` Method in the `PluginsService` Class

```
private const string PluginsFolderName = "Plugins/";

public void ProcessRequest(HttpContext context)
{
    var pluginFolder = new DirectoryInfo(
        HttpContext.Current.Server.MapPath(
        PluginsFolderName));
    var response = new StringBuilder();

    if (pluginFolder.Exists)
    {
        foreach (var xap in pluginFolder.GetFiles("*.xap"))
        {
            response.AppendLine(
                PluginsFolderName + xap.Name);
```

```
            }
        }
        context.Response.ContentType = "text/plain";
        context.Response.Write(response);
}
```

4. Add a new folder to the web project and name it **Plugins**.

Preparing a Plug-in

In Step 1 in the preceding section, you downloaded and extracted two zip files. The first is the main application we modified earlier. The second is another plug-in that also implements the `ISearchEngine` interface. We can modify it to be loaded by MEF with the following steps:

1. Open the MefPlugins.BingImageSearch.sln solution in the MefPlugins.BingImageSearch folder.
2. Copy the Bing App ID into BingImageSearch.xaml.cs, where the text `"Copy your App ID here"` is found.
3. Expand the Service References folder.
4. Right-click the BingSearchService reference and select Configure Service Reference from the context menu.
5. In the Service References Settings dialog, in the Address field, enter the same App ID in the URL, where the text `ENTERAPPID` is found.
6. Select the MefPlugins.BingImageSearch.Web project as Startup Project and the index.html page as Start Page. Then run the application, enter a query and see the result. The application is automatically loading a query for the search term *silverlight*.

The plug-in is quite similar to the `BingTextSearch` that was used before, but instead of a web search, an image search is performed. Note that this is a normal Silverlight application with a MainPage.xaml, App.xaml, and so forth. When the application is built, a XAP file is created, which is what MEF needs to dynamically download the code.

Strictly speaking, the MainPage.xaml and App.xaml pages are not needed when the plug-in is loaded by the MefPlugins application, and could be safely removed. However, leaving them in the application is convenient because it allows testing the plug-in as a standalone application. Now we can convert this plug-in to MEF as follows:

1. In the MefPlugins.BingImageSearch project, add a reference to the System.ComponentModel.Composition DLL.
2. Add an `Export` attribute to the `BingImageSearch` class, exactly as was done in Listing 20.30 for the `BingTextSearch` class.
3. Build the application.

4. Right-click the MefPlugins.BingImageSearch project (not the Solution!) and select Open Folder in Windows Explorer from the context menu.

5. Copy the file MefPlugins.BingImageSearch.xap from the Bin\Debug folder and paste this file into the Plugins folder that was created in the web application earlier.

Modifying the Application to Load Plug-ins

Finally, the MefPlugins application needs to trigger the loading of the plug-ins with the following steps:

1. In the MefPlugins project, modify the `MainPage` constructor as shown in Listing 20.32. Instead of using the `CompositionInitializer.SatisfyImport` shortcut, we are using a catalog to scan the plug-in assembly. Later, other catalogs will be added to load the additional XAP files over the wire.

LISTING 20.32 Modifying the `MainPage` Constructor

```
private static AggregateCatalog _aggregateCatalog;
private CompositionContainer _container;
private string _baseAddress;
private Dictionary<string, DeploymentCatalog> _catalogs
    = new Dictionary<string, DeploymentCatalog>();

public MainPage()
{
    InitializeComponent();

    _aggregateCatalog = new AggregateCatalog();
    _aggregateCatalog.Catalogs.Add(
        new AssemblyCatalog(
            typeof(BingTextSearch.BingTextSearch).Assembly));
    _container = new CompositionContainer(_aggregateCatalog);

    var xapUri = App.Current.Host.Source;
    _baseAddress = xapUri.AbsoluteUri.Substring(
        0, xapUri.AbsoluteUri.IndexOf(xapUri.AbsolutePath))
        + "/";

    _container.ComposeParts(this);
    Compose();
    LoadPlugins();
}
```

2. Implement the `LoadPlugins` method as shown in Listing 20.33. This method uses a `WebClient` to ask the `PluginsService` implemented before what XAP files are found in the Plugins folder. When the service returns the list of XAP files, the `Result` is parsed, and the `AddXap` method is called for each XAP file.

LISTING 20.33 LoadPlugins Method

```
private void LoadPlugins()
{
    var serviceAddress = _baseAddress
        + "PluginsService.ashx?"
        + DateTime.Now.Ticks;

    var client = new WebClient();
    client.DownloadStringCompleted += client_DownloadStringCompleted;
    client.DownloadStringAsync(new Uri(serviceAddress));
}

void client_DownloadStringCompleted(
    object sender,
    DownloadStringCompletedEventArgs e)
{
    var plugins = e.Result.Split(
        new string[] { Environment.NewLine },
        StringSplitOptions.RemoveEmptyEntries);
    foreach (var plugin in plugins)
    {
        AddXap(_baseAddress + plugin);
    }
}
```

3. Implement the AddXap method in Listing 20.34.

LISTING 20.34 AddXap Method

```
1  private void AddXap(string uri)
2  {
4      DeploymentCatalog catalog;
5       if (!_catalogs.TryGetValue(uri, out catalog))
6      {
7          catalog = new DeploymentCatalog(
8              new Uri(uri, UriKind.Absolute));
9          _aggregateCatalog.Catalogs.Add(catalog);
10         catalog.DownloadCompleted += (s, e) =>
11         {
12             if (e.Error == null
13                 && !e.Cancelled)
14             {
15                 Compose() ;
16             }
17         } ;
```

```
18             catalog.DownloadAsync();
19
20             _catalogs[uri] = catalog ;
21         }
22         _aggregateCatalog.Catalogs.Add(catalog) ;
23     }
```

- Line 4 declares an instance of type `DeploymentCatalog`. This is a catalog able to load classes dynamically over the network.
- The new `DeploymentCatalog` is added to the `AggregateCatalog` on line 9. The `AggregateCatalog` has a list composed of the `AssemblyCatalog` created on Step 2 as well as one `DeploymentCatalog` instance for each remote XAP file.
- Line 5 makes sure that the corresponding XAP file has not been loaded already. All the catalogs are saved in a `Dictionary` to avoid loading the same plug-in twice.
- Lines 12 to 16 are executed when the remote XAP file is loaded. This is the `Completed` event handler, expressed here as a lambda expression. If everything went well, the `Compose` method is called.
- Finally, the asynchronous download is triggered on line 18.

4. Modify the `RefreshClick` event handler as shown in Listing 20.35.

LISTING 20.35 `RefreshClick` Event Handler

```
private void RefreshClick(object sender, RoutedEventArgs e)
{
    LoadPlugins();
}
```

5. The initial download will be triggered when the application starts, but it can also be re-executed at any time later. To demonstrate this, in the Plugins folder in the MefPlugins.Web application, rename MefPlugins.BingImageSearch.xap to **MefPlugins.BingImageSearch.bak**.
6. Run the MefPlugins.Web application. Only the Web search plugin is found.
7. Without exiting the application, rename MefPlugins.BingImageSearch.bak to MefPlugins.BingImageSearch.xap on the server.
8. In the application, click the Refresh button. The Image plug-in is shown in the `TabControl` now. Enter a query and click the Search button to execute the query in both plug-ins.

Reducing the Size of the XAP File

With the steps executed in this chapter, the System.ComponentModel.Composition DLLs is downloaded to the web client multiple times: once with the main application, and then each time that a plugin (remote XAP file) is downloaded. This causes unneeded costs (because of the wasted bandwidth) and is not necessary. It is easy to optimize this with the following steps:

1. In the folder containing the MefPlugins.BingImageSearch project, find the Bin\Debug folder and write down the size of the MefPlugins.BingImageSearch.xap file.
2. Open the MefPlugins.BingImageSearch solution in Visual Studio and expand the References folder.
3. Find the reference to the System.ComponentModel.Composition assembly. Select this assembly and press F4 to display the properties.
4. Change the value of CopyLocal to false. Then build the application again. Do the same for the MefPlugins.Contracts assembly.
5. Build the application and check the size of the XAP file: It should have shrunk by a good 90KB.
6. Copy the smaller XAP file from the MefPlugins.BingImageSearch\Bin\Debug folder to the MefPlugins.Web application's Plugins folder.
7. For consistency, set CopyLocal to false on the System.ComponentModel.Composition and MefPlugins.Contracts assemblies in the References folder of the MefPlugins.BingTextSearch project, too.
8. Run the application again. The functionality should work in exactly the same way.

This is possible because the System.ComponentModel.Composition DLL is already loaded by the main application. When the plug-in's DLL is added to the application, the Silverlight runtime engine looks for this DLL (from the list of references) and finds it. To the Silverlight framework, it makes no difference where this DLL comes from, so long as its name and version are correct.

If your application and its plug-ins need multiple assemblies, if you have multiple plug-ins and a large number of users, the amount of bandwidth (and money) saved can be very consequent.

What About Prism?

Prism is a guidance developed by Microsoft to create composite UI. It is supported by a framework named the Composite Application Library CAL, which fulfills similar goals by providing extensibility mechanisms for an application. While Prism is for UI applications only, MEF and Unity can be used to create any kind of extensible applications.

Prism is more complex to use than MEF. In fact, the next version of Prism (v4) will use MEF under the covers for its modularity infrastructure. Although Prism absolutely makes sense in certain situations, it may be too complex to use it to implement simple decoupled applications. It is recommended to carefully evaluate the use of Prism in an application and to consider starting with MEF and an MVVM framework as a possible simpler alternative.

Using an MVVM Framework

When working with MVVM a lot, it can be valuable to use a framework to avoid repetitive tasks, whether you implement the framework yourself based on the recommendations and samples in this book or choose an existing framework developed by members of the Silverlight community.

Discovering the Components

Quite a large number of MVVM frameworks are available developed by the community. A few frameworks seem to emerge as the community's choice: Caliburn (a powerful framework developed over many years in a very professional way by Rob Eisenberg), nRoute (an innovative framework exploring new ways to solve issues), Prism (of which some components can be used specifically for MVVM), MVVM Light Toolkit (a small and easy-to-use framework aimed at improving the work with Blend), and more.

Most frameworks offer the following components helping to build decoupled applications:

- A base class for view-models, making it easier to raise the `PropertyChanged` event
- A messaging system to send messages in a decoupled manner from one object to another
- A command helper such as the `RelayCommand` class that we used often in this book
- Helper classes to enable cross thread access
- Mechanisms to facilitate the communication between the view-model and the view

In addition, each framework brings its own components, functions, and concepts that often go beyond MVVM.

Sending Messages

When working with plug-ins (like in the section about MEF), it can be quite complex to let these plug-ins communicate together. In this section, we show how a messaging system can make this painless and easy. The framework used here is the MVVM Light Toolkit mentioned a few times in this book and developed by this author. You can find more information about the MVVM Light Toolkit at http://www.galasoft.ch/mvvm/getstarted and at http://mvvmlight.codeplex.com.

In this sample, we extend the MefPlugins application by providing a mechanism for the plug-ins to pass information to the main application in a decoupled manner with the following steps:

1. Install the MVVM Light Toolkit's binaries by following the procedure described at http://galasoft.ch/mvvm/installing.
2. Open the MefPlugins solution that was edited in the previous section. If you didn't keep it, the start state for this section can be downloaded from http://www.galasoft.ch/sl4-messaging. Make sure to download, unblock and extract both the Messaging-Start.zip and Messaging.BingImageSearch-Start.zip files.
3. In the MefPlugins project, right-click the References folder and add a reference to the GalaSoft.MvvmLight.SL4.dll located in C:\Program Files\Laurent Bugnion (GalaSoft)\Mvvm Light Toolkit\Binaries\Silverlight4. This is the DLL in which the `Messenger` class is located.
4. Add a new class in the MefPlugins.Contracts project named **Notifications.cs.**
5. Edit the `Notifications` class as shown in Listing 20.36. In the current state there is only one notification, but additional ones can be added as needed.

LISTING 20.36 Adding Notifications

```
public static class Notifications
{
    public static readonly string NumberOfMessages
        = Guid.NewGuid().ToString();
}
```

6. Open MainPage.xaml and modify the `LayoutRoot` `Grid`'s `RowDefinitions` and add a `TextBlock`, as shown in Listing 20.37.

LISTING 20.37 Adding a Row and a `TextBlock`

```
<Grid.RowDefinitions>
    <RowDefinition Height="50" />
    <RowDefinition />
    <RowDefinition Height="100" />
    <RowDefinition Height="50" />
</Grid.RowDefinitions>

<TextBlock x:Name="MessageTextBlock"
           Margin="10,0,10,0"
           Grid.Row="3"
           FontSize="14" />
```

7. In MainPage.xaml.cs, add a private attribute to keep track of the number of results for a given query, as shown in Listing 20.38.

LISTING 20.38 Counting the Results

```
private int _numberOfMessages;
```

8. At the end of the `MainPage` constructor, add the code shown in Listing 20.39.

LISTING 20.39 Registering to Receive Messages

```
Messenger.Default.Register<int>(
    this,
    Notifications.NumberOfMessages,
    n =>
    {
        _numberOfMessages += n;
        MessageTextBlock.Text
            = string.Format(
            "There are {0} search results",
            _numberOfMessages);
    });
```

- The code in Listing 20.39 instructs the default `Messenger` instance to watch for messages where the payload is an `int` and the `token` is set to `Notifications.NumberOfMessages`. If such a message is transmitted, the method defined as a lambda expression should be executed: The number of messages is increased, and a status message is shown.

9. In MefPlugins.BingTextSearch, add a reference to the same GalaSoft.MvvmLight.SL4.dll as in Step 3 above.
10. With the GalaSoft.MvvmLight.SL4 DLL selected in the References folder, press F4 to show the properties and set CopyLocal to false.
11. Open BingTextSearch.xaml.cs. At the end of the `HandleResponse` method, after the `Results` collection is created, add the code shown in Listing 20.40.

> **TIP**
>
> **Communicating with Objects**
>
> In addition to sending targeted messages with a token as in this sample, the `Messenger` class can also broadcast messages to everyone (registration based on the type of the payload) or send messages to all instance of a given type (or interface). You can find more information about the `Messenger` class at http://www.galasoft.ch/sl4-messenger.

LISTING 20.40 Sending a Message

```
Messenger.Default.Send(
    Results.Count,
    Notifications.NumberOfMessages);
```

12. Build the MefPlugins solution.
13. Open the MefPlugins.BingImageSearch solution.
14. Repeat the Steps 9 to 11 for the `BingImageSearch` class in the MefPlugins.BingImageSearch project.
15. Build MefPlugins.BingImageSearch; then copy the new XAP file from the Bin\Debug folder into the Plugins folder of the MefPlugins.Web application.
16. Build everything, and then view the MefPluginsTestPage.html page of the MefPlugins.Web application inside the web browser. After both plug-ins are loaded, enter a query and click the Search button. You should see the number of results being updated.

The MVVM Light Toolkit Messenger class is a very powerful way to enable loose communication between an application's elements. It is also implemented in a way that does not create a strong link between the sender and the receiver, and enables garbage collection even if an element omits to unregister before being disposed. Use it with care, however, because a very loose coupling between elements is also more difficult to understand for less-experienced people working on the code.

The MVVM Light Toolkit's components and concepts were used at various occasions in this book and in this chapter. The `Messenger` class, in particular, allows sending messages in a much decoupled manner, without putting any constraint on the sender or the receiver. The `RelayCommand` class was used in other samples in this book, and is a very precious helper class when working with commands. In addition, the MVVM Light Toolkit places a lot of importance in the Blendability and the creation of design-time data.

Other frameworks are also available, each with their strengths and community. Here, too, informing oneself before adopting one or the other framework is very important. More information about MVVM in general and the MVVM Light Toolkit can be found at http://www.galasoft.ch/sl4-understanding (video presentation).

Summary

In this chapter, we demonstrated the use of three frameworks used to create loosely coupled, extensible applications in Silverlight 4.

- The Unity DI container allows registering and resolving objects in a simple manner and without creating complicated dependencies.

- The Managed Extensibility Framework is a fantastic and innovative framework to build decoupled and extensible applications. It exports and imports objects to combine them in a loose manner. It also allows loading parts of the application on demand, to enhance the download time and to create pluggable applications. A big strength of MEF is that it is part of the Silverlight framework and easy to add. It would not be surprising at all to see MEF become mainstream and be added to most applications in the future.
- Finally, the MVVM Light Toolkit offers components to help with the creation of and the communication within loosely coupled applications.

We also talked about other frameworks that fulfill the same functionality in a different manner. This offers interesting alternatives for the developer to build modern applications that are easy to maintain and extend.

In the next chapter, we talk about ways to optimize the performance of your Silverlight applications to offer an even more enjoyable experience to your users.

CHAPTER 21

Optimizing Performance

IN THIS CHAPTER, WE WILL:

- See how we can improve the download time of a Silverlight application to make the initial experience more enjoyable for the user.
- Improve the way that data is displayed on the screen by virtualizing the user interface.
- Accelerate the user interface to speed up and smoothen animations.
- Talk about profiling and how to avoid memory leaks.

Silverlight applications are deployed over the Internet and running on all kind of computers, from high-end desktop machines to Windows Phone 7 devices. To guarantee a pleasant user experience, some areas should be optimized for performance:

- Reducing the size of the material (code, media, and other assets) being downloaded
- Optimizing the speed of the application as it runs
- Reducing the size of the memory used and, most important, avoiding losing memory

In this chapter, we explore techniques to improve these areas.

Improving the XAP Download Time

A Silverlight application needs to be downloaded to run. When a user navigates to a HTML page containing a Silverlight application, the following happens:

1. The web browser sends a request to the web server for the HTML page.
2. When the HTML page is received, the web browser parses it and sees that an object tag is embedded. The Silverlight plug-in is started.

3. (If available) The plug-in downloads a custom splash screen for the user to see while the XAP file is downloaded. You saw how to create custom splash screens in Chapter 18, "Drag and Drop, Full Screen, Clipboard, COM Interop, Duplex Polling, Notification Windows, and Splash Screens."
4. The splash screen is displayed in the plug-in, and the XAP download starts.
5. The download process uses the web browser's network stack, so the cache is checked first. If a file corresponding to the XAP's URL is found in the cache, the download doesn't take place but the cached file is displayed instead.
6. If the XAP file is not found in the cache, it is downloaded from the web server. Depending on the size of the XAP file, it can take a moment.
7. The Silverlight application is started and the user can interact with it.

Obviously, things are different for an out-of-browser application, where the XAP file and all needed material are installed on the client computer. For an in-browser application, however, files are cached in a temporary location that is cleaned periodically (either when the user deletes his browsing history, or when the web browser cleans up to avoid filling the hard drive).

A few things can be done to improve this experience:

- Make sure that the XAP is cached correctly, and that the cached version is used. During development, it is common to force the web browser to reload the XAP file every time that the web page is refreshed (for example, by using JavaScript to append a unique number to the XAP's URL, as a query string). Make sure that such mechanisms are disabled for production!
- Reduce the size of the XAP file. We already saw in Chapter 20, "Building Extensible and Maintainable Applications," how a Silverlight application can be split in multiple XAP files and loaded on demand with the Managed Extensibility Framework. In this chapter, we will see how commonly used DLLs can be externalized so that the web browser caches them and avoids downloading them every time that another XAP file is loaded (see the "Caching Common Assemblies" section, later in this chapter).
- Make sure that all the content packed into a XAP file is really needed. You can inspect the content of a XAP file by renaming a copy to *.zip and then opening it in Windows Explorer. Alternatively, tools like SilverlightSpy (http://www.galasoft.ch/sl4-slspy) have a friendlier interface to inspect the content of a XAP file.
- Avoid packing content (such as large pictures, videos) in the XAP file. You will see in the "Loading Content on Demand" section how pictures and videos can be loaded separately.

Remember that bandwidth is still an issue in many places. It is possible to simulate low bandwidth and various critical cases by using software such as the open source Wanem (http://wanem.sourceforge.net). It is recommended to test your Silverlight application's download experience in such difficult conditions.

Loading Content on Demand

When content must be displayed by a Silverlight application, it is better not to include it inside the XAP file to avoid long download times, as explained in the "Reducing the Download Time" section.

Making Sure That the Content Is Not in the XAP

In case the content (images, videos, and so on) is referenced by the project file, it will probably end up in the DLL or in the XAP file unless Visual Studio is instructed differently. To change this, use the following steps:

1. In Visual Studio, click the content that you want to exclude from the XAP file.
2. Show the file's properties by pressing F4.
3. Check the Build Action and the Copy to Output Directory properties.

Content is typically added to a project with one of the three following settings:

- **Build Action = Content**: This is the most common setting. In this case, Copy to Output Directory should be set to Copy If Newer (recommended) or Copy Always. The content file will be packed inside the XAP file, but outside of the DLL. It can be referenced using a simple relative URI, in XAML, or in source code.
- **Build Action = Resource**: For this action, Copy to Output Directory should be set to Do Not Copy. The content file will be embedded inside the DLL. This is useful in certain cases, although in general the Content action is preferred.
- **Build Action = None**: In this case, the content file is not included in the DLL or in the XAP file. It should be uploaded to the web server separately, and will be downloaded on demand by setting the `Source` property or using a `WebClient`, as shown later in this section.

> **WARNING**
>
> **Referencing a Content File with a Relative URI**
>
> Remember that when a content file is not packed in the XAP file, using a relative URI to reference it is dangerous because the path is resolved relatively to the location of the XAP file. It is preferable to construct an absolute URI for example, with the code shown in Listing 21.1.

LISTING 21.1 Constructing an Absolute URI

```
var xapUri = Application.Current.Host.Source;
var baseAddress = xapUri.AbsoluteUri.Substring(
    0, xapUri.AbsoluteUri.IndexOf(xapUri.AbsolutePath))
    + "/";
var imageUri = new Uri(baseAddress + "images/myimage.jpg");
```

Setting the Source Property

The easiest way to start a download without any fuss is to simply set the `Source` property of a `BitmapImage` element or of the `MediaElement` control as shown in Listing 21.2. This triggers an asynchronous download of the desired media file.

LISTING 21.2 Setting the Source Property

```
private void LoadNextMedia(bool picture)
{
    if (picture)
    {
        var image = new BitmapImage(
            new Uri("http://www.mydomain.com/myimage.jpg"));
        MyMediaElement.Visibility = Visibility.Collapsed;
        MyImage.Visibility = Visibility.Visible;
        MyImage.Source = image;
    }
    else
    {
        MyMediaElement.Visibility = Visibility.Visible;
        MyImage.Visibility = Visibility.Collapsed;
        MyMediaElement.Source
            = new Uri("http://www.mydomain.com/myvideo.wmv");
    }
}
```

However, consider the following:

- For images, there is no way to inform the user about the download progress. There is, however, a `DownloadProgressChanged` event on the `MediaElement` class.
- Once a download has been started, it cannot be stopped.

For large videos, it is better to use video streaming if possible. This optimizes the bandwidth consumption. In addition, if the video is stopped, the download is immediately interrupted and does not put strain on the video server. Combined with the smooth streaming features of the Internet Information Services (IIS) Media Services, this ensures an optimal user experience even with low bandwidth. You can find more information about smooth streaming at http://www.galasoft.ch/sl4-smooth.

WARNING

Solving Cross-Schema Issues

When testing on-demand download, remember that a Silverlight application executed in `file://` mode may not access content from `http://`. To test, make sure to use a web application set as Startup object! On the other hand, there are no cross-domain restrictions for pictures and videos.

Downloading Using the WebClient

Another possibility is to download the bytes using a `WebClient` instance. This provides more fine-grained control on the download operation. For example, it is possible to download one media file from the Internet while another one is playing in the `MediaElement`.

Initiating a download with the `WebClient` uses the same code for pictures and videos as shown in Listing 21.3.

LISTING 21.3 Initiating Media Download with the `WebClient`

```
private bool _isPicture;

private void LoadNextMedia(bool picture)
{
    _client = new WebClient();
    _client.DownloadProgressChanged += ClientDownloadProgressChanged;
    _client.OpenReadCompleted += ClientOpenReadCompleted;

    _isPicture = picture;

    if (picture)
    {
        _client.OpenReadAsync(
            new Uri("http://www.mydomain.com/myimage.jpg"));
    }
    else
    {
        _client.OpenReadAsync(
            new Uri("http://www.mydomain.com/myvideo.wmv"));
    }

    _isPicture = picture;
}
```

Once the download is completed, a `MediaElement` or an `Image` can load the bytes from memory to display them, as shown in Listing 21.4. In this listing, `Progress` is a `DependencyProperty` of type `double`, `MyImage` is an `Image` control, and `MyMediaElement` is a control of type MediaElement. Also, content can be saved in the isolated storage for later consumption, which makes it perfect for offline use, for example.

Note, however, that downloading a whole video in memory might lead to issues if it is big. For these scenarios, video streaming is really recommended instead.

LISTING 21.4 Handling the DownloadProgressChanged and OpenReadCompleted Events

```
private void ClientDownloadProgressChanged(
    object sender,
    DownloadProgressChangedEventArgs e)
{
    Progress = e.ProgressPercentage;
}

private void ClientOpenReadCompleted(
    object sender,
    OpenReadCompletedEventArgs e)
{
    MyMediaElement.Stop();

    if (_isPicture)
    {
        var image = new BitmapImage();
        image.SetSource(e.Result);
        MyImage.Source = image;
        MyImage.Visibility = Visibility.Visible;
        MyMediaElement.Visibility = Visibility.Collapsed;
    }
    else
    {
        MyMediaElement.SetSource(e.Result);
        MyMediaElement.Play();
        MyImage.Visibility = Visibility.Collapsed;
        MyMediaElement.Visibility = Visibility.Visible;
    }
}
```

Using the WebClient, it is also possible to abort a download with the code shown in Listing 21.5.

LISTING 21.5 Aborting the Download

```
public void Stop()
{
    if (_client != null)
    {
```

```
        _client.CancelAsync();
        _client.DownloadProgressChanged
            -= ClientDownloadProgressChanged;
        _client.OpenReadCompleted
            -= ClientOpenReadCompleted;
        _client = null;
    }

    MyMediaElement.Stop();
}
```

Whichever mechanism you choose, by downloading the media content on demand, the size of the XAP file is much smaller than if the content was embedded, and the experience is more enjoyable for the user.

Caching Common Assemblies

Another measure that can be taken to reduce a XAP file's size and to speed up its download is to externalize some of the assemblies it contains. With this process, when the XAP is loaded, the Silverlight plug-in sends additional requests for the external assemblies, and downloads them separately. The advantage is that if these assemblies are already in the web browser's cache, they do not need to be redownloaded for another Silverlight application, but instead they will be loaded directly from the cache, which is much faster. The disadvantage is, however, that sending multiple requests may take more time if the assemblies are not available in the cache (on the first load, or if the cache has been cleared).

Reducing Your XAP File's Size

To externalize assemblies from the XAP file, and make them cachable, follow these steps.

1. Open the MefPlugins solution that was created in Chapter 20 about the Managed Extensibility Framework. If you did not keep this application, it can be downloaded from http://www.galasoft.ch/sl4-externalize. Make sure that you unblock the file before extracting it to your hard drive.
2. Build the application.
3. Right-click the ClientBin folder in the MefPlugins.Web project and select Open Folder in Windows Explorer.
4. Write down the size of the MefPlugins.xap file. This is the file that is downloaded to the Silverlight plug-in.
5. Make a copy of the XAP file and rename it the copy with the .zip extension. Then open it in Windows Explorer or in your favorite zip application. Inside the zip file, you should see DLLs and a few other files. Among them, notice four System.*.dll components accounting for about 1MB uncompressed.
6. Go back to Visual Studio, right-click the MefPlugins project, and select Properties.

7. In the Silverlight tab, check the Reduce XAP Size by Using Application Library Caching check box.
8. Build the application again.
9. Go again to the ClientBin folder again and check the size of the XAP file now.

The XAP file has shrunk and three DLLs have been externalized as zip files, and placed in the ClientBin folder, too. When the Reduce XAP Size check box is checked and the application is built, Visual Studio looks into each referenced assembly's folder if it can find a file named <AssemblyFileName>.extmap.xml. For example, for the system assemblies, the compiler looks into C:\Program Files\Microsoft SDKs\Silverlight\v4.0\Libraries\Client.

If the extmap.xml file can be found, the indications in the file are used to pack the DLL separately as a zip file. Because it is a separate file, the plug-in will send a separate request for this file; if the same file is found in the web browser's cache, the download is not necessary. If multiple applications use the same cached assemblies, the gain in download time can be very noticeable.

Making Your Own Assemblies Cacheable

It is possible to make your own assemblies cacheable by creating your own extmap.xml file. This can be useful for class libraries that are used by multiple applications. Tim Heuer (Microsoft Silverlight Program Manager) has a very good explanation of the process to follow to create an extmap.xml file at http://www.galasoft.ch/sl4-extmap.

In this article, Tim explains that not only can assemblies be externalized in their own zip file, but in addition it is possible to host these applications on a third-party web server. This allows having a central server delivering class assemblies (for example, framework components, utility classes). Obviously, this is a gain only if the third-party web server is fast, reliable, and reachable through firewalls.

Not Externalizing Assemblies in OOB

It is not possible to use this feature for out-of-browser (OOB) applications. Trying to check both the Reduce XAP Size check box and the Enable Running Application Out of the Browser check box will cause Visual Studio to display a warning that asks you to uncheck one or both. In fact, OOB applications do not need assemblies to be cached, since the whole application and all its components are downloaded to the client computer when the application is installed out-of-the-browser.

For in-browser applications, however, this feature can be an interesting way to reduce the amount of data transmitted over slow connections, and to make the experience more enjoyable.

Virtualizing the User Interface

When a Silverlight user interface is rendered, the number of objects created in memory can be huge if the developer (and the designer!) is not careful. To visualize this, follow these steps:

1. Download the file named VirtualizationSample.zip from http://www.galasoft.ch/sl4-virtualize. Unblock the file using the file properties' Unblock button (if available) and extract the content to your hard drive.
2. Open the VirtualizationSample.sln solution in Visual Studio.
3. Select the Output window. If you cannot see this window in Studio, select the menu View, Output.
4. Run the application in debug mode by pressing the F5 key.
5. In the Output window, notice the debug messages written by the application. The rendering of the items on the screen starts after the message `"Assigned"` is shown and ends when the last message `"One template loaded"` is shown. Calculate the difference between the time shown for the last template and the time shown for the Assigned message. (Note that times are shown in MM:ss:mmm format, where mmm are milliseconds.)
6. Open MainPage.xaml.
7. Add comment signs around the `ListBox` tag, and then remove the comment signs around the `ItemsControl` tag.
8. Run the application again in debug mode with the F5 key.
9. Again, calculate the time difference between the `"Assigned"` message and the last `"One template loaded"` message.

The time needed for the `ItemsControl` is much larger than for the `ListBox`. The problem is that the `ItemsControl`'s items panel is not *virtualized*. The number of `"One template loaded"` messages is very much larger. In fact, there is exactly one such message per item loaded in the `MainViewModel` class. On the other hand, the `ListBox` control shows only a handful of these messages.

When the `ListBox` renders items, it takes in account the visible surface and only creates items until that surface is filled (plus a small buffer on the top and on the bottom of the scroll viewer). If you scroll down when the items are rendered in the `ListBox`, new `"One template loaded"` messages are added to the Output window all the time. Templates that get out of sight are recycled and new templates are created for the items that come in sight. There is no such mechanism by default for the `ItemsControl`.

Virtualizing the `ItemsControl`

`ItemsControl` is the base class for data controls in Silverlight, including the `ListBox`. It has the same ability than the `ListBox` to display a collection of items by applying a `DataTemplate`, but lacks the selection mechanism, the `ScrollViewer` and the virtualization.

This last function can, however, be added to an `ItemsControl` with the markup shown in Listing 21.6.

LISTING 21.6 Virtualizing the ItemsControl

```
1  <ItemsControl Margin="10"
2               ItemsSource="{Binding Items}"
3               ItemTemplate="{StaticResource MyDataTemplate}"
4               x:Name="MyListControl">
5      <ItemsControl.Template>
6          <ControlTemplate TargetType="ItemsControl">
7              <ScrollViewer>
8                  <ItemsPresenter />
9              </ScrollViewer>
10         </ControlTemplate>
11     </ItemsControl.Template>
12     <ItemsControl.ItemsPanel>
13         <ItemsPanelTemplate>
14             <VirtualizingStackPanel />
15         </ItemsPanelTemplate>
16     </ItemsControl.ItemsPanel>
17 </ItemsControl>
```

- Lines 5 to 11 define a new `ControlTemplate` for the `ItemsControl`. This uses an `ItemsPresenter` control, in charge of presenting a list of items without adding any chrome to these items. This is the equivalent of the `ContentPresenter` used often when creating a `ControlTemplate` for a `ContentControl` such as a `Button`.
- Note that the `ItemsPresenter` is wrapped into a `ScrollViewer` (lines 7 to 9). The default `ItemsControl` `ControlTemplate` does not have a `ScrollViewer`. However, in Silverlight, virtualization is turned on only when the content can be scrolled.
- Lines 12 to 16 set the `ItemsPanel` property of the `ItemsControl` to a `VirtualizingStackPanel`. The default `ItemsPanel` for this control is normally a `StackPanel` without virtualization.

The VirtualizationSample solution enables you to experiment with different virtualization settings for a `ListBox` and an `ItemsControl`. Note that even with a very simple `DataTemplate` and only 1,000 items in the collection, the difference in the loading time is very noticeable.

> **WARNING**
>
> **(Not) Setting IsVirtualizing**
>
> In Windows Presentation Foundation (WPF), an attached property named `VirtualizingStackPanel.IsVirtualizing` can be set to true or false on controls using a `VirtualizingStackPanel` such as the `ListBox` control. In Silverlight, however, this property is read-only.

Unvirtualizing the ListBox

In some cases, the application may require virtualization to be turned off on a `ListBox` control (for example, in the following scenarios):

- The content of a `DataTemplate` executes a long-lasting operation when it is loaded (for example, a `UserControl` connects to a web service). Because virtualizing items recycles the `DataTemplate` when it is brought out of sight, and creates a new one when it is in sight again, this might cause more delays and unnecessary connections.
- A scrolling operation must be extremely fast and the content of the `DataTemplate` is very complex. In this case, creating and rendering new `DataTemplate` elements while scrolling might render the movement less smooth. It may be preferable to make the user patient while the `DataTemplate` elements are initially rendered, and avoid delays later.

These are marginal cases; in general, it is safe to leave the virtualization turned on the `ListBox` control. Should that really be needed, however, the virtualization can be removed from the `ListBox` by using the markup in Listing 21.7.

LISTING 21.7 `ListBox` Without Virtualization

```
<ListBox Margin="10"
         ItemsSource="{Binding Items}"
         ItemTemplate="{StaticResource MyDataTemplate}"
         x:Name="MyListControl">
    <ListBox.ItemsPanel>
        <ItemsPanelTemplate>
            <StackPanel />
        </ItemsPanelTemplate>
    </ListBox.ItemsPanel>
</ListBox>
```

Simplifying the DataTemplate

A simple measure when working with list controls is to try and simplify the `DataTemplate`'s tree that will be created and rendered *for each item in the list.*

Sometimes, a compromise has to be found between the amount of markup needed to obtain the exact rendering that the designers have created in comps, and a minimum amount of XAML to keep the user experience optimal. Optimizing templates is a common task when working in XAML, and Silverlight developers should keep this in mind when creating a `DataTemplate`.

Creating Items in Batches

Working with large quantities of data can introduce delays in the application, as you saw in the "Virtualizing the User Interface" section. To improve the user experience, you saw how simplifying the `DataTemplate` and turning virtualization on can help speed up the rendering process.

However, even with these improvements, loading the items can take quite some time, during which, if nothing is done to prevent it, the user interface is blocked. Observe this effect by following these steps:

1. Download the file VirtualizationSample-Start.zip from http://www.galasoft.ch/sl4-batches. Unblock the file by displaying the file properties and pressing the Unblock button (if available). Then, extract the content of the file on your hard drive.
2. Open the VirtualizationSample.sln solution in Visual Studio.
3. The class named `ItemsService` is in charge of creating the items. To simulate a long lasting operation, this class sleeps 10 milliseconds after creating each item as shown in Listing 21.8.

LISTING 21.8 `ItemsService` Creating the Items

```
public static IEnumerable<Item> GetItems(int numberOfItems)
{
    var list = new List<Item>();

    for (var index = 0; index < numberOfItems; index++)
    {
        list.Add(
            new Item
            {
                Message = "This item was created at "
                  + DateTime.Now.ToLongTimeString()
            });

        Thread.Sleep(10);
    }

    return list;
}
```

4. The `MainViewModel` class calls the `GetItems` method to create 10,000 items. Because each item takes at least 10 milliseconds to create, the complete collection will need at least 100 seconds to create. During this long time, the user interface is blocked because everything happens on the same thread.

5. Run the application and wait until the items appear in the `ListBox`. The wait is very long and the animation is blocked. (The sphere in the bottom-right corner should be rotating instead of just sitting there.)

This is obviously a very bad way to handle a long-lasting operation. Instead, two things can be improved:

- The `GetItems` method should be called in a background thread to avoid blocking the UI.
- The items should be created in smaller batches so that the user has something to see without waiting so long. For example, if items are created in batches of 100, the user only has to wait one second before something appears on the screen. The total loading time will be the same eventually, but the user will have the feeling that he didn't wait that long.

This technique has one small disadvantage: The vertical `ScrollBar` on the side of the `ListBox` will gradually change until all the items are loaded. This is not very noticeable, but can be disturbing, especially if the user attempts to drag the `ScrollBar`'s cursor before all the items are loaded.

Working in Threads

Starting background threads in fairly easy in Silverlight. However, multithreading is a very complex programming style because every operation is asynchronous and it is hard to keep the overview on what is happening. You'll learn more about multithreading in Chapter 22, "Advanced Development Techniques."

Note that for web service requests (such as a Windows Communication Foundation (WCF) request, WCF RIA Services operation, or any other web-based service call), the request is already happening on a background thread (asynchronous operation), and it is not necessary to manually start a background thread like we do with the following step:

1. Modify the `MainViewModel` constructor as shown in Listing 21.9.

LISTING 21.9 Getting the `Dispatcher` and Starting the Background Operation

```
1  private const int BatchSize = 100;
2  private readonly Dispatcher _dispatcher;
3
4  public MainViewModel()
5  {
6      Items = new ObservableCollection<Item>();
7      _dispatcher = Deployment.Current.Dispatcher;
8      ThreadPool.QueueUserWorkItem(CreateItems);
9  }
```

- Line 2 declares a private attribute of type `Dispatcher`. You'll learn more about this type later in this section and also in Chapter 22.

- Line 7 saves the Dispatcher from the Deployment.Current object for later.
- Line 8 calls the static method QueueWorkItem on the ThreadPool class and passes to it the CreateItems method that will create the 10,000 items.

Storing the Current Dispatcher

The Dispatcher class is crucial for threading operations. There is exactly one Dispatcher per Thread. This class can be used to communicate (*dispatch messages*) from one Thread to another, as you will see in a moment. The Deployment.Current object happens to store the current Thread's Dispatcher (in this case, it is the UI thread), so we can easily access it and save it for later.

Starting a Background Thread

There are multiple ways to start a background thread n Silverlight. For operations that are very local (such as the call to CreateItems), the ThreadPool class is a good alternative because it doesn't require creating or storing any object. All that is needed is a call to the static QueueUserWorkItem method.

Another good way to perform work on a background thread is to use the BackgroundWorker class. You'll learn more about this class in Chapter 22.

1. Insert the CreateItems method as shown in Listing 21.10

LISTING 21.10 Creating the Items

```
1  private void CreateItems(object state)
2  {
3      // This method runs in a background thread!
4
5      int itemsCounter = 0;
6
7      while (itemsCounter < NumberOfItems)
8      {
9          IEnumerable<Item> batchItems;
10         if (itemsCounter + BatchSize < NumberOfItems)
11         {
12             batchItems = ItemsService.GetItems(BatchSize);
13         }
14         else
15         {
16             batchItems = ItemsService.GetItems(
17                 NumberOfItems - itemsCounter);
18         }
19
20         foreach (var item in batchItems)
21         {
22             Items.Add(item);
```

```
23            }
24
25            itemsCounter += batchItems.Count();
26        }
27    }
```

- Lines 7 to 26 are executed in a loop until all the items have been created.
- Line 10 checks how many items remain to be created. If more than 100 items remain, the `GetItems` method is called for a batch of 100.
- If fewer than 100 items remain, lines 16 and 17 call `GetItems` for the remaining items.
- Then, on lines 20 to 23, the items from the batch are added to the `Items` `ObservableCollection` before the `itemsCounter` is incremented on line 25.

2. Place a breakpoint on line 22 of Listing 21.10 and run the application in debug mode by pressing F5.
3. When the debugger reaches the breakpoint, press F10 to step one operation further. The application crashes and an exception message is shown like in Figure 21.1.

The cause of the exception is a rule that every multithreaded application must respect: When an object is created on a `Thread`, it may only be accessed by other objects from the same `Thread`. In our case, the `Items` `ObservableCollection` is data bound to a `ListBox` that belongs to the UI thread, and therefore the background thread may not save items in the `ObservableCollection` without causing an exception. You'll learn more about this issue in Chapter 22.

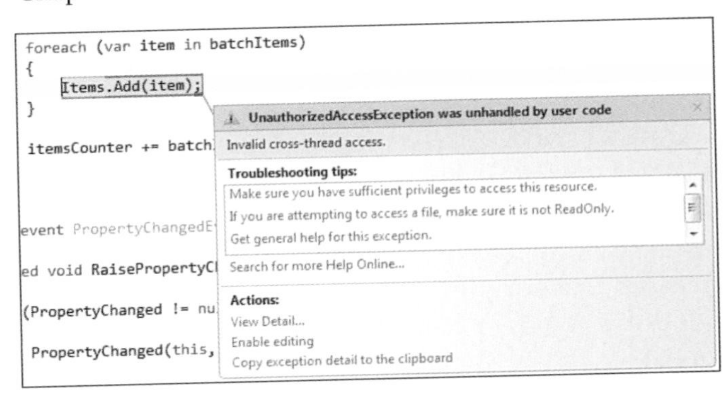

FIGURE 21.1 *UnauthorizedAccessException* in *CreateItems* method.

To correct the issue, follow these steps:

1. Modify lines 20 to 23 of Listing 21.10 as shown in Listing 21.11.

LISTING 21.11 Dispatching the Operation

```
1  foreach (var item in batchItems)
2  {
3      _dispatcher.BeginInvoke(() => Items.Add(item));
4  }
```

- Line 3 now uses the `Dispatcher` instance that was saved before (on line 7 of Listing 21.9) to pass the operation to its `Thread`. Because Listing 21.10 was executed on the UI thread, this `Dispatcher` may access the `ObservableCollection` and the `ListBox`, and the application doesn't crash.

2. Run the application. After about one second, 100 items have been created and added to the `ListBox`. You can start scrolling down. After another second, notice how the `ScrollBar` is reacting: The cursor is shrinking. This is because 100 more items were added, and the scrolling area is larger. The cursor will continue to shrink and move a little until all the items are created. This is the side effect that was mentioned in the beginning of this section.

On the other hand, the wait is much shorter before something happens on the screen. Also, the animation is not blocked because the creation of the items happens on the background thread, and the UI thread is not blocked.

Accelerating the User Interface

Modern computers have multiple processors, some of them specialized to execute certain tasks only, and to execute them well. The best known is the graphic processor unit (GPU) that is in charge of rendering the graphic elements to the screen. Depending on the age and power of the graphic card on the client computer, this processor can be extremely efficient for this task.

In the opposite, rendering graphics in the central processing unit (CPU) is slower. When possible, complex graphic operations should be delegated to the specialized GPU, which gives the CPU more cycles to take care of other tasks such as handling data, performing calculations, running threads, and so forth.

Silverlight (from Version 3) can use the GPU to perform certain tasks and speed them up, giving a smoother experience to the user. However, there are certain caveats with hardware acceleration, as you will see in this section.

Enabling Hardware Acceleration in the Browser

To test hardware acceleration, download the file HardwareAcceleration-Start.zip at http://www.galasoft.ch/sl4-gpuacceleration. Open the zip file properties and unblock it using the Unblock button (if available), then extract the content to your hard drive. Follow these steps:

1. Open the HardwareAcceleration.sln solution file in Visual Studio.

2. Set the HardwareAcceleration.Web application as Startup project, and HardwareAccelerationTestPage.html as Startup page.

3. Run the application. The scene shown in Figure 21.2 is shown, with a half transparent video playing. This video is used to "paint" (with a `VideoBrush`) a series of ellipse that are animated (scale and rotation animations).

4. When the `TextBlock` with the text set to `"Some text"` is at its largest, notice that the rendering of the text is crisp even though it is scaled at 200%.

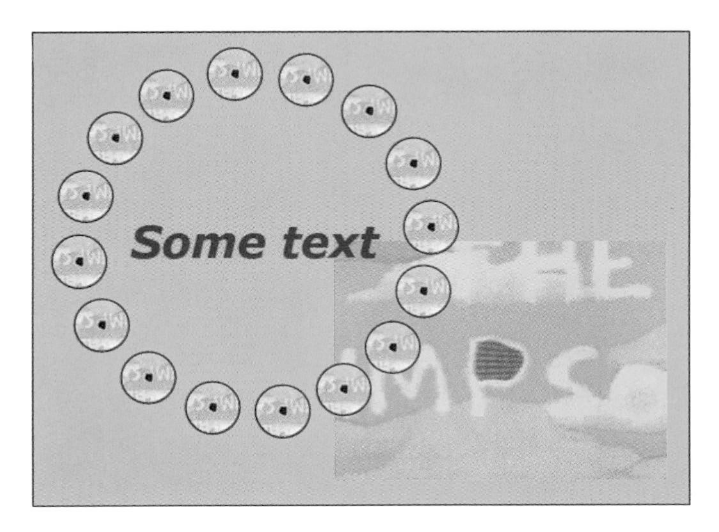

FIGURE 21.2 Scene for hardware acceleration.

5. Right-click the Windows taskbar and select Start Task Manager from the context menu.

6. In the Windows Task Manager window, select the Performance tab and then click Resource Monitor.

7. In the Resource Monitor window shown in Figure 21.3, in the Overview tab, check the check box next to the process named iexplore.exe. This is the Internet Explorer process in which the Silverlight plug-in runs the application. Note that depending on the configuration of the computer, the Silverlight application might be running in a different web browser (see the "Finding the Right Process" box).

8. Wait for a moment and write down the value of the column titled Average. This shows, in average, how much CPU time the Silverlight application requires. Remember that if your computer is a dual core, a value of 50% means that one core is working 100% of the time to render the animations. Depending on your hardware configuration, the animation might be choppy.

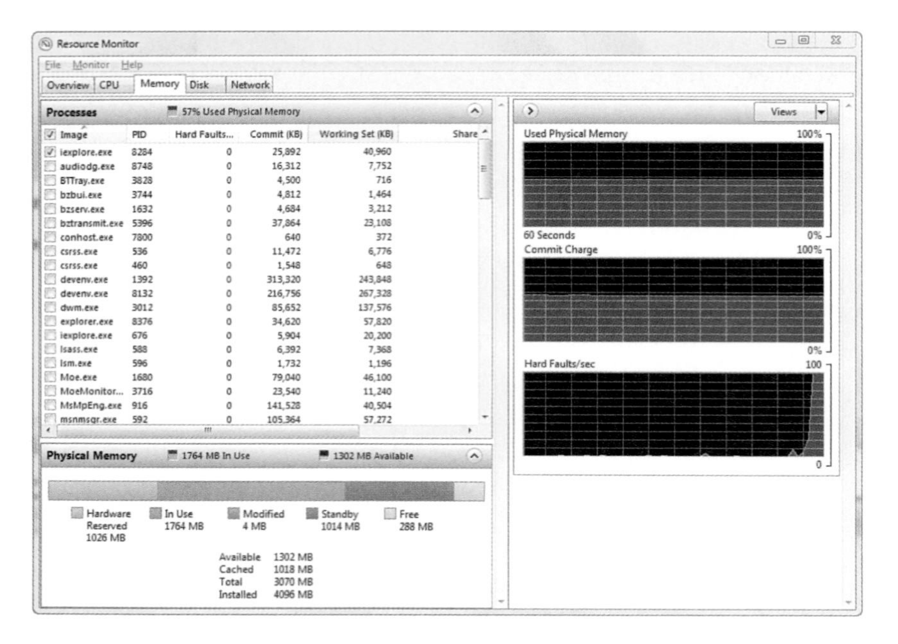

FIGURE 21.3 Resource monitor.

TIP

Finding the Right Process

Finding the right process to monitor depends on how the Silverlight application is running. For in-browser applications, the Silverlight plug-in is hosted by the web browser in which it is running. To find out which web browser is selected by Visual Studio as default browser, right-click in the Solution Explorer on HardwareAccelerationTestPage.html and select Browse With from the context menu. In the Browse With dialog, one of the choices is marked as (default). This is the web browser that Visual Studio is picking to run the Silverlight application. Note that you can also select a different web browser without changing the default thanks to this dialog.

When running out-of-browser, the Silverlight application is hosted in a process named sllauncher.exe.

If multiple instances of the web browser (or multiple OOB applications) are running at the same time, multiple processes with the same name are found in the Task Explorer. In that case, it is preferable to close the other windows to keep it simpler.

The most recent versions of Internet Explorer and the Chrome web browser run one process for the window, and an additional process for each open tab (including the one in which the Silverlight application is running). In general, it is easy to differentiate the tab's process from the window's process (which should not be monitored) because it is using more CPU and more memory.

Switching Acceleration On

By default, hardware acceleration is not enabled for a Silverlight application. To switch it on, follow these steps:

1. To instruct the plug-in to be ready for hardware acceleration, a parameter must be set in the HardwareAccelerationTestPage.html page on the `object` tag as shown in Listing 21.12.

LISTING 21.12 Setting Hardware Acceleration on the Object Tag

```
<object data="data:application/x-silverlight-2,"
        type="application/x-silverlight-2"
    width="100%" height="100%">
    <param name="source" value="ClientBin/HardwareAcceleration.xap" />
    <param name="enableGPUAcceleration" value="true" />
    ...
</object>
```

2. In MainPage.xaml, locate the `Grid` named `Container` and modify its tag as shown in Listing 21.13. The `CacheMode` property governs the way that the element (in this case, the `Grid` with the text and the `Ellipse` elements) is cached. Note that Silverlight 4 supports only the `BitmapCache` mode.

LISTING 21.13 Switching On Hardware Acceleration in XAML

```
<Grid x:Name="Container"
        Margin="50,47,252,95"
        RenderTransformOrigin="0.5,0.5"
        CacheMode="BitmapCache">
```

3. Run the application again and check the iexplore.exe process in the Resource Monitor. The Average column should display a much lower value than before, and depending on your hardware configuration, the animation may run much more smoothly.

4. When the `TextBlock` with the text set to “Some text” is at its largest, notice that some pixels are visible. It is not as smooth as it was without hardware acceleration. The same can be observed on each `Ellipse`. This effect is explained in the “Accelerating with Care” section.

By turning on hardware acceleration, the load on the CPU was reduced (and for some hardware configurations almost set to zero). This leaves much more time to this processor to perform other tasks and lets the specialized GPU handle the heavy rendering operations.

Checking What Is Hardware Accelerated

Mixing accelerated and nonaccelerated surfaces can, in fact, create a worse performance than not using acceleration at all. Because the surfaces are rendered by different processors, intertwining them complicates the rendering process and slows down the whole scene.

To visualize what surfaces are hardware accelerated, the Silverlight plug-in can be set in a visualization mode with the following steps. Note that this feature should be used during development only.

1. Open HardwareAccelerationTestPage.html.
2. Set an additional parameter on the object tag as shown in Listing 21.14.

LISTING 21.14 Enabling Cache Visualization

```
<param name="enableCacheVisualization" value="true" />
```

3. Run the application again. The surfaces that are *not* hardware accelerated are rendered through a colored layer as shown in Figure 21.4. Only the surfaces that are rendered in GPU are not colored. Note that the pixilation is visible in this figure for the text and the `Ellipse` elements.

FIGURE 21.4 Hardware accelerated surfaces without coloring.

Enabling Hardware Acceleration Out of the Browser

Applications running out of the browser (OOB) are not hosted in a HTML page. Instead, they are rendered in a window host, as shown in Chapter 14, “Enhancing Line-of-Business Applications and Running Out of the Browser.” In these applications, a setting is found in the project properties, as shown by the following steps:

1. Open the HardwareAcceleration Silverlight project properties.
2. In the Silverlight tab, check the Enable Running Application Out of the Browser check box.
3. Open the Out-of-Browser Settings and check the Use GPU Acceleration check box.
4. Run the application again, and then right-click its surface and select Install HardwareAcceleration Application onto this Computer.
5. In the OOB application, notice that the text is still pixilated, which is the case when `BitmapCache` is used.

Accelerating with Care

Hardware acceleration works especially well on certain animations affecting a transform as well as when working with opacity (for example, to create a reveal effect between two surfaces). There are, however, a few things that one needs to consider when using hardware acceleration:

- Because the scene on which `BitmapCache` is enabled is converted to a bitmap, it can get pixilated. This is the effect that we noticed when the blue `TextBlock` is scaled to 200%. Although hardware acceleration works great on scale animations, it is preferable to avoid using it if the `ScaleX` and/or `ScaleY` properties are set to more than 100%. Instead, start with a large scene in XAML and use the animation to shrink it to less than 100%.
- As you saw earlier, it is best to avoid mixing accelerated and nonaccelerated surfaces too much. This can be counterproductive.
- Some elements and effects cannot be hardware accelerated:

  `OpacityMask` and nonrectangular clips. (We talked about `OpacityMask` and about clips in *Silverlight 2 Unleashed*, Chapter 6.) Note that if a rectangular clip is rotated, it is not accelerated either.

  The `WriteableBitmap` class renders its content through a different medium and does not benefit from hardware acceleration.

Contrary to Silverlight 3, elements with the following effects are hardware accelerated in Silverlight 4:

- Perspective transforms
- DeepZoom scenes (discussed in *Silverlight 2 Unleashed*, Chapter 16)

> **TIP**
>
> **Accelerating Children**
>
> Even though an element with `CacheMode="BitmapCache"` cannot be accelerated if a nonrectangular clip or an `OpacityMask` is applied to it, the same is not true from its children. The children of an accelerated UI element can be clipped or have their `OpacityMask` set.

Accelerating in the Windows Phone 7

In a Silverlight application running in a Windows Phone 7 device, a notable difference is that most animations are running on a specialized thread named the *render thread*. This is interesting because it allows smoother and faster animations on a platform with less power than a desktop or laptop computer.

Also, the Silverlight application does not run in a HTML page, and the `EnableGPUAcceleration` parameter is always true.

When the application runs in the Windows Phone 7 emulator, it is only accelerated on computers sporting a graphic card compatible with DirectX10 with WDDM 1.1. Failing this, the rendering will fall back to the CPU. On the Windows Phone 7 devices, however, hardware rendering is always enabled.

Using a Code Profiler

If after the measures mentioned earlier in this chapter your Silverlight application still runs slow, it is a good idea to use a profiler to find out which parts of the application should be sped up. There are multiple types of profilers:

A code profiler attaches to an *instrumented* application and measures the time that various parts of the applications require to run to completion. This type of profilers is preferred to find issues with I/O (writing and reading files), memory related issues, etc.

> **TIP**
>
> **Instrumenting an Assembly**
>
> Instrumenting an assembly is the process of adding some hooks within the assembly to which a utility can attach and perform calculation. For the profiler, the hooks are used to determine how long a given portion of the code is taking to run. The profiler typically takes care of this during a preliminary step.

Another type of profiler is called *sample based profiler* and does not require instrumenting the assemblies. Instead, they take a sample periodically (such as a stack trace, reading a performance counter, and so on). This kind of profilers is preferred to investigate issues related to the CPU (for example, what methods need more time to perform). For Silverlight applications, it is generally recommended to use a sample based profiler to find issues.

After the application runs, the code profiler prepares a report where it is visible which portions of the code need more time to be executed. The developer can dive deeper in this portion and try to optimize, to let the application run faster.

Optimizing the performance of an application is a long and sometimes difficult process. It is practically impossible to tune an application to the perfection, especially in the case of cross platform frameworks such as Silverlight, where the available hardware can range from quite old and slow computers without hardware acceleration to very fast top-of-the-line machines. It is good to remember during development that many users have less powerful computers than a developer typically owns, and to test often on slow computers to find out areas where issues might arise later. As usual, the rule of developing in small increments and testing these increments often applies here, too.

At the time of this writing, Visual Studio Premium and Ultimate editions come with a sample based profiler for Silverlight 4. Instructions can be found at http://www.galasoft.ch/sl4-vs10profiler. Also, the firm EQATEC has a commercial code profiler available at http://www.galasoft.ch/sl4-profiler.

Avoiding Memory Leaks

Next to saving CPU and trying to speed up applications, another critical resource of computers is the random access memory (RAM). Even though modern desktops and even laptops are equipped with an amount of RAM that seemed just impossible just a few years ago, applications have also become more complex, and the risk of memory leak is still present and must be taken care of.

Saving an Object on the Stack or the Heap

In Silverlight and in .NET, there are two kinds of objects: Those held *by value* and those held *by reference*. To make things a little more complicated, there are also two kinds of memory in a computer: the *stack* and the *heap*.

Value types are simple types such as `int`, `bool`, `double` and other primitive types. These values belong to the object that created them, but no other object can reference them. Instead, if an object attempts to access them, a copy is created for this consumer.

Reference types on the other hand can be referenced by multiple objects, as shown in Figure 21.5. A reference to such an object is sometimes known as *a pointer* (as it was called in the C++ programming language), although nowadays C# developers rather speak of a *reference* to an object.

Reference types are always stored on the heap memory. This kind of memory is optimized for larger objects that have a longer lifetime. On the other hand, the stack is a kind of memory that is optimized for faster access and frequent cleanups. Although the stack is easy to clean up, the heap requires special attention, with the help of the so-called garbage collector (GC).

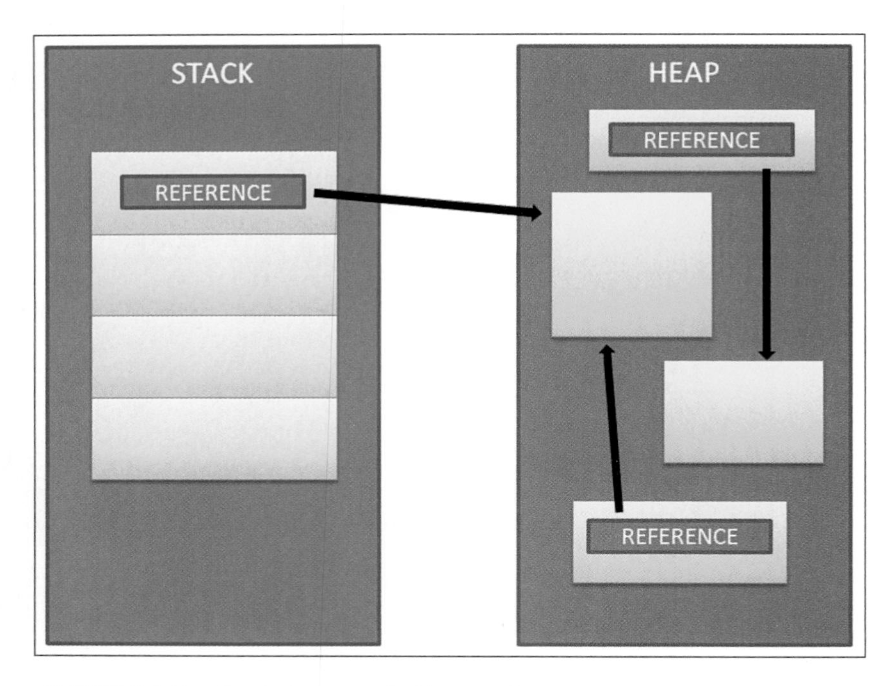

FIGURE 21.5 Stack, heap, and objects references.

Collecting Garbage and Leaking Memory

.NET is a *managed environment,* which means that the .NET application does not typically access the computer's hardware directly. Instead, application programming interfaces (APIs) are used. For the developer, this is interesting because the risk of crashes is reduced compared to older technologies such as unmanaged MFC applications written in C++ for instance.

A good example of this is memory management. Developers writing in non-managed languages such as C/C++ had to manage memory manually, deleting unused objects explicitly and freeing the memory. In the contrary, the garbage collector used by .NET monitors periodically which objects are not used anymore, and removes them from memory. Garbage collection is a very fascinating topic: On one hand, the garbage collection must occur from time to time to avoid that the computer runs out of memory. On the other hand, collecting garbage is a slow process, and running the GC too often will slow down the application and the computer. A lot more information about the garbage collector in .NET can be found at http://www.galasoft.ch/sl4-gc (video with Patrick Dussud, who was at the origin of the .NET garbage collector at Microsoft).

Finding Which Objects Can Be Collected

On every cycle, the garbage collector is looking for objects that the application is not using anymore. In the great lines, here is how GC works:

- Starting at a root object, all the children, then the children's children (and so on) are marked (typically by setting a flag on the objects). For instance, if an object has an array of other objects, these other objects are reachable and thus are marked.
- Of course, certain objects are marked multiple times because more than one object is keeping a reference to them. This is not a problem because if there is at least one reference to this object, it will be spared.
- Then, all objects are inspected. Those without the flag set are unreachable by any other object. They are collected, and the memory they were using is freed.

One can see why this process is taking time. Also, during the inspection, it is crucial that the tree of objects is not modified. During the garbage collection time, no other operation may run.

In the past few years, GC has been very much optimized and improved with new algorithms. Concepts like this of *generation* help the GC to identify faster which objects are more likely to be unused by the application. Fundamentally, however, one fact remains true: If an object holds a reference to another child object, the child is considered in use by the application. Note that this is the case even if the object has been forgotten and is not actually needed by the application anymore. It is easy to understand that keeping track of these references and attempting to free them when possible will help to optimize memory.

> **TIP**
>
> **Sorting Objects in Generations**
>
> In short, the concept of *generation* specifies that objects that "survived" garbage collection a first time will be assigned to generation 1, and will be visited less often by the garbage collector than new objects (in generation 0). Similarly, objects that survived a generation 1 garbage collection will be assigned to generation 2, and will be visited even less often. This speeds up the garbage collection by assuming that older objects are less likely to be modified often than new objects.

Freeing an Object

For the developer, freeing an object amounts to making sure that all the references to that object are set to `null`:

- For local variables inside a block (such as a loop, a method, and so on), the reference will automatically be set to `null` when the block is exited.
- For global variables, the reference should be set to `null` manually to make sure that the object can be garbage collected (given of course that no other references to that object are found in the application). For example consider the classes in Listing 21.15.

LISTING 21.15 Class Hierarchy

```
 1  public class MyCustomObject
 2  {
 3      private MyChildObject _child;
 4      public MyCustomObject(MyChildObject child)
 5      {
 6          _child = child;
 7      }
 8      // ...
 9  }
10
11  public class MyOtherObject
12  {
13      private MyChildObject _child;
14      public MyOtherObject(MyChildObject child)
15      {
16          _child = child;
17      }
18      // ...
19  }
20
21  public class MyChildObject
22  {
23      // ...
24  }
```

Creating and freeing the classes can occur as in Listing 21.16.

LISTING 21.16 Creating and Freeing the Classes

```
 1  public partial class MainPage : UserControl
 2  {
 3      private MyCustomObject _custom;
 4      private MyOtherObject _other;
 5
 6      public MainPage()
 7      {
 8          InitializeComponent();
 9
10          var child = new MyChildObject();
11          _custom = new MyCustomObject(child);
12          _other = new MyOtherObject(child);
13
14          // ...
15
```

```
16            _other = null; // free the reference
17        }
18    }
```

- Both _custom and _other are kept as reference by the MainPage class (lines 3 and 4 declares them as private attributes).
- An instance of MyChildObject is created on line 10. Because it is local, this reference will be deleted when the block exits; that is when the constructor finishes execution.
- However, this instance has been passed to the MyCustomObject and to the MyOtherObject constructors who in turn store a reference to that instance (lines 3 and 13 of Listing 21.15).
- On line 16 the reference named _other is set to null explicitly. Because no one else keeps a reference to that instance, it will be collected the next time that the GC runs. However, the instance of MyChildObject is still referenced by the MyCustomObject instance, and therefore it cannot be freed.

Here we see that it is critical to explicitly free large objects by setting all their references to null, so that the GC considers them as unused. Forgetting even just one reference will prevent the memory to be freed.

Living a Shorter Life

In-browser Silverlight applications typically have a shorter life than, for example, WPF applications running on the desktop. Because of this, the risk of getting a really critical memory leak in an in-browser Silverlight application is smaller: When the web page hosting the plug in is either refreshed or navigated away from, the memory is cleaned up and the computer is not at risk.

However, Silverlight 4 and the new advanced OOB applications are much more similar to desktop applications than to web applications. Their lifetime is typically longer, and a memory leak in these applications is much more dangerous. Generally speaking, it is good to remember that Silverlight applications are rich applications, and that regardless of where and how they are running, memory leaks should be avoided absolutely.

Unregistering Event Handlers

A typical mistake done by .NET programmers is related to event handling: Consider the code in Listing 21.17.

LISTING 21.17 Strong Event Handling

```
1  public class MyObjectWithEvents
2  {
3      public event EventHandler<EventArgs> SomethingHappened;
4      // ...
5  }
```

```
 6
 7  public partial class MainPage : UserControl
 8  {
 9      public MainPage()
10      {
11          InitializeComponent();
12
13          var myObject = new MyObjectWithEvents();
14          myObject.SomethingHappened += HandleSomethingHappened;
15          // …
16      }
17
18      private void HandleSomethingHappened(object sender, EventArgs e)
19      {
20          // …
21      }
22  }
```

- On line 13, an instance of `MyObjectWithEvents` is created. Note that it is stored as a local variable, and therefore will be garbage collected as soon as the block (the `MainPage` constructor) is finished executing.
- Line 14 assigns an event handler (the `HandleSomethingChanged` method) to the `SomethingChanged` event of the `MyObjectWithEvents` instance.

This simple operation caused a potential memory leak: An event handler is creating a *strong reference* between the object that raises the event (in that case, the `myObject` instance) and the object that handles the event (`MainPage`). When the constructor exits, `myObject` cannot be collected for deletion by the GC because of this strong reference.

To solve the issue, the event handler must be removed before the block exits with the line of code shown in Listing 21.18, to be placed between lines 15 and 16 of Listing 21.17.

LISTING 21.18 Removing the Event Handler

```
myObject.SomethingHappened -= HandleSomethingHappened;
```

Properly removing all the event handlers on unused references before exiting a block or before a class is deleted is a good practice that reduces the memory leaks and ensures that your application will run more smoothly and provide a better user experience.

Using Commands Instead

In contrast to events, the `Command` property of a `Button` control is set through a `Binding`, which creates a less strong dependency between two objects. Even though the `Command` references another object (for example, a view-model), this does not prevent the view-model object to be garbage collected if needed. Using commands rather than events is a good practice because of the looser dependency that it creates between two objects.

Disposing Objects

Another kind of objects should be cleaned up after the application is done using them: the types implementing the IDisposable interface. When an object is defined as IDisposable by its developer, it is a clear indication that this object might have used resources that should be properly cleaned up. For example, this might be an access to the file system (for the Stream, StreamReader, StreamWriter, and other classes), a connection to a database, and so forth.

Closing and disposing such objects used to be an annoying process but in more recent versions of .NET (and in Silverlight), it has become very easy thanks to the using keyword. For example, a StreamReader and its Stream are automatically closed and disposed by the code in Listing 21.19.

LISTING 21.19 Closing and Disposing a Stream and StreamReader

```
var dialog = new OpenFileDialog();
if (dialog.ShowDialog() == true)
{
    using (var stream = dialog.File.OpenRead())
    {
        using (var reader = new StreamReader(stream))
        {
            // Read the file
        }
    }
}
```

You can find more information about the IDisposable pattern at http://www.galasoft.ch/sl4-idisposable.

Using Weak References

One way to avoid strong references between objects is to use the WeakReference class. This special class keeps a reference to an object but does not prevent it to be garbage collected.

For example, the sample shown in Listing 21.15 can be modified to avoid blocking the MyChildObject instance, as shown in Listing 21.20.

LISTING 21.20 Using a WeakReference

```
1  public class MyCustomObject
2  {
3      private WeakReference _childReference;
4
5      public MyCustomObject(MyChildObject child)
6      {
7          _childReference = new WeakReference(child);
8      }
```

```
 9
10       // ...
11
12       public void UseChild()
13       {
14           if (_childReference != null
15               && _childReference.IsAlive)
16           {
17               (_childReference.Target as MyChildObject).DoSomething();
18           }
19       }
20   }
```

- Line 3 declares a WeakReference instead of storing the instance of MyChildObject as an attribute directly.
- Line 7 constructs a new WeakReference instance and passes it the child.
- Finally, when the child needs to be used, line 15 makes sure that the MyChildObject instance is still alive. Because WeakReference does not prevent the GC to delete the child object, this step is necessary to avoid calling disposed objects.
- If the object is still alive, the Target property of the WeakReference is used to access the stored object.

As Listing 21.20 shows, using a WeakReference is more convoluted than using an attribute directly. Although this class is very useful in some cases, it must be used with care. In many cases indeed, an object referenced by another object should *not* be allowed to be deleted. This is exactly the intent of the reference: to signal that the referenced object is still needed. Instead, the WeakReference class can be used when two objects should have a way to communicate, but neither object is responsible for the other object's lifetime.

Finding a Leak

If, in spite of all the precautions mentioned in this section, a memory leak is suspected in an application, you can use the WinDbg utility to find the cause. A detailed explanation of the process can be found at http://www.galasoft.ch/sl4-windbg.

Also, Visual Studio Premium and Ultimate support some limited profiling of memory garbage collection as well as allocation and object lifetime.

Summary

Although it is easy in Silverlight to create beautiful applications, the topic of performance should not be neglected: A smooth-running application participates as much to a beautiful user experience than the user interface itself. This chapter showed some techniques and tools that can be used to improve the application's performance in multiple places: When the application is downloaded, when it runs, and when it stores items in memory. Applying these few rules should take care of many risks, but eventually tuning an application is a process that requires time and experience. Make sure to plan enough time in your projects to test the performance of the application and to find ways to make it run faster and more smoothly.

In the next and last chapter, we talk about a few advanced software development techniques related to .NET and especially Silverlight.

CHAPTER 22

Advanced Development Techniques

IN THIS CHAPTER, WE WILL:

- Study new features of the C# language such as lambda expressions, the `dynamic` keyword, and named parameters.
- Localize applications to prepare it for users of other cultures.
- Encrypt and decrypt text to store it or send it securely.
- Talk about multithreading and understand how Silverlight applications can be enhanced with background workers.
- Use unit tests to develop our applications

In this last chapter, we will study advanced techniques that Silverlight developers can use to solve programming problems, extend their applications, or make them perform better.

Using New C# and .NET Features

C# as a language and the .NET framework have been continuously enhanced since they were first released in 2001. Early versions of C# were extremely static and type safe: If the application didn't show errors at compilation, it meant that most errors had been already avoided. The downside to this approach was that static languages are limited in their abilities to be extended, to communicate with interfaces that are not defined in advance, and so forth. In the opposite, dynamic languages (such as JavaScript, Ruby, Python, and so on) are very extensible and flexible, but they are also more risky to program against.

Using Modern Programming Syntax

To improve the situation and make C# more dynamic, a few improvements were brought into C# in the latest versions.

Using Lambda Expressions

We already used lambda expressions in this book. They are a neat way to define anonymous delegates that can be passed as argument to another method, for instance, or to create event handlers as shown in Listing 22.1.

LISTING 22.1 Lambda Expressions

```
1  MouseMove += (s, e) =>
2  {
3      DoSomething(s);
4      DoSomethingElse(s, e);
5  };
6
7  MouseLeftButtonDown += (s, e) =>
8      HandleMousePosition(e.GetPosition(this));
```

- Lines 1 to 5 define an anonymous event handler for the `MouseMove` event. Because the anonymous method's body has more than one line, the block syntax is used.
- Lines 7 and 8 define another anonymous event handler for the `MouseLeftButtonDown` event. Here, only one line of code is executed, so the block can be left out, allowing for a very compact and elegant syntax.

Using Action and Func

The introduction of the `Action` and `Func` classes allow considering a method just like an object. Such instances can be passed to another object, stored, and executed later. This reduces the need for more complex object-oriented mechanisms such as defining interfaces, as shown in Listing 22.2.

LISTING 22.2 Action and Func

```
1  private Action<bool> _callback;
2
3  public void CallAsynchronousService(Action<bool> callback)
4  {
5      this._callback = callback;
6      var client = new WebClient();
7
8      client.DownloadStringCompleted
9          += ClientDownloadStringCompleted;
10     client.DownloadStringAsync(
11         new Uri("http://www.silverlight.net"));
12 }
13
14 void ClientDownloadStringCompleted(
15     object sender,
16     DownloadStringCompletedEventArgs e)
17 {
18     if (_callback != null)
19     {
20         _callback(e.Error == null);
21     }
22 }
```

- Line 1 declares a callback that will be passed to the `CallAsynchronousService` method, and executed later when the asynchronous service call is completed.
- On lines 20, the callback is actually executed. The `CallAsynchronousService` method can be called by a consumer, as shown in Listing 22.3.

LISTING 22.3 Calling the `CallAsynchronousService` Method

```
 1  public void Test()
 2  {
 3      CallAsynchronousService(
 4          result => MessageBox.Show(result ? "Success" : "Error"));
 5
 6      CallAsynchronousService(HandleResult);
 7  }
 8
 9  public void HandleResult(bool result)
10  {
11      // Do something
12  }
```

- Lines 3 and 4 call the asynchronous method by providing an anonymous delegate for the callback (expressed as a lambda expression).
- Line 6 uses a different syntax and passes a so-called method group, which is in fact a named reference to the method defined on lines 9 to 12.

`Func` delegates are similar to the `Action` delegate, but they return a value as shown in Listing 22.4.

LISTING 22.4 Using a `Func` to Filter Items

```
1  public IEnumerable<Customer> GetCustomers(string lastName)
2  {
3      return Customers.Where(c => c.LastName == lastName);
4  }
```

- On line 3, a `Func<Customer, bool>` is used as a filter for the `Where` query method. This very compact syntax (again) is equivalent to the code shown in Listing 22.5.

LISTING 22.5 Verbose Syntax to Filter Items

```
public IEnumerable<Customer> GetCustomers(string lastName)
{
    var foundCustomers = new List<Customer>();
    foreach (var customer in Customers)
    {
        if (customer.LastName == lastName)
```

```
        {
            foundCustomers.Add(customer);
        }
    }
    return foundCustomers.AsEnumerable();
}
```

Note that multiple overloads exist for the `Func` and `Action` constructors, allowing using delegates with multiple parameters.

Chaining Methods

More attention has been put into creating classes that allow a *fluent syntax* such as the one creating LINQ queries. Each method's result can be *chained* to the next method. This is a very elegant way to write code. Note that in the case of LINQ, another syntax is available, using keywords such as `select`, `from`, `where`, `orderby` and so forth. You are free to choose which syntax you prefer.

Other frameworks allow using fluent syntax, too. The key to creating an object allowing fluent syntax is to always return an instance that can be used by the next call. For example, Listing 22.6 shows methods that can be chained.

LISTING 22.6 Fluent Syntax

```
public class Item
{
    private int _counter;

    public Item Increment()
    {
        _counter++;
        return this;
    }

    public Item Execute()
    {
        if (_counter % 2 == 0)
        {
            // Do something...
        }
        return this;
    }
}

//...

public void IncrementAndExecuteItem()
{
```

```
    var item = new Item();
    item.Increment().Execute()
        .Increment().Execute();
}
```

In Listing 22.6, notice how each method returns the current `Item` instance, allowing the next method to be called directly. For more information about fluent interfaces, check out this article: http://www.galasoft.ch/sl4-fluent. Note that, as Martin Fowler underlines, building a good fluent interface is quite hard, which is why this programming style is not available frequently.

Creating Extension Methods

Extension methods were already mentioned a few times in this book. They are a way to add functionality to a class that cannot be modified (because you don't have the source code, or because you want the changes to be applied only in certain cases). Such a method is shown in Listing 22.7.

LISTING 22.7 Creating an Extension Method

```
namespace ExtensionMethodSample.Helpers
{
    public static class CustomerHelper
    {
        public static string GetFullName(
            this Customer caller)
        {
            return caller.FirstName
                + " "
                + caller.LastName;
        }
    }
}
```

The method in Listing 22.7 adds functionality to a WCF proxy object named `Customer` (such as we used in Chapter 7, "Understanding the Model-View-ViewModel Pattern"). This class has a `FirstName` and a `LastName` properties, but it lacks the `FullName` property. Since the `Customer` class is generated by Visual Studio, it cannot be modified. Using an extension method is a convenient way to add the desired property.

Note that extension methods can have additional parameters (but the `this` parameter must always be first). They can be added in external assemblies too. Also, extension methods can be added not only to classes, but also to interfaces (just like LINQ adds extension methods to the `IEnumerable` interface as well as others).

Using the Extension Method

To use the extension method in your code, you must take care of referencing the DLL that hosts the method (if needed), and to add a `using` directive at the top of the page, pointing to the namespace in which the helper method is defined. The extension method will only appear in IntelliSense after you add the `using` directive, as shown in figure 22.1.

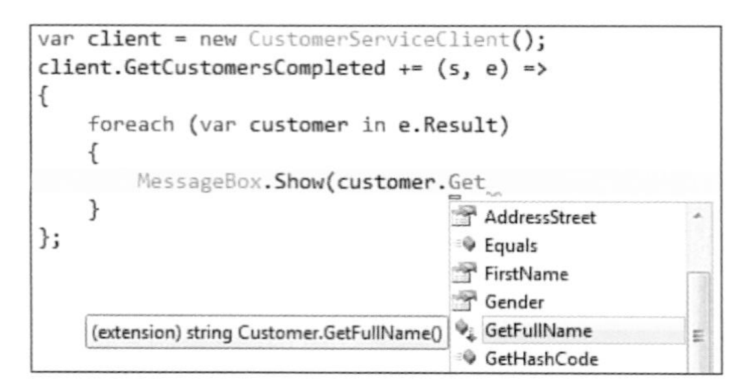

FIGURE 22.1 The extension method in IntelliSense.

Using Extension Methods with Care

Extension methods can be confusing, especially for inexperienced programmers who may have difficulties to understand why a method is available in some situations, but not in others. While certain parts of the Silverlight frameworks (such as LINQ) make extensive use of extension methods, you may want to think twice before adding such methods to your libraries.

Consuming Dynamic Objects

The `dynamic` keyword is an addition that enables more flexibility in the C# language. For example, this keyword can be used with the COM automation that we covered in Chapter 18, "Drag and Drop, Full Screen, Clipboard, COM Interop, Duplex Polling, Notification Windows and Splash Screens," to interact with applications such as Word, Excel, or even the Windows operating system.

Another usage for the dynamic keyword is with dynamic languages such as IronRuby and IronPython (the .NET versions of the languages Ruby and Python). This enables loading and executing script files at runtime; for example, the user may be asked to load a script file that will be read and executed. Or, Ruby/Python scripts may be embedded inside the HTML file and used at runtime to customize the Silverlight experience.

More information about dynamic languages can be found at http://www.galasoft.ch/sl4-dynamic. A very interesting experiment with dynamic languages using Silverlight as an engine is called Gestalt and exposed at http://www.galasoft.ch/sl4-gestalt.

Using Named/Optional Parameters

Another really nice improvement in C# 4.0 that is also available in Silverlight 4 is the possibility to define named parameters in methods. This answers an issue that is often found into frameworks: The need to define multiple overloads for a method, to allow for different sets of parameters. In C# 4.0, this can be replaced by the code in Listing 22.8.

LISTING 22.8 Using Named Parameters

```
 1  public void Execute(
 2      bool flag = false,
 3      string firstName = string.Empty)
 4  {
 5      // Do something
 6  }
 7
 8  public void Test()
 9  {
10      Execute(firstName: "Laurent");
11  }
```

- Line 2 specifies that a `bool` parameter can be passed to the method. However, it is optional. If the parameter is missing, its value is set to `false`.
- Similarly, a second optional parameter is defined, named `firstName` and its default value set to `string.Empty`.
- Line 10 shows how the method can be called with only the `firstName` parameter.

With these improvements, C# 4.0 is a more dynamic and friendlier programming language. The fact that Silverlight can execute script files in Python or Ruby and that it can communicate with COM interfaces (on Windows and with elevated permissions only) opens new possibilities in creating powerful applications. However, more power means more responsibility, and there is a risk to create more unstable applications at runtime.

Localizing Applications

Localization is the process used to adapt an application to various regions of the world and various cultures. This goes beyond translating the texts of the application! In some cultures, colors have different meanings than in others. Icons can be interpreted very differently. Also, some cultures use right-to-left languages.

Adding a Resource File

In .NET, resources are stored in RESX files (that is, files named *.resx). When the application is compiled, the resources are parsed and embedded inside the assembly. Visual Studio also provides easy access to these resources through a generated class. In most cases, the localized resources stored in the RESX file are strings, but the file can also handle icons, images, audio files, and so forth.

> **WARNING**
>
> **There Are Resources and Resources**
>
> Do not get confused! The resources we store in a `ResourceDictionary` in XAML and the resources used to localize an application are quite different. In this section, we are not talking about XAML resources.

Making an Application Localizable

In this sample, we take a simple application and localize it with the following steps:

1. Download LocalizationSample-Start.zip from http://www.galasoft.ch/sl4-localize. As always, unblock the file and extract the content to your hard drive. Then open LocalizationSample.sln in Visual Studio.
2. Make LocalizationSample.Web the Startup project and LocalizationSampleTestPage.html the Startup page.
3. Run the application. A single `TextBlock` displays a text in English.
4. Right-click the Silverlight project and select Add, New Item from the context menu.
5. In the Add New Item dialog, under General, select a Resources file and name it **Resources.resx**.
6. In Resources.resx, add a new text with the name `"TestString"` and the value `"This is a test string"`. It is a good idea to use the same text for the Value and for the Comment columns.
7. Still in Resources.resx, make sure that the Access Modifier combo box is set to Public, as shown in Figure 22.2.

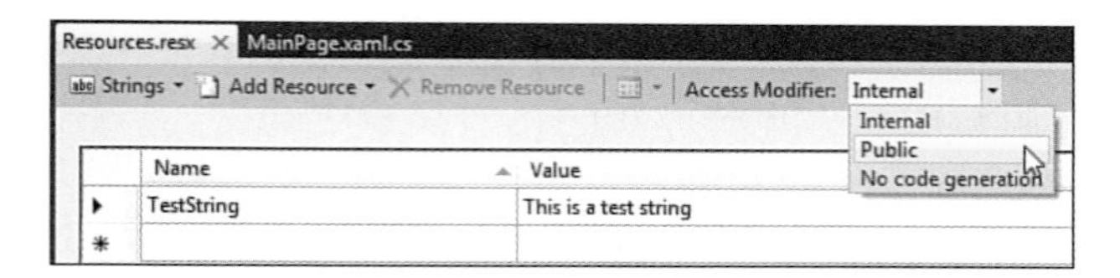

FIGURE 22.2 Changing the access modifier.

8. Close Resources.resx. Then, copy this file in the Solution Explorer and paste it. Rename the copy Resources.fr-FR.resx.
9. Open the new file and replace the value with the translation **C'est une chaîne de caractères pour tests**.
10. It is better to keep RESX files into the Properties folder, so select both and move them into this folder in the Solution Explorer.

Including the Resource DLL in the XAP

When the application is built, the fr-FR resources are placed in an external assembly in the folder bin\Debug\fr-FR. This assembly is called LocalizationSample.resources.dll and contains only resources. For the assembly to be placed in the XAP file and made available to the Silverlight application, the project file needs to be edited manually with the following steps:

1. Right-click the Silverlight project and select Unload Project from the context menu.
2. Right-click the unloaded project and select Edit LocalizationSample.csproj.

3. Look for the SupportedCultures tag and modify it to <SupportedCultures>fr-FR</SupportedCultures>. If you have multiple cultures, enter their code separated with commas.

4. Save and close the CSPROJ file.

5. Right-click the unloaded project and select Reload Project.

When the application is built next, the satellite DLL will be added to the XAP file. Note that if you need to support multiple cultures, this can add quite a lot of bulk to the XAP file, which is annoying. To improve this, check the "Downloading Resources on Demand" section.

Using a ResourceManager for Data Binding

Visual Studio generates a class named LocalizationSample.Properties.Resources that allows easy access to the embedded localized resources. For example, this class in the current sample has a property named TestString that can be used to access the localized string. Depending on the current culture, the framework will try to find a corresponding resource. For example, if the culture is set to fr-FR, the Resources.fr-FR.resx file will be used. If the culture is set to it-IT, no corresponding file is found. In that case, the Resources.resx file is used. This is called the *fallback resources*. Note that if traditionally fallback resources are localized in American English (en-US), this is by no means an obligation.

In a perfect world, it would be possible to use the Properties.Resources class to directly data-bind a UI element's property to a localized value. Unfortunately, there is a small bug in the current version of Visual Studio that needs a quick workaround with the following steps:

1. Add a new class to the Silverlight project and name it Localizer.cs.

2. Implement the Localizer class as shown in Listing 22.9. This class is exposing an instance of the Resources class so that we can indirectly data bind to its properties. This takes care of the small bug previously mentioned.

LISTING 22.9 Localizer Class

```
public class Localizer
{
    private static readonly Properties.Resources _resources
        = new Properties.Resources();

    public Properties.Resources Localize
    {
        get { return _resources; }
    }
}
```

3. Open App.xaml and add an instance of the `Localizer` class to the `Application.Resources` as shown in Listing 22.10.

LISTING 22.10 Adding a `Localizer` to the Global Resources

```
<Application.Resources>
    <local:Localizer x:Key="Localizer"
        xmlns:local="clr-namespace:LocalizationSample"/>
</Application.Resources>x
```

4. Then, in MainPage.xaml, change the `Text` property of the `TextBlock` as shown in Listing 22.11.

LISTING 22.11 Binding Through a `Localizer`

```
Text="{Binding Source={StaticResource Localizer},
               Path=Localize.TestString}"
```

5. Run the application. The string should appear just like before.

TIP

Changing the Neutral Language

If you decide to change the fallback culture, it is good to also set the corresponding value in the assembly information by opening the Silverlight project properties, selecting Silverlight, Assembly Information, and then choosing the correct neutral culture.

Changing the Culture

In this sample, we use the URL of the HTML page to select a different culture. To do this, open App.xaml.cs and modify the `App` constructor as shown in Listing 22.12.

LISTING 22.12 Loading the Culture

```
private const string QueryParameter = "culture=";

public App()
{
    var query = HtmlPage.Document.DocumentUri.Query;
    if (!string.IsNullOrEmpty(query)
        && query.IndexOf(QueryParameter) > -1)
    {
        var queryParameters = query.Split(new char[] { '&' });

        foreach (var parameter in queryParameters)
        {
            if (parameter.StartsWith(QueryParameter)
                || parameter.StartsWith("?" + QueryParameter))
            {
```

```
                var values = parameter.Split(new char[] { '=' });

                Thread.CurrentThread.CurrentCulture
                    = Thread.CurrentThread.CurrentUICulture
                    = new System.Globalization.CultureInfo(values[1]);
            }
        }
    }

    this.Startup += this.Application_Startup;
    this.Exit += this.Application_Exit;
    this.UnhandledException += this.Application_UnhandledException;
    InitializeComponent();
}
```


The code in Listing 22.12 checks the query string in the URL of the HTML page and detects whether a parameter named `culture` was passed. Then, it sets the `Thread.CurrentThread.CurrentCulture` (for numbers formats, dates, phone numbers, and so on) and the `Thread.CurrentThread.CurrentUICulture` (for UI elements).

To test this, make sure that the web project is set as StartUp Project and the page LocalizationSampleTestPage.html is set as Startup page, run the application, add **?culture=fr-FR** after the .html extension in the location bar and press Enter. You should now see the string displayed in French.

There are multiple ways to instruct the Silverlight application to select a different current culture, including the following:

- The culture set by the operating system should be picked automatically by the Silverlight framework. It is also available in `System.Globalization.CultureInfo.CurrentUICulture` and `CurrentCulture`.
- You can define an additional initialization parameter in the HTML page's `object` tag. We saw how to do that in *Silverlight 2 Unleashed*, Chapter 21, in the "Setting Initialization Parameters and Retrieving Initialization Parameters" section.

Unfortunately, it is not possible to change the culture during runtime. To do this, when the user selects a different culture, save the state of the application and then reload the HTML page with a different query string.

Using Tools

Not many tools are available to automate the process of localizing Silverlight assemblies. One promising tool seems to be Alchemy Catalyst, of which version 8.0 supports Silverlight. More information about this tool can be found at http://www.galasoft.ch/sl4-catalyst.

Downloading Resource Applications on Demand

As mentioned before, adding multiple resource assemblies to a XAP file increases its size, even though only one such DLL is needed for the application to work. The solution is to load these assemblies on demand.

Unfortunately, describing the whole process would take too much space, but a working sample is provided at http://www.galasoft.ch/sl4-localize. Download the zip file named LocalizationSample-OnDemand.zip, unblock it, and extract the content. Then you can open the solution file in Visual Studio and check how the on-demand loading is done in App.xaml.cs. Note that if you want to download resource assemblies on demand, you must *not* include them in the XAP file, so the step described in "Including the Resource DLL in the XAP" section must be avoided!

Encrypting and Decrypting

Silverlight provides everything needed for strong encryption/decryption directly in the framework. We will not go too deep in the details here because this is a very complex topic for the time that we have. However, a sample is included at http://www.galasoft.ch/sl4-encrypt. Download this file, unblock it, and extract the content to your hard drive. Then open EncryptionSample.sln in Visual Studio and run the application.

To test the encryption/decryption, enter some text in the `TextBox` on the left. Then, enter a password in the `PasswordBox` directly beneath and click the Encrypt button. Select a name and location for the file and save it. Then end the application.

Open the file you just saved in a text editor. As expected, the result should is unreadable. The content has been encrypted.

To decrypt the file, run the application again. Enter the same password you used in the encryption phase and then click the Decrypt button. The decrypted content appears in the `TextBox` on the right.

You can also try what happens when the password is not valid: Enter a different password and click Decrypt: A message is shown warning you that it is impossible to decrypt the file.

Understanding the Encryption/Decryption Mechanism

There are a few classes able to encrypt and decrypt text in Silverlight, located within the `System.Security.Cryptography` namespace. Each class corresponds to a different encryption algorithm, such as Advanced Encryption Standard (AES), Data Encryption Standard (DES), Elliptic Curve Diffie-Hellman (ECDH), Hash-based Message Authentication Code (HMAC), and more.

To encrypt a text, a key is prepared using the password you provided as well as a piece of text named the "salt" (hard coded in the application) which creates additional randomization of the key. Upon decryption, the password and the salt must be provided in the exact same spelling and capitalization.

The actual encryption/decryption is done using a class named `CryptoStream`, which is a specific implementation of the `Stream` base class. This can be used to write to (or read from) any place that a `Stream` can be used for, such as isolated storage, memory, file system, or of course, sending requests on the web and receiving responses to protect the web traffic.

Studying the provided sample should provide enough material to get started with encryption. You can find more information about the `Cryptography` namespace at http://www.galasoft.ch/sl4-crypto.

Multithreading

When an application needs to wait for a long time before continuing to perform an operation, it would be impractical to block the whole user interface and simply let the user wait. This is what happens in traditional websites (which do not use advanced JavaScript functionalities known as AJAX). For example, when a user performs a search on a search engine, he has to wait until the search results return. Granted, search engines are very much optimized for speed, but the experience could be better nonetheless.

Similarly, when a long-lasting operation needs to be performed (for example, a calculation involving a large number of data rows), the user should get information about the progress. This can be done only if the user interface is not blocked during the operation. This also provides a possibility to let the user start a different operation, for example, or to show him something to let the time go faster (animation, video, even advertisement).

To handle this, modern application frameworks such as Silverlight have the possibility to start multiple *threads*.

What Is a Thread?

Normally, desktop applications run in a *process*. This is what you can see when you open the Task Explorer by right-clicking on the taskbar in Windows and selecting the corresponding context menu item. This can be, for example, Word.exe (for Microsoft Word), iexplore.exe (for Internet Explorer), chrome.exe (for Google Chrome), and so forth.

For Silverlight, it is slightly more complex because all Silverlight instances run within the process named iexplore.exe (for in-browser applications) or sllauncher.exe (for out-of-browser applications). This process is just a host for the Silverlight application, which runs in its own isolated environment.

Each application (and each Silverlight application as well) has, in addition, the possibility to *spawn* one or more threads. Note that there is always at least one thread, often called the *main thread*. For Silverlight, the main thread is also often called the *UI thread*, because this is the thread which is responsible for rendering all the UI elements.

In addition to the UI thread, Silverlight is able to spawn threads automatically (for example, when an asynchronous web request is sent). We noted already that the user interface is not blocked while the application waits for the response. The Silverlight framework takes care of everything here, and the developer does not need to explicitly start this new thread. For other *multithreaded* operations, however, Silverlight must be told exactly what to do, when to start and when to stop doing it.

Using the ThreadPool

One way to spawn new threads is to use the `ThreadPool` static class. When it is started, each Silverlight application creates a small number of threads and places them in the `ThreadPool`. These threads can be consumed by the application, and returned automatically to the `ThreadPool` when the task is completed.

The `ThreadPool` class is useful typically when a large number of threads are needed for a short time. The Silverlight framework takes care of managing the resources, and creates new threads on demand if enough memory is available. If resources become too sparse, the requests are queued, and will get processed as soon as one thread becomes available again.

Although starting a threaded operation on the `ThreadPool` is the easiest method from a syntax point of view, it is recommended to use a `BackgroundWorker` instead for longer operations, as you will see in the "Creating a BackgroundWorker" section.

The following sample creates an application calculating all prime numbers from 0 to 10,000. Such a calculation is a small "unit of work" that can be delegated to a background thread. This is a good usage for a `ThreadPool`, a large amount of short-lived threads. Follow these steps:

1. Create a new Silverlight application in Visual Studio and name it **ThreadPoolSample**.
2. Modify the MainPage.xaml as shown in Listing 22.13.

LISTING 22.13 Modifying the UI

```
<ScrollViewer>
    <StackPanel x:Name="PrimeNumbersPanel"
                Background="White">
    </StackPanel>
</ScrollViewer>
```

3. Modify the `MainPage` constructor (in MainPage.xaml.cs) as shown in Listing 22.14.

LISTING 22.14 `MainPage` Constructor

```
1  private const int NumberOfPrimes = 10000;
2
3  public MainPage()
4  {
5      InitializeComponent();
6
```

```
 7      for (var index = 0; index < NumberOfPrimes; index++)
 8      {
 9          CalculatePrime(index);
10      }
11  }
```

22

- Line 1 defines how many numbers must be tested to find prime numbers.
- Lines 7 to 10 call the `CalculatePrime` method 10,000 times. This method (defined in Listing 22.16) tests whether a number is a prime number.

4. Define the `DisplayPrimeNumber` method as shown in Listing 22.15.

LISTING 22.15 Preparing the Display and Testing the Numbers

```
 1  private void DisplayPrimeNumber(int prime)
 2  {
 3      var text = new TextBlock
 4      {
 5          Foreground = new SolidColorBrush(Colors.Red),
 6          FontSize = 24,
 7          Text = prime.ToString()
 8      };
 9
10      PrimeNumbersPanel.Children.Add(text);
11  }
```

- Lines 3 to 8 create a new `TextBlock` and assign the prime number found to its `Text` property.
- Then the new `TextBlock` is added to the `StackPanel`.

5. Add the new method to calculate prime numbers as shown in Listing 22.16.

LISTING 22.16 Calculating a Prime Number

```
 1  private void CalculatePrime(int index)
 2  {
 3      ThreadPool.QueueUserWorkItem(
 4          o =>
 5          {
 6              Thread.CurrentThread.Name
 7                  = "Worker # " + index;
 8              var root = (int) Math.Ceiling(Math.Sqrt(index));
 9              var isPrime = false;
10
11              while (root > 1)
```

```
12              {
13                  if (root != index
14                      && index % root == 0)
15                  {
16                      isPrime = false;
17                      break;
18                  }
19                  else if (!isPrime)
20                  {
21                      isPrime = true;
22                  }
23
24                  root--;
25              }
26
27              if (isPrime)
28              {
29                  Dispatcher.BeginInvoke(
30                      () => DisplayPrimeNumber(index));
31              }
32          });
33  }
```

Because the `CalculatePrime` method is called 10,000 times, and because each calculation can take a different time, blocking the user interface during the operation would provide a very bad user experience. Instead, spawning multiple background threads as we do here provides a better experience: The user interface is not blocked, so it is possible to provide user information. Also, the computer's resources are optimized: The `ThreadPool` class takes care of reusing and recycling existing `Thread` instances, of creating new ones when needed, and of queuing incoming requests to process them as soon as possible.

The following happens in Listing 22.16:

- Line 3 requires the `ThreadPool` class to start an operation in a `Thread`. The parameter of the `QueueWorkItem` method is an instance of the `WaitCallback` class. In many cases, however, an anonymous delegate can be used for this task, as provided on lines 4 to 30 (as a lambda expression).
- When resources are available to actually start the thread, the content of the anonymous delegate is executed on a background thread. This starts on lines 6 to 23 by checking whether the provided number is a prime number. We won't go into explaining the algorithm here; it is available in multiple places online.
- A name is given to the current `Thread` on lines 6 to 7. We will see why it is important in the "Enhancing Multithreaded Code" section.

- If the number is indeed a prime, the method `DisplayPrimeNumber` needs to be called. This is done on lines 27 and 28. Note, however, that a direct call to this method will cause an exception to occur. Instead, a `Dispatcher` is used. We already talked about the `Dispatcher` object as early as Chapter 5, "Understanding Dependency Properties," and will explain it in details in "Dispatching Back to the UI Thread" section.

> **WARNING**
>
> **Synchronizing the Threads**
>
> The code in this section does not take care of synchronizing the threads. This can lead to unexpected results: Because each threaded operation can take a various length of time to execute (depending on the complexity of the task, on the CPU's load, and so on), there is no guarantee that the prime numbers will be displayed in order. If the output needs to be in ascending order, the `DisplayPrimeNumber` method will need to take care of checking the already displayed numbers and inserting the new one at the correct location.

Typically, the `ThreadPool` class is rather used on servers, where resource management is critical, and where applications are typically very long lived. They can have their usage in Silverlight, too, as shown in this example. For other threading scenarios, the `BackgroundWorker` class that we will study in the "Creating and Using a BackgroundWorker" section is typically preferred.

Dispatching Back to the UI Thread

In Listing 22.16, lines 27 and 28 are using the `BeginInvoke` method of a `Dispatcher`. This is needed, because the `DisplayPrimeNumber` method (defined in Listing 22.15) creates a `TextBlock` element and adds it to an existing `StackPanel`. However, in Silverlight an instance of a control belongs to the `Thread` on which it was created (in that case, the UI thread). If another `Thread` attempts to access and modify it, this causes an `UnauthorizedAccessException` to be thrown with the message "Invalid cross-thread access." To try this, just replace lines 27 and 28 in Listing 22.16 with `DisplayPrimeNumber(index);` Then run the application and see how the exception is displayed.

To make sure that a method has the right to access another object, and to perform the actual call safely, the `Dispatcher` class can be used. There is exactly one instance of a `Dispatcher` per `Thread`. This instance is accessible through a number of ways, including the following:

- Each `DependencyObject` has a property named `Dispatcher`. (Do not get confused by the fact that the property has the same name as the class it holds.) This property can be used to access the `BeginInvoke` method. However, it is not always possible to use this property, as explained in the "Using the RootVisual's Dispatcher" box.

- The UI dispatcher is also accessible through the `System.Windows.Deployment` class. This is probably the most convenient way to access the `Dispatcher`.

As a rule of thumb, if multithreaded code is executed within a DependencyObject (such as within the MainPage class like in Listing 22.16, or within a custom Control), using the object's own Dispatcher property is the most convenient way to execute code on the UI thread. For other cases, the System.Windows.Deployment class as shown in Listing 22.17.

LISTING 22.17 Using System.Windows.Deployment's Dispatcher

```
System.Windows.Deployment.Current.Dispatcher.BeginInvoke(
    () => DoSomething());
```

WARNING

Using the RootVisual's Dispatcher

It is tempting to try and access the UI thread's Dispatcher through accessing the static property called Application.Current.RootVisual. This property holds the element that is set as the RootVisual of the application, typically in App.xaml.cs, in the Application_Startup event handler.

However, access to this property will throw the same UnauthorizedAccessException that we are trying to avoid. This happens because the RootVisual belongs to the UI Thread, and may not be accessed by the worker Thread.

Checking Access Before Dispatching

Using the BeginInvoke method is needed to enable cross-thread access, as we saw, but it also has a side effect: It adds the call into a queue on the destination Thread. The code will be executed only when the queue reaches this particular entry. Depending on what is currently running on the main thread, this can take some time.

If the call should be executed as soon as possible, it is possible to check whether a direct call is possible, without passing through the BeginInvoke method, by using the undocumented CheckAccess method on the Dispatcher class. It may seem a little weird that this method is not documented in the official Silverlight documentation and that it does not appear in IntelliSense. However, it is perfectly safe to use it as shown in Listing 22.18.

LISTING 22.18 Checking Access

```
1  if (Deployment.Current.Dispatcher.CheckAccess())
2  {
3      DoSomething();
4  }
5   else
6  {
7      Deployment.Current.Dispatcher.BeginInvoke(
8          () => DoSomething());
9  }
```

- Line 1 uses the Dispatcher to check whether the current Thread has access to its objects.
- If access is okay, the DoSomething method can be called directly. It will be executed synchronously, without any delay.
- If CheckAccess returns false, however, the BeginInvoke method is used. This causes the DoSomething method to be executed asynchronously, with a small delay.

Using BeginInvoke on the Current Thread

In some occasions, it can be useful to use BeginInvoke on the current thread to add asynchronicity to the current operation. For example, before starting a lengthy calculation, you may want to finish the current method first. Consider the code in Listing 22.19.

LISTING 22.19 Initializing a Page

```
 1  public MainPage()
 2  {
 3      Items = new ObservableCollection<string>();
 4      InitializeComponent();
 5
 6      Loaded += (s, e) => MessageBox.Show("Loaded");
 7      OutputMany();
 8      OutputOne();
 9  }
10
11  private void OutputOne()
12  {
12      Items.Add("One");
13  }
14  private void OutputMany()
15  {
16      for (var index = 0; index < 10; index++)
17      {
18          Items.Add(index.ToString());
19      }
20  }
```

With the code in Listing 22.19, the ListBox in MainPage.xaml displays numbers from 0 to 9 first, then the string "One", and only then will the MessageBox be displayed. The OutputMany method is blocking the initialization of the page, and if it lasts for a long time (unlike here), it can be disturbing. Instead, it is possible to modify line 7 of Listing 22.19 to render the call to OutputMany asynchronous, as shown in Listing 22.20.

LISTING 22.20 Making an Asynchronous Call on the Current Thread

```
Dispatcher.BeginInvoke(() => OutputMany());
```

After modifying the application and running it, we first see the string "One", then the MessageBox is displayed, and only after the MessageBox is closed will the numbers 0 to 9 appear. Note, however, that all the operations occur on the UI thread, so this is not multi-threaded code!

Dispatching to Other Thread Instances
Every Thread has a Dispatcher, not just the UI Thread. The techniques detailed here work between two background Thread instances, too.

Creating and Using a BackgroundWorker

As mentioned earlier, a BackgroundWorker instance is preferred in certain scenarios: When one Thread instance may be invoked multiple times; when it might be running long-lasting operations; when a reference to the running Thread is needed in multiple places in the application.

BackgroundWorker is a higher-level class than ThreadPool, and it provides a few advantages to the programmer:

- An ongoing operation can be cancelled by calling the CancelAsync method. This is very handy and less complicated than with the ThreadPool class.
- A special event named ProgressChanged is available to report the progress of the ongoing operation.
- A property named IsBusy indicates whether the ongoing operation is still running or is completed already.
- Some events of the BackgroundWorker class (ProgressChanged, RunWorkerCompleted) can be handled on the UI thread directly, without having to use the Dispatcher. This makes the code more legible and easier to implement and test.

The following sample is a Silverlight application that checks periodically whether the site it originates from is active. This can be useful, for example, if you want to monitor the outage of a web server. Follow these steps:

1. Download the start application from http://www.galasoft.ch/sl4-backgroundworker. Unblock the downloaded file, and then extract the content to your hard drive. Open WebServerMonitor.sln in Visual Studio.
2. This application has a web server running at http://localhost:60000. The Silverlight application will periodically "ping" the web server by attempting to download a very small text file named ping.txt. Note that we could have used any file on the server (including index.html), but using a small text file minimizes the traffic.
3. Open MainPage.xaml.cs and add a property as shown in Listing 22.21.

LISTING 22.21 Adding a BackgroundWorker

```
public BackgroundWorker Worker
{
    get;
    private set;
}
```

4. Implement the StartMonitoring method as shown in Listing 22.22.

LISTING 22.22 StartMonitoring Method

```
1  private void StartMonitoring()
2  {
3      Worker = new BackgroundWorker
4      {
5          WorkerReportsProgress = true
6      };
7
8      Worker.DoWork += (s, e) =>
9      {
10         var client = new WebClient();
11         client.DownloadStringCompleted
12             += client_DownloadStringCompleted;
13
14         while (true)
15         {
16             Worker.ReportProgress(0,
17                 "Pinging at " + DateTime.Now.ToString());
18             client.DownloadStringAsync(_pingFileUri);
19             Thread.Sleep(PingDelay);
20         }
21     };
22
23     Worker.ProgressChanged += (s, e) =>
24         Entries.Add(e.UserState.ToString());
25
26     Worker.RunWorkerAsync();
27 }
```

- Lines 3 to 6 create the new BackgroundWorker and enable progress report. If this property is not set, the ProgressChanged event will never fire.
- Lines 10 to 20 are executed when the RunWorkerAsync method is called. A new WebClient is created on line 10, and its DownloadStringCompleted event is handled on line 11. The actual event handler is shown in Listing 22.23.

- Line 14 starts an endless loop. This could cause the thread to hog the CPU and not let any calculation time to any other task, which is why the Thread is put to sleep for 5,000 milliseconds on line 19.
- Line 16 calls the ReportProgress method, which in turn raises the ProgressChanged event on the UI thread. We use this to save a message into the Entries collection, as you will see in Listing 22.23.
- A request is sent to the web server on line 18 before the Thread sleeps for five seconds.
- Lines 23 and 24 handle the ProgressChanged event by adding the message into the Entries collection. A ListBox is data bound to this collection in MainPage.xaml to display the result. Notice that there is no call to Dispatcher.BeginInvoke here because the ProgressChanged event is already raised on the UI thread.
- Finally, line 26 calls RunWorkerAsync, which causes the DoWork event to be raised, and the whole process can begin.

5. Handle the DownloadStringCompleted event as shown in Listing 22.23. This is where the code can find out whether the web server is running, by looking at the Error property of the DownloadStringCompletedEventArgs parameter.

LISTING 22.23 DownloadStringCompleted Event Handler

```
void client_DownloadStringCompleted(
    object sender,
    DownloadStringCompletedEventArgs e)
{
    if (e.Error == null)
    {
        Worker.ReportProgress(0, "Ping OK");
    }
    else
    {
        Worker.ReportProgress(0,
            "Ping Error: " + e.Error.Message);
    }
}
```

6. Build the application to make sure that all the files are available.
7. Right-click the WebServerMonitor.Web project and select View in Browser from the context menu. This starts the web server in a window (or tab) of your favorite web browser.
8. Open another window (or tab) and navigate to the URL http://localhost:60000/index.html. The ListBox starts recording entries showing that the web server is running.

9. Use the small icon shown in Figure 14.3 (in Chapter 14, "Enhancing Line-of-Business Applications and Running Out of the Browser," the icon is located in the Windows taskbar's Notification area) to stop the web server. Immediately, some error messages are shown in the `ListBox`. Even though the web server stops running, the client application continues to work independently, and registers that the file ping.txt is not returned anymore.

10. Repeat Step 6. The web server restarts, and the `ListBox` registers success messages again.

Because the `BackgroundWorker` instance is exposed as a property, another object could register for the `ProgressChanged` event (for example, to input the entries into a text file and save it to isolated storage). Of course, in this sample, we should take care of removing entries from the `ListBox` after a certain time, or else the memory consumption of the application will grow too big and crash the application eventually.

Locking Critical Resources

When multiple threads need access to a resource (for example, a collection of objects), and especially when these threads might be modifying the resource, some unexpected side effects may happen. In this case, we talk about a *critical resource*, and its access should be safeguarded. For example, implement a sample with the following steps:

1. Create a new Silverlight application and name it **LockingResources**.

2. Set the `MainPage`'s `x:Name` to `"MyPage"` in MainPage.xaml.

3. Still in MainPage.xaml, add a `ListBox` to the `LayoutRoot Grid` as shown in Listing 22.24.

LISTING 22.24 Adding a ListBox

```
<Grid x:Name="LayoutRoot" Background="White">
    <ListBox ItemsSource="{Binding ElementName=MyPage, Path=Items}" />
</Grid>
```

4. Add a new `ObservableCollection` to MainPage.xaml.cs and initialize the page as shown in Listing 22.25.

LISTING 22.25 Adding a Collection and Initializing

```
public ObservableCollection<string> Items
{
    get;
    private set;
}
```

```
public MainPage()
{
    Items = new ObservableCollection<string>();
    InitializeComponent();
    StartThreadedOperation();
}
```

5. Implement the `StartThreadedOperation` and the threads as in Listing 22.26.

LISTING 22.26 Starting the Threaded Operations

```
 1  private void StartThreadedOperation()
 2  {
 3      for (var index = 0; index < 3; index++)
 4      {
 5           CreateAndStartWorker(index);
 6      }
 7  }
 8
 9  private void CreateAndStartWorker(int workerIndex)
10  {
11      var worker = new BackgroundWorker
12      {
13          WorkerReportsProgress = true
14      };
15
16      worker.DoWork += (s, e) =>
17      {
18          Thread.CurrentThread.Name
19              = "Worker # " + workerIndex;
20          for (var index = 0; index < 10; index++)
21          {
22              Thread.Sleep(100);
23              worker.ReportProgress(
24                  index * 10,
25                  string.Format(
26                     "Worker # {0}, Operation # {1}",
27                     workerIndex, index));
28          }
29      };
30
31      worker.ProgressChanged += (s, e) =>
32      {
33          Items.Add(e.UserState.ToString());
34      };
```

```
35
36         worker.RunWorkerAsync();
37     }
```

- The CreateAndStartWorker method is called three times.
- On lines 11 to 14, this method creates a new BackgroundWorker and enabled progress report.
- Lines 20 to 28 are executed 10 times. First the Thread sleeps for 100 milliseconds on line 22. Then, an item is sent to the UI thread through the ProgressChanged event.
- This event is handled on line 33: The sent item is simply added to the ObservableCollection. Through the data binding set in Listing 22.24, the display will automatically be updated.

6. Run the application and observe the result. Results may vary depending on the computer's configuration, but typically some of the threads are competing for the access to the Items collection: The items are intermingled, as shown in Figure 22.3.

```
Worker # 0, Operation # 5
Worker # 1, Operation # 5
Worker # 0, Operation # 6
Worker # 1, Operation # 6
Worker # 2, Operation # 0
Worker # 0, Operation # 7
Worker # 1, Operation # 7
Worker # 2, Operation # 1
Worker # 0, Operation # 8
```

FIGURE 22.3 Uncontrolled access to a critical resource.

The operation implemented here is completely unpredictable. Running the application 10 times will likely create 10 different results. Depending on the actual operation, this can lead to very annoying or even catastrophic results. For example, if a Thread modifies a collection while another iterates through it, the application will crash. To avoid these side-effects, critical resources should be locked for access, for example, with the following step:

1. Modify the worker.DoWork event handler as shown in Listing 22.27.

LISTING 22.27 Locking the Critical Resource

```
worker.DoWork += (s, e) =>
{
    Thread.CurrentThread.Name = "Worker # " + workerIndex;
    lock (Items)
    {
        for (var index = 0; index < 10; index++)
        {
            Thread.Sleep(100);
            worker.ReportProgress(
                index * 10,
                string.Format(
                    "Worker # {0}, Operation # {1}",
                    workerIndex,
```

```
                        index));
            }
        }
};
```

The change in Listing 22.27 from Listing 22.26 is that the access to the Items collection is now protected by a lock. When a Thread reaches this statement, it checks whether the instance is locked already. If that is not the case, it locks it and then proceeds with the operation. If the collection is locked, however, the Thread has to wait until the collection becomes unlocked. The result is that the output of worker # 0 will appear grouped together, followed by worker # 1 and worker # 2's outputs. Note that depending on the circumstances, it is possible that worker # 1 appears first, or worker # 2. But all the entries belonging to one worker will appear together anyway.

Any reference type can be used in a lock statement, but not value types. In fact, nothing forces you to use the critical resource itself as the lock. Instead, it can be any object that all the threads can access, for example, as shown in Listing 22.28.

LISTING 22.28 Using an object as lock

```
private object _lock = new object();

private void CreateAndStartWorker(int workerIndex)
{
    var worker = new BackgroundWorker
    {
        WorkerReportsProgress = true
    };

    worker.DoWork += (s, e) =>
    {
        lock(_lock)
        {
            // ...
        }
    };

    // ...
}
```

Enhancing Multithreaded Code

Programming multithreaded operations is probably one of the most complex coding styles, but at the same time, it is the future of programming because of the increased availability of multicore computers. It is important to understand what happens inside the thread, how multiple threads influence each other, and to take a few measures to make it easier to code and debug multithreaded applications:

- Always give a name to the worker thread. We saw how to do that in the earlier examples. This is important when the code is not working correctly and the developer needs to debug the code: If multiple threads run the same code asynchronously, it becomes very hard to know which `Thread` is currently active. By setting the thread's name, you can open the Threads window while debugging in Visual Studio (Debug, Windows, Threads). The current thread is indicated with its name, as shown in Figure 22.4.

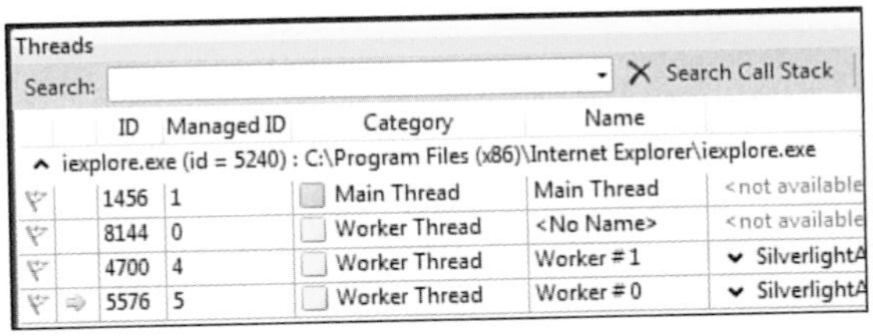

Threads

Search: [ ] ✕ Search Call Stack

		ID	Managed ID	Category	Name	
^ iexplore.exe (id = 5240) : C:\Program Files (x86)\Internet Explorer\iexplore.exe						
		1456	1	Main Thread	Main Thread	<not available
		8144	0	Worker Thread	<No Name>	<not available
		4700	4	Worker Thread	Worker #1	SilverlightA
	⇨	5576	5	Worker Thread	Worker #0	SilverlightA

FIGURE 22.4 Threads window in Visual Studio.

- Always lock critical resources. If any unexpected result appears, the first suspect is usually an unplanned concurrent access of a critical resource by multiple threads.
- In a worker thread, especially for long operations, give a little time to the other threads by letting the current one sleep for a few milliseconds, as shown in Listing 22.26, line 22.
- Remember that when a background thread is active, it uses the CPU, which needs power. Especially on mobile devices where battery life is critical, use background threads with care.
- Test, test, and test some more. If possible, automate the tests by using a unit test framework as shown in the "Unit Testing Silverlight Code" section. Note that testing asynchronous code can be especially difficult.

Multithreading is a very complex topic, hard to debug, hard to understand exactly what happens, and easy to make mistakes that can cause an application to run fine thousand times and suddenly to start crashing. On the other hand, with the current trend in multi-core computers, parallel programming becomes more and more important, and can really enhance the speed of your application. In Silverlight (Version 4 but also for Windows Phone 7), spawning new threads is quite simple, as you saw in this section, and Visual Studio (with its Threads debug window) provides modern tools to debug multithreaded code. Do not hesitate to enhance your code with threads, but proceed with care.

Unit Testing the Application

With ever-more complex applications, some mechanisms are needed to ensure that the code runs in reproducible conditions with reproducible results. Most important, it must be ensured that changes to the code do not break anything that was running before.

Such reproducible, automated tests are called *unit tests*. We already talked about this in *Silverlight 2 Unleashed*, Chapter 24, and implemented a functionality using a development process named *test-driven development (TDD)*. In this section, we dig a little deeper and see how to use the new Silverlight Unit Test framework distributed with the Silverlight Toolkit. Finally, we will talk about unit testing for a Windows Phone 7 application.

Installing a Unit Test Framework

Currently, the main unit test frameworks for Silverlight 4 are NUnit and the Silverlight Unit Test framework. NUnit is a well-known, well-respected unit test framework. Unfortunately, there is not much documentation about making it run for Silverlight.

The Silverlight Unit Test framework is a private initiative by Microsoft employee Jeff Wilcox that was already available for Silverlight 2 and improved since then. Nowadays, this framework is available as a part of the Silverlight toolkit. When the toolkit is installed, the Silverlight Unit Test framework is automatically available, which is very convenient. Note that much of the Silverlight framework itself is tested using Jeff's unit test framework.

In case this was not done already, download and install the latest version of the Silverlight toolkit from http://silverlight.codeplex.com/.

Adding Functionality with TDD

In this section, we extend an existing application by testing it in various edge conditions, to make it more robust. As a starting point, the dependency injection sample that was developed in Chapter 20, "Building Extensible and Maintainable Applications," is used. If you didn't keep this project, the file UnitTesting-Start.zip can be downloaded from http://www.galasoft.ch/sl4-unittest. As usual, after the zip file is downloaded, it needs to be unblocked in the file's Properties dialog in Windows Explorer. Click the Unblock button on the General tab (if available). Then, extract the files on your hard drive and open WhyDependencyInjection.sln in Visual Studio.

Creating a Test Case

This application was not developed using TDD so far, and we will not start by adding test cases for the existing features as we would in a real-life project. Instead, we will move directly to the edge cases. True TDD requires a test to be written first, and to fail. Then, the application should be modified to make the test pass. Follow these steps:

1. With the WhyDependencyInjection solution open in Visual Studio, right-click the solution in the Solution Explorer, and select Add, New Project from the context menu.
2. In the Silverlight category, select Silverlight Unit Test Application from the Add New Project dialog. Name the new project **WhyDependencyInjection.UnitTests**.
3. In the New Silverlight Application dialog, choose to create a new website for the unit test application. This avoids common permission issues, for example, when trying to access Internet resources.
4. The Silverlight Unit Test application is an almost normal Silverlight application with a few changes:

- There is no MainPage.xaml. In fact, the `RootVisual` is generated automatically in App.xaml.cs, in the `Application_Startup` event handler.
- There is a reference to the DLLs named Microsoft.Silverlight.Testing and Microsoft.VisualStudio.QualityTools.UnitTesting.Silverlight. The former contains the unit test framework itself, whereas the latter contains the attributes (compatible with the .NET version of the unit test framework) used to define test classes and test methods.

5. Into the WhyDependencyInjection.UnitTests project, add a reference to the WhyDependencyInjection project. Use the Projects tab into the Add Reference dialog.
6. Rename the file Tests.cs into ViewModelTests.cs. If Visual Studio asks if you want to rename the class too, say yes. Otherwise, rename the class manually to **ViewModelTests**.
7. Rename the method `TestMethod1` to **TestViewModelInjectionNull**.
8. Implement this method as shown in Listing 22.29.

LISTING 22.29 Implementing the `TestViewModelInjectionNull` Method

```
[TestMethod]
public void TestViewModelInjectionNull()
{
    var vm = new ViewModelWithDependencyInjection(null);
    Assert.IsNotNull(vm);
}
```

9. Set the WhyDependencyInjection.UnitTests.Web as StartUp project and the WhyDependencyInjection.UnitTestsTestPage.html page as Startup page, and then run the application.
10. The dialog shown in Figure 22.5 is displayed when a new test run is started. You can either click No, Run All Tests or wait until the test run starts.
11. The test fails. For more information, click the TestViewModelInjectionNull entry in Figure 22.6 to display the test results. The issue is a `NullReferenceException`.

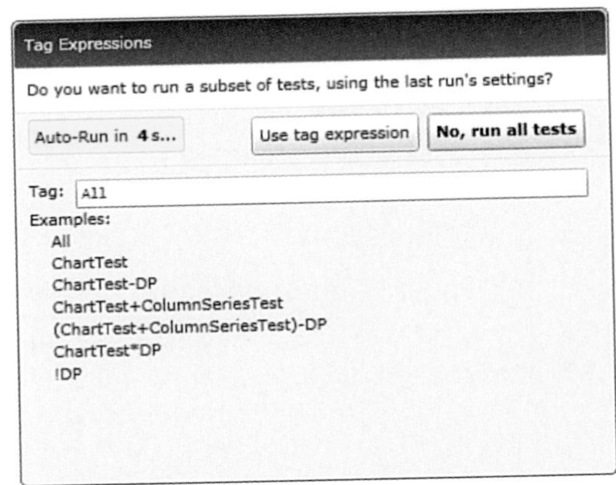

FIGURE 22.5 Starting a new test run.

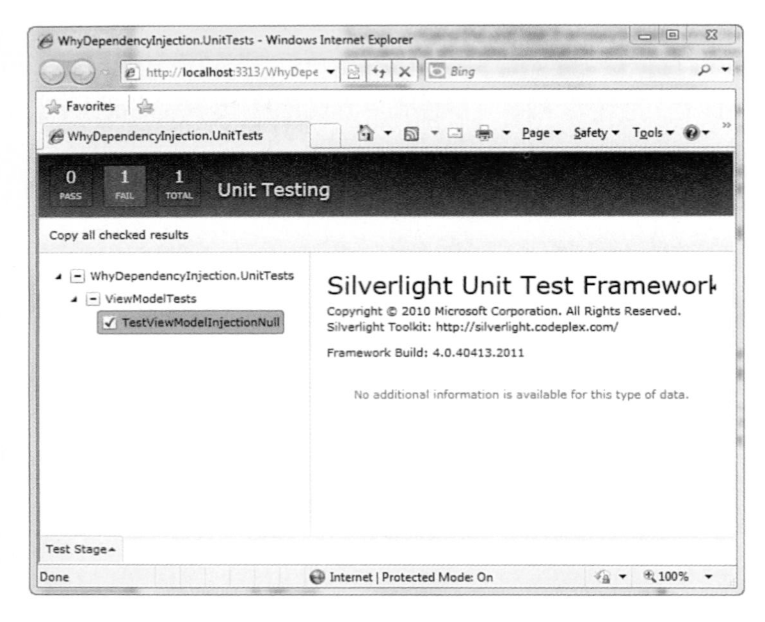

FIGURE 22.6 Failed test.

12. To make the test pass, open ViewModelWithDependencyInjection.cs in the WhyDependencyInjection application and modify the code as shown in Listing 22.30.

LISTING 22.30 Making the Test Pass

```
public ViewModelWithDependencyInjection(IDataService service)
{
    if (service == null)
    {
        return;
    }

    service.GetItems(items =>
    {
        Items = new ObservableCollection<Item>(items);
    });
}
```

13. Run the test again. This time, the run is successful.

Creating a Test Service and Injecting it

Now, we will test what happens when the service returns `null` instead of the `IEnumerable<Item>` that is expected in the callback. To do this, we need an implementation of `IDataService` that is predictable, and that can be controlled. Follow these steps:

1. Create a new class in WhyDependencyInjection.UnitTests, name it **TestDataService.cs**, and implement it as shown in Listing 22.31.

LISTING 22.31 Returning a `null` Collection

```
public enum TestCase
{
    ReturnNull = 0
}
public class TestDataService : IDataService
{
    private TestCase _whichTest;

    public TestDataService(TestCase whichTest)
    {
        this._whichTest = whichTest;
    }

    public void GetItems(
        Action<IEnumerable<Item>> callback)
    {
        switch (_whichTest)
        {
            case TestCase.ReturnNull:
                callback(null);
                break;
        }
    }
}
```

2. Implement a new test method in the `ViewModelTests` class as shown in Listing 22.32. If the service returns `null`, it is expected that the `Items` collection is not `null`, but that it has zero items.

LISTING 22.32 `TestGetItemsNull` Method

```
[TestMethod]
public void TestGetItemsNull()
{
    var service = new TestDataService(TestCase.ReturnNull);
```

```
    var vm = new ViewModelWithDependencyInjection(service);
    Assert.IsNotNull(vm.Items);
    Assert.AreEqual(0, vm.Items.Count);
}
```

3. Run the application to see the test fail.
4. Modify the `ViewModelWithDependencyInjection` constructor as shown in Listing 22.33. Then run the application again to see the test pass. Note that if you need to understand better what happens, you can also place breakpoints in the code and run the debug mode instead.

LISTING 22.33 Making the Test Pass

```
public ViewModelWithDependencyInjection(IDataService service)
{
    if (service == null)
    {
        return;
    }

    service.GetItems(items =>
    {
        if (items == null)
        {
            Items = new ObservableCollection<Item>();
            return;
        }

        Items = new ObservableCollection<Item>(items);
    });
}
```

TIP

Customizing the Test Run

It is possible to avoid running all tests with every test run by passing tags to the dialog shown in Figure 22.5. When the dialog is displayed, interrupt the countdown by clicking anywhere on it. Then, enter the name of the method you want to test and click the Use Tag Expression button. You can also enter multiple names of methods, or exclude one or more methods. You can find more information at http://www.galasoft.ch/sl4-tests4.

Additional test cases are easy to write now (for instance, testing what happens if the returned items collection is empty).

Using Code Coverage

The current version of the Silverlight Unit Test framework does not support test coverage. However, because this framework uses the same syntax (`TestClass`, `TestMethod`, `Assert`, and so on) as the desktop version (MSTest), it is possible to create a WPF application, share the source code, and the test files and to run code coverage on the WPF assemblies. This is not always possible, however, especially when using some Silverlight-only features.

Unit Testing Windows Phone 7 Applications

Jeff Wilcox also made the Silverlight Unit Test framework available for Windows Phone 7 applications. Using the same syntax, it is possible to run the tests directly into a Windows Phone device.

The latest assemblies are available at http://www.galasoft.ch/sl4-testsphone. Unfortunately, at the time of this writing, there are no unit test project templates for Windows Phone 7, so “hooking up” the test framework must be done manually. More information on this is available on Jeff Wilcox’s blog.

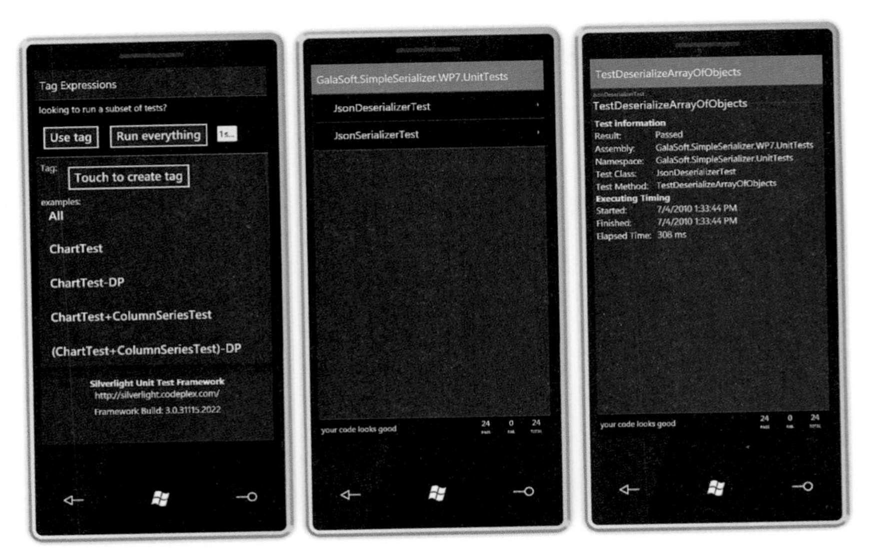

FIGURE 22.7 Unit test results in Windows Phone 7.

Unit tests are widely recognized as a best practice when the goal is to create stable, robust applications that perform well in a variety of scenarios and can be modified and extended easily without risking breaking existing functionality. Although not all the code can be tested (some user interface specific code is really difficult to test automatically), most of the lower layers of the application (view-model, model, data access, and so on) should be unit tested. Although some functionality available in .NET unit test frameworks is not available yet in Silverlight (especially code coverage), the existing infrastructure allows creating unit tests and gathering information about the application in multiple test scenarios.

Summary

This last chapter in our long journey exposed some advanced techniques to enhance Silverlight applications in a professional manner. Such techniques require a good understanding of the way that .NET and especially Silverlight work. Hopefully, this chapter gives you a good head start in that direction. Be sure to exercise these techniques (as well as everything you learned in this book) over and over again until you really understand what is happening. In programming, just like in other arts, practice is the only way to become a better craftsman.

CONCLUSION

This concludes our journey through the Silverlight framework. As you have seen, it is now a very powerful and mature framework, able to cover multiple requirements for your rich applications. In fact, it is wise to think of Silverlight not as a web technology anymore, but rather as a rich application development framework available on multiple platforms (and this is just a start).

In a time when user experience is breaking its traditional boundaries, when fingers are replacing the mouse and keyboard devices, when users are expecting more from their applications than the usual battleship gray and square buttons, Silverlight offers a great way to build flexible, decoupled, extensible applications. It also improves the collaboration between designers and developers, which allows building more beautiful applications at a fraction of the effort (and the cost) that was necessary with classic technologies.

You reaching the conclusion of this book (and kudos on that, by the way) does not mean that you are done learning Silverlight. The best way to consolidate this knowledge is to build applications and to publish them. You saw how to do that, so now is the time to dig out that project you always wanted to implement and to build it. You have the choice between Silverlight for the Web, for the desktop, for the Windows Phone, or all of them! And by all means, when you are ready to show it to the world, let me know; I am really anxious to see what you are going to build!

The End

A

B

C

D

E

F

G

H

J–K

L

M

P

Q–R

T

U

V

W

X–Z